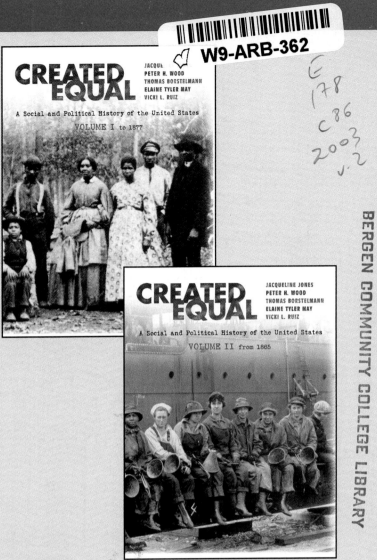

Jacqueline Jones, *Brandeis University*
Peter H. Wood, *Duke University*
Thomas Borstelmann, *Cornell University*
Elaine Tyler May, *University of Minnesota*
Vicki L. Ruiz, *University of California, Irvine*

With its sweeping inclusive view of American history, *Created Equal* emphasizes social history — including the lives and labors of women, immigrants, working people, and persons of color in all regions of the country — in the context of political and economic history. This new text from Longman Publishers acknowledges and reflects the diversity of class, race, culture, region, and gender that has always been part of the American story, and pays unique attention to the large middle class that has been central to the development of American society.

SVE • ©2003 • 1168 pages • Hardcover • ISBN 0-321-05296-X
Volume I • ©2003 • 656 pages • Paper • ISBN 0-321-05298-6
Volume II • ©2003 • 640 pages • Paper • ISBN 0-321-05300-1

Outstanding Features in *Created Equal*

▶ **Part Openers and Timelines.**

Part Openers preview the key issues and the political, cultural, ethnic, and regional diversity characteristic of the distinctive historical period covered in each three-chapter part. **Illustrated timelines** highlight significant events and trends and serve as a convenient preview/review for students. Each part covers approximately the era of a single generation of Americans.

1900	U.S. troops sent to China to crush Boxer Rebellion
1901	McKinley is assassinated; Vice President Theodore Roosevelt becomes President
1902	Newlands Act spurs dam building and irrigation in the Southwest
1903	First motorized flight by Orville and Wilbur Wright
	Henry Ford founds Ford Motor Company
1904	Roosevelt Corollary to the Monroe Doctrine
1905	Industrial Workers of the World founded
	Japan defeats Russia
1906	San Francisco Earthquake
	Sinclair Lewis, The Jungle
	Pure Food and Drug Act
	Indiana becomes first state to pass compulsory sterilization law
1907	"Gentlemen's Agreement" with Japan
	Oklahoma (former Indian Territory) becomes a state
1908	Muller v. Oregon upholds maximum hours for working women
1909	New York City garment workers' "Uprising of the 20,000"
	Peary/Henson Expedition reaches North Pole with four Greenland Inuit
1910	Mexican Revolution begins
	National Association for the Advancement of Colored People (NAACP) founded
1911	Triangle Shirtwaist fire, New York City
	Society of American Indians founded
1912	Theodore Roosevelt helps form Progressive Party
1913	Federal Reserve Act
	Sixteenth Amendment (federal personal

P A R T   S E V E N

Reform at Home, Revolution Abroad, 1900-1929

M ANY AMERICANS GREETED THE FIRST YEARS OF THE TWENTIETH century with optimism. Developments at home and abroad seemed to promise a new era of prosperity and progress. The mass manufacturing of automobiles proved a boon to the economy and transformed patterns of travel, leisure, and consumption. The beginning of commercial air flights heralded a revolution in communication and transportation. Moving pictures and new musical forms such as jazz delighted millions.

Focused on the new challenges of urbanization and industrialization, Progressive reformers sought to use science to solve a wide range of problems related to public health and welfare. Some advocated overhauling the system of public education; others pressed for legislation affecting the sale and distribution of alcohol. Some lobbied for worker health and safety legislation, while still others sought to exercise social control through eugenics and state-mandated sterilization.

A variety of social groups challenged white men's exclusive claim to civil rights. African Americans took the national stage to argue for equality under the law and for freedom from state-sanctioned violence in the form of lynching and debt peonage. Beginning with the "Great Migration" of World War I, southern blacks abandoned the southern cotton fields to seek jobs in northern cities

The changing roles of women bolstered the women's suffrage movement. Growing numbers of women were becoming labor organizers, reformers, and college professors. Rising divorce rates and the emergence of birth control as a political as well as medical issue signaled challenges

---

Systems of Unfree Labor

T he controversy over slavery ultimately precipitated the Civil War, the bloodiest conflict in the nation's history. Yet the abolition of slavery (with the ratification of the Thirteenth Amendment in 1865) did not eradicate forms of coerced labor. Indeed, systems of unfree labor—in which individuals are forced to work without compensation and for the benefit of someone else—have characterized the whole sweep of American history.

In the seventeenth century, most tobacco field workers in the Chesapeake region were indentured servants. These young men and women received passage from Europe to the colonies. In return, they bound themselves to a master for a stipulated amount of time (usually 7 years). Apprentices, children and young people, labored for a master artisan until they reached age 21.

Beginning in the late seventeenth century, the institution of slavery spread throughout the colonies. This system, which depended on the labor of Africans and their descendants, differed in crucial ways from indentured servitude and apprenticeship. Slaves remained slaves for life, and they had no rights under law. Children took the status of their enslaved mother.

States outside the South had emancipated their slaves by the mid-

Shackled inmates work to clear brush along a highway near Prattville, Alabama. A 1996 settlement prevented the state from shackling prisoners together on a "chain gang" but shackling of individual convict laborers was still permissible.

such as growing crops, spinning thread, weaving cloth, and producing handicrafts. In some cases, ship captains kidnapped sailors and forced them to work for no pay on long voyages. Indian and African American children remained at risk as labor-hungry whites forcibly "apprenticed" them with the aid of the courts.

By the late nineteenth century, peonage characterized the southern staple crop economy as well as the rural extractive sector (logging, sawmills, turpentine production, and

men) into the rough and dangerous work of building roads through swamps and digging coal out of the earth. Convict labor officials often demonstrated a reckless disregard for human life. Unlike slave owners, prison officials and the private individuals who leased convicts had few incentives to treat these workers in a humane way.

In the early twenty-first century, coerced labor persists. Some illegal immigrants continue to indenture themselves to smugglers and remain indebted to these smugglers for many

▶ **"Connecting History"** features demonstrate the relationship between the ways we experience and the ways we remember history. These short essays examine a specific topic related to the chapter content tracing it both forward and backward in time, showing students how the issues and concerns relevant to one period of American history reverberate in other eras.

Martin Luther King, Jr., and the Vietnam War

Most Americans approved of the war in Vietnam until at least 1968. Appreciative of Lyndon Johnson's commitment to reduce poverty and end racial discrimination at home, African Americans generally supported the president's policies in Southeast Asia. However, younger, more radical civil rights workers were among those who opposed the first insertion of U.S. combat troops in 1965. Within 2 years, the nation's most prominent black leader, Martin Luther King, Jr., decided that he could no longer keep quiet about his growing unease with the American war effort. A storm of criticism greeted his public denunciation of the war, most of it suggesting that he should limit himself to domestic civil rights work. But King no longer believed that events at home and abroad could be separated. The following excerpt is from his speech at Riverside Church, New York City, April 4, 1967:

A few years ago there was a shining moment in that struggle [against poverty and discrimination]. It seemed as if there was a real promise of hope for the poor—both black and white—through the Poverty Program. There were experiments, hopes, new beginnings. Then came the build-up in Vietnam and I watched the program broken and eviscerated as if it were some idle political plaything of a society gone mad on war. . . . I was increasingly compelled to see the war as an enemy of the poor and to attack it as such. . . .

We were taking the black young men who had been crippled by our society and sending them 8,000 miles away to guarantee liberties in Southeast Asia which they had not found in Southwest Georgia and East Harlem. So we have been repeatedly faced with the cruel irony of watching Negro and white boys on TV screens as they kill and die together for a nation that has been unable to seat them together in the same schools. . . .

As I have walked among the desperate, rejected and angry young men [in the ghettos of the North the last three summers] I have told them that Molotov cocktails and rifles would not solve their problems. I have tried to offer them my deepest compassion while maintaining my convictions that social change comes most meaningfully through non-violent action. But they asked—and rightly so— what about Vietnam? They asked if our own nation wasn't using massive doses of violence to solve its problems, to bring about the changes it wanted. Their questions hit home, and I knew that I would never again raise my voice against the violence of the oppressed in the ghettos without having first spoken clearly to the greatest purveyor of

His birthday now a national holiday, Martin Luther King, Jr., has become widely accepted as a heroic figure in the American past. But in the last few years of his life, King's increasingly sharp criticisms of injustice in American society disturbed many fellow citizens.

violence in the world today—my own government. . . .

[Our troops in Vietnam] must know after a short period there that none of the things we claim to be fighting for [such as freedom, justice, and peace] are really involved. Before long they must know that their government has sent them into a struggle among Vietnamese, and the more sophisticated surely realize that we are on the side of the wealthy and the secure while we create a hell for the poor. ■

"Interpreting History" features help students critically analyze source documents related to the issues discussed in each chapter. Providing students with the opportunity to "do history" on their own, these boxes encourage readers to examine primary documents in their socio-historical context to see how people — both famous and obscure — have reflected on and interpreted the historical developments of their time and their particular role in history.

"Sites to Visit" at the end of each chapter list both actual historical sites and Web sites with URLs relevant to the chapter content.

Sites to Visit

Secession Era Editorial Project
history.furman.edu/~benson/docs/
Furman University is digitizing editorials about the secession crisis and already includes scores of them on this site.

John Brown trial links
www.law.umkc/edu/faculty/projecs/ftrials/Brown.html
For information about the John Brown trial, this site provides a list of excellent links.

Abraham Lincoln and Slavery
odur.let.nl/~usa/H/1990/ch5_p6.html
This site discusses Lincoln's views and actions concerning slavery, especially the Lincoln–Douglas debate.

The Compromise of 1850 and the Fugitive Slave Act
www.pbs.org/wgbh/aia/part4
From the series on Africans in America, an analysis of the Compromise of 1850 and the effect of the Fugitive Slave Act on black Americans.

The 1850s: An Increasingly Divided Union
nac.gmu/mmts/50proto.html
A tutorial skill development site of the Multi-Media Thinking Skills project that focuses on events in the 1850s leading to the Civil War.

Words and Deeds in American History
leweb2.loc.gov/ammem/mcchtml/corhome.html
A Library of Congress site containing links to Frederick Douglass; the Compromise of 1850; speeches by John C. Calhoun, Daniel Webster, and Henry Clay; and other topics from the Civil War era.

Harriet Beecher Stowe and Uncle Tom's Cabin
xroads.virginia.edu/~HYPER/STOWE/stowe.html
This site provides both text and descriptions of Stowe's important books and information about the author's life.

For Further Reading

General Works

Foner, Eric. *Free Labor, Free Soil, Free Men: The Ideology of the Republican Party Before the Civil War.* 1970.
Freehling, William W. *The Road to Disunion.* 1990.
Hine, Robert V. and John Mack Faragher. *The American West: A New Interpretive History.* 2000.
Horton, James Oliver and Lois E. Horton. *In Hope of Liberty: Culture, Community and Protest Among Northern Free Blacks, 1700–1860.* 1997.
Isenberg, Nancy. *Sex and Citizenship in Antebellum America.* 1998.

Regional Economies and Conflicts

Montejano, David. *Anglos and Mexicans in the Making of Texas, 1836–1986.* 1987.

Shifting Collective Identities

Almaguer, Tomás. *Racial Faultlines: The Historical Origins of White Supremacy in California.* 1994.
Anderson, Bonnie S. *Joyous Greetings: The First International Women's Movement, 1830–1860.* 2000.
Blewett, Mary H. *Men, Women, and Work: Class, Gender, and Protest in the New England Shoe Industry, 1780–1910.* 1988.
Chen, Yong. *Chinese San Francisco, 1850–1943: A Trans-Pacific Community.* 2000.
Levine, Frances. *Our Prayers Are in This Place: Pecos Pueblo Identity over the Centuries.* 1999.

Supplements

For Qualified Adopters:

Instructor's Resource Manual
Yvonne Johnson, *Central Missouri State University* • Jason Tetzloff, *University of Wisconsin – Eau Claire*
0-321-10856-6
Each chapter contains a chapter outline, significant themes, learning objectives, lesson enrichment ideas, discussion suggestions, and questions for discussing the primary source document in the text.

Test Bank
D. Niler Pyeatt, *Wayland Baptist University*
0-321-10840-X
This supplement contains over 1200 multiple-choice, true/false, and essay questions. Multiple-choice and true-false questions are referenced by topic and text page number.

TestGen EQ Computerized Testing System
0-321-10736-5
This flexible, easy-to-master computerized test bank on a dual-platform CD includes all of the items in the printed test bank and allows instructors to select specific questions, edit existing questions and add their own items to create exams. Tests can be printed in several different fonts and formats and can include figures, such as graphs and tables.

Companion Website for Created Equal
Download the Instructor's Manual, maps and figures from the book, and the *Created Equal* PowerPoint™ Presentations
Website address: http://www.ablongman.com/jonescreatedequal

CourseCompass
www.ablongman.com/coursecompass
Combines the strength of the content from *Created Equal* with state-of-the-art eLearning tools. CourseCompass is an easy-to-use online course management system that allows professors to tailor content and functionality to meet individual course needs. Every CourseCompass course includes a range of pre-loaded content — all designed to help students master core course objectives. Organized by era, CourseCompass allows you to access maps, map exercises, and primary sources from several of our best-selling supplements. The course can also be quickly and easily customized to include the test questions from the printed test bank, interactive quizzes from the companion website, or other book specific resources.

BlackBoard and WebCT
The American history course in CourseCompass is also available in BlackBoard and WebCT.

Visual Aids:

Comprehensive American History Transparency Set
0-673-97211-9
This collection includes more than 200 four-color American history map transparencies on subjects ranging from the first Native Americans to the end of the Cold War, covering wars, social trends, elections, immigration, and demographics.

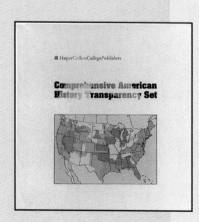

Discovering American History Through Maps and Views Transparency Set
0-673-53766-8
Created by Gerald Danzer, the recipient of AHA's James Harvey Robinson Prize for his work in using maps — including primary source maps — to teach American history, this set of 140 four-color acetates is a unique instructional tool. The collection includes cartographic and pictorial maps, views and photos, urban plans, building diagrams, and works of art.

Text-specific Transparency Set
0-321-10855-8
A set of four-color transparency acetates showing maps, graphs, and charts from the text selected to complement our other general American history transparencies sets.

For Students:

Multimedia Edition CD-ROM
0-321-11246-6

This electronic version of *Created Equal* contains the entire text with hundreds of images, maps, interactive maps, and audio/video clips integrated throughout. Electronic versions of the Study Guide and numerous supplementary books as well as links to interactive review quizzes for each chapter are also included. *Free when bundled.*

Study Guide
William Pelz, *Elgin Community College*
Volume I: 0-321-10838-8; Volume 2: 0-321-10839-6

This two-volume supplement for students contains activities and study aids for every chapter in the text. Each chapter includes a thorough summary; learning objectives; identification, completion, multiple-choice, and thought questions; and critical thinking questions based on primary source documents included in the text.

Companion Website for Created Equal

Popular features of the Website include interactive practice tests, summaries, flash cards, and web links for every chapter of the book. The site also includes a comprehensive glossary and an online appendix.
Website address: http://www.ablongman.com/jonescreatedequal

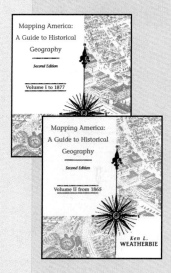

Mapping American History
Gerald A. Danzer
0-673-53768-4

A workbook created for use in conjunction with *Discovering American History Through Maps and Views* and designed to teach students to interpret and analyze cartographic materials as historical documents. *Free when bundled.*

Mapping America: A Guide to Historical Geography, 2/e
Ken L. Weatherbie, *Del Mar College*
Volume I: 0-321-00487-6; Volume II: 0-321-00488-4

A two-volume workbook that presents the basic geography of the United States and helps students place the history of the United States into spatial perspective.
Free when bundled.

Longman American History Atlas
0-321-00486-8

A four-color reference tool and visual guide to American history that includes almost 100 maps and covers the full scope of history. Atlas overhead transparencies available to adopters.
$3.00 when bundled.

iSearch Guide for History (with ContentSelect)
0-321-14282-9

The most practical, indispensible guide to the Internet available. This guide book contains exercises and tips specific to using the Internet for the study of history. It also includes access to the History ContentSelect Research Database. The database is a customized, searchable collection of 25,000+ discipline-specific articles from top-tier academic publications and journals. *Free when bundled.*

America Through the Eyes of Its People
0-673-97738-2

A comprehensive anthology that makes primary sources widely available in an inexpensive format, balancing social and political history and providing up-to-date narrative material.
Free when bundled.

The partnership between Penguin-Putnam USA and Longman Publishers offers your students a discount on the titles below when you bundle them with any Longman survey.

Available titles

Horatio Alger, *Ragged Dick & Struggling Upward*

Louis Auchincloss, *Woodrow Wilson*

Edward Bellamy, *Looking Backward*

Willa Cather, *O Pioneers!*

Alexis De Tocqueville, *Democracy in America*

Frederick Douglass, *Narrative of the Life of Frederick Douglass*

Gordon Hutner, *Immigrant Voices*

Martin Luther King, Jr., *Why We Can't Wait*

L. Jesse Lemisch (Editor), *Benjamin Franklin: The Autobiography & Other Writings*

Sinclair Lewis, *Babbitt*

Wendy Martin (Editor), *Colonial American Travel Narratives*

Tony Morrison, *Beloved*

Thomas Paine, *Common Sense*

Clinton Rossiter (Editor), *The Federalist Papers*

Upton Sinclair, *The Jungle*

Harriet Beecher Stowe, *Uncle Tom's Cabin*

Mark Twain, *Adventures of Huckleberry Finn*

U.S. History Readers

Historical Viewpoints, 9/e

John A. Garraty

Volume One — ISBN 0-321-10299-1
Volume Two — ISBN 0-321-10211-8

This collection of secondary source readings features articles adapted from the popular magazine *American Heritage.* Accessible, interesting, and significant, *Historical Viewpoints,* introduces students to a broad spectrum of historical issues and opinions from many of the world's foremost historians.

The Social Fabric, 9/e

Thomas L. Hartshorne
Robert A. Wheeler
John H. Cary
Julius Weinberg

Volume One — ISBN 0-321-10139-1
Volume Two — ISBN 0-321-10140-5

An engaging collection of secondary sources oriented to social history, this reader leads students to consider the role of women, ethnic groups, and laboring Americans in the weaving of the nation's social fabric.

Retracing the Past, 5/e

Gary B. Nash
Ronald Schultz

Volume One — ISBN 0-321-10137-5
Volume Two — ISBN 0-321-10138-3

This anthology of readings — both secondary and primary ("Past Traces") — describes the lives of ordinary Americans and examines the diversity of the American people, from the earliest settlement of America to the present day.

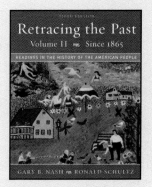

U.S. History Readers continued

Women and the National Experience, 2/e

Ellen Skinner, *Pace University*

ISBN 0-321-00555-4

This brief, affordable primary source reader contains over one hundred different sources that describe the history of women in the United States. Combining classic and unusual sources, this anthology explores the private voices and public lives of women throughout U.S. history.

20th Century U.S. Foreign Policy

Gary A. Donaldson, *Xavier University*

ISBN 0-321-10506-0

With full-length primary source documents, including several contemporary opposing viewpoints, this collection is intended as a supplement to a U.S. Foreign Policy course that covers the 20th Century.

American History in a Box

Julie Roy Jeffrey, *Goucher College*
Peter J. Frederick, *Wabash College*

Volume One — ©2002 • Boxed Set • 12 folders • ISBN 0-321-03005-2
Volume Two — ©2002 • Boxed Set • 13 folders • ISBN 0-321-03006-0

American History in a Box takes your students on a fascinating journey through our nation's past. Containing a wealth of facsimiles of original documents – poems, photographs, speeches, cartoons, advertisements, sheet music, letters, and much more – these two volumes allow your students to learn first-hand what history is and what historians actually do.

CREATED EQUAL

CREATED EQUAL

A SOCIAL AND POLITICAL HISTORY OF THE UNITED STATES

VOLUME II ▪ FROM 1865

Jacqueline Jones
Brandeis University

Peter H. Wood
Duke University

Elaine Tyler May
University of Minnesota

Thomas Borstelmann
Cornell University

Vicki L. Ruiz
University of California, Irvine

Longman

New York San Francisco Boston
London Toronto Sydney Tokyo Singapore Madrid
Mexico City Munich Paris Cape Town Hong Kong Montreal

To our own teachers, who helped set us on the historian's path, and to our students, who help keep us there. You have touched our intellects, our hearts, and our lives.

A nuestros propios maestros, quienes nos ayudaron a seguir en el sendero de historiador, y a nuestros estudiantes que ayudan a mantenernos alli. Usted ha tocado nuestros intelectos, nuestros corazones, y nuestras vidas.

Vice President and Publisher: Priscilla McGeehon
Acquisitions Editor: Ashley Dodge
Director of Development: Lisa Pinto
Development Manager: Betty Slack
Executive Marketing Manager: Sue Westmoreland
Media Editor: Patrick McCarthy
Supplements Editor: Kristi Olson
Director of Market Research: Laura Coaty
Production Manager: Ellen MacElree
Project Coordination, Electronic Page Makeup, and Cartography: Electronic Publishing Services Inc., NYC
Interior Design: Pearson Education Development
Cover Designer/Manager: Wendy Ann Fredericks
Photo Researcher: Photosearch, Inc.
Manufacturing Buyer: Lucy Hebard
Printer and Binder: Webcrafters
Cover Printer: Phoenix Color Corps.
Cover/Frontispiece Photo: Women rivet heaters and passers on ship construction work in the Navy Yard at Puget Sound, Seattle, Washington, 1919 © Hulton/Archive

Credits for literary selections, selected maps and figures, and timeline photos appear on pages C-1–C-2.

Library of Congress Cataloging-in-Publication Data
Created equal : a social and political history of the United States / Jacqueline Jones ... [et al.].
    p. cm.
  Includes bibliographical references and index.
  ISBN 0-321-0-5296-X
  1. United States—History. 2. United States—Social conditions. 3. United States—Politics and government. 4. Pluralism (Social sciences)—United States—History. 5. Minorities—United States—History. 6. Pluralism (Social sciences)—United States—History—Sources. 7. Minorities—United States—History—Sources. I. Jones, Jacqueline, 1948–
E178 .C86 2003
973—dc21
                                  2002069476

Please visit our website at www.ablongman.com

ISBN: 0-321-05296-X (Complete Edition)
ISBN: 0-321-05298-6 (Volume I)
ISBN: 0-321-05300-1 (Volume II)

1 2 3 4 5 6 7 8 9 10—WC—05 04 03 02

Brief Contents

Detailed Contents

List of Maps

List of Figures and Tables

Figures

Tables

List of Features

Connecting History

Interpreting History

Preface

> *"We hold these truths to be self-evident: That all men are created equal; that they are endowed by their Creator with certain unalienable rights; that among these are life, liberty, and the pursuit of happiness. . . . "*

Ever since the Continental Congress approved the Declaration of Independence on July 4, 1776, the noble sentiments expressed in the document have inspired people in the United States and around the world. The Founding Fathers conceived of the new nation in what we today would consider narrow terms—as a political community of white men of property. Gradually, as the generations unfolded, diverse racial and ethnic groups, as well as women of all backgrounds, cited the Declaration in their struggle to achieve a more inclusive definition of American citizenship. American history is the story of various groups of men and women, all "created equal" in their common humanity, claiming an American identity for themselves.

In fact American history consists of many stories—the story of territorial growth and expansion, the story of the rise of the middle class, the story of technological innovation and economic development, and the story of U.S. engagement with the wider world. *Created Equal* incorporates these traditional narratives into a new and fresh interpretation of American history, one that includes the stories of diverse groups of people and explores expanding notions of American identity.

The book's basic framework focuses on the political events and economic structures discussed in most American history textbooks. *Created Equal* aims not to overturn the familiar chronology of American history, but to incorporate into it a variety of groups and individuals whose stories help us to provide an accurate, comprehensive, and compelling view of the past.

Four Themes

We have chosen to highlight four significant themes that run throughout American history.

- **Diversity.** In considering the theme of diversity, we acknowledge that the formation of social identity is a central element of the American story. We examine how individual Americans have understood and identified themselves by gender, religion, region, income, race, and ethnicity, among other factors. Native Americans, African Americans, Spanish-speaking inhabitants of the Southwest, Chinese immigrants, members of the laboring classes, women of all groups—all of these people have played a major role in defining what it means to be an American. At the same time, diverse forms of identity are by no means fixed or static. For example, in the early twentieth century, a Russian immigrant garment worker on New York's Lower East Side might think of herself in any number of ways—as a Jew, an employee, a union member, a single woman, a resident of a thriving city—and these forms of identity might change over time, depending on the woman's circumstances.

- **Class and systems of power.** These have also shaped American society in profound ways and an understanding of them is fundamental to understanding events in American history. Those systems take many forms. The institution of slavery denied people of African descent basic human freedoms. Class differences based on income and formal education mocked broader ideals of social equality. Some groups used the law to deny other groups the right to participate in the political system. Popular ideas related to alleged social differences and innate inferiority served to justify the treatment of certain groups as second-class citizens. U.S. military leaders launched military campaigns against vulnerable peoples within and outside the nation's borders. By the end of the nineteenth century, the United States boasted the largest and most comfortable middle class in the world—and yet the most substantial political and economic power was distributed among a relatively small contingent of white men. During the twentieth century, Americans dismantled the legal system of inequality that reduced blacks, women, and other groups to second-class citizenship. Nevertheless, a growing gap between the rich and poor continued to mock the notion of true equality.

- **Environment.** The role of the environment in American history has been significant. The physical landscape has profoundly shaped American society, and has in turn been shaped by it. The theme of the environment is key to understanding cultural, political, and economic developments. Many Native American groups shared a sense of oneness with the land; for them, the material and spiritual worlds were intimately related. In contrast, many European Americans saw the land as a means of making a living or making money, or as the source of valuable raw materials—in other words, as a thing to be bought, sold, and used. The vast richness of the American landscape has provoked violent conflict over the years, even as it has formed a key component in American wealth and power. We examine regional differences in all geographical areas—not just the eastern seaboard.

- **Globalization.** Finally, the increasing globalization of the United States' economy and society in recent decades reminds us of how deeply the country has always been engaged with the rest of the world. Since the earliest days of colonial settlement, Americans have traded goods, cultural practices, and ideas with peoples outside their borders. As an immigrant nation and the modern world's superpower, America's foreign and domestic relations have always been intertwined. After World War II, Americans' fears of Communism and the Soviet Union exerted a profound effect upon the country's politics and society. In the wake of the attacks of September 11, 2001, all Americans were forced to confront the role of the United States in the larger world, with all the opportunities and dangers that role entailed.

These four themes serve as the lenses through which we view the traditional narrative framework of American history. Readers of *Created Equal* will understand the major political developments that shaped the country's past, as well as the role of diverse groups in initiating and reacting to those developments. Chapter 13, for example, which focuses on the 1850s, includes a detailed account of the effects of the slavery crisis on Congress and the political party system, as well as a discussion of shifting group identities affecting Indians, Latinos, northern women, and enslaved and free blacks. Chapter 18, focusing on the 1890s, covers the rise of the Populist Party and stirrings of American imperialism, as well as a discussion of barriers to a U.S. workers' political party and challenges to traditional gender roles. Thus *Created Equal* builds upon the basic history that forms the foundation of most major textbooks and offers a rich and comprehensive look at the past by including the stories of all Americans, in addition.

Chronological Organization

One of the challenges in writing *Created Equal* has been to emphasize the way in which the four major themes come together and influence each other, affecting specific generations of Americans. Thus, the text is organized into ten parts, most of these covering a generation. Many textbooks organize discussions of immigrants, cities, the West, and foreign diplomacy (to name a few topics) into separate chapters that cover large time periods. In contrast, *Created Equal* integrates material related to a variety of topics within individual chapters. Although the text adheres to a chronological organization, it stresses coherent discussions of specific topics within that framework. This provides students with a richer understanding of events. Chapter 15, for example, which covers the dozen or so years after the end of the Civil

War, deals with Reconstruction in the South, Indian wars on the High Plains, and the rise of the women's and labor movements, stressing the relationships among all these developments. To cite another example: Many texts devote a chapter exclusively to America's post–World War II rise to global power; *Created Equal* integrates material related to that development in a series of six chapters that cover the period of 1945 to 2000. Each of these chapters illustrates the effects of dramatic world developments on American social relations and domestic policy on a decade-by-decade basis. This approach allows readers to appreciate the rich complexity of any particular time period and to understand that major events occur not in a vacuum, but in a larger social context.

Special Features

The book includes a number of features designed to make American history clear and engaging to the reader, and to encourage students to "do" history on their own. These features include:

- **Parts and timelines.** *Created Equal* consists of ten parts covering three chapters each. An opening section that lays out the basic themes of the period introduces each part. Each part opener also includes an illustrated timeline highlighting major events covered in the three chapters that follow.

- **Chapter introductory vignettes and conclusions.** Each chapter begins with a story that introduces the reader to groups and individuals representative of the themes developed in the chapter. Among the chapter introductory vignettes are the stories of a Norwegian immigrant woman in Wisconsin (Chapter 12), a group of runaway slaves accused of treason by Confederate authorities in wartime (Chapter 14), Spanish-speaking inhabitants of Northern New Mexico struggling to retain their culture in the face of an onslaught of European American settlers (Chapter 17), and a Sioux Indian boy at a government boarding school (Chapter 18). At the end of each chapter, a concluding section sums up the chapter's themes and points the reader toward the next chapter.

- **"Connecting History."** *Created Equal* encourages students to think outside the boundaries of specific periods by including in each chapter a boxed feature called "Connecting History." A topic is examined at two different periods, or as it evolved over time. Several of these mini-essays span the entire sweep of American history. Topics include the history of naval navigation, civil liberties, education, advertising, the Ku Klux Klan, and the Internet.

- **"Interpreting History."** This feature consists of a primary document on a topic relevant to the chapter's themes. Through this feature we hear the voices of a variety of Americans—a seventeenth-century slave, a sail maker in post-Revolutionary New York City, a Mexican lawyer visiting New Mexico in the early nineteenth century, a group of Cherokee women in early nineteenth-century Georgia, an antebellum southern professor, industrial titan Andrew Carnegie, and the environmental activist Rachel Carson. The "Interpreting History" feature takes many different forms—letters, sermons, court decisions, labor contracts, Congressional hearings, and songs. Students thus have an opportunity to analyze primary documents and to better appreciate the historian's task—to read materials critically and to place them in their larger sociohistorical context.

- **Maps, charts, pullout quotes, and artifacts.** Illustrations—photographs, tables, pictures of objects from the time period, and figures—enhance the narrative. Large maps offer greater geographical detail and invite students to see the relationship between geography and history. Highlighted quotes help the reader grasp the chapter's major themes.

- **"Sites to Visit" and "For Further Reading."** At the end of each chapter is a list of "Sites to Visit," identifying sites on the World Wide Web relevant to the chapter and occasionally listing the location of important historical sites and landmarks as well. There is also a list of suggested works related to each section of the chapter. These features encourage students to follow up on major topics on their own—either on the computer or in the library.

Created Equal introduces students to recent scholarship in social history as well as providing a firm grounding in the traditional political narrative. In recent decades social identity has emerged as a central theme of American history. However, exclusive attention to cultural and social diversity can overshadow the political and economic structures of American society. Students should gain an understanding of our nation's social diversity but also learn about the power relations that have shaped that past—which groups have had influence and how they have maintained and wielded that influence. Placing these issues at the forefront, *Created Equal* tells the dramatic, evolving story of America in all its complexity—a story of a diverse people "created equal" yet struggling to achieve equality.

The Authors

Meet the Authors

Jacqueline Jones was born in Christiana, Delaware, a small town of 400 people in the northern part of the state. The local public school was desegregated in 1955, when she was a third grader. That event, combined with the peculiar social etiquette of relations between blacks and whites in the town, sparked her interest in American history. She attended the University of Delaware in nearby Newark and went on to graduate school at the University of Wisconsin, Madison, where she received her Ph.D. in history. Her scholarly interests have evolved over time, focusing on American labor, and women's, African American, and southern history.

One of her biggest challenges has been to balance her responsibilities as teacher, historian, wife, and mother (of two daughters). One of her proudest achievements is the fact that she has been able to teach full-time and still pick up her daughters at school every day at 2:30 in the afternoon (thanks to a flexible professor's schedule). She is the author of several books, including *Soldiers of Light and Love: Northern Teachers and Georgia Blacks* (1980); *Labor of Love, Labor of Sorrow: Black Women, Work, and Family Since Slavery* (1985), which won the Bancroft Prize and was a finalist for a Pulitzer Prize; *The Dispossessed: America's Underclasses Since the Civil War* (1992); and *American Work: Four Centuries of Black and White Labor* (1998). In 2001, she completed a memoir that recounts her childhood in Christiana: *Creek Walking: Growing Up in Delaware in the 1950s.*

She teaches American history at Brandeis University, where she is Harry S. Truman Professor. In 1999, she received a MacArthur Fellowship.

Peter H. Wood was born in St. Louis (before the famous arch was built). He recalls seeing Jackie Robinson play against the Cardinals, visiting the courthouse where the Dred Scott case originated, and traveling up the Mississippi to Hannibal, birthplace of Mark Twain. Summer work on the northern Great Lakes aroused his interest in Native American cultures, past and present. He studied at Harvard (B.A., 1964; Ph.D., 1972) and at Oxford, where he was a Rhodes Scholar (1964–1966). His pioneering book, *Black Majority* (1974), concerning slavery in colonial South Carolina, won the Beveridge Prize of the American Historical Association. Since 1975, he has taught early American history at Duke University, where he also coached the women's lacrosse club for three years. The topics of his articles range from the French explorer LaSalle to Gerald Ford's pardon of Richard Nixon. He coauthored *Winslow Homer's Images of Blacks,* and he has written *Strange New Land,* a book about early African Americans. In 1989, he coedited *Powhatan's Mantle: Indians in the Colonial Southeast.* His demographic essay in that volume provided the first clear picture of population change in the eighteenth-century South. Dr. Wood has served on the boards of the Highlander Center, Harvard University, Houston's Rothko Chapel, the Menil Foundation, and the Institute of Early American History and Culture in Williamsburg. He is married to colonial historian Elizabeth Fenn; his varied interests include archaeology, documentary film, and growing gourds. He keeps a baseball bat used by Ted Williams beside his desk.

Thomas Borstelmann, the son of a university psychologist, has taught at the elementary, high school, and college levels. He taught second-grade physical education, taught and coached high school lacrosse, soccer, and basketball, and since 1991 has taught American history at Cornell University. In addition to his teaching experience, he also served as "Head Maid" of a conference center near Lake Tahoe. He lives with his wife and two sons in Syracuse, New York, where his greatest challenge—and delight—is doing the bulk of childcare while commuting 60 miles to Cornell. An avid bicyclist, runner, and cross-country skier, he earned his B.A. from Stanford University in 1980 and Ph.D. from Duke University in 1990.

He became a historian to figure out the Cold War and American race relations, in part because he had grown up in the South. His first book, concerning American relations with southern Africa in the mid-twentieth century, won the Stuart L. Bernath Book Prize of the Society for Historians of Foreign Relations. His second book, *The Cold War and the Color Line*, appeared in 2002. His commitment to the classroom remains clear at Cornell University, where he has won a major teaching award: the Robert and Helen Appel Fellowship. He found writing *Created Equal* a natural complement to what he does in the classroom, trying to provide both telling details of the American past and the broad picture of how the United States has developed as it has. A specialist in U.S. foreign relations, he is equally fascinated with domestic politics and social change. He is currently working on a book about the 1970s.

Elaine Tyler May grew up in the shadow of Hollywood, performing in neighborhood circuses with her friends. She went to high school before girls could play on sports teams, so she spent her after-school hours as a cheerleader and her summer days as a bodysurfing beach bum. Her passion for American history developed in college when she spent her junior year in Japan. The year was 1968. The Vietnam War was raging, along with turmoil at home. As an American in Asia, often called on to explain her nation's actions, she yearned for a deeper understanding of America's past and its place in the world. She returned home to study history at UCLA, where she earned her B.A., M.A., and Ph.D. She has taught at Princeton and Harvard Universities and since 1978 at the University of Minnesota. She has written four books examining the relationship between politics, public policy, and private life. Her widely acclaimed *Homeward Bound: American Families in the Cold War Era* was the first study to link the baby boom and suburbia to the politics of the Cold War. The *Chronicle of Higher Education* featured *Barren in the Promised Land: Childless Americans and the Pursuit of Happiness* as a pioneering study of the history of reproduction. *Lingua Franca* named her coedited volume *Here, There, and Everywhere: The Foreign Politics of American Popular Culture* a "Breakthrough Book." She served as president of the American Studies Association in 1996 and as Distinguished Fulbright Professor of American History in Dublin, Ireland, in 1997. She is married to historian Lary May and has three children who have inherited their parents' passion for history.

Vicki L. Ruiz is a professor of history and Chicano/Latino studies at the University of California, Irvine. For her, history remains a grand adventure, one that she began at the kitchen table listening to the stories of her mother and grandmother and continued with the help of the local bookmobile. She read constantly as she sat on the dock catching small fish ("grunts") to be used as bait on her father's fishing boat. As she grew older, she was promoted to working with her mother selling tickets for the *Blue Sea II*. The first in her family to receive an advanced degree, she graduated from Gulf Coast Community College and Florida State University, then went on to earn a Ph.D. in history at Stanford in 1982, the fourth Mexican American woman to receive a doctorate in history. Her first book, *Cannery Women, Cannery Lives*, received an award from the National Women's Political Caucus, and her second, *From Out of the Shadows: Mexican Women in 20th-Century America*, was named a *Choice* Outstanding Academic Book of 1998 by the American Library Association. She is coeditor with Ellen Carol Dubois of *Unequal Sisters: A Multicultural Reader in U.S. Women's History*. She and Virginia Sánchez Korrol coedit *Latinas in the United States: A Historical Encyclopedia*, and both were recognized by *Latina Magazine* as Latinas of the Year in Education for 2000. Active in student mentorship projects, summer institutes for teachers, and public humanities programs, Dr. Ruiz served as an appointee to the National Council of the Humanities. She has also served on the national governing bodies of the American Historical Association, the Organization of American Histories, and the American Studies Association. The mother of two grown sons, she is married to Victor Becerra, urban planner and gourmet cook extraordinaire.

A Conversation with the Authors

> Created Equal *tells stories across generations, regions, and cultures, integrating the lives of individuals within the economic, political, cultural, global, and environmental vectors shaping their lives. These tales of simple courage breathe life into history, bringing an immediacy and vibrancy to the past. We cherish the telling of stories for it is within these tales that we remember the* ánimo y sueños *(spirit and dreams) of the American people.*
>
> VICKI RUIZ

How Did This Project Begin?

PETER: It started with a videocassette. The Longman history editor taped a lively conversation with a dozen exceptional history teachers from very different backgrounds. They were all energized about teaching U.S. history in new ways, but they felt frustrated by their current texts. Then Longman sent the video to me. The video was not great cinematography, just talking heads. But their voices were so articulate, and I shared so many of their concerns. I remember watching the cassette on a Sunday night, and it set my mind spinning. I couldn't get much sleep. Here were real teachers like me who wanted a dramatically different text. And here was a major publisher, Longman, saying, "What do you think?"

At the time, I was teaching one of those special classes, a group of history majors that really clicked. Four of the best students had parents from other countries—South Africa, Mexico, Haiti, Vietnam—and all four were fascinated by American history. I remember thinking, "I'd love to be part of a team of historians who developed a text that would excite Darlene Aquino from Texas and Minh-Thu Pham from North Carolina." I called Longman and said, "Let's find a way to do it."

How Did You Come to the Decision to Write This Book?

JACKIE: I thought that writing a new kind of text would be a real intellectual challenge. We have the opportunity to rethink and reconfigure the traditional American history narrative, and that's exciting.

PETER: I was not eager to write a "feel good" text. American history has not been a big happy rainbow. I was convinced that we could be much more open and inclusive than most current texts. We could also be more direct and matter-of-fact in many areas. It is important to be frank about differences and contradictions in the American story in a way that actually helps explain things.

THOMAS: Writing a textbook was attractive because it's so complementary to what I do in the classroom, particularly teaching the introductory American history survey. Having the chance to try to tell the entire story of the American past was exciting as a balance to the other work we do.

How Did the Author Team Come Together, Work Together?

PETER: The Longman videotape circulated. Eventually, we had a team of people who felt that they could answer, collectively, the challenge presented by those articulate teachers. Obviously, no one could do it alone, but the right combination might be able to pull it off.

Having watched the Duke basketball team for two decades, I know what five very different people can do if they pay attention to each other, and if they all have the same goal in mind. An author team is like a basketball team: The players have to complement one another. (Sometimes we *compliment* each other, too!) And each person gets better and contributes more through practice and hard work. This team works hard.

VICKI: I joined the *Created Equal* team out of the profound respect I have for the scholarship of my colleagues. I had met Elaine and Jackie previously at conferences and knew Peter and Thomas only from their scholarship. The first brainstorming meeting I attended in New York City was intellectual magic, pure and simple. From the first hour onward, we exchanged our separate visions and expectations, debated periodization and conceptual frames, and began the process of intellectual coalescence that marks this truly collaborative enterprise. I left New York exhilarated and exhausted.

> *I joined the* Created Equal *team out of the profound respect I have for the scholarship of my colleagues.*
> *VICKI RUIZ*

ELAINE: I joined this project because I was excited about the challenge of writing a textbook that would convey the drama and excitement of the nation's history. It offered an opportunity to work with a team of scholars who I have long admired, and it has been a joy and a privilege to collaborate with them. We have become a close group of friends and colleagues, and our text reflects the lively exchanges, debates, and brainstorming sessions we've had over email, phone calls, and gatherings when we have come together to work on the project.

Tell Us About the Title—*Created Equal.*

JACKIE: The title reflects our commitment to be inclusive in our coverage of different groups and the part they played in shaping American history. Of course, we are invoking the Declaration of Independence: "We hold these truths to be self-evident, that all men are created equal." That document, and those words, have inspired countless individuals, groups, and nations around the world.

PETER: We all recognize the phrase, "created equal" from the Declaration of Independence, but we rarely ponder it. For me, it represents an affirmation of humanity, the family of mankind. But it also raises the deepest American theme—the endless struggles over defining whose equality will be recognized. I suppose you could say that there is equality in birth and death, but a great deal of inequality in between.

Many of those inequities—and their partial removal—drive the story of American History. Thomas Paine understood this in 1776 when he published *Common Sense.* Months before the Declaration of Independence appeared, Paine put it this way: "Mankind being originally equal in the order of creation, the equality could only be destroyed by some subsequent circumstance."

How and Why Did You Choose the Themes that Structure the Text?

THOMAS: The themes that we chose to highlight in *Created Equal* reflect what we see as the current and future state of the field of U.S. history, as well as the needs of future generations of students.

The prominence of multiculturalism in recent decades made clear that identity remains a central piece of the American story: how individual Americans understand and identify themselves (by religion, class, region, sex, race, ethnicity, etc.). But too much attention to cultural issues has often led to a discounting of the political and economic structure of American society: Who has material wealth and power, and how they use it, is fundamental for determining the course of the past and present. The increasing globalization of the U.S. economy and American society (e.g., through rising immigration) in recent decades has reminded us of how deeply the United States has always been engaged with the rest of the world—as an immigrant nation and the modern world's superpower, America's foreign and domestic affairs have always been intertwined. And the deepening awareness in recent decades of the fragility of the earth's environment has stimulated a whole subfield of American environmental history, which we try to tap into—in a sense, the environment represents the clearest example of the interconnectedness of American and international history.

JACKIE: It was time to integrate recent scholarship related to the many different groups that have been part of the American story, and to open up that story to include all geographical areas (and not just the eastern seaboard). The theme of the environment is key to understanding American history; we explore the ways American cultural, political, and economic developments influence and are shaped by the nation's natural resources and landscape. The theme of power relations helps students to understand that differences of class, and differences in political and material resources, are significant aspects of the country's history. We balance this perspective by showing how America emerged as a uniquely open and middle-class nation—one that has attracted immigrants from all over the world throughout its history.

> Created Equal *brings together aspects of the nation's story that are usually examined separately.*
> ELAINE TYLER MAY

ELAINE: *Created Equal* brings together aspects of the nation's story that are usually examined separately. It demonstrates that the people who make change are not only those in major positions of power—they are also ordinary Americans from all backgrounds. We illuminate ways that ordinary Americans have seized opportunities to improve their lives and their nation. In *Created Equal*, the land itself is a major player in the story—the environment, the different regions, and the ways in which people, businesses, public policies, and the forces of nature have shaped it. We also address the ongoing interaction between the United States and the rest of the world, examining the nation in a truly global context.

How Is the Book Organized?

PETER: History is the study of change over time, so chronology becomes extremely important. We wanted to emphasize central themes, but we wanted to explore and explain how they related to one another at any given moment. So we made a conscious decision to be more chronological than many recent texts in our presentation. It makes for less confusion, less jumping back and forth in time, than when broad themes are played out separately. After all, this is the way we lead our own lives—sequentially.

JACKIE: Most of the 10 separate parts in the book each cover about a generation. The parts give students a sense of the big picture over a longer period—the way our themes fit together and the impact of major developments on a particular generation of Americans. The chronological organization of the book forces us to understand the "wholeness" of any particular period—to consider links among political, social, economic, and cultural developments. By maintaining a strictly chronological focus, we hope to show students how the events and developments of any one period are intertwined with each other. For example, for coverage of the period after the end of the Civil War, it is important to show links between the Indian wars in the West and the process of Reconstruction in the South. In most texts, those regional perspectives are separated into different chapters, but, in *Created Equal*, these connections are presented together in Chapter 15.

Each of the Chapters Has Two Feature Essays: "Interpreting History" and "Connecting History." What are the Benefits of These Features?

JACKIE: The "Interpreting History" feature provides students with an opportunity to "do history" on their own. These are brief primary documents related to the issues presented in a particular chapter. We have chosen documents that are particularly rich in terms of providing material for discussion and analysis. By working with this material, students will learn how to balance the close reading of a text with an understanding of the larger historical context of the document.

The "Connecting History" feature follows a particular subject backward and forward in time, suggesting ways that a topic discussed in a particular chapter has evolved through American history. These mini-essays encourage students to consider change over long periods of time.

What Did You Enjoy Most About Writing this Text?

JACKIE: The intellectual stimulation and the opportunity to work with a wonderful group of people.

PETER: Three things. My teammates and their different energies, for sure. Also, the staff at Longman. I had never worked on a big collective effort like this, and I still marvel at the intricacies and coordination of the whole operation.

But most of all, writing this text has reinforced my sense of the intense relevance of history. We were hard at work when the World Trade Center attack occurred. Suddenly our entire society was on a new footing. A culture oriented to the present and the future had to re-examine the past, both locally and globally, recent and distant. In reconnecting to our history in new ways—examining it openly and fearlessly and critically—we find a story that is more relevant than most of us imagined. It is complex, dramatic, sobering, and uplifting all at once . . . like life itself.

> *Writing this text has reinforced my sense of the intense relevance of history.*
>
> PETER WOOD

THOMAS: It's been a pleasure to work as a team. When I first joined the project in its early phases, I was lured by the prospect of working with Peter—and then I got that much more excited as the rest of the team was filled in. I've been deeply impressed by how well we communicate, especially the combination of serious intellectual challenges to each other and our great personal support for each other. I simply learn a lot every time we communicate, and I'm grateful for the friendships that have emerged out of our joint endeavor.

What Do You Hope Students Will Get Out of the Book?

PETER: I want readers to connect. As a child, you connect to your family, your neighbors, your schoolmates. As you get older, that circle expands; you begin to relate to people in other places and other times. In a good history class, or a strong history book, that relationship becomes close. You start to care about, argue with, and connect to the persons you are studying. Pretty soon, their tough choices and surprising experiences in life start to resemble our own in ways we never expected, even though their worlds are dramatically different from ours.

JACKIE: By presenting an inclusive view of the past, we give students a more accurate account of American history. Many texts only pay lip service to diversity. Non-elite groups are tacked on, marginalized, or segregated from the "real" story of America. In contrast, we believe that the history of all groups constitutes the real story of America.

Acknowledgments

As authors, we could not have completed this project without the loving support of our families. We wish to thank Jeffrey Abramson, Lil Fenn, Lynn Borstelmann, Lary May, and Victor Becerra for their interest, forbearance, and encouragement over the course of many drafts. Our children, now ranging in age from 6 to 32, have been a source of inspiration, as have our many students, past and present. We are grateful to scores of colleagues and friends who have helped shape this book, both directly and indirectly, in more ways than they know.

Special thanks are due to Pam Gordon for pulling this team together and launching the project, to Dan Usner and Jay O'Callaghan for their useful involvement in the early stages, and to Steve Fraser for his insightful midcourse corrections, which came at a crucial time in the process. Along the way, Matt Basso, Chad Cover, Eben Miller, Andrea Sachs, Mary Strunk, and Melissa Williams provided useful research and administrative assistance; their help was invaluable. Louis Balizet provided careful reading of several chapter drafts. Thanks to Deborah Anderson for a stellar job in locating images, and to Jennifer Mazurkie for all her terrific work in overseeing the layout.

Our friends at Longman have shown their belief in this project from the beginning. They supported an invaluable two-day retreat at Truro, on Cape Cod, and they worked hard to smooth out numerous bumps along this long road. We thank all the creative people at Longman (and there are many) who have had a hand in bringing this book to life. We are especially grateful to Priscilla McGeehon, Lisa Pinto, Betty Slack, and Sue Westmoreland for their enthusiastic devotion to this project and their expertise and friendship from start to finish. Ashley Dodge, joining the Longman team recently, has embraced *Created Equal* and given it her full and timely support.

From the beginning, we knew that we wanted a unique and distinctive look for this book. For their comments and feedback on sample design material, we thank the following reviewers:

Scott Barton
East Central University

Keith Pacholl
California State University–Fullerton

Rachel Standish
Foothill College

Constance M. McGovern
Frostburg State University

Robert E. Rook
Fort Hays State University

Michael M. Topp
University of Texas–El Paso

Finally, we wish to express our deep gratitude to the following people who read and commented on the manuscript as it went through its several drafts. Collectively they pushed us hard with their high standards, tough questions, and shrewd advice. The thoughtful criticisms and generous suggestions from these colleagues have helped improve the book.

Ken Adderley
Upper Iowa University

Leslie Alexander
Ohio State University

John Andrew
Franklin and Marshall College

Abel Bartley
University of Akron

Donald Scott Barton
Central Carolina Technical College

Mia Bay
Rutgers University

Chris Bierwith
Treasure Valley Community College

Charles Bolton
University of Arkansas at Little Rock

Susan Burch
Gallaudet University

Tommy Bynum
Georgia Perimeter College

Robert B. Carey
Empire State College–SUNY

Todd Carney
Southern Oregon University

Kathleen Carter
Highpoint University

Jonathan Chu
University of Massachusetts

Amy E. Davis
University of California–Los Angeles

Judy DeMark
Northern Michigan University

James A. Denton
University of Colorado

Joseph A. Devine
Stephen F. Austin University

Margaret Dwight
*North Carolina Agricultural
   and Technical University*

Nancy Gabin
Purdue University

Lori Ginzberg
Pennsylvania State University

Gregory Goodwin
Bakersfield College

Amy S. Greenberg
Pennsylvania State University

Nadine Isitani Hata
El Camino College

James Hedtke
Cabrini College

Fred Hoxie
University of Illinois

Tera Hunter
Carnegie Mellon University

David Jaffe
City College of New York

Jeremy Johnson
Northwest College

Yvonne Johnson
Central Missouri State University

Kurt Keichtle
University of Wisconsin

Anne Klejment
University of St. Thomas

Dennis Kortheuer
California State University–Long Beach

Joel Kunze
Upper Iowa University

Joseph Laythe
Edinboro College of Pennsylvania

Chana Kai Lee
Indiana University

Dan Letwin
Pennsylvania State University

Gaylen Lewis
Bakersfield College

Kenneth Lipartito
Florida International University

Kyle Longley
Arizona State University

Edith L. Macdonald
University of Central Florida

Lorie Maltby
Henderson Community College

Sandra Mathews-Lamb
Nebraska Wesleyan University

Constance M. McGovern
Frostburg State University

Henry McKiven
University of South Alabama

James H. Merrell
Vassar College

Earl Mulderink
Southern Utah State University

Steven Noll
University of Florida

Jim Norris
North Dakota State University

Elsa Nystrom
Kennesaw State University

Keith Pacholl
California State University–Fullerton

William Pelz
Elgin Community College

Melanie Perrault
University of Central Arkansas

Delores D. Petersen
Foothill College

Robert Pierce
Foothill College

Louis Potts
University of Missouri–Kansas City

Sarah Purcell
Central Michigan University

Niler Pyeatt
Wayland Baptist University

Steven Reschly
Truman State University

Arthur Robinson
Santa Rosa Junior College

Robert E. Rook
Fort Hays State University

Steven Ruggles
University of Minnesota

Christine Sears
University of Delaware

Rebecca Shoemaker
Indiana State University

Howard Shore
Columbia River High School

James Sidbury
University of Texas

Arwin D. Smallwood
Bradley University

Margaret Spratt
California University of Pennsylvania

Rachel Standish
Foothill College

Jon Stauff
St. Ambrose University

David Steigerwald
Ohio State University–Marion

Kay Stockbridge
Central Carolina Technical College

Daniel Thorp
Virginia Tech University

Michael M. Topp
University of Texas–El Paso

Clifford Trafzer
University of California–Riverside

Deborah Gray White
Rutgers University

Scott Wong
Williams College

Bill Woodward
Seattle Pacific University

Nancy Zens
Central Oregon Community College

David Zonderman
North Carolina State University

CHAPTER 15

In the Wake of War: Consolidating a Triumphant Union, 1865–1877

Edward Lamson Henry, *Kept In*, 1889. Fenimore Art Museum, Cooperstown, New York (N-309.61). Photo by Richard Walker

■ The artist Edward L. Henry titled this 1888 painting *Kept In*. A pupil endures her punishment while her classmates frolic outside during recess. Former slaves of all ages eagerly embraced the opportunity to learn to read and write, and many African American communities established their own schools after the war. Some Northerners, mostly young white women, traveled south to teach the freedpeople.

I N SAVANNAH, GEORGIA, IN MID-DECEMBER 1864, AFRICAN AMERICAN MEN, WOMEN, AND children rejoiced when the troops of Union General William Tecumseh Sherman liberated the city: the day of jubilee had come at last! The city's black community immediately formed its own school system under the sponsorship of a new group, the Savannah Education Association (SEA). The association owed its creation to the desire of freedpeople of all ages to learn to read and write. A committee of nine black clergy began by hiring 15 black teachers and acquiring buildings (including the Old Bryan Slave Mart) for use as schools. By January 1, 1865, Savannah blacks had raised $800 to pay teachers' salaries, enabling several hundred black children to attend classes free of charge.

Following hard on the heels of the Union army, a group of northern white missionaries arrived in Savannah to seek black converts for two Protestant denominations, the Presbyterians and the Congregationalists. On the first day of school, in January 1865, these northern newcomers watched a grand procession of children wend its way through the streets of Savannah. The missionaries expressed amazement that the SEA was an entirely black-run organization; these whites had believed the former slaves incapable of creating such an impressive educational system.

Charleston, South Carolina, after Sherman's 1865 siege.

In March 1865, the federal government, under the auspices of the newly formed Bureau of Refugees, Freedmen, and Abandoned Lands (Freedmen's Bureau), agreed to work with missionaries in opening schools for black children throughout the former Confederate states. In Georgia, missionaries and government officials soon became alarmed that black leaders were willing to accept financial aid from them but not willing to relinquish control of SEA schools to the whites in return. The Northerners were also distressed by the militancy of certain local black leaders. One of these leaders was Aaron Bradley, who, armed with a pistol and bowie knife, was urging other black men to vote as a bloc in all elections.

In an effort to wrest control of the SEA from Savannah blacks, northern missionaries and agents of the Freedmen's Bureau decided to withhold funds from the association. By March 1866, these efforts had paid off: The city's black community, swollen by a refugee population, was no longer able to support its own schools. Northern whites took over SEA operations, and the association ceased to exist.

Postwar political interest in the South unleashed a major conflict between supporters of African American rights and supporters of southern privilege. Republican congressmen hoped to *reconstruct* the South by enabling African Americans to own their own land and to become full citizens. Southern freedpeople sought to free themselves from white employers, landlords, and clergy and to establish control over their own workplaces, families, and churches. In contrast, President Andrew Johnson appeared bent on *restoring* the antebellum

THIRD READER.   249

LESSON CXXXVIII.

church	as-sign	com-mun-ion	ar-range-ment
stretch	oys-ter	pro-ces-sion	op-por-tu-ni-ty
through	shoul-der	ex-am-ine	or-gan-i-za-tion

SCHOOLS IN SAVANNAH.

Rev. Mr. Alvord, whose picture is on this page, was in Savannah when the first colored schools were formed, and assisted in organizing the "Educational Association." We
give his description of the scene when the members were admitted to the Association.
The admission-fee was three dollars.

THE large church was full; and, as soon as opportunity was offered, the crowd came forward.
About the communion-table they pressed, stretching

Courtesy, American Antiquarian Society

■ The Boston wing of the American Tract Society, an abolitionist group, published a series of reading primers for the newly freed slaves. The primers provided moral lessons as well as reading lessons for the pupils. This page from *The Freedman's Third Reader* focuses on the work of John W. Alvord, the Freedmen's Bureau general superintendent of education. The authors suggest (wrongly) that Alvord played a major role in organizing the Savannah Education Association in Savannah, Georgia, in early 1865.

power relations that made southern black people field laborers dependent on white landowners. For their part, many southern whites were determined to prevent black people from becoming truly free. Most former rebels remained embittered about the outcome of the war and vengeful toward the freedpeople.

The Civil War hardened the positions of the two major political parties. The Republicans remained in favor of a strong national government, one that promoted economic growth. The Democrats tended to support states' efforts to manage their own affairs, which included regulating relations between employers and employees, whites and blacks.

After the war, western economic development presented new challenges for men who had fought for the Union. In order to open the West to European American miners and homesteaders, the U.S. army clashed repeatedly with Native Americans. On the Plains and in the Northwest, Indians resisted white efforts to force them to abandon their nomadic way of life and take up sedentary farming. William Tecumseh Sherman, Philip H. Sheridan, and George Custer were among the U.S. military officers who had commanded troops in the Civil War and now attempted to subdue the Plains Indians and further white settlement. Sherman declared, "We must act with vindictive earnestness against the Sioux, even to their extermination, men, women and children." The former head of the Freedmen's Bureau, General Oliver O. Howard, oversaw the expulsion of Chief Joseph and his people, the Nez Perce, from their homeland in Washington's Walla Walla Valley in 1877.

U.S. soldiers also contributed to the building of the transcontinental railroad. A former Union military officer, Grenville Dodge, served as chief civil engineer for the Union Pacific Railroad, supervising huge workforces of immigrant laborers. The railroad industry was a potent symbol of postwar U.S. nationalism. It also represented a robust, Republican-sponsored partnership between private enterprise and the federal government. Between 1862 and 1872, the government gave the industry subsidies that included millions of dollars in cash and more than 100 million acres of land. On the Plains, U.S. soldiers protected Union Pacific Railroad land surveyors against the retaliatory raids conducted by Indians who were enraged by this incursion into their territory and by the government's failure to abide by its treaties.

The Civil War, and the economic growth unleashed after the conflict, transformed the physical landscape of the nation. In the South the scars of war were everywhere, in the form of ruined crop fields, pillaged forests, and smoldering cities. Pursuing a strategy of "total war" in the final months of the war, Sherman's troops had destroyed many of the towns and farms that lay in their path on their famous march from Atlanta to Savannah and then north into South Carolina. New train trestles, wharfs, and warehouses stood as monuments to the recent efforts of both rebel and Union forces to move and supply their troops. In the West, construction of new towns and railroad tracks demanded tremendous amounts of lumber. Some observers warned of an impending timber famine, spurring interest in the conservation of natural resources of all kinds.

The Republicans' triumph prompted dissent from diverse people who feared that the victorious Union would serve the interests of specific groups such as men, employers, and white property owners. Some women's rights activists, for example, felt betrayed by the suggestion that this was "the hour of the Negro [man]." These women were not willing to wait indefinitely for their own voting rights. At the same time, in the bustling workshops of the nation's cities, many workers realized that they remained at the mercy of employers bent on using cheap labor. The founding of the National Labor Union in 1866 revealed that members of the laboring classes had a national vision of their own, one that valued the efforts of working people to earn a decent living for their families.

At great cost of human life, the Civil War decisively settled several immediate and long-standing political conflicts. The southern secessionists were defeated, and slavery as a legal institution was destroyed. Nevertheless, the relationship between federal power and group rights remained unresolved, leading to continued bloodshed between whites and Indians on the High Plains, as well as in the former Confederate states between Union supporters and diehard rebels. During the postwar period, federal government officials attempted to complete the political process that the military defeat of the South had only begun: the consolidation of the Union, North and South, East and West. This process encompassed the nation as a whole.

The Struggle over the South

The Civil War had a devastating impact on the South in physical, social, and economic terms. The region had lost an estimated $2 billion in investments in slaves; modest homesteads and grand plantations alike lay in ruins; and gardens, orchards, and cotton fields were barren. Along the seacoast and riverways, fish stocks were depleted. More than three million former slaves eagerly embraced freedom, but the vast majority lacked the land, cash, and credit necessary to build family homesteads for themselves. At the same time, landowning whites considered black people primarily as a source of agricultural labor; these whites resisted the idea that the freedpeople should be granted citizenship rights. This conflict—between blacks as family members determined to control their own lives and whites as landowners determined to reassert authority over blacks—assumed immense proportions.

In the North, Republican lawmakers disagreed among themselves how best to punish the defeated but defiant rebels. President Abraham Lincoln had indicated early that after the war the government should bring the South back into the Union quickly and painlessly. However, his successor wanted to see members of the southern planter elite humiliated, but resisted the notion that freedpeople should become independent of white landowners. In Congress, moderate and radical Republicans argued about how far the government should go in ensuring the former slaves' freedom.

Southern and northern blacks, staunch defenders of the Republican party, hoped to achieve social and economic self-determination. After the war, southern whites condemned what they called the freedpeople's "noxious liberty": their tendency to move around. In fact, all over the South, African American men and women had set out to claim what they believed was rightfully theirs. They traveled great distances, usually on foot, in efforts to locate loved ones and reunite families that had been separated during slavery. They also went to great lengths to resist attempts by white employers to bind them out as apprentices, a new form of bondage. Freed parents turned their energies toward providing for their families, cultivating food crops for their own consumption, and trying to buy land whenever possible. Just as black people had proved to be a military and political force during the war, so they became major actors in the reconstruction of the postwar South.

Wartime Preludes to Postwar Policies

The political and social complications of a northern victory became apparent long before the Confederates laid down their arms at Appomattox Courthouse. Wartime experiments with African American free labor in Union-occupied areas foreshadowed bitter postwar debates. As early as November 1861, Union forces had occupied the Sea Islands off Port Royal Sound in South Carolina. In response, wealthy cotton planters fled to the mainland. As many as 10,000 slaves stayed behind on the islands to fish and to cultivate corn for themselves.

Over the next few months, three groups of northern civilians landed on the Sea Islands with the intention of guiding blacks in the transition from slave to free labor. Teachers arrived intent on creating schools, and missionaries hoped to start churches. A third group, representing Boston investors, had also settled on the Sea Islands to assess economic opporunities; by early 1862, they decided to institute a system of wage labor that would reestablish a staple crop economy and funnel cotton directly into northern textile mills. The freed slaves gave a cautious welcome to the teachers and missionaries, but they resisted growing cotton for the wartime market. They preferred to grow crops for their families to eat rather than cotton to sell, relying on a system of barter and trade among networks of extended families. Their goal was to break free of white landlords, suppliers, and cotton merchants.

Not all Union military men relished the prospect of forcing blacks to work on the plantations where they had been enslaved.

Meanwhile, in southern Louisiana, the Union capture of New Orleans in the spring of 1862 enabled northern military officials to implement their own free (that is, nonslave) labor system. General Nathaniel Banks, the Union officer in charge of occupied New Orleans, outlined the plan. Many blacks had fled from their former owners when the Union army occupied the area. Banks proclaimed that U.S. troops should forcibly relocate blacks to plantations "where they belong"; there they would continue to work for their former owners in the sugar and cotton fields, but now for wages supposedly negotiated annually. The Union army would compel blacks to work if they resisted doing so. Furthermore, said Banks, black men, women, and children must "work diligently and faithfully for one year, respectful of their employers." In defiance of these orders, however, some blacks went on strike for higher wages, and others refused to work at all. Moreover, not all Union military men relished the prospect of forcing blacks to work on the plantations where they had been enslaved. Thus, federal policies returning blacks to plantations remained contested even within the ranks of the army itself. These disputes—between blacks and planters, and among Union officials—would continue throughout the postwar period.

The Port Royal and southern Louisiana precursors to Reconstruction offered variations on two themes: the Republicans' insistence on preserving the southern plantation economy and the former slaves' efforts to achieve freedom from white control.

The Lincoln administration had no hard-and-fast Reconstruction policy to guide congressional lawmakers looking toward the postwar period. In December 1863 the president outlined his Ten Percent Plan. This plan would allow former Confederate states to form new state governments once 10 percent of the men who had voted in the 1860 presidential election had pledged allegiance to the Union and renounced slavery. Congress never acted on Lincoln's plan because many Republicans felt the need for harsher measures.

Instead, at the end of their 1864 session, legislators passed the Wade-Davis Bill, which would have required a majority of southern voters in any state to take a loyalty oath affirming their allegiance to the United States. By refusing to sign the bill before Congress adjourned, Lincoln vetoed the measure (the so-called pocket veto). However, the president approved the creation of the Freedmen's Bureau in March 1865. The Bureau was responsible for coordinating relief efforts on behalf of blacks and poor whites loyal to the Union, for sponsoring schools, and for implementing a labor contract system on southern plantations. Congress also created the Freedman's Savings and Trust Bank in the hope that the former slaves would save a part of their earnings. At the time of his assassination, Lincoln seemed to be leaning toward giving the right to vote the southern black men.

■ Freedmen's Bureau agents distributed rations to former slaves and southern whites who had remained loyal to the Union. Agents also sponsored schools, legalized marriages formed under slavery, arbitrated domestic disputes, and oversaw labor contracts between workers and landowners. This photo shows the bureau office in Petersburg, Virginia.

Presidential Reconstruction, 1865–1867

When Andrew Johnson, the seventeenth president of the United States, assumed office in April 1865, he brought his own agenda for the defeated South. Throughout his political career, Johnson had seen himself as a champion of poor white farmers in opposition to the wealthy planter class. A man of modest background, he had been elected U.S. senator from Tennessee in 1857. He alone among southern senators remained in Congress and loyal to the Union after 1861. Lincoln first appointed Johnson military governor of Tennessee when that state was captured by the Union in 1862 and then tapped him as his running mate for the election of 1864.

Soon after he assumed the presidency, Johnson disappointed congressional Republicans who hoped that he would serve as a champion of the freedpeople. He welcomed back into the Union those states reorganized under Lincoln's 10 percent plan. On May 29, 1865, Johnson announced his own plan for Reconstruction. He advocated denying the vote to wealthy Confederates, though he would allow individuals to come to the White House to beg the president for special pardons. Johnson also outlined a fairly lenient plan for readmitting the other rebel states into the Union. Poor whites would have the right to vote, but they must convene special state conventions that would renounce secession and accept the Thirteenth Amendment abolishing slavery. Further, they must repudiate all Confederate debts—that is, they must default on any loans made by banks or private individuals to finance the southern war effort. The president opposed granting the vote to the former slaves; he believed that they should continue to toil as field workers for white landowners.

Johnson failed to anticipate the speed and vigor with which former Confederate leaders would move to reassert their political authority. In addition, he did not gauge accurately the resentment of congressional Republicans, who thought his policies toward the defeated South were too forgiving. A warning came in December 1865, when Carl Schurz, a German immigrant and former Union brigadier general, issued his "Report on the Condition of the South." In it, he warned that the Freedmen's Bureau was "very unpopular" among white Southerners, who would no doubt fill a power vacuum left by federal weakness and indecision.

> By January 1865, both houses of Congress had approved the Thirteenth Amendment to the Constitution, abolishing slavery.

Several developments quickly proved Schurz right. The southern states that took advantage of Johnson's reunification policies passed so-called Black Codes. These state laws were an ill-disguised attempt to institute a system of near-slavery. They aimed to penalize "vagrant" blacks, defined as those who did not work in the fields for whites, and to deny blacks the right to vote, serve on juries, or in some cases even own land. The Black Code of Mississippi barred blacks from marrying whites and from owning land "except in incorporated towns or cities" and restricted the rights of a freedperson to "keep or carry fire-arms," ammunition, and knives and to "quit the service of his or her employer before the expiration of his or her term of service without good cause." The vagueness of this last provision threatened any blacks who happened not to be working under the supervision of whites at any given moment. People arrested under the Black Codes faced imprisonment or forced labor.

At the end of the war, congressional Republicans were divided into two camps. Radicals wanted to use strong federal measures to advance black people's civil rights and economic independence. In contrast, moderates were more concerned with the free market and private property rights; they took a hands-off approach regarding former slaves, arguing that blacks should fend for themselves and avoid dependence on federal aid. But members of both groups reacted with outrage to the Black Codes. Moreover, when the legislators returned to the Capitol in December 1865, they were in for a shock: among their new colleagues were four former Confederate generals, five colonels, and other high-ranking members of the Confederate elite, including former Vice President Alexander Stephens, now under indictment for treason. All of these rebels were duly elected senators and representatives from southern states. In a special session called for December 4, a joint committee of 15 lawmakers (6 senators and 9 members of the House) voted to bar these men from Congress.

By January 1865, both houses of Congress had approved the Thirteenth Amendment to the Constitution, abolishing slavery. The necessary three-fourths of the states ratified the measure by the end of the year. Unlike the Emancipation Proclamation (1863), which freed only slaves in Confederate territory, the Thirteenth Amendment abolished slavery wherever it existed. The federal government now guaranteed freedom for all black people.

However, President Johnson was becoming more openly defiant of his congressional foes who favored aggressive federal protection of black civil rights. He vetoed two crucial pieces of legislation: an extension and expansion of the Freedmen's Bureau and the Civil Rights Bill of 1866. This latter measure, a precursor to the Fourteenth Amendment, was an unprecedented piece of legislation. It called on the federal government—for the first time in history—to protect individual rights against the willful indifference of the states (as manifested, for example, in the Black Codes). Congress managed to override both vetoes by the summer of 1866.

In June of that year, Congress passed the Fourteenth Amendment. This amendment guaranteed the former slaves citizenship rights, punished states that denied citizens the right to vote, declared the former rebels ineligible for federal and state office, and voided Confederate debts. This amendment was the first to use gender-specific language, guarding against denying the vote "to any of the male inhabitants" of any state. The amendment, also, for the first time legally defined the rights of American citizenship and empowered the federal government to protect those rights.

Even before the war ended, Northerners had moved south; and the flow increased in 1865. Black and white teachers volunteered to teach the former slaves to read and write. Some white Northerners journeyed south to invest in land and become planters in the staple crop economy. White southern critics called all these migrants carpetbaggers. This derisive term suggested that the Northerners hastily packed their belongings in rough bags made of carpet scraps and then rushed south to take advantage of the region's devastation and confusion.

Former Confederates were not the only people suspicious of the newcomers. In 1865 a black abolitionist Union officer, Martin R. Delany, condemned the northern white people recently arrived in South Carolina. These Northerners, Delany told a group of freedpeople, had "come down here to drive you as much as ever. It's slavery again: northern, universal U.S. slavery." To many freedpeople, whether they worked for a white Northerner or Southerner, laboring in the cotton fields was but a continuation of slavery.

Freedmen and white Southerners sometimes differed within their own camps about political and economic aims. For example, southern blacks united in their demands for land and the vote but disagreed among themselves over the necessity of political cooperation with whites in general. Some former southern (white) Whigs, who had been reluctant secessionists, now found common ground with northern Republicans who supported government subsidies for railroads, banking institutions, and public improvements. This group consisted of some members of the humbled planter class as well as men of more modest means. Southern Democrats, who sneered at any alliances with the North, scornfully labeled these whites "scalawags" (the term referred to a scrawny, useless type of horse on the Scottish island of Scalloway).

Soon after the war's end, southern white vigilantes launched a campaign of violence and intimidation against freedpeople who dared to resist the demands of white planters and other employers. In 1866 former Confederate General Nathan Bedford Forrest, who had led the massacre of African American soldiers at Fort Pillow, founded a social club composed of Tennessee war veterans. Calling itself the Ku Klux Klan, this group soon became a white supremacist terrorist organization and spread to other states. In May 1866 violence initiated by white terrorists against blacks in Memphis, Tennessee, left 46 freedpeople and 2 whites dead, and in July, a riot in New Orleans claimed the lives of 34 blacks and 3 of their white allies. These bloody encounters demonstrated the lengths to which ex-Confederates would go to reassert their authority and defy the federal government.

Back in Washington, Johnson was not content to veto Republican legislation. In the summer of 1866, he also began to lobby against the Fourteenth Amendment, traveling around the country and urging the states not to ratify it. He argued that policies related to black suffrage should be decided by the states. The time had come for reconciliation between the North and South, maintained the president. (The amendment would not be adopted until 1868.)

Congressional Republicans fought back. In the election of November 1866, they won a two-thirds majority in both houses of Congress. These numbers allowed them to claim a mandate from their constituents and to override any future vetoes by the president. Taking heart from their newfound legislative successes, moderates and radicals together prepared to bypass Johnson to shape their own Reconstruction policies.

The Southern Postwar Labor Problem

Throughout the South, black people aspired to labor for themselves and gain independence from white overseers and landowners. Yet white landowners persisted in regarding blacks as field hands who must be coerced into working. With the creation of the Freedmen's Bureau in 1865, Congress intended to form an agency that would mediate between these two groups. Bureau agents encouraged workers and employers to sign annual labor contracts designed to eliminate the last vestiges of the slave system. All over the South, freed men, women, and children would contract with an employer on January 1 of each year. They would agree to work for either a monthly wage, an annual share of the crop, or some combination of the two.

The Bureau established elementary schools and distributed rations to southerners who had remained loyal to the Union, blacks and whites alike. Agents also conducted wedding ceremonies for the former slaves, who had been denied the right to legalize their unions as marriages. Yet the agency's most formidable challenge was its effort to usher in a new economic order in the South—one that relied on nonslave labor but also returned the region to prewar productivity levels in terms of planting and harvesting cotton.

In April 1866, a white planter in Thomson, Georgia, wrote to a local Freedmen's Bureau official and complained that the black wives and mothers living on his land had refused to sign labor contracts. The planter explained, "Their husbands are at work, while they are nearly idle as it is possible for them to be, pretending to spin—knit or something that really amounts to nothing." These "idle" women posed a threat to plantation order, the white man asserted.

Women who stayed home to care for their families were hardly idle. Yet Freedmen's Bureau agents and white planters alike tended to define productive labor (among blacks) as work carried out under the supervision of a white man in the fields or a white woman in the kitchen. During the postwar period, a struggle ensued. Who should toil in the fields of the South? And under what conditions should they labor?

The physical devastation wrought by the war gave these questions heightened urgency. Most freedpeople understood they must find a way to provide for themselves first and foremost. They thought of freedom in terms of welfare for their family rather than just for themselves as individuals. Men and women embraced the opportunity to live and work together as a unit. For many couples, their first act as free people was to legalize their marriage vows. Black women shunned the advice of Freedmen's Bureau agents and planters that they continue to pick cotton. These women withdrew from field labor whenever they could afford to do so. Enslaved women had been deprived of the opportunity to attend to family life. Now freedwomen sought to devote themselves to caring for their families.

The Freedmen's Bureau's functions in the areas of labor and education represented a new and significant federal role in the realm of social welfare. Yet the agency did not have the staff or money necessary to effect meaningful change.

According to the Northerners, the benefits of this system were clear. Employers would have an incentive to treat their workers fairly—to offer a decent wage and refrain from physical punishment. Disgruntled workers could leave at the end of the year to work for a more reasonable landowner. In the postbellum South, however, labor relations were shaped not by federal decree but by a process of negotiation that pitted white landowners against blacks who possessed little but their own labor.

For instance, blacks along the Georgia and South Carolina coast were determined to cultivate the land on which their forebears had lived and died. They urged General Sherman to confiscate the land owned by rebels in the area. In response, in early 1865, Sherman issued Field Order Number 15, mandating that the Sea Islands and the coastal region south of Charleston be divided into parcels of 40 acres for individual freed families. He also decreed that the army might lend mules to these families to help them begin planting. Given the provisions of this order, many freed families came to expect that the federal government would grant them "40 acres and a mule."

As a result of Sherman's order, 20,000 former slaves proceeded to cultivate the property once owned by Confederates. Within a few months of the war's end, however, the War Department bowed to pressure from the white landowners and revoked the order. The War Department also provided military protection for whites to return and occupy their former lands. In response, a group of black men calling themselves Commissioners from Edisto Island (one of the Sea Islands)

H.P. Moore/Collection of The New-York Historical Society, Neg. #37497

■ Residents of Edisto Island, off the coast of South Carolina, pose with a U.S. government mule cart immediately after the Civil War. U.S. troops captured the island in November 1861. The following March, the government began to distribute to blacks the lands abandoned by their former masters. In October 1865 President Andrew Johnson halted the program. A group of angry and disappointed blacks appealed to the president, claiming, "This is our home, we have made these lands what they are." After meeting with the group, General Oliver O. Howard noted, "I am convinced that something must be done to give these people and others the prospect of homesteads."

met in committee to protest to the Freedmen's Bureau what they considered a betrayal. Writing from the area in January 1866, one Freedmen's Bureau official noted that the new policy must be upheld but regretted that it had brought the freedpeople in "collision" with "U.S. forces."

During its brief life (1865 to 1868), the Freedmen's Bureau compiled a mixed record. The individual agents represented a broad range of backgrounds, temperaments, and political ideas. Some were former abolitionists who considered northern-style free labor to be "the noblest principle on earth." These men tried to ensure safe and fair working arrangements for black men, women, and children. In contrast, some agents had little patience with the freedpeople's drive for self-sufficiency. Some bureau offices became havens for blacks seeking redress against abusive or fraudulent labor practices, but other offices had little impact on the postwar political and economic landscape. For agents without means of transportation (a reliable horse),

A Southern Labor Contract

After the Civil War, many southern agricultural workers signed labor contracts. These contracts sought to control not only the output of laborers but also their lives outside the workplace.

On January 1, 1868, the planter John D. Williams assembled his workers for the coming year and presented them with a contract to sign. Williams owned a plantation in the Lower Piedmont county of Laurens, South Carolina. He agreed to furnish "the said negroes" (that is, the three black men and two black women whose names were listed on the document) with mules and horses to be used for cultivating the land. The workers could receive their food, clothing, and medical care on credit. They were allowed to keep one-third of all the corn, sweet potatoes, wheat, cotton, oats, and molasses they produced. Presumably, they would pay their debts to Williams using proceeds from their share of the crop.

According to the contract, Williams's workers promised to

bind them Selves to be steady & attentive to there work at all times and to work at keeping in repair all the fences on Said plantation and assist in cuting & taking care of—all the grain crops on Said plantation and work by the direction of me [Williams] or my Agent. . . .

And should any of them depart from the farm or from any services at any time with out our approval they shall forfeit one dollar per day, for the first time and for the second time without good cause they shall forfeit all of their interest in the crop their to me the enjured person—they shall not be allowed to keep firearms or deadly wapons or ardent Spirits and they shall obey all lawful orders from me

or my Agent and shall be honest—truthful—sober—civel—diligent in their business & for all wilful Disobedience of any lawful orders from me or my Agent drunkenness moral or legal misconduct want of respects or civility to me or my Agent or to my Family or any elce, I am permitted to discharge them forfeiting any claims upon me for any part of the crop. . . .

Moses Nathan	1 full hand
Jake Chappal	" "
Milly Williams	½ " "
Easter Williams	" "
Mack Williams	" "

At the end of the contract is this addition:

We the white labores now employed by John D. Williams on his white plains plantation have lisened and heard read the foregoing Contract on this sheet of paper assign equal for the black laborers employed by him on said place and we are perfectly Satisfied with it and heare by bind our selves to abide & be Governed & Controwed by it

Wm Wyatte	1 full hand
John Wyatte	1 full hand
Packingham Wyatte	½ " "
Franklin Wyatte	½ " "
R M Hughes	1 full hand
B G Pollard	1 full hand
George Washington Pollard	1 full hand

To sign the contract, all of the blacks and two of the whites "made their marks"; that is, they signed with an "X" because they were illiterate. ■

Source: Rosser H. Taylor, "Postbellum Southern Rental Contracts" [from Furman University library, Greenville, South Carolina], *Agricultural History* 17 (1943):122–123.

After the Civil War, many rural southern blacks, such as those shown here, continued to toil in cotton fields owned by whites.

Library of Congress

plantations scattered throughout the vast rural South remained outside their control. Because white landowners crafted the wording and specific provisions of labor contracts, the bureau agents who enforced such agreements often served the interests of employers rather than laborers.

In fact, for the most part, postwar freed people pressed for their labor rights independently of the federal government. In the cotton regions of the South, freedpeople resisted the near-slavery system of gang labor that planters tried to enforce right after the war. Instead, extended families came together in groups called squads to negotiate collectively with landowners. Gradually, squads gave way to sharecropping families.

The outlines of sharecropping, a system that defined southern cotton production until well into the twentieth century, were visible just a few years after the Civil War. Poor families, black and white, contracted annually with landlords, who advanced them supplies, such as crop seed, mules, plows, food, and clothing. Fathers directed the labor of their children in the fields. At the end of the year, many families remained indebted to their employer and, thus, entitled to nothing and obliged to work another year in the hope of repaying the debt. If a sharecropper's demeanor or work habits displeased the landlord, the family faced eviction.

Single women with small children were especially vulnerable to the whims of landlords in the postbellum period. Near Greensboro, North Carolina, for example, planter Presley George, Sr., settled accounts with his field worker Polly at the end of 1865. For her year's expenses, Polly was charged a total $69.00 for corn, cloth, thread, and board for a child who did not work. By George's calculations, Polly had earned exactly $69.00 for the labor she and her three children (two sons and a daughter) performed in the course of the year, leaving her no cash of her own. Under these harsh conditions, freedpeople looked to each other for support and strength.

Building Free Communities

Soon after the war's end, southern blacks set about organizing themselves as an effective political force and as free communities devoted to the social and educational welfare of their own people. As early as summer 1865, groups of freedpeople met in convention to press for their rights as U.S. citizens. A group calling itself Colored Citizens of Norfolk, Virginia, issued an address to the people of the United States, warning that the Emancipation Proclamation was insufficient to check the power of diehard rebels. Mass arrests of blacks had been authorized by "the rebel Mayor." Former slaveholders were bent on keeping the blacks "in a state of serfdom," charged the Norfolk petitioners.

Differences among blacks based on income, jobs, culture, and skin color at times inhibited institution-building. Some black communities found themselves divided by class, with blacks who had been free before the war (including many literate and skilled light-skinned men) assuming leadership over illiterate field hands. In New Orleans, a combination of factors contributed to class divisions among people of African heritage. During the antebellum period, light-skinned free people of color, many of whom spoke French, were much more likely to possess property and a formal education compared to enslaved people, who were dark-skinned English speakers. After the Civil War, the more privileged group pressed for public accommodations laws, which would open the city's theaters, opera, and expensive restaurants to all blacks for the first time. However, black churches and social organizations remained segregated according to class. Yet, citywide black conventions held in 1864 and 1867 brought together all groups of African descent in common cause, defined as "the actual liberation from social and political bondage."

For the most part, postbellum black communities united around the principle that freedom from slavery should also mean full citizenship rights: the ability to vote, own land, and educate their children. These rights must be enforced by federal firepower: "a military occupation will be absolutely necessary," declared the blacks of Norfolk, "to protect the white Union men of the South, as well as ourselves." Freedpeople in some states allied themselves with white

TABLE 15-1

Comparison of Black and White Household Structure in 27 Cotton-Belt Counties, 1870, 1880, 1900

1870 (N = 534)

Single Person %	Nuclear %	Ext. %	Aug. %	Ext./Aug. %	Adults %	Total	
3.1	80.7	14.4	1.4	.3	.3	290	Black
2.1	71.3	7.4	17.6	1.2	.4	244	White
2.6	76.4	11.0	8.8	.7	.4	534	

1880 (N = 679)

Single Person %	Nuclear %	Ext. %	Aug. %	Ext./Aug. %	Adults %	Total	
3.7	74.2	13.6	5.9	1.7	.8	353	Black
3.1	62.7	13.5	15.7	5.0	.0	319	White
3.4	68.8	13.5	10.6	3.3	.4	672	

1900 (N = 644)

Single Person %	Nuclear %	Ext. %	Aug. %	Ext./Aug. %	Adults %	Total	
5.7	64.9	22.9	4.0	1.7	.8	353	Black
3.4	65.2	19.0	.7	1.7	.0	290	White
4.7	65.0	21.2	7.0	1.7	.5	643	

Single person: one person living alone.
Nuclear: father, mother, and children.
Ext.: extended family consisting of parents, children, and kin.
Aug.: augmented household consisting of family and nonfamily members (boarders, servants, hired hands).
Ext./aug.: combination of extended and augmented.
Unrelated adults: more than one unrelated adult living together.

Source: Based on information from a sample of households (located in selected cotton staple counties in Alabama, Florida, Georgia, Louisiana, Mississippi, North Carolina, South Carolina, and Texas) listed in the 1870, 1880, and 1900 federal population manuscript censuses.

yeomen who had long resented the political power of the great planters and now saw an opportunity to use state governments as agents of democratization and economic reform.

Networks of freedpeople formed self-help organizations. Like the sponsors of the Savannah Education Association, blacks throughout the South formed committees to raise funds and hire teachers for neighborhood schools. Small Georgia towns, such as Cuthbert, Albany, Cave Spring, and Thomasville, with populations no greater than a few hundred, raised up to $70 per month and contributed as much as $350 each for the construction of school buildings. Funds came from the proceeds of fairs, bazaars, and bake sales; subscriptions raised by local school boards; and tuition fees. In the cash-starved postbellum South, these amounts represented a great personal and group sacrifice for the cause of education.

Black families sought to care for people who could not care for themselves. Freedmen's Bureau agents scoffed at blacks who took in "improvident" and "lazy" elderly kin: how could

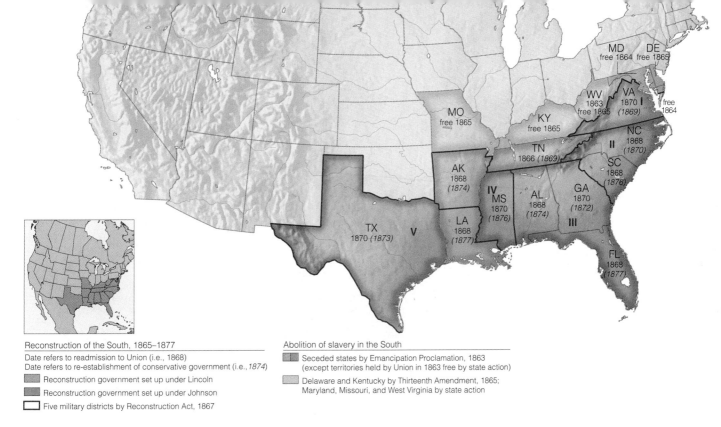

Reconstruction of the South, 1865–1877

Date refers to readmission to Union (i.e., 1868)
Date refers to re-establishment of conservative government (i.e., *1874*)

■ Reconstruction government set up under Lincoln

■ Reconstruction government set up under Johnson

□ Five military districts by Reconstruction Act, 1867

Abolition of slavery in the South

■ Seceded states by Emancipation Proclamation, 1863
(except territories held by Union in 1863 free by state action)

■ Delaware and Kentucky by Thirteenth Amendment, 1865;
Maryland, Missouri, and West Virginia by state action

■ **MAP 15.1**

RADICAL RECONSTRUCTION Four of the former Confederate states, Louisiana, Arkansas, Tennessee, and Virginia, were reorganized under President Lincoln's 10 Percent Plan in 1864. Neither this plan nor the proposals of Lincoln's successor, Andrew Johnson, provided for the enfranchisement of the former slaves. In 1867 Congress established five military districts in the South and demanded that newly reconstituted state governments implement universal manhood suffrage. By 1870 all of the former Confederate states had rejoined the Union, and by 1877 all of those states had installed conservative (i.e., Democratic) governments.

the former slaves hope to advance their own interests if they had to support such unproductive people? All over the South, black families charted their own course. They elected to take in orphans, to pool resources with neighbors, and to arrange for mothers to stay home with their children. These choices challenged the power of former slaveholders and the influence of Freedmen's Bureau agents and northern missionaries and teachers. At the same time, in seeking to attend to their families and to provide for themselves, southern blacks resembled members of other mid-nineteenth-century laboring classes who valued family ties over the demands of employers and landlords.

Tangible signs of the new emerging black communities infuriated southern whites. A schoolhouse run by blacks proved threatening in a society where most white children had little opportunity to receive an education. Black communities were also quick to form their own churches, rather than continue to occupy an inferior place in white churches. Other sights proved equally unsettling: on a main street in Charleston, an armed black soldier marching proudly or a black woman wearing a fashionable hat and veil, the kind favored by white women of the planter class. These developments help to account for the speed with which whites organized themselves in the Klan and various other vigilante groups, such as Young Men's Democratic Clubs, White Brotherhood, and Knights of the White Camellia. Members of this last group took an initiation oath that stated, "Our main and fundamental object is the maintenance of the supremacy of the white race in this Republic."

Congressional Reconstruction: The Radicals' Plan

The rise of armed white supremacist groups in the South helped spur congressional Republicans to action. On March 2, 1867, Congress seized the initiative. A coalition led by two

■ This drawing by famous political cartoonist Thomas Nast depicts the first black members of Congress. Left to right, front row: Senator Hiram Revels of Mississippi (the first African American to serve in the U.S. Senate), Representatives Benjamin S. Turner of Alabama, Josiah T. Walls of Florida, Joseph H. Rainey of South Carolina, Robert B. Elliott of South Carolina. Back row: Representatives Robert G. DeLarge of South Carolina, Jefferson Long of Georgia.

radicals, Senator Charles Sumner of Massachusetts and Congressman Thaddeus Stevens of Pennsylvania, prodded Congress to pass the Reconstruction Act of 1867. The purpose of this measure was to purge the South of disloyalty once and for all. The act stripped thousands of former Confederates of voting rights. The former Confederate states would not be readmitted to the Union until they had ratified the Fourteenth Amendment and written new constitutions that guaranteed black men the right to vote. The South (with the exception of Tennessee, which had ratified the Fourteenth Amendment in 1866) was divided into five military districts. Federal troops were stationed throughout the region. These troops were charged with protecting Union personnel and supporters in the South and with restoring order in the midst of regional political and economic upheaval.

Congress passed two additional acts specifically intended to secure congressional power over the president. The intent of the Tenure of Office Act was to prevent the president from dismissing Secretary of War Edwin Stanton, a supporter of the radicals. The other measure, the Command of the Army Act, required the president to seek approval for all military orders from General Ulysses S. Grant, the army's senior officer. Grant also was a supporter of the Republicans. Both of these acts probably violated the separation of powers doctrine as put forth in the Constitution. Together, they would soon precipitate a national crisis.

The radicals' call for the redistribution of land from former slaveholders to freedpeople won few supporters among moderates in Congress. In contrast, both Republican factions threw their support behind an emerging southern Republican party, a move that had a significant impact on postwar politics. Alert to the designs of the "irritated, revengeful South," Thaddeus Stevens, the leading House radical, urged Republicans, black and white, to assume control of the South; otherwise, "all our blood and treasure will have been spent in vain." Giving the vote to black men spurred the growth of southern Republican party organizations, called Union Leagues, that provided a political forum for a host of black leaders.

During Reconstruction, approximately 2000 black men served as local elected officials, sheriffs, justices of the peace, tax collectors, and city councilors. Many of these leaders were of mixed ancestry, and many had been free before the war. They came in disproportionate numbers from the ranks of literate men, such as clergy, teachers, and skilled artisans. In Alabama, Florida, Louisiana, Mississippi, and South Carolina, black men constituted a majority of the voting public. Throughout the South, 600 black men won election to state legislatures. However, nowhere did blacks control a state government, although they did predominate in South Carolina's lower House. Sixteen black Southerners were elected to Congress during Reconstruction. Most of those elected to Congress in the years immediately after the war were freeborn. However, among the nine men elected for the first time after 1872, six were former slaves. All of these politicians exemplified the desire among southern blacks to become active, engaged citizens.

Among this group of black leaders was war hero Robert Smalls of South Carolina, who early in the war had seized a Confederate gunboat and escaped from Charleston Harbor. Other prominent leaders included Tunis G. Campbell, a native of New Jersey who served as a Georgia state senator and justice of the peace; and the Reverend Henry M. Turner of Georgia, who warned against political divisions between dark- and light-skinned blacks. In Mississippi, in February 1870, Hiram Revels became the first black man to serve in the U.S. Senate. Another Mississippi politician, Blanche K. Bruce, dominated the political scene in Bolivar County, where he served as sheriff, tax collector, and superintendent of education all at the same time. In 1875 Bruce was elected to the U.S. Senate.

Newly reconstructed southern state legislatures provided for public school systems, fairer taxation methods, bargaining rights of plantation laborers, racially integrated public transportation and accommodations, and public works projects, especially railroads. Nevertheless, the legislative coalitions forged between Northerners and Southerners, blacks and whites, were uneasy and, in many cases, less than productive. Southern Democrats (and later, historians sympathetic to them) claimed that Reconstruction governments were uniquely corrupt, with some carpetbaggers, scalawags, and freedpeople vying for kickbacks from railroad and construction magnates. In fact, whenever state legislatures sought to promote business interests, they opened the door to the bribery of public officials. In this respect, northern as well as southern politicians were vulnerable to charges of corruption. In the long run, southern Democrats cared less about charges of legislative corruption and more about the growing political power of local black Republican party organizations.

In Washington in early 1868 President Johnson forced a final showdown with Congress. He replaced several high military officials with more conservative men. He also fired Secretary of War Stanton, in apparent violation of the Tenure of Office Act. Shortly thereafter, in February, a newly composed House Reconstruction Committee impeached Johnson for ingnoring the act, and the Senate began his trial on March 30. The president and Congress were locked in an extraordinary battle for political power.

During the House debate and the Senate trial, political rhetoric verged on the melodramatic. Representative Stevens condemned Johnson as "the nightmare that crouched on the heaving breast of the nation." Nevertheless, the president managed to avoid conviction. The final vote was 35 senators against Johnson, one vote short of the necessary two-thirds of all senators' votes needed for conviction. Nineteen senators voted to acquit Johnson of the charges. The president celebrated his victory by sharing a round of whiskey with his lawyers. Nevertheless, to win acquittal, he had had to promise moderates that he would not stand in the way of congressional plans for Reconstruction. Johnson essentially withdrew from policymaking in the spring of 1868.

TABLE 15-2			
The Election of 1868			
Candidate	**Political Party**	**Popular Vote**	**Electoral Vote**
Ulysses S. Grant	Republican	3,013,421	214
Horatio Seymour	Democratic	2,706,829	80

That November, Republicans urged Northerners to "vote as you shot" (that is, to cast ballots against the former Confederates) and elected Ulysses S. Grant to the presidency. Grant defeated the Democratic nominee, Horatio Seymour, a former governor of New York. An estimated half a million former slaves cast their ballots for Grant, whom they hailed as a liberator.

Two Presidents Impeached

The president, a Democrat, had humble roots in the South. He was raised by a hard-working single mother. His tenure as a state governor ill prepared him for the hostility he encountered as chief executive in Washington, where people persisted in gossiping about his personal life. The Republicans, firmly in control of Congress, despised him and managed to impeach him. At the same time, many observers questioned whether his misdeeds rose to the level of "high crimes and misdemeanors." With the aid of skillful lawyers, members of his own party, and a core of Republican moderates, he avoided conviction in the Senate. Nevertheless, the political battle diminished his capacity to lead forcefully for the rest of his term in office.

Andrew Johnson in 1868 or Bill Clinton 130 years later? The answer, of course, is both. Yet these superficial similarities in the careers of the two men mask dramatic differences between them. Andrew Johnson was charged with violating the Tenure of Office Act, a law that probably was unconstitutional in any case. His impeachment took place against the backdrop of a national debate over the course of Reconstruction, a debate that was intensely ideological.

In contrast, Bill Clinton was charged with lying and obstructing justice, charges that stemmed from an

President Andrew Johnson (1865–1868). Library of Congress

President Bill Clinton (1992–2000). White House Historical Association

extramarital affair the president had conducted with a young White House intern, Monica Lewinsky. His impeachment reflected the bitter partisanship and personal animosity between Democrats and Republicans in the 1990s. (See Chapter 29.)

Andrew Johnson was born in Raleigh, North Carolina, in 1808. At age 13, he was apprenticed to a tailor. As a young man, he moved to Tennessee. There he came to identify with the state's yeoman farmers and artisans in opposition to the great planters. Although he served as governor of Tennessee and later U.S. senator, he had little formal education; his wife, the daughter of a Scottish shoemaker, taught him how to write and do arithmetic.

In contrast, Bill Clinton attended Georgetown University and went on to graduate from Yale Law School. Clinton

also appreciated the help and support of his wife, but Hillary Rodham Clinton was a unique First Lady. She possessed impressive skills as a political campaigner and maintained a keen interest in policy issues. In 2000, just as her husband was leaving office, she was elected U.S. senator from the state of New York.

Generations of historians have disagreed about Johnson's case. In the early twentieth century, pro-South scholars sympathized with Lincoln's successor. Yet many scholars later in the century looked more favorably on the radical Republicans; influenced by the Civil Rights movement, these historians focused on Johnson's anti–civil rights stance. Therefore, it is difficult to predict how history will judge Bill Clinton and his battle with congressional Republicans. Historians themselves are an unpredictable lot. ■

The general had proved himself a brilliant strategist during the war, but he lacked political experience, a shortcoming that soon became abundantly clear.

Political reunion was an uneven process, but one that gradually eroded the newly won rights of former slaves in many southern states. By the end of 1868, Arkansas, North Carolina, South Carolina, Louisiana, Tennessee, Alabama, and Florida had met congressional conditions for readmission to the Union, and two years later, Mississippi, Virginia, Georgia, and Texas followed. The Fifteenth Amendment, passed by Congress in 1869 and ratified by the necessary number of states a year later, granted all black men the right to vote.

The National Archives

■ At Promontory Point near Ogden, Utah, workers joined the tracks linking the Central Pacific (its wood-burning locomotive, Jupiter, is on the left) with the Union Pacific's coal-burning engine No. 119. This photo was taken during the May 10, 1869, celebration marking the completion of the transcontinental railroad. According to one eyewitness, the crowd included Indians, Chinese and Irish immigrants, European Americans, and Mexicans "grouped in picturesque confusion." Yet this official photo shows little evidence of the Chinese workers who helped to engineer and build the Central Pacific line.

However, in some states, such as Louisiana, reunification gave Democrats license to engage in wholesale election fraud and violence toward freed men and women. In 1870–1871, a congressional inquiry into the Klan exposed pervasive and grisly assaults on Republican schoolteachers, preachers, and prospective voters, black and white. The Klan also targeted men and women who refused to work like slaves in the fields. In April 1871, Congress passed the Ku Klux Klan Act, which punished conspiracies intended to deny rights to citizens. But Klan violence and intimidation had already taken their toll. Republican voting strength began to decline in rural areas where blacks were the majority population and freedmen had attempted to assert their citizenship rights.

Claiming Territory for the Union

In 1871 poet Walt Whitman wrote an essay titled "Democratic Vistas." In it he celebrated the "manly and courageous instincts" that propelled a brave, adventurous people west. Whitman hailed the march across the prairies and over the mountains as a cavalcade of progress. He and other Americans believed that the postbellum migration fulfilled a mission of national regeneration begun by the Civil War. Kansas's population grew by 240 percent in the 1860s, Nebraska's by 355 percent.

To unite the entire country together as a single economic and political unit was the Republican ideal. Achieving this ideal entailed both technological and military means. The railroads in particular served as vehicles of national integration. When the Central Pacific and Union Pacific Railroads met at Promontory Point, Utah, in 1869, the hammering of the spike that joined the two roads produced a telegraphic signal received simultaneously on both coasts, setting off a national celebration. In Philadelphia, the Liberty Bell tolled.

Meanwhile, regular units of United States cavalry, including two regiments of blacks, were launching attacks on Indians on the Plains, in the Northwest, and in the Southwest. Between

■ With this 1870 photograph, the Kansas Pacific Railroad advertised the opportunity for western travelers to shoot buffalo from the comfort and safety of their railroad car. The company's official taxidermist shows off his handiwork. Railroad expansion facilitated the exploitation of natural resources while promoting tourism.

DeGolyer Library, Southern Methodist University

1865 and 1890, U.S. military forces conducted a dozen separate campaigns against western Indian peoples and met Indian warriors in battle or attacked Indian settlements in more than 1000 engagements. The war for the West pitted agents of American nationalism against Indian groups that battled to maintain their distinctive way of life in a rapidly changing world. In contrast to African Americans, who adamantly demanded their rights as American citizens, defiant western Indians battled a government to which they owed no allegiance.

Federal Military Campaigns Against Western Indians

In 1871 the U.S. government renounced the practice of seeking treaties with various Indian groups. This change in policy opened the way for a more aggressive effort to subdue native populations. It also hastened the expansion of the reservation system, an effort begun in the antebellum period to confine specific Indian groups to specific territories.

In the Southwest, clashes between Indians and U.S. soldiers persisted after the Civil War. In 1867 at Medicine Lodge Creek in southern Kansas the United States signed a treaty with an alliance of Comanche, Kiowa, Cheyenne, Arapaho, and Plains Apache. This treaty could not long withstand the provocation posed by the railroad. The year before, the Seventh U. S. Cavalry, under the command of Lieutenant Colonel George Custer, had been formed to ward off native attacks on the Union Pacific, snaking its way across the central Plains westward from Kansas. In November 1868 Custer destroyed a Cheyenne settlement on the Washita River, in present-day Oklahoma. The settlement's leader was Black Kettle, who had brought his people to reservation territory after the Sand Creek Massacre in Colorado in 1864. Custer's men murdered women and children, burned tepees, and destroyed 800 horses. Sickened by the scene, one army officer later wrote sarcastically of the "daring dash" on the part of "heroes of a bloody day." The soldiers left piles of corpses scattered among the smoldering ruins of the village.

A series of peace delegations to Washington, several led by Red Cloud of the Sioux, produced much curiosity among whites but no end to the slaughter of people or animals in the West.

■ MAP 15.2

PLAINS INDIAN WARS, 1865–1900   This map reveals that between 1865 and 1890, many of the conflicts between Indians and U.S. troops occurred along either railroad lines or trails used by European American settlers. For example, the Sioux, Cheyenne, and Arapaho fiercely resisted travelers along the Bozeman Trail running from Colorado to Montana.

Indians continued to attack the surveyors, supply caravans, and military escorts that preceded the railroad work crews. Lamenting the loss of his people's hunting grounds to the railroad, Red Cloud said, "The white children have surrounded me and have left me nothing but an island."

The Apache Indians managed to elude General George Crook until 1875. Crook employed some of these Apaches to track down the war chief Geronimo of the Chiricahuas. Like many other Indian leaders, Geronimo offered both religious and military guidance to his people. He believed that a spirit would protect him from the white man's bullets and from the arrows of Indians in league with government troops. Yet Geronimo was tricked into a momentary surrender in 1877. Sorrowfully, he agreed to bring his followers into the San Carlos reservation in eastern Arizona. There he was held in irons for several months before gaining his release and challenging authorities for another nine years.

In 1874 Custer took the Seventh into the Black Hills of the Dakotas, so-called unceded Indian territory. Supposedly, the 1868 Treaty of Fort Laramie had rendered this land off-limits to whites. Custer's mission was to offer protection for the surveyors of the Northern Pacific Railroad and to force Indians onto reservations as stipulated in the 1868 treaty. However, the officer lost no time trumpeting the fact that Indian lands were filled with gold. This report prompted a rush to the Black Hills, lands sacred to the Sioux. Within two years, 15,000 gold

Bettmann/CORBIS

■ During the morning of June 25, 1876, General George Custer and his force of 264 soldiers attacked a Sun Dance gathering of 2500 Sioux and Cheyenne on the banks of the Little Big Horn River in Montana. This European American version of the battle illustrated a book celebrating the life of Custer. The book was published soon after the battle, which took place in June 1876. At the time, the country was in the midst of a celebration marking the centennial of the nation's birth. The engraving portrays Custer and his men making a courageous "last stand."

miners had illegally descended on Indian lands to seek their fortunes. The federal government proposed to buy the land, but leaders of the Sioux, including Red Cloud, Spotted Tail, and Sitting Bull, spurned the offer. "The Black Hills belong to me," declared Sitting Bull. "If the whites try to take them, I will fight."

Indians throughout the West maintained their distinctive ways of life during these turbulent times. Horse holdings, so crucial for hunting, trading, and fighting, varied from group to group, with the Crow wealthy in relation to their Central Plains neighbors the Oglala and the Arikara. Plains and Plateau peoples engaged in a lively trading system. They exchanged horses and their trappings (bridles and blankets) for eastern goods such as kettles, guns, and ammunition. Despite their differences in economy, these groups held similar religious beliefs about an all-powerful life force that governed the natural world. People, plants, and animals were all part of the same order.

Even in the midst of brutal repression, Indian cultural traditions survived and in some cases flourished. On the West Central Plains and the Plateau, among the Crow, Shoshone, Nez Perce and other tribes, women developed a new, distinctive style of seed beadwork characterized by variations of triangular patterns. These designs, made of beads selected for their quality and consistency, adorned leggings, gauntlets, and belt pouches. In these ways, the decorative arts were endowed with great symbolic meaning. When wives embellished moccasins with patterns signifying their husband's military achievements, handicrafts assumed political as well as artistic significance.

The Postwar Western Labor Problem

In the eyes of many European Americans, the West offered vast challenges and opportunities. To construct a railroad across the plains and mountains, to extract rich reserves of timber and minerals, to harvest immense crops of wheat—all of these tasks demanded large numbers of willing workers. But such workers were in short supply. Moreover, available workers wanted employers to pay and treat them fairly.

In 1865 the owners of the Central Pacific Railroad seemed poised for one of the great engineering feats of the nineteenth century. In the race eastward from California, they would construct trestles spanning vast chasms and roadbeds traversing mountains and deserts. Government officials in Washington were eager to subsidize the railroad. What the owners lacked was a dependable labor force. The Irish workers who began the line in California struck for higher wages in compensation for brutal, dangerous work. These immigrants dropped their shovels and hammers at the first word of a gold strike nearby—or far away. As a result, in 1866 the Central Pacific had decided to tap into a vast labor source by importing thousands of Chinese men from their native Guandong province.

The Chinese toiled to extend the railroad tracks eastward from Sacramento, California, up to ten miles a day in the desert, only a few feet a day in the rugged Sierra Nevada Mountains. They alternately loaded and dumped millions of tons of earth and rocks to clear the land and construct the roadbed. In nerve-wracking feats of skill, they lowered themselves in woven baskets to implant nitroglycerine explosives in canyon walls. Chinese

Kicking Bear, *Battle of Little Big Horn*, c.1890. Southwest Museum, Los Angeles

■ Custer foolishly launched his attack without adequate backup, and he and his men were easily overwhelmed and killed by Indian warriors, led by the Oglala Sioux Crazy Horse and others. Reacting to this defeat, U.S. military officials reduced the Lakotas and Cheyennes to wardship status, ending their autonomy. This version of the Battle of the Little Big Horn, by Sioux artist Kicking Bear, highlights the aesthetic and ritualistic elements of the Indian's costume and the decorations attached to his horse. In this picture, warrior and soldier meet face to face. Unarmed and on foot, the soldier is at the mercy of his foe.

laborers toiled through snowstorms and blistering heat to blast tunnels and cut passes through granite mountains. Journalists marveled at the ability of a squad of Chinese to unload 200 tons of iron and 10 tons of spikes from railroad cars in just ten minutes. These reporters also commented on the strange sight of men in their native dress and traditional broad straw hats, taking afternoon tea breaks.

Charles Crocker, the general superintendent of the Central Pacific, observed of the Chinese, "Wherever we put them, we found them good." Paid $1 a day (less than the wage paid to whites), the Chinese had little leverage with which to press for higher compensation. In the spring of 1867, 5000 (out of a workforce of 12,000) walked off the job. They demanded $1.50 a day and an eight-hour day. Crocker responded by withholding rations, and the laborers were forced to return to work within a week. With the final linking of the railroad in Utah in 1869, many Chinese returned to California.

Signed in 1868, the Burlingame Treaty, named for Anson Burlingame, an American envoy to China, had supposedly guaranteed government protection for Chinese immigrants as visitors, traders, or permanent residents. Most immigrants were men. (Six out of ten California Chinese women were listed in the 1870 census as prostitutes, most the victims of their compatriots.) Yet the treaty did not inhibit U.S. employers, landlords, and government officials from discriminating against the Chinese.

By 1870, 40,000 Chinese lived in California and represented fully one-quarter of the state's wage earners. They found work in the cigar, woolen-goods, and boot and shoe factories of San Francisco; in the gold mining towns, now as laundry operators rather than as miners as

■ Chinese construction workers labor on the Central Pacific Railroad, c. 1868. Many Chinese immigrants toiled as indentured laborers, indebted to Chinese merchant creditors who paid for their passage to California. Isolated in all-male work camps, crews of railroad workers retained their traditional dress, language, and diet. After the completion of the transcontinental railroad in 1869, some immigrants returned to China, and others dispersed to small towns and cities throughout the West.

Carleton Watkins/Union Pacific Historical Collection

they had before the Civil War; and in the fields as agricultural laborers. White workers began to cry unfair competition against this Asian group that was becoming increasingly integrated into the region's economy.

As a group, Chinese men differed from California Indians, who remained trapped in the traditional agricultural economy of unskilled labor. Whites appropriated Indian land and forced many men, women, and children to work as wage earners for large landowners. Deprived of their familiar hunting and gathering lands, and wracked by disease and starvation, California Indians had suffered a drastic decline in their numbers by 1870, from 100,000 to 30,000 in 20 years.

By the early 1870s western manufacturers were faltering under the pressure of cheaper goods imported from the East by rail. At the same time, the growth of fledgling gigantic agricultural businesses opened new avenues of trade and commerce. Located in an arc surrounding the San Francisco Bay, large ("bonanza") wheat farmers grew huge crops and exported the grain to the East Coast and to England. These enterprises stimulated the building of wharves and railroad trunk lines and encouraged technological innovation in threshing and harvesting. Western enterprises showed a growing demand for labor whatever its skin color or nationality.

Land Use in an Expanding Nation

The end of the Civil War prompted new conflicts and deepened long-standing ones over the use of the land in a rich, sprawling country. In the South, staple crop planters began to share political power with an emerging elite, men who owned railroads and textile mills. Despairing of ever achieving antebellum levels of labor efficiency, some landowners turned to mining the earth and the forests for saleable commodities. These products, obtained through extraction, included phosphate (used in producing fertilizer), timber, coal, and turpentine. Labor in extractive industries complemented labor in the plantation economy. Sharecroppers alternated between tilling cotton fields in the spring and harvesting the crop in the fall, while seeking employment in sawmills and coal mines in the winter and summer.

As European Americans settled in the West and Southwest, they displaced natives who had been living there for generations. For example, the U.S. court system determined who could legally claim property. Western courts also decided whether natural resources such as water, land, timber, and fish and game constituted property that could be owned by private interests. In the Southwest, European American settlers, including army soldiers who had come to fight Indians and then stayed, continued to place Hispanic land titles at risk. Citing prewar precedents, American courts favored the claims of recent squatters over those of long-standing residents. In 1869 with the death of her husband (who had served as a general in the Union army), Maria Amparo Ruiz de Burton saw the large ranch they had worked together near San Diego slip out of her control. The first Spanish-speaking woman to be published in English in the United States, de Burton was a member of the Hispanic elite. Nevertheless, she had little political power. California judges backed the squatters who occupied the ranch.

As they controlled more land and assumed public office, some European Americans in the Southwest exploited their political connections and economic power. In the process they managed to wield great influence over people and vast amounts of natural resources. In the 1870s the so-called Santa Fe Ring wrested more than 80 percent of the original Spanish grants of land from Hispanic landholders in New Mexico. An alliance of European American lawyers, businesspeople, and politicians, the Santa Fe Ring defrauded families and kin groups of their land titles and speculated in property to make a profit. Whereas many ordinary Hispanic settlers saw land—with its crops, pasture, fuel, building materials, and game—as a source of livelihood, groups, such as the Santa Fe Ring, saw land primarily as a commodity to be bought and sold.

Seemingly overnight, boom towns sprang up wherever minerals or timber beckoned: southern Arizona and the Rocky Mountains west of Denver, Virginia City in western Nevada, the Idaho–Montana region, and the Black Hills of South Dakota. In all these places, increasing numbers of workers operated sophisticated kinds of machinery, such as rock crushers, and labored for wages. When the vein was exhausted or the forests depleted, the towns went bust.

Railroads facilitated not only the mining of minerals but also the growth of the cattle-ranching industry. By 1869 a quarter of a million cattle were grazing in Colorado Territory. Rail connections between the Midwest and East made it profitable for Texas ranchers to pay cowboys to drive their herds of long-horned steers to Abilene, Ellsworth, Wichita, or Dodge City, Kansas, for shipment to stockyards in Chicago or St. Louis. Large meatpackers, such as Swift and Armour, prepared the carcasses for the eastern market.

Cattle drives were huge; an estimated 10 million animals were herded north from Texas alone between 1865 and 1890. They offered employment to all kinds of men with sufficient skills and endurance. Among the cowhands were African American horsebreakers and gunmen and Mexicans skilled in the use of the *reata* (lasso). Blacks made up about 25 percent and Hispanics about 15 percent of all cowboy outfits. Tracing the evolution of the Chisholm Trail, which

TABLE 15-3

Estimates of Railroad Crossties Used and Acres of Forest Cleared, 1870–1910

Year	Miles of Track	Ties Renewed Annually (millions)	Ties Used on New Construction (millions)	Total Ties Annually (millions)	Acres of Forest Cleared (thousands)
1870	60,000	21	18	39	195
1880	107,000	37	21	58	290
1890	200,000	70	19	89	445
1900	259,000			91	455
1910	357,000			124	620

Source: Michael Williams, *Americans and Their Forests* (1989), 352.

linked southern Texas to Abilene, from Indian path to commercial route, one observer wrote in 1874, "So many cattle have been driven over the trail in the last few years that a broad highway is tread out, looking much like a national highway." Yet this new "national highway" traversed Indian Territory (present-day Oklahoma), lands supposedly promised to Indians forever.

In knitting regional economies together, federal land policies were crucial to the Republican vision of a developing nation. Yet a series of land use acts had a mixed legacy. The Mineral Act of 1866 granted title to millions of acres of mineral-rich land to mining companies, a gift from the federal government to private interests. In 1866 Congress passed the Southern Homestead Act to help blacks acquire land, but the measure accomplished little and was repealed in 1876. The Timber Culture Act of 1873 allotted 160 acres to individuals in selected western states if they agreed to plant one-fourth of the acreage with trees. Four years later, the Desert Land Act provided cheap land if buyers irrigated at least part of their parcels.

The exploitation of western resources raised many legal questions: Must ranchers pay for the prairies their cattle grazed on and the trails they followed to market? How could one "own" a stampeding buffalo herd or a flowing river? What was the point of holding title to a piece of property if only the timber, oil, water, or minerals on and in it (but not the soil) were of value?

The Apex Mining Act of 1872 sought to address at least some of these issues. This law legalized traditional mining practices in the West by validating titles approved by local courts. According to the law, a person who could locate the apex of a vein (its point closest to the surface) could lay claim to the entire vein beneath the surface. The measure contributed to the wholesale destruction of certain parts of the western landscape as mining companies blasted their way through mountains and left piles of rocks in their wake. It also spurred thousands of lawsuits as claimants argued over what constituted an apex or a vein.

It was during this period that a young Scottish-born naturalist named John Muir began to explore the magnificent canyons and mountains of California. Viewing nature as a means for regenerating the human spirit, Muir emphasized a deep appreciation of the natural world. He contrasted nature's majesty with the artificial landscape created by and for humans. In the wilderness, there is nothing "truly dead or dull, or any trace of

Colorado Historical Society (CHS.J 2067)

■ Chicago photographer Thomas J. Hine titled this stereograph "Old Faithful in Action, Fire Hole Basin." It is the first photograph of the eruption of the famous Yellowstone geyser. Costing 15–25 cents each, stereographs were a popular form of entertainment in middle-class households beginning in the 1860s. The stereoscope merged two identical photos to form a single three-dimensional image. Widely distributed stereographs of scenic natural wonders boosted western tourism.

what in manufactories is called rubbish or waste," he wrote; "everything is perfectly clean and pure and full of divine lessons." Muir believed that the need to protect breathtaking vistas and magnificent stands of giant redwoods compelled the federal government to act as land policy regulator.

Muir was gratified by the creation of the National Park system during the postwar period. By this time, pressure had been building on the federal government to protect vast tracts of undeveloped lands. Painters and geologists were among the first Easterners to appreciate the spectacular vistas of the western landscape. In 1864 Congress set aside a small area within California's Yosemite Valley for public recreation and enjoyment. Soon after the war, railroad promoters forged an alliance with government officials in an effort to block commercial development of particularly beautiful pockets of land. In the late 1860s the invention of the Pullman sleeping car—a luxurious hotel room on wheels—helped spur the drive to protect these areas from farming, lumbering, stock raising, and mining. Northern Pacific railroad financier Jay Cooke lobbied hard for the government to create a two-million-acre park in what is today the northwest corner of Wyoming. As a result, in March 1872, Congress created Yellowstone National Park. Tourism would continue to serve as a key component of the western economy.

Muir and others portrayed the Yosemite and Yellowstone Valleys as wildernesses, empty of human activity. In fact, both areas had long provided hunting and foraging grounds for native peoples. Yellowstone had been occupied by the people now called the Shoshone since the fifteenth century. This group, together with the Bannock, Crow, and Blackfeet, tried to retain access to Yellowstone's meadows, rivers, and forests after it became a national park. However, U.S. policymakers and military officials persisted in their efforts to mark off territory for specific purposes, while Indians were confined to reservations.

Buying Territory for the Union

Before the war, Republicans had opposed any federal expansionist schemes that they feared might benefit slaveholders. However, after 1865 and the outlawing of slavery, some Republican lawmakers and administration officials advocated the acquisition of additional territory. Secretary of State William Seward led the way in 1867 by purchasing Alaska from Russia and trying unsuccessfully to buy the Danish West Indies.

The purchase of Alaska immeasurably enriched the nation's natural resources. For $7.2 million (about 2 cents an acre), the United States gained 591,004 square miles of land. Within the territory were diverse indigenous groups—Eskimos, Aleuts, Tlingit, Tsimshian, Athabaskan, and Haida—and a small number of native Russians. Though derided at the time as "Seward's icebox," Alaska yielded enough fish, timber, minerals, and water power in the years to come to prove that the original purchase price was a tremendous bargain.

The impulse that prompted administration support for the Alaska purchase also spawned other plans for territorial acquisitions. In 1870 some Republicans joined with Democrats in calling for the annexation of the Dominican Republic. These congressmen argued that the tiny Caribbean country would make a fine naval base, provide investment opportunities for American businesspeople, and offer a refuge for southern freedpeople. Frederick Douglass, who had visited the country, claimed that annexing the Dominican Republic would "transplant within her tropical borders the glorious institutions" of the United States.

However, Charles Sumner, chairman of the Senate Foreign Relations Committee, opposed ratification of the annexation treaty. He warned against a takeover without considering the will of the Dominican people, who were currently involved in their own civil war. Some congressmen, in a prelude to foreign policy debates of the 1890s, suggested that the dark-skinned Dominican people were incapable of appreciating the blessings of American citizenship. In 1871 the treaty failed to win Senate approval. A firm supporter of annexation, President Grant felt personally betrayed by the Republicans who opposed him on this issue.

The Republican Vision and Its Limits

After the Civil War, victorious Republicans envisioned a nation united in the pursuit of prosperity. All citizens would be free to follow their individual economic self-interest and to enjoy the fruits of honest toil. In contrast, some increasingly vocal and well-organized groups saw the expansion of legal rights, and gving black men the right to vote in particular, as only initial, tentative steps on the path to an all-inclusive citizenship. Women, industrial workers, farmers, and African Americans made up overlapping constituencies pressing for equal political rights and economic opportunity. Together they challenged the mainstream Republican view that defeat of the rebels and destruction of slavery were sufficient to guarantee all people prosperity.

Government–business partnerships also produced unanticipated consequences for Republicans committed to what they believed was the collective good. Some politicians and business leaders saw these partnerships as opportunities for private gain. Consequently, private greed and public corruption accompanied postwar economic growth. Thus, Republican leaders faced challenges from two very different sources: people agitating for civil rights and people hoping to reap personal gain from political activities.

Postbellum Origins of the Woman Suffrage Movement

After the Civil War, the nation's middle class, which had its origins in the antebellum period, continued to grow. Dedicated to self-improvement and filled with a sense of moral authority, many middle-class Americans (especially Protestants) felt a deep cultural connection to their counterparts in England. Indeed, the United States produced its own "Victorians," so called for the self-conscious middle class that emerged in the England of Queen Victoria during her reign from 1837 to 1901.

At the heart of the Victorian sensibility was the ideal of domesticity: a harmonious family living in a well-appointed home, guided by a pious mother and supported by a father successful in business. Famous Protestant clergyman Henry Ward Beecher and his wife were outspoken proponents of this domestic ideal. According to Eunice Beecher, women had no "higher, nobler, more divine mission than in the conscientious endeavor to create a *true home*." Her husband added, "The laborer ought to be ashamed of himself who in 20 years does not own the ground on which his house stands . . . who has not in that house provided carpets for the rooms, who has not his China plates, who has not his chromos [decorative photographs], who has not some books nestling on the shelf."

Yet the traumatic events of the Civil War only intensified the desire among a growing group of American women to participate fully in the nation's political life. They wanted to extend their moral influence outside the narrow and exclusive sphere of the home. In countless everyday, unsung ways, Union women had supported the Union cause. They had managed farms, raised money for the U.S. Sanitary Commission, and sponsored patriotic rallies. Many women believed that they deserved the vote and that the time was right to demand it.

In 1866 veteran reformers Elizabeth Cady Stanton, Susan B. Anthony, and Lucy Stone founded the Equal Rights Association to link the rights of white women and African Americans. Nevertheless, in 1867, Kansas voters defeated a referendum proposing suffrage for both blacks and white women. This disappointment convinced some former abolitionists that the two causes should be separated—that women should wait patiently until the rights of African American men were firmly secured. Frederick Douglass declined an invitation to a women's suffrage convention in Washington, D.C., in 1868. He explained, "I am now devoting myself to a cause [if] not more sacred, certainly more urgent, because it is one of life and death to the long enslaved people of this country, and that is: negro suffrage."

Douglass left African American women out of his call for "negro suffrage." He implied that the chief advocates of women's suffrage were white and middle class. As a result, Douglass failed to gauge the way in which the issue of universal suffrage connected all black people with all women. African American activist and former slave Sojourner Truth warned white women not to presume to speak for all women, and she also urged black men not to speak for themselves only. At a meeting of the newly formed Equal Rights Association, Truth pointed out, "There is a great stir about colored men getting their rights, but not a word about the colored women; and if colored men get their rights, and not colored women get theirs, there will be a bad time about it."

In 1869 two factions of women parted ways and formed separate organizations devoted to women's rights. The more radical wing, including Cady Stanton and Anthony, bitterly denounced the Fifteenth Amendment because it gave the vote to black men only. In 1868 the two leaders had attempted to organize a Working Women's Party, which they hoped would appeal to female wage earners and serve as the foundation of a new political party dedicated to broad-based reform.

The following year they helped to found the National Woman Suffrage Association (NWSA). Members of NWSA argued for a renewed commitment to the original Declaration of Sentiments passed in Seneca Falls, New York two decades earlier. They favored married women's property rights, liberalization of divorce laws, opening colleges and trade schools to women, a new federal amendment to allow women to vote. In 1869, women's rights proponents Lucy Stone and her husband, Henry Blackwell, founded the rival American Woman Suffrage Association (AWSA). This group downplayed the larger struggle for women's rights and focused on the suffrage question exclusively. Its members supported the Fifteenth Amendment and retained ties to the Republican party. The AWSA focused on state-by-state campaigns for women's suffrage.

In 1871 the NWSA welcomed the daring, flamboyant Victoria Woodhull as a vocal supporter, only to renounce her a few years later. Woodhull's political agenda ranged from free love and dietary reform to legalized prostitution, working men's rights, and women's suffrage. (In the nineteenth century, free love advocates denounced what they called a sexual double standard, one that glorified female chastity while tolerating male promiscuity.) Woodhull's speeches gained her a great deal of publicity; in one political cartoon she was labeled "Mrs. Satan." This was hardly the kind of publicity the NWSA craved. At the group's 1871 convention Woodhull startled many of the old guard with her declaration, "We mean treason! We mean secession. . . . We are plotting Revolution! We will overthrow this bogus republic and plant a government of righteousness in its stead."

In 1872 one of Woodhull's critics successfully challenged her. Woodhull spent a month in jail as a result of the zealous prosecution by vice reformer Anthony Comstock, a clergyman

Library of Congress

■ New York City newspaper *The Daily Graphic* carried this caricature of Susan B. Anthony on its June 5, 1873, cover. The artist suggests that the drive for women's suffrage has resulted in a reversal of gender roles. Titled "The Woman Who Dared," the cartoon portrays Anthony as a masculine figure. One of her male supporters, on the right, holds a baby, while women activists march and give speeches. On the left, a female police officer keeps watch over the scene.

who objected to her public discussions and writings on sexuality. Comstock assumed the role of an outspoken crusader against vice. A federal law passed in 1873, and named after him, equated information related to birth control with pornography, banning this and other "obscene material" from the mails.

Also in 1872, Woodhull formed what she called the Equal Rights Party. This new party nominated its founder for the U.S. presidency. However, Woodhull's proposed vice presidential running mate, Frederick Douglass, declined the honor. He announced that he planned to vote for Grant again.

For her part, Susan B. Anthony used the 1872 presidential election as a test case for women's suffrage. She attempted to vote and was arrested, tried, and convicted as a result. By this time, most women suffragists, and most members of the NWSA for that matter, had become convinced that they should focus on the vote exclusively; they therefore accepted the AWSA's policy on this issue. In the coming years, they would avoid other causes with which they might have allied themselves, including black civil rights and labor reform.

Workers' Organizations

Many Americans benefited from economic changes of the postwar era. Railroading, mining, and heavy industry helped fuel the national economy and in the process boosted the growth of the urban managerial class. In the Midwest, many landowning farmers prospered when they responded to an expanding demand for grain and other staple crops. In Wisconsin, wheat farmers cleared forests, drained swamps, diverted rivers, and profited from the booming world market in grain. Yet the economic developments that allowed factory managers and owners of large wheat farms to make a comfortable living for themselves did not necessarily benefit agricultural and manufacturing workers.

Several organizations offered laborers an alternative vision to the Republicans' brand of individualism and nationalism.

Indeed, during this period growing numbers of working people, in the countryside and in the cities, became caught up in a cycle of indebtedness. In the upcountry South (above the fall line, or Piedmont), formerly self-sufficient family farmers sought loans from banks to repair their war-damaged homesteads. To qualify for these loans, the farmer had to plant cotton as a staple crop, to the neglect of corn and other foodstuffs. Many sharecroppers, black and white, received payment in the form of credit only; for these families, the end-of-the-year reckoning yielded little more than rapidly accumulating debts. Midwestern farmers increasingly relied on expensive threshing and harvesting machinery and on bank loans to purchase the machinery. In cities all over the country, the mass production of shoes and textiles meant that members of the laboring classes depended more than ever on cash to buy such necessities, yet depressed wages and irregular employment put families at risk.

Several organizations founded within five years of the war's end offered laborers an alternative vision to the Republicans' brand of individualism and nationalism. In 1867 Oliver H. Kelly, a former Minnesota farmer now working in a Washington office, organized the National Grange of the Patrons of Husbandry, popularly known as the Grange. This movement sought to address a new, complex marketplace increasingly dominated by railroads, banks, and grain elevator operators. The Grange encouraged farmers to form cooperatives that would market their crops and to challenge discriminatory railroad rates that favored big business.

Founded in Baltimore in 1866, the National Labor Union (NLU) consisted of a collection of craft unions and claimed as many as 600,000 members at its peak in the early 1870s. The group welcomed farmers as well as factory workers and promoted a general program of social reform. The group also favored legislation for an eight-hour workday and the arbitration of industrial disputes.

William Sylvis, a leader of the Iron Molders' International Union in Philadelphia and the second president of the NLU, sounded twin themes that would mark national labor

State Historical Society of Wisconsin, WHi (D32) 821

■ A Norwegian immigrant extended family in the town of Norway Grove, Wisconsin, poses in front of their imposing home and up-to-date carriage in this photograph taken in the mid-1870s. Linking their fortunes to the world wheat market, these newcomers to the United States prospered. Wrote one woman to her brother back home in Norway, "We all have cattle, driving oxen, and wagons. We also have children in abundance."

union organizing efforts for generations to come. He called for an alliance of black and white workers. Yet at the same time, Sylvis defended the practice of excluding blacks from positions of leadership on the job and in the union. Impatient with such pronouncements, Isaac Myers, a black ship caulker from Baltimore, helped found the short-lived Colored National Labor Union in Washington, D.C., in 1868. (This association remained small and disbanded within three years.) Myers offered a view of citizenship that differed from white Republicans' exclusive emphasis on the franchise: "If citizenship means anything at all," the black labor leader declared, "it means the freedom of labor, as broad and as universal as freedom of the ballot."

In 1873 a nationwide depression threw thousands out of work and worsened the plight of debtors. Businesspeople in agriculture, mining, the railroad industry, and manufacturing had overexpanded their operations. The free-wheeling loan practices of major banks had

TABLE 15-4

National and International Union Members of the National Labor Union (with dates of each union's founding)

National Typographical Union (printers and typesetters) (1850)
Iron Molders' I.U. (1859)
Machinists' and Blacksmiths' I.U. (1859)
American Miners' Association (1861)
  Miners' National Association (1873)
Sons of Vulcan (steel workers) (1862)
National Telegraphic Union (1863)
  Telegraphers' Protective League (1868)
Brotherhood of Locomotive Engineers (1863)
Ship Carpenters' and Caulkers' I.U. (1864)
Cigar Makers' I.U. (1864)
N.U. of Journeyman Curriers (tanners) (1864)
Plasterers' N.U. (1864, again 1871)
Iron and Steel Heaters' I.U. (1865, again 1872)
Coachmakers' I.U. (1865)
Dry Goods Clerks' Early Closing Ass'n. (1865)
Tailors I.U. (1865)
Carpenters' and Joiners' I.U. (1865)
Bricklayers' I.U. (1865)
Journeyman Painters' I.U. (1865, again 1871)
Stationary Engineers' N.U. (1866?)
Mule Spinners' I.U. (textile workers) (1866)
Knights of St. Crispin (shoemakers) (1867)
Conductors' Brotherhood (1868)
Workingmen's Benevolent Association (1868)
Wool Hat Finishers' N.U. (1869)
Daughters of St. Crispin (shoemakers) (1869)
Coopers' I.U. (barrel makers) (1870)
Morocco Dressers' N.U. (hide processors) (1870)
American Bricklayers' N.U. (1871)
N.U. of Woodworking Mechanics (1872)
Sons of Adam (cloth cutters) (1872)
Brotherhood of Locomotive Firemen (1873)
Boilers', Roughers', Catchers', and Hookers', N.U. (1873)

Note: I.U.= International Union; N.U. = National Union.

contributed to this situation. The inability of these businesspeople to repay their loans led to the failure of major banks. With the contraction of credit, thousands of small businesses went bankrupt. The NLU did not survive the crisis.

However, by this time, a new organization had appeared to champion the cause of the laboring classes in opposition to lords of finance. Founded in 1869 by Uriah Stephens and other Philadelphia tailors, the Knights of Labor began as a secret fraternal society. Extending their reach, the Knights aimed to unite industrial and rural workers, the self-employed and the wage earner, blacks and whites, and men and women. The Knights were committed to private property and to the independence of the farmer, the entrepreneur, and the industrial worker. The group banned from its ranks "nonproducers," such as liquor sellers, bankers, professional gamblers, stockbrokers, and lawyers. Both the Knights and the Farmers' Grange would enjoy their greatest successes in the 1880s.

This period of depression also laid the foundation for the Greenback Labor Party, organized in 1878. Debtors feared that government policies were leading to a contraction of the money supply. Within three years after the end of the Civil War, the Treasury had withdrawn from circulation $100 million in wartime, paper currency ("greenbacks"). With less money in circulation, debtors found it more difficult to repay their loans. The government also ceased coining silver dollars in 1873, despite the discovery of rich silver lodes in the West. "Cheap-money men" protested what they called the "Crime of '73." To add insult to injury, the Resumption Act (1875) called for the government to continue to withdraw paper "greenbacks." Thus, hard money became dearer, and debtors became more desperate. In 1878 the new Greenback Labor Party managed to win one million votes and elect 14 candidates to Congress. The party laid the foundation for the Populist Party that emerged in the 1890s.

Federal money policies had a great impact on diverse groups of workers, whether they toiled in the fields, the factory, or the workshop. However, several factors made coalition building among these groups difficult. One was the nation's increasingly multicultural workforce. Unions, such as the typographers, were notorious for excluding women and African Americans, a fact publicized by both Frederick Douglass and Susan B. Anthony, to no avail. In 1869 shoe factory workers (members of the Knights of St. Crispin) went on strike in North Adams, Massachusetts. They were soon shocked to see 75 Chinese strikebreakers arrive by train from California. Their employer praised the new arrivals for their "rare industry." The shoemakers' strike collapsed quickly after the appearance of what the workers called this "Mongolian battery." Employers would continue to manipulate and divide the laboring classes through the use of ethnic, religious, and racial prejudices.

Political Corruption and the Decline of Republican Idealism

Out of the new partnership between politics and business emerged an extensive system of bribes and kickbacks. Greedy politicians of both parties challenged the Republicans' high-minded idealism.

News related to the corrupt intertwining of government power and private economic interests burst upon the headlines in the early 1870s. In New York City, the *New York Times* exposed the schemes of William M. "Boss" Tweed. Tweed headed Tammany Hall, a political organization that courted labor unions and contributed liberally to Catholic schools and charities. Tammany Hall politicians routinely used bribery and extortion to fix elections and bilk taxpayers of millions of dollars. One plasterer employed on a city project received $138,000 in "payment" for two days' work. Political cartoonist Thomas Nast portrayed Tweed with a bulging stomach and a sneering face, taunting the public, "As long as I count the votes, what are you going to do about it?" After the *Times* exposé, Tweed was prosecuted and convicted. His downfall attested to the growing influence of newspaper reporters.

Another piece of investigative journalism rocked the political world in 1872. In 1867 major stockholders of the Union Pacific Railroad had formed a new corporation, called the Crédit Mobilier, to build railroads. Heads of powerful congressional committees received shares of stock in the new company. These gifts of stock were bribes to secure the legislators' support for public land grants favorable to the new corporation. The *New York Sun* exposed a number of the chief beneficiaries in the fall of 1872, findings confirmed by congressional investigation. Among the disgraced politicians was Grant's vice president Schuyler Colfax, who had lied under oath to a Congessional Committee investigating the scandal. Colfax denied accepting Crédit Mobilier stock, although bank records show he had deposited $1200 in cash from one of the finance company's supporters.

The 1872 presidential election pitted incumbent Grant against the Democratic challenger, *New York Tribune* editor Horace Greeley. Republicans, disillusioned with congressional corruption and eager to press forward with civil service reform, endorsed the Democratic candidate. Greeley and his Republican allies decried the patronage (or "spoils")

PLATE 17

Harper's Weekly, September 16, 1871

■ In 1871 Thomas Nast drew a series of cartoons exposing the corruption of New York City Democratic boss William M. Tweed and his political organization, Tammany Hall. In this drawing, published in *Harper's Weekly* in 1871, Nast depicts Tweed and his cronies engaging in a "wholesale" looting of the New York City treasury with the assistance of compliant police officers. Those same officers stand ready to crack down on the impoverished father who robs a bakery to feed his family. By portraying Tweed as an enemy of the poor, Nast ignored the fact that the political boss gained a large following among immigrant voters.

TABLE 15-5

The Election of 1872

Candidate	Political Party	Popular Vote	Electoral Vote
Ulysses S. Grant	Republican	3,596,745	286
Horace Greeley	Democratic Liberal		
	Republican	2,843,446	66

system by which politicians rewarded their supporters with government jobs. Nevertheless, Grant won the election.

In an 1872 article titled "The State of the South," a writer for the *Nation* magazine decried northern whites' apparent indifference toward the stalled process of Reconstruction. After four bloody years of war and seven squandered years of postwar opportunity, the federal government seemed prepared to hand the South back to unrepentant rebels. Together, the southern states readmitted to the Union would demonstrate little regard for black people as citizens or as workers. In 1874 the Freedman's Savings Bank failed, taking with it the dreams of many depositors who had saved, on average, $25 out of their hard-won earnings. Neither Congress nor the president attempted to save the bank or reimburse the depositors. Meanwhile, the North showed what one House Republican called "a general apathy among the people concerning the war and the negro." The Civil Rights Act of 1875 guaranteed blacks equal access to public accommodations and transportation. Yet this act represented the final, half-hearted gesture of radical Republicanism. The measure was never enforced, and the Supreme Court declared it unconstitutional in 1883 on the grounds that the government could protect only political and not social rights. White Southerners reasserted their control over the region's political economy.

Grant remained preoccupied by political problems plaguing his administration. In 1875 the so-called Whiskey Ring further tarnished his presidency. The St. Louis–based association consisted of the manufacturers of distilled liquors. Aided by Treasury Department officials and Grant's own private secretary, General Orville E. Babcock, these manufacturers avoided paying sales taxes. With influential friends, members of the ring had eluded detection for years.

The presidential election of 1876 intensified public cynicism about deal making in high places. A dispute over election returns led to what came to be known as the Compromise of 1877. The Republican nominee, Rutherford B. Hayes, a former three-term governor of Ohio, ran against Democrat Samuel J. Tilden. In the popular vote, Tilden outpolled Hayes. However, when the electoral votes were counted, the Democrat had only 184, one short of the necessary number. Nineteen of the 20 votes in dispute came from Louisiana, South Carolina, and Florida, and these three states submitted two new sets of returns, one from each of the two main parties. A specially appointed congressional electoral commission, the Committee of Fifteen, was charged with resolving the dispute. It divided along partisan lines. The eight Republicans outvoted the seven Democrats to accept the Republican set of returns from Florida.

TABLE 15-6

The Election of 1876

Candidate	Political Party	Popular Vote	Electoral Vote
Rutherford B. Hayes	Republican	4,036,572	185
Samuel J. Tilden	Democrat	4,284,020	184

To break the logjam, the Democrats agreed that Hayes could assume office in return for the withdrawal of all remaining federal troops from the South. The Republicans tacitly agreed that their work there was finished and that blacks in the region should fend for themselves. Hayes declined to enforce the Civil Rights Act of 1875. White Southerners were free to uphold the principle of states' rights that had been traditionally invoked to deny blacks their rights in the region.

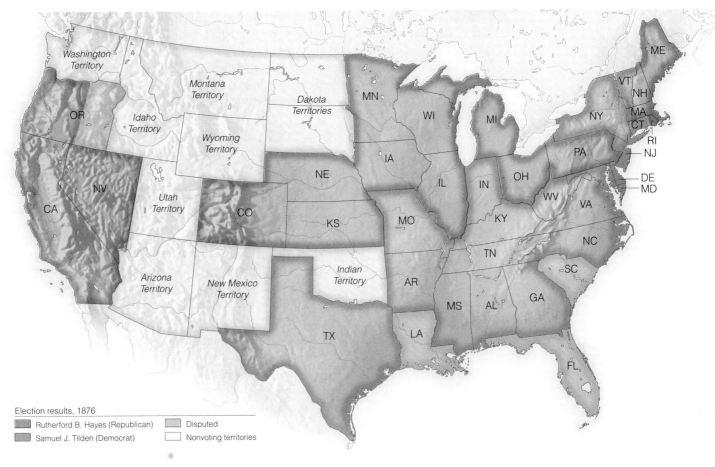

Election results, 1876

- ▮ Rutherford B. Hayes (Republican)
- ▮ Samuel J. Tilden (Democrat)
- ▯ Disputed
- ▯ Nonvoting territories

■ **MAP 15.3**
THE COMPROMISE OF 1877   During the presidential election of 1876, returns from South Carolina, Florida, and Louisiana (the only states that remained under Republican control) were disputed. Under a compromise reached by Republicans and Democrats in Congress, Republican Rutherford B. Hayes became president, and Congress removed all federal troops from the South. As a result, in many areas of the South, the Republican party all but disappeared.

Conclusion

During the dozen or so years after the Civil War, both northern Republicans and southern Democrats registered a series of spectacular wins and crushing losses. Though humiliated by the Union victory, southern white supremacists eventually won for themselves the freedom to control their own local and state governments. As landlords, sheriffs, and merchants, these men defied the postwar federal amendments to the Constitution and deprived African Americans of basic citizenship rights. By the end of Reconstruction, northern Republicans had conceded local power to their former enemies. Apparently, even an aggressive nationalism could accept traditional southern hierarchies: white over nonwhite, rich over poor.

On the other hand, at the end of Reconstruction, Republicans remained in firm control of national economic policy. The white South had secured its right to conduct its own political affairs, but the Republican vision of economic growth and development had become the law of the land. This vision was a guiding principle of historic national and, increasingly, international significance. Economic innovation in particular proved to be a force of great unifying power, stronger even than all the federal military forces deployed during and after the Civil War.

Sites to Visit

The Impeachment of Andrew Johnson

www.impeach-andrewjohnson.com/

This HarpWeek site about the impeachment includes images and text from the Reconstruction period.

Diary and Letters of Rutherford B. Hayes

www.ohiohistory.org/onlinedoc/hayes/index.cfm

The Rutherford B. Hayes Presidential Center in Fremont, Ohio, maintains the searchable database of his writings.

Freedmen and Southern Society Project (University of Maryland, College Park)

www.inform.umd.edu/ARHU/Depts/History/Freedman/home.html

This site contains a chronology and sample documents from several collections or primary sources about emancipation and freedom in the 1860s.

History of the Suffrage Movement

www.rochester.edu/SBA

This site includes a chronology, important texts relating to women's suffrage, and bibliographical information about Susan B. Anthony and Elizabeth Cady Stanton.

Indian Affairs: Laws and Treaties, compiled and edited by Charles J. Kappler (1904)

www.library.okstate.edu/kappler

This digitized text at Oklahoma State University includes pre-removal treaties with the five Civilized Tribes and other tribes.

National Museum of the American Indian

www.si.edu/nmai

The Smithsonian Institution maintains this site, providing information about the museum.

The Northern Great Plains, 1880–1920: Photographs from the Fred Hulstrand and F. A. Pazandak Photograph Collections

www.memory.loc.gov.ammem/award97/ndfahtml/ngphome.html

This American Memory site from the Library of Congress contains two collections from the Institute for Regional Studies at North Dakota State University with 900 photographs of rural and small-town life at the turn of the century. Included are images of sod homes and the people who built them, farms and the machinery that made them prosper, and one-room schools and the children who were educated in them.

For Further Reading

General Works

Ellen Carol DuBois, *Feminism and Suffrage: The Emergence of an Independent Women's Movement in America, 1848–1869* (1978).

Eric Foner, *Reconstruction: America's Unfinished Revolution, 1863–1877* (1988).

David Montgomery, *Beyond Equality: Labor and the Radical Republicans, 1862–1872* (1967).

Amy Dru Stanley, *From Bondage to Contract: Wage Labor, Marriage, and the Market in the Age of Slave Emancipation* (1998).

Ronald Takaki, *A Different Mirror: A History of Multicultural America* (1993).

Robert M. Utley, *The Indian Frontier of the American West, 1846–1890* (1984).

Richard White, *"It's Your Misfortune and None of My Own": A History of the American West* (1991).

The Struggle over the South

Peter Bardaglio, *Reconstructing the Household: Families, Sex and the Law in the Nineteenth-Century South* (1995).

Ira Berlin and Leslie S. Rowland, eds., *Families and Freedom: A Documentary History of African-American Kinship in the Civil War Era* (1997).

Dwight B. Billings, *Planters and the Making of a "New South": Class, Politics, and Development in North Carolina, 1865–1900* (1979).

Lucy M. Cohen, *Chinese in the Post–Civil War South: A People Without a History* (1984).

Frederick Cooper, Thomas C. Holt, and Rebecca J. Scott, eds., *Beyond Slavery: Explorations of Race, Labor, and Citizenship in Post-Emancipation Societies* (2000).

Michael W. Fitzgerald, *The Union League Movement in the Deep South: Politics and Agricultural Change During Reconstruction* (1989).

Michael Golay, *A Ruined Land: The End of the Civil War* (1999).

Thomas C. Holt, *Black over White: Negro Political Leadership in South Carolina During Reconstruction* (1977).

Jacqueline Jones, *Soldiers of Light and Love: Northern Teachers and Georgia Blacks, 1865–1873* (1980).

Leslie Schwalm, *"A Hard Fight for We": Women's Transition from Slavery to Freedom in South Carolina* (1997).

Claiming Territory for the Union

Stephen E. Ambrose, *Nothing Like It in the World: The Men Who Built the Transcontinental Railroad, 1863–1869* (2000).

Orin G. Libby, ed., *The Arikara Narrative of the Campaign Against the Hostile Dakotas, June, 1876* (1998).

Ruth B. Moynihan, Susan Armitage, and Christiane Fischer Dichamp, eds., *So Much to Be Done: Women Settlers on the Mining and Ranching Frontier* (1990).

Richard West Sellars, *Preserving Nature in the National Parks: A History* (1997).

Larry Sklenar, *To Hell with Honor: Custer and the Little Bighorn* (2000).

Robert Wooster, *The Military and United States Indian Policy, 1865–1903* (1988).

Judy Yung, *Unbound Feet: A Social History of Chinese Women in San Francisco* (1995).

The Republican Vision and Its Limits

Leon Fink, *Workingmen's Democracy: The Knights of Labor and American Politics* (1983).

Barbara Goldsmith, *Other Powers: The Age of Suffrage, Spiritualism, and the Scandalous Victoria Woodhull* (1998).

Lyde Cullen Sizer, *The Political Work of Northern Women Writers and the Civil War* (2000).

Irwin Unger, *The Greenback Era: A Social and Political History of American Finance, 1865–1879* (1964).

C. Vann Woodward, *Reunion and Reaction: The Compromise of 1877 and the End of Reconstruction* (1956).

Online Practice Test

Test your understanding of this chapter with interactive review quizzes at

www.ablongman.com/jonescreatedequal/chapter15

Additional Photo Credits

Page 501: Library of Congress

Page 507: Antique Textile Resource, Bethesda MD

Page 517: William T. Garrell Foundry, San Francisco, *The Golden Spike*. The Iris & B. Gerald Cantor Center for Visual Arts at Stanford University (1998.115). Gift of David Hewes

1877	All federal troops withdrawn from the South, ending Reconstruction.
	"Great Uprising" of railroad employees and other workers.
1878	Thomas Edison patents the phonograph.
	San Francisco Workingmen's party stages anti-Chinese protests.
1879	First telephone line connects two American cities (Boston and Lowell, Massachusetts).
1880	New York City streets lit by electricity.

1881	Charles Guiteau assassinates President Garfield.
1882	Standard Oil Trust is created.
	Chinese Exclusion Act.
1883	Pendleton Act (civil service reform).
1884	Mark Twain, *The Adventures of Huckleberry Finn.*
1885	Geronimo leads Apaches to Sierra Madres in Mexico.
1886	Accused Haymarket bombers tried and convicted.
	Geronimo and his followers are sent to Fort Marion, Florida; the children are sent to the government Indian school in Carlisle, Pennsylvania.
1887	Interstate Commerce Act creates Interstate Commerce Commission.
	Dawes Severalty Act.
	United States claims right to Pearl Harbor, leases it as a coaling and repair station.
1888	Edward Bellamy, *Looking Backward.*
1889	First All-American football team, consisting of players from Yale, Harvard, and Princeton.
	National Farmers' Alliance is founded.
1890	Sherman Anti-Trust Act.
	Wyoming admitted to the Union, first state to enfranchise women.
	National American Woman Suffrage Association is formed.
	Wounded Knee Massacre.

PART SIX

The Emergence of Modern America, 1877–1900

THE UNITED STATES BECAME A MODERN NATION DURING THE LAST quarter of the nineteenth century. Vast reserves of coal, timber, and water helped fuel a growing industrial economy. Railroad lines criss-crossed the nation and knit together regional economies. Large numbers of immigrants, many from eastern Europe, arrived in the United States, drawn by America's rising standard of living, high demand for labor, and religious and political freedom.

To raise the money needed to purchase expensive equipment and machinery, coal and oil producers and railroad owners formed modern corporations, businesses that were owned by stockholders rather than individuals. The largest businesses sought to dominate the marketplace by eliminating their competitors. Managers could cut production and operating costs by slashing the wages of workers or by installing labor-saving machinery. Either way, workers paid the price.

The generation that came of age after the Civil War witnessed a series of violent confrontations between workers and employers. Standards of industrial work discipline required workers to labor for long hours at dangerous, disagreeable jobs. Some workers formed new kinds of labor unions to combat the power of big business. Some organizations, such as the Knights of Labor, were national in scope and inclusive in their membership; others represented the interests of specific groups of workers. Employers, local and state law enforcement officials, and judges used a variety of means to suppress strikes and other forms of collective action among workers. Nevertheless, local communities often supported the strikers, who were their friends and neighbors.

During the late nineteenth century, the national economy began to shift to the production of consumer goods. New products gave Americans new ways to spend their money. Manufacturers of everything from toothpaste to bathtubs advertised their goods to a mass market. In cities, department stores offered a dazzling array of goods.

Even as the country was becoming more ethnically diverse, advertisers promoted a single standard of physical beauty and material well-being. At the same time, some scholars and politicians seized on a revolutionary new theory of natural history to argue for the superiority of white, middle-class Americans. Social Darwinism served as the intellectual justification for unfettered economic growth and for the subjugation of darker-skinned peoples, at home and abroad.

Many Americans rejected the trends toward economic standardization and cultural homogeneity. Native Americans in the West continued to resist the railroad and its profound threat to their way of life. By 1890 the U.S. military had forcefully subdued most of these Indians, relegating many to reservations. Together with industrial workers throughout the nation, Hispanic villagers in the Southwest and African American sharecroppers in the South disputed the notion that progress could be defined exclusively in terms of economic growth and development.

Middle-class reformers sought to mediate between what they perceived to be two dangerous groups: arrogant industrialists and discontented workers. These reformers feared that rapid urban and industrial growth would cause rifts in the social fabric. Middle-class women pioneered in the founding of social settlements and other urban institutions to ease the transition of immigrants into modern American society.

The lines between national standards and local cultural interests often blurred. For example, for a short time Sioux chief Sitting Bull (Tatanka Iyotake) appeared with William ("Buffalo Bill") Cody's "Wild West" show, which played to enthusiastic audiences in the United States and Europe. Yet this Indian leader also led the Plains Indians as they attempted to resist U.S. military authorities. Some groups of Americans who sought to preserve their own cultural traditions nonetheless aspired to a middle-class way of life and its material comforts. Elite Hispanic families in the Southwest remained devoted to their Roman Catholic faith and at the same time followed up-to-date clothing fashions marketed by East Coast department stores.

The promise and the conflicts inherent in the emerging modern social order met head on in the 1890s. A new political party called the Populists mounted a brief but potent challenge to entrenched economic and political power. The Populists failed in their attempt to capture the presidency in 1896, but they offered a vision of a new kind of political party, one that would bring black and white farmers and industrial workers together in opposition to landlords, employers, and bankers.

In 1898, in an effort to protect its interests in the Western Hemisphere and to extend those interests into the Pacific, the United States went to war with Spain. This imperialist venture suggested the links among several impulses, including missionary outreach, commercial expansion, and white supremacist racial ideologies. By 1900 the United States was fast becoming a world leader in terms of manufacturing, technological innovation, and the rapid growth of its prosperous middle class.

1891 Populist Party formed.
Eleven Italian immigrants are lynched in New Orleans.

1892 Ellis Island opens as screening site for immigrants.
Miners strike in Coeur d'Alene, Idaho.
Steelworkers strike at Carnegie's Homestead plant near Pittsburgh.

1893 Columbian Exposition opens in Chicago.
Pro-American interests stage a successful coup against Queen Liliuokalani of Hawaii.
Worst nationwide depression to date.

1894 Coxey's Army marches on Washington, D.C.
Pullman workers strike.

1896 Supreme Court decides *Plessy v. Ferguson*, upholds segregation.
W. E. B. DuBois is first black person to receive a Ph.D. from Harvard.

1898 U.S. annexes Hawaii.
Maine blows up in Havana Harbor.

U.S. defeats Spain in Spanish–American–Cuban–Filipino War.
Spain cedes Guam and Puerto Rico to U.S., turns over Philippines in return for $20 million.

1899 Gen. Emilio Aguinaldo leads Filipino revolt against 70,000 U.S. occupying forces.

1900 U.S. troops sent to China to crush Boxer Rebellion.

CHAPTER 16

Standardizing the Nation: Innovations in Technology, Business, and Culture, 1877–1890

Courtesy, Transcendental Graphics

■ A late nineteenth-century crowd enjoys a baseball game on a summer day. These fans show some of the same characteristics of their twenty-first-century counterparts—men and women cheer lustily for the home team, and at least one spectator is enjoying a mug of beer. During this period, the number of professional baseball teams multiplied. Games such as this one turned athletic competitions into forms of mass entertainment.

THOMAS A. SCOTT'S EARLY LIFE PROVIDED FEW CLUES THAT HE WOULD SOMEDAY BECOME a powerful industrialist. Born in 1823 in a small town in south central Pennsylvania, he was the seventh of 11 children. After his father died in 1835, the youth went to live with relatives. Over the next few years, he worked in country stores, learning and developing bookkeeping skills. His clerking abilities eventually landed him a series of railroad jobs. As an employee of the Pennsylvania Railroad, he supervised the transfer of passengers and freight between trains. In 1858 Scott was promoted to the position of general superintendent of the railroad, and in 1874 he became president of the line.

During his career, Scott gained a reputation as a tenacious defender of the railroad's interests; in the words of one politician, Scott could "engineer" almost any bill through the Pennsylvania state legislature. For example, in 1864, Scott lobbied legislators to repeal the charter of a rival line and to grant a new charter to a trunk line of his own company. After the vote, a lawmaker rose to his feet and asked, "Mr. Speaker, may we now go Scott free?"

In the summer of 1877, Scott and other railroad officials were forced to contend with a workers' strike that spread throughout the country. Trying to cut costs in what had become a bitterly competitive business, many of the railroads had demanded that workers labor for longer hours for 10 percent less pay. Managers instituted the practice of "double-heading"—adding more cars to a train but not hiring more men to tend them, placing added burdens on engineers and other workers. In response, beleaguered rail workers walked off the job. Men and women in other struggling industries—from laundresses and longshoremen in Galveston, Texas, to coal miners in Scranton, Pennsylvania, to packinghouse laborers in Chicago—also went on strike during what came to be known as the Great Labor Uprising of 1877. That July the federal government deployed army troops as a strike-breaking force in Chicago, East St. Louis, and Terre Haute, among other cities.

In 1890, commercial establishments lined the riverbanks of Pittsburgh, Pennsylvania.

In a letter to the *North American Review* magazine in August 1877, Thomas Scott justified his railroad's wage cuts and charged that the strikers were under the sway of vicious criminals. Scott hailed the railroads as truly national enterprises, "closely interwoven with the interests not only of our own but other countries." During the Civil War, Union forces had commandeered private rail lines, Scott pointed out. Now it was appropriate that the federal government protect the railroads in this time of crisis. Indeed, according to Scott, "this insurrection," the strike, presented a national emergency "almost as serious as that which prevailed at the outset of the Civil War."

By 1877 the emergence of a national rail system signaled the rise of big business. The railroad industry produced America's first business bureaucracies, employing gigantic workforces to maintain, schedule, operate, and staff trains that traversed 93,000 miles of

■ The "Great Labor Uprising" of July 1877 was the first national strike in U.S. history. As railroad lines proliferated, owners slashed wages in a bid to remain competitive. Railroad workers in some cities destroyed trains, tracks, and other equipment. Spreading eventually to 14 states, the conflict claimed the lives of more than 100 people and resulted in the loss of millions of dollars worth of private property.

Carnegie Library of Pittsburgh (#P-1987)

track. By 1890 the Pennsylvania Railroad had become the nation's largest employer, with 110,000 workers on its payroll. About one out of seven people worked in the rail industry. The personnel in charge of coordinating these vast operations were among the country's first professional, salaried managers.

Andrew Carnegie, a young Scottish immigrant, absorbed critical lessons about the industry's accounting and managerial procedures. A youthful assistant to Thomas Scott in the 1850s, Carnegie labored as a telegrapher and then as a superintendent for the Pennsylvania Railroad's western division. In 1875 he began building the greatest steel empire in the country, using business principles that he learned while working for the railroad.

The railroad industry was both a great centralizer and a great standardizer. Trains ran on schedules that were set by a central office, and those schedules relied on definitions of actual time that were standard throughout the nation. Moreover, trains broke down regional boundaries by transporting goods to all areas of the counry. For the first time, trains carried brand-name goods and commodities to a national market. A California wheat farmer could purchase replacement parts for his McCormick reaper manufactured in Chicago. An Iowa farm family ordered a new cookstove through a mail-order catalogue. Levi-Strauss, a small clothier in San Francisco, shipped its famous denim pants to cowboys in Texas. Pillsbury Flour of Minnesota distributed its products to bakeries throughout the Midwest. Armour Meatpacking of Chicago sent its sausages to the East Coast. With the introduction of the new refrigerated railroad car, trains also began carrying larger loads of fruits and vegetables over longer distances. The new traffic in produce stimulated commercial agriculture in the South and on the West Coast.

Few Americans amassed the fabulous fortunes of rich industrialists like Scott and Carnegie, yet most people aspired to a better life, even in modest terms. Proprietors, managers, and office workers filled the ranks of the comfortable middle class, men and women freed of the danger and drudgery of manual labor. Between 1880 and 1900, clerical workers tripled in number, and business managers increased from 68,000 to more than 318,000. Enjoying steady work and cash salaries, middle-class employees began to move their families out of the city. Urban areas were becoming increasingly befouled by smokestacks and congested with new factories and workshops.

Providers of goods and services celebrated a "standard" American viewed as white, native-born, middle-class, heterosexual, and Protestant. This image assumed special significance in the marketing of consumer products and in the appeal of new forms of leisure activities. With technical innovations came novel ways for people to spend their money. Athletic contests, traveling road shows, and amusement parks provided exciting sensory experiences for young and old alike. At the same time, the mass marketing of goods gave rise to a consumer culture that valued newness, fashion, and luxury.

Mass advertising techniques heightened distinctions that European Americans drew between themselves and people they considered inferior, exotic, or foreign. Yet the energy and vitality associated with American popular culture served as a magnet for people all over the world. Beginning in the 1880s, eastern European immigrants streamed to the United States. They were also eager to partake of the country's plentiful jobs, material prosperity, and democratic openness. Well into the twentieth century, the nation still showed the ethnic and cultural diversity that was shaped by patterns of immigration during the late nineteenth century.

Economic growth produced contradictory effects. Blessed with abundant and diverse natural resources, American industries became competitive in the world marketplace. However, miners and loggers tended to "cut and run," despoiling streams and forests in the process. Economic growth and development transformed natural landscapes throughout the United States. Citizens in general benefited from the proliferation of new technological marvels, but consumers bore the brunt when big business raised prices and eliminated competition within an industry. Certain workers suffered when new machines displaced them from their jobs.

During the last third of the nineteenth century, the rise of big business, the mass production of consumer goods, and innovations in transportation produced national standards that shaped the economic and social life of the nation. Placing advertisements in newspapers and popular magazines, large companies sought to market their products to all parts of the country. These products, from bathtubs to new fashions in dress, helped to set the standard for middle-class life. In addition, advertising conveyed to the buying public an image of "American" beauty; this standard was narrow by definition but supposedly universal in its appeal. New kinds of commercialized leisure activities, such as shows, athletic competitions, and amusement parks, promoted the idea that all Americans, regardless where they lived or what they did for a living, valued spectacles and thrilling forms of entertainment. At the same time, not all people embraced these standards or the assumption that underlay them—the notion that new kinds of goods and entertainment represented progress in American life.

The New Shape of Business

In 1882 prospectors discovered gold in the creeks of Idaho's Coeur d'Alene region (in Indian territory, about 90 miles east of Spokane, Washington). Multiethnic boomtowns mushroomed in the region, as they had in the California gold fields three decades earlier. Yet this new gold rush differed substantially from its predecessor. First, technology had already powerfully shaped the early history of Coeur d'Alene. The Northern Pacific Railway had promoted settlement, and the primitive techniques that had been used in surface mining soon yielded to far more efficient hydraulic methods of extraction (a process in which powerful water hoses wash the soil away to expose gold deposits).

Second, the mining industry in the region soon emerged as a big business. In 1885 an unemployed carpenter named Noah S. Kellogg set in motion a dramatic chain of events. Kellogg discovered a lode containing not only gold but also zinc and lead. In short order, he sold his mines to a Portland businessman, who paid a whopping $650,000 for them. A group of eastern and

California investors, and finally several large corporations, soon controlled major interests in the mines. Meanwhile, new railroad lines were lacing the area. With the advent of electrification across the region, lamps glowed in saloons and mining shafts. Finally, the miners themselves were not solo prospectors, seeking to make their own fortune, but wage-earning employees paid by the mining corporation. By the mid-twentieth century, mining companies had dug more than a billion dollars' worth of metal out of Noah Kellogg's original stake.

Population growth spurred the growth of industries that expoited nature. Between 1880 and 1890, the U.S. population grew from 50 million people to almost 63 million, and six new states entered the Union: North Dakota, South Dakota, Montana, and Washington (all in 1889) and Idaho and Wyoming (both in 1890). Increased demand in turn hastened large-scale commercial mining, logging, and fishing.

> *Advocates of standardized industrial processes and mass marketing hoped to break down regional barriers and create an integrated national economy.*

Crucial to the process of innovation were engineers, who mastered the technical aspects of construction and design. Many American engineers were trained in Germany, but others attended such schools as the Massachusetts Institute of Technology (MIT) or Cornell University, in New York state, both of which introduced electrical engineering into their curricula in 1882. Engineers were in the forefront of professional associations: civil engineers banded together in 1852, mining engineers in 1871, mechanical engineers in 1880, and electrical engineers in 1884 (chemists formed their own association in 1908). American engineers, such as those who worked in Mexico under the auspices of mining companies and the railroads, served as the vanguard of American capitalism throughout the world. Most engineers were men; however, Ellen Swallow Richards, a graduate of MIT and the first female member of the American Institute of Mining Engineers (in 1875), pioneered in home economics.

Advocates of standardized industrial processes and mass marketing hoped to break down regional barriers and create an integrated national economy. Whether they specialized in railroads or shoes, wheat or steel, business owners and managers who possessed the necessary resources and resourcefulness pursued similar goals: to mine, grow, manufacture, or process large quantities of goods and then market them as widely, cheaply, and quickly as possible. Business put a premium on technological innovation, on the efficient use of workers, and on the reduction of uncertainties that accompanied a competitive marketplace. These guiding principles, formulated during the late 1870s and 1880s, laid the foundations of economic progress in late nineteenth-century America.

Yet not all businesses during this period were big. The entrepreneurial spirit flourished, especially within local markets. In the 1880s, even the newest towns, such as Central City, Colorado, west of Denver, supported a rich mix of financiers, professionals, merchants, storekeepers, and skilled artisans. Central City supplied nearby mining and milling operations, but the trade and service industries patronized by those operations accounted for 52 percent of the city's total wealth and more than a quarter of its population. Thus, the history of American enterprise during this period exhibited two seemingly contradictory impulses: one toward consolidation of industries, the other toward a proliferation of small businesses serving their immediate neighborhoods and regions.

New Systems and Machines—and Their Price

The free enterprise system thrived on innovation. Indeed, during the 1880s, new machines, new technical processes, new engineering feats, and new forms of factory organization fueled the growth and efficiency of U.S. businesses. Many devices that became staples of American life appeared during this period. Alexander Graham Bell invented the telephone in 1876. Thomas A. Edison developed the phonograph in 1877 and the electric light in 1879. Cash registers, stock tickers, and typewriters soon became indispensable tools for American businesses. Beginning in the 1880s, railroad cars installed steam heat and electric lights, boosting the comfort of passengers.

Lesser-known inventions revolutionized specific industries. In 1883 Jan Ernest Matzeliger, a young mechanic who was the son of a Dutch man and a Surinamese woman, developed a successful shoe-lasting machine in Lynn, Massachusetts. (A last was a wooden model of a human foot that shoemakers used to attach and shape the shoe leather.) The prototype of Matzeliger's lasting machine consisted of old cigar boxes wired with pieces of wood. Massachusetts shoe manufacturers embraced the device once he had perfected it, for their highly skilled but poorly paid hand lasters were beginning to form a union. The Yankee lasters' concerns had merit, for patent Number 274,207 ultimately spelled doom for them. Matzeliger's machine had eliminated the need for skilled shoe laborers.

During this period, more and more businesses perfected the so-called American system of manufacturing, which dated back half a century and relied on the mass production of interchangeable parts. Factory workers made large numbers of a particular part, each part exactly the same size and shape. This system enabled manufacturers to assemble products more cheaply and efficiently, to repair products easily with new parts, and to redesign products quickly. In the early 1880s the Singer Sewing Machine Company was selling 500,000 units a year. McCormick was producing 21,600 reapers annually. The American system also spurred technological innovation. For example, in 1884 the twine binder used in wheat harvesting was modified with new parts for use in harvesting rice.

The engineers who designed the modern bicycle (which has wheels of equal size) used the American system to make their product affordable to almost anyone who wanted one. The bicycle craze of the late nineteenth century resulted from the novelty and cheapness of this new form of transportation and recreation, one enjoyed by males and females of all ages. Production techniques used to make bicycles were later adapted to the manufacture of automobiles.

New technical processes also facilitated the manufacture and marketing of foods and other consumer goods. Distributors developed pressure-sealed cans, which enabled them to market agricultural products in far-flung parts of the country. Innovative techniques for sheet metal stamping and electric resistance welding transformed a variety of industries. Eager to satisfy a demand for steel (an alloy that was stronger and harder than iron), U.S. manufacturers stepped up production of the versatile metal. For the first time, they broke free of European suppliers. By 1880, 90 percent of American steel was made by the Bessemer process (named after its English inventor but developed in this country by William Kelly), which injected air into molten iron to yield steel.

Oregon Historical Society, OrHi 92918

■ Bonanza farms were huge agricultural enterprises, ranging in size from 15,000 to 50,000 acres. This photo shows a bonanza wheat farm in Oregon, c. 1890. Many of these farms relied not only on sophisticated machinery but also on transient labor forces (up to 1000 men at a time) to help plow, plant, harvest, and thresh the crop. Some of the largest landowners abandoned farming when they had an opportunity to sell their vast holdings for a profit.

■ **MAP 16.1**

AGRICULTURAL REGIONS OF THE MIDWEST AND NORTHEAST   By 1890 several Midwestern cities served as shipping centers, getting wheat and corn to the growing metropolitan areas of the Northeast and Mid-Atlantic. Farmers complained that the railroads gave discounts to large shippers, such as Standard Oil, and discriminated against small producers.

The agriculture business benefited from engineering innovations as well. These techno-logical advances included improvements in irrigation and new labor-saving devices, such as the self-binding harvester (1878) and the first self-steering, self-propelled traction engine (1882). These innovations and devices reached across national boundaries. As just one exam-ple, the first modern irrigation systems in the Southwest were constructed by Native Ameri-cans and *mestizos* (people of both indigenous and Spanish ancestry). And in the 1870s, Japan began importing American farm implements and inviting U.S. engineers to construct dams and canals for new steam- and water-powered gristmills and sawmills. Technology was a uni-versal language, one that many peoples around the globe sought to master.

Long active in territorial exploration and land surveying, the federal government con-tinued to assume a leading role in applied science. In 1879 the U.S. Geological Survey (USGS) was formed, charged with compiling and centralizing data describing the natural landscape, an effort that had originated in 1804 with the Lewis and Clark expedition. In the 1880s, the federal government also began to systematize and disseminate information useful to farmers through the United States Department of Agriculture. Created in 1864, the department orig-inally consisted of several divisions organized around scholarly disciplines, such as chemistry and horticulture. Gradually, administrators looked for ways to solve specific problems faced by farmers. In 1881, for example, the department's Entomology Bureau began to combine cur-rent research on insects with practical techniques for pest control.

Like factory machines, new agricultural machinery benefited consumers but also dis-rupted traditional labor patterns. As farm productivity boomed, the need for hired hands evaporated. Early in the nineteenth century, producing an acre of wheat took 56 hours of labor; in 1880, that number dropped to 20 hours. Machines, such as the self-binding harvester, reduced labor needs by as much as 75 percent. One agricultural worker in Ohio observed, "Of one thing we are convinced, that while improved machinery is gathering our large crops, mak-ing our boots and shoes, doing the work of our carpenters, stone sawyers, and builders,

TABLE 16-1

Amount of Forest Clearing Each Decade, by Major Region, 1850–1909 (in thousands of acres)

	1850–1859	1860–1869	1870–1879	1880–1889	1890–1899	1900–1909	Total
Northeast	1,417	619	1,339	62	80	228	3,745
Mid-Atlantic	4,283	2,811	4,278	295	646	87	12,400
Southeast	6,822	1,869	7,612	6,213	5,410	3,712	31,638
Northcentral	8,245	5,566	9,199	2,420	3,804	1,200	30,434
Southcentral	9,025	1,803	9,156	8,168	7,489	5,767	41,408
Lake	5,093	4,188	7,347	3,131	4,575	2,497	26,831
Southwest	3,018	1,422	7,796	7,148	8,020	7,832	35,236
Pacific	1,774	1,188	2,590	1,166	983	1,063	8,764
Total	39,677	19,466	49,317	28,603	31,007	22,386	190,456

Northeast: Maine, New Hampshire, Vermont, Massachusetts, Connecticut, Rhode Island.
Mid-Atlantic: New York, Pennsylvania, New Jersey, Delaware, Maryland.
Southeast: West Virginia, Virginia, North Carolina, South Carolina, Georgia, Florida.
Northcentral: Minnesota, North Dakota, South Dakota, Nebraska, Kansas, Iowa, Montana, Wyoming, Colorado.
Southcentral: Missouri, Arkansas, Louisiana, Mississippi, Alabama, Tennessee, Kentucky, Oklahoma.
Lake: Ohio, Michigan, Indiana, Illinois, Wisconsin.
Southwest: Nevada, Utah, Arizona, New Mexico, Texas.
Pacific: Washington, Oregon, California.

Source: Michael Williams, *Americans and Their Forests* (1989), 36.

thousands of able, willing men are going from place to place seeking employment, and finding none. The question naturally arises, is improved machinery a blessing or a curse?"

Alterations in the Natural Environment

Innovation altered the natural landscape and hastened the depletion of certain natural resources. By the mid-1870s, Texas had new steam-powered lumber mills equipped with saw rigs that could produce up to 30,000 board feet a day. This capacity made Texas lumbering a big business, especially when it was combined with infusions of capital and the expansion of railroad lines into the piney woods region, along the eastern edge of the state. Texas lumber mills were poised to benefit from the exhaustion of the great forests of the eastern and Great Lakes states.

In the Chesapeake Bay, dredge boats were becoming more efficient in harvesting oysters, and shellfish reserves began to decline. In the mid-1880s oyster harvesters took a record 15 million bushels from the bay; the shellfish simply could not replenish themselves. New means of commercial fishing also reduced supplies of salmon in the Northwest.

In 1884 in California, a federal court issued a permanent injunction against hydraulic mining, because it contributed to soil erosion and water pollution. Hydraulic mining had washed an estimated 12 billion tons of earth into San Francisco Bay, raising the floor of the bay several feet. At the same time, mercury flowing into nearby streams from gold mines in the San Jose hills was poisoning fish in the bay, creating pollution that would be felt well into the twentieth century. Similar cases of industrial pollution despoiled other parts of the country. In the absence of any laws to restrain them, Chicago meatpackers befouled the Chicago River with the byproducts of sausage, glue, and fertilizer.

By stimulating manufacturing and extractive enterprises alike, the railroads powered these great environmental transformations, for better or worse. Trains enabled entrepreneurs to develop large-scale copper mines in Arizona, gigantic herds of longhorn cattle in Kansas, and vast textile mills in Georgia. Every western town clamored for a railroad station; they knew that places bypassed by the rails withered and died. The railroads enabled tourists to enjoy the

■ Following the wholesale slaughter of buffalo on the Great Plains, settlers earned money by gathering the skeletons. "The bones are shipped East by the carloads," reported the Dodge City *Times,* "where they are ground and used for fertilizing and manufactured into numerous useful articles." This mound of buffalo bones at the Michigan Carlson Works in Detroit, c. 1880, suggests the extent of the devastation.

Courtesy, the Burton Historical Collection, Detroit Public Library

beauty of western wilderness areas. Yet the railroads had an insatiable demand for lumber. Between the late 1870s and 1890, U.S. railroads accounted for 20 to 25 percent of all lumber consumed in the nation. They used wood for fuel, fences, trestles, and stations, along with countless railroad ties. In 1890 scientists estimated that the railroads would need 73 million board feet each year to make new ties to lay beneath expanding lines and to replace ties eaten by pests and decayed with age.

Since buffalo herds impeded rail travel, railroads promoted the shooting of buffalo from trains, a "sport" that almost eradicated the species. By the mid-1880s, the great herds had disappeared, victims of ecological change (the incursion of horses into grazing areas), disease (brucellosis spread by domestic livestock), and commercial enterprise. Eastern consumers prized buffalo-hide coats, and eastern factories used the hides to make steam-engine drive belts. Sioux leader Black Elk decried the slaughter and the "heaps of bones" left to rot in the sun.

Innovations in Financing and Organizing Business

As agents of economic development and cultural change, the railroads knew no peer. As private enterprises, however, they faced the same challenges that all big businesses ultimately must address. The proliferation of independent lines and the high fixed costs associated with the industry made profits slim and competition intense. As a result, railroad companies began to come together in informal pools to share equipment and set prices industrywide. In the 1880s these pools gave way to consolidation, a process by which several companies merged into one large company. Jay Gould's Erie Railroad was a consolidated railroad business.

In these years U.S. businesses grew larger and more quickly compared with their western European counterparts. This difference stemmed in large part from America's astonishing population growth and its rich natural resources. (For example, American coal and iron, the ingredients necessary for making steel, existed in proximity.) Equally significant, the United States possessed a social and legal culture favorable to big business. The absence of an entrenched, conservative elite, along with the spread of state and national laws that protected

TABLE 16-2

How Indians Used the Buffalo

Meat	Food and ceremonial use	Hide	Tipis, robes, dresses, gloves, breech cloth, shirts, leggings, moccasins, bedding, dolls, regalia, cradleboards, implements, drums, tipi furnishings
Fat and marrow	Food, paint, and cosmetics		
Bones	Tools, weapons, knives, pipes, soup, sleds		
Brain	Food, used to tan hides	Skull	Ceremonial use
Intestine	Cord	Horns	Implements, ornaments, ceremonial use, games
Hoofs	Implements, utensils, glue, jewelry, food, ceremonial use		
		Hair	Rope, stuffing, ornaments, ceremonial use
Bladder	Storage pouches	Dung	Fuel
Rawhide	Moccasin soles, shields, containers, ornaments, rattles, snow shoes, mortars, lariats, bridles, boats, luggage, food boiling, medicine bundle, saddles, thongs, stirrups	Sinew and muscle	Thread, cord bow strings
		Tail	Flu brush
		Stomach	Cooking vessel, container for carrying/storing water

Source: Adapted from Arlene Hirschfelder and Martha Kreipe de Montaño, *The Native American Almanac: A Portrait of Native America Today* (New York: Prentice Hall, 1993), p. 18.

private property, stimulated the entrepreneurial spirit. The U.S. government refrained from owning industries, although it heavily subsidized the railroad industry. It taxed business lightly and did not tax individual incomes at all until 1913. Finally, American bankers aggressively promoted growth through their lending practices and bond sales. For example, John Pierpont Morgan, a member of the banking firm of Drexel, Morgan, and Company in the 1880s, reorganized the firm under his own name in 1895 and played a leading role in financing a number of major American businesses.

Several large enterprises began to conquer not just local but also national markets. Examples include Bell Telephone (founded in Boston), the Kroger grocery business (Cincinnati), Marshall Field Department store (Chicago), and Boston Fruit Company. In the South, Midwest, and West, investors rushed to finance gigantic agribusinesses, such as the 1.5 million acres devoted to rice cultivation in southeastern Louisiana and bonanza wheat farms (as large as 38,000 acres) in the Red River Valley of North Dakota. In 1886, a single enterprise, the Calumet and Hecla Mining Company, in Montana, was producing 25,000 tons of copper each year, an amount that exceeded the total national output for every year before 1879.

Owners of these enterprises devised new forms of business organization that helped them grow and survive in a dynamic economy. By combining, or integrating, their operations, manufacturers cut costs and monopolized an entire industry in the process. Unable to withstand the ruthless competition that favored larger enterprises, smaller companies folded. The two icons of American big business in the 1880s—Andrew Carnegie in steel and John D. Rockefeller in petroleum—proved master innovators in both the managerial and technical aspects of business.

In 1875 Carnegie opened the Edgar Thomson Steelworks in Pittsburgh. Within a year, he was producing steel at half the prevailing market price. Carnegie excelled at vertical integration, in which a single firm controls all aspects of production and distribution. Carnegie employed miners in the rich iron and copper deposits in northern Minnesota's Mesabi Range and Michigan's Upper Peninsula (the Lake Superior region) to mine the raw material, and he owned the ships and railroads that brought the ore to the mills in Pittsburgh. Within the mills, he saved money by keeping fuel costs to a minimum (molten steel flowed easily from one processing stage to the next), by maintaining huge outputs, and by cutting labor costs to the bone. His personal connections to his former employer, the Pennsylvania Railroad, ensured a large and stable customer for his steel.

Another form of business consolidation was horizontal integration, in which a number of companies producing the same product merge to reduce competition and control prices. In 1882 John D. Rockefeller, a former bookkeeper, horizontally integrated the petroleum industry by forming Standard Oil Trust. Stockholders in small companies turned over their shares to Standard Oil, which then coordinated operations and eliminated competition from other smaller firms. Standard Oil also practiced vertical integration. Like Carnegie, Rockefeller controlled not only a raw material (in this case, crude oil) but also processing plants, or refineries. He managed to keep transportation costs low by negotiating discount rates from rail shippers. Soon he had positioned himself to buy out his rivals—or ruin them. Trusts placed a premium on efficient production, but they also worked to the disadvantage of consumers, who were hostage to high prices within industries that lacked competition.

For the growing managerial class, trusts helped to eliminate some of the uncertainty associated with an unstable marketplace. They ensured industries' access to raw materials, cheap transportation, expansive markets, and reliable credit institutions. This new form of business cropped up in other industries besides steel and oil. In 1887, the so-called Sugar Trust comprised 17 of the 21 U.S. sugar refiners and monopolized sugar refining east of the Mississippi River.

New Labor Supplies for a New Economy

To operate efficiently, expanding industries needed expanding supplies of workers to grow crops, extract raw materials, and produce manufactured goods. Many of these workers came from abroad. The year 1880 marked the leading edge of a new wave of immigration to the United States. Over the next ten years, 5.2 million newcomers entered the country, almost twice the previous decade's level of 2.8 million.

In the mid-nineteenth century, most immigrants hailed from western Europe and the British Isles—from Germany, Scandinavia, England, and Ireland. Between 1880 and 1890, Germans, Scandinavians, and the English kept coming, but they were joined by numerous Italians, Russians, and Poles. In fact, these last three groups predominated among newcomers for the next 35 years, their arrival rates peaking between 1890 and 1910. At the same time, immigrants from Asia, especially from China, were making their way to the Kingdom of Hawaii, which was annexed by the United States in 1898. Between 1852 and 1887, 26,000 Chinese arrived on the islands. Almost 40 percent of all immigrants to the United States during this period were known as "birds of passage," men who were recruited by American employers and who, after earning some money, migrated back to their native land.

Many of the new European immigrants sought to escape oppressive economic and political conditions in Europe, even as they hoped to make a new life for themselves and their families in the United States. Russian Jews fled discrimination and violent anti-Semitism in the form of pogroms, organized massacres, conducted by their Christian neighbors and Russian authorities. Southern Italians, most of whom were landless farmers, suffered from a combination of declining agricultural prices and high birth rates. Impoverished Poles chafed under cultural restrictions imposed by Germany and Russia. Hungarians, Greeks, Portuguese, and Armenians, among other groups, also participated in this great migration; members of these groups too were seeking political freedom and economic opportunity.

Immigrants replenished America's sense of itself as a haven for the downtrodden, a place where opportunity beckoned to hard-working and

William E. Wilson Photographic Collection/Historic Mobile Preservation Society

■ A burst of technological innovation characterized many American businesses during the last quarter of the nineteenth century. Nevertheless, some, like southern cotton plantations, remained largely unmechanized. Commanding large numbers of (sometimes resistant) black and white workers, southern planters refrained from investing in labor-saving technology. This woman, working at the Savannah Cotton Exchange in 1880, carries a basket of cotton on her head, just as her enslaved foremothers did.

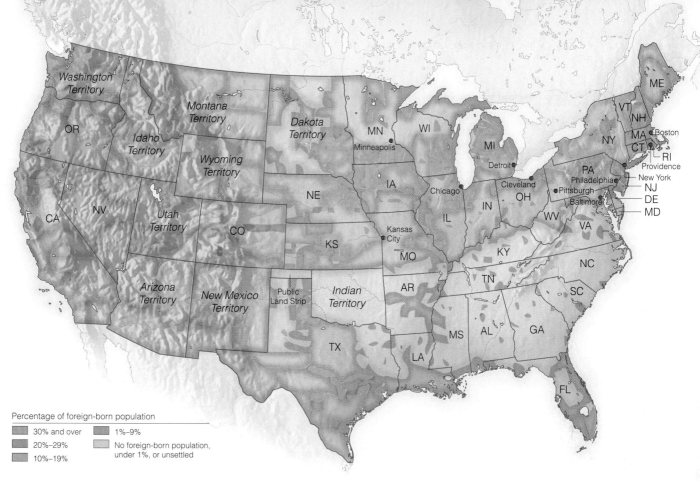

Washington Territory · OR · Idaho Territory · Montana Territory · Dakota Territory · MN · WI · MI · ME · VT · NH · MA · Boston · NY · CT · RI · Providence · New York · NJ · DE · MD · Minneapolis · Detroit · Cleveland · PA · Philadelphia · Pittsburgh · Baltimore · CA · NV · Utah Territory · Wyoming Territory · CO · NE · IA · Chicago · IL · IN · OH · WV · VA · KS · Kansas City · MO · KY · NC · Arizona Territory · New Mexico Territory · Public Land Strip · Indian Territory · AR · TN · SC · TX · MS · AL · GA · LA · FL

Percentage of foreign-born population

- 30% and over
- 20%–29%
- 10%–19%
- 1%–9%
- No foreign-born population, under 1%, or unsettled

■ **MAP 16.2**

POPULATION OF FOREIGN-BORN, BY REGION, 1880 After the Civil War, large numbers of immigrants settled in northeastern cities. In addition, the Upper Midwest and parts of the western mining frontier drew many newcomers from western Europe. The area along the country's southwestern border was home to immigrants from Mexico. Cuban cigar makers established thriving communities in southern Florida.

ambitious people. "The New Colossus," written by American poet Emma Lazarus in 1883, pays tribute to the "huddled masses yearning to breathe free"—people from all over the world who sought refuge in the United States. The words of her poem are inscribed on the Statue of Liberty at the entrance to New York Harbor. (The people of France presented the statue, called "Liberty Enlightening the World," to America in 1884.)

Most of the newcomers found work in the factories, mills, and sweatshops of New York, Philadelphia, and Chicago. At the same time, large numbers of these fresh arrivals dispersed to other areas of the country to work in a wide variety of enterprises. Scandinavians populated the prairies of Iowa and Minnesota and the High Plains of the Dakotas. Immigrants from Mexico found work in the mines and beet fields of Colorado.

In the South, some planters began to recruit immigrants—especially western Europeans of "hardy peasant stock"—to take the place of blacks who resisted working for whites. Nevertheless, planters' experiments with recruiting immigrants amounted to little. Given the opportunity, many immigrants sought to flee from the back-breaking labor and meager wages of the cotton staple crop economy. A group of Germans brought over to toil in the Louisiana swamps soon after the Civil War quickly slipped away from their employers; they had agreed to the arrangement only to gain free passage to America. Thirty Swedes who arrived in Alabama also deserted at an opportune moment, declaring that they were not slaves. South Carolina planters who sponsored colonies of Germans and Italians gave up in exasperation. The few Chinese who began work in the Louisiana sugar fields soon abandoned the plodding work of the plantations in favor of employment in the trades and shops of New Orleans. Still, in 1890, immigrant worker

TABLE 16-3

Immigration by Country of Origin, 1831–1940

	1831–1840	1841–1850	1851–1860	1861–1870	1871–1880	1881–1890	1891–1900	1901–1910	1911–1920	1921–1930	1931–1940
Austria-Hungary			7,800	72,060	353,722	502,707	2,145,266	806,342	65,548	3,469[a]	
Belgium	22	5,094	4,738	6,734	7,221	20,174	18,167	41,635	33,746	15,846	12,189
Bulgaria							160	39,280	22,533	2,945	375
Czechoslovakia									3,426	102,194	8,347
Denmark	1,063	539	3,749	37,094	31,771	88,132	50,231	65,285	41,083	32,430	5,393
France	45,575	77,202	70,358	35,984	72,201	50,403	30,770	73,730	61,897	49,610	38,800
Germany	152,454	434,626	951,667	787,468	717,182	452,970	505,152	341,498	143,945	412,202	226,578[b]
Greece						2,053	15,079	167,519	184,201	51,084	8,973
Italy	2,253	1,870	9,231	11,728	55,762	307,310	651,893	2,045,877	1,109,524	455,315	57,661
Netherlands	1,412	8,251	10,789	9,102	16,541	53,701	26,758	48,262	43,718	26,946	14,860
Norway	1,201	13,903	20,931	109,298	95,323	176,586	95,012	190,505	66,393	68,531	10,100
Sweden					115,922	391,776	226,266	249,534	95,074	97,249	10,665
Poland[c]	—	—	1,164	2,027	12,970	51,806	96,720	—	4,813	227,734	7,571
Romania						5,938	12,750	53,008	13,311	67,646	1,076
Russia[d]	646	656	1,621	4,536	52,254	265,080	602,011	1,597,306	921,957	78,433	548
Spain	2,954	2,759	10,353	8,493	5,206	4,418	8,731	27,935	68,611	28,958	2,898
Portugal					4,627	11,017	28,323	69,149	89,732	29,994	7,423
Switzerland	4,821	4,644	25,011	23,286	28,293	81,088	31,179	34,922	23,001	29,676	10,547
Turkey in Europe						1,185	3,786	119,256	77,210	14,659	580
United Kingdom											
England	7,611	32,002	247,125	222,277	437,706	644,680	216,726	388,017	249,944	157,420	112,252
Ireland	207,381	780,719	914,119	435,778	456,871	655,482	388,416	339,065	146,181	220,501	25,377
Scotland	2,667	3,712	38,331	38,768	87,564	149,869	44,188	120,469	78,357	159,781	16,131
Wales	183	1,261	6,319	4,313	6,631	12,640	10,557	17,464	13,107	13,012	3,209
Not specified	63,347	229,979	132,199	349,538	16,142	186	67				
Other Europe	96	155	116	210	658	1,346	122	665	18,238	22,983	11,813
Total Europe	495,686	1,597,522	2,453,821	2,074,434	2,274,874	4,783,413	3,655,673	8,175,296	4,407,336	2,427,787	621,704
Canada and Newfoundland[e]			59,304	153,878	383,640	393,304	3,311	179,226	742,515	924,185	171,718
Central America			449	95	157	404	549	8,102	17,159	15,769	21,665
Mexico[e]			3,078	2,191	5,162	1,913	971	49,642	219,004	459,287	60,589
South America			1,224	1,397	1,128	2,304	1,075	17,280	41,899	42,215	21,831
West Indies			10,660	9,046	13,957	29,042	33,066	107,548	123,424	74,899	49,725
Total America			74,715	166,607	404,044	425,967	38,972	361,888	1,143,671	1,516,685	354,804[f]
China	8	35	41,397	64,301	123,200	61,711	14,799	20,005	21,270	29,907	16,709
Japan							25,942	129,797	83,837	33,462	1,555
Turkey in Asia							26,799	77,393	79,389	19,165	218
Other Asia	40	47	61	308	603	6,669	3,696	15,772	8,055	14,866	13,298
Total Asia	48	82	41,458	64,609	123,803	65,380	71,236	243,567	192,559	97,400	31,780
Africa			210	312	358	857	350	7,368	8,443	6,286	7,367
Australia, Tasmania, New Zealand			36	9,886	7,017	2,740	11,975	12,348	8,299	13,805
Pacific Islands				1,028	5,557	1,225	1,049	1,079	427	5,437
All other countries			29,169	17,969	700	789	14,063	33,523[g]	1,147	228	142
Total Immigration	495,736	1,597,604	2,599,373	2,323,967	2,814,793	5,292,980	3,794,259	8,832,666	5,766,593	4,057,112	1,035,039

[a]Hungary only.
[b]Includes Austria 1938–1940
[c]From 1890–1919, Poland is included with Austria-Hungary, Germany, and Russia.
[d]Including Finland 1831–1920.
[e]No reports from 1886–1893.
[f]Includes other Americas.
[g]Includes 32,897 people returning to their homes in U.S. After 1906, such aliens were considered nonimmigrants.

Source: Lord & Lord, *Historical Atlas of the U.S.* (New York: Henry Holt).

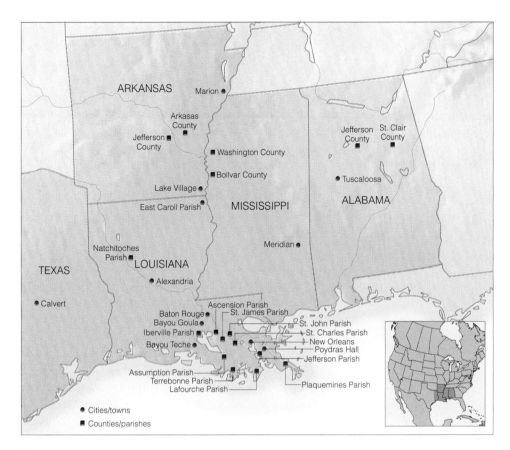

■ MAP 16.3
SOME PLACES WHERE CHINESE LOCATED, 1865–1880 Immediately after the Civil War, some southern whites believed that immigrants would prove to be more reliable and efficient workers than the freedpeople. Planters in Mississippi and Louisiana imported a small number of Chinese from California and others directly from Hong Kong. However, by the early 1870s most of these workers had deserted the fields and moved to nearby towns and cities to work as artisans, grocers, and laundry operators.

enclaves were scattered throughout the South. Irish, Polish, and Italian men were swinging pick-axes in Florida railroad camps. Italian men, women, and children were picking cotton on Louisiana plantations. Hungarian men were digging coal out of mines in West Virginia.

The story of Rosa Cassettari, a young woman who emigrated from northern Italy to the United States in 1884, suggests the challenges that faced many newcomers during this period. Rosa's husband, Santino, had preceded her to America. He had settled in an iron mining camp in Missouri. Leaving her son with relatives, Rosa received the assurances of friends and relatives: "You will get smart in America. And in America you will not be so poor."

In the steerage section of a steamship bound for the United States, Rosa found herself surrounded not only by *paesani* (fellow Italians) but also by Germans, Swedes, Poles, and French—"every kind," she remembered later. After arriving at Castle Garden (an immigration processing center at the tip of Manhattan and a predecessor of Ellis Island), Rosa and her *paesani* were approached by a smooth-talking, well-dressed, Italian-speaking man. Overcharging them for the train trip to Missouri, he left them with no money for food.

Life in the iron camp proved harsh—nothing like what Rosa had expected. Her husband, who was much older than she, neglected her; he preferred the company of prostitutes in the town. The iron was almost depleted, and some workers and their wives had moved on to a new mine in Michigan. Rosa's days centered on caring for her new baby and cooking for 13 of the miners.

Despite these realities, within a couple of years, Rosa grew used to America and considered herself an American. She returned briefly to her hometown in Italy but expressed impatience with the rigid social etiquette that separated the rich from the poor. She also yearned for the hearty meals that had become her staple in the iron camp. Back in Missouri, she mustered enough courage to leave Santino, traveling to Chicago and making a new life for herself in the Italian *colonia* (community) there. She eventually married another Italian man (the two had fallen in love in Missouri) and found work as a cleaning woman at Chicago Commons, a social settlement house. Her new husband alternated between working in construction and peddling bananas and cranberries. Rosa herself gained a reputation as a storyteller; later she said, "Me, I was always crazy for a good story."

These ethnic niches proved crucial for the well-being of many immigrant communities. They provided newcomers with an entrée into the economy.

The influx of so many foreign-born workers transformed the American labor market. Native-born Protestant men moved up the employment ladder to become members of the white-collar (that is, professional) middle class, while recent immigrants filled the ranks in construction and manufacturing. By 1890 Italian immigrants accounted for 90 percent of New York's public works employees and 99 percent of Chicago's street construction and maintenance crews. Women and children, both native and foreign-born, predominated in the textile, garment-making, and food processing industries.

Specific groups of immigrants often gravitated toward particular kinds of jobs. For example, many Poles found work in the vast steel plants of Pittsburgh, and Russian Jews went into the garment industry and street-peddling trade in New York City. California fruit orchards and vegetable farms employed numerous Japanese immigrants. Cuban immigrants rolled cigars in Florida. In Hawaii, the Chinese and Japanese labored in the sugar fields; after they had accumulated a little money, they became rice farmers and shopkeepers. In Boston and New York City, second-generation Irish took advantage of their prominent place in the Democratic party to become public school teachers, firefighters, and police officers.

These ethnic niches proved crucial for the well-being of many immigrant communities. They provided newcomers with an entrée into the economy; indeed, many men and women got their first jobs with the help of kin and other compatriots. Niches also helped immigrants advance within an industry or economic sector. Finally, they enriched immigrant communities by keeping profits and wages within those communities.

The experience of Kinji Ushijima (later known as George Shima) graphically illustrates the power of immigrant niches. Shima arrived in California in 1887 and, like many other Japanese immigrants, he found work as a potato picker in the San Joaquin Valley. Soon, Shima moved up to become a labor contractor, securing Japanese laborers for the valley's white farmers. With the money he made, he bought 15 acres of land and began his own potato farm. Eventually he built a large potato business by expanding his holdings, reclaiming swampland, and investing in a fleet of boats to ship his crops up the coast to San Francisco. Taking advantage of a Japanese niche, Shima had prospered through a combination of good luck and hard work.

Efficient Machines, Efficient People

Just as whole industries consolidated to achieve new milestones in efficiency, productivity, and reliability, so did individual workplaces. Well-oiled machines helped entrepreneurs manufacture mass quantities of uniform parts. Employers now pushed workers to strive for the same level of performance.

By the late nineteenth century, the typical industrial employee labored within an immense, multistory brick structure and operated a machine powered by water or steam. Smoky, smelly kerosene lamps gave way to early forms of electric lighting, first arc and then incandescent light bulbs. Long-standing industries, such as textiles and shoes, were now fully mechanized. The new products flooding the economy—locomotives and bicycles, cash registers and typewriters—streamed from factories designed to ensure maximum efficiency from both machines *and* the people who tended them.

In the 1880s a few factory managers hired efficiency experts. The experts' goal was to cut labor costs in the same way that industry barons had shaved the costs of extracting raw materials or distributing final products. With huge quantities of goods flowing from factories, even modest savings in wages could mean significant profits in the long run. As early as the 1880s, efficiency experts, such as Frederick Winslow Taylor, chief engineer for the Midvale Steel Plant outside Philadelphia, were pioneering in the techniques of "scientific management." These techniques stressed uniform, plantwide procedures for routine machine operation and maintenance and labor organization.

Southern textile mill owners devised their own strategies for shaping a compliant workforce. They employed only white men, women, and children as machine operators, but threatened to hire blacks if the whites protested low wages and poor working conditions. During the prewar period, enslaved workers—males and females, adults and children—had been forced to labor in the small textile mills that dotted the Piedmont region of South Carolina and Georgia. But after the Civil War, employers decided to reserve jobs in the expanding textile industry for whites only in order to preserve and extend divisions within the southern labor force. Poor whites lived in company housing, their children attended company schools, and they received cash wages. In contrast, blacks remained in the countryside, impoverished and without the right to vote. In 1874 the manager of a textile mill in Columbus, Georgia, rationalized his company's exclusive policy: "We do not think the negroes adapted to the labor of cotton-mills. Their lack of quickness, sensitiveness of touch, and general sleepy characteristics disqualify them. . . . Being far better fitted for outdoor labor, they will no doubt always be kept so employed." Prewar textile mill owners, who had used slave labor so profitably, would have been shocked by this later view. In the cities of the North as well as the textile villages of the South, factory workers remained exclusively white until well into the twentieth century.

TABLE 16-4

Number of Firms by Number of Employees per Firm, 1850 and 1880

	Number of Firms							
	1850				1880			
	No. of Employees				No. of Employees			
Industry	0–5	6–50	50+	Total	0–5	6–50	50+	Total
Iron and Steel	6	13	3	22	6	20	17	43
Textiles	46	87	53	186	25	59	8	92
Hardware	76	42	7	125	114	122	27	263
Machines and tools	42	44	6	92	96	113	19	228
Printing	36	60	10	106	105	148	36	289
Building construction	83	59	3	145	588	227	18	833
Clothing	165	294	43	502	301	255	93	649
Furniture	84	66	3	153	185	105	20	310
Metal	83	11	1	95	166	47	5	218
Meat	81	3	0	84	458	23	2	483
Harness	32	15	3	50	96	21	2	119
Baking	384	29	0	413	910	73	8	991
Shoes	339	224	20	583	441	139	34	614
Blacksmith	141	18	1	160	187	12	0	199

Note: Because the census recorded only firms producing more than $500 per year, there may be serious undercounting of firms with one or no employees.

Source: Census of the United States, 1850 and 1880.

The Birth of a National Urban Culture

In the 1880s visitors to the territory of Utah marveled at the capital, Salt Lake City, where Mormon pioneers had made the desert bloom. Situated at the foot of the magnificent snow-covered Wasach Range, this oasis in the Great Salt Basin boasted a built landscape almost as impressive as the natural beauty that surrounded it. In the heart of Salt Lake City lay Temple Square. This broad plaza contained the Mormon Tabernacle, a huge domed structure. Next to it stood the Mormon Temple, a soaring six-spired granite cathedral still under construction. The city had the advantage of rail service (Promontory Point, where the transcontinental railroad was joined, was not far away). Mines in nearby Bingham Canyon yielded rich lodes of silver and large local smelters refined copper ores. Irrigation systems made the city self-sufficient in the production of foodstuffs. A settlement inspired by religious faith, Salt Lake City was at the same time thoroughly modern.

Not just Salt Lake City, but other cities around the country began to assume monumental proportions. In New York, the 1880s marked the completion of Central Park and the Brooklyn Bridge and the arrival of the Statue of Liberty from France. Chicago, rebuilding after a disastrous fire in 1871, became a sprawling rail hub dotted with yards for western cattle, northern timber, and the trains that hauled them. In 1885 Chicago also became the location for a major architectural breakthrough by engineer William LeBaron Jenney. He designed the ten-story Home Insurance Building, the world's first metal frame skyscraper. The steel skeleton weighed only one third as much as the thick stone walls needed to support a similar masonry building, and the design left room for numerous windows. Urban architecture would never be the same again.

Cities in general represented American notions of progress and prosperity; they were places where innovation, consumer culture, and new forms of entertainment grew and flourished. From 1875 to 1900, American cities developed increasingly sophisticated systems of communications and transportation. Streetlights, transportation networks, and sewer lines provided basic services to swelling populations of immigrants and rural in-migrants. Experts in the fields of urban design and architecture and ambitious entrepreneurs in the fields of entertainment and professional sports all left their mark on cities. In a country fascinated with new and bigger and better things, cities set the standard by defining a desirable way of life for a "typical" middle-class American.

In their social and physical configurations, cities also represented a new cultural diversity in American life. At times uneasily, they accommodated immigrants from around the world. San Francisco's Chinatown formed a "city within a city" as hostile European Americans sought to circumscribe its residents. Politics, prejudice, and technology came together to shape the urban landscape.

Economic Sources of Urban Growth

Northeastern and mid-Atlantic cities emerged as centers of concentrated manufacturing activity. Yet, with the aid of eastern capital, western cities also flourished. New York's Wall Street and Boston's State Street, home to the nation's largest investment bankers, financed the Main Streets of the Midwest and West. Some urban areas prospered through milling, mining, or other enterprises, such as lumber and flour milling in Minneapolis and ore smelting in Denver. Others focused on manufacturing to serve a growing western population. Chicago was rivaled only by New York in terms of its industrial economy and the vast territory that it supplied with raw materials, processed food, and manufactured goods. Salt Lake City produced goods for the so-called Mormon Corridor of settlements that stretched west from the city to southern California. By the 1880s San Francisco had a commercial reach that encompassed much of the West as well as Hawaii and Alaska. Writer Henry George noted, "Not a settler in all the Pacific States and Territories but must pay San Francisco tribute. Not an ounce of gold dug, a pound of ore melted, a field gleaned, or a tree felled in all their thousands of square miles, but must add to her wealth."

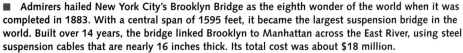

Museum of the City of New York/CORBIS

■ Admirers hailed New York City's Brooklyn Bridge as the eighth wonder of the world when it was completed in 1883. With a central span of 1595 feet, it became the largest suspension bridge in the world. Built over 14 years, the bridge linked Brooklyn to Manhattan across the East River, using steel suspension cables that are nearly 16 inches thick. Its total cost was about $18 million.

No trend supported urban growth more than the arrival of newcomers from abroad. To stoke its furnaces, mill its lumber, and slaughter its cattle, Chicago relied on immigrants from Ireland, Slovakia, Germany, Poland, and Bohemia. Of the three cities with the highest percentage of foreign-born residents in 1880, San Francisco (45 percent) ranked higher than both Chicago (42 percent) and New York (40 percent). Yet all large cities also attracted migrants from America's own countryside, as native-born men and women fled the hardship of life on the farm. The use of increasingly efficient agricultural machines meant that rural workers had fewer job opportunities. Most of the immigrants from rural areas to the cities were young women; they included Yankee girls from the hardscrabble homesteads of New England, daughters of Swedish immigrants in Minnesota, and native-born farm tenants in Indiana.

Rural folk sought the steady work and wages afforded by jobs in the city, but they were also drawn to the excitement that had become the hallmark of the urban scene. In the early nineteenth century, Thomas Jefferson had located the heart of America in its sturdy yeoman farmers; by the late nineteenth century, that heart had shifted to the city.

Building the Cities

In 1886 the Reverend Josiah Strong, a proponent of Protestant missionary efforts abroad, condemned the American city as a "menace" to civilization. However, in decrying what he saw the evils of urban life, Strong described its appeal to people of all ages and both sexes: "It is the city where wealth is massed; and here are the tangible evidences of it piled many stories high. . . . Here are luxuries gathered—everything that dazzles the eye or tempts the appetite; here is the most extravagant expenditure." Strong was right that this conspicuous display of wealth would have profound implications for American politics and culture.

Center for Southwest Research, University of New Mexico

■ Many southwestern cities, such as Albuquerque, were laid out on an Old Town–New Town plan. The original center of settlement, Old Town was characterized by flat-roofed adobe buildings clustered on narrow streets. This photo shows Albuquerque's New Town in the 1880s. Located a mile and a half from Old Town plaza, it consists of Victorian-style buildings. The plan of New Town followed straight lines and right angles, "adapted to the railroad, the regenerator," in the words of one observer.

In these years the American city was emerging as a technological marvel. Through a combination of money and engineering skill, cities managed to provide an adequate water supply for private and commercial purposes, move large numbers of people and goods efficiently, get rid of waste materials, and illuminate thoroughfares at night. Professionals, such as landscape contractors, construction architects, and civil engineers, designed the parks, bridges, public libraries, and museums that made the city so attractive.

Throughout the country, new towns emerged as industrialists and factory owners sought to lure and retain workers. George M. Pullman, who manufactured railroad sleeping cars, built a town outside Chicago and named it after himself. In the South, company towns dotted the Piedmont region (textiles), the steep slopes of the Appalachian Mountains (coal and lumber), the piney woods of Texas (lumber), and the coast of Florida (phosphates). In the West, towns grew up around copper, coal, iron ore, and silver mines. These communities shared a unique characteristic: they directly linked housing, education, and commerce to a particular company.

Cities grew upward and outward as a result of developments in mass production and technology. The availability of factory-assembled building materials accelerated the construction of private dwellings and office buildings. Elevators extended living and office spaces upward (in the Reverend Strong's words, "wealth is massed . . . piled many stories high"). The invention of the electric streetcar in 1888 permitted cities to spread out. Soon, residential suburbs cropped up many miles from urban commercial cores. Wealthy and middle-class urban residents followed the streetcar lines out of the city, hoping to find a green refuge from the grime and noise of downtown while maintaining a manageable commute to work.

As cities expanded, the challenges associated with providing services also grew more complex and expensive. A polluted water supply, for example, meant epidemics of diptheria and cholera, so city taxpayers demanded waterworks that delivered drinkable water through intricate systems of dams, pumps, reservoirs, and pipes. Chicago had long pumped its sewage into Lake Michigan, the source of its drinking water. In the 1880s the city financed the building of a canal and the reversal of the flow of the Chicago River. These changes sent the city's sewage away from Lake Michigan and into the Mississippi River instead. Begun in 1889, the 28-mile Chicago Sanitary and Ship Canal was completed seven years later. One awed observer marveled at the "powerful machinery for digging and hoisting, steam shovels, excavators, inclines, conveyors, derricks, cantilevers, cableways, channelers, steam drills, pumps, etc." The cost: $54 million.

Local Government Gets Bigger

These new systems of services, combined with the mushrooming immigrant neighborhoods, changed both the quality and the quantity of urban problems. Zoning issues—who could build what, where, and when—became flashpoints for conflict as the interests of homeowners, developers, and municipal engineers collided. These controversies called for new forms of local government. Specifically, urban political leaders struggled to improve the city's public works while meeting the needs of multiple ethnic groups. Governing a big city was becoming a big business.

Rising tax rates and ballooning municipal debts told an even larger story. In 1845, the city of Boston spent $8.29 per resident and owed its creditors $748,000. Thirty years later, per capita annual expenditures had risen fivefold, and the city's debt had multiplied several times to more than $27 million. Clearly, running a city was an expensive, full-time enterprise and one that had the potential to be very lucrative to businesspeople and politicians alike.

Although New York's "Boss" Tweed had been convicted on charges of corruption in the early 1870s, the infamous Tammany Hall gang carried on his legacy. The Democratic officials associated with this social and political organization perfected a system of kickbacks linked to municipal construction projects. Under this system contractors paid politicians for city construction contracts. For example, a New York City courthouse that was supposed to cost a quarter of a million dollars ended up costing taxpayers 52 times that amount, or twice as much as the United States paid Russia for Alaska! In the 1880s secretive networks of corruption linking law enforcement personnel, city officials, and construction contractors flourished in many cities. These webs, or "machines," characterized urban life for decades to come.

Local officials went out of their way to support the provision of illegal services demanded by their constituents.

Urban machines existed to secure jobs for their loyal supporters and line the pockets of those at the highest levels of power. Deal-making blurred the lines between private enterprise and public service as everyone from mayors to local ward organizers benefited from the modernization of the American city. In the process, urban bosses ensured that the streets were paved, tenement buildings erected, sewer lines laid, and trolley tracks extended. But taxpayers footed the bill, which included outrageous amounts of money used for bribes and kickbacks.

Local officials went out of their way to support the provision of illegal services, such as prostitution and gambling, demanded by their constituents. Money-grubbing politicians and police extorted "hush money" from brothels, gambling parlors, and unlicensed taverns. In turn, these places became absorbed into the bosses' local empire. Extorted fees greased the palms of the cop on the beat and the judge on the take.

Urban bosses had a vested interest in sponsoring new money-making venues for professional sports and supporting other forms of commercialized leisure activity. Baseball parks, boxing rings, and race tracks yielded huge sums in the form of kickbacks from contractors. Once built, stadiums and boxing rings generated profits indefinitely. Sporting events themselves also gave a city's political, legal, and judicial leaders a chance to meet each other and seal business deals.

Thrills, Chills, and Bathtubs: The Emergence of Consumer Culture

On a hot summer day in 1890, a young mother named Emily Scanlon, with her three-year-old daughter in tow, paid the five-cent admission fee to a popular ride called the Toboggan Slide at the Brandywine Springs Amusement Park near Wilmington, Delaware. The two of them ascended a stairwell to the top of the three-story-high structure and then stepped into a car that ran on a wooden trough. When the attendant released the brakes, the car descended, pulled by gravity. It moved slowly at first, then picked up speed around a curve. Suddenly, Emily Scanlon stood up in the car (perhaps to retrieve her hat, which had blown off), and she and her daughter were thrown from the car. Mrs. Scanlon died instantly of a broken neck, but the youngster survived. Significantly, the tragedy did not provoke a shutdown of the ride or the installation of safety measures. Instead, park managers simply posted a sign that read, "Passengers must keep their seats." Patrons continued to enjoy the thrills of the toboggan.

Brandywine Springs boasted an ornate gateway that proclaimed "Let All Who Enter Here Leave Care Behind." In cities around the country, amusement parks brought men and women, girls and boys together to enjoy merry-go-rounds, prizefights, and circus sideshows. By 1880, railroads and steamships were transporting crowds out of Manhattan to Coney Island, where working-class people mingled with the self-proclaimed "respectable" middle classes.

Late in the century, Americans of all kinds began to sample a new realm of sensual experience—one of physical daring, material luxury, and visual fantasy—either as participants or as observers. The ride at Brandywine Springs was an early prototype of the modern roller coaster. The park afforded patrons not only the thrill of riding the Toboggan Slide but also the sights and sounds of a carnival. The calliope (pipe organ) music and the brightly colored signs beckoned visitors to an exciting world apart from the routine of everyday life.

Ticket holders at Brandywine Springs were participating in an emerging consumer culture. With economic growth and high rates of productivity came the two ingredients necessary to a culture of consumption: industries that catered to the demand for novel experiences, or ready-made goods and people with enough money to buy them. Central to this culture was mass advertising, a form of appeal that sought to instill in consumers the desire for things that were new and visually attractive. Colorful spectacles of all kinds—whether in the form of a department store window or a well-publicized athletic event—became an integral part of American life.

Shows as Spectacles

Public officials, college administrators, and ambitious entrepreneurs alike discovered that Americans craved new and stimulating forms of entertainment and were willing to pay for them. Athletic events began to draw large crowds, revealing their potential as big business. Traveling road shows promoted new products and services by charming their audiences with exotic performances. Though modest by today's standards, such spectacles found a ready market in the United States and other countries.

In the quarter-century after Reconstruction, three major sports began to attract large national audiences. Organized baseball had existed since 1846, when the Knickerbocker Base Ball Club of New York met the New York Nine in Hoboken, New Jersey. (The score was 23 to 1, in favor of the Nine.) The National Baseball League, consisting of eight professional teams, was founded in 1876, the American League in 1900. In the 1880s, several new regulations—those governing the overhand pitch, foul balls, and swingless strikes—helped to standardize the game.

Also in the 1880s, Walter Camp, a former Yale University football player, introduced rules—for instance, the system of downs and the center snap to the quarterback—that made

Courtesy, Transcendental Graphics

KEEFE, (P. NEW YORK).

OLD JUDGE & GYPSY QUEEN CIGARETTES

Courtesy, Transcendental Graphics

CHAMPIONS

Base Ball.		Isaac Murphy,	Jockey.
Andrews, (C.F. Philadelphia).		Charles Wood,	do.
Anson, (1st Base, Chicago).		Beeckman,	Lawn Tennis
Brouthers, (1st Base, Detroit).		Dwight,	do.
Caruthers, (P. Brooklyn).		Sears,	do.
Dunlap, (Capt., Pittsburgh).		Taylor,	do.
Glasscock, (S. S. Indianapolis).		Marksman,	
Keefe, (P. New York).		Captain Bogardus.	
Kelly, (C. Boston).		Beach,	Oarsman.
Prince,	Bicyclist.	Jake Gaudaur,	do.
Rowe,	do.	Hanlan,	do.
Stevens,	do.	Teemer,	do.
Wood,	do.	James Albert,	Pedestrian.
Daly,	Billiards.	Pat Fitzgerald,	do
Schaefer,	do.	Rowell,	do
Sexton,	do.	D'oro,	Pool.
Slosson,	do.	Jack Dempsey,	Pugilist
Vignaux,	do.	Jake Kilrain,	do.
Broadswordsman,		Mitchell,	do.
Duncan C. Ross.		Jem Smith,	do
Capt. Mackenzie,	Chess.	Sullivan,	do.
Steinitz,	do.	Myers,	Runner.
Zukertort,	do.	Strongest Man in the World,	
Foot Ball.		Emil Voss,	
Beecher, (Capt. of Yale Team).		Wild West Hunter,	
W. Byrd Page, High Jumper.		"Buffalo Bill".	
"Snapper" Garrison, Jockey.		Joe Acton,	Wrestler
McLaughlin,	do.	Muldoon,	do.

**GOODWIN & CO.
NEW YORK.**

CARD COLLECTOR'S CO.
REPRINT

■ Baseball cards, like this one featuring New York Giants player Tim Keefe, were sold at department stores. On the back of the card are listed other national athletes featured in the series. One "Wild West Hunter" is identified as "Buffalo Bill" Cody. This card was also a cigarette advertisement.

that sport quicker and more competitive. Camp was also behind the selection of the first "All America" team (1889) to stimulate fan interest. By this time towns, high schools, and colleges were fielding football teams.

Likewise, boxing emerged as a national, regulated sport. John L. Sullivan, an American, won renown as the world's bare-knuckled champion in 1882, even as more and more fighters had started wearing gloves. Sullivan then joined a traveling theatrical group and demonstrated gloved boxing to enthusiastic crowds all over the country. These exhibitions revealed the fine line between displays of physical prowess and theatrical performances. In 1889, Sullivan defeated an opponent in a 75-round match, the last heavyweight, bare-knuckled championship.

Performances based on skills of all kinds gained national audiences, as the career of William "Buffalo Bill" Cody reveals. Born in Iowa in 1846, Cody parlayed his early years as a Pony Express postal rider, cavalry scout, Indian fighter, and buffalo hunter into a form of mass entertainment. In his "Buffalo Bill Combination" show, cowboy and Indian actors performed skits depicting dramatic events in western history (from a European American point of view, at least). In 1876, Cody briefly left the stage to join a U.S. cavalry skirmish against the Sioux and Cheyenne. Soon he returned to the show to exhibit the dried scalp of the Cheyenne warrior Yellow Hand, whom he claimed he had killed in battle. Cody thus presented the subjugation of the Indians as a form of high drama, a scripted performance that audiences applauded from the comfort of their seats.

In 1882 Cody produced "Buffalo Bill's Wild West," a traveling road show that featured sharpshooter Annie Oakley, cowboy musicians, and Sioux warriors performing authentic Native American dances. Sioux leader Sitting Bull (Tatanka Iyotake), long an admirer of Annie Oakley (he called her "Little Sure Shot"), joined the show in 1885. Like other Indians who

The Denver Public Library/Western History/Genealogy Department (Neg. #B-133)

■ "Buffalo Bill" Cody and Sitting Bull pose for a promotional photo for the 1885 season of the "Wild West." Cody refrained from calling the production a "show," maintaining that it demonstrated frontier skills and recreated historical encounters (such as Custer's Last Stand and stagecoach robberies). The "Wild West" toured Canada and Europe and inspired many imitators.

worked for Cody, Sitting Bull took advantage of the opportunity to escape the confines of the reservation (in his case, Standing Rock in North Dakota). As a member of the "Wild West" troupe, he also enjoyed decent food and accommodations. At a time when whites were denigrating Indian culture, Sitting Bull affirmed that culture by demonstrating his shooting and riding skills. However, white audiences jeered him—they saw him as less an entertainer and more an enemy warrior—and he left after just a year. By the 1890s, Cody was playing to audiences in Europe as well as the United States, dramatizing a West that was fast disappearing. Still, the sight of Annie Oakley shooting glass balls and clay pigeons out of the air, as well as mounted cowboys leading "Custer's last charge," gave customers their money's worth.

One type of traveling road spectacle, the medicine show, had a single purpose: the selling of specific health-related products. In the 1880s N. T. ("Nevada Ned") Oliver hawked an all-purpose remedy called Hindoo Patalka to gullible audiences in New Jersey and Pennsylvania. An ensemble of actors bedecked in Oriental costumes, with a live elephant as a prop, enthralled spectators. Nevada Ned himself testified to the increasing popularity of such presentations, noting that medicine shows were playing in "opera houses, halls, storerooms, ball parks, show boats, and tents, as well as doorways, street corners, and fairs." Increasingly, entrepreneurs saw that many aspects of the American experience—sports, myths about western settlement, anxieties about health and public appearance—could generate profits for shrewd businesspeople.

Mass Merchandising as Spectacle

During the late nineteenth century, the act of shopping in cities for goods, especially luxury goods, became an adventure in itself. A new piece of the cityscape, the department store, welcomed customers into a world of luxury and abundance, a place of color, light, and glamour. These "palaces of consumption" showcased a variety of technological innovations. In Marshall Field's "Grand Emporium" (Chicago), Wanamaker's (Philadelphia), and Lord & Taylor (New York), shoppers glided from story to story on escalators and in elevators. Warmed by central heating, they browsed display cases, racks, and tables laden with enticing goods and illuminated by arc lighting. Their money streamed into cash registers or to a central clerk through cash conveyors.

Thus, department stores not only offered a dazzling array of goods but also made shopping an exciting experience. This appealed particularly to middle-class women, who had the leisure time and the cash to indulge in day-long shopping excursions. In 1880 a New Yorker could arrive at Macy's by taking the Sixth Avenue elevated train and spend the morning exploring any number of specialized departments: ribbons, women's and children's muslin underwear, toys, candy, books, men's furnishings, china and glassware, and so on. Fatigued at noon, she might visit the lunchroom to partake of a modest meal and then devote the rest of her day to examining the colored dress silks, a new department established the year before.

During the 1880s, Macy's expanded its line of goods, introducing items as varied as dog collars and telescopes, mirrors, seeds and garden tools, and Goodyear's rubber boots. The store sold brand names and products manufactured by the company itself, including Red Star silk and Red Star velveteen (a soft, plush fabric). One New York newspaper marveled

Persuading People to Buy: Advertising in American History

Over the last four centuries, American advertisers have become increasingly creative in using new media to reach potential customers. During the colonial period, inns and taverns identified themselves by hanging sideboards easily recognizable to pedestrians. Early newspapers, such as Benjamin Franklin's *Philadelphia Gazette* (founded in 1728), pioneered in print advertising. Franklin's paper included descriptions of runaway slaves wanted by their owners as well as ads for slaves offered for sale.

In the streets, peddlers called to passersby. Chimney sweeps hawked their services with their distinctive "Sweep O!" refrain. Dry goods merchants distributed cards (handbills) that listed their wares, from corduroy cloth to colorful ostrich feathers. The Stamp Act of 1765 imposed a two-shilling tax on every print advertisement. Colonial merchants rightly feared that this tax would hinder commercial development.

In the antebellum period, mass circulation newspapers featured advertisements as prominently as news stories. In 1833 the *New York Sun* announced that it would provide "ALL THE NEWS OF THE DAY, and at the same time afford an advantageous medium for advertising."

After the Civil War, advertising served as the engine of an emerging consumer economy that depended on the marketing of large quantities of packaged goods. In the 1880s the Proctor & Gamble company initiated an aggressive marketing campaign, touting

Fair Street Pictures

This ad suggests that the soap Soapine is powerful enough to bleach the black shine out of a whale's hide. Soapine's "scrubbed whale" logo became a familiar sight to late-nineteenth-century consumers.

its brand of Ivory Soap ("99 and 44/100 percent pure") with full-page ads in monthly magazines. (In 1890 the company sold 30 million cakes of the soap.) Traveling road shows advertised patent medicines and at the same time entertained young and old.

The retail sales concerns Montgomery Ward and Sears, Roebuck took advantage of Rural Free Delivery offered by the U.S. Postal Service and sent lavishly illustrated catalogues to households all over the country. In the fall of 1908, Sears distributed 3.7 million copies of its catalogue.

An African American businesswoman, Madame C. J. Walker, built a successful cosmetics company through a variety of modern means; she used print advertising, attractive packaging, endorsements by such celebrities as dancer Josephine Baker, and door-to-door saleswomen called "Walker agents," to enhance her own fame and sell more products.

By the 1920s large advertising agencies were drawing on research in the field of psychology in an effort to create ads that appealed to people's deepest desires as well as their deepest insecurities. In 1957, in *The Hidden Persuaders,* author Vance Packard argued that advertisers used subtle psychological techniques to persuade people to buy goods and services they did not need.

In its 1976 *Virginia State Board of Pharmacy v. Virginia Citizens Council, Inc.* decision, the Supreme Court ruled that advertising was a form of free speech, protected under the Constitution. As a result, professionals such as physicians and lawyers began to advertise their services.

Innovations in communication and transportation opened new channels of advertising. As early as the 1920s, billboards and the sides of barns were used to advertise products to automobile passengers. Radio advertisers specialized in catchy slogans and jingles. In the 1950s television ads became increasingly sophisticated in their use of music and striking visuals. By the late twentieth century, movies and orbiting space capsules provided opportunities for product placement. Airplanes flew advertising banners over crowded summertime beaches and packed football stadiums. Telemarketers pitched their wares over the telephone. Channel One, a closed-circuit television outlet, offered corporate-sponsored educational programming for public school students.

In 1999, U.S. companies, entrepreneurs, and individuals spent more than $200 billion to advertise. By this time, advertising represented a blend of traditional and high-technology methods. The World Wide Web was full of ads, but passersby on city streets were still receiving a barrage of handbills advertising a variety of goods and services. ∎

at the selection and pronounced the store "a bazaar, a museum, a hotel and a great fancy store all combined."

The department store was an exclusively urban phenomenon, but mass merchandising reached far beyond cities. The material riches of American society became accessible to rural people through the mail-order catalogue. This marketing device was pioneered in 1872 by the Chicago company Montgomery Ward, the official supply house for the Farmers' Grange. On homesteads throughout the Midwest, family members gathered to pore over the thousands of items displayed in "The Great Wish Book." The company's motto? "Satisfaction guaranteed or your money back." Farm wives delighted in the latest Parisian fashions, their husbands pondered the intricacies of McCormick threshing machinery, and the children studied the newest line of toys and fishing rods.

Late in the decade, a competitor appeared on the scene in the form of the Sears, Roebuck Catalogue. A former mail-order watch salesman, Richard Sears soon gained a reputation as a man who could "sell a breath of fresh air." Sears helped pioneer the field of modern advertising hyperbole, claiming, for example, that the sewing machine he offered was the "Best on Earth." Selling was fast becoming a circus sideshow.

The mass production needed to satisfy eager customers itself depended on mass advertising, an enterprise still in its infancy in the 1880s. Yet, some of the principles that would shape the future of this business were in place even at this early date. For instance, soon after the Civil War, the makers of Sozodont dentifrice (toothpaste) plastered the name of their product all over weekly religious magazines and more mainstream publications, such as *Harper's* and *Scribner's*. They labeled the natural landscape as well. Indeed, the word *Sozodont* on Maiden's Rock in Red Wing, Minnesota, was so large that steamboat passengers on the Mississippi River three miles away could plainly read it.

The career of L. Frank Baum illustrates the convergence of modern ideas about theatrical performances and sales spectacles. Born to a wealthy German American family in 1856, Baum grew up in upstate New York. His father had made a great deal of money from the oil industry, particularly Pennsylvania gushers that yielded a distinctive emerald green oil. The younger Baum was drawn to what he called the "dream life," with its guilt-free indulgence in pleasure. Together with his wife, he founded a theater troupe that toured the Midwest in the 1880s. He then made a brief foray into merchandising. He marketed Baum's Castorine (axle grease) and opened his own department store, Baum's Bazaar, in Aberdeen, South Dakota, in the northeast corner of the state. There, he also became editor of the town newspaper, the *Aberdeen Saturday Pioneer*.

Baum eventually moved his family to Chicago, where he embarked on a career as a department store window designer. He founded the National Association of Window Trimmers in 1898 and started a trade magazine, *The Show Window*. The magazine encouraged designers to strive for a "sumptuous display" of goods and to highlight their rich textures and colors. Baum went on to become a popular writer of children's fiction. His famous book *The Wizard of Oz* (1900), an allegory of late-nineteenth-century life, covered themes as diverse as feminism and rural poverty. An accomplished and successful showman, Baum understood that Americans were eager to buy fantasy wherever they could find it: in a theater, department store, or children's book.

Whether positioned behind a department store display case or in a show window, featured in a magazine advertisement or in a mail-order catalogue, the face of modern mer-

Refugio Amador and her five daughters, Emilia, Maria, Clotilde, Julieta, and Corina, were members of an elite Hispanic family in Las Cruces, New Mexico. Her husband, Martin Amador, was a prominent politician, merchant, hotel owner, and freighter. A subcontractor for the U.S. government, he supplied military troops in the area. The family shopped by mail-order catalogue from Bloomingdale's Department Store in New York City.

■ This advertisement for a Standard bathtub appeared in the May 1890 issue of *Century Magazine*. Early on, advertisers used sophisticated psychological techniques to convince consumers that a wide array of products, formerly considered luxuries, were necessities. This ad suggests that a husband can show his affection for his wife by buying her a new bathtub.

chandising was bound to be young, white, and well-to-do, brimming with health and material well-being. The new consumer culture was marked by a glaring double standard: Although advertisers marketed to the millions, they established a very narrow standard of the "normal" American.

Defending the New Industrial Order

By the late 1870s, intense conflict over fundamental issues had all but evaporated from national politics. Although ethnic and cultural loyalties continued to inflame local and state elections, Republicans and Democrats at the national level disagreed about little except the tariff. Adhering to tradition, Republicans favored a higher tariff that would benefit domestic businesses by making imported goods more expensive. In contrast, Democrats argued that a higher tariff, and resulting higher prices for goods produced in the United States, would harm consumers. Members of the Republican Party called themselves the Grand Army of the Republic; they "waved the bloody shirt"—that is, reminded voters that many of their Democratic opponents, especially those in the South, had supported secession a generation before. Still, the two major parties openly shared a similar goal: to win as many jobs as possible for their respective supporters. Politics served as a vehicle for patronage and favors rather than as a conduit for ideas and alternative visions of the nation's future.

Many politicians also shared a belief in the idea of *laissez-faire* (a French phrase meaning to leave alone, referring to the absence of government interference in the economy). Laissez-faire was actually a flexible concept, invoked to justify government indifference in some areas but government intervention in others. Indeed, politicians tended to favor laissez-faire in social matters more than in the economy. Thus, support for manufacturers and railroads in the form of tariff protection and land grants, for example, was justified. At the same time, however, Congress, the president, and the Supreme Court were reluctant to enact bold measures to redress the growing gap between rich and poor. In fact, certain clergy, businesspeople, and university professors sought to explain and defend the inequality between the captains of industry and the masses of ill-paid laborers. They argued that the system of industrial capitalism was desirable because it was "natural."

Nevertheless, many advocates of laissez-faire in social welfare policy supported government intervention in the economy. These observers argued that the government was justified in providing tangible support (in the form of tariff protection and land grants, for example) to businesses such as manufacturers and railroads.

In 1873 writer Mark Twain (Samuel Clemens) published his first novel, which he cowrote with friend and fellow writer Charles Dudley Warner. Titled *The Gilded Age,* the book satirized the trend toward corruption in public affairs and the wild financial speculation that produced both poverty and great wealth. The growth of large businesses that received economic and political support from government officials served to enrich employers, investors, and politicians at the expense of workers and farmers. The term *Gilded Age* became synonymous with the excess and extravagance on the part of politicians and businessmen alike during the last quarter of the nineteenth century.

The Contradictory Politics of Laissez-Faire

In 1880 the undistinguished President Rutherford B. Hayes chose not to run for office again. That summer the Republicans nominated James A. Garfield of Ohio, a former mule driver who had become a Civil War general. To counter the "bloody-shirt" effect, Democrats put forth their own former Union general: Winfield S. Hancock, who had been wounded at Gettysburg. (Hancock had nevertheless garnered the support of southern whites while presiding over a military Reconstruction district.) The campaign itself was notable for its lack of attention to victims of the recent nationwide depression, such as industrial laborers and southern and midwestern farmers. Garfield won the popular vote by a narrow margin but overwhelmed Hancock in the Electoral College.

TABLE 16-5

The Election of 1880

Candidate	Party	Popular Vote	Electoral Vote
James A. Garfield	Republican	4,453,295	214
Winfield S. Hancock	Democratic	4,414,082	155
James B. Weaver	Greenback-Labor	308,578	0

Garfield's arrival in the White House set off a race for patronage jobs among loyal Republicans. Indeed, overwhelmed by office-seekers, the new president remarked, "My God! What is there in this place that a man should ever want to get into it?" Then on July 2, 1881, disaster struck. Charles J. Guiteau, who had unsuccessfully sought the position of U.S. consul in Paris, shot Garfield in a Washington, D.C., train station. Garfield languished for a few months, finally dying on September 19. Guiteau tried to finance his own legal defense by asking for contributions from politicians who might enjoy political gains as a result of the president's death. This audacious strategy did not prevent him from being convicted and executed.

Vice President Chester A. Arthur, a former New York politician, assumed the reins of government. Arthur's administration supported certain forms of government intervention in society, or "social engineering." Arthur and others believed that laissez-faire policies had their limits; strong measures were needed to counter what they and other conservatives considered immoral personal behavior. In 1882 Congress passed the Edmunds Act. Targeting Mormons, the act outlawed polygamy (the practice of having more than one spouse at a time), took the right to vote away from the law's offenders, and sent a five-member commission to Utah to oversee local elections. That same year, Congress responded to pressure from West Coast

European American politicians, the San Francisco's Workingmen's Party in particular, and approved the Chinese Exclusion Act. The act became the first piece of legislation to bar a particular group from entering the United States. Supported by congressmen from other areas of the country as well, this measure was approved after a series of hearings in California and on Capitol Hill. In a petition to Congress, California legislators had charged that Chinese men posed a direct threat to "the most needy and most deserving of our people—those who are engaged, or entitled to be engaged, in industrial pursuits in our midst."

In fact, most Chinese immigrants took jobs that native-born whites shunned. Moreover, unemployment among California white manufacturing workers in the 1870s was caused not by Chinese competitors, but by the flood of cheap eastern-made goods carried into the state by the transcontinental railroad. As eastern goods entered California, manufacturers in the West laid off workers and closed factories. The Chinese, thus, became scapegoats for groups hit hard by larger economic changes. At the national level, then, members of both political parties sought to use congressional power to shape the size and ethnic composition of the domestic workplace.

In 1883 the Supreme Court hurt the cause of blacks' civil rights by declaring the Civil Rights Act of 1875 unconstitutional. (The act had guaranteed blacks equal rights to public accommodations and facilities.) This decision, called the Civil Rights cases, involved five separate cases from Kansas, California, Missouri, New York, and Tennessee. The main issue focused on exclusions of blacks from hotels, railroad cars, and theaters. The court held that state governments could not discriminate on the basis of race but that private individuals could do so. This decision put an official stamp of approval on racist practices of employers, hotels, restaurants, and other providers of jobs and services.

Arthur surprised his critics by embracing the cause of civil service reform. This movement sought to inject professional standards into public service and rid the country of the worst excesses of the corrupt "spoils system," where political victors put loyal supporters into public jobs regardless of their qualifications. In response to Garfield's assassination by Guiteau, the disappointed patronage-seeker, Congress passed the Pendleton Act (1883). This measure established a merit system for federal job applicants and created the Civil Service Commission, which administered competitive examinations to candidates in certain classifications. Within a year, the new regulations covered 10 percent of all federal offices, or about 14,000 jobs.

In 1884 Arthur fell ill (he would die shortly), and the Republicans nominated James G. Blaine of Maine as their candidate for the presidency. Blaine, who had benefited from corrupt deals in the past, offended the sensibilities of a group of reform-minded Republicans, who called themselves Mugwumps. (The term reportedly had its roots in an Indian word that meant "holier than thou.") As a result, Blaine was bested in the national election by the former mayor of Buffalo, Grover Cleveland, who became the first Democratic president in 28 years. Both nominees had avoided making

TABLE 16-6

The Election of 1884

Candidate	Party	Popular Vote	Electoral Vote
Grover Cleveland	Democratic	4,874,986	219
James G. Blaine	Republican	4,851,981	182

controversial pronouncements on policy issues. Instead, the campaign had a markedly personal tone. Cleveland publicly accepted responsibility for a son born out of wedlock, although apparently there was more than one candidate for paternity of the child. Still, he was unable to avoid the taunts of his rivals, "Ma, ma, where's my pa?" The Democrats countered with a prophetic chant: "Gone to the White House, ha, ha, ha."

Throughout the 1880s, Congress and the chief executive applied the laissez-faire principle selectively—for example, to the status of Indians. Critics of federal Indian policy had come forward to expose, as writer Helen Hunt Jackson put it, the "cheating, robbing, breaking promises" that had devastated the native population since the nation's founding. Published in 1881, Hunt's book *A Century of Dishonor* called for the "protection of the law to the Indian's rights of

Smithsonian National Anthropological Archives

■ Dakota Indians gather at the Standing Rock Reservation to receive government rations, c. 1880. To counter the Indians' increased dependence on the government for food, Congress passed the Dawes Severalty Act of 1887. U.S. agents cited the act in their efforts to ban crucial aspects of Indian culture, including native practices related to religion, education, language, and even dress and hair styles.

property." Moved to act, Congress passed the Dawes General Allotment (Severalty) Act. The new act was intended to improve the economic condition of Indians by eliminating common ownership of tribal lands in favor of a system of private property. Presumably, the government would withdraw from protecting and supplying Indians (on reservations) and let the free market based on private property run its course. The law distributed plots of land to individual Indians who renounced traditional customs. Such people could gain American citizenship, and their families could receive land grants of up to 160 acres. The law also encouraged these landowners to become sedentary farmers and to adopt "other habits of civilized life." In the end, however, the act amounted to little more than a land-grab on the part of whites; between 1887 and 1900, Indian-held lands decreased from 138 million acres to 78 million acres. The Dawes Act intensified the deep distress of Plains Indians, now deprived of their vast hunting grounds.

By the 1880s, local citizens, through the Grange and their elected public officials, were calling for the states to restrict the monopolistic practices of the railroads. Nevertheless, in *Wabash v. Illinois* (1886), the Supreme Court invalidated a state law regulating railroads, ruling that only Congress, and not the states, could control interstate transportation. The next year Congress took the initiative and passed the Interstate Commerce Act of 1887. This legislation outlawed secretive combinations, such as pools, and mandated that the railroads charge all shippers the same rates and refrain from giving rebates to their largest customers. The act also established the Interstate Commerce Commission to oversee and stabilize the railroad industry. Congress, thus, acknowledged that the public interest demanded some form of business regulation, although enforcement of the act was less than vigorous.

Cleveland invoked laissez-faire principles in 1887 when he vetoed legislation that would have provided seeds for hard-pressed farmers in Texas. As the president put it, "Though the people support the government, the government should not support the people." Furthermore, with his insistence on lower tariff rates, Cleveland alarmed members of his own party, who feared he was handing the Republicans an advantage for the 1888 campaign. As it turned out, most Americans favored government protection of domestic manufacturing in the form of higher tariffs. The Republicans exploited Cleveland's unpopular views on this issue, nominating Benjamin Harrison, grandson of President William Henry ("Tippecanoe") Harrison. The younger Harrison defeated his rival in the electoral college but not in the popular vote.

The principle of government laissez-faire was of little use in addressing a central paradox of the late nineteenth century: The free enterprise system was being undermined by the very

TABLE 16-7			
The Election of 1888			
Candidate	Party	Popular Vote	Electoral Vote
Benjamin Harrison	Republican	5,447,129	233
Grover Cleveland	Democratic	5,537,857	168
Clinton B. Fisk	Prohibition	249,506	0
Anson J. Streeter	Union Labor	146,935	0

forms of business organization it had spawned and nourished. Trusts and combinations were inherently hostile to competition. In 1890 Congress passed a piece of landmark legislation, the Sherman Anti-Trust Act, designed to outlaw trusts and large business combinations of all kinds. However, the act lacked adequate enforcement mechanisms, and many industrialists simply ignored it. Nevertheless, together with its predecessor, the Interstate Commerce Act, the Sherman Act acknowledged that the largest businesses routinely fixed prices, to the detriment of smaller rival businesses and consumers alike. In the coming years, lawyers and government officials would find the act effective primarily as a tool against another form of "combination": labor unions. The Standard Oil Company, which boldly defied the provisions of the act and continued its trust-building, would not be called to account (and dissolved) until 1911.

Social Darwinism and the "Natural" State of Society

In the late nineteenth century, human-made devices and engineering feats helped create a new social order, one marked by a few very wealthy industrialists, a growing middle class, and an increasingly diverse workforce of ill-paid field and factory hands. Brazenly borrowing from the theories of Charles Darwin, a British naturalist who had pioneered the study of evolution, some prominent clergy, businesspeople, journalists, and university professors sought to defend this new order as God-ordained, or "natural." These observers drew parallels between Darwin's theory of "survival of the fittest" and the workings of modern society. (In his book *Origin of the Species,* Darwin had discussed the study of animals, not people or societies.) In the United States, Social Darwinists warned that "unnatural" forms of intervention—specifically, labor unions or social welfare legislation—were misguided, dangerous, and ultimately doomed to failure. In essence, Social Darwinists distorted a sound scientific theory, misusing it to justify exploitation of the poor and laboring classes.

The ideology of Social Darwinism evolved in response to class conflict and other forms of social turbulence in the 1870s and 1880s. For example, Thomas A. Scott invoked its language when he argued that railroad industry wage cuts were the result of a policy "founded on sound business principles" and that those principles merely reflected "the instincts of humanity."

About the same time, famed Brooklyn minister Henry Ward Beecher cited what he called "the great laws of political economy" to preach the virtues of poverty ("it was fit that man should eat the bread of affliction") and the evils of labor unions. In Beecher's view, unions amounted to "tyrannical opposition to all law and order." Thus, they "could not be defended" and should not be tolerated.

However, Beecher and like-minded thinkers agreed that the government had the right and the obligation to come to the rescue of private companies threatened by angry workers or consumers. These observers also made a distinction between public subsidies to railroads and tariff protection for domestic manufacturers on one hand and public intervention on behalf of workers on the other.

Yale sociologist William Graham Sumner declared that society was like a living organism. For the species to remain healthy, individuals must prosper or decline according to their inherent characteristics. "Society, therefore, does not need any care or supervision,"

Andrew Carnegie and the "Gospel of Wealth"

In an article titled "Wealth," published in the North American Review *in 1889, steel manufacturer Andrew Carnegie defended the amassing of large fortunes on the part of a few. He hailed this trend as a sign of progress.*

"Wealth," *North American Review*

The conditions of human life have not only been changed, but revolutionized, within the past few hundred years. In the former days there was little difference between the dwelling, dress, food, and environment of the chief and those of his retainers. The Indians are to-day where civilized man then was. When visiting the Sioux, I was led to the wigwam of the chief. It was just like the others in external appearance, and even within the difference was trifling between it and those of the poorest of his braves. The contrast between the palace of the millionaire and the cottage of the laborer with us to-day measures the change which has come with civilization.

This change, however, is not to be deplored, but welcomed as highly beneficial. It is well, nay, essential for the progress of the race, that the houses of some should be homes for all that is highest and best in literature and the arts, and for all the refinements of civilization, rather than that none should be so. Much better this great irregularity than universal squalor. . . . Whether the change be for good or ill, it is upon us, beyond our power to alter, and therefore to be accepted and made the best of. It is a waste of time to criticise the inevitable.

Carnegie believed that wealthy people had the responsibility to give away their money before they died, although he had distinct ideas about to whom—or to what—such money should be given. He

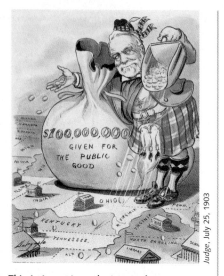

This *Judge* cartoon depicts Andrew Carnegie dispersing his fortune. Many of his donations were used for the establishment of public libraries, a worthy cause according to Carnegie's "gospel of wealth."

Judge, July 25, 1903

elaborated on what came to be called the "gospel of wealth":

There remains, then, only one mode of using great fortunes; but in this we have the true antidote for the temporary unequal distribution of wealth, the reconciliation of the rich and the poor—a reign of harmony—another ideal, differing indeed, from that of the Communist in requiring only the further evolution of existing conditions, not the total overthrow of our civilization. . . . Under its sway we shall have an ideal state, in which the surplus wealth of the few will become, in the best sense, the property of the many, because it is administered for the common good, and this wealth, passing through the hands of the few, can be made a much more potent force for the elevation of our race than if it had been distributed in small sums to the people themselves. Even the poorest can be made to see this, and to agree that the great sums gathered by some of their fellow-citizens and spent for public purposes, from which the masses reap the principal benefit, are more valuable to them than if scattered through the course of many years in trifling amounts.

In 1901, Carnegie sold his steel company to banker J. P. Morgan for $480 million. By the time of his death, Carnegie had given away an estimated $350 million to a variety of causes and institutions. ■

Source: Andrew Carnegie, "Wealth," *North American Review* (1889).

Sumner wrote in his 1883 treatise, *What the Social Classes Owe to Each Other*. These views rationalized not only the hierarchies of the workplace but also the triumph of "Anglo Saxons" on the North American continent and beyond. Editors of the *New York Times* interpreted Darwin's ideas as suggesting that "the red man will be driven out, and the white man will take possession. This is not justice, but it is destiny." In his book *Our Country* (1885), the Reverend Josiah Strong also drew on the ideas of Social Darwinism to claim that just as the fittest plants and animals endure in the natural kingdom, so "civilized" whites would eventually displace "barbarous," dark-skinned peoples, whether on the High Plains of South Dakota or on the savannas of Africa.

Not all Americans studied or debated the theories of Charles Darwin, of course. Nevertheless, middle-class opinion-makers, many of them Victorian Protestants, believed that their own religious and cultural values remained culturally superior to those of other groups of people, at home and abroad. The United States was becoming increasingly diverse in both economic and ethnic terms. At the same time, white, prosperous, native-born Protestants contended that they set the standards for the rest of the nation. These standards revolved around the middle-class domestic ideal, with its rigidly proscribed gender roles, devotion to personal achievement (for men at least), and commitment to moral suasion (that is, regulating a person's behavior by appealing to his or her conscience). Agents of the Victorian middle class included schoolteachers, clergy, magazine editors, business leaders, and other well-educated people able and willing to influence the beliefs of others.

Conclusion

Some historians suggest that the great captains of industry were the chief representatives of widely held values in late-nineteenth-century America. Men such as Carnegie and Rockefeller had the vision and personal ambition necessary to build large corporate enterprises. They became fabulously wealthy by providing the United States with the ingredients necessary to an economic revolution: steel, oil, and other materials. Their ideology of unbridled individualism encouraged many people to aspire to entrepreneurial independence: the tailor's hope that he would someday own his own store, the waiter's dream of opening his own restaurant. The explosion of economic activity during this period—a second American industrial revolution—widened the middle class and lent credence to the notion of widespread upward mobility, modest though it was in most cases.

Nevertheless, a case can be made that engineers were the true representatives of the age. As designers of railroad routes, gravity-defying skyscrapers, and new systems of shop floor management, they oversaw the technical aspects of economic growth and development.

Engineers melded science with mass production to yield a form of capitalism that thrived on consumers' deepest desires and anxieties. That enterprise was not without complications. Throughout the nation, various groups rejected standardization in favor of local tradition or new forms of collective action. Thus, politicians and the Social Darwinists were forced to defend their outlook on life. Some of their critics advanced the idea that society was not a living organism at all. Rather, it was like a machine, a creation of people who had the ability—and the duty—to repair or adjust it. Around the country, in fact, the standardizers met with stiff resistance.

Sites to Visit

Alexander Graham Bell Family Papers
at the Library of Congress
www.memory.loc.gov/ammem/bellhtml/
bellhome.html

This site contains papers from 1862 to 1839 as well as a chronology, images, selected documents, and interpretive essays about Bell.

John D. Rockefeller and the Standard Oil Company
www.micheloud.com/FXM/SO/

This study with accompanying images by François Micheloud tells of the rise of Rockefeller and his mammoth company.

The Transcontinental Railroad
www.sfmuseum.org/hist1/rail.html

This Museum of the City of San Francisco site has excellent information on the railroad.

Touring Turn-of-the-Century America: Photographs from the Detroit Publishing Company, 1880–1920

www.memory.loc.gov/ammem/detroit/dethome.html

> This Library of Congress collection has thousands of photographs from turn-of-the-century America.

Shadow Ball: The Negro Baseball Leagues

www.negro-league.columbus.oh.us/jimcrow1.htm

> This Harlan William article examines the African American baseball leagues.

African American Perspectives: Pamphlets from the Daniel A. P. Murry Collections, 1818–1907

www.memory.loc.gov/ammem/aap/aaphome.html

> This collection includes writings of famous African Americans, including Frederick Douglass, Booker T. Washington, Ida B. Wells-Barnett, Benjamin W. Arnett, Alexander Crummel, and Emanuel Love.

The Evolution of the Conservation Movement, 1850–1920

www.memory.loc.gov/ammem/amrvhtml/conshome.html

> This American Memory site brings together scores of primary sources and photographs about the historical formations and cultural foundations of the movement to conserve and protect America's natural heritage.

Inside an American Factory: The Westinghouse Works, 1904

www.lcweb2.loc.gov/ammem/papr/west/westhome.html

> Part of the American Memory Project at the Library of Congress, this site provides a glimpse inside a turn-of-the-century factory.

For Further Reading

General Works

Alfred D. Chandler, *The Visible Hand: The Managerial Revolution in American Business* (1977).

Jon Gjerde, *The Minds of the West: Ethnocultural Evolution in the Rural Middle West, 1830–1917* (1997).

Andrew C. Isenberg, *The Destruction of the Bison: An Environmental History, 1750–1920* (2000).

T. Jackson Lears, *Fables of Abundance: A Cultural History of Advertising in America* (1994).

Walter Licht, *Industrializing America: The Nineteenth Century* (1995).

Carroll Pursell, *The Machine in America: A Social History of Technology* (1995).

Alan Trachtenberg, *The Incorporation of America: Culture and Society in the Gilded Age* (1982).

C. Vann Woodward, *Origins of the New South, 1877–1913* (1951).

The New Shape of Business

James R. Barrett, *Work and Community in the Jungle: Chicago's Packinghouse Workers, 1894–1922* (1987).

Ron Chernow, *Titan: The Life of John D. Rockefeller, Sr.* (1998).

Thomas C. Cochran, *Two Hundred Years of American Business* (1977).

Wendy Gamber, *The Female Economy: The Millinery and Dressmaking Trades, 1860–1930* (1997).

Thomas Parke Hughes, *American Genesis: A Century of Invention and Technological Enthusiasm, 1870–1970* (1989).

A. J. Millard, *Edison and the Business of Innovation* (1990).

Daniel Nelson, *Managers and Workers: Origins of the New Factory System in the United States, 1880–1920* (1975).

David E. Nye, *Electrifying America: Social Meanings of a New Technology, 1880–1940* (1990).

Donald J. Pisani, *Water, Land, and Law in the West: The Limits of Public Policy, 1850–1920* (1996).

C. J. Schmitz, *The Growth of Big Business in the United States and Western Europe, 1850–1939* (1993).

George Rogers Taylor and Irene D. Neu, *The American Railroad Network, 1861–1890* (1956).

David O. Whitten, *The Emergence of Giant Enterprise, 1860–1914* (1983).

The Birth of a National Urban Culture

Gunther Paul Barth, *City People: The Rise of Modern City Culture in Nineteenth-Century America* (1980).

Edwin G. Burrows and Mike Wallace, *Gotham: A History of New York City to 1898* (1999).

Howard P. Chudacoff and Judith E. Smith, *The Evolution of American Urban Society*, 5th ed. (2000).

William Cronon, *Nature's Metropolis: Chicago and the Great West* (1991).

Robert V. Hine and John Mack Faragher, *The American West: A New Interpretive History* (2000).

Eric Monkkonen, *America Becomes Urban: The Development of U.S. Cities and Towns, 1780–1980* (1988).

David Nasaw, *Going Out: The Rise and Fall of Public Amusements* (1993).

Steven A. Riess, *City Games: The Evolution of American Urban Society and the Rise of Sports* (1989).

Stanley K. Schultz, *Constructing Urban Culture: American Cities and City Planning, 1800–1920* (1989).

Robert Twombly, *Louis Sullivan: His Life and Work* (1986).

Thrills, Chills, and Bathtubs

Boris Emmet and John E. Jeuck, *Catalogues and Counters: A History of Sears, Roebuck and Company* (1950).

Allen Guttmann, *A Whole New Ball Game: An Interpretation of American Sports* (1988).

John F. Kasson, *Amusing the Million: Coney Island at the Turn of the Century* (1978).

Joy S. Kasson, *Buffalo Bill's Wild West: Celebrity, Memory and Popular History* (2000).

William Leach, *Land of Desire: Merchants, Power, and the Rise of a New American Culture* (1993).

Kathy Lee Peiss, *Cheap Amusements: Working Women and Leisure in New York City, 1880 to 1920* (1986).

Robert C. Toll, *On with the Show! The First Century of Show Business in America* (1976).

Defending the New Industrial Order

Thomas L. Haskell, *The Emergence of Professional Social Science: the American Social Science Association and the Nineteenth-Century Crisis of Authority* (1977).

Richard Hofstadter, *Social Darwinism in American Thought, 1860–1914,* rev. ed. (1955).

Morton Keller, *Affairs of State: Public Life in Late Nineteenth-Century America* (1977).

Valerie S. Mathes, *Helen Hunt Jackson and Her Indian Reform Legacy* (1990).

Louis Menand, *The Metaphysical Club: A Story of Ideas in America* (2001).

Online Practice Test

Test your understanding of this chapter with interactive review quizzes at

www.ablongman.com/jonescreatedequal/chapter16

Additional Photo Credits

Challenges to Government and Corporate Power: Resistance and Reform, 1877–1890

The Collection of Christopher Cardozo, Inc.

■ The Ute chief Sevara poses with his family. In the mid-nineteenth century, European American miners began to push the Utes out of their territory in eastern Utah and western Colorado. Although many Utes resisted government pressure to give up hunting and become farmers, even engaging in gun battles with U.S. troops in 1879, they were gradually forced to yield their remaining lands to whites.

IN THE SPRING OF 1889 MEN IN SAN MIGUEL COUNTY, NORTHERN NEW MEXICO TERRITORY, armed themselves and donned masks. Mounting their horses, they rode out to attack their enemies. As members of a secret organization called *las Gorras Blancas* (the Whitecaps), they banded together in the dead of the night and destroyed the fences of local cattle ranchers, chopping the wooden posts to pieces and scattering the barbed wire. In some of their raids, the rebels shot and wounded ranchers. Over the next year and a half, *las Gorras Blancas* broadened their targets. They burned bridges, haystacks, and piles of lumber; cut telegraph wires; and took axes to electric light poles and to railroad ties belonging to the Atcheson, Topeka, and Santa Fe Railroad. The membership of the group overlapped with that of the Knights of Labor, a national labor union that boasted 20 local assemblies in San Miguel County, east of Santa Fe. On the night of March 11, 1890, *las Gorras Blancas* nailed pieces of paper to the buildings of East Las Vegas, the largest town in the county. These pages, copies of the insurgents' "platform," declared, "Our purpose is to protect the rights and interests of the people in general; especially those of the helpless classes."

Who were these determined nightriders? They consisted of Hispanos—Spanish-speaking natives of the area. Their movement began when Juan Jose Herrera, together with his two brothers, Pablo and Nicanor, organized their neighbors in an effort to block European American ranchers from fencing their land. Labeled *las masas de los hombres pobres* (the masses, the poor people) by a local newspaper, *las Gorras Blancas* were desperately struggling to preserve a traditional way of life that was rapidly disappearing. Fenced lands prevented the area's Hispanic settlers from grazing their stock herds in the customary, open-range manner.

By 1889, Santa Fe had seen several centuries of cultural conflict.

The fence-cutters believed they were upholding American principles of justice and fair play. Released from jail in the town of Las Vegas, New Mexico, a group of them marched down the main street. At the head of their procession, women waved the American flag and sang "John Brown's Body," a song beloved by Union supporters during the Civil War.

Many Hispanos lived in adobe (baked-clay) dwellings in small river valley villages surrounded by breathtaking mesas, ponderosa pine forests, and high dry plains. In addition to raising chickens and grazing sheep, families grew chiles, pinto beans, squash, and wheat. Together, villagers relied on the common lands that had come down to them from their ancestors—land originally bestowed through grants from Spain and then Mexico. After the Civil War, European American interlopers—sheep and cattle ranchers, lawyers, speculators, commercial lumberers, and the railroads—began to encroach on these common lands. Through local courts, the newcomers installed a system of private property that granted exclusive ownership to single individuals. It was these groups, with their fences and their laws governing land title registration, that *las Gorras Blancas* targeted.

Northern New Mexico had long witnessed battles between successive waves of settlers; for example, *Mexicanos* had fought Comanches and Jicarilla Apaches for the land in earlier generations. Yet the upheaval in San Miguel County in 1889 and 1890 did not simply pit Hispanic subsistence farmers against European American "land grabbers." The Spanish-speaking population itself was divided between poor villagers and elite *ricos* (merchants and landowners). Members of *las Gorras Blancas* quarreled among themselves over whose fences to cut and whose barns to burn. They also broke with European American members of the Knights, insisting that, as Hispanos, they had the right and the obligation to protect their common lands, by force if necessary. The insurgents even renounced some of their own Hispanic political leaders. These men, they charged, had become corrupted by greed and were willing to do the bidding of European American interlopers.

Las Gorras Blancas had only mixed success. They managed to discourage new European Americans from settling in the area, and they prevented the railroads from buying more rail ties in northern New Mexico. Yet the nightriders could not stem the tide of land loss throughout the Southwest. The Court of Private Land Claims, established in 1891 by the U.S. government, resolved land disputes between Hispanic and European American claimants. Of the more than 35 million acres of land in dispute in the early 1890s, Hispanic claimants received title to little more than 2 million acres—barely one-twentieth of the land they had held in common.

Las Gorras Blancas represented a unique response to local conditions. But it was also part of a growing, nationwide movement against the standards imposed by industrialization and capitalism. Around the country, a wide variety of individuals and organizations emerged in the late 1870s and the 1880s to challenge employers, landlords, and military and government officials. Members of these latter groups responded with a challenge of their own: Business, they proclaimed, must be allowed to develop fully and freely without "unnatural" intervention in the form of regulatory legislation or grassroots rebellions such as that of *las Gorras Blancas*.

> **Las Gorras Blancas** *had only mixed success. The nightriders could not stem the tide of land loss throughout the Southwest.*

It is difficult to generalize about those who contested the emerging order. Even their own names could be misleading. In the early 1890s, another group called "white caps," this one in Mississippi, consisted of whites who terrorized black landowners and mill workers. And although the Knights of Labor was a national union, it shaped its program in accordance with local issues. In San Miguel County, for instance, the issue was land—who controlled it and under what conditions. In Washington, D.C., the Knights' concern was the welfare of workers in the building trades. The Richmond, Virginia, Knights pioneered interracial organizing, living up to the group's motto, "An injury to one is an injury to all." In contrast, the San Francisco Knights spearheaded the move to bar Chinese laborers from the United States and to limit job opportunities for those who remained. Indeed, groups that challenged the authority of government and large business interests often disagreed among themselves about goals and strategies for change.

Rejecting new business principles that favored aggressive profit-seeking above all else, nightriders, union organizers, machine breakers, visionary prophets, investigative journalists, and settlement house workers all offered alternative visions for America. Members of these groups debated among themselves the changes overtaking American society and the means to control them. Some wielded pens or typewriters to effect change; others took photographs, collected data, or conducted interviews. Still others shouldered arms or torched haystacks. In some cases they sought to preserve local religious and social customs; in others they promoted the health and welfare of factory workers.

Some proponents of change advocated radical action that challenged the very foundations of American society. Others stressed the need to reform, but not change radically, certain elements of society and politics. Radicals and reformers alike derived both ideas and inspiration from their European counterparts, for the issues confronting a rapidly industrializing society were not unique to the United States during this period. Nevertheless, Americans remained divided in their vision of the good and just society—a vision that would require the commitment of more than any one political party, labor union, reform association, or band of rebels to become reality.

Resistance to Legal and Military Authority

America's march toward national economic centralization and integration was not steady. On the battlefield and in the courts, European Americans pressed their advantage, but these efforts met with stiff resistance from a variety of aggrieved groups. Members of these groups rightly believed they had much to lose from so-called progress. Often the term was used to protect the interests of white men of property and did not result in any real progress for people of color.

Violent prejudice characterized the tactics of elites in expanding and preserving their privileges; vulnerable groups used various strategies to protect themselves and assert their own interests. European Americans repeatedly used the notion of "racial" difference as a justification for depriving darker-skinned peoples of their claims to land, jobs, and even life itself. For example, California lawmakers at both the state and local levels approved legislation that discriminated against the Chinese as workers and as parents of school-aged children. In an effort to seek redress, some Chinese took their claims to court.

In a similar vein, prejudice against African Americans assumed the form of discriminatory legislation and random violence. Blacks chafed under restrictions intended to bar them from good jobs and from associating with white people on an equal basis. Varieties of black resistance to white authority included migration out of the South, creation of community institutions, and violent retaliation.

For their part, during the late 1880s the Plains Indians responded to encroaching railroads, settlers, and military regiments by embracing a movement of spiritual regeneration. On the Plains, whites, and especially U.S. military officers, perceived this movement as more dangerous than an armed uprising, and they reacted accordingly.

Chinese Lawsuits in California

In San Francisco in 1878 Irish-born Denis Kearney founded the Workingmen's Party of California, composed primarily of unemployed whites. Kearney and others agitated for the violent expulsion of Chinese from jobs. They blamed Chinese shoemakers, tailors, and cigarmakers for the distress that native-born factory workers and tradespeople were suffering. One critic remarked that the temperance Kearney "practiced and preached as to liquor and tobacco did not extend to opinions or their expression."

In rural California, job-hungry whites formed anti-Chinese groups such as the American and European Labor Association, founded in Colusa County in 1882. The association also included employers who resented Chinese demands for equal pay. (Most of these immigrants received two-thirds the wages of their white counterparts for the same work.) Yet despite all the personal and legal discrimination, the Chinese resisted.

Opposition to the Chinese hardened in the 1880s. In San Francisco, the Knights of Labor and the Workingmen's Party of California helped to engineer the passage of the Chinese Exclusion Act, approved by Congress in 1882. This measure denied any additional Chinese laborers entry into the country while allowing some Chinese merchants and students to immigrate. (Put to the voters of California in 1879, the possibility of *total* exclusion of Chinese had garnered 150,000 votes for and only 900 against.) In railroad towns and mining camps, vigilantes looted and burned Chinese communities, in some cases murdering or expelling their inhabitants. In 1885 in Rock Springs, Wyoming, white workers massacred 28 Chinese and drove hundreds out of town in the wake of an announcement by Union Pacific officials that the railroad would begin hiring the lower-paid immigrants. While white women cheered from the sidelines, their husbands and brothers burned the Chinese section of the town to the ground. Such attacks erupted more and more frequently throughout the West in the late 1880s and into the 1890s. White men contended that they must present a united front against all Chinese, who, they claimed, threatened the economic well-being of white working-class communities.

Whites held that the Chinese, with their distinctive customs, would never fit into American life. Nevertheless, early on the Chinese demonstrated an understanding and appreciation of American political and legal processes. Beginning in Gold Rush days, Chinese immigrants had taken their grievances to court. Chan Young sued for citizenship in San Francisco's federal district court in 1855. In 1862 in the same city, Ling Sing protested the $2.50 personal tax levied on Chinese exclusively. The California Supreme Court agreed (in *Ling Sing v. Washburn*) that the group could not be singled out for special taxes. In the 1870s Chinese merchants used the provisions of the Civil Rights Act to challenge state and local laws that forbade them from holding certain jobs, living in white neighborhoods, and testifying in court, among other legal liabilities. In the fall of 1885 Chinese residents of Rock Springs, Wyoming, wrote a lengthy appeal to the Chinese consul in San Francisco, relating their story of the massacre and appealing for justice; 559 people signed the document.

In San Francisco in 1885 laundry operator Yick Wo was convicted under an 1880 municipal law prohibiting the construction of wooden laundries without a license. A native of China, Yick Wo had arrived in the United States in 1861. By the time of his arrest, he had operated a legal laundry for 22 years. When he applied for a license, the board of supervisors turned

■ In the West, Chinese mining companies used water management techniques based on traditional Chinese machinery such as the waterwheel. This photo shows a Chinese river-mining operation in Siskiyou, California, c. 1890. Chinese workers also constructed flumes, dams, canals, tunnels, and pumps to drain areas efficiently.

■ Some Chinese made a prosperous life for themselves in the United States. This photo shows Ah Sue, her husband, Ah Quin, and their 12 children. Ah Sue found refuge in the San Francisco Chinese Mission Home in 1879. Two years later she and Ah Quin celebrated their Christian wedding in the Mission Home. Ah Quin rose from the position of cook to become a successful railroad contractor and merchant in San Diego.

him down. His prominent European Americans lawyers soon learned that the board had denied licenses to all Chinese laundry operators who applied. However, it had granted licenses to almost all of their white counterparts. In 1885 the lawyers petitioned the California Supreme Court, which upheld Yick Wo's arrest. The lawyers continued their appeal to the U.S. Supreme Court, maintaining that the board of supervisors intended to bar Chinese from independent laundry work altogether.

In *Yick Wo v. Hopkins* (1886), the Supreme Court reversed the state court's decision. The higher court held that the San Francisco laundry-licensing board had engaged in the discriminatory *application* of a law that on the surface was nondiscriminatory. (The local board had admitted favoritism toward white license applicants but offered no justification for its actions.) The majority opinion noted, "The very idea that one may be compelled to hold his life, or the means of living, or any material right essential to the enjoyment of life, at the mere will of another" has been considered "intolerable in any country where freedom prevails, as being the essence of slavery itself." (In 1954, the Supreme Court cited this case [*Hernandez v. Texas*] when it overturned the criminal conviction of a Mexican American defendant who showed that the county judicial system systematically excluded people of his background from jury service.)

Still, many cases challenging discriminatory laws never made it to the nation's highest court. And state and local courts in general often refused to acknowledge that Chinese immigrants had any civil rights at all. (Chinese immigrants were not granted citizenship until World War II, although their children born in this country qualified as citizens.) In 1885 the California Supreme Court heard the case *Tape v. Hurley,* brought by Joseph and Mary Tape on behalf of their daughter Mamie. Joseph Tape was a Chinese immigrant with some standing in the San

Francisco Chinese community. Mary Tape had been raised in a Shanghai orphanage and had come to the United States with missionaries when she was 11 years old. She grew up to speak English fluently and dressed as a European American. Their daughter Mamie was quite westernized as well.

Even so, Mamie Tape was barred from the city's public school system. The school board claimed that Mamie's presence in the classroom would be "very mentally and morally detrimental" to her classmates. The Tapes sued the city and won (*Tape v. Hurley*), but the school board retaliated by creating a separate school for children of Asian descent within Chinatown. Mary Tape wrote an angry letter to the board: "Dear Sirs, Will you please to tell me! Is it a disgrace to be Born a Chinese? Didn't God make us all!!! What right! have you to bar my children out of the school?" In the end, the Tapes decided to enroll their two children in the segregated school. Yet their legal protest kept alive the ideal of equality under the law.

In other instances, local white prejudice overwhelmed even Chinese who sought legal redress from violence and discrimination. In 1886 the Chinese living in the Wood River mining district in southern Idaho faced down a group of whites who had met and announced that all Chinese had three months to leave town. Members of the Chinese community promptly hired their own lawyers and took out an advertisement in the local paper stating their intention to hold their ground. As a community they managed to survive. Still, their numbers dropped precipitously throughout Idaho as whites managed to hound many of them out of the state.

Blacks in the "New South"

In 1886 Henry Grady, the young editor of the Atlanta *Constitution,* traveled north to deliver a speech to the New England Society of New York. A graduate of the University of Georgia, the 36-year-old Grady had achieved prominence in Georgia politics. In his speech that day Grady hailed what he called the "New South." The former Confederate states, he claimed, were now forward-looking, prepared to embrace industrialization and promote the reconciliation of blacks and whites. According to the journalist, it was time for the South to march forward and join with a larger, modernizing America.

■ This bustling New Orleans waterfront scene, c. 1885, suggests the commercial vitality often associated with the "New South." However, a closer look reveals that all of the activity revolves around loading and unloading bales of cotton. In fact, the so-called New South remained locked in a low-wage, staple crop economy based on the production of cotton.

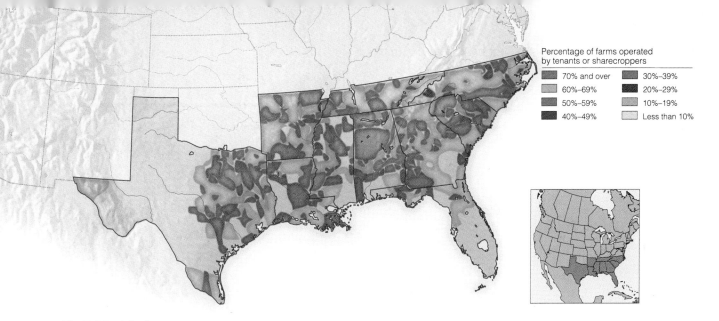

■ **M A P   1 7 . 1**

SOUTHERN TENANCY AND SHARECROPPING, 1880   Tenants and sharecroppers were landless families who worked for a landowner. Tenant families usually owned a mule (to pull a plow); sharecropping families depended on their employers for food and farm supplies. This map shows that rates of tenancy and sharecropping were highest in the areas dominated by the cotton staple crop economy, the same areas where slavery prevailed in the antebellum period.

Grady's speech about the "New South" provided a label that stuck. Yet he doubtless spoke too soon and in terms too grandiose. True, he could point with pride to some dramatic industrial developments in the South. The eastern Piedmont (foothills region), for example, was undergoing a fledgling industrial revolution in the 1880s. Soon after James Bonsack invented a cigarette-rolling machine in 1880 James Buchanan Duke pioneered the production of machine-made cigarettes. In 1884 Duke's Durham, North Carolina, company was selling 400,000 of them each day. The southern textile labor force more than doubled between 1880 and 1890, from 17,000 men, women, and children to 36,000, many of them concentrated in the Carolinas and Georgia.

In the mid-1880s, with the backing of the Tennessee Coal, Iron, and Railway Company, the city of Birmingham, Alabama, specialized in pig iron production. Local manufacturers remained at the mercy of high shipping rates imposed by northern-owned railroads, which provided discounts only to raw materials going north and manufactured goods coming south. However, in 1889 even Andrew Carnegie acknowledged the formidable challenge posed by Birmingham blast furnaces to iron and steel producers in the North and abroad.

Factory and professional work in towns and cities offered new opportunities in the South as industry developed. However, these jobs were dominated by white men. Low-paid heavy labor, primarily in rural areas, continued to be the primary source of work for black men. After they finished harvesting cotton in the fall, many black men worked at sawmills or in railroad construction camps during the winter.

The hardest and lowest-paid jobs, such as digging ore out of a hill in northern Alabama or constructing a railroad through the swamps of Florida, often went to convicts whom private employers had leased from the state. Most of these "convict lease" workers were black men who had been arrested on minor charges and then bound out when they could not pay their fines or court costs. In Mississippi a black man could be picked up for "some trifling misdemeanor," in the words of one observer, fined $500, and compelled to work off the fine (at a rate of 5 cents a day) for a local planter. With an almost unlimited supply of such workers, employers had little incentive to ease the brutal living and working conditions endured by these convicts.

Patterns of migration within and outside the South reveal blacks' efforts to resist discrimination. Some blacks fled the countryside and settled in southern cities where good jobs were limited but personal freedom was greater. In 1890, 15 percent of the southern black population lived in towns and cities; they represented a third of the South's total urban population.

TABLE 17-1

Percentage of Farms Operated by Tenants or Sharecroppers

	1880	1890	1900	1910	1920
North	19.2	22.1	26.2	26.5	28.2
New England	8.5	9.3	9.4	8.0	7.4
Middle Atlantic	19.2	22.1	25.3	22.3	20.7
East North Central	20.5	22.8	26.3	27.0	28.1
West North Central	20.5	24.0	29.6	30.9	34.2
South	36.2	38.5	47.0	49.6	46.9
South Atlantic	36.1	38.5	44.2	45.9	46.8
East South Central	36.8	38.3	48.1	50.7	49.7
West South Central	35.2	38.6	49.1	52.8	52.9
West	14.0	12.1	16.6	14.0	17.7
Mountain	7.4	7.1	12.2	10.7	15.4
Pacific	16.8	14.7	19.7	17.2	20.1
U.S.	25.6	28.4	35.3	37.0	38.1

Source: U.S. Special Committee on Farm Tenancy, *Farm Tenancy* (1937), pp. 39, 36.

Gradually, a new black elite arose. These physicians, lawyers, insurance agents, and undertakers reached out to an exclusively black clientele. They also nourished a sense of community. Black men and women continued to sustain their own institutions, such as schools, lodges, benevolent societies, burial organizations, and churches. Black men formed fraternal organizations such as the Colored Masons and the Colored Odd Fellows. Black women created social and service organizations, such as the United Daughters of Ham and the Order of the Eastern Star.

Despite Henry Grady's pronouncements, clearly the South had not abandoned its historical legacy of white supremacist ideologies. In fact, in the late 1880s white Democrats feared the assertiveness of the new black elite. According to whites, this generation of men and women born as free persons and not as slaves must be "put in their place," quite literally. As a result, new state and local laws mandated separate water fountains for blacks and whites, restricted blacks to separate railroad cars and other forms of public transportation, and excluded them altogether from city parks and other public spaces. Long-standing customs barring black people from white-owned theaters, restaurants, and hotels now carried the weight of law. Taxpayers' money went into state school funds, which were then sent back to local districts. There the money was used to support two separate school systems, one white and well funded, one black and starved of cash. Legal discrimination against blacks came to be called the Jim Crow system. The term itself (a reference to a minstrel show character named Jim Crow) had originated during the antebellum period.

Black leaders throughout the country tried to keep a national spotlight on the Jim Crow system, its legal and violent manifestations. A rising tide of lynching (it would crest in the 1890s) engulfed the South, but white officials did little or nothing to halt it. Black men, women, and children were all vulnerable to the fury of the white lynch mob—on the most flimsy pretext. Perpetrators of these atrocities were rarely if ever apprehended and punished. Other blacks throughout the segregated South rightly feared that they too would be targeted if they spoke out against lynching. Yet northern blacks did not hesitate to highlight the hypocrisy of the federal government, which turned a blind eye toward this practice. Frances Ellen Watkins Harper, an educator and writer living in Philadelphia, issued the following challenge to an audience of white club women: "A government which has the power to tax a man in peace, draft him in war, should have the power to defend his life in the hour of peril." Harper condemned "the government which can protect and defend its citizens from wrong and outrage and does not."

William Katz Collection

■ Among the "buffalo soldiers" who served with the U.S. military were these Seminole scouts. The Seminoles traced their history to the eighteenth century, when Creek Indians and runaway slaves of African descent established communities together in Florida. After the Seminole Wars (1818–1858), many Seminoles were relocated to Indian Territory (present-day Oklahoma). Some fled to Mexico before the Civil War. In 1870 they were recruited by U.S. Army officers to serve as scouts. Their unit was disbanded 11 years later. Racist policies of the military caused some to return to Mexico.

"Jim Crow" in the West

Racial segregation was not limited to the South. The U.S. military enforced its own set of Jim Crow regulations. In 1869 Congress created the 24th and 25th Infantries (Colored) composed of African American soldiers. White officers were appointed to lead these segregated units; consequently, black men who aspired to positions of military leadership found their way blocked. (Before 1900, only three black men received commissions from West Point, and they faced systematic harassment at the academy and after graduation.) Some white officers, such as George Custer, refused to command black troops at all.

Military officials assigned black soldiers to the West, where they became known as buffalo soldiers. (The origins of the term are unclear. It may refer to the buffalo robes worn by many of the soldiers or to Plains Indians' respect for the black men's skills on horseback.) Many of these men were proud to wear a U.S. soldier's uniform, an emblem of their newly won citizenship rights. Organized in two cavalry and two infantry regiments, the soldiers stationed in western outposts found that military duty entailed a combination of new opportunities and old forms of humiliation.

Within their garrisons, they performed a variety of tasks related to everyday military drills and maintenance. Black soldiers helped to construct new roads and forts, protect wagon trains of settlers, and patrol the border between the United States and Mexico. They were an integral part of campaigns to subdue the Cheyenne, Comanche, Sioux, Ute, Kiowa, and Apache Indians. They were among the soldiers deployed to quash strikes among workers (silver miners in Idaho, for example) and to fight forest fires in the Northwest. As members of a novel, all-black regimental musical band, one group played for white audiences from Montana to Texas.

Often the buffalo soldiers encountered hostility from local townspeople, who resented their patronage of local establishments. In 1881 Tenth Cavalry troops stationed at Fort Concho near San Angelo, Texas, reacted angrily when a local white man killed a black soldier in a saloon. Another soldier had died at the hands of a local white within the previous two weeks. In the absence of justice for the murderers, the soldiers blanketed San Angelo with handbills. Signed "U.S. soldiers," the message read, "If we do not receive justice and fair play . . . someone will suffer, if not the guilty, the innocent. It has gone far enough." When some of the soldiers attacked

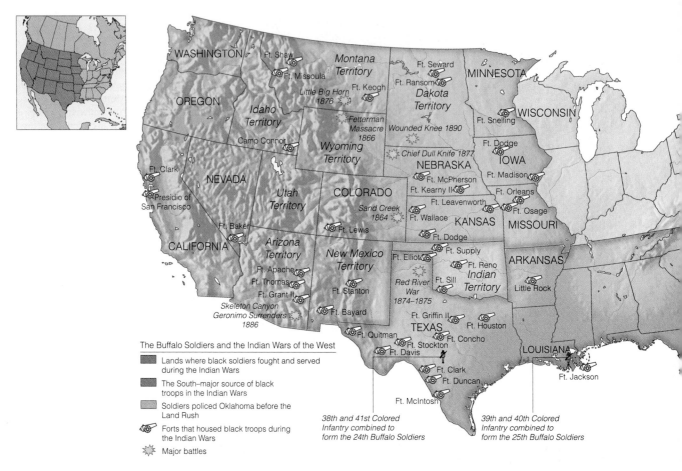

The Buffalo Soldiers and the Indian Wars of the West

- Lands where black soldiers fought and served during the Indian Wars
- The South—major source of black troops in the Indian Wars
- Soldiers policed Oklahoma before the Land Rush
- Forts that housed black troops during the Indian Wars
- Major battles

38th and 41st Colored Infantry combined to form the 24th Buffalo Soldiers

39th and 40th Colored Infantry combined to form the 25th Buffalo Soldiers

■ **MAP 17.2**
BUFFALO SOLDIERS In 1866 Congress authorized the creation of four permanent military units consisting of African American Civil War veterans. These soldiers played a prominent role in the Indian wars of the West from 1866 to 1890. They were stationed in federal forts scattered throughout the western states.

one of the men they believed guilty, the Texas Rangers entered the town to restore order. The army transferred the black companies out of the area and disciplined the leaders of the protest.

Once they were mustered out of the army, some black soldiers decided to settle permanently in the West. There they joined thousands of black migrants who were fleeing the Jim Crow South. In the late 1870s, 20,000 blacks from Tennessee, Mississippi, and Louisiana, called "Exodusters," migrated into western Kansas. The migrants cited the South's convict lease system, poor schools, and pervasive violence and intimidation as reasons for their flight. Henry Adams, a native of Shreveport, Louisiana, and a U.S. army veteran, expanded on the migrants' grievances when he pointed to the failed promise of Reconstruction as the root cause of migration: "The whole South—every State in the South—had got into the hands of the very men that held us as slaves . . . and we thought that the men that held us slaves was holding the reins of government over our heads in every respect almost, even the constable up to the governor."

Some of these migrants established all-black towns in Kansas, Colorado, Nebraska, and New Mexico. Though generally small and poor, such towns were necessarily free of the trappings of Jim Crow. They provided places for blacks to live life on their own terms.

The Ghost Dance on the High Plains

Their lands and way of life threatened by whites, western Indians sought desperately to revitalize their culture and protect themselves. In 1889 an Indian named Wovoka offered the Plains Indians a mystical vision of the future, a vision that promised a return to the beloved past. A leader of the Paiute in Nevada, Wovoka preached what came to be called the Ghost Dance, part religion and part resistance movement. In 1889 a solar eclipse occurred while Wovoka was wracked by fever, and he claimed that the conjunction of the two events enabled him to glimpse the afterworld. The Indians themselves could usher in a new day of peace, Wovoka proclaimed, and this new day would be a time free of disease and armed conflict. The buffalo would return, he promised, and the Indian men and women who had died would come back to replenish depleted villages.

Wovoka's call found its warmest reception among the Plains Indians. In 1890 an anthropologist recorded an exhortation that Wovoka (called Jack Wilson by whites) delivered to the Cheyennes and Arapahos: "When you get home you must make a dance to continue five days. Dance four successive nights, and the last night keep up the dance until the morning of the fifth day, when all must bathe in the river and then disperse to their homes. You must all do in the same way." Some Indians donned so-called ghost shirts, made of white muslin and adorned with images of the sun, moon, stars, and various animals. They believed these garments would provide them with magical powers and protect them from the white men's bullets.

Many of the Indians who performed the Ghost Dance fell into a trance-like state, bringing inspiration to impoverished and disheartened reservation communities. However, as the ritual spread across the Plains, U.S. military officials panicked. In November 1890, E. B. Reynolds, a Special U.S. Indian Agent, described to his superiors in Washington the strange, seemingly dangerous behavior that had gripped the Indians on Pine Ridge Reservation in South Dakota: "The religious excitement aggravated by almost starvation is bearing fruits in this state

Frederic S. Remington, *The Ghost Dance by the Ogallala Sioux at Pine Ridge Agency, Dakota*, 1890. Amon Carter Museum, Fort Worth, Texas

■ A popular artist featured in leading magazines of his time, Frederic Remington drew a scene from the Oglala Sioux Ghost Dance of 1890. Throughout the Great Plains and the Rocky Mountain region, men, women, and children participated in the ritual dance, moving in a circle and singing. The strange sight frightened many whites. In December 1890 U.S. troops attacked and killed several hundred Indians on the Pine Ridge Reservation in South Dakota. The Wounded Knee Massacre marked the end of the Indian wars of the nineteenth century.

Joslyn Art Museum, gift of Mrs. A.H. Richardson (Neg. #JAM.1984.38)

■ A map drawn by John Crazy Mule, a Cheyenne warrior-turned U.S. Army scout, illustrates several historic encounters between Indians and soldiers. Places and events are designated with pictographs. For example, the Missouri River is marked with a steamboat (center right). Among the events depicted is the capture of Chief Joseph of the Nez Percé in the Bear Paw Mountains in 1877.

of insubordination; Indians say they had better die fighting than to die a slow death of starvation, and as the new religion promises their return to earth, at the coming of the millennium, they have no fear of death."

As tensions between whites and Indians mounted, a Sioux named Sitting Bull emerged as a leader. Born in the early 1830s, he had gained respect among his people as a Wichasa Wakan ("holy man"). At the Battle of the Little Big Horn, he helped protect Indian women and children from Custer's soldiers. Wooden Leg, a Northern Cheyenne, later described Sitting Bull as "altogether brave, but peaceable. He was strong in religion—the Indian religion." After leading his followers into Canada, Sitting Bull returned to the United States in 1881. He surrendered at Fort Buford, Dakota Territory, where he was held prisoner for two years. His brief stint as a performer in Buffalo Bill Cody's "Wild West" show left him disgusted with the ways of white people.

Sitting Bull offered a pointed critique of the sedentary, materialistic way of life promoted by whites:

> White men like to dig in the ground for their food. My people prefer to hunt buffalo as their fathers did. White men like to stay in one place. My people want to move their tepees here and there to different hunting grounds. The life of white men is slavery. They are prisoners in towns or farms. The life my people want is a life of freedom. I have seen nothing that a white man has, houses or railways or clothing or food, that is as good as the right to move in open country, and live in our own fashion.

Sitting Bull rejected white notions of "progress" in favor of his people's traditions.

In mid-December 1890 military officials ordered Indian police to arrest Sitting Bull at his cabin on the Standing Rock Reservation in South Dakota. Alarmed by what they perceived as rising Indian military, white settlers in Nebraska and South Dakota pressured the government to rid the area of the "savages . . . armed to the teeth," men who were "traitors, anarchists, and assassins." While arresting Sitting Bull, his Indian captors killed him. The great man's followers, who had revered him as a prophet, decried the murder.

A week later, on December 28 and 29, soldiers of the 7th Cavalry under Colonel James Forsyth, agitated by the tensions over Sitting Bull's death, attacked and killed 146 Indians at Wounded Knee Creek, South Dakota. More than 60 women and children were among those slain as they fled the oncoming troops. Of the 25 U.S. soldiers who perished, most apparently died from shots fired by their own comrades; according to a government eyewitness, the Indian men were unarmed when the cavalry attacked.

The massacre at Wounded Knee proved the last major violent encounter between Plains Indians and U.S. cavalry forces. By this time, many Indians throughout the Midwest lived on reservations and engaged in farming. In Oklahoma, for example, the Cheyenne learned how to grow cotton and watermelons. Government agents, eager to create independent farmers, instructed Indian men in the use of the plow. But John Stands-in-Timber, a Cheyenne, later recalled how plowing became a collective effort. It engaged the energies of Indian men from Oklahoma to Montana, he noted, as bands would work together until their task was done. Thus some Indian groups attempted to maintain customs of collective endeavor in opposition to the European Americas glorification of ambition and individualism.

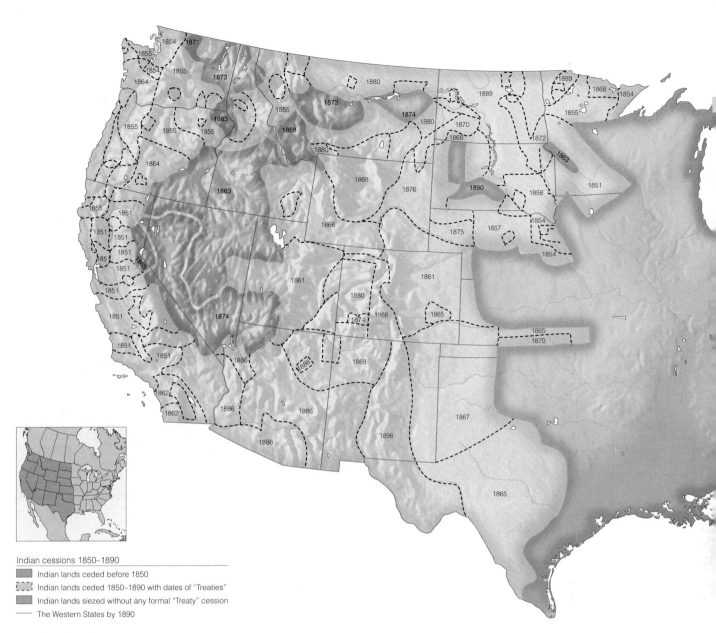

Indian cessions 1850–1890

▨ Indian lands ceded before 1850

⣿ Indian lands ceded 1850–1890 with dates of "Treaties"

▨ Indian lands siezed without any formal "Treaty" cession

— The Western States by 1890

■ **MAP 17.3**

INDIAN LANDS LOST, 1850–1890 Between 1850 and 1890, many "treaties" signed by Indian groups and the U.S. government provided that Indians turn over land in exchange for cash payments. Yet U.S. military forces seized a large portion of western Indian lands by force, without signing any treaty agreements at all. By 1890 many Indians lived on reservations, apart from European American society.

Revolt in the Workplace

During the late nineteenth century, workers challenged employers and the new industrial order for many reasons. Factory operatives objected to long hours and to low pay in return for tending dangerous machines. Miners labored daily under hazardous conditions, often without necessary safety equipment or precautions. Field hands worried that they would soon be displaced by machines such as the giant threshers that were far more efficient— quicker and cheaper—than human labor. Small farmers resented their dependence on bankers and owners of grain elevators and railroads. Throughout the country, many different kinds of workers feared that the large influx of immigrants would provide a vast reserve of cheap labor that would serve to depress the wages of and threaten the job security of everyone.

■ A Nebraska farm family poses proudly with their new windmill, c. 1890. Such devices powered water pumps that reached deep into the earth. Though expensive, windmills were necessities for drought-stricken farmers on the Plains, especially during the harsh years of the mid-1880s to the mid-1890s.

Workers launched different kinds of challenges against the system of industrial capitalism, which, many charged, enriched a few industrialists and bankers at the expense of the vast majority of laboring people. Workers joined together in unions, and in many cases they fought the violence of private company security forces with violence of their own. Some men and women destroyed the machinery that threatened to replace them in the workplace. By the early 1890s, critics of the new industrial order—a system driven by technological innovation—had come together in the form of a new political group, the People's Party. This organization aimed to bring together urban and rural, male and female, agricultural and industrial workers to protest the hardships suffered by laborers of all kinds and to demand that the federal government take strong action in rectifying social ills.

Nevertheless, in workplace conflicts, the lines were not always strictly drawn between employees and employers. For example, the late-nineteenth-century laboring classes never achieved the level of unity called for by the Populists. White workers often expressed intense hostility toward their African American and Chinese counterparts. Within small towns, shopkeepers and landlords at times showed solidarity with striking workers; in these cases community ties were stronger than class differences. Also, despite their critique of big business, workers often embraced the emerging consumer culture. In fact, many of them fought for shorter work days and higher wages so that they could enjoy their share of the material blessings of American life—in department stores, movie theaters, and amusement parks.

Trouble on the Farm

In the late summer of 1878 the combined effects of the recent national depression and the loss of jobs to labor-saving technology catalyzed a rash of machine breaking throughout rural

TABLE 17-2

Estimated Membership, by State, of the National Farmers' Alliance, 1890

Alabama	75,000	New Jersey	500
Arkansas	100,000	New Mexico	5,000
California	1,000	New York	500
Colorado	5,000	North Carolina	100,000
Florida	20,000	North Dakota	40,000
Georgia	100,000	Ohio	300
Illinois	2,000	Pennsylvania	500
Indiana	5,000	South Carolina	50,000
Kansas	100,000	South Dakota	50,000
Kentucky	80,000	Tennessee	100,000
Louisiana	20,000	Texas	150,000
Maryland	5,000	Virginia	50,000
Mississippi	60,000	West Virginia	2,000
Missouri	150,000		
		Total	1,271,800

Source: *Appleton's Annual Cyclopedia and Register of Important Events of the Year 1890* (New York: D. Appleton & Co, 1891), p. 301.

Ohio. The tactics of the machine-breakers bore some resemblance to those of *las Gorras Blancas* in northern New Mexico. In the Midwest, displaced farmhands burned the reapers, mowers, and threshers of their former employers. By autumn the violence had spread to Michigan and Indiana. Scattered reports of torched reapers, mowers, barns, and crops emanated from Illinois, Iowa, Wisconsin, and Minnesota also. Some wealthy farmers responded by abandoning their machinery and rehiring their farmhands. Technology, one noted, "ought to be dispensed with in times like these." Critics charged the machine-breakers with "short-sighted madness." True, seasonal farmhands were fast losing their usefulness in the new machine age. However, the protests revealed that even family farming had become a business. Now farmers needed to secure bank loans, invest in new machinery, and worry about the price of crops in the world market. These changes had profoundly altered labor relations between farm workers and farmers and between farmers and their creditors.

On the Northern Plains, farmers endured extremes of weather and the anxiety of uncertain harvests. This area was home to immigrants from Scandinavia and Russia, drawn to the region by abundant rainfall and cheap land prices in the late 1870s and early 1880s. These men and women concentrated on ranching and farming and built sod houses out of rectangular bricks cut from the hard prairie soil. Warm in winter and cool in summer, the houses nevertheless had roofs that needed shoring up after every rainfall. In Madison County, Nebraska, a family of five lived in a dirt-floor sod house built into the side of a ravine. Their furnishings consisted of a cookstove, a bed, a milk cooler, "and a few other articles."

In the mid-1880s the plight of these Plains farmers worsened when a series of natural disasters highlighted their vulnerability to the elements. No form of modern technology could prevent the drought of 1886, which dragged on for a decade. Combined with declining wheat prices, the prolonged dry weather drove fully half the population of western Kansas and Nebraska back east to Iowa and Illinois during 1888 to 1892. Meanwhile, the bitterly cold winter of 1886–1887 decimated cattle herds throughout the region. The resulting "great die up" ended the days of the huge herds that ranged the Plains. Thereafter, ranchers would concentrate on smaller stock holdings and selective breeding.

Some American writers captured the bleakness of prairie life, highlighting the condition of farmers dependent on predatory institutions and machines, such as banks and railroads.

Writing from first-hand experience of his native Wisconsin, Hamlin Garland portrayed the harsh life endured by men and women who toiled "under the lion's paw" of scheming creditors and landlords. Other chroniclers of life on the Plains portrayed nature as a pitiless adversary that promised bountiful harvests one day but rained plagues of locusts the next.

Things took a radical turn in the 1880s, when a national movement of farmers emerged and tapped into a wellspring of anger and discontent in farming regions throughout the nation. Men and women from the Plains states (organized in the National Farmers' Alliance, or Northern Alliance) joined with their counterparts in Louisiana, Texas, and Arkansas (the National Farmers Alliance and Industrial Union, or Southern Alliance). The Colored Farmers' Alliance was formed in 1886.

The Southern Alliance pressed for an expanded currency, taxation reform, and government ownership of transportation and communication lines. Its members tended to ally with the Democratic party. The Northern Alliance also focused on the expansion of the currency supply—specifically, the coinage of silver—but advocated the formation of a third political party to advance its interests. Both of these large regional groups found adherents in the mountain West. There, miners and farmers joined together to protest the monopolistic powers of the railroads, privately owned water companies, and silver mining interests. These monopolies drove up consumer prices and depressed workers' wages.

Most alliance men and women farmed modest parcels of land. As small producers, they felt powerless to influence the businesspeople and politicians who affected their livelihoods and their life possibilities. Members of the alliance also presented themselves as the last line of defense for the noble yeoman in the face of the corrupting influences of modern capitalism. In rural Alabama, where the Farmers' Alliance had links with local schools and churches, the group's newspapers railed against the "filthy city," a "wicked place" of vice, crime, and dissipation. Farm folk thus distanced themselves from the "New South Creed," which promoted materialism and industrialization.

In many local groups, or suballiances, women stepped forward to claim their due as wives, mothers, and workers. In Tennessee, farm wives who raised chickens and produced milk and butter for market encountered middlemen who set unfair prices for both producers and consumers. Women argued that they were more than their husbands' helpmeets; they were partners in a family enterprise. As such, they demanded respect and a political voice. Wrote one woman to *The Weekly Toiler*, the paper of the state's Farmers' Alliance, "It would be better, methinks, if the men would say, 'come join us in the fight against your enemy' with as bold a front as he says, 'come Betsy, help me hang the meat, and drop the corn and potatoes.'"

Suffering from a recession in the late 1880s, farmers in the Dakotas, Nebraska, Kansas, and Texas began to mobilize into a new political party. Organizing work among Alliance members at the local level laid the foundation for the creation of the People's, or Populist, party. In Johnson County, Wyoming, in 1890, small farmers joined the Populist Party in response to attacks on their property by gunmen hired by the Wyoming Stock Growers Association, a monopoly of large cattle ranchers.

Clay County Historical Society, Moorhead, MN (Neg. #F/W 12971)

■ In the Midwest, farmers had to contend with monopolies that charged high prices for goods and services. Farmers depended on grain elevators (such as this one in Minnesota in 1879) to store their harvests for shipment by rail. In the early 1890s the Populist party exploited the image of the small family farmer at the mercy of powerful industrialists, merchants, banks, and railroads.

Yale collection of Western Americana, Beinecke Rare Book and Manuscript Library

◼ Mining was one of the most hazardous occupations in the United States. Below-surface miners worked with explosives and sophisticated kinds of machinery. As a result, the chances of explosions, cave-ins, rockslides, and fires increased. These conditions help to account for the labor militancy of miners throughout the country. This photo shows a mining operation at Marysville, near Helena, Montana, c. 1885.

Although the Farmers' Alliance identified itself primarily with agricultural interests, it made some notable forays into coalition-building. In 1889 the northern and southern groups attempted to combine with the Colored Farmers' Alliance. Together, these groups claimed more than 4 million members. They also sought to join with the Knights of Labor and thus bring all members of the "producing classes" together. By representing the financial interests of all farmers and highlighting the vulnerabilities of debtors, the organization foreshadowed the wider national appeal of the Populist party in the 1890s.

Militancy in the Factories and Mines

The new economy wrought profound hardship on members of the urban laboring classes as well as on small farmers. Many industrial workers faced layoffs and wage cuts during the depressions of the 1870s and 1880s. The great railroad strikes of 1877 (see Chapter 16) foreshadowed an era of bitter industrial conflict. Because no laws regulated private industry, employers could impose 10- to 15-hour workdays, six days a week. (By the 1890s, bakers were working as long as 65 hours a week.) Industrial accidents were all too common, and some industries lacked safety precautions. Steelworkers labored in excessive heat, and miners and textile mill employees alike contracted respiratory diseases. With windows closed and machines speeded up, new forms of technology created new risks for workers. The Chicago meatpackers, who wielded gigantic cleavers in subfreezing lockers, and the California wheat harvesters, who operated complex mechanical binders and threshers, were among those confronting danger on the job.

Women wage-earners also faced dangerous working conditions. In 1884 the Massachusetts Bureau of Statistics of Labor issued a report outlining the occupational hazards for working women in the city of Boston. In button-making establishments, female workers often got their fingers caught under punch and die machines. Employers provided a surgeon to dress an employee's wounds the first three times she was injured; thereafter, she had to pay for her own medical care. Women operated heavy power machinery in the garment industry and

Rural Protests and Rebellions

In New Mexico in the 1880s, *las Gorras Blancas* expressed the grievances of Hispanic farmers against commercial interests. Throughout American history, groups of farmers have protested government policies they considered unfair and harmful to their own interests. Specific farmers' grievances, and the strategies used to express those grievances, have varied through the generations.

In the seventeenth and eighteenth centuries, impoverished backcountry settlers charged that colonial authorities were indifferent to their plight. Some settlers turned their wrath on the Indians in their midst and on government officials located in eastern towns. Sometimes, protest turned into organized uprising as in Bacon's Rebel-

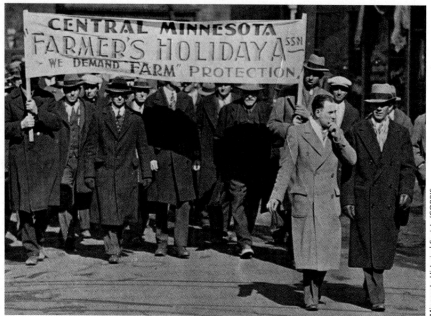

Minnesota Historical Society/CORBIS

■ In Midwestern states during the Depression of the 1930s, some farmers formed "holiday associations" to withhold crops from the market and to prevent creditors from seizing farm homesteads.

lion in Virginia in 1676 and Culpeper's Rebellion in North Carolina the following year.

In 1763 farmers of backcountry Pennsylvania staged a revolt, claiming that the government promoted trade

exposed themselves to dangerous chemicals and food-processing materials in paper-box making, fish packing, and confectionery manufacturing.

Some women workers, especially those who monopolized certain kinds of jobs, organized and struck for higher wages. Three thousand Atlanta washerwomen launched such an effort in 1881 but failed to get their demands met. Most women found it difficult to win the respect not only of employers but also of male unionists. Leonora Barry, an organizer for the Knights of Labor, sought to change all that. Barry visited mills and factories around the country. At each stop, she highlighted women's unique difficulties and condemned the "selfishness of their brothers in toil" who resented women's intrusion into the workplace. Barry was reacting to men such as Edward O'Donnell, a prominent labor official who claimed that wage-earning women threatened the role of men as family breadwinners.

For both men and women workers, the influx of 5.25 million new immigrants in the 1880s stiffened job competition at worksites throughout the country. To make matters worse, vast outlays of capital needed to mechanize and organize manufacturing plants placed pressure on employers to economize. Many of them did so by cutting wages. Like the family farmer who could no longer claim the status of the independent yeoman, industrial workers depended on employers and consumers for their physical well-being and very survival.

Not until 1935 would American workers have the right to organize and bargain collectively with their employers. Until then, laborers who saw strength in numbers and expressed an interest in a union could be summarily fired, blacklisted (their names circulated to other employers), and harassed by private security forces. The Pinkerton National Detective Agency, founded in 1850 by a Scottish immigrant named Allan Pinkerton, initially found eager clients with Indians over the safety of settlers. The so-called Paxton Boys attacked the nearby Conestoga Indians, although their real grievances lay with the colonial legislature. In 1770 the Green Mountain Boys in Vermont disrupted local courts to protest the proprietary rights of large landowners. In all of these cases, a lack of available land, plus official policies that appeared to favor entrenched political and economic interests, fueled resentment among farmers.

Many farmers believed that the American Revolution failed to go far enough in securing their rights. During the postwar monetary crisis, they faced foreclosures on their property and long sentences in debtors' prison. Shays's Rebellion in the Connecticut River Valley and western Massachusetts in 1786–1787 and the Whiskey Rebellion in western Pennsylvania in 1793–1794 pitted local farmers against militia mobilized by the new national government.

The Civil War represents the country's most dramatic agrarian revolt against the central government. With the election of Abraham Lincoln, wealthy southern planters claimed that Washington was in the hands of Republicans who favored free, as opposed to slave, labor. The Confederates' uprising cost the country more than 600,000 lives and culminated in the abolition of the institution that they were seeking to defend.

Postwar national economic development put family farmers at risk. In the 1890s the Populist Party appealed to farmers in the South, the Midwest, and the Rocky Mountain region. Faced with rising costs and the monopolistic power of railroads and banks, these farmers called for government policies that would be more responsive to the needs of the small landowner. The party achieved some success at the local and state levels.

In the 1930s a number of different farmers' groups protested government policies that drove down crop prices. In the Midwest the Farmers' Holiday Association sought to intimidate local bankers and judges. The Sharecroppers' Union in Alabama and the Southern Tenant Farmers Union in Missouri, like the Populist Party of the 1890s, represented biracial coalitions of farmers.

In 1979, the Nevada state legislature seized 49 million acres of federal land within the state. This measure ushered in the so-called Sagebrush Rebellion, a political coalition of western ranchers who opposed government regulation of the land. Elected to the presidency in 1980, Ronald Reagan served as an advocate of western business interests.

In 1999 the U.S. Department of Agriculture settled a class action suit brought by southern African American farmers, the largest class action civil rights settlement in U.S. history, worth $2 billion. The claimants, most of whom came from Mississippi, Arkansas, Georgia, and Tennessee, successfully charged that for decades the government had engaged in racial discrimination in its farm lending program. ■

among the railroads. The Pinkertons, as they were called, served as industrial spies and policemen during some of the most bitter and violent strikes of the late nineteenth century.

For example, in 1876 a Pinkerton detective, James McParlan, was hired by railroad operators to infiltrate a local union of Irish immigrant miners in Schuylkill County, Pennsylvania. The miners, members of a secret society called the Molly Maguires, were determined to do battle against the mine owners, who not only suppressed union activity but also controlled local courts and law enforcement agencies. In 1875 the Mollies had called a strike, but their leaders were arrested and charged with waging a guerrilla war against the mines (and their Welsh and English superintendents). In court McParlan offered testimony against the men, evidence that led to the conviction and execution (by hanging) of 20 of them. In the coming years, employers in a number of industries justified their repressive tactics by claiming that all unions represented a threat to law and order.

In small towns where one or two large industries predominated, workers often could count on their middle-class neighbors as allies. In many cases, shopkeepers, tradesmen, clergy, and landlords objected to the arrival of out-of-town strikebreakers, Pinkerton detectives, or federal troops during labor disputes. Local politicians solicited the support of their working-class constituents. As members of churches and voluntary associations, middle-class and working-class people together upheld community values of family welfare in opposition to large industrialists concerned only with profits and worker productivity. During a boycott of anti-union hat factories in Orange, New Jersey, in 1885, the community rallied around the workers. Brewers and bakers refused to supply establishments that opposed the boycott. Service providers of all kinds, from owners of roller-skating rinks to "knights of the razor" (barbers), closed their doors to patrons who expressed sympathy with what was generally called "the foul." In Orange and other towns, then, coalitions of middle-class and working-class residents severely curtailed the industrialists' power.

The Knights of Labor, a secret fraternal order founded in 1869, came under the leadership of Terence V. Powderly a decade later. With this Irish American at the helm (he was called Grand Master Workman), the labor union made impressive gains in the 1880s. Under Powderly, the Knights launched a concerted effort to organize European American, African American, and Hispanic men and women workers.

In the late 1880s the Knights attempted to organize the laboring classes of San Miguel County, New Mexico, and the other parts of the Southwest. The Knights welcomed cowboys into their organization at the same time they were urging railroad workers to join their ranks. One cowhand said, "No class is harder worked, none so poor paid for their services." A cattle drive north from Texas could last for three months and cover more than a thousand miles. On such drives, a single cowboy would be responsible for keeping 250 to 300 head of cattle in line. Wages remained miserable, and unrest spread.

In the spring of 1883, an extensive strike among cowboys enraged the owners of large ranches in the Texas panhandle. To quell the uprising, ranchers paid gunmen to intimidate the strikers and enlisted the support of the state's law enforcement agency, the Texas Rangers. It was a year before the strikers gave up.

In appealing to many different kinds of workers around the country, the Knights blended a critique of the late-nineteenth-century wage system with a belief in the dignity of labor and a call for collective action. According to the Knights, business monopolies and corrupt politicians everywhere shared a common interest in exploiting the labor of ordinary men and women. The Knights advocated a return to the time when workers controlled their own labor and received a just price for the products they made. "We declare an inevitable and irresistible conflict between the wage system of labor and republican system of government," the Knights proclaimed.

> *According to the Knights, business monopolies and corrupt politicians shared an interest in exploiting the labor of ordinary men and women.*

In condemning the concentration of wealth in the hands of a few, the Knights drew on the ideas of popular social critics of the day. In New York City, Henry George, an economist and land reformer, gained the Knights' support when he ran for mayor on the United Labor party ticket in 1886. (He came in second, with 31 percent of the vote, ahead of a young, up-and-coming Republican named Theodore Roosevelt.) George had achieved national prominence with his book *Progress and Poverty* (1879), in which he advocated a single tax on property as a means of distributing wealth more equally.

Journalist-turned-novelist Edward Bellamy echoed these themes. In his popular novel titled *Looking Backward* (1888), Bellamy envisioned a "cooperative commonwealth" in the year 2000, a socialist paradise in which poverty and greed had disappeared and men and women of all classes enjoyed material comfort and harmonious relations with their neighbors. This utopia was within reach, the author argued, if Americans could simply share in the nation's abundance.

The Nationalist movement, a network of clubs inspired by Bellamy's book, included Terence Powderly as a member. Powderly declared, "We work not selfishly for ourselves alone, but extend the hand of fellowship to all mankind." Between 1885 and 1886, the Knights undertook the difficult task of organizing black workers. Many blacks remained suspicious of white-led unions, and for good reason. Historically, the white labor movement had conceived itself as a way to exclude black men and women from stable, well-paying jobs.

In the city of Richmond, Virginia, where workplaces were strictly segregated by race, the Knights made great gains. African American women there found their job opportunities limited to domestic service, laundry work, and unskilled jobs in tobacco factories. Black men were almost entirely excluded from the artisan crafts. By the mid-1880s, the Richmond Knights boasted a total membership of 7000, with a ratio of four blacks to three whites. Yet members were organized into two district assemblies, one for blacks, the other for whites.

In early 1886 a wave of strikes hit Richmond as painters, coopers (barrel makers), typographers, cotton press workers, and foundry workers, among others, all decried their low wages.

A coalition between the Knights and black Republicans posed a formidable threat to the entrenched Democratic leadership. That spring, labor Republican candidates won a majority of seats on the Richmond city council and gained half the board of aldermen slots. Yet the issue of racial equality proved the undoing of the Knights' fragile biracial coalition. Throughout the South, a generation of blacks and whites had allied themselves with different political parties (the Republicans and Democrats, respectively). Moreover, white workers widely perceived blacks as potential strikebreakers. In Richmond, mutual distrust, combined with pressure from white groups such as the local Law and Order League, fragmented the Knights.

Throughout the South, segregation was the norm within biracial unionism. Whites, whether New Orleans dockworkers, Birmingham District coal miners, or lumber workers in East Texas and Louisiana, insisted on separate locals from blacks. Yet African Americans did not necessarily acquiesce to this arrangement. In 1886 Jere A. Brown, a member of the Carpenter and Joiners' Union of Cleveland, wrote to the *New York Freeman,* declaring to readers of the black newspaper, "For years I have been importuned to enter into the formation of an assembly to be composed exclusively of colored men, but have persistently refused, believing as I do in mixing and not in isolating and ostracizing ourselves, thereby fostering and perpetuating the prejudice as existing today."

In 1886 workers around the country began to mobilize on behalf of the eight-hour day. "Eight hours to constitute a day's work" was their slogan. The issue had broad appeal, but the growing diversity of the labor force made unity difficult. For example, among the white workers of the Richmond Knights were leaders with names such as Kaufman, Kaufeldt, Kelly, and Molloy, suggesting the ethnic variety of late-nineteenth-century union leadership. This diversity paralleled the composition of the general population. In 1880, between 78 and 87 percent of all workers in San Francisco, St. Louis, Cleveland, New York, Detroit, Milwaukee, and Chicago were either immigrants or the children of immigrants. Most hailed from England, Germany, or Ireland, although the Chinese made up a significant part of the laboring classes on the West Coast. By 1890 Poles and Slavs were organizing in steel mills, and New York Jews were providing leadership in the garment industry. Italians were prominent in construction and the building trades. In many places, the laboring classes remained vulnerable to divisive social and cultural animosities. The diversity of ethnic groups, coupled with the fact that many newcomers adopted racist ideas to become "Americans," drove wedges between workers.

The Haymarket Bombing

The year 1886 marked the end of an era dominated by the Knights of Labor as the organization experienced first-hand the difficulties of overcoming its members' diverse crafts, racial loyalties, and political allegiances. In 1886 the Knights suffered serious setbacks in their efforts to organize railroad workers. Industrialists dug in their heels and, with the aid of hired detectives, took union leaders to court on charges of sabotage, assault, conspiracy, and murder.

On May 1, 1886, 350,000 workers in 11,562 business establishments went out on a one-day strike as part of the eight-hour workday movement. In Chicago, home to militant labor anarchists (men and women who opposed government authority of any kind), 40,000 workers participated in the strike. Among the Chicago leaders was Albert Parsons. A descendant of New England Puritans and a printer by trade, Parsons had lived in Waco, Texas, where he met his future wife, Lucia Gonzalez, an Afro-Latina (probably born a slave). In 1873 the Parsonses had moved to Chicago to avoid Texas laws against "race mixing," which prohibited interracial marriage. There Albert joined the International Typographical Union, and Lucia took up dressmaking. They were counted among the most famous and feared radicals in the city.

On May 4, things took a bloody turn. Strikers called a rally in Chicago's Haymarket Square to protest the murder of two McCormick Reaper strikers the day before. During the rally, a bomb went off, killing a police officer and wounding seven others, who later died. Although the identity of the culprit was never discovered, eight anarchists, including Albert Parsons, were arrested. All eight (several of whom were German immigrants) were tried and sentenced to death for conspiring to provoke violence. Parsons was not even present when the bomb exploded. Nevertheless, in November 1887, he and three other detainees were hanged. Another committed suicide in his cell, and the rest received pardons years later. After her husband's death, Lucia ("Lucy") Parsons remained active in Chicago anarchist circles. In 1905 she became a founding member of a new, radical labor union called the Industrial Workers of the World.

The Haymarket hangings demoralized the labor movement nationwide. Now associated in the minds of the middle class with wild-eyed bomb throwers, the Knights suffered repercussions from employers and local police forces alike. After reaching a membership high of 700,000 in 1886, the Knights saw their ranks plummet to 100,000 by the end of the decade. Still, the execution of the Haymarket anarchists inspired young radicals, among them a recent Russian immigrant named Emma Goldman, to devote their lives to the cause of working people.

With the demise of the Knights of Labor, the American Federation of Labor (AFL) emerged to become the most powerful national labor movement. Samuel Gompers, an English immigrant cigarmaker, had founded the new group in 1886 partly in response to the Knights' attempts to usurp the Cigar Makers' International Union with a socialist-dominated local. The AFL garnered the allegiance of skilled trade workers (most of them white men) and promoted basic goals such as better wages and working conditions. The AFL emphasized the walkout and boycott as strategies of labor protest. By the mid-1890s, the AFL had embraced a narrow base: skilled trades dominated by white men.

Yet the radical labor tradition persisted. Meeting in Paris in 1889, a congress of world Socialist parties voted to commemorate the American workers who had marched in support of the eight-hour day during the turbulent year of 1886. The congress voted to set aside May 1, 1890, as a day of worldwide celebrations in support of labor and demonstrations in favor of the eight-hour workday. (May 1 became an international labor day, celebrated annually.) In the United States, the United Mine Workers (founded in 1890) and the American Railway Union (1893) followed the radical labor-organizing principles of the Knights of Labor long after the AFL had attained its ascendancy.

Crosscurrents of Reform

In the 1880s a young Danish-born journalist named Jacob Riis prowled New York's East Side slum district in search of stories for the New York *Tribune* and the Associated Press bureau. In this part of the city, more than 37,000 tenement buildings housed more than 1 million people–newcomers from the far reaches of Europe and Asia. As a result of Riis's stories documenting the inhuman living conditions endured by so many men, women, and children, the city formed the Tenement House Commission in 1884. Riis persisted in his exposés. In 1890 he published a collection of his own photographs, along with explanatory notes, under the title *How the Other Half Lives*.

Reformers later called Riis "the most useful citizen of New York." His book galvanized the public in support of slum clearance and housing codes. *How the Other Half Lives* is a powerful indictment of greedy landlords, indifferent city officials, and rapacious sweatshop owners. The photos of sleeping street urchins huddled around sidewalk heating grates, of impoverished English coal heavers and Indian needleworkers, are powerful even today.

During the last decades of the nineteenth century, reformers adopted a range of causes. Some, like Riis, focused on the plight of the urban poor. Others challenged the Indian reservation system, which, they charged, left Indians poor and dependent on the federal government. Settlement house workers aimed to improve the lives of immigrant families. Middle-class women sought to protect and empower women by aiding abused or vulnerable wives and mothers, promoting temperance in alcohol use, and supporting women's suffrage. Many reformers participated in a trans-Atlantic community of ideas, learning about reform strategies and

■ Jacob Riis titled this photograph *Street Arabs in Sleeping Quarters [Areaway, Mulberry St.].* Riis's photos, collected in his book *How the Other Half Lives,* exposed the poverty and wretched living conditions endured by many immigrants in New York's Lower East Side. In certain cases, Riis carefully positioned his subjects before photographing them. It is doubtful that these little boys were sleeping while the photographer noisily set up his equipment a few feet away.

institutions from their European counterparts. They stressed legislation, education, and moral rewards over coercion in their efforts to change society.

One factor leading to reform was middle-class Americans' fear that the poor would lash out in angry frustration in order to call attention to social injustice. The reformers reasoned that even modest improvements in the lives of the poor would stave off violent conflict between the classes. Dramatic labor disputes, from the railroad workers' "great uprising" of 1877 to the Haymarket bombing of 1886, frightened many well-to-do people, especially in the nation's largest cities. Yet many reformers were also motivated by a genuine sense of concern for less privileged groups—including American Indians, the country's earliest inhabitants.

Although reformers professed to favor the full integration of various ethnic groups into American life, at times they could hardly help but look down on the people they aimed to help. (*How the Other Half Lives,* for all its sympathetic portrayals of the poor, reinforces negative stereotypes of many immigrants.) Some of the people whom reformers hoped to help rejected part of their benefactors' package of values—Protestantism, for example—while accepting forms of concrete aid, such as shelter from abusive husbands. Thus the history of late-nineteenth-century reform reveals the values and goals of not just middle-class Americans, but the values and goals of a wide variety of other social groups as well.

The Goal of Indian Assimilation

In the mid-nineteenth century many European Americans, including government officials, believed that the reservation system was itself a much-needed reform to protect western Indians. Reservations were tracts of land set aside for the exclusive use of Indians. Whites reasoned that reservation Indians would remain separate from the rest of American society, to the benefit of everyone. Indians could preserve their own culture, and they would remain safe from the attacks of both homesteaders and U.S. army troops. By segregating this group, European Americans were free to settle on rich farmlands, mine for gold and silver, and take advantage of timber resources in the West.

By the 1870s the harsh reality of the reservation system had prompted a group composed of both Native Americans and European Americans to call for reform. The reformers pointed out that most western Indians had previously roamed the Plains in search of buffalo and other sources of food, clothing, and shelter; confining whole tribes to reservations meant that they lost not only their traditional means of feeding and housing themselves but their entire way of life. Reservation lands were often unsuitable for farming, leaving the residents on them without jobs or any other means to make a living. They depended on supplies of food, blankets, and clothing provided by the federal government. Kept apart from the rest of American society, denied the rights of citizenship such as education and the vote, many Indians fell victim to self-destructive behavior, including alcoholism and suicide.

Convinced that the reservation system was a failure, in 1879 reformers began to call for the assimilation of Native Americans into American life. This cause was promoted by some Indians as well as Protestant missionaries. In 1879, Ponca chief Standing Bear toured the East Coast, speaking before large, receptive audiences in Chicago, Boston, New York, Philadelphia, and Washington.

> *The reformers believed that the values of white middle-class Protestants provided the best guide for Indians.*

The chief had already received national attention for his role in the case *Standing Bear v. Crook* (1879). Attempting to leave Indian Territory and return to his homeland in Dakota Territory, to bury his son and daughter who had recently died, the chief and 30 warriors were captured by a U.S. cavalry force commanded by General George Crook. The Indians were imprisoned in Omaha, Nebraska. Two European American lawyers offered to represent the aging Indian. They argued, "In time of peace, no authority, civil or military, exists for transporting Indians from one section of the country to another . . . nor to confine them in any particular reservation against their will." In his decision, the judge ruled that Indians were indeed persons under the law, with inalienable rights. The decision called into question the government's attempts to force Indians onto reservations and to keep them there.

On tour, addressing well-to-do listeners, Standing Bear criticized the federal Indian Office and demanded that Indians be granted full citizenship rights. When he spoke, he was accompanied by two young Omaha Indians who themselves seemed to represent the promise of assimilation. Susette LaFlesche, of French and Indian heritage, assumed the name Bright Eyes for the purpose of the tour. She announced that her people "ask you for their liberty." Her brother Joseph, attired in European American clothing, served as translator for Standing Bear, who appealed to crowds saying, "We are bound, we ask you to set us free."

Standing Bear's appeal helped to galvanize eastern reformers. The Boston Indian Citizenship Committee, the Women's National Indian Association, and the Indian Rights Association, all founded between 1879 and 1882, proclaimed the need to abolish the reservation system, much as their antebellum predecessors had called for the abolition of slavery. Indeed, the campaign for Indian assimilation bore a marked resemblance to the antislavery crusade before the Civil War. Both movements focused on the wrongs perpetrated by the U.S. government (slavery and the Indian reservation system). Both argued that the group in question deserved full citizenship rights. And both promoted the ideal of group self-sufficiency: blacks and Indians tilling the soil, embracing mainstream Christianity, and learning trades.

Beginning in 1883, advocates of Indian assimilation sponsored annual conferences at Lake Mohonk, New York, to plot strategy for the coming year. These conferences brought together scholars, clergy, reformers, and politicians, all of whom considered their cause as part of the tradition of Protestant missionary outreach work.

■ Susan LaFlesche was the first Indian woman to become a physician in the United States. Together with her sisters Marguerite and Lucy, Susan attended Hampton Institute in Virginia, a vocational school for African Americans and Indians. This photo, c. 1885, shows Hampton students performing in a pageant at the school. Susan, center, and the woman to her left represented "Indians of the Past." The other students represented "Indians of the Present." Hampton's mission was to prepare its students for farming and the skilled trades.

The reformers believed that the values of white middle-class Protestants provided the best guide for Indians seeking to rid themselves of the hated reservation system. The Women's National Indian Association promoted "civilized home-life" on Indian reservations throughout the West. The Connecticut Branch organized a medical mission to the Omaha tribe in the 1880s. Branch members also paid for the education of another LaFlesche sibling, Susan (a graduate of Hampton Institute) at the Woman's Medical College of Philadelphia. Although LaFlesche's sponsors believed that Indian women could serve as effective agents of civilization, they had less faith in the capacity of Indian men to abandon their traditions and embrace the ways of whites.

Advocates of assimilation received support from people who simply wanted the Plains Indians removed from their land to make way for European American settlers. The *New Orleans Times–Picayune* agreed that the reservation system was flawed, but not because Indians had suffered hardships under the system. The editorialist charged that Indians should not "any longer be permitted to usurp for the purpose of barbarism, the fertile lands, the products of mines, the broad valleys and wooded mountain slopes," which the dominant white society needed.

Out of these conflicting impulses—one on behalf of the Indians' welfare, the other in support of the destruction of Indians' claims to large tracts of land—came two major initiatives that would shape federal Indian policy in the years to come. The first was the Indian boarding school movement, begun in 1879 with the founding of a school near Carlisle, Pennsylvania. The purpose of the movement was to convert Indian children to Christianity, and to force them to abandon their native culture and learn literacy skills. The second was Dawes Severalty Act, passed by Congress in 1887 with the intention of encouraging Indians to farm and apply for citizenship. By allowing reservation land to be divided into separate farms for individual Native American families, the federal act attacked the Indian tribal way of life directly. Moreover, ambitious land speculators and corrupt government officials sought to enrich themselves from the provisions of the act which allowed the sell-off of Indian lands to white buyers.

Trans-Atlantic Networks of Reform

American reformers derived ideas and inspiration from their European counterparts. This trans-Atlantic exchange of ideas was greatly facilitated by improvements in sea transportation. During the 1870s and 1880s, ocean travel became cheaper and safer as well as more efficient and comfortable. The great shipping lines, such as Cunard, began to offer intermediate fares for middle-class passengers who did not want to travel in steerage but could not afford first-class compartments. In 1890 a tourist embarking from New York could cross the Atlantic in just 10 days for about $30.00 (the price of a bicycle) on a well-appointed steamship. Writer Henry James (1843–1916) traveled extensively in Europe before making his home in London in the mid-1870s. In his 1881 novel, *Portrait of a Lady,* the heroine, Isabel Archer, replies to an English gentleman who says he finds her motives for touring Europe "mysterious": "Is there anything mysterious in a purpose entertained and executed every year, in the most public manner, by fifty thousand of my fellow countrymen—the purpose of improving one's mind by foreign travel?"

> *Contacts between European and American scholars enriched the intellectual life of the United States and bolstered the reform impulse.*

Contacts between European and American scholars, students, artists, clergy, writers, and reformers enriched the intellectual life of the United States and bolstered the reform impulse. American women's rights supporters conferred with their counterparts in London. American college students attended classes at German universities. For example, American scholars at German universities absorbed ideas related to "reform Darwinism," the notion that state and private charitable intervention could improve modern social relations. Out of these ideas came the Social Gospel, a moral reform movement that stressed the responsibility of Christians to address the ills of modern urban life. Furthering this exchange of ideas, municipal and federal commissions studied labor unions and prisons on both sides of the Atlantic. Popular journals such as the *Nation* and the *New Republic* reported on social policy initiatives of European governments.

An idealistic graduate of Rockford (Illinois) Female Seminary, Jane Addams journeyed to Europe for the first time in 1883. The sight of large numbers of poor people in London's East End made a lasting impression on her. She returned home, searching for a way to be useful, and for "an outward symbol of fellowship . . . some blessed spot where unity of spirit might claim right of way over all differences." In 1888 she went again to England and visited Toynbee Hall, a social settlement founded to alleviate the problems of the laboring classes. Back in Chicago, she and her friend and fellow classmate Ellen Gates Starr decided to open a settlement house of their own. Called Hull House, it was located in the Nineteenth Ward, home to 5000 Greek, Russian, Italian, and German immigrants.

Social settlement houses—so-called because their goal was to help immigrants with the transition of settling in the United States—provided a variety of services for immigrants, including English language classes, neighborhood health clinics, after-school programs for children, and instruction in personal hygiene and infant care. In 1891, six settlements were in operation, including the Neighborhood Guild of New York City (1886) as well as Addams's Hull House in Chicago (1889). By 1900, the number stood at 200.

Later, Addams recalled that, with the opening of Hull House, she hoped to counter the anarchists and strikers. Like other reformers, Addams believed that social-welfare activities would improve the lot of the poor and thus diffuse their radical, violent impulses. Moreover, she hoped to offer a sphere of useful work for young, well-educated women. Within the settlement house, she believed, these women reformers "might restore a balance of activity along traditional lines and learn of life from life itself." This was a place "where they might try out some of the things they had been taught."

Women Reformers: "Beginning to Burst the Bonds"

Like the Indian assimilation movement, women's reform work in general during this period had a strong missionary strain. In San Francisco, the Occidental Branch of the Women's Foreign Missionary Society enlisted the aid of well-to-do women in sponsoring a rescue home for Chinese prostitutes. Without the protection of traditional kin ties, these immigrants remained vulnerable to sexual and physical abuse. The rescue home enabled the young women to escape the men who exploited them and, in some cases, to reenter society, now as married women or factory wage-earners or small merchants.

In Salt Lake City, a group of women challenged the Mormon practice of plural marriage. In 1886 their Industrial Christian Home Association received a subsidy from Congress to provide shelter for "women who renounce polygamy and their children of a tender age." That same year some Denver women founded the Colorado Cottage Home, a rescue home for pregnant girls and women. Many women sought out by these reformers welcomed services such as job training and shelter from abusive men. However, some women declined to embrace other aspects of these charitable organizations, such as religious lessons.

May Wright Sewall Collection/The Library of Congress

■ **Frances Willard (1839–1898) grew up on a farm in Wisconsin Territory. She served as the first dean of women at Northwestern University in Illinois. In the mid–1870s, she decided to devote her life to the cause of temperance. From 1879 until her death, she was president of the Woman's Christian Temperance Union. Willard developed what she called a "Do-Everything policy." Under her leadership, the WCTU addressed a range of issues, including woman suffrage and workers' rights.**

The Women's Christian Temperance Union (WCTU) is an apt example of the missionary impulse behind late-nineteenth-century reform. Though best known for its antialcohol crusade, the WCTU also sponsored homes for unwed mothers and day and night nurseries for the children of working women. It also stressed the need for women's "purity," claiming that women and children were the chief victims of men's alcohol consumption. But the group went further to denounce women's victimization at the hands of men in general.

Like national labor unions at the time, the WCTU organized African American women into local chapters separate from those of whites. Frances Ellen Watkins Harper served as head of the black division of the organization between 1883 and 1890. Harper, much in demand as a lecturer, also organized Sunday schools for black children and enlisted the aid of black clergy in her campaign against juvenile delinquency in Philadelphia. In 1887 middle-class black women in Atlanta formed the West Atlanta chapter of the WCTU. The group reached out to the students of Atlanta University with talks on topics with titles like "Character Building," "Mother's Influence," and "Unfermented Wine."

Frances Willard proved a popular national speaker from the time she founded the WCTU in 1879 until her death in 1898. She served as the organization's first president during those years and in 1883 formed a world temperance union. Willard believed in the power of direct

Platform Statement of Presidential Candidate Belva Lockwood, 1884

In 1884 a group of women calling themselves the National Equal Rights Party convened in California and nominated Belva Lockwood for president of the United States. Born in Royalton, New York, in 1830, Lockwood was the first woman admitted to practice law before the Supreme Court (in 1879). She was a staunch proponent of woman suffrage and of equal pay for equal work. Lockwood believed that her presidential candidacy would bring much-needed publicity to the cause of women's rights. She accepted the nomination by outlining her platform:

"Two Unpublished Letters from Belva Lockwood"

It will be my earnest effort to promote and maintain equal political privileges to every class of our citizens irrespective of sex, color or nationality, and to make of this great and glorious Country in truth what it has been so long in name, "the land of the free and the home of the brave."

I shall seek to insure a fair distribution of the public offices to women as well as to men, with a scrupulous regard to civil service reform after the women are duly installed in office.

I am also in accord with the platform of the party in the desire

Belva Lockwood.

to protect and foster American industries, and in my sympathy with the working men and women of the country, who are organized against free trade, for the purpose of rendering the laboring classes of our country more comfortable and independent.

I sympathize with the soldier and the soldier's widow; . . . believing that the surplus revenues of the country cannot be better used than in clothing the widows and educating the orphans of our Nation's defenders . . . .

I am opposed to monopoly in the sense of the men of the country monopolizing all of the votes and all of the offices, and at the same time insisting upon having the distribution of all of the money both public and private . . . .

I am in full sympathy with the Temperance advocates of the country, especially the W.C.T.U.,

but believe that Woman Suffrage will have a greater tendency to abolish the liquor traffic, than prohibition will to bring about woman suffrage. If the former is adopted, the latter will be its probable sequence.

If elected, I shall recommend in my Inaugural speech, a uniform system of laws as far as practicable for all the States, and especially for marriage, divorce, and the limitation of contracts, and such a regulation of the laws of descent and distribution of estates as will make the wife equal with the husband in authority and right, and an equal partner in the common business.

I favor an extension of our commercial relations with foreign countries, and especially with the Central and South American States, and the establishment of a high Court of Arbitration to which shall be referred all differences that may arise between these Several States, or between them and the United States.

My Indian policy would be, to break up their tribal relations, distribute to them their lands in severalty, and make them citizens, amenable to the laws of the land as other white and colored persons are . . . .

Again thanking you Ladies for your expression of esteem.

Lockwood received 4149 votes cast in six states in the 1884 election. In the late 1880s and 1890s she devoted her energies to the cause of world peace. Belva Lockwood died in Washington, D.C., in 1917. ■

Source: Madeleine B. Stern, "Two Unpublished Letters from Belva Lockwood," *Signs* 1 (Autumn 1975):274–275.

action. She exhorted groups of women to descend on taverns and rum shops and to shame customers into taking the "cold water pledge." The pledge required its adherents to quench their thirst with cold water, not alcohol.

An enthusiastic advocate of woman suffrage, Willard was instrumental in bringing women's issues into the political realm. In her speeches, she quoted women such as "a

Presbyterian lady" who declared, "For my part, I never wanted to vote until our gentlemen passed a prohibition ordinance . . . and a month later . . . chose a saloon keeper for mayor."

By the 1870s the issue of woman suffrage had captured the attention of men and women throughout the country. And in fact, the issue had special resonance in the West for several reasons. When European American women overcame the hardships associated with the challenge of settling the trans-Mississippi West, they considered themselves worthy of having an equal voice in the polling booth. Reflecting on her hard life as a settler in Circle Valley, Utah, Mrs. L. L. Dalton wrote in 1876 that she was "proud and thankful" to see women "beginning to burst the bonds of iron handed custom" and asserting their "co-heirship" with fathers, brothers, and husbands. Abigail Scott Duniway, who sympathized with the plight of overworked and lonely farm wives, published a women's rights journal, *New Northwest*, in Portland, Oregon, from 1871 to 1887. In 1873 she had helped found the Oregon Equal Suffrage Association and served as its president.

Western politics pitted cattle ranchers against farmers and religious and cultural groups against each other. These conflicts prompted the men of various groups to seek allies wherever they could find them—within their own households if necessary. The territorial legislature of Wyoming granted women the right to vote in 1869. Utah Territory followed suit in 1870, and Washington Territory in 1883. Territorial governments facilitated the enactment of woman suffrage, for they required only that the measure win the approval of a majority of the legislature and the approval of the governor. In contrast, states had to approve a constitutional amendment, which required support of two-thirds of the legislators and a majority of the voters. The states of Wyoming (in 1890), Colorado (1893), and Utah and Idaho (both in 1896) approved suffrage for women. Colorado's victory was the only one resulting from a successful statewide referendum.

The nature of the western suffrage movement points to the need to view women's rights, and women's activism in general, in their historical and regional contexts. For example, African American women also pressed for the right to vote, and their demands assumed special urgency amid violence and terrorism. Ida B. Wells-Barnett would later lead an African American women's suffrage club in Chicago and play a pivotal role in the national suffrage movement. She began her public career as a crusading journalist in Memphis in the 1880s. In the early 1890s she clashed with Frances Willard over the issue of lynching, charging that the WCTU president refused to condemn the barbaric practice. Although Willard had been an active abolitionist and a steadfast campaigner for women's suffrage, according to Wells-Barnett, she was "no better or worse than the great bulk of white Americans on the Negro question." Thus women's political issues reflected tensions between blacks and whites as well as between women and men.

Conclusion

In the 1870s and 1880s the Americans who challenged the power of government and big business represented a wide spectrum of ideologies, tactics, and goals. Some resisted violently, smashing the machines, trains, and telegraph poles that were transforming American society. The Ohio machine-breakers and southwestern *Gorras Blancas* destroyed property in an effort to assert their claims to a traditional way of life. Others formed new institutions such as settlement houses, reform associations, or political parties to advance their agenda on the national scene. Some people hoping to effect social change used the language of evangelical Protestantism, echoing the reform activities of persons who called for the abolition of slavery before the Civil War. Others collected data and interviewed specific groups of workers, women, or immigrants in an effort, first, to expose the conditions under which these groups lived and labored and second, to propose specific legislation to remedy those conditions. Plains Indians embraced religious mysticism in a failed attempt to halt the incursion of European

Americans into their ancient hunting grounds. Thus, powerful groups encountered much resistance from people opposed to their narrow idea of progress—the idea that bigger factories, more efficient farm machinery, and a nationwide network of railroad lines would bring prosperity to all Americans.

As Americans began to think more broadly about their place in the world, some men and women hoped to apply the principles of moral and civic reform to other countries west of the United States. The 1880s thus laid the foundations not only for a trans-Atlantic republic of cultural exchange, but also for a trans-Pacific empire of missionary work and trade. In the process, a new ideology of expansionism emerged, one that blended elements of economic gain, national security, and Christian missionary outreach to peoples in far-off lands.

Sites to Visit

Anarchist Archives at Pitzer University

http://dwardmac.pitzer.edu/Anarchist_Archives/
archivehome.html

This archive includes classic anarchist texts, especially information about and graphics of the Haymarket Riot.

Labor–Management Conflict in American History

www.history.ohio-state.edu/projects/laborconflict/

This Ohio State University site includes primary accounts of some of the major events in the history of the labor–management conflict in the late nineteenth and early twentieth centuries.

Samuel Gompers Papers at the University of Maryland

www.inform.umd.edu/HIST/Gompers/web1.html

This site includes information about the papers project. It also has a photo gallery, selected documents, and a brief history of the first president of the American Federation of Labor.

African American Perspectives: Pamphlets from the Daniel A. P. Murry Collections, 1818–1907

http://lcweb2.loc.gov/ammem/aap/aapone.html

This collection includes writings of famous African Americans, including Frederick Douglass, Booker T. Washington, Ida B. Wells-Barnett, Benjamin W. Arnett, Alexander Crummel, and Emanuel Love.

Coal Mining During the Gilded Age and Progressive Era

www.history.ohio-state.edu/projects/Lessons_US/
Gilded_Age/Coal_Mining/default.htm

This Ohio State University site examines the development of the coal industry, including the sometimes violent labor–management conflict.

African American Women Writers of the Nineteenth Century

digital.nypl.org/schomburg/writers_aa19/

The New York Public Library's Schomburg Center for Research in Black Culture maintains this site, which contains a large number of digital texts by African American women of the nineteenth century.

For Further Reading

General Works

Edward L. Ayers, *The Promise of the New South: Life After Reconstruction* (1992).

Sarah Deutsch, *No Separate Refuge: Culture, Class, and Gender on an Anglo-Hispanic Frontier, 1880–1940* (1987).

Lawrence Goodwyn, *Democratic Promise: The Populist Moment in America* (1976).

Patricia N. Limerick, *The Legacy of Conquest: The Unbroken Past of the American West* (1987).

David Montgomery, *The Fall of the House of Labor: The Workplace, the State, and American Labor Activism, 1865–1925* (1987).

Elizabeth Sanders, *Roots of Reform: Farmers, Workers, and the American State, 1877–1917* (1999).

Resistance to Legal and Military Authority

Tomás Almaguer, *Racial Fault Lines: The Historical Origins of White Supremacy in California* (1994).

Dee Brown, *Bury My Heart at Wounded Knee: An Indian History of the American West* (1970).

Arlen L. Fowler, *The Black Infantry in the West, 1869–1891* (1971).

Alex Lichtenstein, *Twice the Work of Free Labor: The Political Economy of Convict Labor in the New South* (1996).

Leon Litwack, *Trouble in Mind: Black Southerners in the Age of Jim Crow* (1998).

Robert J. Rosenbaum, *Mexicano Resistance in the Southwest: The Sacred Right of Self-Preservation* (1981).

Alexander Saxton, *The Indispensable Enemy: Labor and the Anti-Chinese Movement in California* (1971).

Robert M. Utley, *The Lance and the Shield: The Life and Times of Sitting Bull* (1993).

Revolt in the Workplace

Paul Avrich, *The Haymarket Tragedy* (1984).

Leon Fink, *Workingmen's Democracy: The Knights of Labor and American Politics* (1983).

Philip S. Foner, *The Great Labor Uprising of 1877* (1977).

Jacquelyn Dowd Hall, James Leloudis, Robert Korstad, Mary Murphy, LuAnn Jones, and Christopher B. Daly, *Like a Family: The Making of a Southern Cotton Mill World* (1987).

Stuart B. Kaufman, *Samuel Gompers and the Origins of the American Federation of Labor, 1848–1896* (1973).

Theodore R. Mitchell, *Political Education in the Southern Farmers' Alliance, 1887–1900* (1987).

Bruce Nelson, *Beyond the Martyrs: A Social History of Chicago's Anarchists, 1870–1900* (1988).

Crosscurrents of Reform

Jean Bethke Elshtain, *Jane Addams and the Dream of American Democracy* (2001).

Barbara L. Epstein, *The Politics of Domesticity: Women, Evangelism, and Temperance* (1980).

Paula Giddings, *When and Where I Enter: The Impact of Black Women on Race and Sex and America* (1984).

Frederick E. Hoxie, *A Final Promise: The Campaign to Assimilate the Indians, 1880–1920* (1984).

Jane Taylor Nelsen, ed., *A Prairie Populist: The Memoirs of Luna Kellie* (1992).

Peggy Pascoe, *Relations of Rescue: The Search for Female Moral Authority in the American West, 1874–1939* (1990).

Jacob Riis, *How the Other Half Lives: Studies Among the Tenements of New York* (1971).

Daniel T. Rodgers, *Atlantic Crossings: Social Politics in a Progressive Age* (1998).

Online Practice Test

Test your understanding of this chapter with interactive review quizzes at

www.ablongman.com/jonescreatedequal/chapter17

Additional Photo Credits

Page 573: Ben Wittick, Museum of New Mexico, Palace of the Governors (Neg. #15821 & #58591)
Page 593: Fair Street Pictures
Page 595: Jacob Riis, *Street Arabs at Night*, c. 1890. Museum of the City of New York, The Jacob A. Riis Collection, #123
Page 600: Culver Pictures
Page 601: Courtesy, Janice L. and David Frent

CHAPTER

18

Political and Cultural Conflict in a Decade of Depression and War: The 1890s

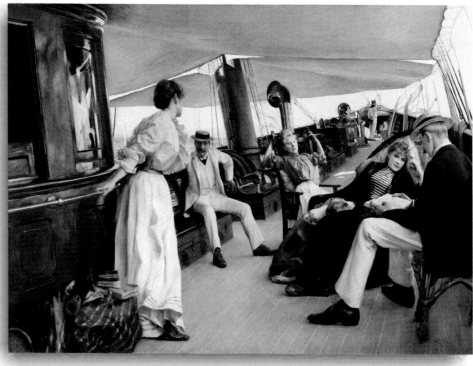

Julius L. Stewart, *On the Yacht "Namouna," Venice*, 1890. The Wadsworth Atheneum Museum of Art, Hartford, CT. The Ella Gallup Sumner and Mary Catlin Sumner Collection Fund, 1965.32

■ Several Americans relax on the yacht *Namouna* as it sails in the waters off the coast of Venice, Italy. By the late nineteenth century, innovations in ocean transportation had made travel cheaper and faster. Wealthy Americans flocked to Europe, contributing to a trans-Atlantic culture of ideas, literature, and fashion.

IN THE EARLY 1890S, LUTHER STANDING BEAR, A YOUNG MAN OF LAKOTA SIOUX ORIGIN, found himself suspended between two worlds. Born in 1868 in South Dakota, he had learned to hunt buffalo in the traditional manner of the Western Sioux. In 1879 he bowed to the wishes of his father, Standing Bear (not to be confused with the Ponca leader of the same name), who insisted that he learn the ways of "Long Knives," or whites. And so the youth was among the first pupils to attend the new federal Indian boarding school in Carlisle, Pennsylvania. En route to Carlisle, the 11-year-old regarding his journey—by boat and train—as an ordeal that he must endure with honor. Once at the school, he discovered that he was to become an "imitation of a white man"—and quickly.

Called Ota Kte, or Plenty Kill, at home, now he was required to pick a new first name from among those listed on a classroom blackboard. He chose Luther. His teachers took away his blanket and moccasins and gave him a coat, pants, and vest to wear. They forbade him to speak his native language, and they cut his long hair. One of his classmates protested, "If I am to learn the ways of the white people, I can do it just as well with my hair on." Like most other youths at Carlisle, Standing Bear learned to read and write English and to practice a craft (in his case, tin-smithing). His teachers encouraged him to embrace Christianity.

In 1884, as part of his government-sponsored training, Luther Standing Bear traveled to Philadelphia to work at the Wanamaker department store. The head of Carlisle, Captain Richard Henry Pratt, had sent the youth on his way with the words, "You are to be an example of what this school can turn out. Go, my boy, and do your best. Die there if necessary, but do not fail." After spending a year stocking shelves and performing other tasks at the famous store, Standing Bear returned to South Dakota. There he taught Sioux children in a school near the place of his birth, now the Rosebud Indian Reservation. He married the daughter of an Indian mother and a white father.

This group of Chiricahua Apache students arrived at the Carlisle Indian boarding school in 1890. Government-sponsored Indian education included dressing them in European American clothing and cutting their hair.

The massacre at Wounded Knee, South Dakota in December 1890, which was not far from his home, left the young man fearful for the safety of his family. He subsequently moved with them to the nearby Pine Ridge Reservation, where he began work as a shopkeeper and postal clerk. In the late 1890s, Luther Standing Bear served as an interpreter for Buffalo Bill's "Wild West" show during its tour in London.

By 1912 he had become an American citizen and settled in southern California, where he began his acting career in the new motion picture industry. He appeared in some of the first movie westerns together with famous actors Douglas Fairbanks and William S. Hart. At the same time, Luther Standing Bear also became an Indian activist, serving as president of the Los Angeles American Indian Progressive Association and speaking out against the "government prison" known as the reservation. Standing Bear died in 1939 while working on a film called *Union Pacific*.

In the 1890s, Luther Standing Bear's journey took place amid the depression, civil strife, and war of the era. Throughout the decade, workers challenged the idea that the United States was immune to the bloody class conflict that had long plagued Europe. Some scholars lamented the closing of the western frontier, prompting fears that America's unique dynamic of growth and social improvement had come to an end.

> *Native-born whites began to seize upon new categories of "racial" difference.*

Domestic developments had a profound effect on American foreign policy. Native-born whites began to seize upon new categories of racial difference to draw distinctions between various groups in the United States and around the world. Faced with declining consumer demand at home, politicians and businesspeople joined forces to expand American markets and American influence abroad. Economic and humanitarian interests often went hand in hand. Reformers claimed that the blessings of American consumer society would "civilize" darker peoples everywhere. In 1896 Merrill Gates, a philanthropist and advocate of Indian boarding-school education, described the goal of such education: "We need to *awaken in him* [the Indian] *wants.* . . . Discontent with the tepee and the starving rations of the Indian camp in winter is needed to get the Indian out of the blanket and into trousers—and trousers with a pocket in them, and with a *pocket that aches to be filled with dollars!*" America's imperialistic ventures would reveal a similar blend of economic interests and missionary outreach.

Thus, the 1890s was a time of stark contrasts. The same year the depression hit, the Chicago World's Fair, called the Columbian Exposition, celebrated American architectural and technological progress. Among the exhibits was an early motion picture camera. This was a decade when bicycling became a craze, and the syncopated rhythms of a new form of music called ragtime became all the rage. But during the same decade, southern lynch mobs burned alive black men and women and American military forces pursued a brutal war in Cuba and the Philippines.

Whereas some Americans tried to define rigid racial and nationalistic boundaries, others sought avenues of connections. A new political party, the Populist, or People's, party, aimed to bring together men and women of all backgrounds and regions. By advocating grassroots democracy as well as government action to regulate the economy, the party paved the way for the Progressive reforms of the early twentieth-century.

Relying on a variety of means, from new legal and educational systems to commercial expansion and the deployment of military might, American elites attempted to consolidate their political power and cultural influence. In the process, the United States confronted not only the domestic challenges of sustaining a modern industrial society but also the worldwide challenges that pitted the enduring ideal of democracy against the emerging reality of colonialism.

Frontiers at Home, Lost and Found

In 1893 historian Frederick Jackson Turner wrote an essay titled "The Significance of the Frontier in American History." Delivered as an address to a group of historians at the Columbian Exposition in Chicago, the essay presented a new way of thinking about American history. According to Turner, the process of settling the West had shaped all of American history. He argued that during the colonial period, the rigors of taming the land had transformed English colonists into more resourceful, more democratic people—in other words, into Americans. With each successive wave of western settlement, American society renewed itself. In his view, the West served as a "safety valve," a place of opportunity that beckoned people out of crowded eastern cities. However, Turner noted, an 1890 Census Report had concluded that the frontier—the unsettled area of the western part of the country—had recently disappeared. The historian sounded an ominous note at the end of his address: "And now, four centuries from the discovery of America, at the end of a hundred years of life under the Constitution, the frontier has gone, and with its going has closed the first period in American history."

Turner's thesis promoted the idea of American "exceptionalism": the idea that its individualism and democratic values made the United States unique among the nations of the world. Yet his association of geography with an "American character" was simplistic at best. In his celebration of the sturdy frontiersman, Turner ignored the bloody legacy of western settlement and its devastating effects on native peoples and Spanish-speaking settlers.

Nevertheless, at the end of the nineteenth century, Turner and others were asking questions. Did America need to conquer new lands and "tame" certain peoples to preserve its distinctive character? Now that the frontier had disappeared, what was to prevent the United States from becoming more like Europe? These urgent concerns led to efforts to assimilate and Americanize certain groups of people and to tighten systems of legal discrimination against others.

■ Frederick Jackson Turner's 1893 announcement that the western frontier had disappeared was premature. Here, homesteaders in Washington State cut down trees to carve a farm out of the forest, c. 1900. Felling gigantic hardwoods in the Northwest was a formidable challenge to family farmers.

Claiming and Managing the Land

As less and less land was available for cultivation, grazing, and mining, the politics of rural development entered a new phase. In the early 1890s, the last great parcel of Indian land was opened to European American farmers. The Indian Removal Act of 1830 had authorized the federal government to use force in relocating the Five Civilized Tribes from the Southeast to newly designated "Indian Territory." Survivors of the "trail of tears" reestablished native political and cultural institutions in the territory. Between 1830 and 1880, representatives of as many as 50 native groups had settled in this area, including tribes forced out of the Upper Midwest and refugees of the Plains Indian wars.

European American ranchers and farmers in nearby states coveted the fertile lands in Indian Territory. In 1889 President Benjamin Harrison opened to white settlement the unoccupied lands in the present state of Oklahoma. (The name combines two Choctaw words: *okla,* meaning "people," and *humma,* meaning "red.") On April 22 of that year, as many as 60,000 settlers rushed in to claim parcels of land amounting to 2 million acres of the territory.

Congress established the Territory of Oklahoma in 1890, and three years later, the Cherokee Outlet in the north central part of the territory, combined with Tonkawa and Pawnee reservations, was thrown open to settlers and oil developers. On September 16, 1893, 100,000 people claimed 6.5 million newly opened acres in a single day. The "sooners," people who rushed to claim the land, gave the state of Oklahoma its nickname. The "Sooner State" was admitted to the Union in 1907.

Congress took other steps to manage western lands during the 1890s. The Court of Private Land Claims (1891) oversaw land disputes in New Mexico, Colorado, and Arizona. This court favored recent European American claimants over the Hispanic settlers who had received title to the lands from either Spain or Mexico generations earlier. Dispossessed of their land, many Hispanic sheep sharecroppers (*partidarios*) became dependent on European Americans for land and credit. Some were forced to earn a living as wage workers in the mines and beet fields of Colorado.

Land courts were only one example of an expanded federal role in the settlement of the West and management of the land. During the 1890s, the federal government continued to provide information and services for farmers through the U.S. Department of Agriculture (USDA). Among other programs, the USDA encouraged Texas cotton planters to diversify their crops in response to damage caused by the boll weevil, a pest that entered the state from Mexico in 1892. A forerunner of the National Weather Service, the Weather Bureau supplied farmers with forecasts and information related to rainfall and temperatures. The Division of Road Inquiries, formed in 1893 in response to pressure from bicyclists and farmers, aimed to study road building and sponsor pilot projects, including concrete roads. The Division of Biological Survey catalogued and classified species of plants that were disappearing as the population increased and the wilderness disappeared.

Government policymakers argued over the proper balance between conserving natural resources for use by farmers, loggers, and oilmen and preserving the beauty of unspoiled panoramas for the enjoyment of all. In 1890 Congress established a national park in California's spectacular Yosemite Valley. The Yosemite Indians had lived in the valley for hundreds of years, fishing, hunting, and foraging for sustenance. Nevertheless, park officials were determined to create "frontier-like" conditions. These officials stocked local lakes with both native and nonnative fish. The 1891 Forest Reserve Act set aside forest reserves in the public domain; (that is, vast tracts of land still owned by the federal government). Logging companies were allowed to exploit these areas for their timber.

With his appointment as chief of the Division of Forestry in 1898, Gifford Pinchot sought to bring the issue of natural resource conservation to national attention. He believed that a managed forest could provide lumber and then renew itself. His approach suggested that conserving natural resources and using them commercially could be compatible goals.

■ MAP 18.1

INDIAN TERRITORY AND THE STATE OF OKLAHOMA, 1885–1907 In the early 1890s, the federal government began to purchase land from the so-called Five Civilized Tribes and other Indian groups to open Indian Territory to European American settlement. The lands of the Potawatomi, Shawnee, Iowa, Sauk, and Fox were opened in 1891; Cheyenne and Arapaho in 1892; the Cherokee Outlet in 1893; Kickapoo in 1895; and Kiowa, Comanche, Apache, and Wichita between 1901 and 1906. In 1907, Indian Territory and Oklahoma Territory merged to become the state of Oklahoma.

Pinchot found his views challenged by John Muir and others who argued that uninhabited regions should be preserved in their natural state, unmarred by dams, mines, or logging operations. In 1892 Muir founded the Sierra Club, a group devoted to preserving wilderness. In 1899 both Muir and the Northern Pacific Railroad lobbied successfully for two new national parks, Mount Rainier in Washington and Glacier in Montana, highlighting the ongoing significance of railroad tourism. The philosophical disagreements between Pinchot and the conservationists on one hand and Muir and the preservationists on the other shaped a wider debate between conservationists and preservationists in the early twentieth century.

"Rusticating," or hiking and enjoying the beauty of nature, became a popular pastime for many Americans in the 1890s. By 1890, tourists from Boston could board a train and, eight hours later, reach the rocky coast of Maine's Frenchman's Bay, where large hotels provided comfortable accomodations and breathtaking views. Throughout northern New England, religious groups and extended families established summer colonies on the coast and in the mountains so that they could live close to "the great outdoors," renewing social ties and refreshing the spirit. Although the frontier of the cattle rancher and farmer was receding, the frontier of recreational tourism was growing by leaps and bounds, as excursion trains provided greater access to beach resorts and mountain retreats.

The Tyranny of Racial Categories

The supposed closing of the western frontier, and with it the disappearance of the "safety valve" for restless Easterners, highlighted urban America's increasing class and cultural diversity. In an effort to categorize social groups, many national opinion-makers—scholars, journalists, and politicians—claimed that people should be distinguished from one another by their inborn, "natural" characteristics, ranging from skin color to facial bone structure and intelligence. Supposedly, these differences defined specific racial categories, such as Caucasoid, Mongoloid, and

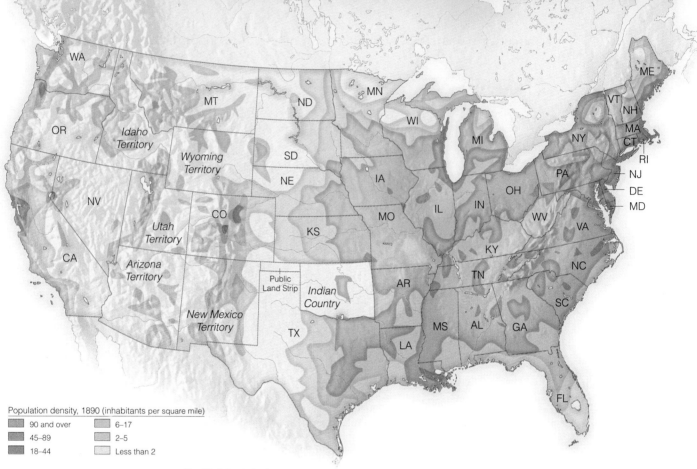

Population density, 1890 (inhabitants per square mile)

- 90 and over
- 45–89
- 18–44
- 6–17
- 2–5
- Less than 2

■ MAP 18.2

POPULATION DENSITY, 1890   In 1890 the United States still contained vast tracts of wilderness. Some Americans worried that the Northeast was overpopulated and that, as a result, the country would face the same problems as Europe—class conflict, poverty, and urban ills.

Negroid. In fact, so-called racial differences between groups were cultural differences. Prewar nativists had opposed foreign immigration because they considered native-born Protestants to be superior to people born in other countries. In contrast, late-nineteenth-century scientific racists ranked "superior" and "inferior" races on an elaborate hierarchy encompassing all groups, native and foreign-born.

Several factors account for this renewed obsession with race in the 1890s. European and American efforts to colonize and explore the far reaches of the globe brought whites face-to-face with darker-skinned peoples, whom scholars in the new discipline of anthropology studied and classified. The "New Immigration" from Eastern Europe raised concerns about conferring citizenship on non-Anglos, such as Russian Jews, Poles, and Italians. Persistent violence along the U.S.–Mexican border, combined with the resistance of Indians and African Americans to the authority of white people, alarmed local and federal officials. Theories of "racial difference" were used to justify attempts to subordinate these groups, by violence if necessary.

Identification of racial categories pervaded the nation's popular, political, and legal cultures. Scientists filled scholarly journals and books with "evidence" of the superiority of the "white race," citing the size and weight of bones of various groups and comparing blacks and Jews in the United States with each other and with Eskimos in Greenland and Tapuyan Indians in Brazil. Based on poor science, this scholarship revealed the researchers' fascination with factors irrelevant to intelligence, such as the size of the skull and jaw projection. First published in 1895, the *Encyclopedia Britannica* listed the physical characteristics that allegedly distinguished the races from each other, including jaw projection and facial angles. Most people did not read these highly technical reports, but images in advertising and other forms of popular culture portrayed blacks and Asians as inferior, servile people.

In the South, the doctrine of white supremacy had disastrous consequences for African Americans. Beginning with Mississippi in 1890, over the next 20 years, white Democrats in all the southern states met in state constitutional conventions and imposed restrictions on the voting rights of African American men, using a variety of means: literacy requirements, poll taxes (fees that people had to pay to vote), and "grandfather clauses." These last measures stipulated that only men whose grandfathers had been eligible to vote before ratification of the Fifteenth Amendment could vote themselves. In some instances, the literacy requirements and poll taxes disenfranchised poor white men as well.

In 1896 the Supreme Court put its stamp of approval on segregated schools, trains, and streetcars in its *Plessy v. Ferguson* opinion. Four years earlier in New Orleans, a black man named Homer Plessy had refused to sit in a segregated railroad car. By a seven-to-one majority, the Supreme Court ruled that states could exercise "reasonable" authority by segregating public accommodations. Such Jim Crow laws, according to the court, did "not necessarily imply the inferiority of either race." Justice John Marshall Harlan dissented from the majority view, pointing out the obvious: "The white race deems itself to be the dominant race," a view that conflicted with the "colorblind" U.S. Constitution.

Between 1882 and 1901, more than 100 people, most of them black men, were lynched every year in the United States; the year 1892 set a record of 230 deaths. In the South, lynch mobs targeted black men and women who refused to subordinate themselves to whites. In 1892 a black woman born in slavery, newspaper editor Ida B. Wells, incurred the wrath of whites in her native Memphis when she condemned the killings of three black men. They had operated a Memphis store, the People's Cooperative Grocery Store, which competed for black customers with a nearby white-owned establishment. While defending their store from a mob of whites, the three men were lynched, their bodies mutilated. In the words of a friend, "They were succeeding too well. They were guilty of no crime but that."

■ A middle-class Powhatan Indian family in Virginia poses for the camera, c. 1900. Since the seventeenth century, the Powhatans had intermarried with the Nanticokes of Delaware as well as African Americans of the Mid-Atlantic region. Communities such as these defied the efforts of scientists and others to rigidly categorize people according to race.

Smithsonian National Anthropological Archives

Many black men victimized by lynch mobs were falsely accused of raping white women. In her newspaper *Free Speech,* Wells charged (correctly) that accusations of rape were merely a pretext for the murder of black men. The southern white man, wrote Wells, "had never gotten over his resentment that the Negro was no longer his plaything, his servant, and his source of income." Death threats forced the editor to move north.

In Wilmington, North Carolina, in November 1898 whites again attacked assertive black men and women, those "out of their place," especially professionals and property owners. Alex Manly, an African American newspaper editor, had labeled white men "a lot of carping hypocrites." He charged that white men who exploited black women sexually felt free to call for the murder of alleged black rapists. In retaliation, a mob destroyed Manly's offices and then turned on the city's black residents, driving them into the swamps and chasing them out of town at gunpoint. At least ten blacks were killed in the violence.

Yet even in the South, racial definitions were never as clear-cut or self-evident as racists, scientific or otherwise, claimed. For example, Italians and Jews occupied a middle ground between black and white, as class issues intermingled with racial categories. In 1891 in New Orleans the lynching of a group of 11 Italian prisoners accused of conspiring to murder the city's chief of police met with no public outcry. Instead, a local newspaper condemned the "lawless passions" and "the cutthroat practices" that it claimed were characteristic of all Italian immigrants. However, the Italian government protested loudly against the incident. Armed conflict between the two nations was averted only when the United States agreed to compensate the victims' families.

■ As a region, the South lacked the ethnic diversity characteristic of the rest of the country. However, small numbers of Jewish immigrants did settle in the South, and some managed to turn modest dry goods establishments into major urban department stores. Atlanta's Rich & Brothers Dry Goods store, shown here in the 1880s, was founded and owned by Jews.

At the same time, Jewish shopkeepers and merchants in the South gained a conditional entry into the ranks of "whites." In Natchez, Mississippi, the small but prosperous Jewish community owned 45 businesses, about a third of all in the town. Merchant Simon Moses and others like him built grand, Victorian-style houses and worshiped in an imposing synagogue, Temple B'Nai Israel. However, anti-Jewish feeling manifested itself in subtle ways. Living in an overwhelmingly Protestant region of the country, many southern Jews found themselves barred from local social organizations.

A variety of organizations sought to enforce the notion of Anglo superiority in the workplace and in the courts. In 1890 the San Francisco Boot and Shoemakers' White Labor League convinced a shoe manufacturer to fire 15 Japanese workers. The 1891 lynching of the New Orleans Italian workers (deemed nonwhites) was organized by the White League, a terrorist group similar to the Ku Klux Klan. In 1893 the newly formed Immigration Restriction League launched a campaign to impose a literacy test on incoming aliens. Thus definitions of race served as political strategies to limit the power of blacks and other minorities as workers and as voters.

New Roles for Schools

Between 1890 and 1899, nearly 3.7 million immigrants entered the United States, fewer than 1.4 million of them English speakers from the United Kingdom and Ireland, compared to nearly 2.3 million non-English speakers from Germany, Italy, Austria–Hungary, and Russia. During this period, public displays of patriotism became increasingly characteristic of American life. The recitation of the Pledge of Allegiance was introduced into public classrooms and courtrooms in the 1890s.

Victorians (in England and the United States) saw formal education as a great equalizer of social groups. Moreover, many younger immigrants and the children of immigrants eagerly embraced American schooling as a means of upward mobility. However, schools did not always fulfill their promise as agents of equal opportunity for all. Increasingly, schools separated and grouped children according to their culture, religion, and class as well as race.

Reformers, missionaries, philanthropists, and government officials alike extolled the virtues of schooling tailor-made for particular groups. Presbyterian missionary women founded the Presbyterian College of the Southwest to instruct Spanish-speaking girls in both English and Protestantism. European American teachers taught young Indian women at the Cherokee Female Seminary near the Cherokee Nation capital at Tahlequah, Oklahoma.

Whether designed for Indians, Hispanics, or African Americans, boarding schools enabled teachers to exercise authority over pupils day and night. The head of Carlisle, Captain Richard Henry Pratt, expressed the school's principles this way: "I am a Baptist, because I believe in immersing the Indians in our civilization and when we get them under holding them until they are thoroughly soaked." At the school, boys learned to make harnesses, tin pots and pans, wagons, and carriages, among other products, many of which were sold to local residents to raise money for the school. Girls took in laundry and ironed, also part of the school's money-making effort. The goal of such activities was to enable the pupils to become self-supporting upon graduation.

Indians who taught in Indian schools tried to counter the message that whites had nothing to learn from Indian culture. Born on the Yankton Sioux Reservation in Dakota Territory, Gertrude Bonnin chose the pen name Zitkala-Sa to write about her experiences as a teacher at the Carlisle school. She recounted the shame she felt when one of the white

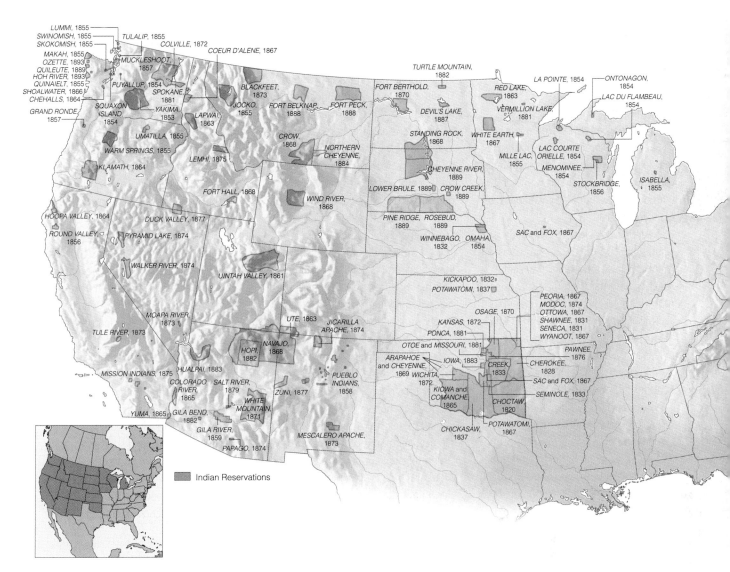

■ MAP 18.3

INDIAN RESERVATIONS, 1900   The Dawes Severalty Act, passed by Congress in 1887, intended to abandon the reservation system and integrate Indians into mainstream American society. Nevertheless, many reservations remained intact. As a group, Indians remained apart from European Americans. By the early twentieth century, the Indian as a "vanishing American" had become a stock character in novels and films. Yet Indian activists continued to press the cause of their people: to preserve native cultures and, at the same time, protest persistent poverty.

teachers taunted a young man by reminding him "that he was nothing but a 'government pauper.'" She lamented, "I wished my heart's burdens would turn me to unfeeling stone. But alive, in my tomb, I was destitute!"

The school as a vehicle for vocational instruction also found support among northern philanthropists concerned about education for southern black children and young people. A generation after the Civil War, the persistent poverty of many rural southern blacks convinced northern reformers that this group of Americans should be educated for a distinct form of second-class citizenship. Philanthropists, such as Julius Rosenwald of Chicago, upheld the notion of segregated public education. They created new institutions, or modified existing ones, to stress the trades and "domestic arts" at the expense of such subjects as philosophy, mathematics, and foreign languages. Embracing the "industrial education movement," the white

Systems of Education

Efforts to educate and socialize young people assume many forms. Americans have transmitted skills and moral and religious values to younger generations at home, in the workplace, at school, and through religious institutions.

America's history of religious instruction is as old and as varied as the history of the land itself. In ancient America, in what is now New Mexico, native peoples built kivas, underground ceremonial chambers. There men initiated their sons in the customs and beliefs of their society.

European settlers adhered to and adapted their own distinctive traditions. Catholics and many Protestant denominations offered religious instruction, culminating in a young person's confirmation in the church. Beginning in the 1920s, Jewish girls in reform synagogues celebrated their *bat mitzvah,* a coming-of-age ritual for 13-year-olds.

In Europe, such rituals had been reserved for boys (the *bar mitzvah*).

Much secular instruction took place within the family or workplace. Traditionally, native youth learned from their parents—the boys to hunt and fish; the girls to raise crops, process food and hides, and make garments. In the British colonies, children learned a trade, embraced Christianity, and became responsible community members by participating in a thick web of family, church, and town activities.

In the early nineteenth century, literacy assumed political significance. Southern planters feared that literate blacks would learn of the work of northern abolitionists and communicate among themselves to foment rebellion. Nat Turner's revolt in 1831, in Virginia, led many southern states and towns to crack down on clandestine black schools.

In the North at the same time, Horace Mann and other reformers were promoting tax-supported schools that would provide a "common" (i.e., standard) education for all children. The purpose of the common school system was to educate efficiently the large numbers of immigrants arriving in the United States. The result was the growth of municipal and state educational bureaucracies in the Northeast and Midwest.

Challenges to the reformers came from several quarters. Roman Catholics objected to the use of the King James version (that is, the version favored by Protestants) of the Bible in the public schools. In the early twentieth century, adherents of Progressive education criticized public school instruction as "rigidly prescribed" and "mechanical." The Progressives urged teachers to appeal to their pupils' natural sense of curiosity and love of learning.

Some formal instruction took place outside schools. For example, founded in 1891, the International Correspondence Schools of Scranton, Pennsylvania, boasted more than 2 million students by the 1920s. The schools offered mail-order lessons for land surveyors and mining engineers among others.

Meanwhile, class and racial distinctions had become institutionalized in the public school system. In 1954 trustees of the state-sponsored North Carolina Agricultural and Mechanical College (a segregated black college) voted to exclude women from the school altogether. They reasoned that "neither the girls or boys wanted to engage in the harder kinds of manual labor in the presence of the other sex, but would strive to dress up in fine clothes to impress the other."

This emphasis on vocational training evoked varied reactions from African American leaders. Born a slave in 1858, Booker T. Washington had labored in a West Virginia coal mine before attending Hampton Normal (teacher-training) and Agricultural Institute in Virginia. In 1881 he assumed the leadership of Tuskegee Institute, an Alabama school for blacks founded on the Hampton model. Speaking at the Cotton States Exposition, a fair held in Atlanta in 1895, Washington urged southern blacks to "Cast down your buckets where you are"—in other words, to concentrate on acquiring manual skills that would bring a measure of self-sufficiency to black families and communities. In the same address, Washington proposed that blacks refrain from agitating for civil rights, such as the vote. In return, whites should refrain from attacking innocent men, women, and children. Ignoring this last part of the speech, whites hailed Washington's "Atlanta Compromise" proposal as one that endorsed racial segregation and second-class citizenship for blacks. Nevertheless, in the coming years, Washington worked secretly to undermine the legal foundations of some of the white South's most cherished institutions, including segregated railroad cars and rural forced labor.

team and its retinue of doctors, trainers, cooks, and coaches from one game to the next. The game of basketball was invented in 1891, and, soon after, many colleges formed teams that played the new sport.

Connections Between Consciousness and Behavior

In the 1890s some scholars and writers proposed that, although America's geographic frontier was closed, the "interior" frontier (of the human will and imagination) still attracted the curious. In Vienna, professor–physician Sigmund Freud pioneered the study of the human unconscious, the mysterious realm of thought and feeling that lies hidden beneath the mundane activities of everyday life. Freud's *The Interpretation of Dreams* (1900) suggested that dreams reveal the dreamer's unconscious desires and that these desires shape routine behavior.

In the United States, the new discipline of psychology owed much to the work of Harvard University professor William James. In his *Principles of Psychology* (1890), James described the human brain as an organism constantly adjusting itself to its environment; people's surroundings profoundly influence their behavior, he argued. In *The Will to Believe* (1897), he explored the psychology of religious faith. According to James, religion, science, and philosophy all have immediate relevance to the way people live their lives, and these ways of thinking and believing can cast light on social problems and their possible solutions.

Henry James, William's brother, explored the psychological dimensions of class, gender, and national identities in his short stories, plays, and literary criticism. In much of his fiction Henry James probed the consciousness of his subjects and experimented with methods of controlling points of view. Such works as *Daisy Miller* (1878), *The Wings of the Dove* (1902), *The Ambassadors* (1903), and *The Golden Bowl* (1904) reveal his intense interest in encounters between European and American elites and the clash of cultures between the two groups.

Novelist Stephen Crane combined an unflinching look at reality—a blood-soaked Civil War battlefield or the slums of New York City—with a sensitive probing of human psychology. In *The Red Badge of Courage* (1894), Crane explores the fears and self-delusions of a Union soldier, basing his account on first-hand descriptions of the fighting a generation before. By stripping the story of all ideology—northern soldiers are hardly distinguishable from southern soldiers, and political issues are never mentioned—Crane suggests that the real war was that of the combatants battling their own private demons.

The new discipline of psychology owed much to the work of Harvard University professor William James.

Kate Chopin wrote about gender roles in New Orleans Creole, or French-influenced, society. Her novel *The Awakening* (1899) prompted outrage among critics. They objected to the sympathetic portrayal of the wealthy married heroine, Edna Pontellier, who anguishes over her inability to reconcile her artistic, free-spirited temperament with her roles of wife and mother. At the end of the story, she chooses to commit suicide rather than submit to a life of convention. The novel focuses on Edna's reaction to the expectations other people have of her and on her gradual awakening to the idea that she must live life—or die—on her own terms.

Psychologists and novelists were not the only people to explore the uncharted territory of the mind. Some religious leaders saw human consciousness as the key to understanding spiritual growth and development. In the late nineteenth century, the Church of Christ, Scientist, founded by Mary Baker Eddy in 1879, prospered and grew. Eddy held that physical illness was a sign of sin and that such illness could be healed by Christian faith and prayer. By linking religious life to physical health, Eddy affirmed a crucial link between belief and personal well-being. She also suggested that reality was spiritual in nature and not bounded by the material, or physical, realm. In 1892 she reorganized her Christian Science faith around a mother church in Boston. Through branch churches, the American-born sect has now spread to more than 60 countries throughout the world.

The Search for Alliances

In the 1890s, groups of Americans seemed to be estranged from each other as they never had been before. A few were enjoying the fruits of astonishing wealth, building for themselves magnificent, multimillion-dollar "summer cottages" reminiscent of glittering European palaces. In 1899 University of Chicago sociologist Thorstein Veblen coined the term *conspicuous consumption* to describe the expensive tastes of the ostentatious rich. Meanwhile, working men and women toiled long hours under dangerous conditions—when they had jobs. In 1895 the average worker was unemployed for three months of the year. Categories of race pitted various groups, native-born and immigrant, against one another. Self-styled sophisticated city folk derided the "hayseeds" on the farm.

Still, the prosperous middle class believed that certain unifying forces would connect different classes and ethnic groups. Members of the elite, including businessmen, lawyers, and other professionals, placed their faith in public schools, such cultural institutions as public museums and libraries, and the consumer impulse to instill "American" values in newcomers and the poor. The 1890s also witnessed some remarkable alliances between groups of people who had never before found common ground. Some of these alliances were tentative and temporary, others widespread and enduring. The Populist party had a profound impact on the nation's political landscape in the 1890s. And women, through their local and national organizations, helped to blend domestic concerns with politics, offering a new model of civic involvement. Their activities suggested that the boundary separating the household from the wider world had blurred.

Class Conflict

Under President Benjamin Harrison, the Fifty-First, or "Billion-Dollar," Congress earned its nickname by becoming the first body in peacetime to spend that much money on new initiatives. The Pension Act of 1890 provided pensions for all disabled men who had served in the Union army during the Civil War. By the middle of the decade, 970,000 pensioners were receiving a total of more than $135 million in cash annually. The Sherman Silver Purchase Act became law in 1890. This measure received congressional support when western interests agreed to a high tariff (tax) on a wide variety of imported goods (named the McKinley Tariff after Representative William McKinley of Ohio). In return, the federal government promised to buy a total of 4.5 million ounces of silver each month and to issue banknotes for that amount redeemable in gold or silver. As a result, Westerners paid more for home-produced manufactures, but their region benefited from the infusion of federal cash used to purchase silver mined in the West. The northeastern states, more dependent on domestic manufacturing, traditionally supported a high tariff.

The tariff was necessary to pay for the Pension Act, but the pairing of a high tariff with the purchase of silver produced explosive political and economic results. The tax on imported manufactured goods hurt consumers, and when wages did not keep pace with prices, workers revolted. Some employers exploited the vulnerability of workers in this era of rising prices. For example, in 1892 steel magnate Andrew Carnegie and his company chairman Henry Clay Frick launched an all-out assault on the Amalgamated Iron, Steel and Tin Workers, a craft union affiliated with the American Federation of Labor. Called the "aristocrats of labor," members of the Amalgamated took pride in their skills and the strength of their union. Carnegie and Frick initiated a drastic wage cut at the Carnegie Steel Company's Homestead plant, near Pittsburgh. Workers struck in June. They armed themselves with rifles and dynamite and engaged in a pitched battle with some 300 detectives from the Pinkerton agency, men hired by Frick to break the strike. (Homestead town officials had refused Frick's request to subdue the strikers.) Ten people died, and 60 were wounded. In response to the violence, the governor of Pennsylvania mobilized the state's National Guard. The troops escorted strikebreakers to work. The company cut its workforce by 25 percent and reduced the wages of the strikebreakers. All over the country, the Amalgamated Union lay in ruins. Gloated Frick, "Our victory is now complete and most gratifying."

In the West, gold, copper, and silver miners faced daunting barriers to labor organization from within and outside their ranks. Protestants harbored suspicions of Roman Catholics. Ancient hatreds prevented the Irish from cooperating with the English. European Americans disdained Mexicans and the Chinese. However, the workers in Idaho's Coeur d'Alene mines managed to overcome these animosities and strike for union recognition. In March 1892 mine owners in the region formed a "protective association" and slashed wages. When workers walked off the job, the owners imported strikebreakers from other areas of the West. The strikers retaliated by blowing up a mine with dynamite. Fifteen hundred state and federal troops arrived on the scene, and the resulting clash left seven miners dead. The troops confined 300 striking miners in bullpens, where they remained for several weeks before their trials. In this case, too, the strikers met with defeat. However, out of this conflict came a new organization, founded in Butte, Montana, in 1893: the Western Federation of Miners.

Widespread discontent over the tariff and simmering resentment on the part of debtors clamoring for unlimited coinage of silver helped unseat President Harrison in the election of 1892. The victorious Democratic candidate, Grover Cleveland, took office once more in 1893 (the only defeated president to be reelected). A new and noteworthy player in the election of 1892 was the People's (Populist) party, which nominated an old Greenback Labor party man, James B. Weaver. Weaver polled more than 1 million votes, putting both the Republicans and Democrats on notice that the Populists had the potential to swing future national elections.

The first national convention of the Populist party took place in Omaha, Nebraska, in the summer of 1892. The party had emerged from the Farmers' Alliances that had so effectively organized black and white midwestern and southern farmers in the 1880s. In the 1890s the plight of western farmers reflected the state of American agriculture in general. On the Plains, farmers incurred ever deeper debts as they bought more land and invested in expensive machinery to raise pigs, cattle, wheat, and fruit for market. But to put food on their own tables, they had to pay cash for bacon, beef, bread, and canned peaches at the store. The price of wheat had been a dollar a bushel in 1870, but it was only 35 cents 20 years later. Dakota farmers lost 15 cents on every bushel of wheat they sent to market.

As early as 1890 the Populist party was making gains in state legislatures, and a number of Populist orators were making their mark on the political scene. In Nebraska, party activist Luna Kellie explained the fine points of international finance to her listeners, denouncing foreign investors in the state economy and at the same time extolling the opening of foreign markets for the state's crops. "Stand up for Nebraska, so fertile and fair," she urged farmers.

The Populist party platform endorsed at the Omaha convention supported "free and unlimited coinage of silver and gold at the present legal

TABLE 18-1

The Election of 1892

Candidate	Political Party	Popular Vote	Electoral Vote
Grover Cleveland	Democratic	5,555,426	277
Benjamin Harrison	Republican	5,182,690	145
James B. Weaver	Populist	1,029,846	22
John Bidwell	Prohibition	264,133	

TABLE 18-2

Work Hours Needed to Produce Specified Amounts of Wheat, Corn, and Cotton, 1880 and 1900

	1880	1900
Wheat		
Work hours per acre	20	15
Yield per acre (bu)	13.2	13.9
Work hours per 100 bushels	152	108
Corn		
Work hours per acre	46	38
Yield per acre (bu)	25.6	25.9
Work hours per 100 bushels	180	147
Cotton		
Work hours per acre	119	112
Yield of lint per acre (bl)	179	191
Work hours per bale[a]	318	280

[a] Yields are five-year averages, centered on year shown. For statistical purposes, a bale of cotton is 500 pounds gross weight or 480 pounds net weight of lint. Actual bale weights vary widely.

Source: Historical Statistics of the United States, Colonial Times to 1957 (1961) 281.

ratio of sixteen to one"; a graduated income tax; government ownership of railroad, telegraph, and telephone companies; and an end to land speculation. The delegates also condemned government subsidies to private corporations (for example, land grants to railroads) and called for the direct election of U.S. senators. Populists supported other measures designed to make the political process more open and democratic, such as provisions for voters to recall corrupt elected officials and public referenda on pressing policy issues of the day.

The Populists sought to extend their reach beyond the cotton fields of the South and the plains of the Midwest to working men and women in the nation's cities. Though separated by geography and history, farmers and wage earners could lay claim to certain common interests. The Populists' 1892 platform included resolutions sympathizing "with the efforts of organized workmen to shorten the hours of labor" to an eight-hour work day (many workers were forced to toil 12–14 hours daily) and expressing solidarity with the Knights of Labor in their struggles against "tyrannical" employers. Although the Populist platform sounded radical in comparison to its Democratic and Republican counterparts, it foreshadowed both the substance and spirit of the early-twentieth-century Progressives and the New Deal of the 1930s.

The Populists gained strength when a national depression hit in 1893. This dramatic downturn stemmed from several causes. As debtors clamored for "free silver," foreign investors in the United States became nervous, and European bankers began to call in their loans. A bubble of overbuilding and land speculation burst.

The effects of the depression were widespread. Within six months, 8000 businesses failed, throwing thousands of men and women out of work. As many as 20 percent of all workers lost their jobs. Some took to the road as tramps or hoboes to seek employment; others begged for handouts. In 1894, Jacob S. Coxey, an Ohio quarry owner, dubbed himself a "general" and mobilized his own "army" of 5000 men to march to Washington, D.C. There, the marchers protested the failure of the federal government to provide relief, now that the country was in the midst of the worst depression ever. "Coxey's Army" petitioned Congress to create extensive public works projects at the federal and local levels. However, the "army" met with an abrupt end when Coxey and his men were arrested for trampling the grass on Capitol Hill.

> *Though separated by geography and history, farmers and wage earners could lay claim to certain common interests.*

Also in 1894, Eugene V. Debs, head of the American Railway Union (ARU), inspired the union's 150,000 members to protest conditions at the Pullman Palace Car Company. Employees in the company town of Pullman near Chicago felt squeezed when Pullman cut their wages by one-third but left intact the rents on their company-owned houses. The resulting strike crippled railroads from Chicago to California. The U.S. attorney general, Richard Olney, a former attorney for the railroads, urged President Cleveland to intervene in the strike. Cleveland heeded Olney's advice, declaring that he could not stand by while the strikers interfered with the delivery of the U.S. mail. The president sent troops to quell the uprising, crushing the strike. For the first time, a federal court issued an injunction to force workers to go back to their jobs. Debs and other ARU leaders defied the order and went to jail.

To workers all over the country, the response to the Pullman strike signaled a troublesome alliance between government and big business, two powerful forces that the poor and the unemployed could not hope to counter. That alliance seemed to be solidified in 1895 when federal gold reserves fell to a dangerous low of $41 million (it was widely believed that a minimum of $100 million in gold was necessary to sustain the paper currency in circulation). Cleveland authorized the sale of government bonds for gold, but he also turned to J. P. Morgan, a Wall Street banker, for a loan. Morgan and a group of bankers agreed to lend the government $65 million, earning a $7 million commission for themselves in the process.

Judicial decisions confirmed the belief of many farmers and workers that all branches of the federal government were conspiring to favor the rich at the expense of the poor. In 1895 the Supreme Court rendered two opinions that favored big business and the wealthiest Americans. In *United States v. E.C. Knight,* the court ruled that the Sherman Anti-Trust Act of 1890

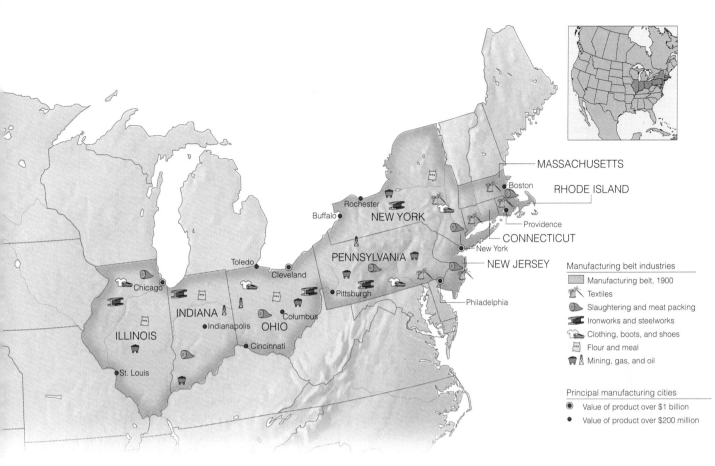

MASSACHUSETTS
RHODE ISLAND
CONNECTICUT
NEW JERSEY

Boston
Providence
New York

Rochester
Buffalo
NEW YORK
Toledo
Cleveland
PENNSYLVANIA
Pittsburgh
Philadelphia

Chicago
INDIANA
Indianapolis
OHIO
Columbus
Cincinnati

ILLINOIS

St. Louis

Manufacturing belt industries

- Manufacturing belt, 1900
- Textiles
- Slaughtering and meat packing
- Ironworks and steelworks
- Clothing, boots, and shoes
- Flour and meal
- Mining, gas, and oil

Principal manufacturing cities

- ◎ Value of product over $1 billion
- • Value of product over $200 million

■ **MAP 18.5**

MANUFACTURING IN THE UNITED STATES, 1900 During the late nineteenth century, most manufacturing took place in the northeastern United States. Exceptions included flour milling in Minneapolis, the growing textile industry in the southern Piedmont, and the emergence of steel production in Birmingham, Alabama, thanks to rich local deposits of iron and coal ore.

applied only to interstate commerce and not to manufacturers. The court had decided in favor of the subject of the suit, the sugar trust that controlled 98 percent of the industry. In *Pollock v. Farmers' Loan and Trust Company,* the court struck down a modest federal income tax (2 percent on incomes over $4,000 per year). These decisions helped set the stage for the showdown between the Populists and the two major parties in 1896.

Demise of the Populists

In 1896 the Republicans nominated Congressman William McKinley of Ohio, whose name had graced the widely unpopular tariff bill of 1890. The Democrats turned their back on Cleveland, regarded as a pariah by members of his own party for his deal with Morgan and his high-handed tactics against the Pullman strikers. Without an obvious presidential candidate at their convention in Chicago in July, the Democrats seemed at loose ends. Then, out of the audience, a young man rose to address the 15,000 delegates. William Jennings Bryan, a 36-year-old Populist from Nebraska, electrified the assembly with his passionate denunciation of arrogant industrialists and indifferent politicians. The country must abandon the gold standard once and for all, he thundered: "You shall not press down upon the brow of labor this crown of thorns, you shall not crucify mankind upon a cross of gold." One awestruck listener, an alternate member of the Nebraska delegation, later said of Bryan's "Cross of Gold" speech, "There are no words in our language to picture the effect it produced upon the vast multitude which heard it." The next day, the Democrats chose Bryan as their candidate for president.

TABLE 18-3

The Election of 1896

Candidate	Political Party	Popular Vote	Electoral Vote
William McKinley	Republican	7,102,246	271
William J. Bryan	Democratic	6,492,559	176

By nominating this eloquent upstart, the Democrats took on the Populist cause of free silver. Conservative Democrats bolted the party or sat out the election. Meanwhile, some Populists were appalled that the Democrats had picked conservative Maine banker Arthur Sewall as Bryan's vice-presidential running mate. Meeting in their own convention later in the summer, the Populists chose Bryan as their candidate for president and Thomas E. Watson of Georgia for vice president. Thus, during his presidential campaign in the fall, Bryan had to contend with two different running mates from two different parties.

In the general election, McKinley received much support from his friend and political supporter, Marcus (Mark) Hanna. A wealthy iron magnate and chair of the Republican National Committee, Hanna coordinated an effort to raise large sums of money for the Republicans ($16 million in total, compared with the Democrats' $1 million). He also fueled a nationwide hysteria over the possibility that Bryan would become president, blanketing the country with leaflets declaring "In God we trust, in Bryan we bust." Hanna charged that Bryan as president would mean disaster for businessmen, bankers, and other creditors, who would now be at the mercy of working people, small farmers, and other debtors. Benefitting from Hanna's strategy and from divisions between the populists and Democrats, McKinley triumphed in November. As a national force, the People's Party rapidly disintegrated after the election of 1896.

Yet as a political movement encompassing disparate elements, the Populists left a mixed legacy. In some areas of the country, the party yielded some remarkable, if short-lived, interracial coalitions. In Grimes County, Texas, in the cotton-growing eastern part of the state, the Populist spirit survived for a few years beyond 1896. Some whites had split from the Democratic party, and some blacks had renounced their traditional allegiance to the Republican party. The alliance brought together blacks, such as school principal Morris Carrington, and whites, such as Garrett Scott, a Populist sheriff.

In the fall of 1899, the White Man's Union (WMU) emerged to oppose this biracial coalition. A member of the WMU tried to put its aims to poetry:

Twas nature's laws that drew the lines
Between the Anglo-Saxon and African races,
And we, the Anglo-Saxons of Grand Old Grimes,
Must force the African to keep his place.

The WMU made good on its vow to rid the county of "Negro rule." A November 1900 shootout at Anderson, the county seat, left Garrett Scott wounded and his brother Emmett and two other men dead. The gun battle effectively ended the Populist presence in Grimes County.

The Populists were unable to sustain a regionwide biracial coalition in the South. This failure suggests the power of white supremacist beliefs. The threat of cooperation between Republican and Populist voters was powerful, especially in such states as North Carolina. In that state, Republican–Populist fusion had captured the state legislature in 1894 and the governorship in 1896. Throughout the South, the black population was growing—a total of 10 million people in 1890 compared with 4.5 million on the eve of the Civil War. Frightened by this development, white southern Democrats campaigned to disfranchise black men, beginning in the 1890s. Landless blacks and whites would find no common political ground again until the 1930s.

Barriers to a U.S. Workers' Political Movement

In the 1890s, workers in Europe were forging new political parties to represent their interests and, in some cases, to press a bold socialist agenda, in the forum of national politics. Although late-nineteenth-century America showed dramatic evidence of bitter class conflict, it produced no viable workers' party or socialist movement. Why? The answer is not simple. Together, farmers and members of the industrial laboring classes aspired to self-sufficiency, a life free of debt that released their wives and children from unremitting toil and provided some measure of material comfort. Nevertheless, both groups found it difficult to ally with each other.

The large influx of immigrants meant that competition for even low-paying jobs remained fierce among wage-earning men and women. Employers manipulated racial, ethnic, and religious prejudices among workers to keep them estranged. Between 1890 and 1900, at least 29 major strikes—primarily in the iron, steel, coal-mining, meatpacking, railroad, and longshore industries—prompted management to employ African American strikebreakers.

White Protestant workers seized on ethnic and religious distinctions to win for themselves advantages in the workplace. Their unions excluded certain racial and ethnic groups altogether. Even somewhat egalitarian unions fell prey to racial prejudice. For example, the United Mine Workers (UMW) professed to welcome both black and white workers into its ranks. However, an 1892 report from an African American organizer in Jellico, Tennessee, stated that "the whites declare that they won't work" under an African American boss. At best, whites relegated their black and female coworkers to segregated unions and enforced a discriminatory division of labor within the workplace.

Moreover, the pace and processes of mechanization and technological development varied from job to job, making it difficult for workers in one industry to form alliances with workers in another. By 1900 the steel, shoe, and textile industries were fully mechanized. In contrast, skilled craft workers dominated the cigar, garment, and glass-blowing industries, although women machine operatives were beginning to challenge male cigarmakers. Taking pride in their craft and its traditions, skilled workers distanced themselves from those who tended machines.

Many American workers, regardless of ethnicity, religion, or industry, continued to believe that they could eventually own their own businesses; thus, they resisted casting their lot

■ In 1896 Charles H. Epps, the city sergeant of Richmond, Virginia, ran for reelection. He distributed these cards to prospective voters. The cards suggest the masculine nature of politics at this time. This one doubled as a scorecard for the city's professional baseball team and carried advertisements for a local whiskey manufacturer and liquor and tobacco store.

TABLE 18-4

Categories of Employment, 1880–1910

Occupation	1880	Percentage	1890	Percentage	1900	Percentage	1910	Percentage
Agriculture, forestry, and fishing	8,705	50.1	10,170	42.8	10,920	37.6	11,590	31.6
Extractive industries	310	1.8	480	2.0	760	2.6	1,050	2.9
Manufacturing	3,170	18.2	4,750	20.0	6,340	21.8	8,230	22.4
Construction	830	4.8	1,440	6.1	1,660	5.7	2,300	6.3
Commerce and finance	1,220	7.0	1,990	8.4	2,760	9.5	3,890	10.6
Transportation and communications	860	4.9	1,530	6.4	2,100	7.2	3,190	8.7
Services	2,100	12.1	3,210	13.5	4,160	14.3	5,880	16.0
Other	195	1.1	170	0.7	370	1.3	600	1.6
Total	17,390	100	23,740	100	29,070	100	36,730	100

Numbers given in thousands.

Source: International Historical Statistics, 154.

California Views Historical Photo Collection, Monterey, CA

■ The diversity of the American workforce and the American economy inhibited the development of a national workers' political party. By the 1890s, some industries were fully mechanized. Others relied on traditional forms of manual labor. In California, Asian workers faced persistent discrimination from labor unions. These immigrants are picking oranges near Santa Ana, c. 1895.

permanently with unions or other working-class organizations. High rates of geographic mobility also prevented workers from committing themselves to a particular union in a particular place. The power of antistrike forces proved daunting. Private security agencies, such as the Pinkertons, as well as state-deployed National Guard troops, backed up the authority of employers, judges, mayors, and governors. And finally, unlike European parliamentary systems, U.S. politics was based on a "winner-take-all" principle. In America, the two major parties tried to capture the political center, discouraging coalition-building among smaller parties. Such alliances might have pushed the country farther to the left or right.

These factors help to account for the success of the American Federation of Labor (AFL) in attracting and retaining members. By the end of the nineteenth century, the AFL had rejected the rhetoric of radical labor leaders in favor of organizing a select group of workers, mostly skilled white men. Leaders of AFL union affiliates denounced "cheap labor" competitors, whether women workers or Japanese or Chinese immigrants. In the coming years, the AFL would prove that it had staying power, although it represented primarily the interests of white male craftsmen.

Challenges to Traditional Gender Roles

In the 1890s the women's suffrage, club, missionary, and social settlement movements emerged as significant political forces. Nevertheless, for the most part, white women in these movements remained steadfast in their refusal to embrace their nonwhite counterparts.

In 1890 the two major national woman suffrage associations, the National Woman Suffrage Association and the American Woman Suffrage Association, merged to form the National–American Woman Suffrage Association (NAWSA). Elizabeth Cady Stanton served as the new group's first president for two years. The suffrage movement exhibited contradictory impulses. On one hand, it brought together supporters from around the country and yielded striking examples of international cooperation. Beginning in 1890 and every year thereafter until 1920, members of NAWSA branches scattered throughout the United States met in convention to debate strategy. American women consulted with their counterparts in England and western Europe to advance their cause.

On the other hand, in an effort to become "respectable," white native-born Protestant American suffragists sought to distance themselves from the poor, immigrants, African Americans, and the laboring classes within their own country. When NAWSA leaders called for an "educated franchise," they implicitly left out immigrant and poor women. They also refused to admit black women's suffrage clubs into their umbrella organization. In the process, the white women turned their backs on some of the most committed supporters of their own cause.

Identifying themselves primarily as wives and mothers, some women entered the political realm through local women's clubs. They believed that personal intellectual development and group political activity would benefit both their own families and society in general. In the 1880s, the typical club focused on self-improvement through reading history and literature. By the 1890s, many clubs had embraced political activism. They lobbied local politicians for improvements in education and social welfare and raised money for hospitals and playgrounds.

The General Federation of Women's Clubs (GFWC), founded in 1892, united 100,000 women in 500 affiliate clubs throughout the nation.

Yet the GFWC specifically excluded African American clubs. Black women formed their own national federation, the National Association of Colored Women (NACW), in 1896. Through club work, they spoke out against lynch mobs and segregationists and worked to improve their local communities. In 1899 the first president of NACW, Mary Church Terrell, appeared before a mostly white organization, the National Congress of Mothers. She minced no words in contrasting the resources available to white mothers and children with the inferior medical care afforded their African American counterparts. Declared Terrell, "So rough does the way of her infant appear to many a poor black mother that instead of thrilling with the joy which you feel, as you clasp your little ones to your breast, she trembles with apprehension and despair."

In some areas of the country, black and white women did make common cause—to further the goals of temperance, for example—although white women embraced these alliances uneasily. At the end of the century, black women in North Carolina sought to circumvent the sometimes violent political realm dominated by white men. They worked with middle-class white women through voluntary organizations, such as the Young Women's Christian Association and the Women's Christian Temperance Union.

In the West, Protestant-sponsored "mission homes" ministered to women in need. The San Francisco Presbyterian Chinese Mission Home offered a safe haven for Chinese women fleeing abuse and exploitation. In 1898 a young Chinese woman, Lee Yow Chun, appeared before a government official and testified to the poverty of her family in Hong Kong and to the web of deception that had led to her arrival in the United States as a prostitute. Encountering an immigration official in San Francisco, Lee "fell in a lump on the floor and cried loudly, saying I did not want to be landed by those people [who had tricked her]; that I would jump into the sea rather than be taken by them." As a result, she was allowed to go to the mission home. In response to stories such as Lee's, eastern women opened their pocketbooks to further not only the San Francisco mission but also shelters for unwed mothers and abused girls in other cities, in the name of virtuous womanhood.

The daily operations of the settlement house reflected the priorities of its founders.

Religious beliefs inspired some women to go beyond national boundaries in their efforts to reach out to like-minded people. In the 1880s and 1890s, a group of American women participated in an interdenominational, international campaign to support the work of Pandita Ramabai, a native of India who had converted to Christianity and worked to challenge the subordinate role of women in her own country. In 1890 almost 60 "Ramabai Circles" claimed more than 4000 members in the United States and Canada. Ramabai chose not to ally herself with the growing Indian nationalist movement (in opposition to Great Britain, the colonial power that ruled India); in her view, Christianity, not nation-state loyalties, should shape the identities of both men and women.

Social settlements were unique institutions, founded and staffed by well-educated women, many of whom had attended elite women's colleges. The daily operations of the settlement house reflected the priorities of its founders, who often brought activists, public health officials, journalists, and laboring men and women together around the dinner table to discuss problems of the poor. Settlement house workers hoped to instill in poor women the values of domesticity and pride in American citizenship. By 1900 more than 200 social settlement houses were helping to acculturate immigrants by offering classes in a variety of subjects, including English, health, and personal hygiene. In 1893 the women social workers of Hull House successfully lobbied Illinois state legislators for the passage of anti-sweatshop legislation that would protect female employees and prohibit child labor. Florence Kelley, who served for three decades as the general secretary of the National Consumer League, was a resident of Hull House in the early 1890s. In 1899 she moved to New York's Henry Street Settlement (founded by a nurse named Lillian Wald in 1893). The settlement's neighbors included the 500,000 people packed into the Lower East Side, many of them from Italy, Russia, Germany, Greece, and Hungary.

Culver Pictures

■ To the modern eye, the Victorian parlor looks cluttered. Yet to late-nineteenth-century middle-class people, the parlor was a place to display possessions that testified to their comfortable way of life. Books, family photographs, and musical instruments had great social and symbolic value. Families gathered to read aloud, pore over photo albums, and sing old favorites. Some men, worried that their opportunities for "manly" activity were vanishing with the western frontier, considered parlors to be female spaces.

Although often associated with immigrants in the largest cities, settlement houses reached diverse populations. In the late 1890s, a coalition of the Kentucky Federation of Women's Clubs and other organizations sponsored several teachers who organized a summer settlement called Camp Cedar Grove in the eastern part of the state. This venture provided the foundation for the Hindman Settlement School. The school, still in existence, initially aimed to acculturate mountain people to middle-class ways in dress, eating habits, and manners and to preserve traditional mountain music and crafts.

Sensitive to the racial prejudices of their clients and their neighbors, most early settlements failed to reach out to African Americans. This policy stimulated the development of black-led settlements, such as the Phyllis Wheatley Settlement in Minneapolis and the Neighborhood Union in Atlanta. Founded by Lugenia Burns Hope in 1908, the Neighborhood Union aimed "to bring about a better understanding between the races."

In the tradition of Frances Wright and Victoria Woodhull, some women challenged traditional gender relations that relegated women to dependence on men. Emma Goldman, a Russian immigrant and self-proclaimed anarchist, paired the sexual liberation of women with the rights of workers to live a decent life. A radical by any measure, Goldman was, nevertheless, not alone in rejecting the idea that marriage should always be permanent. Between 1890 and 1900, the divorce rate increased from 1 out of every 17 new marriages to 1 out of 12. More and more couples, middle-class and working-class, native-born and immigrant, were seeking means to dissolve marriages that had failed.

■ This interior of a Tlingit Indian chief's house in Chilkat, Alaska, c. 1900, suggests that the Victorians were not the only group of people to arrange crowded displays of art and other cultural artifacts in central living spaces. Indians of the Northwest coast enjoyed an abundance of marine foods. They had time to devote to making intricate wood carvings in the form of masks and totem poles. Social status was based on inheritable wealth, as revealed by works of art and other material goods.

Charlotte Perkins Gilman was among the most prolific and well-known critics of the conventional division of labor in the home. Through fiction, nonfiction, and poetry, she claimed that humankind had progressed beyond the point where brute strength was the determinant of social status. Gilman proclaimed that women, no longer content to remain dependent on men, must take their rightful place within the economy, working as equals with their brothers and husbands. In *Women and Economics: A Study of the Economic Relations Between Men and Woman as a Factor in Social Evolution* (1898), she proposed that housework be divided into its specialized tasks to be performed by professionals. This system would free women from the unpaid, mind-numbing task of combined "cook–nurse–laundress–chambermaid–housekeeper–waitress–governor." In her critique of gender conventions, Gilman anticipated the feminist movement of the 1960s.

Men also pondered the effects of industrializing society on their own roles. Some elite men revolted against the trappings of Victorian culture. These men worked every day in business offices, not out of doors. Some yearned for "manly" activities such as courageous exploits against nature or other men. They believed that overstuffed parlors represented "feminine" interiors. Life indoors—singing religious hymns around the piano or reading aloud to family members—stifled men's "natural" instincts for bravery and adventure, they claimed. They yearned to embrace the outdoors and prove their masculinity in the process. As assistant secretary of the Navy in the late 1890s, Theodore Roosevelt worried that, in this age of machines, young men lacked the opportunities for "the strenuous life" their grandfathers had

■ Crushed when his mother and wife both died on the same day in 1884, Theodore Roosevelt abandoned New York politics and spent several years ranching in South Dakota and hunting in Montana. This photo served as the frontispiece for Roosevelt's 1897 book, *Hunting Trips of a Ranchman*. TR believed that the West promoted "the qualities of hardihood, self-reliance, and resolution." In 1886 he returned to New York City and resumed his political career.

enjoyed. He argued that unapologetic masculine bravado provided the key to American strength and rejuvenation on both a national and personal level. In his multivolume history, *The Winning of the West* (1889–96), Roosevelt extolled America's relentless march to the Pacific: "The rude, fierce settler who drives the savage from the land lays all civilized mankind under a debt to him." Imperialism at home and abroad, he declared, was a "race-important work," one that should claim the energies of men as politicians and soldiers.

American Imperialism

In the 1890s the United States began to extend its political reach and its economic dominance to other parts of the world. Americans looked beyond their borders and saw exotic peoples who represented a variety of opportunities—as consumers of American goods, producers of goods Americans wanted to buy, and objects of American benevolence. This view represented an extension of the reform impulse at home. Indeed, broader thinking about the United States' place in the world reflected a new desire among those who benefited from prosperity to spread American standards—in behavior, productivity, and quality of life—to other peoples.

The country's mighty industrial manufacturing sector demanded new markets and a wider consumer base. The depression of 1893, in particular, raised fears that manufacturers would have to contend with surpluses of goods that Americans could not afford to buy. American businesspeople and state department officials established a partnership that combined private economic self-interest with national military considerations. Some molders of public opinion used the new languages of race and masculine virility to justify an "Anglo-Saxon" mission of conquest of "childlike" peoples. Meanwhile, European countries were carving up Africa and making economic inroads into China. Many Americans believed their own country should join the "race" for riches and "march" to glory as part of the international competition to exploit the natural resources and trade potential of weaker countries.

Cultural Encounters with the Exotic

In early October 1897, 30,000 spectators paid their 25-cent fee to enter New York's Excursion Wharf and observe the strange cargo of the recently arrived steamship *Hope*. Arctic explorer Robert Peary had returned from Greenland, bringing with him six Greenland Eskimos and a 37.5-ton meteorite dislodged from the Cape York region. Among the native Greenlanders were Qisuk and his seven-year old son, Minik. The American public hailed the intrepid explorer Peary as a hero. The American Museum of Natural History put the Eskimos on display, and New Yorkers regarded their odd clothing, language, and eating habits with intense curiosity. But their curiosity was only superficial and did not extend to protection for the young Minik.

Over the next year, four of the Eskimos (including Qisuk) died, and one other returned to his native land. The orphaned Minik survived and remained in the United States. Within a few years, he was abandoned by Peary and museum officials who had initially touted him as a significant scientific discovery. Minik returned to Greenland when he was a young man, but he was restless and unhappy there. He returned to the United States in 1916, eventually finding some peace with a New Hampshire farm family. He died in 1918, a victim of a worldwide flu epidemic.

Minik's short, tragic life reveals certain aspects of Americans' encounter with "exotic" peoples in the late nineteenth century. The Museum of Natural History subjected him and the other members of his group to close study. When Qisuk died, the museum conducted a mock burial for the benefit of his son but then created a public exhibit of Qisuk's bones. (Nearly 100 years later, the passage of the Native American Grave and Burial Protection Act provided an incentive for museum authorities to send the remains of the four Eskimos back to Greenland for burial.)

During the late nineteenth century, Americans were fascinated by artifacts and images dealing with far-away places, especially Africa, the Middle East, and Asia. This impulse, revealed in high art as well as popular culture, stereotyped darker-skinned, non-Christian peoples as primitive, sensual, and inscrutable. Chicago's Columbian Exposition of 1893 featured exhibits depicting harems, spice merchants, and turbaned warriors and performances of "hootchy kootchy dancers," scantily clothed young women writhing to the music of exotic instruments.

Throughout the late nineteenth century, photographers took pictures of Middle Eastern nomads and African villagers. American artists, such as Frederic Edwin Church and John Singer Sargent, traveled abroad to render romantic scenes of deserts, ancient ruins, and mysterious peoples in oils and in watercolors. Painter Eric Pape arranged to have himself tied to a pyramid so that he could partake of an "Egyptian experience"; he produced a painting called *Site of Ancient Memphis* in 1891.

These cultural tendencies could be used to sell products and entertainment. The glassmaker–jeweler Tiffany and Co. evoked Islamic art in its tea services and silver patterns. Tobacco companies marketed mass-produced cigarettes with "Oriental" brand names: "Fatima," "Omar," and "Camel." Thus, a fascination with the exotic encompassed a wide range of impulses in American life and letters, bringing together explorers, scientists, artists, and advertising agents.

Initial Imperialist Ventures

The opening of Asia to American trade, combined with the military challenges posed by the major European imperial powers, stimulated the growth of the U.S. Navy in the 1880s. In 1883, Congress appropriated funds to build 90 small ships, one-third made of wood, the rest out of steel. Seven years later, Captain Alfred Thayer Mahan argued for a modern force of large seagoing battleships. In his book *The Influence of Sea-Power in History, 1660–1763* (1890), Mahan contended that if the United States aspired to be a world power, it must control the seas.

Seeking way stations for its ships, the United States negotiated control over both Pearl Harbor in Hawaii and the harbor at Pago Pago in Samoa in 1887. The state department even achieved a voice in Samoan foreign relations to stave off rivals Great Britain and Germany, which also coveted Pago Pago. In 1889 warships of these three powers gathered in the Samoan harbor. Fortunately, a hurricane thwarted a showdown. The powers, unnerved by their near brush with war, agreed to establish joint control over the islands for the next ten years.

In October 1890, Secretary of State James G. Blaine hosted the first Pan-American Conference in Washington, D.C. a gathering of representatives from 19 independent Latin American republics. Topics included the adaptation of standardized weights and measures for all participants in the conference and a possible intercontinental railroad. These developments suggested the blurring of military, diplomatic, strategic, and economic interests—a mix that characterized American foreign policy for decades to come.

In 1895 the United States signaled to Great Britain that it was prepared to go to war to bar Europeans from colonizing or intervening in the Americas, a policy outlined in the Monroe

American Museum of Natural History Library, Image No. 220-545

■ The Greenland Eskimo Minik is shown here soon after his arrival in New York City in 1897. Minik was devastated by the death of his widowed father, Qisuk; the two were among six Eskimos brought to New York by Arctic explorer Robert E. Peary. Later in his life, Minik spoke of his father to a newspaper reporter, saying, "He was dearer to me than anything else in the world, especially when we were brought to New York, strangers in a strange land."

Doctrine more than 70 years before. Britain had persisted in its long-standing claims to the jungle boundary between its colony of British Guiana and the country of Venezuela on the north central coast of South America. President Cleveland made clear his intention to enforce the Monroe Doctrine. Britain, sensitive to other threats posed by European imperial powers on the far-flung British empire, backed down. Thereafter, Britain began to concentrate on strengthening its diplomatic ties with the United States.

Meanwhile, in the South Pacific, the Hawaiian Islands seemed to pose both a threat and an opportunity for American interests. Located 2000 miles from the California coast, Hawaii had a population of 150,000 in 1890. When English explorer James Cook had landed there in 1778, the islands were inhabited exclusively by the descendants of ancient seafaring Polynesians. Protestant missionaries began to arrive in 1820, and the first sugar plantation appeared 15 years later. In 1875 sugar planters and merchants, many of whom were related to missionaries, negotiated a treaty with the United States that let them ship the crop to the United States duty-free. Production of Hawaiian sugar increased from less than 10,000 tons in 1870 to 300,000 tons 30 years later.

In 1895 the United States signaled to Great Britain that it was prepared to go to war to bar Europeans from colonizing or intervening in the Americas.

By this time, the Chinese, Koreans, Filipinos, Puerto Ricans, the Japanese, and the Portuguese had made their way to the Hawaiian Islands. These groups formed the bulk of the plantation labor force, for disease had decimated the native population. In the fields and in their barracks, immigrant contract workers followed a disciplined regimen under the supervision of mounted, whip-wielding overseers called *lunas*. Indeed, these laborers' workday bore a marked resemblance to that of sharecroppers on the largest cotton plantations of the U.S. South.

Not surprisingly, both clergy and growers were alarmed by the laborers' resistance to regimentation in the fields and in the quarters. Some men and women workers drank on Saturday night, smoked opium, and gambled. Worse, in the eyes of their employers, many grabbed any opportunity to flee the plantation in search of jobs as wage earners or shopkeepers in the city of Honolulu. Some even became rice farmers on their own. Planters were forced to suspend operations to accommodate traditional festivals, such as the Chinese New Year, when workers decorated their barracks and cottages with colorful flags and lanterns. Missionaries and sugar planters alike hoped to transform the workers into more stable, predictable employees.

The McKinley Tariff of 1890 raised duties on imports of the islands' sugar. This served to overturn the 1875 pro-planter treaty, causing planters (mostly Americans) to panic about their livelihood. They received no support from the islands' native leader, Queen Liliuokalani, who believed foreigners should be barred from running the country. In 1893 the planters, backed by American Marines, launched a successful revolt that deposed the queen. They then called for the United States to annex the islands as a territory. Upon investigation, President Cleveland discovered that native Hawaiians opposed annexation and so refused to agree to the move. His refusal incurred the wrath of American imperialists, who claimed that the "Hawaiian pear" had been "ripe for the plucking."

The Spanish–American–Cuban–Filipino War of 1898

In the Caribbean, Cuban nationalists staged an uprising against the Spanish in 1895. The leader of the insurrection was José Julian Martí. He had lived in exile in the United States from 1881 to 1895. Rebelling against the repressive Spanish colonialists who had ruled the island for more than 400 years, native *insurrectos* under the leadership of Martí burned crops of sugar cane and attacked passenger trains. American companies with large investments in the Cuban sugar industry (a total of about $50 million) were outraged at the destruction of their property; they had no sympathy for the *insurrectos*. Yet the arrival of Spanish military officials, who herded the rebels into barbed-wire concentration camps, inflamed public opinion in the United States. Both businesspeople and humanitarians urged McKinley to intervene in Cuba.

Two American newspaper publishers, William R. Hearst and Joseph Pulitzer, seized the chance to boost their respective circulations by highlighting Spanish atrocities against Cubans. Pulitzer owned the St. Louis *Post Dispatch* and the *New York World,* and Hearst challenged him with the *San Francisco Examiner* and the *New York Journal.* On February 9, 1898, Hearst published a letter written by the Spanish minister in Washington, D.C. Dupuy de Lôme, in which de Lôme denounced President McKinley as a spineless politician. Six days later, the American battleship *Maine,* which had been sent to Havana harbor to evacuate Americans should the need arise, exploded and sank. Two hundred sixty officers and men were killed. Subsequent investigations concluded that the heat from one of the coal bins had ignited an adjacent powder magazine. But the Hearst papers implied that the Spanish were responsible for the blast.

Attempting to expand their readership, the Hearst and Pulitzer newspapers engaged in "yellow journalism": sensational news reporting that blurred the line between fact and fiction, spontaneous reality and staged theater. War sold papers. During the crisis in Cuba, the *Journal* was selling at a rate of a million copies a day.

McKinley responded to American businesspeople who feared for their interests in Cuba and to other Americans who decried Spain's brutality toward the *insurrectos.* On April 11, 1898, McKinley called on Congress to declare a U.S. war against Spain. His own assistant secretary of the Navy, Theodore Roosevelt, had reportedly called the president a "white-livered" poor excuse for a man. To Roosevelt and other pro-warriors, much was at stake: the large American sugar investment, trade with the island, and American power and influence in the Western Hemisphere. Congress responded to McKinley's message by adopting the Teller Amendment, which declared that the United States would guarantee Cuba its independence once the Spanish were driven from the island. America went to war on April 29.

McKinley hoped to hobble the Spanish navy by making a preemptive attack on the fleet in the Philippines. Commodore George Dewey, stationed with the American Asiatic Squadron in Hong Kong, was dispatched with his ships to Manila Bay, where on May 1, 1898, his force of four battleships sank all ten rickety Spanish vessels, killing 400, with only a few minor American casualties.

The Granger Collection, NY

■ **The battleship *Maine* exploded and sank in Havana harbor on February 15, 1898.**

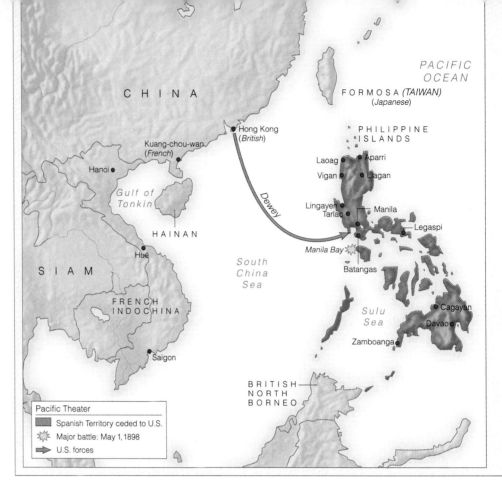

■ MAP 18.6
THE SPANISH–AMERICAN–CUBAN–FILIPINO WAR OF 1898
In Cuba, the United States combined a blockade of the island with an army invasion to defeat Spanish forces. In the Philippines, the U.S. triumph over the Spanish opened a wider war between American occupying forces and native Filipinos.

Dewey waited in the harbor until American reinforcements arrived in August. Then, with the help of Filipino nationalists led by Emilio Aguinaldo, U.S. forces overran Manila on August 13.

Meanwhile, congressional Republicans had found the necessary votes to annex Hawaii. They claimed that the United States needed the Pacific islands to secure a refueling way station for Dewey's troops. McKinley signed the congressional resolution on July 7, 1898. Hawaiian residents were granted citizenship rights, and the islands became an official U.S. territory in 1900.

Earlier in the summer of 1898, halfway around the globe, 17,000 American troops traveled to Tampa, Florida, in preparation for their incursion into Cuba. Among them were the Rough Riders, a crew of volunteers organized by Lieutenant Colonel Theodore Roosevelt, who had resigned his post as assistant secretary of the Navy to serve as an officer. The troops, woefully unprepared for combat in the tropical heat, landed near Santiago, Cuba, in late June.

On July 1, Roosevelt and his men engaged an unprepared Spanish force of about 2000 men at El Caney and San Juan Hill. The Rough Riders charged up nearby Kettle Hill (they were on foot, not on horses) and into American legend. Later in speeches, Roosevelt boasted of shooting a Spanish soldier at point-blank range. But Roosevelt neglected to mention that he and his men had received crucial backup support from two African American regiments that day. Blacks had formed a skirmish line at the bottom of the hill, and, according to an eyewitness, "with an unearthly yell, charged up it" in company with the white soldiers. Federal military authorities had assigned African American men prominent combat roles in Cuba and the Philippines, believing that blacks were better able than whites to withstand the withering heat of the tropics.

By late July, American warships had destroyed the Spanish fleet in Santiago Bay. Again, Spanish losses were high (500 men killed) and American losses slight (1 man killed). According to Secretary of State John Hay, it had been "a splendid little war," just 113 days long. Battles claimed 385 American lives (although many times that number died from disease—malaria, typhoid, dysentery, and yellow fever—and from the rotten meat the soldiers ate). On August 12, 1898, Spain signed an armistice and later in the year ceded its claim to remnants of its empire, including Cuba and Puerto Rico in the Caribbean and the island of Guam in the Pacific.

The United States forced Cuba to incorporate into its constitution (written in 1901) the so-called Platt Amendment, which guaranteed continuing U.S. influence over the country, including the stationing of American troops at a naval station on Guantanamo.

Meeting with Spanish negotiators in Paris, the United States agreed to pay $20 million for the Philippines. McKinley's motives in acquiring the islands stemmed from both commercial interests (the Philippines as a gateway to China) and religious concerns (the opportunity for Protestants to convert Spanish-speaking Roman Catholics).

But Filipino rebels were not about to bow to a new colonial power. Over the next two years, the United States committed 100,000 troops to subdue the rebels, using tactics that foreshadowed the U.S. war in Vietnam 70 years later. Hunting down guerrillas hiding in the jungle, American soldiers torched villages and crops. They forced water down the throats of suspected rebel leaders—in a form of torture known as the "water cure"—in an effort to extract information. Four thousand Americans and 20,000 Filipinos died in combat. As many as 600,000 Filipino civilians succumbed to disease and starvation. Not until 1901 could the Americans claim victory over their "little brown brothers," as future president William Howard Taft referred to the Filipino people.

Ownership of the Philippine Islands gave the United States a foothold in Asia. In 1894–1895, Japan had waged a successful war against China, and European traders rushed in to China to monopolize local markets and establish their own spheres of influence. Secretary of State John Hay issued a communication called the Open Door note in the summer of 1899; in it, he urged the imperial powers to respect the trading interests of all nations. The Europeans were reluctant to cede anything to their international competitors, and only Italy agreed to the terms of Hay's policy. But in 1900, the Boxer Uprising in China prompted cooperation between the western powers. The Boxers, Chinese ultranationalists, killed 200 foreign missionaries and other whites in an effort to purge China of outsiders. Together, the Germans, Japanese, British, French, and Americans sent 18,000 troops to quell the revolt. The United States and European nations continued to compete for the China market well into the twentieth century.

Proceedings of the Congressional Committee on the Philippines

In January 1900, Congress established the Committee on the Philippines. Senator Henry Cabot Lodge of Massachusetts was appointed chair of the committee. Its task was to review the American conduct of the war. The testimony of two U.S. officers, which follows, foreshadows the difficulties faced by the United States in fighting a guerilla war in Vietnam six decades later.

Brigadier General Robert P. Hughes testified in response to questions posed by committee members:

Q: In burning towns, what would you do? Would the entire town be destroyed by fire or would only offending portions of the town be burned?

GEN. HUGHES: I do not know that we ever had a case of burning what you would call a town in this country; but probably a *barrio* or a *sitio*; probably a half dozen houses, native shacks, where the *insurrectos* [rebels] would go in and be concealed, and if they caught a detachment passing they would kill some of them.

Q: What did I understand you to say would be the consequence of that?

GEN. HUGHES: They usually burned the village.

Q: All of the houses in the village?

GEN. HUGHES: Yes, every one of them.

Q: What would become of the inhabitants?

GEN. HUGHES: That was their lookout. . . . The destruction was as a punishment.

Q: The punishment in that case would fall, not upon the men, who would go elsewhere, but mainly upon the women and little children.

GEN. HUGHES: The women and children, are part of the family, and where you wish to inflict a punishment you can punish the man probably worse in that way than in any other.

Q: But is that within the ordinary rules of civilized warfare? Of course you could exterminate the family, which would be still worse punishment.

GEN. HUGHES: These people are not civilized. . . .

Sergeant Charles S. Riley also testified in response to the following questions:

Q: During your service there [in the Philippine Islands] did you witness what is generally known as the water cure?

A: I did.

Q: When and where?

A: On November 27, 1900, in the town of Igbaras, Iloilo Province, Panay Island. . . .

[Riley describes a Filipino man, 40–45 years of age, stripped to the waist, with his hands tied behind him.]

Q: Do you remember who had charge of him?

A: Captain Glenn stood there beside him and one or two men were tying him. . . . He was then taken and placed under the tank, and the faucet was opened and a stream of water was forced down or allowed to run down his throat; his throat was held so he could not prevent swallowing the water, so that he had to allow the water to run into his stomach. . . . When he was filled with water it was forced out of him by

Critics of Imperialism

Theodore Roosevelt seemed to personify the late-nineteenth-century idea of American manifest destiny: the notion that the core of the nation's history was a militant mission to expand its territorial reach. However, not all Americans agreed with Roosevelt. New York financier Mark Hanna called him a "madman" and "that damned cowboy." Writer Mark Twain believed him "clearly insane" and "insanest upon war and its supreme glories." Twain and other prominent people founded the Anti-Imperialist League in 1898 in an attempt to stem the rising tide of militarism.

It is difficult to generalize about the politics of anti-imperialists during this period. AFL president Samuel Gompers and industrialist Andrew Carnegie both considered themselves members of the anti-imperialist camp, but clearly that stance did not mean they agreed on much, or even on anti-imperialism. Some critics of imperialism advocated a hands-off policy toward other nations in the belief that all peoples were entitled to self-determination. In contrast, other anti-imperialists used arguments about racial hierarchies to justify their opposition to expansion. Yale sociology professor William Graham Sumner, a proponent of Social Darwinism, argued that "uncivilized and half-civilized peoples" were hostile to democratic self-government and unprepared for its rigors. Thus, Sumner believed that American efforts to "civ-

Philippine civilians encounter U.S. army troops during the war of 1898. Resisting attempts to colonize the islands, Filipinos battled American forces in a war that lasted four years. A soldier in the Third Regiment wrote of the indiscriminate killing of civilians, "I am probably growing hard-hearted for I am in my glory when I can sight my gun on some dark-skin and pull the trigger."

pressing a foot on his stomach or else with their hands. . . .

Q: What had been his crime?

A: Information had been obtained from a native source as to his being an insurgent officer. After the treatment he admitted that he held the rank of captain in the insurgent army—an active captain. . . .

Q: His offense was treachery to the American cause?

A: Yes, sir. . . . ■

Source: Proceedings of the Congressional Committee on the Philippines, in Harvey Graff, ed., *American Imperialism and the Philippine Insurrection* (Boston, 1969), pp. 64–79.

ilize" and colonize foreign peoples would inevitably fail because those peoples were incapable of embracing American values.

Recent newcomers to the United States resented the idea that the "march of the flag" was an enterprise to be led by Anglo-Saxons (that is, people of English descent), as some imperialists claimed. German immigrants invoked their heritage of conquest, and the Irish juxtaposed their native culture with what they called the historic "brutal savagery" of the English. Nevertheless, supporting imperialism was one way for immigrants to proclaim their own Americanness and distance themselves from allegedly inferior peoples.

In the summer of 1900, the Democrats and Republicans prepared for the upcoming presidential election. Receiving the Democratic nomination once again, William Jennings Bryan was eager to press the outdated cause of free silver. He also condemned the American presence in the Philippines, although this issue, too, was rapidly losing the attention of the electorate. At the Republican convention, Roosevelt's supporters managed to win for him the slot as McKinley's running mate. That fall, the former Rough Rider waged an exuberant campaign. Accompanied by a retinue of gun-toting cowboys, he wrapped the Republicans in the American flag. When McKinley swept back into office in the fall, few Americans could have anticipated how central Roosevelt's vision would become to the country over the next two decades.

635

Conclusion

As Americans greeted the twentieth century, they might have marveled at the dramatic changes that had occurred in their country over the last 100 years. In 1800 the United States was home to 5.3 million people who lived in 16 states. One hundred years later, the country included 45 states and boasted a population of 76 million people. Many workplaces, fields as well as factories, were dominated by machines and the people who tended them. The economy was shifting toward the mass production of consumer goods.

In 1900 the United States exerted control over the land and peoples of Alaska, the Hawaiian and Samoan Islands, the Philippines, Guam, Puerto Rico, and (through the Platt Amendment), Cuba as well. These holdings, notable for their strategic significance, illustrated the growing willingness of the United States to extend its influence and economic reach—by armed force if necessary—to the far corners of the earth.

The 1890s foreshadowed many of the major themes of the twentieth century. The Populists looked to the federal government to address social ills, paving the way for Progressives in the early twentieth century and New Dealers in the 1930s. Conversationists provided the foundation for the environmentalist movement of the 1970s. And suffragists were the foremothers of the modern women's movement. Yet for Americans, a generations-old contradiction lingered between prosperity and political equality for some groups and poverty and political subordination for others. On the international stage, the United States was quick to take advantage of weaker nations if such action was deemed crucial to the "national interest." The new drive for worldwide economic and political power was fast eclipsing America's revolutionary heritage, with its values of democracy and self-determination.

Sites to Visit

The Spanish–American War
www.loe.gov/rr/hispanic/1898

This site provides resources and documents about the Spanish-American War, the period before the war, and the people who participated in the fighting or commented on it.

Imperialism Web Page
www.smplanet.com/imperialism/toc.html

Focusing on the late nineteenth and early twentieth centuries, this site includes much information about American imperialism.

Hispanic Voices/Voces Hispanas
www.lib.berkeley.edu/BANC

This interactive site on Latinos in California is maintained by the Bancroft Library in Berkeley. The autobiographical narratives include late-nineteenth-century oral histories with Latinos.

Late Nineteenth-Century Authors
xroads.virginia.edu/~HYPER/hypertex.html

This University of Virginia site includes material on prominent nineteenth-century writers, including William Dan Howells, Mark Twain, and Joel Chandler Harris.

Mary Baker Eddy
www.tfccs.com/GC/MBE/MBEmain.jhtml

This site looks at the founding of Christian Science.

National Arts and Crafts Archives
www.arts-crafts.com/index.html

This site serves as a guide to materials related to the Arts and Crafts movement, which lasted from about 1890 to 1929.

Samuel Gompers Papers
www.inform.umd.edu/HIST/Gompers/page4.html

This site includes information about the Samuel Gompers Papers project at the University of Maryland. It also has a photo gallery, selected documents, and a brief history of the first president of the American Federation of Labor.

The Era of William McKinley
www.history.ohio-state.edu/projects/mckinley/

This Ohio State University site contains a bibliography and numerous images from various periods of McKinley's career. It also includes a section with an excellent collection of McKinley-era cartoons.

For Further Reading

General

Glenda Elizabeth Gilmore, *Gender and Jim Crow: Women and the Politics of White Supremacy in North Carolina, 1896–1920* (1996).

Matthew Frye Jacobson, *Barbarian Virtues: The United States Encounters Foreign Peoples at Home and Abroad, 1876–1917* (2000).

Walter LaFeber, *The New Empire: An Interpretation of American Expansion, 1860–1898* (1963).

Emily S. Rosenberg, *Spreading the American Dream: American Economic and Cultural Expansion, 1890–1945* (1982).

Robert W. Rydell, *All the World's a Fair: Visions of Empire at American International Expositions, 1876–1916* (1984).

Frontiers at Home, Lost and Found

David Wallace Adams, *Education for Extinction: American Indians and the Boarding School Experience, 1875–1928* (1995).

Willard B. Gatewood, Jr., *Black Americans and the White Man's Burden, 1898–1903* (1975).

Matthew Frye Jacobson, *Whiteness of a Different Color: European Immigrants and the Alchemy of Race* (1998).

Neil R. McMillen, *Dark Journey: Black Mississippians in the Age of Jim Crow* (1989).

Donald J. Pisani, *From the Family Farm to Agribusiness: The Irrigation Crusade in California, 1850–1931* (1984).

Barbara M. Solomon, *In the Company of Educated Women: A History of Women and Higher Education in America* (1985).

Mark David Spence, *Dispossessing the Wilderness: Indian Removal and the Making of the National Parks* (1999).

David B. Tyack, *Managers of Virtue: Public School Leadership in America, 1820–1980* (1982).

The Search for Alliances

Paul Buhle, *From the Knights of Labor to the New World Order: Essays on Labor and Culture* (1997).

Sarah Deutsch, *Women and the City: Gender, Space, and Power in Boston, 1870–1940* (2000).

Patricia R. Hill, *The World their Household: The American Woman's Foreign Mission Movement and Cultural Transformation, 1870–1920* (1985).

Elisabeth Lasch-Quinn, *Black Neighbors: Race and the Limits of Reform in the American Settlement House Movement, 1890–1945* (1993).

Seymour Martin Lipset and Gary Marks. *It Didn't Happen Here: Why Socialism Failed in the United States* (2000).

Vicki L. Ruiz and Ellen Carol DuBois, eds., *Unequal Sisters: A Multicultural Reader in U.S. Women's History* (2000).

David E. Whisnant, *All That Is Native and Fine: The Politics of Culture in an American Region* (1983).

American Imperialism

Robert L. Beisner, *Twelve Against Empire: The Anti-Imperialists, 1898–1900* (1968).

H. W. Brands, *Bound to Empire: The United States and the Philippines* (1992).

Paul A. Cohen, *History in Three Keys: The Boxers as Event, Experience, and Myth* (1997).

Kenn Harper, *Give Me My Father's Body: The Life of Minik, the New York Eskimo* (2000).

Thomas J. McCormick, *China Market: America's Quest for Informal Empire, 1893–1901* (1967).

William Appleman Williams, *The Tragedy of American Diplomacy* (1972).

Online Practice Test

Test your understanding of this chapter with interactive review quizzes at

www.ablongman.com/jonescreatedequal/chapter18

PART SEVEN

Reform at Home, Revolution Abroad, 1900–1929

MANY AMERICANS GREETED THE FIRST YEARS OF THE TWENTIETH century with optimism. Developments at home and abroad seemed to promise a new era of prosperity and progress. The mass manufacturing of automobiles proved a boon to the economy and transformed patterns of travel, leisure, and consumption. The beginning of commercial air flights heralded a revolution in communication and transportation. Moving pictures and new musical forms such as jazz delighted millions.

Focused on the new challenges of urbanization and industrialization, Progressive reformers sought to use science to solve a wide range of problems related to public health and welfare. Some advocated overhauling the system of public education; others pressed for legislation banning the sale and distribution of alcohol. Some lobbied for worker health and safety legislation, and still others sought to exercise social control through eugenics and state-mandated sterilization.

A variety of groups challenged white men's exclusive claim to civil rights. African Americans took the national stage to argue for equality under the law and for freedom from state-sanctioned violence in the form of lynching and debt peonage. Beginning with the Great Migration of World War I, southern blacks abandoned the cotton fields to seek jobs in northern cities.

The changing roles of women bolstered the women's suffrage movement. Growing numbers of women were becoming labor organizers, reformers, and college professors. Rising divorce rates and the emergence of birth control as a political as well as a medical issue signaled challenges to the traditional patriarchal family. At the same time, conflicts among reformers emerged. For example, white middle-class suffragists hoped to maintain their "respectability" in an effort to win the support of reluctant male leaders; in the process, these women distanced themselves from members of the working class and even the African American women active in the suffrage movement. Suffragists' efforts paid off in 1920, with the ratification of the Nineteenth Amendment to the Constitution.

With its lively consumer culture and rising standard of living, the United States continued to attract newcomers from abroad. Immigrants from Mexico and eastern Europe sought refuge from poverty, oppression, and civil strife at home. In 1914, 1.2 million immigrants came to America, the largest number in a single year before or since that date. Between 1900 and 1930, more than 1 million Mexicans migrated north, most settling into existing Mexican American communities in the Southwest or creating new communities there or in the Midwest.

World War I shattered the belief among many Progressives that conflicts could be solved in a rational, peaceful way. The end of the war had permanently entangled U.S. interests in European affairs. Moreover, revolutions in Mexico (1910) and Russia (1917) affected the United States directly, the former by spurring immigration across the country's southwest border, the latter by challenging the nation's system of industrial capitalism. Nevertheless, many Americans remained convinced that the country could and should isolate itself from world affairs.

Natural forces also remained beyond the control of reformers and government officials. The San Francisco earthquake of 1906, the great Mississippi flood of 1927, and the Florida hurricane of 1928 exacted devastating tolls in terms of human life and property damage. The local communities that were directly affected struggled for years to recover from these disasters.

But for many Americans, the 1920s was a period of peace and prosperity. New household appliances and conveniences lightened the burdens of housework. Radios and movies proved to be popular forms of entertainment. Traditional social mores gave way to expressions of sexual freedom. Progressive impulses waned as business values rose to take their place.

The decade after the end of World War I revealed both the persistence of old conflicts and the emergence of new conflicts within American society. Conservatives branded labor union organizers and socialists as unpatriotic and subversive. Asian immigrants on the West Coast and blacks in the rural South and urban North faced continued legal discrimination in the workplace and in the courts. Protestant fundamentalists challenged the move toward secularism and rationalism, claiming that religious faith, not science, set the standard for morality in modern life. Responding to those who feared that foreign immigration represented a threat to American society, Congress imposed immigration restrictions in 1924. Put into effect in 1920, the Eighteenth Amendment to the Constitution prohibited the sale and distribution of alcoholic beverages. The three Republican presidents who served during the 1920s—Harding, Coolidge, and Hoover—retreated from the activist stance favored by their predecessors, including Theodore Roosevelt and Woodrow Wilson.

The stock market crash of 1929 revealed fundamental weaknesses in the American economy. A tide of bank failures engulfed individual American families even as it threatened businesses abroad. As the depression deepened, Americans looked to the federal government to address the crisis.

1916 Jeannette Rankin elected first female member of Congress.
U.S. Marines occupy Dominican Republic.

1917 U.S. enters World War I.
U.S. Marines occupy Cuba.
Russian Revolution.
Residents of Puerto Rico granted U.S. citizenship.

1918 Spanish influenza epidemic kills 20 million worldwide.
Sedition Act.
Wilson's "Fourteen Points" speech to Congress.

1919 Versailles Treaty ends World War I.
U.S. Senate rejects League of Nations.
Eighteenth Amendment (prohibition) ratified.

1920 Nineteenth Amendment (women's suffrage) ratified.

1921 Tulsa whites attack black community.
Sheppard–Towner Act.

1922 Five-Power Naval Treaty.

1923 Equal Rights Amendment proposed.

1924 Johnson–Reid Act.
Portable radio introduced.

1925 Scopes Trial, Dayton, Tennessee.
F. Scott Fitzgerald, *The Great Gatsby.*

1926 Gertrude Ederle is first woman to swim across English Channel.

1927 Charles Lindbergh flies nonstop from New York to Paris.
Al Jolson stars in *The Jazz Singer,* first talking movie.
Sacco and Vanzetti executed.
Buck v. Bell upholds compulsory sterilization laws.

1928 Tamiami Trail across Florida Everglades completed.

1929 Stock market crash.

The Promise and Perils of Progressive Reform, 1900–1912

Abraham Walkowitz, "In the Street," 1909. Hirshhorn Museum and Sculpture Garden, Smithsonian Institution, Washington, D.C. (66.5446) Gift of Joseph H. Hirshhorn, 1966. Photograph by Lee Stalsworth

■ Abraham Walkowitz's 1909 painting, *In the Street*, depicts a Jewish immigrant couple on a crowded urban street.

"I AM A WORKING GIRL," DECLARED CLARA LEMLICH IN HER NATIVE YIDDISH, "ONE OF those striking against intolerable conditions." Still in her teens, the petite young woman took the podium on the night of November 22, 1909, in front of thousands of striking workers in New York, and roused them with her passionate, direct call for action: "I am tired of listening to speakers who talk in generalities. What we are here for is to decide whether or not to strike. I offer a resolution that a general strike be declared—now." The next morning, 15,000 garment workers went on strike, demanding that the work week be reduced to 52 hours, with overtime pay and union recognition. Soon, the strikers swelled in number to more than 20,000. Observers at the time were astonished to see lively, fashionably dressed young women filling the picket lines. Ninety percent of the striking workers were women; they were overwhelmingly young Jewish immigrants, with Italian women constituting about 6 percent. Quickly, the strikers drew a wide coalition of support from the International Ladies Garment Workers Union (ILGWU), the Women's Trade Union League (WTUL), and middle-class reformers and activists for women's suffrage.

The strike was a demand for union recognition, reasonable wages and hours, and safe and decent working conditions, including an end to sexual harassment on the job. But at the same time, the strikers insisted that they should be treated as "ladies" and have access to the consumer goods and leisure culture taking shape in American cities. Although the young women were bullied and arrested by police, their high spirits prompted some observers to make light of their struggle. Sarah Comstock, a reporter for *Collier's* magazine, wrote of the strike, "This was a scene of gaiety and flirtation. My preconceived idea of a strike was a somber meeting where somber resolutions were made. . . . But they don't look as if they had any grievances." In response to those who tried to trivialize the women's mobilization and in defense of their desire to be part of the new consumer culture, Lemlich stated, "We like new hats as well as other young women. Why shouldn't we?" Ultimately, the strike ended with a failed compromise when the striking workers overwhelmingly rejected an offer of better wages and working conditions that did not include recognition of their union. Calling the strikers "socialists," their more moderate allies broke from the union and left the young female workers vulnerable to the power of the company owners. The coalition of support fell apart, and most of the strikers eventually went back to work.

Victims of the Triangle Shirtwaist Company fire.

Less than two years later, a fire broke out in the top floors of the Triangle Shirtwaist Company, one of the major centers of the 1909 strike. Eight hundred workers, most of them young Jewish and Italian women, were trapped in the inferno because company officials had locked interior doors to prevent the women from taking unauthorized breaks or leaving work early. The flames tore through the building in less than half an hour, leaving 146 young women dead. Those who did not succumb to flames and smoke jumped to their deaths. "One girl after another fell, like shot birds, from above, from the burning floors," remembered one witness. "They hit the pavement just like hail," reported a firefighter. Parents rushed to the scene to find their young daughters dead, dying, or maimed. "My little girl lies dead, shrouds instead of a wedding gown," cried one of the bereaved. One reporter wrote, "I looked upon the dead bodies and I remembered these girls were the shirtwaist makers. I remembered their great strike of last year in which the same girls had demanded more sanitary conditions and more safety precautions in the shops. Their dead bodies were the answer." In the investigation that followed, the owner of the factory was never charged with a crime or held responsible for the tragedy. He claimed that his building was in full compliance with safety laws, but compliance with the laws did not ensure safety for the workers. No laws required sprinklers, adequate fire escapes, or fire drills. Just a few months before the fire, the building had been inspected and declared "fireproof." Defending himself after the fire against accusations of negligence, the building owner pointed to the sturdy brick structure, which, as the *New York Times* noted, "showed hardly any signs of the disaster."

The "uprising of twenty thousand," as the 1909 strike came to be called, and the tragic factory fire that ignited in its aftermath, are two among many dramatic episodes in the early twentieth century that expose the fractures and tensions within the nation at the time. Immigrants and racial minorities demanded the full promise of American life; workers struggled against the exploitation, poor pay, and dangerous conditions that characterized industrial jobs; young women insisted on respect at work and access to the playful environment of urban fashion and popular culture; female voices called for full citizenship and the vote and claimed their right to be heard by male bosses and union leaders; and activists across the political spectrum tried to control and manage the changes taking place around them in accord with their widely differing values.

During the first years of the twentieth century, the nation began to emerge as something profoundly different than it had been in the past. Even the landscape changed as cities continued to grow not only outward but also upward, with the construction of towering skyscrapers, and downward, with the creation of subway systems. But human enterprise continued to be vulnerable to the forces of nature. On April 18, 1906, an earthquake virtually leveled San Francisco. The nation saw in one deadly instant that human technological genius paled in the face of nature's fury. After the quake, fire devoured the city. In the words of writer Jack London, "All the cunning adjustments of a twentieth century city had been smashed by the earthquake. The streets were humped into ridges and depressions, and piled with the debris of fallen walls. The steel rails were twisted into perpendicular and horizontal angles. The telephone and telegraph systems were disrupted. And the great water mains had burst. All the shrewd contrivances and safeguards of man had been thrown out of gear by thirty seconds' twitching of the earth-crust."

■ An earthquake devastated San Francisco on April 18, 1906. Here a Chinese immigrant watches as the city goes up in flames. Chinatown was destroyed, along with much of the downtown.

Library of Congress

If New York's Triangle Shirtwaist Company building—unscathed after the young women inside perished in flames—was a monument to corporate arrogance, the crumbled buildings of San Francisco offered a lesson in humility. "Never, in all San Francisco's history, were her people so kind and courteous as on this night of terror," noted London. Railroads carried thousands of refugees out of the city, free of

Rose Freedman

(Both photos) Courtesy, Bud Freedman

Rose Rosenfeld Freedman as a young immigrant, and decades later as a labor activist.

Major historical events sometimes take on a life of their own, locked in a single frame of historical memory. The 1911 Triangle Shirtwaist Company fire is one such event. Rose Rosenfeld Freedman, one of the young women working at the factory on that fateful day, provides a reminder that events are not simply frozen in time. The tragic fire that she survived fueled in her a lifelong committment to the rights of workers.

Rose Rosenfeld was not born into a working class community that might have nurtured her committment to workers' rights. The daughter of a prosperous business owner, she emigrated from Vienna to the United States in 1909 at age 15. She did not need a job, but as a young Jewish immigrant, she recalled, "I wanted to show that I'm [a] real American and I want to work like everybody else. And I went on my own, found a job. . . . And then, I almost paid with my life." She was 16 when she went to work at Triangle, sewing buttons at a wage of $3 for a six-day week.

Rose was working on the ninth floor when the fire alarm sounded at 4:43 P.M. on March 25, 1911. Finding the exit doors locked, she ran up to the tenth floor, where the executives worked, but the bosses were gone. "They saved themselves already." She pulled her dress over her head and followed the bosses to the roof, where firefighters hoisted her to safety on top of the adjacent building.

The fire inspired her to action. Nearly a century later, her memory of the fire remained vivid: "The executives with a couple steps could have opened the door. But they thought they were better than the working people. . . . What good is a rich man [if] he hasn't

got a heart? I feel it. Still. I feel very bad about it." Outrage over the fire led to the passage of 36 labor and safety laws in the next three years. Rose Rosenfeld left the garment business and went on to college, but she remained a passionate advocate for workers' rights.

In another dramatic brush with history, Rosenfeld demonstrated her willingness to stand up for others whose rights and safety were threatened. She was visiting Austria just as World War I erupted. A Russian Jew who had been spying for Austria arrived at the house where she was staying, begging for protection from Russian soldiers. She hid him in a coal bin in the basement and when the soldiers arrived, she told them to leave. Weeks later, the wife of the man she hid came to the house to thank her for saving the father of their five children.

In 1927, Rose married Harry Freedman, who ran a typewriter business. During World War II, in the midst of a terrifying polio epidemic, she escaped another tragedy. Two of her children were stricken with the disease but recovered. For Freedman, it was another miracle, like her escape from the Triangle fire. Widowed in 1952,

Freedman entered business school at age 59 and got a job with a pen company in New York. At 64, she lied about her age and got a job in customer relations at the Metropolitan Life Insurance Company. She stayed there for 15 years, retiring at age 79.

Still an active crusader, Freedman moved to Los Angeles when she was in her nineties. At age 100, she went to Mexico to study Spanish. Like the shirtwaist workers who wore hats and stylish clothes on the picket line in 1909, Rose Freedman still wore high heels, had her hair done every week, and did her own shopping. Cherishing her independence, she refused to move in with her children, explaining that "young people belong together and I have a life of my own."

In 2000, at age 106, Rose Freedman lectured on sweatshops to enthralled students at Occidental College in Los Angeles. "She loved her career. . . . She believed quite fully in doing things that make you happy," said her granddaughter Dana Walden, head of 20th Century Fox Television. Rose Freedman died in 2001 at age 107, the last survivor of the Triangle Shirtwaist Company fire. ∎

charge. And the national government stepped in immediately, as it would countless times throughout the twentieth century in the face of disaster.

The San Francisco earthquake symbolized American life at the dawn of the twentieth century in one word: upheaval. When the smoke and dust cleared, Chinatown was destroyed, as were the modest homes of laborers, the new houses of the middle class, the palaces of the wealthy, sturdy banks and businesses, and the brick and steel constructions of modernity. But out of death and destruction, the city and its people came back. San Francisco, along with the rest of the country, grappled with upheaval as the nation continued on its path toward the diverse, urban, industrial society that characterized American life in the twentieth century.

The dramatic changes taking place in the nation at the dawn of the new century, from industry and technology down to the most intimate levels of life, sparked equally dramatic efforts to control, tame, and regulate them. Because of the flurry of reform activity during this period, historians call it the Progressive Era. Politicians from all parties participated in the wide range of reform efforts known as Progressivism, fueled by a faith in progress and a belief in the possibility for social improvement.

Jessie Tarbox Beals, "Women and Children in the Kitchen," 1915. Community Service Society, New York, NY. ©The Jewish Museum

■ An immigrant family manages the daily routines of life in a tenement flat in 1910. Crowded conditions, poor ventilation, and inadequate plumbing made it impossible for impoverished residents such as these to maintain a clean and healthy environment.

Migration and Immigration: The Changing Face of the Nation

Charismatic young labor leader Clara Lemlich was one of millions of immigrants at the time who were changing the face of the nation. This migration, which began in the latter decades of the nineteenth century, resulted largely from international economic and political upheavals. Facing severe hardships in their home countries, many migrants took the desperate action of departing for foreign lands. Between 1900 and 1910, nearly 9 million immigrants entered the United States, by far the largest number for any single decade in the nation's history before or since. The United States was one of several potential destinations for these courageous and hopeful sojourners. It was particularly appealing because of its often exaggerated, but nonetheless real, opportunities for jobs and economic advancement, its official commitment to freedom of religion and political thought, and its reputation as a nation that welcomed newcomers from abroad.

Many immigrants followed kin or fellow townsfolk who had come in the nineteenth century; others were drawn to the promise of a better life, symbolized by the Statue of Liberty. On arrival, many found that the "promised land" was not the paradise they expected. They faced crowded living conditions in urban tenements, jobs in sweatshops and factories with long hours, low wages, and miserable working conditions, and a hostile reception. Many Americans— including some whose own parents or grandparents had come to the United States as immigrants—looked down on the newcomers as "racially inferior" and morally suspect, feared competition for jobs, and worried that the masses of poor foreigners in their midst would become a burden on taxpayers and public institutions. The Statue of Liberty may have held

Pecentage of foreign-born population in 1900

- More than 30%
- 10–30%
- 1–10%
- Less than 1%, or no foreign-born population

■ **MAP 19.1**

FOREIGN-BORN POPULATION, 1900 Although the most famous points of entry for immigrants during the turn-of-the-century decades were New York's Ellis Island for people from Europe, and Angel Island off of San Francisco for people from Asia, most immigrants actually settled in the Upper Midwest and the Southwestern region bordering Mexico.

up the torch of welcome, but many citizens, from union halls to legislative chambers, wanted the newcomers to leave.

Many did leave. One-third of immigrants to the United States returned to their home countries. Some came for only a few years and returned to their native lands, including nearly 90 percent of migrants from the Balkans. Other groups, especially those who faced severe hardships in the lands of their birth, were more likely to make the United States their permanent home, settling with their families and building communities. Only 11 percent of the Irish and 5 percent of the Jews returned between 1908 and 1923.

Although some of the newcomers moved to rural areas and worked in agriculture, most settled in the cities, where they were joined by rural Americans leaving farms for new opportunities in the rapidly growing urban centers. In the first decade of the twentieth century, more than four and a half million Americans moved from east to west, and nearly 80,000 migrated from south to north. Each person who took part in this huge global and national migration brought hopes, anxieties, and fears. But over time, these newcomers transformed almost every aspect of American life: political, economic, cultural, and social.

The Heartland: Land of Newcomers

Known as the nation's heartland, the upper Midwest carries associations of small towns dotted with Protestant churches and inhabited by hardy Anglo-Saxon pioneers and their descendants. But at the dawn of the twentieth century, it was not the coastal cities, with their visible

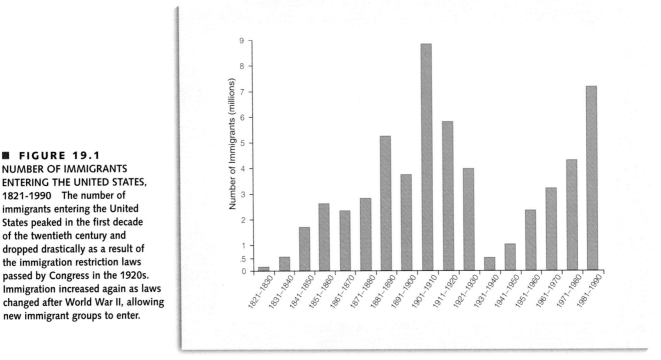

■ **FIGURE 19.1**
NUMBER OF IMMIGRANTS ENTERING THE UNITED STATES, 1821-1990 The number of immigrants entering the United States peaked in the first decade of the twentieth century and dropped drastically as a result of the immigration restriction laws passed by Congress in the 1920s. Immigration increased again as laws changed after World War II, allowing new immigrant groups to enter.

immigrant ghettos, but the settlements in the upper Midwest, along with the lower Southwest, where the greatest concentration of foreign-born residents lived. In the growing towns and cities of the Midwest, newcomers from central Europe and Italy joined the earlier settlers from Germany and Scandinavia to form farming and mining communities on the rich soil and abundant iron deposits of the region.

Immigrants from central and southern Europe settled in the region, which came to be known as the "iron range." In the 1890s, the area was sparsely settled. As a result of the Dawes Act of 1887, which divided tribal lands into individual parcels, much of the land orginally held by Indians had been divided and sold. Most of the Indians who were native to that region were removed to reservations. The iron-rich areas, previously the hunting, fishing, and gathering areas of the Native Americans, were now inhabited by lumberjacks who cut the forests. The harsh climate, ranging from −40°F in the snowy winters to more than 110°F in the sweltering summers, plus aggressive swarms of biting insects made it a difficult place to settle. Nevertheless, mining companies discovered the iron deposits and began recruiting workers, first from northern Europe and then, after 1900, from southern and eastern Europe. By 1910, the iron range was home to 35 European immigrant groups. Gradually, these cohesive working-class communities, like others elsewhere, developed their own brand of ethnic Americanism, complete with elaborate Fourth of July celebrations and other festivities that expressed both their distinctive ethnic identities and their allegiance to their adopted country.

The Southwest: Mexican Borderlands

In 1904 a train carrying Irish orphans from a New York Catholic foundling home chugged westward to deliver its small passengers to waiting Catholic families in Clifton and Morenci in the Arizona territory. Church officials at the New York orphanage had screened the families carefully to be certain that the couples hoping to adopt these children were virtuous church-going Catholics, industrious workers, and respectable members of the community. The local parish priest approved these couples, and on the appointed day, they waited eagerly as the orphans, dressed in their best clothes with their pink cheeks scrubbed clean, departed from the train. Along with the expectant couples, the waiting crowd included many women of the town. But when the Anglo-Protestant residents of the town discovered that Mexican Catholic foster parents claimed these fair-skinned children, they were outraged.

That night, the Anglo women gathered to mobilize their husbands into a vigilante posse. In the middle of the night, during a driving rainstorm, the men went to the homes of the Mexican couples, banged on the doors, and kidnapped the children at gunpoint. The next day, the children were distributed to the vigilantes' wives and other Anglo foster parents. Although the Catholic foundling home that had placed the children with the Mexican couples fought a lengthy legal battle to regain custody of the children, the Anglos managed to keep the orphans. The Arizona Supreme Court validated the kidnapping in the name of the "best interests of the children," and the U.S. Supreme Court let the ruling stand.

The struggle over the orphans reflected tensions and divisions in the region along lines of class as well as race. Longtime residents of this borderland region of Arizona included many Mexicans, mainly farmers, ranchers, and miners. In the early twentieth century Mexico's deteriorating economy prompted large numbers of Mexicans to migrate to California and the Southwest, looking for work. The year before the arrival of the orphans, Mexican mine workers had struck for better wages and working conditions against the Anglo owners of the Arizona Copper Company. The owners put down the strike, and the conflict left bitter feelings on both sides. The vigilante kidnapping of the orphans was, in part, retaliation against the Mexican workers who had organized the strike the previous year.

The upheavals of the Mexican Revolution increased migration after 1911. Most of the migrants to the Southwest found work in mining, railroads, and agriculture, usually as unskilled workers earning meager wages. Excluded from most labor unions until the 1920s, they nevertheless organized strikes from time to time to improve wages and working conditions. During the first decade of the century, and especially after the Mexican Revolution, nativist hostility to the Mexicans intensified. Although the orphan abduction was unique, the conditions and tensions that gave rise to it existed across the region.

Courtesy, Arizona Historical Society/Tucson (#58785)

■ Mexican miners in Arizona struck against their Anglo employers in 1903. The mining company paid Mexican workers less than their Anglo counterparts. In addition to the human toll of death and disease caused by the dangerous conditions in the mines, copper mining also caused permanent damage to the environment.

Asian immigration exclusion

- Immigration restricted by Chinese Exclusion Acts (1882–1943)
- Asiatic barred zone (1917–1952)
- Japanese and Koreans restricted by "Gentleman's Agreement" (1907) and barred in 1924

■ **MAP 19.2**

AREAS EXCLUDED FROM IMMIGRATION TO THE UNITED STATES, 1882–1952 In 1882 the United States barred Chinese immigrants from entering the country; Japanese and Koreans were barred in 1924. In 1917 the exclusion was extended to people from India, Indonesia, and the Arabian Peninsula. Those laws remained in effect until 1943 and 1952, respectively.

Asian Immigration and the Impact of Exclusion

Asians continued to face the most severe restrictions on immigration. The Chinese Exclusion Act of 1882, which prohibited most Chinese from immigrating to the United States, was renewed and extended in 1902. As a result, the mostly bachelor Chinese community in the United States declined by nearly half between 1890 and 1920. Many died or returned to China, reducing the numbers from more than 107,000 to about 61,000. The sex ratio remained severely imbalanced, with about 14 men for every woman.

During the exclusion era, certain categories of Chinese immigrants were allowed entry. Wives of Chinese men already in the United States could enter, as could teachers, students, and merchants. These exceptions made it possible for more than 20,000 Chinese to enter the country during the first decade of the new century. One such emigrant was Sieh King King, an 18-year-old student. In 1902, at a meeting of the Protect the Emperor Society, a reform party that advocated restoring the deposed emperor and establishing a constitutional monarchy in China, she addressed a packed hall in San Francisco's Chinatown. The *San Francisco Chronicle* reported that she "boldly condemned the slave girl system, raged at the horrors of foot-binding [a traditonal Chinese practice in which girls' feet were tightly bound to keep them small] and, with all the vehemence of aroused youth, declared that men and women were equal and should enjoy the privileges of equals." Like Clara Lemlich, her eastern European Jewish peer in New York, Sieh King King expressed ideas that were emerging among urban radicals in the United States but also reflected political movements in their home countries. Sieh King

King's sentiments were directly linked to the women's rights and nationalist movements in China, which were central to efforts to modernize China and strengthen it against further foreign encroachments. The radicalism she brought with her from China called for changes in her native land as well as in her adopted country.

Individual Chinese could also immigrate if they had family members in the United States. As a result, American-born Chinese frequently traveled back and forth, claiming on their return that they left a child in China and requesting permission for their offspring to emigrate. In this way they created spaceholders for imaginary kin, allowing other Chinese to enter the country. The American authorities knew of this system of "paper sons" and "paper fathers" and tried to stop the practice with elaborate and lengthy investigations that could last a year or more while hopeful Chinese immigrants waited as virtual prisoners in wretched conditions on Angel Island, the immigrant gateway off the coast of San Francisco.

Not easily thwarted, Chinese Americans on the mainland smuggled information to their fictional relatives, cleverly providing details of their families and communities back home so that their stories would match. Since it was illegal to transmit such information and letters were read and confiscated, these messages often arrived concealed in walnut shells or other camouflages. These subterfuges provided essential information for the hopeful migrants while also contributing to the stereotype that the Chinese were inscrutable and sneaky. The Chinese resisted their exclusion and their unfair treatment in the United States with open and collective action as well. They persuaded China and other Chinese communities overseas to boycott U.S. goods, which led to some improvements in their treatment. Nevertheless, the restrictions remained.

Before the Chinese Exclusion Act in 1882, more than 332,000 Chinese immigrants had entered the United States, most of them unskilled laborers. White Californians, fearing that the Chinese would compete for jobs and drive down the wages, pressured Congress to prohibit Chinese immigration. Only Chinese immigrants were excluded. At the time, there were only about 3000 Japanese immigrants in mainland United States. Japanese immigrants could still enter the country, and nearly 300,000 did so between 1890 and 1920, when opportunities for high-paying jobs in Hawaii and California offered an alternative to the economic crisis they faced in Japan. As one Japanese immigrant wrote in traditional Haiku poetic form,

> Huge dreams of fortune
> Go with me to foreign lands
> Across the ocean.

When the Chinese Exclusion Act was renewed in 1902, nearly as many Japanese immigrants entered the country as had the Chinese during the peak years before their exclusion in 1882. Most of the men came as workers; most of the women arrived as wives. Marriages in Japan generally were arranged by families, and some men returned to Japan to meet and marry their brides. But cost and distance often prevented those meetings. Some women came to the United States as "picture brides" after an exchange of photographs. Although some women were disappointed with their often much older husbands, most accepted their fate as they would have accepted an arranged marriage in Japan. Others were delighted

California Views Historical Photo Collection, Monterey, CA

■ This young woman was a "picture bride" whose photograph secured her betrothal to her distant future husband. In this way, many men who emigrated from Asia arranged to marry women they had never met. The young fiancée then left her home to join a strange man in a strange land, hoping for the best.

with the opportunity for adventure and life in the new land. As one picture bride explained, many of the people from her village had already gone to the United States, and she wanted to go, too: "I didn't care what the man looked like."

Although the Japanese comprised less than 1 percent of California's population, they faced intense nativist hostility. The Japanese in California protested against the discrimination they faced, and in one case they successfully turned a local case of school segregation into an international incident. In response to the segregation of Japanese children in San Francisco, the Japanese government expressed its extreme displeasure. Hoping to avoid a confrontation with Japan—a significant military power that had just won a war with Russia—President Theodore Roosevelt interceded and convinced the San Francisco school board to rescind its segregation order. This incident led to the "Gentlemen's Agreement" of 1907, in which the Japanese government agreed to limit the number of immigrants to the United States. The numbers of immigrants from Japan dwindled, and Japanese immigrants instead began to settle in Brazil.

Newcomers from Southern and Eastern Europe

Eastern European Jews were among the most numerous of the "new" immigrants in the early twentieth century. In 1880, there were about 250,000 Jews in America; by 1920, there were 4 million, the vast majority from eastern Europe. During those 40 years, a number of factors motivated Jews to leave their small towns, or *shtetls*. Antisemitic policies in Russia and eastern Europe confined them within the Pale of Settlement, an area restricted for Jews. Eco-

International Museum of Photography at George Eastman House, Rochester, New York

■ At Ellis Island this immigrant family received identification tags, indicating that they had been examined and declared healthy. Those who were ill, or youngsters without relatives to meet them, were sent to quarantine houses. Some were refused entry and sent back to their home countries.

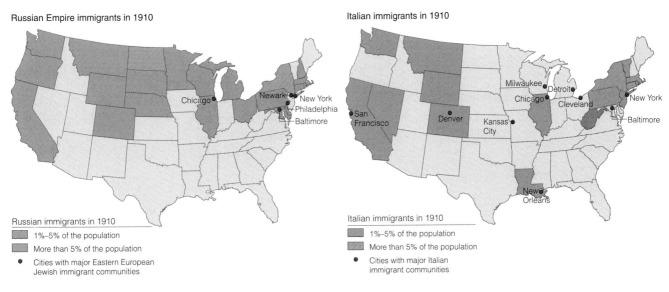

Russian Empire immigrants in 1910

Italian immigrants in 1910

Russian immigrants in 1910
- ▨ 1%–5% of the population
- ▨ More than 5% of the population
- ● Cities with major Eastern European Jewish immigrant communities

Italian immigrants in 1910
- ▨ 1%–5% of the population
- ▨ More than 5% of the population
- ● Cities with major Italian immigrant communities

■ **MAP 19.3**
RUSSIAN AND ITALIAN IMMIGRANTS IN THE UNITED STATES, 1910   Immigrants from Russia and Italy settled across the Northeast, Midwest, and West, with concentrations in large cities. Louisiana was the only southern state with a large concentration of Eastern or Southern European immigrants.

nomic turmoil and restrictions on Jewish land ownership, trade, and business left many Jews impoverished. Even more devastating was the increase in anti-Semitic violence in the form of riots, or *pogroms,* in which Jewish towns were attacked and many Jews were beaten and killed. Although Jews were denied civil rights and faced frequent attacks, they were, nevertheless, subject to the draft. Many young boys emigrated to avoid being conscripted into the czar's army.

One such emigrant was young Morris Bass. At age 12 he left his family and ventured alone across the Atlantic. The uncle who was to meet him forgot about his arrival, stranding Morris in the quarantine building on Ellis Island. Although he was among the lucky ones who passed the medical exam and was declared healthy enough to enter the country, he could not be released until a relative came to claim him and guarantee that the boy would be provided with support. After two weeks, just as immigration officials were preparing to send the boy back to Russia, his uncle appeared. He brought Morris home and showed him where to sleep. But as soon as the boy heard his uncle snoring, Morris ran away, furious at this relative who had left him to suffer two miserable weeks in captivity. He did not wander long in the crowded Jewish ghetto before a butcher offered him a job and a place to sleep on a straw mat behind the shop.

Morris did well in the new land. Although he did not live out the rags-to-riches dream, few immigrants did. Like many others, he prospered modestly. After a few years, he was able to strike out on his own as a pushcart peddler. Eventually, he sent home enough money to bring his parents and siblings to America. Some Jewish immigrants struggled to retain the faith and practices of Jewish orthodoxy that had defined their lives in the *shtetl.* But Morris was among those who wanted to assimilate into American life. He retained Jewish cultural practices but abandoned many religious rituals, such as refraining from work on Saturdays (the Jewish Sabbath) and wearing distinctive clothes. Nevertheless, he lived his life as a Jew among Jews, speaking Yiddish, celebrating the religious holidays, and maintaining a kosher home according to Jewish dietary laws, even though he rarely set foot in a synagogue.

Italian immigration also reached its peak between 1900 and 1914. While 90 percent of the Jews who migrated from Russia came to the United States, Italians ventured to many countries around the world. Turmoil in their home country resulting from the political and economic consequences of unification of the Italian peninsula, prompted 27 million Italians—a third of Italy's population—to migrate between 1870 and 1920. The majority of Italians who came to the United States arrived with their families and settled permanently, establishing strong communities and mutual aid societies. Most Italians were committed Catholics, and they preserved their rituals, festivals, and faith in the new country.

Work, Science, and Leisure

As the nineteenth century gave way to the twentieth, working women and men could increasingly expect to be employed in industry rather than farms, in large organizations rather than small shops, and in enterprises that relied more on efficiency than craftsmanship. Towering skyscrapers began to dot the urban landscape, symbolic of the triumph of commerce and corporate power. Science and technology reigned, changing the nature of work as well as the fruits of production. Professional organizations of educators, social workers, physicians, and scientists emerged, while experts with academic credentials became leaders of many public institutions. It seemed as though science could solve virtually any problem. Advances in medical science contributed to improved public health. But in some cases, experts relied on scientific principles to address social problems rather than confronting the underlying structural causes, such as widespread poverty.

The Uses and Abuses of Science

Breakthroughs in science and medicine led to improvements in public health. Reformers exposed the dangers of potions and remedies sold by street vendors, as standards for medications improved. But crowding and lack of sanitation still fostered the spread of disease, especially among the poor. In 1900 the death rate for African Americans was 69 percent higher than the rate for whites. Lack of access to clean water was one of the major causes of disease, along with crowding, lack of medical care, and other chronic problems of poverty. Public sanitation alleviated the problem considerably in the early years of the twentieth century, reducing the incidence of typhoid fever by 70 percent. Among those who contributed to better conditions were community nurses. In 1900 the New York Charity Organization Society hired Jessie Sleet Scales, the first African American public health nurse, to address problems related to tuberculosis. Scales and other public health professionals implemented sanitation standards and provided care for poor communities, helping to control the spread of disease.

Public sanitation remained a problem, however, especially in crowded cities. An outbreak of typhoid among well-to-do New Yorkers led to Mary Mallon, an Irish immigrant, who had worked as a cook for a number of prominent families. When six members of a household where she worked developed typhoid, she was identified as a carrier of the disease. Later, authorities discovered that typhoid outbreaks occurred in seven of eight households that had employed her. Although Mallon had no symptoms, she was forced to remain in a hospital for people with contagious diseases until she sued for her release in 1909 and was released in 1910. She was instructed not to cook for a living, but as she had no other means to support herself, she went back to work as a cook. In 1915, she was arrested again after more typhoid cases were traced to her, and this time she was placed in isolation on an island virtually as a prisoner for 26 years, until her death in 1939.

The local press vilified Mallon, whom they dubbed "Typhoid Mary," and blamed her for the spread of the illness. As a carrier of the disease, she did indeed infect several people.

But she was not the only source of contagion in the city. Typhoid, like many other diseases, was a public health problem. Although Mallon was not the only healthy carrier of typhoid at this time, she was the only healthy person who had never been accused of a crime but was subjected to what amounted to a life sentence of imprisonment. City officials might have pursued other alternatives, such as helping Mallon find a job in which she would not endanger others and developing a broad-based public health approach that would have improved sanitation in the city.

Reflecting a similar impulse to blame social problems on allegedly flawed individuals or groups was the eugenics movement, which advocated scientific breeding to improve the nation's racial stock. The pseudoscience of eugenics emerged in the nineteenth century in England and spread to the United States, where it gained wide support. Drawing on theories of white racial superiority and unscientific notions of genetic inheritance, eugenicists believed that character traits were inherited, including tendencies toward criminality, sexual immorality, and lack of discipline leading to poverty. Eugenicists claimed that social problems resulted from the high birthrate of immigrants and others they considered to be racially inferior to Anglo-Saxon Americans and the low birthrate of educated middle-class whites.

President Theodore Roosevelt was an outspoken advocate of eugenics reform. One of his major concerns was that Americans were shirking their duty to create a robust citizenry for the future. Alarmed by the dramatic decline in the birthrate of native-born Americans and the tendency of college-educated women to remain single and childless, he feared that the immigrants, with their much higher birthrate, would overrun the nation. Roosevelt called upon Anglo-Saxon women to prevent what he called "race suicide," much as male citizens had an obligation to defend the country if called to military duty. In his sixth annual message to Congress in 1903, Roosevelt warned:

New York American, June 20, 1909, p. 6.

■ "Typhoid Mary" unwittingly mixes death into an omelet in this 1909 poster warning against bad hygiene.

> When home ties are loosened, when men and women cease to regard a worthy family life . . . as the life best worth living, then evil days of the commonwealth are at hand. There are regions in our own land, and classes of our population, where the birth rate has sunk below the death rate. Surely it should need no demonstration to show that willful sterility is, from the standpoint of the nation . . . the one sin for which the penalty is national death, race death. . . . No man, no woman, can shirk the primary duties of life, whether for love of ease and pleasure, or for any other reason, and retain his or her self-respect.

Some eugenics crusaders proposed compulsory sterilization of those they deemed unfit for parenthood. Indiana enacted a eugenic sterilization law in 1907, and other states soon followed. These laws gave legal sanction to the surgical sterilization of thousands of men and even greater numbers of women whom government and medical officials deemed "feeble-minded." The criteria for determining "feeblemindedness" were vague at best; often sexual impropriety or out-of-wedlock pregnancy landed young women—generally poor and often foreign-born—in institutions for the feebleminded, where the operations took place. The Supreme Court upheld compulsory sterilization laws in the 1920s. Increasingly, women of color were targeted, and the practice continued well into the 1980s.

Scientific Management and Mass Production

In 1911 Frederick Winslow Taylor wrote *The Principles of Scientific Management,* his guide to increased efficiency in the nation's industries. Taylor began his career as a laborer in the Midvale

Defining Whiteness

Naturalization laws pertaining to immigrants in the early twentieth century were based on racial categories. Asian immigrants, classified racially as "Mongolians," were not allowed to apply for U.S. citizenship. Naturalization was available only "to aliens being free white persons and to aliens of African nativity and to persons of African descent." Because racial theories were imprecise and fluid, and racial identities were not linked to nationality, immigrants occasionally challenged their racial classification to claim that they were "white." John Svan, who was Finnish, petitioned in federal court to contest the labeling of Finns as Mongolians, claiming that he was white and, therefore, allowed to apply for U.S. citizenship. The petition demonstrates the acceptance of racial definitions based on phenotype—particularly skin color—as well as the imprecise nature of those definitions. The court granted Svan's petition, legally changing his racial identity from Mongolian to white and reclassifying Finns as white people. Here is the court's memorandum, which allowed Svan to become a citizen:

John Svan was born in Finland and calls himself a Finn. . . . According to ethnologists, the Finns in very remote times were of Mongol origin; but the various groupings of the human race into families is arbitrary and, as respects any particular people, is not permanent but is subject to change and modification through the influences of climate, employment, intermarriage and other causes. There are indications that central and western Europe was at one time overrun by the Finns; some of their stock remained, but their racial characteristics were entirely lost in their remote descendants, who now are in no danger of being classed as Mongols. The Osmanlis, said to be of Mongol extraction, are now among the purest and best types of the Caucasian race. Changes are constantly going on and those occurring in the lapse of a few hundred years with any people may be very great.

The chief physical characteristics of the Mongolians are as follows: They are short of stature, with little hair on their body or face; they have yellow-brown skins, black eyes, black hair, short, flat noses, and oblique eyes. In actual experience we sometimes, though rarely, see natives of Finland whose eyes are slightly oblique. We sometimes see them with sparse beards and

Steel Works near Philadelphia in 1878 and rose through the ranks to become the plant's chief engineer. There he developed a system to improve mass production in factories in order to make more goods more quickly. Taylor's principles included analysis of each job to determine the precise motions and tools needed to maximize each worker's productivity, detailed instructions for workers and guidelines for their supervisors, and wage scales with incentives to motivate workers to achieve high production goals. Over the next decades, industrial managers all over the country drew on Taylor's studies. Business leaders rushed to embrace Taylor's principles, and Taylor himself became a pioneering management consultant.

Henry Ford was among the most successful industrialists to employ Taylor's techniques. Born in 1863 on a farm near Dearborn, Michigan, the mechanically inclined Ford became an apprentice in a Detroit machine shop in 1879. Although he did not invent the automobile—the first motor cars were manufactured in Germany—he developed design and production methods that brought the cost of an automobile within the reach of the average worker. Experimenting with the new internal combustion engine in the 1890s, he built his first automobile in 1896. In 1903 Ford established the Ford Motor Company and began a profitable business. He introduced the popular and relatively inexpensive, mass-produced Model T automobile

in 1908, which sold for $850. In 1913 Ford introduced assembly line production, a system in which each worker performed one task repeatedly as each automobile in the process of construction moved along a conveyor. Assembly-line manufacturing increased production while cutting costs. In 1914 Ford increased his workers' wages to $5 per day at a time when industrial laborers averaged only $11 per week. By 1916 the price of the Model T dropped to $360. In this sense Ford was a pioneer not only in production but also in consumption.

Minnesota Historical Society, Negative #93125. Photo by Maki of Virginia, MN

These Finnish men living in Minnesota were among those whose racial classification was changed from "Mongolian" to "White" as the result of one Finnish immigrant's petition. Along with the Jews, Italians, Irish, and other immigrant groups now considered "white," Finns were classified as nonwhite until the laws and customs changed. Racial categories were fluid and imprecise, but whiteness conferred status and privileges.

sometimes with flat noses; but Finns with a yellow or brown or yellow-brown skin or with black eyes or black hair would be an unusual sight. They are almost universally of light skin, blue or gray eyes, and light hair. No people of foreign births applying in this section of the country for the full rights of citizenship are lighter-skinned than those born in Finland. In stature they are quite up to the average. Confessedly, Finland has often been overrun with Teutons and by other branches of the human family, who, with their descendants, have remained within her borders and are now called Finns. They are in the main indistinguishable in their physical characteristics from those of purer Finnish blood. Intermarriages have been frequent over a very long period of time. If the Finns were originally Mongols, modifying influences have continued until they are now among the whitest people in Europe. It would, therefore, require a most exhaustive tracing of family history to determine whether any particular individual born in Finland had or had not a remote Mongol ancestry. This, of course, cannot be done and was not intended. The question is not whether a person had or had not such ancestry, but whether he is now a "white person" within the meaning of that term as usually understood. This is the practical construction which has uniformly been placed upon the law. . . . Under such law Finns have always been admitted to citizenship, and there is no occasion now to change the construction.

The applicant is without doubt a white person within the true intent and meaning of such law.

The objections, therefore, in my opinion should be overruled and it will be so ordered. ∎

Although an industrial genius, Ford was narrow-minded and bigoted. A ferocious anti-Semite, he later became an active supporter of Adolf Hitler. He fought unionization fiercely with a private police force. But his production methods, as well as the Ford motor car, became fixtures of twentieth-century business and consumer culture. Ford embodied many contradictions: he helped to create modern life, but he was also repulsed by it. He created a nostalgic theme park in Deerfield Village, Michigan, where he brought together old houses and artifacts to recreate a small town of the nineteenth century, where there were no cars or factories. Yet Ford's own life's work had contributed to the disappearance of the way of life represented in Deerfield Village.

New Amusements

As Americans increasingly moved from rural to urban areas, and from farms to factories, new institutions of leisure emerged in the growing cities. Consumer culture was the flipside of business culture in the early twentieth century, and it represented a major change not only in leisure time pursuits but also in cultural values. Newcomers and "outsiders" were largely responsible for those changing values. One of the great ironies of American history in the twentieth century is that its popular culture—which more than anything else identifies the United States to the rest of the world—was largely a creation of immigrants and people of color. During the very years when these groups faced intense discrimination, they developed the cultural products that came to define America itself.

The motion picture industry is a case in point. In 1888 Thomas Edison invented the kinetoscope, the early motion picture camera. The pragmatic Edison thought that his new device might be used in education and industry. But he did not see much commercial potential for the gadget. As he wrote in 1893,

> I have constructed a little instrument which I call a Kinetoscope, with a nickel and slot attachment. Some twenty-five have been made, but I am very doubtful there is any commercial feature in it, and fear that they will not earn their cost. These zeotropic devices are of too sentimental a value to get the public to invest in.

Because of his lack of enthusiasm as well as his lack of investors, Edison did not even bother to take out a foreign patent on the kinetoscope or to seek markets for his invention at home. Not until the early twentieth century, when Jewish immigrant entrepreneurs recognized its potential for mass entertainment, did the moving picture begin to reach a wide audience. Moviemak-

ers left the East Coast and moved to the West, taking advantage of the even climate, cheap land, and nonunion labor. Within a few years, the moviemakers, mostly Jewish immigrants from Europe, established the film industry. By the late teens and twenties, Paramount, Metro-Goldwyn-Mayer, and Fox Studios—all founded by Jews—had become leaders in moviemaking. Hollywood emerged as a major center of American popular culture, sending its products across the nation and abroad.

The first audiences for the motion pictures were in the working-class neighborhoods of the growing cities. New York offers a vivid example of the rapid expansion of the movies as well as other urban amusements. In that city alone, by 1910, there were 1000 small storefront theaters and fun houses known as penny arcades where there had been none 20 years earlier. The numbers of saloons also increased from 7000 to 9000, while the Coney Island amusement park drew thousands to its shimmering lights and thrilling rides. During these same years, the sounds of African American music began to attract audiences among immigrants as well as native-born whites. Youths from all ethnic groups flocked to dance halls where they danced to the lively tunes often played by black musicians who "ragged" the beat with new jazz rhythms.

Working-class youth were not the only ones drawn to the new urban amusements. Glamorous night clubs, known as cabarets, also began to appear, offering dining, dancing, music, and entertainment to the wealthy. Jesse Lasky opened the Follies Bergeres in New York in 1911. Lasky filled his cabaret with lavish furnishings, hired black musicians to play ragtime music, and charged high prices. "Everything about the Follies," Lasky wrote, "was unheard of in New York, including the prices." In an effort to render these upper-class cabarets respectable and distinguish them from the rowdy working-class dance halls, owners tamed the erotic dances to express a more moderate sensuality.

"Sex O'Clock in America"

The sexual mores and behavior of Americans seemed to be changing so dramatically that one observer announced that "sex o'clock" had struck. Indeed, the codes of the past were challenged at every turn. Among the middle class, unchaperoned dating began to replace the previous system of a man "coming to call" at the home of a woman he hoped to court. Automobiles gave young couples more freedom and privacy. Physical intimacy became more acceptable, and even unacceptable sexual behavior became more common.

Immigrants often brought traditional courtship patterns to the new world and extended them into the next generation. One Italian man described his thwarted efforts to woo his fiancée in private. When he visited her home, "She sat on one side of the table, and I at the other. They afraid I touch." Finally, less than a month before their wedding, he got permission to take her to the theater. But the family was unwilling to let them go alone. "We came to the aisles of the theater. My mother-in-law go first, my fiancée next, my little sister, my father in law. I was the last one. I had two in between. . . . I was next to the old man." He tried to steal a kiss a few days before the wedding, but his fiancée rebuffed him: "No, not yet."

In spite of efforts by their elders, native-born as well as immigrant youth challenged the sexual codes of the past. Young working women looked forward to fun in their leisure hours and sometimes exchanged physical intimacies for "treats" from men who took them out to a meal or a dance. These women were known as "charity girls" to distinguish them from prostitutes. Increasing sexual intimacy among unmarried men and women reflected heightened expectations for sexual satisfaction—for women as well as men. These years also witnessed a rise in the proportion of brides who were pregnant at marriage, from a low of 10 percent in the mid-nineteenth century to 23 percent by 1910.

> *Marriage increasingly held the promise not only of love, intimacy, and mutual obligation, but of sexual fulfillment and shared leisure pursuits.*

Marriage increasingly held the promise not only of love, intimacy, and mutual obligation, as it had in the nineteenth century, but of sexual fulfillment and shared leisure pursuits. As expectations for marital happiness rose, so did the divorce rate. Liberal divorce laws, combined with expanding opportunities for women to support themselves, prompted increasing numbers of men and women to end unhappy marriages and try again. The rising divorce rate did not signal a decline in the popularity of marriage, however; a greater proportion of Americans married and at increasingly younger ages. Those who divorced were likely to remarry, a pattern that continued through the twentieth century.

Some women did not marry but instead formed lifelong attachments to other women. Rarely identified as lesbian but often described as "Boston marriages," these unions signified long-term emotional bonds between women who lived together. The widely admired reformer Jane Addams shared her life with Mary Rozet Smith for more than thirty years. Meanwhile, lesbians, as well as gay men, gained greater visibility in the cities. They frequented bars and clubs in such places as Greenwich Village and Harlem, hoping to avoid the attention of police, who were likely to arrest them for indecent conduct. Heterosexual men and women also came to these neighborhoods for entertainment. Drag balls became elaborate annual events that drew thousands of spectators and participants, including large numbers of heterosexuals.

Artists Respond to the New Era

Artists, composers, writers, and architects all contributed to enriching, expressing, interpreting, and transforming the urban industrial landscape. Among the most controversial was a group of painters who focused their attention on portrayals of life in the cities—including urban amusements and diverse working-class subjects. Although these artists did not pioneer new styles of painting, their content was revolutionary. Robert Henri painted scenes of the city including ethnic minorities, William Glackens depicted cabarets and night life, Everett Shinn portrayed prostitutes and other "low-life" characters, and John Sloan evoked New York's Lower East Side, immigrants, and theaters. This art exuded the vitality of urban life and conveyed a gritty reality without moral condemnation; these artists treated their subjects with dignity and humanity. Contemptuous critics referred to them as the "Ashcan School," a label they embraced.

The artistic movement known as realism, characterized by a detached and skeptical approach to subject matter, also infused in the writing of fiction. The novelist Theodore Dreiser wrote in this new style. His 1900 novel *Sister Carrie* narrates the story of an independent young woman who comes to Chicago and uses her sexuality to advance her ambition. Contrary to the morality tales popular at the time, Carrie does not suffer for her sins. Rather, she prospers, while her male lovers are destroyed by their infatuation with her. Because of the novel's scandalous content, Dreiser's publisher did not promote the book, although it was revived and republished in later years.

Photography also began to exhibit a new realism in the work of such documentary photographers as Lewis Hine, who photographed immigrants, industrial work, and urban street

George Luks, The Cafe Francis, c. 1909. The Butler Institute of American Art, Youngstown, Ohio

■ *The Café Francis,* by George Luks, c. 1909. Luks was one of the "Ashcan School" artists who celebrated urban street life and popular culture. Their raw and sensual depictions of city entertainments stirred controversy among art critics at the time.

life, and such avant-garde artists as Alfred Stieglitz and Edward Steichen, who drew inspiration from artistic innovations in Europe, such as Cubism. Popular music also flourished in the first decade of the century, especially jazz. From its roots in African musical traditions, slave songs, spirituals, and ragtime, jazz brought together the various strains of African American music and developed new forms. Centered in New Orleans, artists such as pianist Ferdinand "Jelly Roll" Morton and cornet player Charles "Buddy" Bolden played the new syncopated rhythms.

Reformers and Radicals

The broad movement for social reform known as Progressivism included two distinct impulses. On the one hand, many Anglo-Saxon Protestants tried to impose order on a rapidly changing nation. They hoped to stem the tide of immigration, bolster the rapidly eroding sexual codes, and quell the movements for social change. On the other hand, women's rights activists, workers, and African Americans struggled to achieve the rights and privileges available to white men of property and standing. The tensions between these two very different approaches to reform shaped the politics of the era.

Muckrakers, Moral Reform, and Vice Crusades

In the early twentieth century, a group of investigative journalists began to expose the ills of industrial life. President Theodore Roosevelt dubbed them the "muckrakers" in 1906 to signal their tendency to unearth the dirtiest aspects of the nation's political and economic institutions. Although Roosevelt intended the term as an insult, the muckrakers embraced their label. Their best-known works illuminated corruption in business and politics. Ida Tarbell wrote a powerful exposé of ruthless business practices of John D. Rockefeller, who transformed the Standard Oil company into a monopoly. Lincoln Steffens unearthed scandals in city and state politics. By 1912, more than 1000 muckraking articles appeared in widely read and popular magazines such as *McClure's*, *Everybody's,* and *Collier's.*

One of the best-known muckraking novels was Upton Sinclair's *The Jungle,* published in 1906. A dedicated socialist, Sinclair hoped that his novel would illuminate the exploitation of immigrant workers. *The Jungle* tells the story of Jurgis Rudkus, a Lithuanian immigrant, and his family and friends and provides a grim exposé of horrid living and working conditions. Depiction of the meatpacking plant where Rudkus works includes descriptions of the filth, rats, and even the body parts of workers that end up ground into the packages of meat. The book had a powerful impact, but the effect was not what Sinclair had hoped. Rather than spark interest in socialism or even improved wages and working conditions, the novel aroused consumer indignation and, within months of its publication, led to the passage of the Pure Food and Drug Act and a Meat Inspection Act, which prohibited adulterated or fraudulently labeled food and drugs from interstate commerce. Sinclair later wrote with regret, "I aimed at the public's heart and by accident hit it in the stomach." The Pure Food and Drug Act was the first of a series of consumer protection laws passed in the twentieth century.

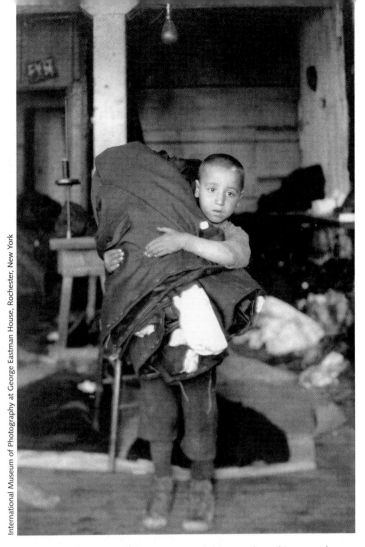

International Museum of Photography at George Eastman House, Rochester, New York

■ In the early twentieth century, many children such as this young boy worked long hours doing hard labor. Photographer Lewis Hine, who took this picture, worked for the National Child Labor Committee. His photographs documented the exploitation of child workers and helped to generate support for child labor laws.

Child labor was another concern of reformers. Children worked in fields and factories across the country, picking cotton in Texas, mining coal in West Virginia, working in the textile mills of North Carolina, and sewing buttons in urban sweatshops. The National Child Labor Committee, organized in 1904, as well as many state committees, endeavored to regulate or eliminate child labor. Children of immigrants and rural migrants often assisted parents on farms or in shops, their labor an accepted part of the household economy. Many parents felt that work also offered children opportunities to learn discipline as well as a trade and to gain a sense of pride and satisfaction as contributors to the family's needs. But the sorts of jobs available to children in the urban industrial world often were dangerous and unhealthy, characterized by long hours, low pay, and miserable working conditions. Reformers attempted to improve the conditions under which children worked and to establish age limits so that children could attend school and spend time in healthful recreation rather than in grim sweatshops and factories. Ultimately, child labor activists succeeded in passing legislation at the state level that restricted child labor, although these efforts were more successful in northern states than in the South.

Protective legislation for women was also controversial. Reformers campaigned for laws that would establish minimum wages, maximum hours, regulations against night work, and restrictions on heavy lifting. When they were unable to secure such safety measures for all workers, they argued that women needed special protections because of their physical frailty and their role as future mothers. Women's rights activists disagreed over these measures. Some argued that they were necessary to protect women from exploitation and dangerous working conditions. Others claimed that women should be treated the same as men, arguing that protective legislation implied that women needed special care and were not suited for particular kinds of work. These debates continued throughout the century.

Women were prominent among Progressive reformers. Jane Addams, founder of Hull House, the immigrant neighborhood center in Chicago, became the most admired woman of her day. But many other influential women left their stamp on the culture and public policies of the era. Florence Kelley, the daughter of a prominent Philadelphia Quaker family, joined Addams's Hull House community and later headed the National Consumers' League (NCL) from 1898 until her death in 1932. Under her leadership, the NCL became the most effective lobbying agency for protective labor legislation for women and children. Kelley was instrumental in the successful defense of the ten-hour working day for women, which was affirmed by the Supreme Court in its 1908 decision, *Muller v. Oregon.*

> *Women were prominent among Progressive reformers and left their stamp on the culture and public policies of the era.*

Another noted reformer was Helen Keller, whose work on behalf of the blind called attention to the needs of the disabled. Keller lost her sight and hearing from an illness at the age of 19 months and learned to communicate through Braille and sign language, which she mastered through touch, with the help of her extraordinary teacher, Anne Sullivan. Keller went on to study at schools for the deaf and graduated with honors from Radcliffe College in 1904. A passionate socialist and advocate of women's rights along with other radical causes, Keller wrote several books and lectured widely all over the world, with the assistance of interpreters.

Most Progressive reformers were prosperous American-born Anglo-Saxon Protestants. Along with their efforts to improve living and working conditions and alleviate the suffering of the poor, they also hoped to eradicate vice from their society. At the level of local government, many reformers promoted zoning laws that would keep commercial entertainments out of residential neighborhoods. Vice crusaders in most of the nation's large cities tried to eliminate prostitution and to patrol dance halls, movie theaters, and saloons. Gay men and lesbians risked arrest if they were discovered mingling in public. At the national level, vice crusading culminated in the passage of the Mann Act in 1910, which made it illegal to transport women across state lines for "immoral purposes." The Mann Act resulted in 1,537 convictions by 1916. Over the years, authorities used the Mann Act not only to police prostitution but also to regulate interracial sex.

One such case garnered national attention. African American boxer Jack Johnson had defeated white fighters in the ring to become the world heavyweight champion in 1910. He was a hero to black Americans but a villain to many whites, who resented not only his athletic success but also his relationships with white women. In 1912, Lucille Cameron, a young white woman from Minnesota, visited Johnson's Chicago nightclub, and the two began an affair. Cameron's mother brought charges of abduction against Johnson, but the young woman refused to testify, so the case was dismissed. The couple later married. Authorities continued their efforts to punish Johnson for his racial and sexual transgressions. When federal agents persuaded one of Johnson's former lovers, a white prostitute, to testify that Johnson had paid for her travel from Pittsburgh to Chicago, he was convicted under the Mann Act and sentenced to one year in prison.

Woman Suffrage

The movement for women's rights, including the effort to gain the vote, was already more than half a century old by 1900. But the movement gained momentum at the dawn of the twentieth century. A new generation of women's rights leaders came together in the suffrage movement. They included working-class women and young college-educated women, some of them with experience in the settlement movement, and others who had participated in socialist and labor circles. They initiated new grassroots strategies, such as door-to-door campaigns, to gather support for woman suffrage. The militance of the suffrage movement in England inspired American activists to develop new tactics and international alliances. These activists achieved legislative success when several western states granted women the right to vote: Washington in 1910, California in 1911, and three more states in 1912. Eventually the movement united around the goal of enacting a federal amendment. The required three-quarters majority of the states ratified the Nineteenth Amendment in 1920, granting women the vote.

The suffrage movement, for all its radicalism, was largely a movement of white middle-class women. White suffrage leaders feared that any alliance with women of color would alienate Southern voters whom they needed for ratification of the Nineteenth Amendment. They also hoped to win over to their cause racist and nativist critics in the North who feared that granting the vote to women would enfranchise "undesirable" voters, specifically immigrant and minority women. Some women's rights leaders argued that granting the vote to women would increase the voting power of white Anglo-Saxons. Belle Kearney, a southern suffragist, saw the ballot for women as a means of keeping African Americans in their place: "The enfranchisement of women would insure immediate and durable white supremacy, honestly attained." The suffrage movement also gained the support of conservatives who believed that women would vote for conservative causes such as prohibition and immigration restriction.

Many minority women, such as Hispana activist Adelina Otero Warren, also supported the suffrage movement even though white leaders kept their distance and refused to embrace the antiracist campaigns of their nonwhite sisters. The African American antilynching activist Ida B. Wells (also known by her married name as Ida B. Wells-Barnett) supported woman suffrage but was unable to convince the white women's rights leaders to denounce lynching. Ultimately, the passage of the suffrage amendment resulted from a combination of factors, including radical activism, strong support of a wide range of reformers, and an alliance with conservative, racist, and anti-immigrant forces.

Radical Politics and the Labor Movement

Progressive reformers believed that American capitalist democracy was a fundamentally sound system that simply needed to be fixed to achieve its full promise. Radicals of the era believed that the system itself was flawed and needed to be fundamentally transformed. Emma Goldman, a Russian Jewish immigrant, was one of many radical activists who gained both fame and notoriety for her outspoken support of radical causes. Like Sieh King King and Clara Lemlich, Goldman was among the growing numbers of women who were leaders in the labor struggles of the day. But women were excluded from most unions. Only 3.3 percent of the 4 million women engaged in nonagricultural jobs in 1900 were members of trade unions. The number doubled in the wake of the successful wave of strikes by young immigrant garment workers in 1909–1910, including the 1909 shirtwaist makers' strike. In 1903 the WTUL brought together elite reformers and female laborers to help working women in their efforts to unionize while also connecting those efforts to the broader movement for women's rights.

Socialism also attracted followers during these years. Socialism was never as strong in the United States as it was in Europe, but it did gain strength at the turn of the century. Socialists promoted labor unions and the rights of women and formed their own political party. Socialist leader Eugene V. Debs gained national fame for his role in the 1894 railroad strike. Radicalized by his involvement in the labor movement, he turned to socialism at the turn of the century as a means for improving the conditions of the working classes. Forging alliances with a number of immigrant socialist groups, he became the spokesperson and leader of the Socialist party. Between 1900

Brown Brothers

■ Elizabeth Gurley Flynn of the Industrial Workers of the World (IWW) addresses a crowd of women in 1913. Flynn was one of the organizers of the IWW, known as the Wobblies, an organization of workers from diverse backgrounds that enrolled nearly 3 million members.

and 1920, he was the party's candidate for president, gaining nearly a million votes, or 6 percent of the electorate, in the 1912 election. Although the socialists never gathered a large enough following to win national elections, they elected hundreds of candidates to local office.

The Industrial Workers of the World (IWW), also known as the Wobblies, offered another possibility for labor radicalism. Organized in 1905 by socialists and labor militants, its founders included Debs, William "Big Bill" Haywood of the Western Federation of Miners, the well-known labor activist Elizabeth Gurley Flynn, and the Tejana of Mexican and African American heritage Lucia Gonzales Parsons, whose husband had been executed as a result of the Haymarket bombing of 1886. The IWW included women, blacks, immigrants, and unskilled and migratory laborers, workers generally shunned by the American Federation of Labor (AFL). The Wobblies organized workers in the mines of the Rocky Mountain states, in the lumber camps of the Pacific Northwest and the South, and in the eastern textile and steel mills. Its membership reached about 3 million people, although no more than 150,000 were members at any one time. Although the Socialist party and the IWW were open to black members, they had no particular interest in combating racism or addressing the unique needs of African American workers. They assumed that labor activism would improve the lives of all workers. To address their unique concerns, black Americans organized on their own behalf.

Resistance to Racism

The Progressive Era was anything but progressive for nonwhite Americans. Although there were notable exceptions, such as Jane Addams, many white Protestant reformers were either indifferent to racial minorities or actively hostile to them. Moreover, most blacks lived in the rural South, not in northern cities where Progressives were most active. Lynching continued into the twentieth century, with nearly 100 lynchings per year between 1900 and 1910. African Americans were the primary targets of lynch mobs, although other minorities were also vulnerable. Black leaders spoke out against lynching and other forms of racial injustice. Ida B. Wells-Barnett, who had launched an international crusade against lynching in the 1890s, worked to establish local and national networks of black women's clubs. As a highly respected national leader, she had a profound impact on black life during these years and formed important alliances with other reformers. Although she was unable to persuade white suffrage leaders to support the cause of racial justice, she worked closely with Jane Addams to prevent the establishment of segregated schools in Chicago.

A number of other black leaders came to prominence in the first decade of the twentieth century as African Americans formed a wide range of organizations that grew and flourished. In 1905 scholar and civil rights leader W. E. B. Du Bois joined with other black leaders to form the Niagara Movement, which called for an end to segregation and discrimination in unions, the courts, and public accommodations, as well as equal economic and educational opportunity. In 1908 black leaders joined with white progressive allies—Hull House founder Jane Addams, philosopher John Dewey, and novelist William Dean Howells, among others— to establish the National Association for the Advancement of Colored People (NAACP). The new organization adopted the platform of the Niagara Movement, and Du Bois became the editor of its journal, *The Crisis*. Wells-Barnett insisted that the organization go on record as opposed to lynching. The NAACP has remained a major voice for African American civil rights and racial justice to this day.

Expanding National Power

Along with flourishing radical and reform movements at the grassroots, the Progressive Era gave rise to a reformist impulse at the national level. The person who most fully embodied the national Progressive movement was Theodore Roosevelt, president from 1901 to 1908. Roosevelt's primary goals as president were to expand the power of the presidency and the federal government and to strengthen American nationalism at home and national power abroad. Roosevelt used his power to regulate big business, intervene in labor disputes, extend the reach of the nation across the world, and control the uses of the natural environment.

Theodore Roosevelt: The "Rough Rider" as President

Theodore Roosevelt rose to prominence in the Republican party in the 1880s and held a number of important political posts, including assistant secretary of the Navy (1897–1898) and governor of New York (1899–1900). In 1900 Republican party leaders selected Roosevelt as William McKinley's running mate, and when McKinley was reelected, Roosevelt became vice president. But in September 1901, McKinley was assassinated, and at age 42, Roosevelt became the youngest person ever to become president.

TABLE 19-1

The Election of 1900

Candidate	Political Party	Popular Vote	Electoral Vote
William McKinley	Republican	7,207,923	292
William Jennings Bryan	Democratic-Populist	6,358,133	155

Roosevelt was a strong proponent of American military and commercial presence in the world. He expanded the power of the federal government both at home and abroad and used the "bully pulpit" of the presidency to exert moral leadership. He favored big government and limitations on corporate power, yet he cooperated with business to foster capitalism and free trade. Using the Sherman Anti-Trust Act of 1890, which gave the federal government the power to break up monopolies, Roosevelt in 1902 ordered the Justice Department to prosecute the Northern Securities Company, a $400-million monopoly that controlled all railroad lines and traffic in the Northwest. Within a year, the company was dissolved. Although this bold act earned Roosevelt the title of "trust-buster," it was not his intention to weaken big business. In fact, he believed that a strong country needed large, powerful industries, and he hoped to regulate them to keep big business strong. His antitrust efforts actually helped big business by fostering competition.

The same year that Roosevelt took on the Northern Securities Company, he also used the powers of the federal government to intervene in a labor dispute. Striking coal miners in eastern Pennsylvania wanted recognition of their union, a 10 to 20 percent increase in wages, and an eight-hour day. But the mine owners refused to negotiate. Roosevelt summoned the mine owners and John Mitchell, president of the United Mine Workers union, to the White House for a meeting. He threatened to send in troops if the mine owners did not agree to the union's request for arbitration. The mine owners backed down, and the arbitrators awarded the miners a 10 percent wage increase and a nine-hour day.

Roosevelt's efforts to strengthen the state and foster American nationalism extended to his attitudes toward immigrants. He believed that discrimination against loyal newcomers harmed the democracy: "It is a base outrage to oppose a man because of his religion or birthplace. . . . A Scandinavian, a German, or an Irishman who has really become an American has the right to stand on exactly the same footing as any native-born citizen in the land, and is just as much entitled to the friendship and support, social and political, of his neighbor." He was proud of appointing a cabinet in which "Catholic and Protestant and Jew sat side by side." But to Roosevelt, becoming an American meant renouncing any loyalties to one's original homeland or culture: "We must Americanize them in every way. . . . [The immigrant] must not bring in his Old-World religious[,] race[,] and national antipathies, but must merge them into love for our common country, and must take pride in the things which we can all take pride in. He must revere our flag; not only must it come first, but no other flag should ever come second. He must learn to celebrate Washington's birthday rather than that of the Queen or Kaiser, and the Fourth of July instead of St. Patrick's Day. . . . Above all, the immigrant must learn to talk and think and be United States." Roosevelt did not believe in cultural pluralism, the idea that the United States could include citizens who retained their ethnic heritage. Rather, he promoted the idea of a melting pot that would blend all diverse cultures into a unique American "race."

Although Roosevelt was a firm believer in Anglo-Saxon superiority, he was the first president to invite an African American leader, Booker T. Washington, to the White House. Roosevelt's meeting with Washington demonstrated his willingness to stand up to southern politicians, but he did not follow that gesture with meaningful policy initiatives such as antilynching or civil rights laws. In the 1904 presidential election, Roosevelt won 57 percent of the popular vote against his Democratic rival, Alton B. Parker.

TABLE 19-2			
The Election of 1904			
Candidate	Political Party	Popular Vote	Electoral Vote
Theodore Roosevelt	Republican	7,623,486	336
Alton B. Parker	Democratic	6,358,133	155
Eugene V. Debs	Socialist	402,283	0

Protecting and Preserving the Natural World

Industrial smoke had long been a problem in both European and American cities, and Progressive Era reformers established organizations in major cities to fight air pollution. At the same time,

■ The Los Angeles Aqueduct opened at the Cascades on November 5, 1913. The aqueduct brought water from the Owens River, allowing the naturally dry terrain of Los Angeles to flourish and sustain a large population. Residents of the Owens Valley protested the diversion of their water supply, to no avail.

Courtesy, the Los Angeles Department of Water and Power

mining and other industries were depleting natural resources while destroying the natural beauty of the land. More than any previous president, Roosevelt used the federal government to control the natural world. Although his actions did not please everyone on all sides of the debate, Roosevelt's environmental efforts were among his most enduring legacies.

Roosevelt advocated both preservation and conservation (see Chapter 18). His preservation policies doubled the number of national parks, created 16 national monuments, such as Muir Woods in California, and established 51 wildlife refuges. At the same time, he shared the view of conservationists that timberlands, areas for livestock grazing, water, and minerals were at risk of being depleted. He believed the federal government should extend its reach into the management of these resources. Roosevelt transferred 125 million acres of public land into the forest reserves to prevent the depletion of timber, and he set aside land for dam sites, oil and coal reserves, and grazing lands. Some of these efforts faced strong opposition from preservationists because of their negative impact on the natural environment.

Conservationists and preservationists battled frequently, and no issue was more divisive than water. Conservationists favored damming rivers to create reservoirs and aqueducts to provide water and electricity for western settlements. John Muir and the Sierra Club campaigned to protect the Hetch Hetchy Valley in Yosemite National Park, but Congress passed the Raker Act in 1913, allowing the city of San Francisco to build a dam and a reservoir, flooding the valley. Residents of the Owens Valley also protested the building of an aqueduct to divert water to the Los Angeles area. Dams, reservoirs, and aqueducts brought water and electricity to arid regions, allowing such cities as Las Vegas and Los Angeles to flourish in environments that would otherwise be unable to support large populations.

Expanding National Power Abroad

The decades surrounding the turn of the twentieth century marked the high point of European and American imperial expansion, bringing 80 percent of the world's land under the control of Europeans or their descendants. Unlike several Western European countries, the United States did not aquire a large colonial empire. Nevertheless, Theodore Roosevelt believed that the United States should be an imperial power with moral and military superiority over what he considered to be less "civilized" lands. He hoped to strengthen the federal government at home, develop the nation's military and commercial might, and extend American power abroad. To further these ends, he sent troops to China as part of the international expedition to crush the Boxer Rebellion in 1900. He also proposed the construction of a canal across the Isthmus of Panama, and Congress approved the Panama Canal project in 1902.

In 1904 Roosevelt increased the authority of the United States to intervene in the affairs of nations in the Western Hemisphere through what came to be known as the Roosevelt Corollary to the Monroe Doctrine. Fearing political uprisings that might threaten American commercial interests, Roosevelt asserted that "chronic wrongdoing" might require the intervention by "some civilized nation" in the affairs of another and that "in the Western Hemisphere the adherence of the United States to the Monroe Doctrine may force the United States, however reluctantly, in flagrant cases of such wrongdoing or impotence, to the exercise of an international police power." The Roosevelt Corollary justified later interventions into the Dominican Republic, Cuba, Nicaragua, Mexico, and Haiti.

Roosevelt also continued the U.S. war against Filipino nationalists that began in 1899. The bloody and costly war lasted four years before the Americans crushed the revolt and established

Yale Collection of Western Americana, Beinecke Rare Book and Manuscript Library

■ Lumberjacks topple a giant spruce tree in a forest in Washington state around 1900. President Theodore Roosevelt believed that the federal government should manage timberlands and other natural resources to prevent depletion while allowing their use. Roosevelt preserved some Pacific Northwest forests in national parks and refuges but allowed others to be cultivated for timber.

firm colonial rule in the Philippines. William Howard Taft, the future American President, became the colony's first governor-general in 1901. As the war against the rebels continued, Taft developed a program of public works that included an infrastructure of roads, bridges, and schools. He also transferred government functions to those Filipinos who cooperated with American colonial powers. Although the United States promised to grant Philippine independence, that promise was deferred until 1946.

William Howard Taft: The One-Term Progressive

A financial panic in 1907 prompted Roosevelt to increase his efforts to overhaul the banking system and the stock market. But the president's critics among Republican conservatives and the business elite blamed Roosevelt's reform policies for the economic downturn. In the face of increasing rifts within his own party, along with his own earlier pledge to step down, Roosevelt declined to run for reelection in 1908. The Republicans selected Roosevelt's hand-picked successor, William Howard Taft, who won the election with 52 percent of the votes against William Jennings Bryan, the Democratic candidate. Prior to his service in the Philippines, Taft had been a federal circuit judge. In 1904 Roosevelt appointed him secretary of war. Taft was a loyal ally who worked closely with Roosevelt on foreign and domestic policies. Roosevelt assumed that Taft would fulfill his reform agenda.

TABLE 19-3			
The Election of 1908			
Candidate	Political Party	Popular Vote	Electoral Vote
William H. Taft	Republican	7,678,908	321
William Jennings Bryan	Democrat-Populist	6,409,104	162
Eugene V. Debs	Socialist	420,793	0

At first glance, the most obvious difference between Roosevelt and Taft was their appearance. The energetic Roosevelt was a proponent and model of physical fitness, compared with the 300-pound Taft. Political cartoonists never tired of mocking the rotund chief executive. The two presidents also differed in their leadership styles: Roosevelt, relishing the rough-and-tumble of politics; Taft, cautious and averse to taking risks. Taft's respect for the separation of powers spelled out in the U.S. Constitution made him dubious about some of Roosevelt's extensions of the powers of the presidency. Nevertheless, Taft initiated far more antitrust suits than Roosevelt had during his presidency. Despite similar political inclinations, Roosevelt's support for his protégé cooled. Although Roosevelt counted major business leaders among his own advisors, he was displeased when Taft appointed corporate lawyers rather than activist reformers to his cabinet. His displeasure increased when Taft abandoned the fight for an inheritance tax and a reduction in tariffs.

Taft departed from Roosevelt's foreign policy as well. In contrast to Roosevelt, who emphasized military might, Taft claimed that "Dollar Diplomacy" was the best way for the United States to exert influence in the world:

> This policy has been characterized as substituting dollars for bullets. It is one that appeals alike to idealistic humanitarian sentiments, to the dictates of sound policy and strategy, and to legitimate commercial aims. It is an effort frankly directed to the increase of American trade upon the axiomatic principle that the government of the United States shall extend all proper support to every legitimate and beneficial American enterprise abroad.

Taft's relationship with the Philippines illustrates both his policy of Dollar Diplomacy and his reinforcement of American imperialism abroad. Taft took Roosevelt's bloody rule of the islands a step further by establishing U.S. business interests there. As *El Renacimiento,* a Filipino newspaper, put it at the beginning of Taft's administration:

> For [Taft] the present generation is a generation of children, incapable of assuming the responsibilities of self-government; and this point of view we can never accept. Yet we recognize

the power that lies in his hands. . . . President Taft, with the avowed purpose of helping the Filipinos, will encourage the introduction into this country of large capital which will buy up and exploit everything here worth having; and the inevitable result will be the complete domination of American commercial interests. When that day comes, of what benefit will be all this policy of education, this long preparation for self government, except to make servitude more intolerable?

When Taft signed the Payne–Aldrich Tariff in 1909, he disappointed progressive Republicans and aligned himself with the conservative old guard of the party, those who had been most critical of Roosevelt. The breach between Taft and the Progressives widened when Taft's secretary of the interior, Richard A. Ballinger, opened up for commercial development 1 million acres of land that Roosevelt had placed under federal protection. In a further affront to conservationists, Gifford Pinchot, still head of the National Forest Service, discovered that Ballinger had sold Alaskan coal deposits to corporate moguls J. P. Morgan and David Guggenheim. When Taft defended Ballinger, Pinchot leaked the news to the press and called for a congressional investigation. Taft subsequently fired Pinchot, but Roosevelt publicly supported Pinchot and signaled his break from Taft.

Roosevelt returned from big-game hunting in Africa to enter the political spotlight once again. He toured the country in 1910, describing his plan for a "New Nationalism," a far-reaching expansion of the federal government to stabilize the economy and institute social reforms. The election of reformers of both parties to Congress in 1910 indicated that Roosevelt's vision had popular support. With that encouragement, Roosevelt challenged Taft for leadership of the Republican party and announced his intention to run in the Republican presidential primary in 1912. Although Roosevelt had wide public support and easily defeated Taft and the other challenger, Robert La Follette, in the 13 states that held preferential primaries, the old guard still dominated the national party, and they nominated Taft at the Republican National Convention.

The day after Taft's nomination, Roosevelt and his supporters withdrew from the Republican party and formed the Progressive party. They nominated Roosevelt for president and California governor Hiram W. Johnson for vice president. Roosevelt boasted, "I am as strong as a bull moose," inspiring his followers to call themselves the "Bull Moosers." Their reformist platform called for extensive controls on corporations, minimum wage laws, child labor laws, a graduated income tax, and woman suffrage. But the Republican vote split between Taft and Roosevelt, and the victory went to the Democratic candidate, Woodrow Wilson, former president of Princeton University and governor of New Jersey. Wilson also ran on a strong reform platform. Eugene V. Debs, the Socialist party candidate vowed reform as well. The three reform candidates, Wilson, Debs, and Roosevelt, all agreed that the large corporations had too much power. But they disagreed as to what to do about it. Debs argued that the national government should take over the trusts. Roosevelt argued for a "New Nationalism," in which a strong federal government would regulate the trusts and, if necessary, curb their power. Wilson, reluctant to vest so much power in the govern-

TABLE 19-4			
The Election of 1912			
Candidate	Political Party	Popular Vote	Electoral Vote
Woodrow Wilson	Democratic	6,293,454	435
Theodore Roosevelt	Progressive	4,119,538	88
William H. Taft	Republican	3,484,980	8
Eugene V. Debs	Socialist	900,672	0

ment, called his approach the "New Freedom," believing that the government should dismantle the trusts and then revert to limited powers. Wilson won the election with 42 percent of the vote, but all three reform candidates together gained 75 percent of the total. Debs won 6 percent, the strongest showing ever for the Socialist party. Wilson took office amid an overwhelming popular mandate for reform.

Conclusion

When Woodrow Wilson took office, the nation looked and behaved differently than it had at the turn of the century. Millions of immigrants from Europe, Asia, and Mexico had arrived in the United States and settled in towns and cities across the nation. Growing urban areas with new amusements and increasingly diverse populations emerged as centers of a national mass culture. New developments in science and technology brought the automobile and the motion picture to American consumers. At the same time, industrial production contributed to environmental damage, pollution, and dangerous working conditions.

Progressive reformers and labor activists mounted efforts to curb the ill effects of urban industrial society. Faith in science and expertise gave rise to pervasive optimism that social problems could be solved. Technological changes converged with the widespread belief that society is the sum of interdependent parts that can work together to mitigate the harmful effects of industrial life. At the local level, as well as through state and national institutions, reformers sought to solve society's ills. Muckrakers exposed corruption, women's rights activists pushed for the vote, and African American leaders organized for civil rights and against lynching. In the West and Southwest, Mexicans and Asians challenged discriminatory laws and labor practices. At the same time, moralists and vice crusaders sought to tame what they considered to be dangerous challenges to the social order.

These years also witnessed a major expansion of national power, within the nation as well as abroad. Presidents Roosevelt and Taft strengthened the role of the federal government through new efforts to regulate big business and by extending American military and economic presence abroad. By 1912 most Americans supported a strong reform agenda. But within a few years, the nation became embroiled in a major world war that would challenge the inherent optimism of Progressivism, signaling the end of an era.

Sites to Visit

Touring Turn-of-the-Century America: Photographs from the Detroit Publishing Company, 1880–1920.
memory.loc.gov/ammem/detroit/dethome.html
> This Library of Congress site includes thousands of photographs from turn-of-the-century America.

Coal Mining during the Gilded Age and Progressive Era
www.history.ohio-state.edu/projects/Lessons_US/
Gilded_Age/Coal_Mining/default.htm
> This Ohio State University site examines the development of the coal industry, including experiences of miners and sometimes violent labor-management conflict.

W.E.B. DuBois Resources
www-unix.oit.umass.edu/%7Ecscpo/db.html
> Included here are writings by and about the great African American intellectual and civil rights leader W.E.B. DuBois.

The Triange Shirtwaist Factory Fire, March 25, 1911
www.ilr.cornell.edu/trianglefire/
> Oral histories, cartoons, images, and essays about the fire are included here.

Inside an American Factory: The Westinghouse Works, 1904
lcweb2.loc.gov/ammem/papr/west/westhome.html
> This site provides a glimpse inside a turn-of-the-twentieth-century factory.

Theodore Roosevelt
www.ipl.org/ref/POTUS/troosevelt.html
> This Internet Public Library site contains biographical information about Theodore Roosevelt and his election to the presidency and links to Internet biographies and resources about him.

William Howard Taft
www.ipl.org/ref/POTUS/whtaft.html
> This Internet Public Library site contains biographical information about William Howard Taft and his election to the presidency and links to Internet biographies and resources about him.

The Emma Goldman Papers
sunsite.berkeley.edu/Goldman/
> This site includes information about the famous immigrant radical and selections of writings by and about her.

For Further Reading

General Works

Gail Bederman, *Manliness and Civilization: A Cultural History of Gender and Race in the United States, 1800–1917* (1995).

John R. Borchert, *America's Northern Heartland: An Economic and Historical Geography of the Upper Midwest* (1987).

Herbert Croly, *The Promise of American Life* (1909).

Steven J. Diner, *A Very Different Age: Americans of the Progressive Era* (1998).

Sara Evans, *Born for Liberty: A History of Women in America* (1989).

Gary Gerstle, *American Crucible: Race and Nation in the Twentieth Century* (2001).

Migration and Immigration: The Changing Face of the Nation

Albert Camarillo, *Chicanos in a Changing Society* (1977).

Linda Gordon, *The Great Arizona Orphan Abduction* (1999).

Matthew Frye Jacobson, *Barbarian Virtues: The United States Encounters Foreign Peoples at Home and Abroad* (2000).

Riv-Ellen Prell, *Fighting to Become Americans: Jews, Gender, and the Anxiety of Assimilation* (1999).

Vicki L. Ruiz, *From Out of the Shadows: Mexican Women in Twentieth-Century America* (1998).

Judith Smith, *Family Connections: A History of Italian and Jewish Immigrant Lives in Providence, Rhode Island, 1900–1940* (1985).

Ronald Takaki, *Strangers from a Different Shore: A History of Asian Americans* (1989).

Work, Science, and Leisure

George Chauncey, *Gay New York* (1994).

John D'Emilio and Estelle Freedman, *Intimate Matters: A History of Sexuality in America* (1988).

Elaine Tyler May, *Great Expectations: Marriage and Divorce in Post-Victorian America* (1980).

Lary May, *Screening Out the Past: The Birth of Mass Culture and the Motion Picture Industry* (1980).

Stephen Meyer, III, *The Five Dollar Day: Labor Management and Social Control in the Ford Motor Company, 1908–1921* (1981).

Leon Stein, *The Triangle Fire* (1962).

Reformers and Radicals

Jane Addams, *Twenty Years at Hull House* (1910).

W. E. B. Du Bois, *The Souls of Black Folk* (1903).

Nan Enstad, *Ladies of Labor, Girls of Adventure: Working Women, Popular Culture, and Labor Politics at the Turn of the Twentieth Century* (1999).

Dorothy Herrmann, *Helen Keller: A Life* (1999).

Louise Michelle Newman, *White Women's Rights: The Racial Origins of Feminism in the United States* (1999).

Viviana A. Zelizer, *Pricing the Priceless Child: The Changing Social Value of Children* (1985).

Expanding National Power

Richard Drinnon, *Facing West: The Metaphysics of Indian-Hating and Empire-Building* (1980).

William H. Harbaugh, *The Life and Times of Theodore Roosevelt* (1975).

Richard Hofstadter, *The Age of Reform* (1955).

Hazel M. McFerson, *The Racial Dimension of American Overseas Colonial Policy* (1997).

George Mowry, *Theodore Roosevelt and the Progressive Movement* (1946).

Robert Weibe, *The Search for Order* (1967).

Online Practice Test

Test your understanding of this chapter with interactive review quizzes at

www.ablongman.com/jonescreatedequal/chapter19

Additional Photo Credits

Page 641: Brown Brothers

Page 645: From the HUC Skirball Cultural Center, Museum Collection, Los Angeles, CA. Gift of Brenda Grossman Spivack in memory of Godina Eisenstein Schwartz. Clothes and Textiles: Gift of Harold Brill and Regina Starr Brill. HUCSM 31.194. Photography by Susan Einstein

Page 654: From the Collections of Henry Ford Museum & Greenfield Village

Page 656: The Advertising Archive Ltd

Page 659: Courtesy, The Lilly Library, Indiana University, Bloomington, Indiana

Page 662: Courtesy, Janice L. and David Frent

War and Revolution, 1912–1920

Jacob Lawrence, "The Migration of the Negro Panel no. 57," 1940–41. Acquired 1942, The Phillips Collection, Washington, D.C. Courtesy, Francine Seders Gallery

■ Two million Americans experienced World War I as soldiers serving in France, while all citizens at home felt the impact of that global conflict. *Migration of the Negro* by painter Jacob Lawrence suggests the burdensome toil of Southern African Americans, and why so many moved to Northern cities after 1914 in search of better jobs.

On the morning of April 6, 1909, six people arrived at the top of the world. They had fulfilled at last the dream of two generations of Arctic explorers to reach the North Pole. Exhausted from a month of walking across the treacherous ice of the Arctic Sea, they rested for 30 hours at their polar camp. Then they turned south—the only direction available—and raced for their lives against the brutal cold that threatened to kill them.

Who were these men? Four were Greenland Inuit ("Eskimos"), for whom the Arctic region was home, even if they rarely ventured out on the frozen sea that covered the last 400 miles to the Pole. Two were American. The leader of the party, Bowdoin College graduate and renowned Arctic adventurer Robert Peary, had already built a reputation as a leading figure in the explorations of the Earth's last remote places. The other American to reach the North Pole that day received no such fame. Yet by the accounts of his fellow travelers, Matthew Henson was the indispensable man on the trip. A skilled dogsled driver, a master carpenter who built the expedition's shelters and fixed its sleds, and the only American on the voyage to learn the Inuit language, Henson was the one person Peary said he could not get along without. Henson was also African American. He had grown up during Reconstruction in rural Maryland and Washington, D.C. As a young man he developed a taste for exotic travel by working as a sailor on ships that took him to east Asia, north Africa, and the Black Sea.

American Robert Peary led the first expedition to reach the North Pole.

Back in Washington, Henson worked as a clerk at an exclusive fur company to which Peary brought furs from his early trips to Greenland. Despite living on opposite sides of the increasingly stark color line of Jim Crow, the two men made strongly positive impressions on each other. Peary, ten years older, hired Henson as his assistant in 1888. Over the next 21 years, as white Americans unleashed a growing torrent of violence against their black fellow citizens, these two men built a relationship of great mutual respect as they pressed northward on several journeys into the icy wilderness of the Arctic. In his intimate working relationship with Henson, Peary acted so much as an equal that he sometimes offended other white Americans on the expeditions.

Twelve years after Henson and Peary stood together to plant the American flag in the Inuit world of the far North, the relations between white and black Americans appeared in a sharply different light in Oklahoma. The former Indian Territory had become a state in 1907 and had more than 50,000 Cherokee and other Native American residents, more than any other state. The discovery at the turn of the century of vast oil reserves along the Arkansas River made Tulsa a boom town, with all the social tensions that accompany rapid growth. The vibrant African American section of the segregated city along Greenwood Avenue offered a strong example of black economic independence.

American Matthew Henson accompanied Peary on the epic 1909 expedition.

That entire community was destroyed on the night of May 31, 1921, in the largest American race riot of the twentieth century. In previous years, similar riots had erupted in St. Louis, Chicago, and elsewhere, when white resentment over black mobility and declining deference exploded around a petty pretext. In Tulsa, a false charge against a young black man of attempted rape of a white elevator operator sparked thousands of angry white Tulsans to descend on the county courthouse to seize the suspect from jail. The city's white newspaper spurred them on with an editorial titled "To Lynch Negro Tonight." But many black Tulsans were determined not to let that happen. Veterans just back from World War I insisted that their sacrifices to make the world "safe for democracy" not be marred by terrorism. A group of 75 African Americans drove down to the courthouse to defend it from the mob. Their leader was a former serviceman who, others remembered, "came back from France with exaggerated ideas of equality."

The two groups exchanged words and then gunfire. Several people fell dead. Enraged, the much larger and better-armed white crowd poured across the railroad tracks into Greenwood, shooting and burning. Rather than restraining them, the Tulsa police force deputized hundreds of the marauders with instructions to kill. In the next few hours, the invaders executed as many as 300 African Americans and burned the entire Greenwood district to the ground. Mary E. Jones Parrish, a Greenwood resident, felt as though World War I had come to her town: "The enemy had organized in the night and was invading our district, the same as the Germans invaded France and Belgium." No white Tulsans were ever punished by the law for their actions that night.

The decade that stretched from the discovery of the North Pole to the Tulsa race riot was marked by unusual turbulence in American life. From 1910 to 1914 optimism about solving the nation's social problems rose as reformers attempted to ameliorate some of the worst aspects of modern industrial life. International developments then turned American attentions abroad. Traumatic social revolutions swept through Mexico, China, and Russia, and the conflagration of the Great War—World War I—consumed all of Europe and eventually drew in the United States. What President Woodrow Wilson called the war "to make the world safe for democracy" encouraged people of color, both in the vast European-ruled colonies of Asia and Africa and in the segregated United States, to claim a place of greater equality. But at home the war also created pressures for conformity and an intolerance for dissent. The events in Tulsa were part of a broad pattern of violence against political radicals and people of color that was rampant by 1920. The United States emerged from the war with great prestige and power, but most Americans were not yet convinced of the nation's obligations abroad, and the Versailles Treaty ending World War I failed to create a lasting structure for world peace.

A World in Upheaval

American politics between 1910 and 1920 and the U.S. involvement in World War I must be understood within the context of change and uncertainty in the international system. While world affairs were still dominated by the wealthy nations of western Europe and North America, the first wave of the great revolutions of the twentieth century was beginning to wash away much of the old order. Tensions also sharpened within the United States over traditional hierarchies of color, gender, and class. The struggle between reform and reaction pervaded public life in the United States and much of the rest of the world.

The Apex of European Conquest

On the eve of World War I, all but a quarter of the world's population lived under the rule of Europeans or their descendants. Explorations of the most remote parts of the globe filled in the last blank spaces on world maps, including the North (1909) and South (1911) poles. A 1913 expedition led by Episcopalian missionary Hudson Stuck reached the top of Alaska's Mt. McKinley, at 20,320 feet the highest peak in North America. The granting of statehood to Arizona and New Mexico in 1912 filled out the 48 mainland states. With U.S. control of the continent complete, its native inhabitants began to seem to white Americans less a current threat than a piece of the past to be preserved. The U.S. Treasury issued the first Indian head nickel the following year.

Technological innovations in transportation and communication tied the world more closely together. Just as the Suez Canal (1870) and the trans-Siberian railroad (1904) linked Europe more directly to Asia, the Panama Canal (1914) cut in half the travel time by water between the East and West coasts of the United States. Cables laid on the floor of the Atlantic Ocean in 1914 inaugurated telephone service between Europe and the United States. The first motorized flight by Orville and Wilbur Wright along the Outer Banks of North Carolina in 1903 led to transcontinental airmail service by 1920.

The competition that arose from the expansion of European power sowed the seeds of World War I. Germany, France, Britain, Italy, and Russia raced each other for new colonies and greater influence across Africa and Asia. Conflicts within Europe over disputed borders (Alsace–Lorraine) and nationalist movements (the Balkans) further heightened tensions. The central rivalry emerged between a newly unified Germany (1871) and traditionally dominant Britain. France had been defeated by Germany in the last armed clash in Europe (the Franco-Prussian War of 1870) and feared a renewed conflict with its larger, stronger neighbor. Anticipating trouble, each of the major European powers sought allies to bolster its position. Britain, France, and Russia formed the Triple Entente against the Triple Alliance of Germany, Austria–Hungary, and Italy (when war came in 1914 Italy switched sides and the Ottoman Empire—modern Turkey—joined Germany and Austria–Hungary as the Central Powers). These unprecedented peacetime alliances between global empires meant that a single spark could ignite a worldwide war.

> *The United States had been born in the first successful revolution by colonies against a European empire.*

The United States emerged as a global power in this same period around the turn of the century. Fifteen years after it seized an overseas empire in 1898, the country's economic growth was stunning. U.S. consumption of energy from modern fuels (coal and oil) in 1913 equaled that of Britain, Germany, France, Russia, and Austria–Hungary combined. The United States brought a different history to the world stage. It had been born in 1776 in the first successful revolution by colonies against a European empire. Americans had long understood themselves as a people who opposed empires and supported self-government. The events of 1898 contradicted this legacy, and Americans remained ambivalent about their country's imperial venture. The U.S. Congress promised eventual independence to the Philippines in 1916 and granted U.S. citizenship to residents of Puerto Rico in 1917.

The American rise to world power came just as the major revolutions of the twentieth century began to shatter the structures of imperialism. The United States became the leading status quo power when much of the globe was beginning to reject that status quo. The great example of anticolonial revolution now stood as one of the foremost counterrevolutionary states. Rather than new colonies, however, Americans sought expanded economic opportunities abroad, and they expected their government to help them. While president of Princeton University in 1907, Woodrow Wilson explained that because "the manufacturer insists on having the world as a market, the flag of his nation must follow him . . . even if the sovereignty of unwilling nations be outraged in the process." Wilson's victory in the election of 1912 brought the first native Southerner to the White House since before the Civil War, a symbol of a reunited majority white population ready to turn outward.

Confronting Revolutions Abroad

More than most people, Wilson feared social upheaval. Born in 1856, he had grown up in Augusta, Georgia, amid the destruction of the Civil War, and he made his career as a political scientist and as governor of New Jersey (1910–1912) during a period of labor strife. Whatever Wilson's hopes for a stable social order at home and abroad, the global process of western capitalist expansion into decentralized, preindustrial societies was producing a widespread backlash by 1910. The first signs had already appeared of a broad rejection of the world order dominated by the white nations of Europe and North America. Ethiopia crushed an invading Italian army in 1896 in the first victory of an African state over a modern European one. In 1905 Japan destroyed the Russian army and naval fleet, putting Europeans on notice that their days of having their way in Asia were over. Harassed across eastern Europe in brutal pogroms, Jews under the leadership of Theodor Herzl founded the Zionist movement in 1897 for a national homeland in Palestine. Blacks organized the African National Congress in 1912 to struggle against racial oppression in South Africa, just as African Americans formed the National Association for the Advancement of Colored People (NAACP) in 1910.

As nationalist movements in China, Russia, and Mexico overturned weak central governments controlled by foreign investors, American economic and security interests seemed to be at stake on three continents. In Asia, the Chinese deeply resented exclusive foreign enclaves that dominated their nation's coastal region and exempted foreigners from the constraints of Chinese laws. Signs in Shanghai reading "No dogs or Chinese" suggested the attitudes that accompanied European and American control of the bulk of China's wealth. In 1911 nationalist revolutionaries inspired by Sun Yat-sen, a Hawaiian-educated democratic reformer, overthrew the Manchu dynasty that had proven unable to resist western incursions.

The American desire for an open door into China's trade—a door that no other powerful nation could close at will—conflicted with the rising imperial power of the region: Japan. The Tokyo government, which had annexed Korea in 1910, responded to the outbreak of World War I by seizing the valuable German-held Shantung Peninsula in northeastern China. In its famous 21 Demands to China, issued in January 1915, Japan made clear its plans to dominate the development of the Chinese economy. The American relationship with both China and Japan was undercut at home by continued discrimination and violence against immigrants from Asia, who remained ineligible for naturalization as U.S. citizens (unlike any children born on American soil, who were U.S. citizens regardless of their race or ethnicity). In 1913 the California legislature passed the Alien Land Act to prevent ownership of land in the state by people "ineligible to citizenship"—people born in Asia, particularly those from Japan.

Revolutionary struggles with implications for America also threatened the monarchs who ruled eastern Europe. For Russians, defeat at the hands of Japan in 1905 helped precipitate a thwarted revolution in 1905 followed by two years of political turmoil. The Czar survived to rule another decade, and thousands of political activists—unionists, anarchists, and socialists—joined a growing wave of immigration from Russia to the United States. The wave crested in 1914 at 1.2 million people, most of them from east or south of the Alps. That same year, the assassination of the heir to the Austro-Hungarian throne by a Serbian nationalist in Sarajevo in June provided the spark that ignited the Great War. Russia's defense of the Serbs put the alliance system into action as the Entente went to war with the Central Powers.

The most important region of the world for the United States before World War I was Latin America, especially Central America and the Caribbean islands. This area guarded the nation's

Tijuana

Columbus, NM

El Paso

MEXICO

Pancho Villa pursued, 1916–1917

Parral

UNITED STATES

ATLANTIC OCEAN

Houston
New Orleans

San Antonio

Gulf of Mexico

Miami

BAHAMA
ISLANDS
(British)

DOMINICAN
REPUBLIC
*Occupied, 1916–1924
Protectorate, 1905–1941*

U.S. VIRGIN
ISLANDS
*Acquired from
Denmark, 1917*

Guantanamo
U.S. Naval Base, 1898

Mexico City

CUBA
*Occupied, 1898–1902,
1906–1909, 1912, 1917, 1922,
Protectorate, 1898–1934*

PUERTO RICO
Annexed, 1898

HAITI
*Occupied, 1915–1934
Protectorate, 1915–1936*

Veracruz
Occupied, 1914

JAMAICA
(British)

*Caribbean
Sea*

BRITISH
HONDURAS

HONDURAS
*Occupied, 1912–1919,
1924–1925*

NICARAGUA
*Occupied, 1912–1925,
1926–1933*

GUATEMALA

EL SALVADOR

Canal Zone
*Seized from Colombia, 1903,
then leased from Panama, 1903*

VENEZUELA

U.S. interests in the Caribbean, 1898–1939
- U.S. and possessions
- Occupied by or protectorate of U.S.
- U.S. assaults

PANAMA
Protectorate, 1903–1939

COLOMBIA

■ **MAP 20.1**

U.S. INTERESTS AND INTERVENTIONS IN THE CARIBBEAN REGION, 1898–1939 By its size, wealth,
and military power, the United States dominated the Caribbean region to its south. American capitalists
invested heavily in Mexico, Central America, and the Caribbean islands, and U.S. troops often intervened
to protect those investments. Puerto Rico (by acquisition from Spain) and the Panama Canal Zone (by lease
from Panama) became particularly important territories ruled by the United States.

strategic southern flank, and American citizens and corporations invested more money in Latin
America than in any other region of the world. President Wilson spoke of the ability of Latin
Americans to govern themselves "when properly directed" and proceeded to provide that direction. U.S. Marines occupied Haiti (1915), the Dominican Republic (1916), and Cuba (1917)
and maintained their earlier presence in Nicaragua to defend American-owned property and
ensure that local debts were paid to American creditors. The Bryan–Chamorro Treaty of 1916
guaranteed that no other nation would build a competitor to the Panama Canal through
Nicaragua. The United States purchased the Danish Virgin Islands in 1917 to keep them out
of German hands.

American anxieties about stability to the south centered on Mexico. "Land for the landless and Mexico for the Mexicans" became the slogan of revolutionaries there between 1910
and 1920. After troops led by Francisco Madero overthrew the long-standing dictatorship of
Porfirio Díaz in 1911, various factions competed to determine the course of the revolution. U.S.

stakes in the Mexican revolution were high. American investors owned 43 percent of all Mexico's wealth (other foreigners owned another 25 percent), and more than half of the country's trade flowed north to the United States. Moreover, by 1921 Mexico became the world's second largest exporter of oil. Washington feared the spread of radical political ideas northward as almost a million Mexicans crossed their northern border during the revolutionary decade, tripling the number of Americans with recent roots south of the Rio Grande.

Many came through El Paso, the "Ellis Island" for immigrants from the south. Fleeing poverty and violence, they found both discrimination and employment. Dam building and irrigation in the American Southwest since the Newlands Act of 1902 had created a boom in commercial agriculture across California and Arizona and a desperate need for farm workers. Employers often recruited south of the border. "I believe that the Mexican laborers are the solution to our common labor problem in this country," one cotton company executive told President Wilson. It was not an easy life, especially for women who had to balance paid employment with taking care of families. Grace Luna remembered picking cotton in Madera, California, where women scaled ladders with 100 pounds of cotton on their backs and "some carried their kids on top of their picking sacks." Whereas most immigrants sought unskilled positions, members of Mexico's professional classes came north for political asylum as well, including teachers, architects, and lawyers. New arrivals of all classes joined Mexican Americans who had lived in the region since it was part of Mexico. They had not crossed the border; in 1848, the border had crossed them.

> *Mexican Americans had lived in the region since it was part of Mexico. They had not crossed the border; in 1848, the border had crossed them.*

Wilson sought unsuccessfully to reestablish in Mexico a political order respectful of the rights of foreign property owners. He refused to recognize the government of Victoriano Huerta, which had deposed and murdered Madero in 1912. Wilson instead supported the forces around Venustiano Carranza while opposing the more radical opposition led by Emiliano Zapata in the south and Francisco ("Pancho") Villa in the north. Wilson twice sent U.S. troops into Mexico, at Veracruz in April 1914 to block a German arms shipment to Huerta's forces and then in pursuit of Villa and his army after their 1916 assault on Columbus, New Mexico. The American forces under General John J. Pershing withdrew in early 1917 as the president prepared to enter the much larger war in Europe. Land redistribution and national control of Mexico's abundant mineral wealth, particularly oil, were written into the new constitution passed a few days later, and the revolutionary upheaval ended by 1920.

Conflicts over Hierarchies at Home

Just as social upheaval threatened monarchies and international investors abroad, less privileged Americans contested traditional lines of hierarchy and control in the United States. For example, racial lines were not always clear. Native-born whites continued to disagree about whether the millions of new immigrants from eastern and southern Europe were also "white." Anthropologists led by Franz Boas at Columbia University began to question the supposed significance of racial differences. Americans of all colors applauded the spectacular successes of Native American athlete Jim Thorpe at the 1912 Olympic Games in Sweden. In 1916 Wilson appointed Louis Brandeis as the first Jewish justice of the Supreme Court, but that same year anxieties about the future of white supremacy found a voice in the popular new book of a conservative New York intellectual named Madison Grant. *The Passing of the Great Race*, a bigoted sociology tract, identified Jesus as "Nordic" to distance the central figure of the Christian faith from the many new Jewish immigrants in America.

The Wilson administration's "New Freedom" slogan did not apply to African Americans, who faced continuing discrimination in employment and housing. The president filled his cabinet with white Southerners who segregated the few federal agencies that had employed

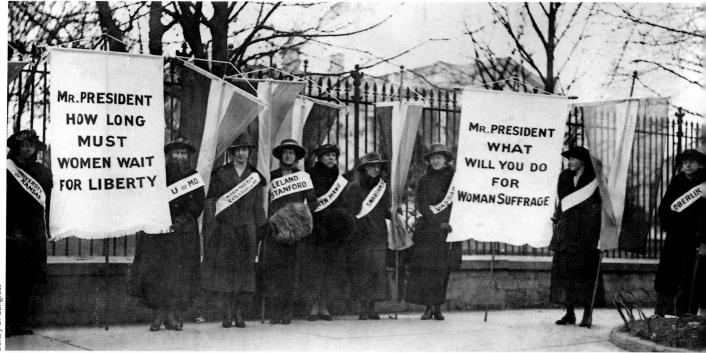

■ In February 1917, as the United States broke relations with Germany and began to prepare to enter World War I, supporters of woman's suffrage continued to picket on the sidewalk outside the White House. College women joined the effort to ensure that winning liberty at home would go hand in hand with fighting for democracy abroad.

blacks. When Wilson took office African Americans continued to be murdered publicly by vigilante mobs across the South at a rate of more than one person per week. But the president ignored requests from the recently formed NAACP for an antilynching law, and the United States remained one of the few societies in which human beings were burned at the stake. Instead, the historian–president endorsed D. W. Griffith's 1915 film *Birth of a Nation* as "history written with lightning." Griffith, a Kentucky-born champion of the "Lost Cause" of slavery in the South, had created a racist blockbuster that celebrated the Ku Klux Klan of the 1860s and helped inspire the Klan's rebirth that fall at Stone Mountain, Georgia.

Women of all colors lived under particular burdens of discrimination. Their uniquely intimate relationships—as daughters, wives, mothers—to those who did not treat them as equals complicated their efforts at reform. So did their dilemma about women's roles in society: some sought full legal equality with men, and others wanted special protections for women on the grounds that they were fundamentally different. At issue was the nature of women's political identity. Was their primary identification in their attachment to individual men or to the nation? American women lost their U.S. citizenship by marrying a foreigner, whereas American men did not. A growing chorus of female activists rejected this kind of double standard and focused on the key issue of suffrage.

American women's long struggle to vote came to a head in this decade. By 1912, a growing number of European nations and nine American states, all in the West, granted the franchise to citizens of both sexes. Jeannette Rankin, a Republican feminist and pacifist from Montana, won election in 1916 as the nation's first female member of Congress. Suffragists varied in the tactics they believed most effective for winning the vote. The more moderate National American Women Suffrage Association under the leadership of Carrie Chapman Catt worked within the political system, building an alliance with President Wilson after he endorsed women's suffrage in 1916 and supporting the U.S. entry into World War I the next year. Alice Paul and other militants formed the National Women's Party and opposed the war effort as inherently undemocratic because half the adult population could not vote. In 1917 five picketers were imprisoned for seven months for obstructing traffic in front of the White House; despite brutal force-feedings, Paul and Rose Winslow persisted in a hunger strike so "that women fighting for liberty may be considered political prisoners." In 1918 suffragist organizers helped elect a more sympathetic Congress that passed the Nineteenth Amendment, ending sex discrimination in voting two years later.

Contention over women's social roles also divided Americans. Traditionalists promoted the declaration of the first Mother's Day in 1913. The desire to provide special protections for women resulted in the Sheppard–Towner Act of 1921, which expanded the role of the new federal Children's Bureau in providing infant and maternal health services. The struggle over contraception foreshadowed the conflict over abortion that dominated women's politics in the last quarter of the twentieth century. Socialist Margaret Sanger campaigned for women's access to contraception, opening the nation's first birth control clinic in Brooklyn in 1916. Sanger's experiences as a public health nurse with working-class New Yorkers convinced her that controlling pregnancy was the central issue for helping women gain greater autonomy. Unable to separate sexual experience from reproduction and facing poverty and unsanitary living conditions, married women in the lower classes suffered frequent pregnancies and the often debilitating and sometimes fatal consequences of abortions, an illegal but common operation. "The menace of another pregnancy hung like a sword over the head of every poor woman I came in contact with," Sanger recalled. She reached a turning point after hearing the joking response of a physician to the desperate plea of one frail 28-year-old mother of three for help in preventing another pregnancy: "Tell Jake to sleep on the roof!" Sanger was appalled, and the young woman's subsequent death as a result of a botched abortion pushed Sanger to begin her crusade for contraception.

Most adult Americans—workers—continued to find themselves in frequent conflict with the owners who employed them. Industrial capitalism's efficiency produced great material wealth, but 60 percent of it belonged to 2 percent of the population, whereas two-thirds of Americans owned only 2 percent of the wealth. President Wilson acknowledged that as factories grew larger, "the individual has been submerged." Skills became less necessary in the assembly-line workplace and workers more interchangeable. The anticapitalist aspirations of the Socialist party and the Industrial Workers of the World (IWW) frightened both industrialists and the more conservative labor leaders of the American Federation of Labor (AFL), especially when the western-based IWW led two major strikes in the East, one a success in Lawrence, Massachusetts, in 1912 and the other a failure in Paterson, New Jersey, in 1913. The campaign against a wage cut at the vast Lawrence textile factory was especially impressive in uniting 20,000 workers of 40 different national backgrounds.

Businesses had long opposed workers' efforts to build unions. Some owners sought to undercut union campaigns by providing better working conditions and even company-run "unions." These carrots of concession were accompanied by the stick of force. Bolstered by sympathetic federal courts and state governors, companies usually refused to negotiate with work-

■ The coal miners' tent colony outside Ludlow stood on the high plains of south central Colorado, at the base of the mountains of the Front Range. Winter snows and cold temperatures made for a difficult life, as did the grueling and dangerous work of mining coal that was common across the state. Strikers along with their wives and children died in the Ludlow massacre on April 20, 1914.

Denver Public Library, Western History Department

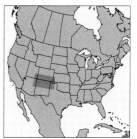

■ **MAP 20.2**
SOUTHERN COLORADO AND NORTHERN NEW MEXICO   The mountainous region of southern Colorado and northern New Mexico in the 1910s had an economy based on mining, ranching, and lumbering—like much of the rural West. A large Indian population included Navajos, Apaches, Pueblos, and Utes. Since the 1920s, Santa Fe and Taos supported important communities of artists enchanted by the area's natural beauty. That same beauty attracted growing numbers of visitors later in the twentieth century, as the tourist trade surpassed older extractive industries as the chief source of employment in much of the mountainous West.

ers who went on strike. This pattern reached a shocking climax on Easter night in 1914 outside Ludlow, Colorado, in a mining camp owned by John D. Rockefeller, Jr.'s Colorado Fuel and Iron Company. State militia and company guards broke a strike there with torches and machine guns, burning the miners' tent colony and killing 2 women and 11 children. A total of 66 strikers and strike supporters died before federal troops eventually restored order. Ludlow recalled the actions of the Colorado militia exactly 50 years earlier, when it had destroyed the Cheyenne Indian camp at Sand Creek. Immigrant coal miners and their families had replaced Native Americans as the apparent threat to Colorado's social order.

Such brutality by owners against workers appalled most Americans. The Wilson administration slowly began supporting the right of laborers to organize for collective bargaining with their employers. Wilson's strong backing from Samuel Gompers and the AFL in the 1912 election initiated the modern Democratic–labor alliance. The president named William B. Wilson, a U.S. congressman from Pennsylvania and a former labor activist with the Knights of Labor and the United Mine Workers, to head the new U.S. Department of Labor, the permanent agency established "to foster, promote and develop the welfare of working people" by improving their working conditions and mediating labor disputes. The president appointed labor lawyer Frank Walsh to chair the separate short-term U.S. Committee on Industrial Relations, which for two years explored the causes of industrial violence in public hearings. Walsh even grilled Rockefeller about the events at Ludlow, embarrassing the corporate titan by revealing his close involvement and clear responsibility for what happened.

The Great War and American Neutrality

Most Americans had roots of some kind in Europe and had long defined themselves in relation to life on "the continent." But they also considered themselves part of the New World that was separate from the Old World of kings, castles, and rigid social classes. When Europe stepped off the precipice in August 1914 into a war larger than any previously fought or imagined, few Americans wanted any part of it. Make "no entangling alliances," George Washington had urged his fellow citizens. Europeans must stay out of our hemisphere, the Monroe Doctrine had declared. For generations, the preoccupation of the United States had been constructing the world's "best" society, however Americans might disagree about its proper contours. But migration and commerce had reduced the nation's isolation. International ties proved too important to the well-being of Americans for the country to remain indefinitely on the sidelines of World War I.

"The One Great Nation at Peace"

"It would be an irony of fate," Wilson told a friend, "if my administration had to deal chiefly with foreign affairs." But so it was for the scholar of American history and politics who entered national office with a large domestic agenda. Just a year and a half into his presidency, Americans were stunned as "civilized" Europe slid into savage conflict. "The lamps are going out all over Europe," British Foreign Secretary Edward Grey observed. "We shall not see them lit again in our lifetime." Following traditional U.S. policy, Wilson urged Americans to remain neutral "in fact as well as in name" to promote an eventual "peace without victory."

Neutrality was profitable. Wilson stoutly defended the rights of neutrals to trade with belligerents, the same principle that had led the United States into the War of 1812 against England. American industries depended on overseas trade, he believed, and "they will burst their jackets if they cannot find a free outlet to the markets of the world." After the recession of 1913–1914, war-related demands from abroad for American farm and factory products jump-started the economy. In the course of World War I, American bankers extended $10 billion in loans to the Entente (primarily Britain and France), and the United States changed from a debtor nation to the world's largest creditor.

The nature of the fighting in Europe bolstered the American determination to avoid being drawn into the conflict. Industrialized warfare brought fiendish new ways to kill human beings, including machine guns and poison gas. Gone were the days of bold maneuvers and dashing cavalry charges; now was the time of trench warfare, with its unrelenting misery, terror, and helplessness. Eight and a half million young men lost their lives and another 21 million were wounded, devastating an entire generation of European society. Eight million civilians also died as a result of the fighting, and an international outbreak of influenza in 1918 killed another 20 million around the world. Continuous shelling rendered whole sections of the landscape of northern France a wasteland. Prewar optimism about human progress swiftly disappeared.

In the United States, neutrality also made political sense. Immigrants from every part of Europe lived and voted in the United States, so Americans had blood ties to all the belligerents. Commercial and political elites tended to identify with Britain and France, as did many other Americans. But among two of the largest groups of Americans, those with roots in Germany and Ireland, many took a different view. Few Irish Americans equated England with the cause of democracy after centuries of British rule in Ireland, and London's severe repression of the 1916 Easter Rising in Dublin underscored their case. The sheer scale of the immigrant stream to the United States between 1900 and 1914 reinforced the need to avoid Europe's conflicts. Native-born white Americans were already concerned with preserving unity in their increasingly varied and urban society. Allowing in the hatreds from Europe's battlefields would only exacerbate the ethnic and class tensions that worried social reformers and many politicians, including President Wilson.

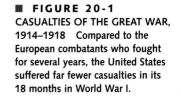

■ **FIGURE 20-1**
CASUALTIES OF THE GREAT WAR,
1914–1918   Compared to the
European combatants who fought
for several years, the United States
suffered far fewer casualties in its
18 months in World War I.

Reform Priorities at Home

Americans traditionally considered powerful government a primary threat to individual liberty, but the rise of mammoth corporations at the start of the twentieth century altered that calculation. Competition was disappearing, particularly in critical sectors of the economy such as oil production and railroads. Laissez-faire policies, by which federal agencies encouraged economic expansion, were no longer adequate; only government could balance the new might of the largest companies. This meant modest regulation of some aspects of the marketplace. Wilson's first term also encouraged such democratic reforms as the ratification of the Seventeenth Amendment for the direct popular election of U.S. senators (1913), previously chosen by state legislatures. Until American entry into the Great War in 1917 turned the nation to a very different task, this period marked the climax of the first chapter of twentieth-century liberalism.

Three areas topped the Wilson administration's reform agenda: taxes, the money system, and monopolies. The Underwood–Simmons Tariff of 1913 cut duties—taxes—on imported goods by almost one-half, helping American consumers and promoting freer trade. The Sixteenth Amendment (1913) allowed a federal income tax, which the 1916 Revenue Act put into effect. This was a progressive tax, one that took a larger percentage of the income of the rich than it took from the poor. The legislation also levied higher taxes on corporate profits and created the first federal estate tax on inheritances. Though small, a tax on inheritances supported the principle of equality of opportunity. It implied that children of the wealthy

■ A former professor and university president, Woodrow Wilson was the only holder of a Ph.D. to become president of the United States. He was also the first native Southerner elected to the Oval Office since before the Civil War. Wilson's self-confidence and tendency toward self-righteousness alienated some citizens, but a majority found him to be a compelling public speaker.

Hulton|Archive/Getty Images

should not receive an enormous head start in life and that Americans growing up without an inheritance should not be handicapped by the large inequalities among past generations.

Congress moved to regulate money in another new way as well. The absence of a centrally managed money system had long contributed to the exaggerated boom-and-bust cycles in the American economy. The Federal Reserve Act of 1913 created a system of 12 Federal Reserve Banks to control the amount of currency in circulation, increasing it in deflationary times and decreasing it when inflation threatened. The system aimed to abolish depressions and prevent bank closures. It did not fully succeed, as the years after 1929 showed, but the Federal Reserve System stabilized the American banking industry and helped position the dollar to become the central global currency.

No issue so dominated American politics between 1913 and 1915 as the tension between huge new corporations and the nation's antimonopoly tradition. The size and market share of companies such as U.S. Steel, American Tobacco, and Du Pont (chemicals) inhibited competition, just as Microsoft dominated computer software at the end of the twentieth century. Investigations by a congressional committee chaired by Arsene Pujo in 1913 revealed the concentration of financial power in the hands of J. P. Morgan and a few other New York bankers, dubbed the Money Trust. Congress created the Federal Trade Commission (1914) to investigate business practices that unfairly prevented competition. The Clayton Antitrust Act of 1914 supplemented the 1890 Sherman Antitrust Act by outlawing specific unfair business practices such as local price cutting and granting rebates to undermine competitors. The Clayton Act also delighted the AFL by declaring that unions should not be "construed to be illegal combinations in restraint of trade." Most federal judges remained unsympathetic to unions, but they could no longer wield the Sherman Act against striking workers rather than against the corporate trusts it had originally intended to target.

The early years after 1910 witnessed the rise of legislation to protect particular groups of citizens, especially women, children, and certain workers. States led the way, with half by 1913 passing workers' compensation laws to provide assistance to workers injured on the job and their

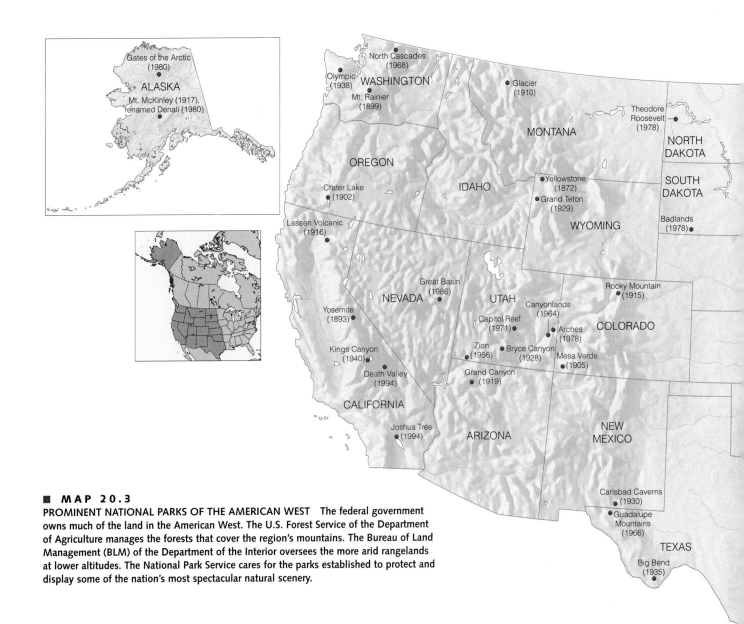

■ MAP 20.3
PROMINENT NATIONAL PARKS OF THE AMERICAN WEST The federal government owns much of the land in the American West. The U.S. Forest Service of the Department of Agriculture manages the forests that cover the region's mountains. The Bureau of Land Management (BLM) of the Department of the Interior oversees the more arid rangelands at lower altitudes. The National Park Service cares for the parks established to protect and display some of the nation's most spectacular natural scenery.

families. In 1916 Congress passed the first federal law limiting child labor, the Keating–Owen Act. The Supreme Court later found it to be unconstitutional, but state child labor laws remained in place. The Adamson Act (1916), providing for an eight-hour day for railroad workers, was the first case of the federal government regulating the hours of workers in the private sector.

Another kind of protective legislation focused on conservation through the preservation of natural landscapes. An increasingly urban, industrial society looked to its most beautiful rural places for solace. Local and state governments set aside parklands throughout the Progressive era. Wilson followed in Roosevelt's conservationist footsteps by creating the National Park Service in 1916 to provide unified management of such new national treasures as Glacier National Park in Montana (1910), Rocky Mountain National Park in Colorado (1915), Lassen Volcanic National Park in California (1916), and Acadia National Park in Maine (1919).

The Great Migration

The so-called Progressive era of 1900–1920 was anything but progressive from the viewpoint of African Americans, who experienced little progress. White mob violence reached its apex in these years, with hundreds of lynchings and dozens of race riots. Most African Americans lived in the South, where segregation and discrimination trapped the majority in poverty. Many therefore seized the unprecedented opportunity offered by the outbreak of the Great

Historical Pictures/Stock Montage, Inc.

■ A migrant family from the South arriving in Chicago, c. 1916. Southerners of all colors, like Europeans, were drawn by the lure of better jobs to the industrial cities of the American Northeast and Midwest. With immigration from Europe slowed to a trickle by the onset of World War I, industry's demand for southern immigrants increased sharply.

War. War-related orders created huge needs for workers in northern factories, and the war also closed the spigot of European immigration, drying up the standard source of new labor. Along with other cities, Chicago and Detroit became centers of the Great Migration of more than half a million African Americans out of Dixie during the war years.

Encouraged by black newspapers such as the *Chicago Defender* and sometimes assisted by northern labor recruiters, black Southerners wanted to go "where a man is a man" regardless of his color. They still found plenty of discrimination in the urban North. But the large black communities of Philadelphia, Cleveland, and New York offered far greater independence than the rural South they left behind. Here "I don't have to humble to no one," one former Southerner wrote home. African Americans could vote, earn higher wages, send their children to better schools, and even sit where they wanted on streetcars. One woman newly arrived in Chicago was stunned the first time she boarded a trolley and saw black people sitting next to whites. "I just held my breath, for I thought any minute they would start something. Then I saw nobody notices it, and I just thought this is a real place for Negroes."

The Great Migration fit in a broader pattern of oppressed peoples seeking greater freedom and opportunity in the industrial workplaces of the American North. African Americans could not change their color and escape from discrimination, as could ethnic Europeans such as Irish, Italians, and Jews who struggled successfully against widespread prejudice to be identified as "white" (while still enduring elements of discrimination). But black Southerners moving north in pursuit of work and liberty acted much as European immigrants had, and they joined other newcomers seeking urban work. The 1920 census showed for the first time a majority of Americans living in towns and cities of at least 2500 people.

When war in Europe shut off most Atlantic immigration after 1914, it opened the door to newcomers who did not have to cross the submarine-infested ocean. Blacks who boarded trains for the North were joined by a similar number of white Southerners leaving rural poverty to look for jobs. A small stream of French Canadians found work in New England factories. A much larger stream of Mexicans and Mexican Americans flowed to jobs across the American Southwest and Midwest. Like African Americans, who had been leaving the South since the Civil War, people of Mexican descent had been moving across the American West for economic reasons since the mid-nineteenth century. World War I and the Mexican Revolution increased their numbers sharply, with the growing cities of Los Angeles, San Antonio, and El Paso remaining particular magnets for new immigrants. The number of Mexican Americans in Los Angeles soared from 6000 in 1910 to nearly 100,000 in 1930.

Limits to American Neutrality

A steady undertow of interests and inclinations pulled against American neutrality after 1914. Most Americans who paid attention to events abroad favored the Entente over the Central Powers. The diversity of Americans' ethnic roots across Europe, Africa, Asia, and Latin America could not mask fundamental cultural and linguistic connections to England, the one-time "mother country." President Wilson deeply admired British political values and institutions, and most influential newspaper editors supported the British cause. Even Americans critical of the British Empire did not want to see the European continent under the autocratic rule of the German Kaiser.

Concrete economic interests also tied the United States to the Allied side. During three years of neutrality, American bankers lent 85 times as much to the Entente nations as to the Central Powers ($2.3 billion versus $27 million). Opponents of American entry into the war later pointed out that bankers and weapon makers had lobbied for joining the British cause, which fattened their wallets. But millions of other Americans also benefited from the nation's trade with Britain and France. Large corporations reaped the bulk of the profits, and agricultural and industrial workers earned decent wages in filling Entente war orders.

Certain powerful Americans, concentrated on the East Coast, tried from the start to prepare the country for entering the war. They emphasized that the U.S. military was much smaller than the forces of European states because of Americans' traditional aversion to large standing armies. Republicans such as Theodore Roosevelt and former Secretary of State Elihu Root led the war preparedness movement, which sought to pressure new immigrants into "100 percent Americanism" and to establish universal military training as "the only way to yank the hyphen out of America."

Progressives themselves split over the war. More radical reformers opposed joining it as a matter of principle. "Let the capitalists do their own fighting and furnish their own corpses," Socialist Eugene Debs wrote in 1914, "and there will never be another war on the face of the earth." Settlement house leader Jane Addams and black labor organizer A. Philip Randolph likewise opposed the war throughout, as did writer Randolph Bourne. They feared, presciently, that going to war would take the wind out of the sails of domestic reform.

TABLE 20-1			
The Election of 1916			
Candidate	Political Party	Popular Vote	Electoral Vote
Woodrow Wilson	Democratic	9,129,606	277
Charles E. Hughes	Republican	8,538,221	254
A. L. Benson	Socialist	585,113	0

Most Progressives followed President Wilson's leadership, opposing U.S. involvement in Europe at first but gradually shifting to support it. Roosevelt's return to mainstream Republicanism and his enthusiasm for war left Wilson the standard-bearer of Progressivism in the 1916 election. This allowed the president to squeak by conservative Republican nominee Charles Evans Hughes, winning a second term in the White House. "He kept us out of war," his supporters declared, but Wilson himself was less optimistic. He knew where German submarine warfare might lead: "Any little German lieutenant can put us into the war at any time by some calculated outrage."

The United States Goes to War

Like Lyndon Johnson in 1964 regarding Vietnam, Wilson won reelection as a liberal reformer and a man of peace, only to go to war within six months. On April 2, 1917, Wilson asked Congress for a declaration of war against Germany "to make the world safe for democracy." Congress agreed by a large majority, and four days later the United States entered the Great War. Mobilization went slowly; it took almost a year before American soldiers in large numbers saw combat in the trenches of northern France. But troops of the Entente took heart from the knowledge that the Yanks were finally coming. American foodstuffs and munitions arrived more quickly, as did American naval ships protecting cargo vessels bound for England. The U.S. entry into the war ultimately provided the narrow margin of victory against the Central Powers.

The Logic of Belligerency

Wilson's insistence on the traditional rights of neutral nations to trade with belligerents clashed with German and British efforts to prevent trade destined for their enemy. The German use of the new submarines or U-boats (from the German *Unterseeboots*) against superior British surface forces pulled Americans into the war. Submarines were extremely vulnerable when not submerged. Before firing on a merchant or passenger ship that might be armed or carrying contraband (war materials), they refused to surface and warn civilian passengers—as required under international law—to evacuate on lifeboats. With Britain arming merchant ships and stowing munitions in the holds of passenger ships, U-boats were the key element in the German campaign to weaken the enemy. The British navy, in turn, seized American goods bound for Germany. But Britain's blockade of the German coastline and neutral ports nearby did not endanger civilians in the same way. "One deals with life; the other with property," Secretary of State Robert Lansing explained.

The deaths of civilians without warning on the high seas shocked and angered the American public, especially the sinking of the magnificent British ocean liner *Lusitania* in May 1915, which killed 128 U.S. citizens and a thousand others. However, some Americans believed Wilson to be less than neutral in negotiating with the British over their offenses while giving ultimatums to Germany. Lansing's predecessor, William Jennings Bryan, resigned in June 1915 to protest the president's manner of defending American trading rights. Bryan found both sides—stalemated and unable to gain victory in the trenches—reprehensible for trying to win by killing "noncombatant men, women, and children." Only their methods differed: Germany drowned innocent civilians; England starved them with its blockade. Hoping not to draw the United States into the war, the German government twice put its unrestricted submarine warfare on hold (the *Arabic* pledge of September 1915 and the *Sussex* pledge of May 1916). By January 1917 the British blockade had reduced German food rations per person to less than half the prewar level. Facing imminent starvation, Berlin decided to take one last chance with unrestricted submarine warfare. The German government calculated that it could force a British and French surrender before enough American assistance arrived. "Not one American will land on the continent," the chief of the German naval staff confidently promised the Kaiser. Two days later, on February 3, the United States broke diplomatic relations with Germany.

Preparing for war with the Americans, German Ambassador Arthur Zimmermann secretly offered German aid to the revolutionary Mexican government "to reconquer the lost territory in Texas, New Mexico, and Arizona" if it joined the Central Powers. Mexico declined, but the Zimmermann telegram leaked to the press on March 1 and outraged Americans. The German threat seemed finally to have reached American soil. One last hindrance to joining the Entente disappeared with the revolution that same month in Russia, which replaced the monarchy with a social democratic government, which Wilson called "a fit partner for a league of

■ The body of a soldier lies caught in barbed wire in the "no-man's-land" between opposing trenches on the western front. Technological advances in weaponry helped make the fighting in World War I vastly more destructive than previous wars. The sheer scale of the slaughter stunned combatants and observers, both in Europe and America, and helped turn many in the postwar generation to deep skepticism regarding the use of military force.

honor." The president could now more genuinely call for a war to make the world "safe for democracy," with France a republic and Britain ruled by Parliament. Politics and economics merged as Lansing underlined the "industrial depression" and "general unrest and suffering among the laboring classes" that an Entente defeat would cause in America.

Still jealous of American autonomy and wary of close identification with the French, British, and Russian empires, however, Wilson took the nation into war as an "Associated" power rather than a full-blown member of the Entente. The president believed that the United States, unique among the belligerents, sought only to defend principles rather than to acquire territory, assuring it of distinctive moral leadership at an eventual postwar peace conference. "We have no quarrel with the German people" themselves but only with the "Prussian autocracy" whose U-boats were engaged in "a warfare against mankind," Wilson declared in calling Americans to a great crusade in Europe. "We desire no conquest, no dominion," but merely to be "one of the champions of the rights of mankind."

Mobilizing the Home Front

Going to war entailed a complete reorientation of the American economy. For the Army and Navy to succeed abroad, mass production of war materials had to be centrally planned, and

Courtesy, Hagley Museum and Library (Neg. #69.170.13,622)

■ European demand for war-related goods brought the U.S. economy out of the deep recession of 1913–1914 and created hundreds of thousands of new jobs. U.S. entry into the war in April 1917 took several million men into the armed forces, opening better-paying opportunities in manufacturing to many women. Four workers at the Westinghouse Electric Company pause from their labors in 1918.

only the federal government could fulfill this role. Such an expansion of government regulation fit with the broader agenda of Progressive reform. Federal agencies could mediate some of the tensions between capital and labor as they focused on ensuring adequate food, clothing, and weapons for the troops at the front.

The Wilson administration created several new agencies to manage the war effort at home. The Selective Service Act established local boards to draft young men into the military. The U.S. Railroad Administration took control of the nation's primary transportation system to solve railroad tie-ups caused by heavy demands for war materials. The War Industries Board supervised all war-related production, allowing large manufacturers to coordinate their schedules without fear of antitrust action. The War Labor Board resolved disputes between workers and employers, providing the most advanced solution to industrial conflict before the New Deal of the 1930s. The Committee on Public Information (CPI), run by Progressive journalist George Creel, provided the government's version of information about the war. The CPI had the crucial task of inspiring and maintaining public support for Wilson's war policies.

The close cooperation between industry and government, combined with strong demand for American goods from the Allied governments, caused corporate earnings to soar. Cost-plus contracts guaranteed profits by eliminating competition and risk. "We are all making more money out of this war than the average human being ought to," one steel company official admitted privately. And some of the war gains were spread, for a collaborative effort entailed keeping workers productive and content. Taking a position unprecedented in the U.S. government, the War Labor Board promoted an 8-hour workday and the right of workers to form unions. But even as the economy bustled, social unity proved elusive, especially when word of American casualties arrived from Europe.

Ensuring Unity

The deaths of U.S. soldiers and sailors made support for the war an emotional issue, and a pattern of repressing dissent took hold that outlasted the war itself. Everything German was particularly suspect. Several states banned teaching the German language (Nebraska briefly banned teaching any foreign language, even Latin, in a preview of the 1980s "English only" campaign). Sauerkraut became "liberty cabbage," frankfurters became hot dogs, and many German Americans anglicized their names. Temperance reformers cited German beer drinking in their successful campaign for a constitutional prohibition of alcohol production. Congress approved the controversial Eighteenth Amendment in December 1917 as a way to save grain for the war effort, and the states ratified it in 1919. Anti-German sentiment led to sometimes deadly violence against Americans of German descent by the summer of 1918. Congress passed sharply restrictive immigration legislation in 1917 as anti-German feelings fed broader prewar fears of new immigrants.

Library of Congress

■ Once the United States joined the Entente side in World War I, dissent against the war became associated for many Americans, including this cartoonist, with aiding the enemy: Germany. Here the antiwar Industrial Workers of the World (IWW) are depicted as allies of the German Kaiser. The IWW's radical politics and fervent opposition to colonialism, capitalism, and monarchy—all features of the German state—made this a particularly ironic portrayal.

A wave of discontent among working Americans redoubled anxieties about national unity. The draft and reduced immigration thinned the ranks of labor as the war created a greater need for workers. For the first time in memory laborers could choose between jobs, and corporations were dismayed by rising employee turnover rates. Workers worried about inflation, which doubled between 1914 and 1920. Seeking better wages and more control over the workplace, they joined unions and went out on 6000 strikes during the year and a half in which the United States was in the war. Working-class women and men identified their cause with the war for democracy abroad by calling for the "de-Kaisering of industry" at home.

Industrialists saw the strikers differently. "All they seem to think of is money," one complained, mirroring what workers often said of employers. Anti-unionists tried to tar all of organized labor with the brush of disloyalty. The government passed the Espionage Act (1917) and Sedition Act (1918) to ban written and verbal organizing against the war. Socialists who encouraged draft resistance, such as Eugene Debs and Wisconsin Congressman Victor Berger, went to prison. The Supreme Court in *Schenck v. United States* (1919) upheld restrictions on free speech in the case of a "clear and present danger" to the nation's security. The Justice Department worked closely with private "patriotic" organizations such as the National Security League, which helped spy on potential dissidents.

Hostility to unions mixed with fervent prowar sentiment to produce a devastating campaign against labor activists in the West. Along the Rocky Mountains from Montana to the Mexican border, striking copper miners under IWW leadership found federal, state, and local police forces as well as vigilantes lined up against them. Sheriff Harry Wheeler of Bisbee, Arizona, arrested more than a thousand strikers, many of them Mexican Americans suspected of sympathies with Pancho Villa. Wheeler, a former Rough Rider with Theodore Roosevelt in Cuba, locked the strikers into boxcars in the July heat of 1917 and towed them into the southern New Mexico desert before releasing them. Federal agents eviscerated the antiwar IWW by raiding its offices two months later and putting 166 of its leaders on trial. A visiting British coal-mining executive found "hostility to a quite unbelievable extent against organized labor."

Most African Americans agreed with W. E. B. Du Bois's call to "close our ranks shoulder to shoulder" with white fellow citizens in support of the war effort, despite escalating antiblack violence. The arrival of 300,000 to 500,000 black Southerners in northern cities increased competition for jobs and housing, causing resentment among many whites. Employers contributed to tensions by recruiting African Americans as strikebreakers and pitting them against white workers. Whites rioted in East St. Louis on July 1, 1917, causing at least 47 fatalities, most of them black. Black soldiers from the North rebelled against the Jim Crow restrictions they found on southern military bases. On August 23, 1917, African American troops from Camp Logan near Houston intervened to protect a black woman being beaten by police on a downtown street. The resulting gunfire killed 16 whites and 4 African Americans. Swift Army court-martials resulted in executions of 19 of the black soldiers and life imprisonment of 63 others.

The War in Europe

When the United States entered the war in Europe in 1917, crisis gripped the Entente. In the east, much of the war effort collapsed in the confusion of Russia's revolution against the Czar. In the west, 49 divisions of the French army mutinied, refusing orders to make further suicidal advances. And in the South, at Caporetto, Austro-Hungarian forces inflicted a disastrous defeat on the Italian army. It was not clear whether the Americans had joined soon enough to stave off Allied defeat.

No battle-ready American army waited at ports for immediate shipment to the trenches of northern France. U.S. commanders instead had to conscript and train nearly 5 million young men for an American Expeditionary Force (AEF) under General Pershing, and 16,000 young women volunteered for service overseas as nurses and Red Cross workers. U.S. troops participated in their first offensive operations in February 1918, although the veteran French and British lines had to stand largely on their own against the final German spring offensive. American soldiers later engaged in fierce combat at Belleau Wood, Château-Thierry, and St. Mihiel, ultimately losing 114,000 men. As the only army growing stronger in 1918, the AEF contributed crucially to the fall offensive that convinced Germany to surrender on November 11.

Fighting with French and British allies gave many American GIs an appreciation for Europeans that balanced the anti-immigrant sentiments common back home. White U.S. soldiers also bonded with each other across ethnic and religious lines while engaged in the supremely dangerous task of deadly combat. One young captain from Missouri, Harry Truman, returned from the war with a stronger appreciation for Europe that would help alter America's role in the world when he became president in 1945. Truman wrote home to his fiancée, Bess Wallace, from Nice on the south coast of France, "There is no blue like the Mediterranean blue." Almost 400,000 African American soldiers served with particular determination to prove their loyalty and courage, despite being segregated and given the hardest and least inspiring work. The French, delighted to have all who would help defend them, treated black GIs with a respect they had rarely known from whites in America. When acceptance led to growing pride among black troops abroad, U.S. commanders reacted with consternation. "It has gone to their heads," President Wilson worried.

Events in Russia provoked the greatest long-term concerns. On April 8, 1917, just two years after the United States entered the war, Vladimir Lenin and 32 fellow Bolshevik refugees from Czarism left their asylum in Zurich, Switzerland, on a train ride into history. They arrived in the Russian capital of St. Petersburg and in October seized control of the government, building a dictatorship of the Communist party in the name of the working class. The Bolsheviks opposed the Great War, condemning the battle for greater wealth and power as a demonstration of pure greed among rival capitalists. In the Czar's archives, they found and published the secret treaties of the Entente for dividing up their prospective conquests after the war,

■ MAP 20.4
WORLD WAR I IN EUROPE AND THE WESTERN FRONT, 1918 By the time the U.S. troops arrived in force on the western front in northern France, the new Bolshevik (Communist) government of Russia had made peace with the Germans and withdrawn from the war. Germany now faced enemies only on one front—the western front—and moved all its troops there. In this dire situation for the French and British, American soldiers helped fill the gap in 1918.

both in Europe and in the colonies overseas. While Wilson spoke of a war for democracy, the Bolsheviks asked Russians, "Are you willing to fight for this, that the English capitalists should rob Mesopotamia and Palestine?"

The answer, as Wilson feared, was no. In January 1918 the president gave the famous "14 Points" speech to the U.S. Congress, outlining his aims of a postwar world built not on expansion and revenge but on national self-determination, open diplomacy, and freedom of commerce and travel, to be guaranteed by a new League of Nations. He hoped to dissuade the Bolsheviks from making a separate peace with Germany that would allow Germany to move

■ Members of the 369th Infantry Regiment wear the Croix de Guerre (Cross of War) awarded to them for bravery by the French government. Like their white fellow soldiers, African American troops often fought bravely and with distinction on the fields of northern France. But they were segregated and given the hardest, most demeaning work by U.S. commanders, following the same pattern at home in the United States.

The National Archives

all its troops to the western front. But Lenin, facing civil war at home, conceded huge swaths of the old Czarist empire in eastern Europe to the Germans to gain peace with the Brest–Litovsk Treaty of March 3, 1918.

The competing visions of Wilson and Lenin for world order contained the roots of the Cold War that would dominate American life after 1945. They agreed that the old diplomacy of imperialist states competing for pieces of property around the globe would no longer work and that only the creation of democratic states would prevent further wars. But they understood democracy very differently. For Wilson, it meant self-governing nations with capitalist economies and republican political practices (at least in Europe and North America, and eventually elsewhere). For Lenin, it meant workers in every land overthrowing the owners of capital and setting up Soviet governments. Whereas Wilson viewed the world as a collection of nations, Lenin saw it as a battleground between two classes.

The Struggle to Win the Peace

World War I killed more than 16 million people and wrought immeasurable physical, social, and psychological damage. Was it worth it? Citizens of the belligerent nations emerged from 1918 convinced that only a guarantee of a future free of war could legitimate such suffering. Some put their hopes in the radical solution unfolding in Russia. Some in the Allied states believed that severe measures against Germany would ensure peace. Most looked to Woodrow Wilson in the winter and spring of 1919 as the world leader whose vision for a more peaceful, democratic postwar order was "all that had made the war

African American Women in the Great War

Just as black American men served in the American Expeditionary Forces in France in 1917–1918, black American women served in auxiliary organizations such as the Red Cross and the Young Men's and Women's Christian Associations (YMCA and YWCA), which worked to boost the soldiers' morale. They staffed canteens set up to provide social and educational support for American troops as an alternative to entertainments such as prostitution and gambling. Addie W. Hunton and Kathryn M. Johnson felt a particular calling to encourage African American soldiers, who suffered from discrimination and segregation even as they fought for democracy. As devout Christians, the two women believed they must model a life of service and compassion, even in the face of persecution. An account of their time in Europe published soon after they returned to the United States suggests some of the complications of a segregated society sending people abroad.

The National Archives

American women supported the war effort in many ways, including working in munitions factories, buying war bonds, single-parenting while husbands were away in the military, and volunteering as nurses for the armed forces in France. Here, African American women entertain black soldiers with music in a service club in Newark, New Jersey, 1918.

Two Colored Women with the American Expeditionary Forces

The relationship between the colored soldiers, the colored welfare workers, and the French people was most cordial and friendly and grew in sympathy and understanding, as their associations brought about a closer acquaintance. It was rather an unusual as well as a most welcome experience to be able to go into places of public accommodation without having any hesitations or misgivings; to be at liberty to take a seat in a common carrier, without fear of inviting some humiliating experience; to go into a home and receive a greeting that carried with it a hospitality and kindliness of spirit that could not be questioned.

These things were at once noticeable upon the arrival of a stranger within the gates of this sister democracy, and the first ten days in France, though filled with duties and harassed with visits from German bombing planes, were nevertheless a delight, in that they furnished to some of us the first full breath of freedom that had ever come into our limited experience.

The first post of duty assigned to us was Brest. Upon arriving there we received our first experience with American prejudices, which had not only been carried across the seas, but had become a part of such an intricate propaganda, that the relationship between the colored soldier and the French people is more or less a story colored by a continued and subtle effort to inject this same prejudice into the heart of the hitherto unprejudiced Frenchman.

[An order posted by white officer of black battalion read:] "Enlisted men of this organization will not talk to or be in company with any white women, regardless of whether the women solicit their company or not."

[Another order read:] "There are two Y.M.C.A.'s, one near the camp, for white troops, and one in town, for the colored troops. All men will be instructed to patronize their own Y."

. . . Quite a bit of unpleasantness was experienced on the boats coming home . . . . On [one] boat there were nineteen colored welfare workers; all the women were placed on a floor below the white women, and the entire colored party was placed in an obscure, poorly ventilated section of the dining-room, entirely separated from the other workers by a long table of Dutch civilians. The writer immediately protested; the reply was made that the southern white workers on board the ship would be insulted if the colored workers ate in the same section of the dining-room with them, and, at any rate, the colored people did not expect any such treatment as had been given them by the French. ∎

Source: Addie W. Hunton and Kathryn M. Johnson, *Two Colored Women with American Expeditionary Forces* (New York: Brooklyn Eagle Press, 1920), 28–30, 182–183, 186.

tolerable to many of us," as one admirer put it. The president sailed for Europe in January to lead the conference that would shape the peace. Vast crowds greeted him enthusiastically as he toured England, Italy, and France.

Peacemaking and the Versailles Treaty

War and revolution destroyed the four great empires of Russia, Germany, Austria–Hungary, and the Ottomans (based in modern Turkey). Meeting in Paris from January to June 1919, the "Big Three" of Wilson, French President Georges Clemenceau, and British Prime Minister David Lloyd George took on two major tasks to shape the postwar order. (The Italian prime minister left the conference after failing to get the new territories he had sought.) First, the three leaders redrew the map of eastern and central Europe to create nation-states out of the vanished empires. Second, they had to decide what to do about a defeated Germany. The possible spread of revolution gave the negotiations a particular urgency. Anticolonial revolts broke out in India and China, and pro-Soviet workers' councils seized power briefly in Hungary and southern Germany. "We are running a race with Bolshevism," Wilson warned, "and the world is on fire."

To put out the fire, the Big Three created a string of new nations running from Finland in the north to Yugoslavia in the south. Eastern Europeans were to be self-governing within the new political boundaries. Ultimately, some of the new states—Czechoslovakia and especially Yugoslavia—lacked the sense of nationhood necessary for success and broke apart into smaller ethnic components in the 1990s. But a major purpose of these new nations for the negotiators in Paris was to establish an anticommunist belt keeping Russian communism out of Europe while satisfying their residents' desire for greater self-determination.

How far would "self-determination" go? Secretary of State Lansing worried that the president's language of democracy was "loaded with dynamite." The world's nonwhite majority wondered whether it applied to them. "Security of Life for Poles and Serbs—Why Not for Colored Nations?" asked one black newspaper in New York. A young nationalist from Vietnam named Ho Chi Minh tried but failed to get an audience with Wilson to ask for the 14 Points to apply to his French-ruled country; a generation later, Ho led the Vietnamese people's armed struggle against France and then the United States. The Big Three instead created the mandate system to provide for eventual self-determination for colonies after a period of tutelage under an established power, and they rejected Japan's proposal to include racial equality as a principle of the new League of Nations.

The German question predominated at the Paris conference. To create a long-term peaceful order in Europe, Wilson wanted lenient terms for Germany. But the French and British had lost much more in the war than the Americans, and they believed Germany must pay for that. French security seemed to depend on keeping its powerful and aggressive neighbor down. The Versailles Treaty (named for the famous estate of King Louis XIV outside Paris, where it was signed) reflected compromises that gave each of the Allies what it most wanted. To satisfy France and England, Germany had to admit guilt for causing the war and pay $33 billion in reparations, while losing much of its eastern territory to the new Polish and Czechoslovakian states. For Wilson the League of Nations was the key: this new and unprecedented global organization would keep the peace by ensuring collective security for all nations. Disputes between nations would be mediated before they escalated to armed conflict, and potential aggressors would be deterred by the promise of collective action in defense of any threatened league member.

The absence of certain crucial players from the Paris negotiations undermined the resulting international order. The Soviets and the Germans did not participate. Wilson took in his entourage no representatives of the Republican party. This proved important, for Republicans had won the congressional elections two months earlier, giving them control of the process for ratifying any treaties. Most Republicans objected on principle to one key aspect of the Versailles Treaty: Article 10 of the League of Nations charter, guaranteeing ahead of time a collective response to defend any member's territory from attack. Treaty opponents were deter-

Changes in European
boundaries after World War I

- Areas lost by Russian Empire
- Areas lost by Austro-Hungarian Empire
- Areas lost by German Empire
- Areas lost by Bulgaria

Names of the newly independent nations created
at the Versailles Conference of 1919 are in bold

■ **MAP 20.5**
EUROPE AFTER WORLD WAR I The outcome of World War I led to
significant changes in the boundaries of Europe, particularly its eastern
parts. Four great empires in the region—Russia, Germany, Austria-Hungary, and the
Ottomans—collapsed. Negotiations at Versailles created a band of new
nations, providing both self-determination and a bulwark against Russian communism.

mined to preserve complete American autonomy, including freedom of action in Latin America. Henry Cabot Lodge, Jr., of Massachusetts, the powerful Republican chair of the Senate Foreign Relations Committee, organized the two Senate votes rejecting American membership in the league. Hoping to stave off defeat for his idealistic plan, Wilson undertook an ill-advised national speaking tour to promote the League. His strenuous effort failed to win American participation in the league, and it ultimately broke his fragile health. Wilson suffered a stroke on October 2, 1919, that left him incapacitated for the rest of his presidency.

The League of Nations and International Security

The experience of World War I stunned Europeans and Americans. Never before had an armed conflict killed and wounded so many people in so brief a time. Observers from outside the Central Powers, like most historians since, placed primary responsibility for the onset of the war on the aggressive actions of German Kaiser Wilhelm II. Other critics noted the expansive empires of every member of the Entente and wondered whether more than just German imperialism was troubling the international system. The sheer scale of the carnage, especially the continuing slaughter of soldiers in indecisive battles on the almost immovable western front for four long years, suggested that something deeper might be wrong with the way nations waged both diplomacy and war.

The intensifying rivalry of the European nations after 1910 created the conditions for the Great War. In the international arena few rules guided how powerful nations behaved, in contrast to the domestic sphere of any particular nation, which had clear guidelines for how its citizens could act. A handful of international conventions created some general expectations for "civilized" actions in peace and war, but no form of effective enforcement backed these up. When a rising power such as Germany (unified in 1871)

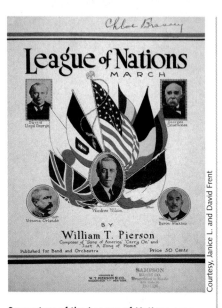

Supporters of the League of Nations even wrote popular sheet music in its honor.

Courtesy, Janice L. and David Frent

chose to upset the existing balance of power between nations, the only recourse available was on the battlefield. The new tools of warfare on display in World War I—machine guns, poison gas, submarines, airplanes—made this a grim prospect.

Woodrow Wilson's original vision for the League of Nations was a bold effort to come to terms with this challenge. Rejecting the amoral old diplomacy of nations strengthening themselves at the cost of weakening others, Wilson called for a new diplomacy of collective security. All nations would agree to protect each other and the status quo, deterring potential aggressors by promising to come to the defense of any nation under attack. Without arms races to destabilize the international order, militarism would subside. The U.S. failure to join the League of Nations undermined its effectiveness, however, as did the competing desire of national leaders to pre-

serve maximum autonomy for pursuing their nations' own interests.

World War II seemed to prove Wilson correct. His vision of substituting collective internationalism for competitive nationalism helped shape the United Nations (UN) in 1945, especially its General Assembly of all nations. However, the UN's powerful Security Council with its five permanent members (Britain, France, Russia, China, and the United States) who each retained the right to veto any action by the organization, limited the degree of collective security that members could depend on. The Cold War (1946–1989) also reduced the UN's effectiveness by dividing the world into two competing collective security systems, one headed by the Soviet Union (Russia) and one by the United States.

In the 1990s the UN gained renewed prominence, first in the international coalition fighting against Iraq in the 1991 Gulf War and subsequently as the source of mediation efforts and peacekeeping forces for civil conflicts around the globe. The growing seriousness of problems that were unarguably international in nature, such as global warming and the proliferation of nuclear weapons, provided a potent argument in favor of collective action. Americans nonetheless remained ambivalent about the UN at the start of the new millennium. As the world's most powerful nation in military and economic terms, the United States expected to lead the UN. But U.S. leaders did not like to be hemmed in by its collective decision-making process. Unilateral freedom of action in the international sphere, like that suggested two centuries earlier by George Washington's warning to avoid "entangling alliances," continued to appeal to many citizens. ∎

Waging Counterrevolution Abroad

Soon after Russia withdrew from the war, the western members of the Entente intervened in the civil war there between the Bolsheviks (the "Reds") and the various counterrevolutionary forces (the "Whites"). The initial military rationale in the summer of 1918 was to reopen the eastern front against Germany. The United States landed 7000 troops in Vladivostock, on Russia's far Pacific coast, to help rescue a large group of former Czech prisoners of war from the Austro-Hungarian army who now wanted to join the Allied side and to deter Japanese expansion into Siberia. In conjunction with the British, 5000 U.S. soldiers went ashore at Archangel in northern Russia to prevent Allied supplies from falling into German hands. They quickly became involved in fighting the Red Army. The Wilson administration meanwhile funneled money and military intelligence to leaders of the White forces.

The Bolsheviks rejected certain values cherished by most Americans: the sanctity of private property and contracts, political liberty, and religious freedom. They liberalized divorce laws and legalized abortion, challenging conservative American attitudes about the relationships between women and men. And they established the Comintern in 1919 to promote similar revolutions around the world. Allied intervention in the Russian civil war failed to overthrow Lenin's government, and American troops pulled out in 1920. They left behind a powerful legacy of anti-American sentiment in Russia, exacerbated by Washington's refusal for the next 13 years to recognize the Soviet government.

Anticommunists used the metaphor of infection to describe Bolshevism. The Kaiser, they said, had allowed Lenin to pass through Germany on a "sealed train," lest the bacillus of revolution leak out and spread through the German population. This image had unusual power in 1918–1919 because of the spread of one of the twentieth century's worst killers. The "Spanish influenza" (named for one of its early victims, the King of Spain) hit the United States much harder than the Great War had, killing six times as many people (675,000). In an era before effective vaccines and antibiotic drugs, little could be done for the 20 million Americans stricken besides comforting them, so nurses were in much greater demand than doctors. Not until the longer-lasting AIDS crisis after 1980 did Americans again live in such fear of a disease.

From Art of the October Revolution, Leningrad, Aurora Art Publishers, 1979

■ **"Comrade Lenin Sweeps the Globe Clean."** This Bolshevik (Communist) drawing shows Vladimir I. Lenin (1870–1924), the leader of the Russian revolution and founder of the world's first Communist government, ridding the world of capitalists and monarchs. But Lenin also sought western trade and investment, especially from the United States, as a stimulus to reconstructing the devastated postwar economy of the new Union of Soviet Socialist Republics (USSR).

The Red and Black Scares at Home

Four million American workers, one out of every five, went out on strike in 1919—the highest proportion of the workforce ever. They sought improved wages and working conditions as well as recognition of the right to collective bargaining. The scale of industrial unrest provoked fears of a Soviet-style revolution. In Seattle a walkout by shipyard workers mushroomed into a general strike that shut down most of the city for a week. In Pittsburgh, the AFL led a bitter strike against U.S. Steel in pursuit of union recognition. The United Mine Workers led walkouts by hundreds of thousands of coal miners, which evolved into open warfare between miners and coal companies in West Virginia over the next two years. In Boston three quarters of the police force went on strike to protest wages lower than those of common laborers. Traditional May 1 (May Day) parades celebrating the dignity of labor featured violent clashes between socialist marchers and heckling veterans in Cleveland, New York, and other cities. Between April and June, anarchists mailed or delivered bombs to 36 prominent public figures, including Attorney General A. Mitchell Palmer. All were defused except two, one wounding the wife and maid of a U.S. senator from Georgia, the other destroying the front of Palmer's house and dismembering its anarchist deliverer.

Whereas many Americans sympathized with struggles for unionization, others viewed them as dangerous to private property and social order. They associated strikes with radical immigrants and anarchists and considered them "un-American." "Unionism is nothing less than bolshevism," declared the National Association of Manufacturers. The "Red Scare" of 1919 associated reform and social justice of any kind with subversion. To break strikes, employers hired private armies from "detective" agencies such as the Pinkertons and the Baldwin–Felts, often staffed by World War I veterans. Private organizations promoting "100 percent Americanism," such as the Ku Klux Klan and the new American Legion, monitored and harassed potential subversives and the foreign-born. Attorney General Palmer directed the deportation to Russia of 249 foreign-born radicals aboard the *Buford* in December 1919, including anarchist and feminist Emma Goldman. "Palmer raids" led to the arrest of thousands more within a month. U.S. Army troops and state militias brought the ultimate force to bear against union organizers, as at the Battle of Blair Mountain on August 31, 1921, against several thousand striking West Virginia miners.

Violence against workers extended to African Americans after World War I. An upsurge in lynching included at least ten black veterans still in uniform and was not limited to the South. In Nebraska white residents of Omaha butchered William Brown with such frenzy that thousands of federal troops had to be called in to restore calm. White mobs burned entire black communities to the ground, including Tulsa's Greenwood neighborhood (1921) and the all-black town of Rosewood, Florida (1923). The Red Scare and the "Black Scare" merged in Phillips County, Arkansas, where black sharecroppers, many of them veterans, formed a union in 1919 to pursue equitable crop settlements from landlords. Fearing insurrection, local white leaders used 2500 federal troops and white vigilantes to massacre more than 200 sharecroppers. But any inclination toward deference in the face of brutality was gone, and African Americans fought back fiercely against white marauders in deadly riots in Washington and Chicago in the summer of 1919. One black woman recalled hearing news that in Washington "our men had stood like men" and crying for joy: "Oh, I thank God, thank God!"

Where was the president during this turmoil? Incapacitated by his stroke, he lay resting in his bed in Washington, the administration managed largely by his wife, Edith, and his secretary, Joseph Tumulty. In any case, Wilson's segregationist policies suggested that he would have been unlikely to provide effective leadership in bridging the nation's racial divides. The only Republican of similar stature, Theodore Roosevelt, had died a few months earlier. "There is no leadership worthy of the name," a veteran reporter lamented. Wilson's breakdown came in the middle of the 1919 baseball World Series, which the heavily favored but poorly paid Chicago White Sox intentionally lost to the Cincinnati Reds, in arrangement with gamblers. Eight "Black Sox" were banned from the sport. With its president out of action and its national pastime corrupted, the nation seemed adrift as the lights dimmed on the Progressive era.

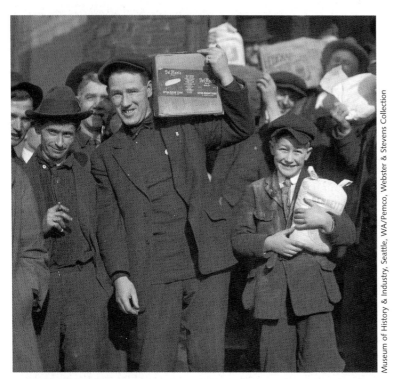

Museum of History & Industry, Seattle, WA/Pemco, Webster & Stevens Collection

■ The Seattle General Strike Committee took on the responsibility of keeping essential services running in the city. Here its members issue groceries to union families, January 1919. The cooperation necessary among organized workers to keep a strike going offered a different model of community interaction than did the individualism often touted by wealthier Americans.

Bettmann/CORBIS

■ **Death by hanging or burning, often preceded by torture, at the hands of a white mob constituted one end of a range of tactics of intimidation and coercion used against black Southerners in the early twentieth century. Outnumbered and outgunned, African Americans fought back fiercely when they could. Lynchings sometimes had a festive air for the white participants, with children often present.**

Conclusion

How much success could a varied generation of Progressive reformers claim? Women had won the vote with the Nineteenth Amendment, in an expansion of democracy second only to the combination of the Emancipation Proclamation of 1863 and the Fifteenth Amendment, outlawing slavery. African Americans who moved north usually could vote as well, unlike those who stayed in Dixie. On either side of the Mason–Dixon line, however, daily life for Americans of darker hue entailed picking one's way through a maze of discrimination. Most union campaigns stalled by 1920, beaten back by the physical force and cleverness of corporate employers and their government sympathizers. When the Red Scare dissipated, Americans did not return to the reform spirit of Progressivism. Many turned away from politics. Voter turnout in 1920 dipped below 50 percent for the first time in a century. Those who did vote that year gave the Republican party a sweeping victory. Promising "not revolution, but restoration," Ohio Senator Warren G. Harding took the White House. His speeches may have been, as one rival said, "an army of pompous phrases moving over the landscape in search of an idea," but most of the nation sought calm after the upheavals of the previous decade.

American contributions to democracy abroad were similarly ambivalent. Whereas eastern Europeans named streets in their newly independent nations for President Wilson, few Latin Americans believed that U.S. invasions of Caribbean and Central American countries promoted self-government. Russians admired much about American society and the U.S. economy while resenting American troops in their land. Above all hung the problem of Germany, still the most powerful single nation in Europe. The Versailles Treaty imposed harsh terms and embittered a generation of German people. "If I were a German, I think I should not sign it," Wilson admitted privately. The Weimar Republic that replaced the abdicated German Kaiser lasted through the 1920s. But the storms of the Great Depression swamped Germany's republican experiment and gave rise to Adolph Hitler.

Sites to Visit

The Great War, 1914–1918
www.pitt.edu/~pugachev/greatwar/ww1.html

This site offers an array of narratives, photos, documents, statistics, maps, and bibliography, plus links to other useful World War I sites.

Women and Social Movements in the United States, 1775–1940
womhist.binghamton.edu

Maintained by two Binghamton University historians, this site has a rich trove of documents on the history of American women as well as excellent links to others.

The Avalon Project at the Yale Law School: Documents in Law, History, and Diplomacy
www.yale.edu/lawweb/avalon/avalon.htm

Researchers can find here the texts of a large number of the most important primary documents illuminating U.S. relations with other countries, including materials on American responses to the Bolshevik revolution in Russia.

Temperance and Prohibition
prohibition.history.ohio-state.edu/Contents.htm

Cartoons, newspaper articles, and other primary documents available here illuminate in fascinating ways the struggle over whether to prohibit the sale of alcoholic beverages.

The Emma Goldman Papers
sunsite.berkeley.edu/Goldman/

This site has photos and excerpts from the writings and speeches of one of America's most influential radicals and feminists from this era.

Divining America: Religion and the National Culture
scriptorium.lib.duke.edu/wlm/

This site has essays by prominent historians on diverse aspects of the religious history of the United States.

Up South: African-American Migration in the Era of the Great War
www.ashp.cuny.edu/video/south.html

Maintained by the American Social History Project at the Graduate Center of the City University of New York, this site offers details of the mass migration of rural black Southerners to the urban north during World War I.

The Influenza Pandemic of 1918
www.stanford.edu/group/virus/uda/

A variety of information, documents, and photos of the deadly global outbreak of the "Spanish flu" can be found here.

For Further Reading

General

Kendrick A. Clements, *Woodrow Wilson: World Statesman* (1987).

John M. Cooper, *Pivotal Decades: The United States, 1900–1920* (1990).

Alan Dawley, *Struggles for Justice: Social Responsibility and the Liberal State* (1991).

Nell Irvin Painter, *Standing at Armageddon: The United States, 1877–1919* (1987).

Daniel T. Rodgers, *Atlantic Crossings: Social Politics in a Progressive Age* (1998).

A World in Upheaval

Friedrich Katz, *The Secret War in Mexico: Europe, the United States, and the Mexican Revolution* (1981).

Paul Kennedy, *The Rise and Fall of the Great Powers: Economic Change and Military Conflict from 1500 to 2000* (1987).

Arthur Link, ed., *Woodrow Wilson and a Revolutionary World* (1982).

Joseph A. McCartin, *Labor's Great War: The Struggle for Industrial Democracy and the Origins of Modern American Labor Relations, 1912–1921* (1997).

George J. Sánchez, *Becoming Mexican American: Ethnicity, Culture, and Identity in Chicano Los Angeles, 1900–1945* (1993).

The Great War and American Neutrality

John W. Coogan, *The End of Neutrality: The United States, Britain, and Maritime Rights, 1899–1915* (1981).

Steven J. Diner, *A Very Different Age: Americans of the Progressive Era* (1998).

James Grossman, *Land of Hope: Chicago, Black Southerners, and the Great Migration* (1989).

Vicki I. Ruiz, *From Out of the Shadows: Mexican Women in Twentieth-Century America* (1998).

Martin Sklar, *The Corporate Reconstruction of American Capitalism, 1890–1916: The Market, the Law, and Politics* (1988).

The United States Goes to War

Edward M. Coffman, *The War to End All Wars: The American Military Experience in World War I* (1987).

Martin Gilbert, *The First World War: A Complete History* (1994).

David M. Kennedy, *Over Here: The First World War and American Society* (1980).

Kathleen Kennedy, *Disloyal Mothers and Scurrilous Citizens: Women and Subversion During World War I* (1999).

Richard Polenberg, *Fighting Faiths: The Abrams Case, the Supreme Court, and Free Speech* (1987).

Nick Salvatore, *Eugene V. Debs: Citizen and Socialist* (1982).

The Struggle to Win the Peace

Alfred W. Crosby, *America's Forgotten Pandemic: The Influenza of 1918* (1989).

Scott Ellsworth, *Death in a Promised Land: The Tulsa Race Riot of 1921* (1982).

David S. Foglesong, *America's Secret War Against Bolshevism: U.S. Intervention in the Russian Civil War, 1917–1920* (1995).

Thomas J. Knock, *To End All Wars: Woodrow Wilson and the Quest for a New World Order* (1992).

Gordon N. Levin, Jr., *Woodrow Wilson and World Politics: America's Response to War and Revolution* (1968).

William M. Tuttle, Jr., *Race Riot: Chicago in the Red Summer of 1919* (1970).

Betty M. Unterberger, *The United States, Revolutionary Russia, and the Rise of Czechoslovakia* (1989).

Online Practice Test

Test your understanding of this chapter with interactive review quizzes at

www.ablongman.com/jonescreatedequal/chapter20

The Promise of Consumer Culture: The 1920s

Florine Stettheimer, *Portrait of My Sister Ettie*, 1923. Columbia University in the City of New York, Gift of the Estate of Ettie Stettheimer, 1967 (Neg. #57675)

■ Florine Stettheimer's *Portrait of Ettie* (1923) conveys the glamour and sensuality of the 1920s "flapper."

IN THE SUPERIOR COURT OF LOS ANGELES IN 1920, LORIMER LINGANFIELD, A RESPECTABLE barber, filed for divorce. Although his wife, Marsha, held him in "high regard and esteem as her husband," there were "evidences of indiscretion" in her conduct. She wore a new bathing suit, "designed especially for the purpose of exhibiting to the public the shape and form of her body." To his further humiliation, she was "beset with a desire to sing and dance at cafes and restaurants for the entertainment of the public." When Lorimer complained about her "appetite for beer and whisky" and extravagant tastes for luxury, she replied that he was "not the only pebble on the beach, she had a millionaire 'guy' who would buy her all the clothes, automobiles, diamonds and booze that she wanted." But the ultimate insult was her refusal to have any sexual intercourse, claiming that she did not want any "dirty little brats around her." The judge was sympathetic, and Lorimer Linganfield won his suit.

The Linganfields's difficulties represent a larger struggle as Americans shifted their sensibilities from the producer economy of the nineteenth century, complete with clearly defined gender roles and sexual mores, to the consumer ethic of the twentieth century with its new amusements, changing sexual behavior, and flamboyant "new women." Marsha Linganfield was a "flapper," one of the young women of the 1910s and 1920s who broke from time-honored conventions. With short, "bobbed" hair, knee-length dresses, and boyish styles unencumbered by layers of petticoats, flappers flirted, petted, and danced "wild" dances like the Charleston, an African American dance brought north from South Carolina juke joints. Flappers blurred the line between "good girls" and "bad girls" that had previously defined proper female behavior.

Marsha was fond of fancy clothes and night life. Lorimer undoubtedly was attracted to the lively young flapper whom he wooed and wed. He was surely anticipating conjugal bliss, as experts at the time approved of female sexual pleasure in marriage. New patterns of courtship allowed couples some intimacy now that chaperones were no longer required when a man "came calling." The widespread availability of automobiles offered increased mobility and privacy. So Marsha's sexual refusal, as well as her scandalous rejection of motherhood, must have been intolerable for Lorimer. The "new woman" of the age was allowed more leeway in her dress, demeanor, and behavior, but she was still expected to be virginal at marriage and eager for marital sex and motherhood.

The Linganfields met and married in Los Angeles, home of Hollywood, the beacon of the new culture. The most successful film director of the era, Cecil B. DeMille, made several films in which modern couples seek the right balance between fun and virtue in marriage. The popular DeMille formula offered a blueprint for couples like the

Gertrude Ederle swims the English Channel.

Linganfields. In the typical DeMille plot, either the husband or the wife becomes bored with a spouse who, unable to shed drab old-fashioned virtue, refuses to take part in the leisure-oriented, sexually charged life of the 1920s.

In *Why Change Your Wife* (1920), for example, the heroine loses her husband by refusing to go dancing with him or to wear the sexy lingerie he buys for her. He abandons his wife for a fun-loving flapper, but he leaves the new flame when he finds that she wants only his money and has no interest in settling down to family life. By this time his ex-wife has discovered the error of her ways and transformed herself into an alluring "new woman." The former husband finds her at a beach resort, wearing a revealing swimsuit and surrounded by admiring men. The two renew their love and settle again into marriage, now combining the virtues of domestic life with the excitement of modern consumer culture and sexuality. The final caption of the film warns, "Ladies, if you want to be your husband's sweetheart, you must simply forget [that] you are his wife."

> *The great heroes of the 1920s were celebrities admired for their individual achievements in sports and adventure.*

New forms of popular entertainment that developed in the 1920s, especially Hollywood movies and jazz music, became defining features of the nation itself. The popular arts offered Jews and blacks a space for innovation. At a time when white, Anglo-Saxon, Protestant men had control of nearly all government and business institutions, Jewish moviemakers and African American musicians were creating the culture that would soon represent the nation. During the years when Congress largely closed off immigration, Jewish immigrants built Hollywood into the most American of all industries. In the midst of the Jim Crow era, African Americans created the music that gave the 1920s its identity as the Jazz Age.

The great heroes of the 1920s were celebrities admired for their individual achievements in sports and adventure. In 1927, the same year that Babe Ruth hit a record 60 home runs, Charles Lindbergh flew his small monoplane, *The Spirit of St. Louis,* nonstop from New York to Paris in 33 1/2 hours, a feat that electrified the world and made him an instant hero. Professional sports came of age in the 1920s, giving rise to new heroes such as baseball's Babe Ruth, football's Red Grange, and boxing's Jack Dempsey. It was also a decade of tremendous visibility in women's sports, with such stars as tennis sensation Helen Wills and swimmer Sybil Bauer. In 1926, 19-year-old Olympic gold medalist Gertrude Ederle became the first woman to swim the English Channel. She broke the world's record with her time of 14 hours and 31 minutes, 2 hours shorter than those of the six men who had preceded her. On her return to the United States 2 million cheering fans lined the streets of New York City to welcome her home. The nation idolized this new generation of heroes, who dominated headlines and drew cheering crowds wherever they went.

The glamorous life, however, was available to few. Often characterized as the "roaring twenties" of giddy prosperity and reckless good times, these were also years of widespread poverty, especially in rural areas and urban ghettos. Much of rural America and an estimated 40 percent of the working class remained mired in poverty, with inadequate food and housing. Few Americans were able to afford the new consumer goods that were being mass-produced and were more widely available. At the end of the decade, fewer than half of all households owned a car or a radio; fewer than one in three owned a washing machine or a vacuum cleaner. Only 1 percent of households earned more than $10,000 per year, and two-thirds lived on an annual income of less than $1999.

Conservative politics at the national level prevailed throughout the decade. Disenchantment after World War I prompted national leaders to emphasize economic ties and foreign trade and to shrink from military entanglements. The politics of the era favored big business, but the disparity between rich and poor left the country vulnerable to the downturn of the economy. Business values of material acquisition spread as the expansion of consumer credit weakened the traditions of saving and frugality. For those with money to invest, Wall Street beckoned. The stock market rose to perilous heights, only to collapse at the end of the decade.

The Decline of Reform

The voices of workers, sharecroppers, and other poor people were muffled in the 1920s, a decade of a booming economy and conservative politics. Reformers who had championed the causes of the marginalized and disadvantaged lost influence. Progressive politics declined precipitously in the wake of World War I. After achieving the vote the women's rights movement splintered as younger women sought new freedoms not through politics but through a social and sexual revolution. Widespread hostility toward immigrants and various ethnic groups were at the root of the outlawing of liquor, new laws restricting immigration, and the rise of the Ku Klux Klan. But progressive political impulses did not entirely disappear, especially among African Americans, who continued to mobilize and organize for civil rights.

Women's Rights in the Aftermath of Suffrage

One indication of the waning of progressive reform was the fragmentation of women's rights activism in the 1920s. The more radical wing of the suffrage movement, the National Women's Party (NWP), under the leadership of Alice Paul, in 1923 launched a campaign for the Equal Rights Amendment (ERA), which was introduced in Congress two decades later with these words: "Equality of rights under the law shall not be denied or abridged by the United States or by any state on account of sex."

The debate over the ERA in the 1920s reflected the fundamental question that would permeate women's rights activism throughout the rest of the twentieth century. On one side were those who believed that women were fundamentally the same as men and deserved equal rights; on the other side were those who argued that women were different and deserved special privileges and protections. Many women's rights activists opposed the ERA because it would undercut efforts to gain special legislative protections for women based on their presumed physical weakness and their potential for childbearing, such as maximum hours, regulations against night work, and limitations on the weights they could lift. These women disapproved of the goals and tactics of the NWP and formed their own nonpartisan organization, the League of Women Voters, which promoted social and political reform.

Legislative gains for women did not entirely disappear in the 1920s. In 1921 Congress passed the Sheppard–Towner bill for maternal and infant health education. The bill provided for public health nurses to educate mothers in prenatal and infant health care to reduce infant mortality. Physicians opposed the legislation because they were consolidating their control over medical practice and did not want nurses functioning as independent health care providers, even though

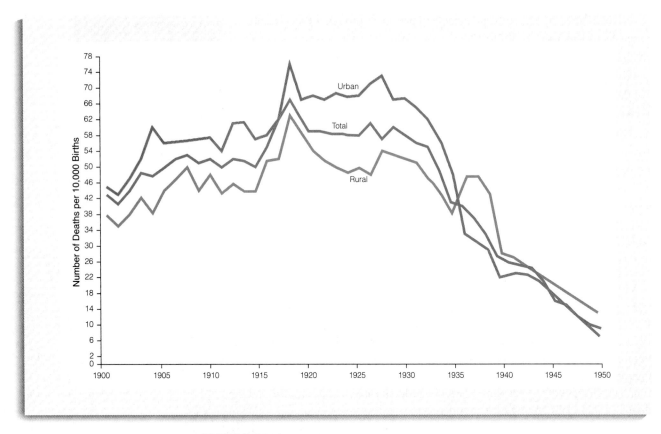

■ FIGURE 21.1
MATERNAL DEATH RATES FROM ALL CHILDBIRTH-RELATED CAUSES, UNITED STATES, 1901–1950
During the early decades of the twentieth century, childbirth increasingly took place in hospitals. But the rate of deaths from childbirth actually increased during those years and did not decline until the 1930s.

the nurses offered only preventive health care and advice. Doctors also worried that government-sponsored programs would compete with their private practices. Nevertheless, Sheppard–Towner remained in force until the end of the decade, when its budget was cut, a casualty of the conservative temperament in Congress that saw such forms of government support as socialistic.

One way in which women continued their political influence was by seeking elective office. In 1922, for example, Adelina Otero Warren ran as a Republican candidate for the U.S. House of Representatives, the first New Mexican woman and the first Hispanic woman to run for national office. During the campaign, a cousin publicly revealed that Warren had lied about her marital status, claiming to be widowed when she was really divorced. That revelation dashed her political ambitions. But neither her divorce nor her effort to pass as a widow was unusual at a time when marital breakdown still carried a heavy negative stigma, especially for women. The divorce rate doubled between 1900 and 1920 and continued to rise throughout the 1920s, in part the result of women's increasing independence. As job opportunities for women increased, more women felt able to abandon unhappy marriages.

Prohibition: The Experiment That Failed

The Eighteenth Amendment, prohibiting the manufacture and sale of alcohol, went into effect in January 1920. Several diverse interests came together to promote the ban on liquor. Temperance crusaders in the Anti-Saloon League and the Women's Christian Temperance Union

The Persistence of the Ku Klux Klan

The Ku Klux Klan promoted itself as a patriotic organization dedicated to preserving American values. The white supremacist hate group first emerged in the South after the Civil War to terrorize the newly freed African Americans, was revived in the North during the 1920s, and continues to this day.

I n the 1920s the Ku Klux Klan became the most powerful white supremacy group in the nation, remaining active throughout the twentieth century. The original Klan emerged during Reconstruction to intimidate the former slaves through terrorism. Klan members used secrecy and violence to maintain white supremacy in the South. Their vigilante activities included threatening cross-burnings, beatings, and lynchings. The original KKK faded in the 1870s. But it revived in the early twentieth century, moving north and targeting not just blacks but other minorities and immigrants. The new KKK was inspired in part by Thomas Dixon's novel, The Clansman, and its film version, D. W. Griffith's The Birth of a Nation, an epic that portrayed the post–Civil War Klan as a hero defending vanquished Southern white womanhood from predatory black men.

The revival remained small until its leaders mounted a recruitment drive. Under the banner of "Americanism," the Klan set itself as a civic group dedicated to uphold the values that Klan members felt were threatened in the nation. Harking back to what they saw as a moral and patriotic tradition, Klan members—farmers, businessmen, and social leaders felt that white, native-born Protestant Americans alone embodied the

evils of modern life, brought on by the influence of morally suspect outsiders.

The women who joined the Klan championed women's rights and worked on behalf of temperance, child welfare measures, public education, good citizenship, morality, and militant Christianity while also supporting white supremacy and initiating whisper campaigns and boycotts against Jewish and Catholic shopkeepers. The Klan used vigilante violence and politically savvy mobilizations to attack African Americans, communists, feminists, Jews, and Catholics who were making economic and social gains in the cities, and divorced or allegedly promiscuous women. The Klan also appealed to voters who were sympathetic to their

views. Growing to 3 million members by the early 1920s, the Klan wielded great power, especially in Texas, Oklahoma, Oregon, and Indiana. Some Klan members continued to engage in vigilante violence, while others held elaborate rallies and parades, burned crosses to intimidate and threaten their foes, and endorsed political candidates. Klan efforts in Oregon persuaded the state's lawmakers to pass a compulsory public schooling bill in 1922 that would have closed private and parochial schools, but the U.S. Supreme Court overturned the law. The Klan-controlled legislature in Oklahoma impeached and removed an anti-Klan governor.

The Klan dwindled and finally disbanded in 1944. But a new Klan emerged barely two years later, once again centered in the South, in reaction to the civil rights movement taking shape after World War II. The membership of this third Klan peaked in the 1960s with about 17,000 members. The Klan's efforts largely backfired as their actions repulsed most white Americans and helped gain support for the civil rights movement. The Klan declined after the 1960s but did not disappear, often joining forces with other white supremacy groups, such as the Aryan Nations and the Skinheads. In 1991 former Klan leader and Nazi sympathizer David Duke ran for governor of Louisiana and garnered 39 percent of the votes. He won 55 percent of the white vote, but Louisiana's African American voters defeated him. At the end of the twentieth century, the Klan still had influence in some localities— running candidates for office, holding rallies and parades, and seeking legitimacy through civic volunteer projects. ■

Courtesy, Janice L. and David Frent

had argued since the late nineteenth century that women and children suffered when men spent their paychecks at the saloon and returned home drunk and violent. World War I prompted others to support a ban on the manufacture of liquor to save grain for the war effort. Anti-immigrant "drys" had political motives for promoting prohibition. They hoped to undercut the power bases of immigrant and ethnic politicians who used local saloons to forge their constituencies and political machines. The "wets" included alienated intellectuals, Jazz Age rebels, and many city dwellers whose social lives revolved around neighborhood pubs, especially in Irish and German communities.

Enforcement was impossible. The 1919 Volstead Act established a Prohibition Bureau within the Treasury Department to allocate funds for enforcement, but budget cuts weakened its effectiveness. Federal agents had responsibility for enforcing the law, but their numbers were inadequate. In order to be effective, federal agents had to work closely with local law enforcement officials. In some urban areas, local officials refused to cooperate with federal agents. New York repealed its prohibition enforcement law in 1923, leaving a small number of federal agents with the daunting task of shutting down illegal clubs where liquor was sold, known as "speakeasies." In sporadic raids, the beleaguered agents closed down some of the speakeasies, only to have them pop up again in new locations. Americans who wanted to drink liquor found many ways to acquire it. Illegal speakeasies abounded where customers could buy drinks delivered by rumrunners who smuggled in liquor from Canada, Mexico, and the West Indies. Many people concocted their own "bathtub gin" or "moonshine whiskey," homemade brews using readily available ingredients and household equipment.

Prohibition was intended to cure society's ills. Instead, it provided vast opportunities for crime and profit, both among criminals and law enforcement agents. Nightclubs and restaurants with an urban middle-class clientele found it difficult to make a profit when they could no longer serve liquor. Many went out of business, opening the way for gangsters and petty criminals to cater to the nightlife crowd. Organized crime received a major boost when violence erupted in the scramble to profit from illegal liquor. Chicago witnessed 550 gangland killings in the 1920s, with few arrests or convictions. Police looked the other way when rival gangs engaged in bloody wars to control the city's liquor business. By 1929 Chicago mob king Al Capone controlled a massive network of speakeasies that raked in $60 million annually.

Those charged with upholding the law often benefited from the illegal trade themselves. Authorities in St. Paul, Minnesota, for example, struck a bargain with gangsters who smuggled in liquor from Canada through the poorly patrolled wilderness in northern Minnesota. After paying a bribe to the local police, the smugglers hid their stash in St. Paul's chalk caves along the banks of the Mississippi River until they were able to transport it down the river.

Prohibition failed to live up to its promise. Within a year of the passage of the amendment, alcohol consumption declined by two thirds. But by 1929 the consumption of alcohol had climbed back up to 70 percent of its pre-Prohibition level. Expenditures for alcoholic beverages actually increased by 50 percent during the Prohibition era, no doubt due in part to higher black-market prices.

■ Speakeasy hostess Mary Louise Guinan appears unrepentant as she is arrested for selling alcohol during the Prohibition era. Law enforcement was futile because speakeasies that were raided and closed simply reopened in new locations.

Bettmann/CORBIS

Nicola Sacco and Bartolomeo Vanzetti, Italian aliens and self-proclaimed anarchists, were accused of murder in May 1920. The men and their supporters claimed they were on trial not for the crime but for their political beliefs and their immigrant status. After all appeals failed, the two were executed in 1927.

Bettmann/CORBIS

■ **FIGURE 21.2**
NUMBER OF IMMIGRANTS AND COUNTRIES OF ORIGIN, 1891–1920 AND 1921–1940   Before the immigration restriction laws passed in the 1920s, most immigrants came from Russia and southern and eastern Europe. After immigration restriction, most came from Western Europe and Canada.

Reactionary Impulses

The Red Scare after World War I (see Chapter 20) inaugurated a decade of hostility to political radicals and foreigners. Shoemaker Nicola Sacco and fish peddler Bartolomeo Vanzetti were both: Italian aliens and self-proclaimed anarchists. In May 1920 the paymaster and guard of a South Braintree, Massachusetts, shoe company was robbed and murdered, and Sacco and Vanzetti were arrested and charged with the crime. Sacco testified that he was in Boston at the time, applying for a passport, and his alibi was corroborated. Both men proclaimed their innocence and insisted that they were on trial for their political beliefs rather than the crime itself. Their Italian accents and advocacy of anarchism in the courtroom did not help their case with many Americans suspicious of foreign radicals, including the judge presiding at their trial. Despite a weak case against them, Sacco and Vanzetti were convicted of first-degree murder and sentenced to death.

Lawyers for the two anarchists appealed the case several times to no avail. The convictions sparked outrage among Italian Americans, political radicals, labor activists, and liberal intellectuals who believed the two men were falsely convicted. The case soon generated mass demonstrations, appeals for clemency, and petitions from around the world. In response the governor of Massachusetts appointed a commission to review the case, but the commission concluded that there were no grounds for a new trial. Finally, on August 23, 1927, Sacco and Vanzetti were executed by electric chair at Charlestown State Prison.

The case of Sacco and Vanzetti underscored the anti-immigrant sentiment that prevailed in the 1920s. Although efforts to curtail immigration since the late nineteenth century had resulted in numerous fed-

eral laws, none were as harsh as those passed in the 1920s, which cut the flow of immigrants down to a tiny trickle. The 1921 immigration restriction act set a limit on the number of European immigrants allowed into the United States. The numbers of immigrants permitted to enter was limited to a percentage of immigrants from each country who lived in the United States in 1910. In that year large numbers of immigrants from southern and eastern European countries lived in the United States, so the quota from each country, while limited, still allowed newcomers from those countries to enter. Then, in 1924, Congress passed the Johnson–Reid Act, imposing a limit of 165,000 immigrants from countries outside the Western Hemisphere and pushing back the quota basis to 1890, a time when British, German, and Scandinavian immigrants dominated the foreign-born population. The Johnson–Reid Act limited entry every year to 2 percent of the total number of immigrants from each country who were present in 1890. This measure effectively barred Jews, Slavs, Greeks, Italians, and Poles because their numbers were so small in 1890. In addition, the 1924 law reaffirmed the exclusion of Chinese immigrants and added Japanese and other Asians to the list, effectively closing the door to all migrants from Asia. Further modification of the immigration laws in 1927 reduced the quota to 150,000 per year, with most slots reserved f northern Europeans. Few Americans objected to these measures, other than the groups w kin and compatriots were excluded.

Agricultural interests in California and Texas lobbied hard to keep the door open to Mexicans because of the low-waged labor they provided. In the aftermath of the Mexican Revolution, many Mexicans hoped to find stability and jobs in th United States. Between 1910 and 1930, more than 1 million Mexicans, nearly c tenth of Mexico's population, migrated to the United States, where they found in the farms, railroads, and mines. Recruiters often stood along the borde ing to sign up laborers. The U.S. Chamber of Commerce noted in 1930 th can agricultural workers picked more than 80 percent of the perish produced in the Southwest.

Marcus Garvey and the Persistence of Civil Rights Activism

In the midst of a decade of reactionary policies toward outsider African Americans continued their struggle for civil right nationalist Marcus Garvey moved to New York City's Ha a branch of his Universal Negro Improvement Associa Garvey's organization had 30,000 members in New Philadelphia and Cincinnati, and 4000 in Detroit. Ga lish their own nation-state in Africa: "Africa was pe men, who were masters in art, science, and litera' peoples of the world." The UNIA staged color itary uniform. His followers proudly wore th port for the movement and joined the parades i. a journal, *The Negro World*, and encouraged the estab nesses such as grocery stores and laundries. The UNIA gam lowers and called for political justice and labor rights for black A

■ **FIGURE 21.3**
PERCENTAGE OF POPULATION FOREIGN
immigration restriction laws had a dramat
population, which reached nearly 15 per
population in the first two decades of
restriction, the percentage dropped p
when new laws allowed more imm

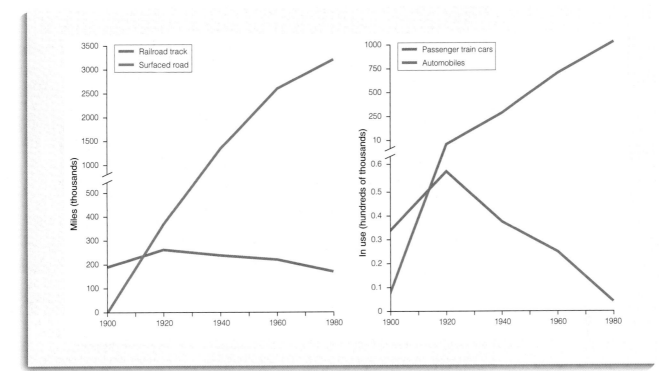

■ FIGURE 21.5
TRAINS AND AUTOMOBILES, 1900–1980   As increasing numbers of Americans acquired automobiles,
roads were built to accommodate all the cars. Starting in 1920, passenger trains decreased, along with
train tracks.

Science on Trial

Although advances in technology and medicine improved the quality of life for many Americans in the early twentieth century, scientific efforts to alter the natural world did not always lead to expected social benefits. One case in point was the engineering project to build levees along the Mississippi River to prevent flooding. These human-made structures were expected to protect the human-built settlements and agricultural developments in the fertile floodplains where the river would normally expand. As it turned out, the engineers were no match for the river. Scientific ideas were tested not only along the banks of the Mississippi River but also in the nation's courtrooms. Two major cases, the Scopes trial and the Supreme Court's decision in *Buck v. Bell,* subjected scientific ideas to judicial and cultural scrutiny. Although decisions in both cases resolved the immediate legal issues, the questions they raised continued to generate controversy and debate throughout the rest of the century.

The Great Flood of 1927

For half a century the engineers of the Mississippi River Commission had adhered to a policy of building levees, assuming that strong barricades against the river's banks would prevent flooding. Presumably, the levees would allow the rich soil of the floodplains along the river to be settled and farmed rather than leaving the basins empty to provide places for the river to expand and contract. But the levee policy proved to be a disastrous example of human efforts to master the natural contours of the land. In March 1927, the rains came, and the river rose.

■ The Mississippi River flood of 1927 devastated 26,000 square miles of prime farmland and homes across seven states. Levees built along the river's banks proved inadequate, despite engineers' assurances that the structures would prevent flooding. More than 900,000 people lost their homes, and crops and livestock worth more than $120 million were destroyed.

Public authorities and river experts assured those who watched and worried that the levees would hold. But they were wrong. Torrential rains caused the river to rage across the levees and the land beyond, submerging 26,000 square miles of prime farmland in 170 counties across seven states. More than 900,000 people were forced from their homes. One-third of the refugees found shelter in ill-equipped and understaffed Red Cross camps, and another third received Red Cross rations. The flood caused more than $100 million in crop losses and $23 million in livestock deaths. Journalists at the time called it "America's greatest peacetime disaster."

With the help of the Department of Commerce and the National Guard, the Red Cross set up 154 relief camps for flood victims. The camps were racially segregated. Refugees in the white camps were free to come and go and had more comfortable and generous accommodations and rations than those in the black camps. Armed guards patrolled the camps for black refugees and restricted people attempting to enter or leave. Black laborers had to register and give the names of their employers to receive any shelter or assistance. Only those planters were allowed to enter the camps and reclaim their workers. Relations between plantation owners and sharecroppers had been strained across the South before the flood, and many black laborers hoped to leave the plantations and find work elsewhere. But when labor agents came to the camps looking for workers to fill northern jobs, those patrolling the camps denied them entry. Federal authorities, including Secretary of Commerce Herbert Hoover, refused to intervene in local camp management. As a result, southern whites were able to force black sharecroppers back to work on their plantations. Despite the prisonlike conditions, many African American refugees managed to escape and made their way north.

The Triumph of Eugenics: *Buck v. Bell*

In 1924 racial theorist Lothrop Stoddard wrote a best-selling book, *The Rising Tide of Color Against White World Supremacy.* In this polemic, Stoddard predicted a war among the "primary" races of the world and warned of the "weakening" of the white race through immigration and "mongrelization." Stoddard wrote, "The melting pot may mix, but does not melt.

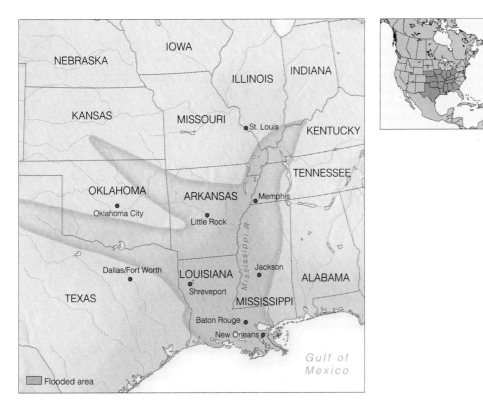

■ **MAP 21.1**
THE MISSISSIPPI RIVER FLOOD OF 1927   The Mississippi River flood in 1927 sent water across a huge area of the South, extending as far west as Texas, covering most of Louisiana, Arkansas, and Mississippi, and reaching north into Kansas, Illinois, and Indiana.

Each race type, formed ages ago . . . is a stubbornly persistent entity. Each type possesses a special set of characters: not merely the physical characters visible to the naked eye, but moral, intellectual, and spiritual characters as well." Stoddard's views were so familiar that F. Scott Fitzgerald placed them in the dialogue of his 1925 novel, *The Great Gatsby*. Fitzgerald's intention was to discredit the theory by showing it to be as ludicrous as other fantasies of his hapless protagonist, Tom Buchanan, who mused, "The idea is if we don't look out the white race will be—will be utterly submerged. It's all scientific stuff; it's been proved."

Fitzgerald may have hoped to discredit Stoddard's ideas, but many Americans, including large numbers of policymakers, believed in white racial superiority. Supposedly scientific theories of race bolstered claims that distinct, biologically based characteristics divided humans into superior and inferior races. These theories had no scientific merit and were later thoroughly discredited. But in the 1920s, these dubious theories of racial superiority supported measures such as immigration restriction and eugenic sterilization laws. Eugenics was a pseudoscience based on notions of racial superiority. Eugenicists claimed that the Anglo-Saxon Protestant "race" was superior to all others, including Jews, Southern Europeans, Catholics, as well as nonwhites. Racial superiority, according to eugenic reformers, might be compromised not only by mixing with inferior groups but also by the propagation of individuals whose mental or moral condition rendered them inferior, and whose offspring would diminish the quality of the Anglo-Saxon "stock."

These ideas were consistent with the theories of social Darwinists, who misused the ideas of Charles Darwin. Darwin's work on evolution focused on the origins of species in the animal world. Darwin found that weaker species died out, while stronger species evolved. Darwin did not study humans. But social Darwinists claimed that Darwin's evolutionary theories were relevant to human society, arguing that only the fittest ought to survive. Social Darwinists argued against government aid to the poor and infirm, claiming that such assistance interfered with "natural selection" of the "fittest." Social Darwinism also supported eugenic theories that provided the rationale for sterilization of the "unfit."

Several states had enacted eugenic laws that allowed the state to sterilize "inferior" individuals without their knowledge or consent. These laws authorized government and medical officials to determine whether or not an individual was inferior, or "feebleminded," and to order that the person be sterilized. Opponents of eugenic sterilization, mostly Catholic activists, challenged these laws in several states. In an effort to put an end to such challenges, eugenic advocates decided to test the constitutionality of the Virginia compulsory sterilization law. Their plan was to bring the case all the way to the U.S. Supreme Court, which they expected to uphold the law. The proponents of the law selected the case of Carrie Buck, in part because she was white. Eugenic advocates did not want race to be at the center of the case, especially because eugenic sterilization laws did not target particular races; they simply targeted the "feebleminded." Feeblemindedness was a loosely defined criterion often used to label poor, immigrant, or minority women who were sexually active. At the age of 17 Carrie Buck was raped and became pregnant; as a result she was sent to a state institution for the feebleminded. Buck was labeled as feebleminded because she had borne a child out of wedlock and was therefore deemed morally unfit for parenthood. The noted eugenicist Harry Laughlin pointed out that Buck herself was born out of wedlock, as was her daughter, and described them as part of the "shiftless, ignorant and worthless class of anti-social whites of the South."

Carrie Buck was sterilized in 1927. The following year, Buck's sister Doris was taken to the Virginia Colony for Epileptics and the Feebleminded and sterilized at age 16. She was told that she had an appendectomy. Later, Doris Buck married and tried to get pregnant. None of the physicians she consulted told her why she could not conceive. She finally learned the truth in 1979. "I broke down and cried. My husband and I wanted children desperately. We were crazy about them. I never knew what they'd done to me."

No evidence established that Carrie Buck, her mother, or her daughter was below normal intelligence. Buck's daughter died as a child, but her teachers described the girl as bright. In writing the majority opinion for the Supreme Court that upheld the law, Justice Oliver Wendell Holmes wrote, "Three generations of imbeciles are enough." Within the next few years, 30 states had compulsory sterilization laws, and the number of operations rose dramatically. In the 1930s the Nazis in Germany modeled their sterilization policies on the California law. Although eugenics in the United States received less publicity during World War II as Nazi sterilization policies became known, the practice continued. Over the next several decades, increasing numbers of coerced sterilizations took place in public clinics and hospitals. Nearly all of these later sterilizations were performed on women of color, including well-known civil rights leader Fanny Lou Hamer in the 1960s. Only the Catholic Church consistently mounted organized opposition to the practice. Finally, in the 1980s, in a rare alliance of traditional Catholics and feminist activists over an issue of reproductive choice, compulsory sterilization laws were repealed.

Science, Religion, and the Scopes Trial

Although there was little organized protest against sterilization laws, many Americans were troubled by eugenics and its corollary, Social Darwinism. The populist leader William Jennings Bryan was among them. Bryan, three times the Democratic candidate for president and Woodrow Wilson's secretary of state, for 30 years had been a powerful voice for reform and social justice. Bryan believed that Social Darwinism was an ill-founded misapplication of scientific theory used to support the subjugation of women, the second-class status of ethnic and racial minorities, the neglect of the poor, and the practice of eugenic sterilization.

In Bryan's last public crusade, he defended his principles in a courtroom in Dayton, Tennessee, in July 1925. Tennessee had recently enacted the Butler Act, which made it illegal to

The Rise and Fall of Man

Primate   **Neanderthal Man**   **Socrates**   **W. J. Bryan**

■ This satiric political cartoon, published during the Scopes trial, depicts the theory of evolution as the development of humans from their origins as apes to the "survival of the fittest," portrayed as William Jennings Bryan. Bryan argued the case against evolution in the famous courtroom drama.

teach the theory of evolution in the schools. The American Civil Liberties Union (ACLU) announced that it would defend any teacher charged with violating the Butler Act. A 24-year-old science teacher from the local high school, John Thomas Scopes, agreed to test the law. Using a state-approved textbook, Scopes taught a lesson on evolutionary theory on April 24 to his Rhea County High School science class. He was arrested on May 7 and quickly indicted by a grand jury. Bryan agreed to represent the prosecution; famed Chicago criminal lawyer Clarence Darrow headed the ACLU's team of defense lawyers.

Bryan did not oppose science, but he objected to its misapplication. Darrow did not oppose religion. But he argued that religious fundamentalists—"creationists" who believed in the literal interpretation of the Bible—should not determine the way science was taught in the schools. Reporters at the time, and since, cast the trial as a struggle between religion and science, with rural and small-town Americans on the side of creationism and secular urbanites supporting evolution. But the divide was not so clear-cut. In a poll taken in Arkansas in 1928, city dwellers were more inclined to support creationism than rural residents. Almost all advocates on both sides of the Scopes trial were Christians who disagreed over how to interpret the Bible. They were also believers in science; those opposed to the teaching of evolution considered it to be an unscientific theory.

In the 1920s evangelical religion did not necessarily represent old-fashioned values resisting the new urban consumer culture. To take just one example, evangelist Aimee Semple McPherson regularly filled the 52,000 seats in her elaborate Angelus Temple in Los Angeles and reached many thousands more via radio, preaching the message of her Foursquare Gospel Church with the style and flair of a Hollywood celebrity. McPherson drew followers to 600 branches of her church using the latest techniques of advertising and mass culture. On one occasion, she used a gigantic electric scoreboard to illustrate the triumph of good over evil. Combining show-biz glitz with faith healing, she gathered a wide urban and rural following.

The Scopes trial also contained elements of popular entertainment. Dubbed "the Monkey trial" because Darwin's theory of evolution demonstrated that humans evolved from an earlier primate form that included monkeys and chimpanzees, the trial was one of the first national media events. The judge invited reporters from around the country, including broadcast journalists. The Scopes trial was the first jury trial broadcast on live radio. More than 900 spectators packed into the courtroom, and hundreds more gathered in the streets, where

> *Almost all advocates on both sides of the Scopes trial were Christians who disagreed over how to interpret the Bible.*

a carnival atmosphere prevailed, complete with souvenir stands, food vendors, itinerant preachers, and hucksters, including numerous chimpanzees accompanied by their trainers.

The trial did not deal with the question of the First Amendment, which guaranteed freedom of speech, nor the matter of who should decide the content of classroom education. Rather, religious fundamentalism was on trial. Although rules of evidence cannot apply to matters of faith, Darrow forced Bryan to defend his religious beliefs in a court of law. Darrow fully expected to lose the case so he could appeal it to the U.S. Supreme Court, and the jury obliged, reaching a guilty verdict in just nine minutes. Scopes was fined $100, but the fine was never imposed. Exhausted by the trial and ill with diabetes, Bryan died a week later.

Bryan technically won the case, but most reporters deemed the spectacle a victory for Darrow and the teaching of evolution. That assessment was premature. The Tennessee Supreme Court overturned the verdict on a technicality, robbing Darrow of his chance to take the case to the U.S. Supreme Court. Before the trial, most science textbooks included discussion of evolution; after the trial, material on evolution began to disappear. Laws against the teaching of evolution remained on the books until the U.S. Supreme Court overturned an Arkansas law in 1968.

The Scopes trial did not resolve the debate between creationists and evolutionists, and the controversy continued throughout the century. As late as 2000, the Board of Education in Kansas ruled that creationism and evolution were both unproven theories and that both could be taught in the schools. The Scopes trial may not have resolved anything, but it did have one significant unintended consequence. The trial generated tremendous interest in nonhuman primates. After the trial, attendance at the nation's zoos skyrocketed, boosting their funding and their prestige. So in the end, the real winners in the "Monkey trial" were the monkeys.

The Business of Politics

In 1924, President Calvin Coolidge declared, "The business of America is business." Despite its many critics, with the support of national political leaders, business reigned. After an initial recession following World War I, the economy grew steadily. The Gross National Product (GNP) increased 5.5 percent per year, from $149 billion in 1922 to $227 billion in 1929. Official unemployment remained below 5 percent throughout the decade, and real wages rose 15 percent. These trends fueled the popularity of the conservative, business-friendly presidents of the 1920s. Economic interests also drove foreign policy during the decade. After World War I, with much of Europe in shambles, the United States made loans to foreign countries, becoming the world's leading creditor nation. International markets opened up for American-made products, leading to a tremendous expansion in foreign trade.

Warren G. Harding: The Politics of Scandal

Warren G. Harding, a former newspaper editor and U.S. senator from Ohio, won the 1920 presidential election by the biggest landslide since 1820. Once elected, he released 66-year-old Socialist party leader Eugene V. Debs from prison. He then appointed a strong cabinet, including Herbert Hoover as secretary of commerce, Charles Evans Hughes as secretary of state, and Andrew Mellon as secretary of the treasury.

Harding established the conservative agenda that would last throughout the decade. His administration favored tariff protection, which placed a tax on goods entering the United States from abroad. Tariffs helped American industries by increasing the cost of imported goods. Harding also supported immigration restriction and opposed labor unions. In the wake of World War I, Harding distanced himself from Woodrow Wilson's peace settlement but promoted international treaties. In 1921 and 1922 Secretary of State Charles Evans Hughes achieved the first major disarmament accord, the Five-Power Treaty, signed by Japan, Britain,

France, Italy, and the United States. The five nations agreed to scrap more than 2 million tons of warships in the first such pact of its kind. Instead of an arms buildup, Hughes extended the power of the United States abroad through economic ties, encouraging banks to provide loans to war-ravaged Europe and using the government to protect such investments.

TABLE 21-1			
The Election of 1920			
Candidate	Political Party	Popular Vote	Electoral Vote
Warren G. Harding	Republican	16,152,200	404
James M. Cox	Democratic	9,147,353	127
Eugene V. Debs	Socialist	919,799	0

But Harding's presidency was marred by scandal. He had built his political base by handing out favors and deals to his friends, and he continued to do so as president. His buddies used their offices and influence for personal gain, while Harding caroused with them, drinking, despite Prohibition, and engaging in notorious extramarital affairs. At first, the press ignored these obvious abuses, but by 1923, the many scandals finally broke. Harding's cronies were exposed for selling government appointments and providing judicial pardons and police protection for bootleggers.

The most serious scandal of Harding's presidency involved the large government oil reserves at Teapot Dome, Wyoming, and Elk Hills, California. At the urging of Secretary of the Interior Albert Fall, Harding transferred control over the reserves from the Navy to the Department of the Interior. After accepting a bribe of nearly $400,000 from two oil tycoons, Harry F. Sinclair and Edward L. Doheny, Fall secretly issued leases to them without opening up the competition to other oil companies, thereby allowing Sinclair and Doheny to pump oil from the wells in exchange for providing fuel tank reserves to the Navy. Fall went to jail for a year as a result. In another scandal, Charles R. Forbes, head of the Veteran's Bureau, went to prison for swindling the government out of $200 million worth of hospital supplies. Forbes's lawyer committed suicide, as did a close associate of Attorney General Harry Daugherty, who was forced out of the Harding administration in disgrace. When he learned of the scandals that occurred in his close circle, Harding grew deeply worried. The stress probably contributed to the illness that killed him in 1923.

Calvin Coolidge: The Hands-Off President

Harding's vice president, Calvin Coolidge, took over the presidency when Harding died in 1923. Sober, serious, and humorless, Coolidge was not vulnerable to scandal as his predecessor had been. Coolidge believed that the government should meddle as little as possible in the affairs of the nation. He took long naps every day and exerted very little presidential leadership. Known mostly for his hostility to labor unions and his laissez-faire attitude toward business, he was a popular president during the complacent mid-1920s.

Not everyone was pleased with Coolidge's probusiness politics, and opposition mobilized for the 1924 election. Progressive Republicans formed a new Progressive party and nominated Robert M. La Follette for president, with Senator Burton K. Wheeler of Montana for vice president. The Progressive platform promoted conservation measures, higher taxes on the wealthy, doing away with the electoral college in favor of direct election of the president, and the abolition of child labor. The Democrats deadlocked between Catholic candidate Alfred E. Smith, an urban politician from New York, and Protestant William G. McAdoo, who had a base of support in the South and West. On the 103rd ballot, the delegates finally chose a compromise candidate, John W. Davis, a corporation lawyer, with Charles W. Bryan of Nebraska (William Jennings Bryan's brother) as his running mate. The Republicans nominated Coolidge, with Charles G. Dawes of Illinois as

TABLE 21-2			
The Election of 1924			
Candidate	Political Party	Popular Vote	Electoral Vote
Calvin Coolidge	Republican	15,725,016	382
John W. Davis	Democratic	8,386,503	136
Robert M. LaFollette	Progressive	4,822,856	13

his running mate. Coolidge claimed responsibility for the nation's prosperity and won easily, receiving more votes than the other two candidates combined.

Coolidge took pride in measures that prevented the government from interfering in the economy, such as his vetoes of the 1926 and 1928 McNary–Haugen bills, which would have provided government subsidies to farmers if farm prices dropped. The passage of the Revenue Act of 1926, a form of trickle-down economics intended to boost the economy, reduced the high income and estate taxes that Progressive reformers had put into place during World

War I. Coolidge also continued Harding's efforts to sustain world peace. In 1928, under the leadership of Secretary of State Frank Kellogg and French Foreign Minister Aristide Briand, delegates from the United States, France, and 13 other nations gathered in Paris to sign the Kellogg–Briand Pact, in which they agreed to resolve conflicts through peaceful means rather than war. Unfortunately, with no means to enforce the agreement, the pact did nothing to alleviate the international hostilities that later erupted into World War II.

Herbert Hoover: The Self-Made President

The 1928 election was a major turning point for the presence of ethnic minorities in politics, for the Democrats broke tradition by selecting an Irish Catholic, Alfred E. Smith, governor of New York, as their candidate. It was the first time a major party had nominated a Catholic for president. Coolidge decided not to run for reelection in 1928, and the Republican party selected Secretary of Commerce Herbert Hoover as its nominee. Prohibition figured prominently in the 1928 presidential campaign. Although the Democratic platform gave lukewarm support to the continuation of Prohibition, Smith made no secret of his support for the repeal of the Eighteenth Amendment. By contrast, Republican Herbert Hoover praised Prohibition as "a great social and economic experiment." The other major issue of the campaign was religion. Anti-Catholic sentiment was strong throughout the country, especially in the South, where Democrats either sat out the election or voted Republican. Smith's opponents attacked his Catholicism, charging that he was more loyal to the Vatican than to the United States. Although Hoover won by a substantial majority, Smith carried the nation's 12 largest cities, indicating the strength of the ethnic vote in urban centers and the political and cultural rift between urban and rural Americans. Smith's candidacy also laid the groundwork for another Irish Catholic, John F. Kennedy, who ran successfully on the Democratic ticket 32 years later.

TABLE 21-3			
The Election of 1928			
Candidate	Political Party	Popular Vote	Electoral Vote
Herbert Hoover	Republican	21,391,381	444
Alfred E. Smith	Democratic	15,016,443	87
Norman Thomas	Socialist	267,835	0

Herbert Hoover epitomized the values of the self-made man. He was orphaned as a child and raised by relatives of modest means. These early hardships fortified Hoover's ambition to overcome adversity, and he set his sights on business success. After graduating from Stanford University, he went into mining and rose through the ranks to become a wealthy corporate leader. By age 40 he was already a millionaire. Hoover began his career in government during World War I, when he earned widespread admiration for handling the distribution of food relief to European war refugees. He then served ably as secretary of commerce in the Harding and Coolidge administrations. President Hoover believed that his government experience rendered him ideally suited to secure prosperity for the nation's future. Shortly after the election, he predicted, "We in America today are nearer to the final triumph over poverty than ever before in the history of any land." But less than a year into his presidency, his optimism, along with the nation's economy, came crashing down.

Consumer Dreams and Nightmares

During the 1920s, spending on recreation nearly doubled. Faith in continuing prosperity promoted the extension of consumer credit to unprecedented heights. Previously, the only major item routinely purchased on credit was a house. But in the twenties, installment buying became the rage for a wide range of consumer goods, from autos and radios to household appliances. Consumer debt rose from $2.6 billion in 1919 to $7.1 billion in 1929. As one official in a midwestern loan company remarked, "People don't think anything nowadays of borrowing sums they'd never have thought of borrowing in the old days. They will assume an obligation for $2000 today as calmly as they would have borrowed $300 or $400 in 1890." This habit of buying on credit boosted the standard of living for many but also left families in a precarious situation and vulnerable to the vagaries of the broader economy.

Marketing the Good Life

Advertising fueled much of the new spending. As one contemporary reporter noted, "Advertising is to business what fertilizer is to a farm." According to advertisers, consumer goods promised health, beauty, success, and the means to eliminate personal and embarrassing flaws, such as bad breath or dandruff. Cigarette companies used advertising to promote smoking as a symbol of independence for women and as a means to achieve beauty. Clever advertising campaigns promised women that if they would "reach for a Lucky Strike" instead of a sweet they would remain slim, healthy, and sexually appealing.

Advertising also fostered a vision of big business as a benevolent force, promoting individual happiness. In his 1925 best-seller, *The Man That Nobody Knows,* advertising executive Bruce Barton portrayed Jesus as a businessman who gathered a group of 12 followers who believed in his enterprise and, through effective public relations and advertising, sold his product to the world. The consumer culture had its temples: movie palaces, department stores, and the 1920s innovation, the shopping center. Kansas City's Country Club Plaza, the first shopping center in the nation, was the brainchild of Jesse Clyde (J. C.) Nichols, who purchased 55 acres of swampland for the project. Like the architects of the movie palaces, Nichols looked to European aristocratic styles for inspiration. He chose a Spanish–Moorish theme for the plaza that included courtyards and stucco buildings with red tile roofs and ornate towers. He adorned the plaza's streets and sidewalks with works of art, columns, wrought iron, and fountains. Most significantly, he designed his shopping center with the car in mind. The shopping center originally boasted eight filling stations and numerous garages and parking lots. Skeptical city leaders called it "Nichols' Folly," but the Country Club Plaza was a commercial success.

A much less successful venture was the Florida land boom, based on fantasies of a consumer paradise. When

JUST GOING ALONG FOR THE RIDE

■ In the 1920s advertisers used sexualized images to sell all sorts of products. This advertisement for automobile tires provides very little information about the product itself but evokes images of fun and romance to capture consumers' attention.

World War I closed off routes to the European playgrounds of the American elites, shrewd developers in Florida began to advertise: "Go to Florida, Where enterprise is enthroned. Where you sit and watch at twilight the fronds of the graceful palm, latticed against the fading gold of the sun kissed sky." These promotional efforts sparked a frenzy of investment in Florida real estate. To create "earthly paradises" and resorts, developers rushed to construct roads and find new land on which to build. Forging the Tamiami Trail across 90 miles of Everglades swamp entailed dredging a canal, blowing up the submerged limestone layer with dynamite, piling the broken limestone beside the canal, and then crushing it into a road surface. The dangerous work claimed the lives of many laborers and severely damaged the sensitive ecology of the vast Everglades wetland. When the road was finally completed in 1928, the land boom had collapsed.

Human folly and nature's fury contributed to the Florida land boom and bust. The boom peaked in 1925 and quickly collapsed. In 1926 a Danish ship, being renovated to become a floating cabaret, sank and blocked the entrance to the Miami harbor, stranding dozens of ships filled with building materials necessary for ongoing construction. Then a hurricane hit Miami, killing 130 people and causing millions of dollars of property damage. Another hurricane in 1928 killed more than 1000 people and destroyed several towns. The destruction wrought by the hurricanes, and the exposure of exaggerated promotional advertisements and inflated prices, quickly put an end to land speculation. The collapse of the Florida land boom foreshadowed the collapse of the stock market in 1929.

Writers, Critics, and the "Lost Generation"

Some social critics claimed that consumerism fostered not only economic disasters such as the Florida land boom but also a stifling conformity. Sinclair Lewis was one of several novelists of the twenties whose books expressed biting criticism of the frantic pursuit of material gain and status. George Babbitt, the protagonist of Lewis's novel *Babbitt* (1922), struggles to become accepted and successful in his small town by conforming to the empty materialism and standardized opinions accepted and prized by his neighbors. In *Main Street* (1920), Lewis explores similar themes through the character of a woman, Carol Kennicott. She resides in Gopher Prairie, a thinly disguised version of Lewis's own hometown, Sauk Centre, Minnesota. But unlike Babbitt, Kennicott rebels against the stifling small-town life that traps her.

F. Scott Fitzgerald wrote not about small-town conformity, as Lewis did, but about the modern urban life that was its antithesis. Fitzgerald glamorized, criticized, and in many ways embodied the giddy nightlife and status seeking of the Jazz Age. Born in St. Paul, Minnesota, into a family of modest means, he grew up admiring and emulating the

■ Writer F. Scott Fitzgerald and his flapper wife, Zelda, personified the glamorous literati of the Jazz Age. In his writing, Fitzgerald both romanticized and criticized the decadent consumerism of the aspiring and upwardly mobile middle class. In this page from a scrapbook, their photos are adorned with autographs of other famous literary figures.

wealthy. He married glamorous flapper Zelda Sayre, daughter of a prominent Alabama judge, and together they embodied the dizzy, indulgent, free-spirited life of the decade. But Fitzgerald's novels, including *This Side of Paradise* (1920), *The Beautiful and the Damned* (1922), and *The Great Gatsby* (1925), criticized the era's obsessions with success, glamour, consumerism, advertising, and the infatuation with status. The Fitzgeralds, along with other writers who were critical of American superficiality and conformity, moved to Paris. Eventually, the life Fitzgerald both lived and criticized caught up with him. By the end of the decade, he—like the nation—was broken by his excesses. In 1931 he came home to Baltimore an alcoholic; Zelda was diagnosed with schizophrenia and spent the rest of her life in mental institutions.

During their years in Paris, the Fitzgeralds often joined other expatriate writers at the salon of Gertrude Stein, a prolific author of novels, plays, operas, poems, and biographies. Born in 1874 to German Jewish parents in Pennsylvania, she grew up in California and attended Radcliffe College in Massachusetts. In 1903 she moved to France, where she remained for the rest of her life, looking back to America for her subject matter. In Paris she met another American, Alice B. Toklas, who became her lifetime partner. Their openly lesbian relationship gave Stein material for her writing, including *The Autobiography of Alice B. Toklas* (1933). In the 1920s, she dubbed the writers who gathered at her salon the "Lost Generation."

Poverty Amid Plenty

Most Americans in the 1920s were neither investing in Florida real estate nor frequenting Gertrude Stein's Paris salon. Even so, they were not immune to the desires and dreams that the consumer society sparked. The middle class and the more prosperous members of the working class enjoyed many of the comforts, amusements, and appliances that the booming economy made available; the poor struggled just to make ends meet. Throughout the twenties, the nation's poorest people continued to be the most mobile, moving in search of jobs, security, and a place they could settle and call home. Henry Crews, son of a white Georgia sharecropper, longed for "that single house where you were born, where you lived out your childhood . . . your anchor in the world." But he never had such a home. Like that of many other hardworking sharecroppers and factory workers, his family moved frequently in search of a better life, a dream that often proved elusive.

If Zelda Sayre Fitzgerald embodied the Jazz Age, Myrtle Terry Lawrence embodied the experience of the sharecropper. Born in Alabama in 1893, she began chopping and hoeing cotton at age six. She spent two weeks in school in the first grade, which was the full extent of her formal education. She married Ben Lawrence when they were both 13 years old and had her first child at 14. With her husband she worked in the cotton fields for nearly three decades, eventually becoming a major organizer of black and white sharecroppers in the Southern Tenant Farmers' Union (STFU), which fought for the rights of tenant farmers.

Myrtle Lawrence was poor, but she did not consider herself a victim. Her children described her as a "lady," although the tough-talking, tobacco-chewing Lawrence was hardly a southern belle. She took pride in vigorous outdoor work, which she preferred to indoor housework. As her daughter-in-law recalled, "She wasn't no housekeeper. Bless her heart." One of her sons boasted that his mother was paid extra to set the pace for the other workers, including the men, because "she was the best man." In the words of one daughter, "Mama wasn't slow at nothing." Myrtle Lawrence's energy and wits, as well as her refusal to be bullied, won her the admiration of her family and the respect of coworkers and propelled her in the 1930s to leadership in the STFU.

Sharecropping required hard work and careful planning to carve out a meager life, but many did so with pride. Ed Brown, a young black sharecropper, had no formal education but considered himself "pretty schemy." He worked on six different plantations, moving about in

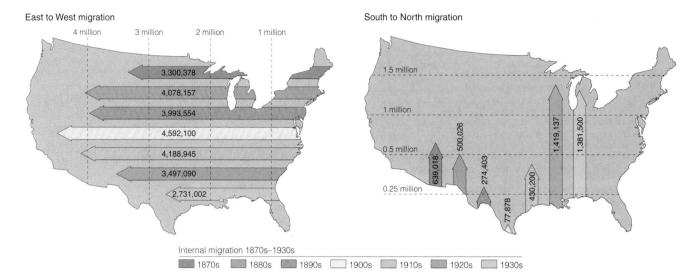

East to West migration

South to North migration

Internal migration 1870s–1930s

1870s 1880s 1890s 1900s 1910s 1920s 1930s

■ **MAP 21.2**
AMERICANS ON THE MOVE, 1870s–1930s   Between the 1870s and the 1930s, millions of Americans moved around the country, mostly from east to west, but also from south to north.

search of better circumstances or to escape from debt or threats of violence. Although he and his wife, Willie Mae, were never able to buy a place of their own, they did improve their circumstances over time. When they finally got out of debt and secured a bit of cash, they used it to adorn their meager cabin. In 1929 they bought an old Model T Ford. But finding it too costly to maintain, they swapped it for a cow and a butter churn and dasher, which provided more practical benefits. Meanwhile, Ed took odd jobs to earn extra money, while Willie Mae took care of the children, picked cotton, took in laundry, and, as Ed noted with appreciation, kept "things . . . lookin very pretty."

Life was a struggle for southern sharecroppers, black and white. But African Americans faced the most difficult jobs and the added insults of racism. Blacks continued to move north in huge numbers in search of improved opportunities. Immigrants had a better chance of moving into semiskilled jobs, while blacks were relegated to unskilled jobs. Many ended up in domestic service, where they worked long hours for low pay. They tried to avoid live-in work, where they had little freedom from the watchful gaze of employers and barely any time with their own families. If they returned to the South, they faced work in the fields or factories for long hours under miserable conditions or in the extracting industries of coal mining, logging, and saw milling, where dangerous working conditions killed thousands of laborers.

Latinos joined African Americans at the bottom of the socioeconomic ladder in the Southwest and Midwest, working in jobs that offered almost no opportunity to save money or acquire property. Plantation owners kept sharecroppers in debt, and mine owners paid their workers in scrip that had to be used in company stores while forcing them to live in company housing.

Immigrants from Asia who arrived on the West Coast also faced difficulty finding stable jobs with decent pay and working conditions. Many ended up in domestic service. A young Japanese woman went to work for a family in Oakland, California, less than a month after arriving in the country. "I had to bring the coal up, all the time I went up and down," she later recalled. "Then I had to wash diapers. Me, I grew up on a farm, so I never had to do that. When I came to America, I didn't know anything. So I just had to cry." Loss of a job also meant loss of housing, creating constant mobility. Nevertheless, the poor maintained strong ties of kinship and community and helped each other survive under difficult conditions.

Industrial workers struggled throughout the decade, especially in a political climate hostile to unions. With the crushing of labor radicalism in the Red Scare after World War I, union organizing and strikes declined. But workers continued to protest low wages and poor working conditions. In March 1929 young women textile workers in Elizabethton, a small town nestled in the Blue Ridge Mountains of eastern Tennessee, closed down the American Glanzstoff plant in protest against low wages, petty rules, and arrogant employers. Soon, the protest spread to textile mills across the region. At Glanzstoff, the strikers returned to work when the company promised better pay and agreed not to discriminate against union members. But the employers broke their promises, so the women struck again. The governor sent in the National Guard, armed with machine guns. More than 1000 people were arrested in confrontations with the troops.

The strikers were young women mostly in their teens and early twenties. They combined labor militance with an air of playfulness. On the picket lines, they expressed their autonomy and independence, but they also found opportunities to flirt and carouse beyond the watchful eyes of parents. Although the strike was ultimately crushed and many of the participants were blacklisted, few expressed regrets. Bessie Edens knew she would not get her job back, but she "didn't care whether they took me back or not. I didn't! If I'd starved I wouldn't of cared, because I knew what I was a'doing when I helped to pull it. And I've never regretted it in any way. . . . And it did help the people, and it's helped the town and the country."

The Stock Market Crash

The symbolic end of the 1920s arrived on "Black Tuesday," October 29, 1929, when the inflated and overextended stock market came crashing down. In one day, stocks fell in value $14 billion. By end of the year, stock prices were down 50 percent; by 1932, they had dropped another 30 percent. In three years, $74 billion of the nation's wealth had vanished. The effect on the economy was catastrophic. Industrial production fell by half. More than 100,000 businesses went bankrupt. Banks failed at alarming rate: more than 2000 banks closed in 1931 alone. Unemployment rose to staggering levels, reaching 25 percent by 1932 and rarely dropping below 17 percent throughout the 1930s.

In keeping with the social policies that had prevailed throughout the 1920s, relief efforts were slim. No federal relief or welfare, no unemployment insurance, no Social Security, no job programs existed to help those who had lost their jobs, their savings, and their homes. Although many wealthy people lost their fortunes, which had been built on speculative investments, the poor suffered the most. People who lost their homes and farms moved into makeshift shelters in shantytowns, which they nicknamed "Hoovervilles" to mock the ineffectual efforts of President Herbert Hoover to respond to their plight.

The causes of the stock market crash and the decade-long depression that followed were complex and varied. Stock prices rose dramatically, especially at the end of the 1920s. Speculators had been purchasing stocks on 10 percent margins, meaning they put down only 10 percent of the cost and borrowed the rest from brokers and banks. The popularity of installment buying in the consumer goods market had devastating effects when applied in this manner to the stock market. Investors expected to get rich quickly by selling their stocks at a higher price and paying back the loans from their huge profits. This system worked for a few years, encouraging investors with limited funds to make risky investments in the hope of gaining large fortunes. When the price of stocks spiraled out of control, far beyond their actual value, creditors demanded repayment of their loans, and investors were unable to pay their debts.

The collapse of the stock market alone would not necessarily have caused such a severe and prolonged depression. Poor decision making by financial and political leaders exacerbated underlying weaknesses in the economy. The Federal Reserve curtailed the amount of money in circulation and raised interest rates, making it more difficult for people to get loans and pay off

Mario Puzo, *The Fortunate Pilgrim*

Italians, like most other European immigrants, established households where almost everyone worked to support the family. Fathers earned wages, mothers often took in boarders or did piecework at home to earn extra money, and sons and daughters found jobs in sweatshops and factories. Young Italian women, along with their Jewish peers, often worked for garment manufacturers, such as the Triangle Shirtwaist Company, scene of the strike of 1909 and the tragic fire that followed. Most immigrants married within their own ethnic groups. Often, immigrant families were torn by fierce generational conflicts, as old-world parents tried to maintain traditional ways while their American children struggled to break free. This generational struggle beset nearly every immigrant group.

Mario Puzo, the Italian American novelist best known for The Godfather, was among the many children of immigrants to express the cultures and experiences of newcomers through the arts. His autobiographical novel, The Fortunate Pilgrim, is a portrait of life in the Italian community of New York City in the early years of the century. The book depicts the struggles and triumphs of an Italian immigrant family. The men work long hours for meager wages while the women struggle to maintain the family. Mothers gather on tenement stoops to bemoan the behavior of their Americanized children, yet they dream the American dream of a better life. At the end of the book the mother's dream comes true, and the family moves to a suburban home in Long Island. Yet it is a bittersweet ending, for she and her family realize the loss of the vibrant

Mario Puzo, author of *The Fortunate Pilgrim* and *The Godfather.*

community that, for all its hardship and poverty, had sustained them in the city.

Each tenement was a village square; each had its group of women, all in black, sitting on stools and boxes and doing more than gossip. They recalled ancient history, argued morals and social law, always taking their precedents from the mountain village in southern Italy they had escaped, fled from many years ago. And with what relish their favorite imaginings! Now: What if their stern fathers were transported by some miracle to face the problems *they* faced every day? Or their mothers of the quick and heavy hands? What shrieks if *they* as daughters had dared as these American children dared? If *they* had presumed.

The women talked of their children as they would of strangers. It was a favorite topic, the corruption of the innocent by the new land. Now: Felicia, who lived around the corner of 31st Street. What type of daughter was she who did not cut short her honeymoon on news of her godmother's illness, the summons issued by her own mother? A real whore. No no, they did not mince words. Felicia's mother herself told the story. And a son, poor man, who could not wait another year to marry when his father so commanded? Ahhh, the disrespect. *Figlio disgraziato.* Never could this pass in Italy. The father would kill his arrogant son; yes, kill him. And the daughter? In Italy—Felicia's mother swore in a voice still trembling with passion, though this had all happened three years ago, the godmother recovered, the grandchildren the light of her life—ah, in Italy the mother would pull the whore out of her bridal chamber, drag her to the hospital bed by the hair of her head. Ah, Italia, Italia; how the world changed and for the worse. What madness was it that made them leave such a land? Where fathers commanded and mothers were treated with respect by their children.

Each in turn told a story of insolence and defiance, themselves heroic, long-suffering, the children spitting Lucifers saved by an application of Italian discipline—the razor strap or the *Tackeril.* And at the end of each story each woman recited her requiem. *Mannaggia America!*—Damn America. But in the hot summer night their voices were filled with hope, with a vigor never sounded in their homeland. Here now was money in the bank, children who could read and write, grandchildren who would be professors if all went well. They spoke with guilty loyalty of customs they had themselves trampled into dust. ∎

Source: Mario Puzo, The Fortunate Pilgrim (New York: Random House, 1997), pp. 10–11.

their debts. These policies had profound worldwide implications and contributed to an international crisis. Banks in Germany and Austria, for example, depended on loans from the United States, and many went bankrupt, causing a ripple effect across Europe. The Tariff Act of 1930, known as the Hawley–Smoot Tariff, also contributed to the downward spiral. The tariff included industrial products as well as agricultural goods and raised duties from 32 to 40 percent. Although industrialists had convinced the Republican-controlled Congress that the tariff would protect American commodities from competition from cheaper foreign goods, they were wrong. Foreign governments retaliated by raising their own tariffs to keep out American goods. These monetary and trade policies backfired, and the economic crisis spread throughout the western industrial world.

Within the United States, the unequal distribution of wealth exacerbated the effects of the economic downturn. The nation may have looked prosperous, but most of the wealth was concentrated in the hands of a small number of people. The gap between the rich and the poor widened during the 1920s, in part because of Coolidge administration policies that lowered taxes on the wealthy. The majority of the population lost purchasing power, resulting in the decline of consumer-oriented industries as the market for their products shrank. Although the wealthy spent money extravagantly, they spent a smaller percentage of their money on consumer goods than wage earners. If average Americans had been able to buy more cars, household appliances, and other products, those industries might have survived, and the economy might have recovered more quickly. Political leaders, and the business-oriented public policies they had promoted throughout the decade, left the country ill prepared to address the crisis and meet the needs of families deprived of their means of livelihood. As the curtain came down on the 1920s, the nation was left suffering.

Conclusion

The stock market collapse, and the prolonged depression that followed, revealed the flaws in the economic system that spurred the apparent prosperity of the 1920s. Beneath the visible affluence was the hidden poverty that prevailed throughout the decade. The aftermath of World War I and the end of Progressive reform led to an era of conservative politics. National leaders promoted business interests and paid little attention to social welfare, the environment, or the need to regulate the economy. By the end of the 1920s, it was clear that Prohibition was a dismal failure and that the federal government was ill equipped to enforce it.

Although political reform withered, cultural vitality flowered. Hollywood emerged as a major industry, and the Jazz Age reflected the widespread appeal of African American music. A black arts movement flourished, centered in Harlem, and writers of the "Lost Generation"—disenchanted with the status quo—gathered in Greenwich Village or moved to France. Across the country, a youth culture challenged the gender and sexual mores of the past. Consumer culture expanded as increasing numbers of families purchased cars, radios, and new fashions.

Few who were involved in the private preoccupations of the decade could have foreseen the disaster ahead. When the stock market crashed and the Depression set in, President Hoover tried to address the crisis by extending the political philosophy that had prevailed throughout the decade: Private enterprise would bring the economy back to health. But Hoover soon discovered that the old formulas would not work in the new reality and that the nation's major economic and political institutions had lost their credibility.

Sites to Visit

Harlem: The Mecca of the New Negro
etext.lib.virginia.edu/harlem/

This site is the on-line text of the March 1925 *Survey Graphic Harlem Number,* which includes writings of many Harlem Renaissance writers.

Calvin Coolidge
www.ipl.org/ref/POTUS/ccoolidge.html

This site contains basic information about Coolidge's election and presidency and online biography.

Warren G. Harding
www.ipl.org/ref/POTUS/wgharding.html

This site contains basic information about Harding's election and presidency and online biography.

Herbert Hoover
www.ipl.org/ref/POTUS/hchoover.html

This site contains basic information about Hoover's election and presidency and online biography.

Harlem 1900–1940: An African American Community
www.si.umich.edu/CHICO/Harlem/

This site of the New York Public Library's Schomburg Center for Research in Black Culture includes information and articles about the history of Harlem as a center of African American cultural life.

The Scopes Trial
xroads.virginia.edu/~UG97/inherit/1925home.html

This site from the University of Virginia's American Studies program includes images, documents, and articles relating to the Scopes Trial.

Temperance and Prohibition
prohibition.history.ohio-state.edu/

This site from Ohio State University covers the history of temperance and prohibition in the United States.

The Flappers
www.geocities.com/flapper_culture/

This site includes images, descriptions, and information on famous "flappers" of the 1920s.

For Further Reading

General

Ann Douglas, *Terrible Honesty: Mongrel Manhattan in the 1920s* (1995).

Lynn Dumenil, *The Modern Temper: American Culture and Society in the 1920s* (1995).

David J. Goldberg, *Discontented America: The United States in the 1920s* (1999).

Robert S. Lynd and Helen Merrell Lynd. *Middletown* (1929).

George Mowry, *The Twenties: Fords, Flappers, and Fanatics* (1963).

The Decline of Reform

Kathleen Blee, *Women of the Klan: Racism and Gender in the 1920s* (1991).

Nancy Cott, *The Grounding of Modern Feminism* (1987).

Kenneth Jackson, *The Ku Klux Klan in the City, 1915–1930* (1967).

Matthew Frye Jacobson, *Whiteness of a Different Color: European Immigrants and the Alchemy of Race* (1998).

Desmond S. King, *Making Americans: Immigration, Race, and the Origins of the Diverse Democracy* (2000).

Nancy MacLean, *Behind the Mask of Chivalry: The Making of the Second Ku Klux Klan* (1994).

Andrew Sinclair, *Prohibition: The Era of Excess* (1962).

Hollywood and Harlem

Beth Bailey, *From Front Porch to Back Seat: Courtship in 20th Century America* (1988).

Ray Batchelor, *Henry Ford, Mass Production, Modernism and Design* (1994).

Nathan Irvin Huggins, *The Harlem Renaissance* (1971).

Angela J. Latham, *Posing a Threat: Flappers, Chorus Girls, and Other Brazen Performers of the American 1920s* (2000).

Virginia Scharff, *Taking the Wheel: Women and the Coming of the Motor Age* (1991).

Science on Trial

John M. Barry, *Rising Tide: The Great Mississippi Flood of 1927 and How It Changed America* (1997).

Richard Hofstadter, *Social Darwinism in American Thought, 1860–1915* (1944).

Daniel Kevles, *In the Name of Eugenics: Genetics and the Uses of Human Heredity* (1985).

Lawrence Levine, *Defender of the Faith: William Jennings Bryan, the Last Decade, 1915–1925* (1987).

Garry Wills, *Under God: Religion and American Politics* (1990).

The Business of Politics

Kendrick A. Clements, *Hoover, Conservation, and Consumerism: Engineering the Good Life* (2000).

John Kenneth Galbraith, *The Great Crash, 1929* (1955).

William E. Leuchtenberg, *The Perils of Prosperity, 1914–1932* (1958, 1993).

Robert K. Murray, *The Politics of Normalcy: Governmental Theory and Practice in the Harding–Coolidge Era* (1973).

Burl Noggle, *Teapot Dome: Oil and Politics in the 1920s* (1962).

Consumer Dreams and Nightmares

William Frazer and John J. Guthrie, Jr., *The Florida Land Boom: Speculation, Money, and the Banks* (1995).

Jacqueline Jones, *The Dispossessed: America's Underclass from the Civil War to the Present* (1992).

Jackson Lears, *Fables of Abundance: A Cultural History of Advertising in America* (1994).

Roland Marchand, *Advertising the American Dream* (1985).

Nancy Milford, *Zelda: A Biography* (1970).

Online Practice Test

Test your understanding of this chapter with interactive review quizzes at

www.ablongman.com/jonescreatedequal/chapter21

PART EIGHT

From Depression and War to World Power, 1929–1953

THE GREAT DEPRESSION AND WORLD WAR II TESTED AMERICANS' FAITH in their federal government to a degree unmatched in the nation's history. Economic collapse in the 1930s and the threat of Nazi and Japanese aggression from 1941 to 1945 presented challenges beyond the reach of ordinary citizens, local communities, and businesses acting alone. The federal government began to take more responsibility for economic and social well-being at home and for the spread of American values around the world.

The Great Depression resulted in a fundamental reordering of American politics. President Franklin Delano Roosevelt (FDR), who took office in 1933, believed that the federal government must assume an active role in banking, agriculture, and social welfare. He sponsored a large number of federal initiatives, known collectively as the New Deal. The New Deal aimed to put people back to work, restore faith in American businesses, boost purchasing power among consumers, and cushion the effects of economic downturns on industrial workers.

The effects of the New Deal were uneven. Many workers, including domestic servants, agricultural laborers, and part-time and seasonal employees, did not qualify for Social Security and other benefits. In the South government policies that discouraged landowners from planting crops led to the displacement of many black and white sharecropping families. On the other hand, employees of many large companies won higher wages and improved job security as a result of militant labor protests. African American civil rights activists, such local communist organizations as urban Unemployed Councils, and southern sharecroppers' and tenants' unions gave voice to the groups hit hardest by the Depression.

The New Deal did not end the Depression. On the morning of December 7, 1941, the Japanese conducted a surprise air attack on the U.S. Pacific naval fleet stationed in Pearl Harbor, Hawaii. Americans reacted with shock and outrage to what the president called this "day of infamy." The U.S. entry into World War II put large numbers of Americans back to work, many of them in the expanding defense industries.

The conflict brought Americans together in shared hardship, sacrifice, and national purpose. At the same time, the war placed strains on the social fabric. All over the country, family members separated from one another to search for work. In the Midwest blacks and whites competed for scarce wartime resources, such as housing. On the West Coast more than 100,000 Japanese immigrants and U.S. citizens of Japanese descent were forced into internment camps.

Elected to an unprecedented fourth term in 1944, Roosevelt proved to be a commanding leader during wartime as well as depression. In the last stages of the war, the president met several times with his British and Soviet counterparts, Winston Churchill and Josef Stalin, to plan for the postwar reconstruction of Europe and Asia. Roosevelt's death in April 1945 catapulted Vice President Harry S. Truman into the presidency. Germany surrendered to the Allies the next month. In August 1945, the new president authorized the dropping of atomic bombs on the Japanese cities of Hiroshima and Nagasaki, effectively ending the war in the Pacific. Together, the two bombs killed 120,000 Japanese civilians and wounded at least 130,000 more. The Atomic Age ushered in a new chapter in the history of human warfare.

Together with its allies, the United States emerged victorious from the war, but unlike its allies, America escaped physical destruction. Yet in many respects the postwar world was radically different from the world of the 1930s. The Soviet Union, an ally in the war against Germany and Japan, emerged as America's greatest enemy. The development of weapons of mass destruction introduced a new and profound threat to the natural environment, as well as to humans. To secure its supremacy in world affairs, the United States helped to form the North Atlantic Treaty Organization (NATO). For the first time, Americans were part of a multination peacetime alliance, one that required them to defend a member of the alliance even if they themselves were not attacked.

World War II also profoundly altered life in the United States. The perceived communist threat led some Americans to suspect domestic groups of internal subversion: African Americans agitating for their civil rights, labor leaders attempting to organize southern factories, and leftists who expressed support for communism in general and the Soviet Union in particular. Supported by government contracts, the defense industry became an integral part of the nation's economy.

Recovering quickly from the disruptions of war, returning soldiers and their wives hoped to settle down to a normal family life. These couples produced the baby boom, a generation that shaped American culture and society in significant ways. In the new and growing suburbs, many (predominantly white) Americans achieved their dream of home ownership, and businesses found plenty of room to expand in new industrial parks. Yet, not all Americans shared in this new found prosperity and security, and not all were willing to forgo their rights to free speech and free assembly in the struggle against communism.

1943 Smith–Connally Act.
Zoot-suit riots in Los Angeles.
Attacks on blacks in Detroit.

1944 Normandy invasion on D-Day (June 6).
Servicemen's Readjustment Act (GI Bill).

1945 Harry S. Truman becomes president upon death of Roosevelt.
First test of atomic bomb, Alamagordo, New Mexico.
Atomic bombs dropped on Hiroshima and Nagasaki.
V-E Day (May 7); V-J Day (Sept. 2).
United Nations created.

1946 *Morgan v. West Virginia* outlaws segregation in interstate transportation.
Winston Churchill gives "Iron Curtain" speech, Fulton, Missouri.

1947 Jackie Robinson joins Brooklyn Dodgers.
Taft–Hartley Act.
Truman Doctrine of containing communism announced.

1948 New Mexico and Arizona grant Indians right to vote.
Modern state of Israel founded.
Armed Services desegregated.
Organization of American States (OAS) founded.

1949 Billy Graham launches his first evangelical crusade in Los Angeles.
Establishment of People's Republic of China.
USSR acquires nuclear weapons.

1950 North Korean troops invade South Korea.
Internal Security Act of 1950.
Sen. Joseph McCarthy accuses State Department of harboring communists.

1951 Ethel and Julius Rosenberg convicted of treason.

1952 McCarran–Walter Act.
Puerto Rico becomes self-governing commonwealth.

1953 Korean War ends.
Soviet leader Josef Stalin dies.

CHAPTER

22

Hardship and Hope in the 1930s: The Great Depression

Joe Jones, *We Demand*, 1934. Gift of Sidney Freedman, 1948.
The Butler Institute of American Art, Youngstown, Ohio (948-0-110)

■ This 1934 painting by Joe Jones, *We Demand*, expresses the increasing strength and militance of
labor unions in the 1930s.

IN 1934, WILL ROGERS COMMENTED ON THE CAUSES OF THE GREAT DEPRESSION DURING HIS weekly radio broadcast. He noted that it was "not the working classes that brought on the economic crisis, it was the big boys that thought the financial drunk was going to last forever, and overbought, overmerged and overcapitalized." As a result, the "difference between our rich and poor grows greater every year. . . . Our rich are getting richer all the time. . . . There was not a millionaire in the country whose fortune did not come from the labor of others. We need to arrange it so that a man that wants work can get work, and give him a more equal division of the wealth the country produces."

Rogers was a Cherokee, a comedian, a plainspoken critic of the nation's rich and powerful, a movie star, journalist, and advisor to President Franklin Delano Roosevelt (FDR). Rogers articulated a new vision of American national identity that took shape in the 1930s. In contrast to an earlier notion of the United States as an Anglo-Saxon country into which newcomers might assimilate, this new Americanism included ethnic minorities, particularly those of European immigrant background. The Great Depression tarnished the status

Presidential candidate Franklin Roosevelt (left) delighted in the support of comic Will Rogers (right) in 1932.

of the nation's business elite and opened up the political process to party realignments and new leaders. The popular culture expressed and reflected this new Americanism; Will Rogers was its most prominent voice. When the *Wall Street Journal* and the *New York Times* condemned him for his criticism of corporate elites, Rogers responded with a humorous assault on the nation's Anglo-Saxon leaders and their myths:

> I have a different slant on things, for my ancestors did not come over on the Mayflower. They met the boat. . . . I hope my Cherokee blood is not making me prejudiced, I want to be broad minded, but I am sure it was only the extreme generosity of the Indians that allowed the Pilgrims to land anywhere. Suppose we reverse the case. Do you reckon the Pilgrims would have ever let the Indians land? Yeah, what a chance, what a chance. The Pilgrims wouldn't even allow the Indians to live after the Indians went to the trouble of letting them land, of course, but they'd always pray. . . . You've never in your life . . . seen a picture of one of the old Pilgrims praying when he didn't have a gun right by the side of him. That was to see that he got what he was praying for.

Born in Oolagah in the Indian Territory of Oklahoma in 1879, Rogers got his start as a rope-twirling Indian cowboy on the vaudeville circuit. Like earlier Indian adventurers, including Sitting Bull, he worked his way through Wild West shows, which offered him an opportunity to demonstrate his impressive riding and roping skills, even though he found the spectacles demeaning to Native Americans, who were always defeated in the shows' mock battles. He came to Hollywood in the 1920s, where his Cherokee identity shaped both his humor and his social criticism.

In the 1930s the Great Depression gave rise to a cultural and political upheaval that helped propel Rogers to stardom and political influence. President Franklin Roosevelt coveted his support, and Rogers obliged by promoting the New Deal, the president's program for economic recovery. However, Rogers also pushed the president to the left by advocating such measures as taxing the rich and redistributing wealth. In 1932 Oklahoma nominated Rogers for president as the state's favorite son; three years later, California Democratic leaders urged him to run for the Senate. But in 1935, before any of these possibilities could come to fruition, Rogers died in a plane crash.

The response to Rogers's death illustrates his stature as a national leader and spokesperson for a new multicultural Americanism. Congress adjourned in his memory, President Roosevelt sent a well-publicized letter to Rogers's family, the governor of California proclaimed a day of mourning, flags flew at half mast, bells rang in Rogers's honor in more than 100 cities, and nearly 100,000 people filed by his coffin at Forest Lawn Cemetery. Radio stations across the country broadcast his memorial service from the Hollywood Bowl, presided over by a Protestant minister and a Catholic priest, while a Yiddish performer sang a Hebrew mourning chant. Across town, Mexican American citizen groups placed a wreath on Olvera Street that read "Nosotros Lamentamos la Muerte de Will Rogers" ("We Mourn the Death of Will Rogers"). In the predominantly black Los Angeles community of Watts, an African American fraternal group called the Friends of Ethiopia joined black performers from Rogers's films in a parade to honor the Cherokee movie star who had spoken out publicly against Italy's 1935 invasion of Ethiopia. Back in his hometown of Claremore, Oklahoma, the Cherokee Indians performed a death dance in memory of their fallen kinsman.

> *The economic crisis opened the door for a politically radical Cherokee Indian to become one of the most popular figures of the Great Depression.*

This massive national grieving reveals not only Rogers's popularity, but also the culture of 1930s America. The economic crisis unleashed changes in society that opened the door for a politically radical Cherokee Indian to become one of the most popular figures of the Great Depression. Millions of Americans experienced poverty—many for the first time. The shared experience of loss and suffering permeated the country.

In the face of widespread hardship, many people felt a common bond and a fresh sense of themselves as Americans. This new type of Americanism was articulated most powerfully by Will Rogers. Those who subscribed to a changing national vision opposed the power of big business, participated actively in the emerging popular culture, and voted Democratic. Many of them came to the polls for the first time to vote for Roosevelt. They included native-born and foreign-born, working class and middle class, Anglo-Saxons and ethnic minorities, and people of color.

Roosevelt drew a new political coalition into the Democratic Party that elected him to the presidency four times. The Depression gave him the opportunity to forge a strong national government and to promote a more representative democracy. His inclusiveness efforts brought citizens of recent immigrant background into the political mainstream but stopped short of the color line. Nevertheless, African American voters abandoned the Republican party to vote for FDR.

The New Deal, a package of remedies put together by Franklin Roosevelt to address the problems of the Depression, provided relief to many Americans in need but did not eradicate poverty or end the Depression. Yet, as American families from every region of the country drew around their radios to hear the president's "fireside chats," as they made heroes of Will Rogers and other outsider celebrities, and as they held onto their faith in the nation's promise in spite of its worst economic crisis, they helped forge a more inclusive nation.

The Great Depression

The Great Depression defined the 1930s in the United States. It shaped the culture, the political life of the nation, the public policies that resulted, and the cultural expressions that reflected the spirit of the people during a time of national crisis. Its effects permeated the lives of Americans from the mansions of the wealthy to the shanties of the poor and from the boardrooms to the bedrooms. But the story is not simply one of despair and hardship. It is also one of strong communities, resourcefulness, and hope.

Causes of the Crisis

The Great Depression of the 1930s was the worst depression in the nation's history. But it was neither the first nor the last. Capitalism, the economic system that forms the basis of the American economy, has cycles of ups and downs. Under capitalism, the free market operates with minimal interference from the government. In the United States, prior to the 1930s, the government stepped in to regulate the economy primarily to protect economic competition. Progressive-era reforms prevented corporations from establishing monopolies, so that competition could flourish and businesses could prosper. In the free market economy, consumers would determine which companies would succeed, based on the quality of their products and services. Because the government did not determine the levels of industrial or agricultural productivity, and did not set the prices, the economy was subject to changing circumstances that led to times of prosperity and times of recession or, in the case of severe economic downturns, depression. The circumstances that affected the up-and-down cycles of the economy included international economic trends, as well as the workings of capitalism itself.

Communism and socialism provide different economic systems, with greater levels of government regulation. Communist countries have state-directed economies in which the government owns and operates the means of production, sets prices, and pays all workers' wages. There is no free market and no competition among businesses. In socialist states, governments own and operate certain industries and services, such as electricity and other utilities, or health care systems. Socialist countries also provide citizens with certain welfare benefits such as medical care, relief from poverty, income for the unemployed, and old age insurance. A number of capitalist countries offer these kinds of benefits to their citizens. These countries operate under a system known as "welfare capitalism," or a "welfare state."

The story of the Depression is not simply one of despair and hardship. It is also one of strong communities, resourcefulness, and hope.

Before the 1930s the United States provided none of these welfare state benefits. Without any policies that would serve as a safety net for workers who lost their jobs, many wage earners and their families fell into poverty during times of economic downturn. In the Great Depression of the 1930s, the economic crisis was so severe that one quarter of the nation's workers, nearly 14 million people, lost their jobs, leaving them and their families—40 million people in all—without any income or security. Many of these people had never known poverty before. Among the newly poor were thousands of middle-class Americans who now faced the loss of their homes and savings. For working-class and poor Americans, the impact of the depression was devastating because they had little economic security to begin with.

The Depression was a global economic catastrophe. Of the major world powers, only the Soviet Union—as a communist society, with state-directed labor, agriculture, and production—was immune to the collapse of the capitalist system after 1929. In fact, its economy grew throughout the 1930s. The relative health of the Soviet economy led many people in troubled capitalist systems to look to communism as an alternative. Socialism gained many converts across Europe, as did communism. The powerful nations of the world all moved toward greater government intervention in their economies. England, France, and the United States moved toward deficit spending to help stimulate the economy and instituted relief programs.

Italy, Germany, and Japan also increased government intervention into the economy, but they used different strategies to address the crisis, particularly military spending. These varied responses to the Depression contributed to the conflicts and alliances that would eventually culminate in World War II.

Within the United States, the business values that had prevailed throughout the 1920s were now suspect. Business practices in every area of the economy, from finance to factories to agriculture, contributed to the disaster. For many Americans the Depression really began in the 1920s. Food production and distribution stumbled along weakly throughout the 1920s, leaving widespread rural poverty in its wake. Large corporations bought up smaller companies, putting many independent shops and manufacturers out of business. During the 1920s, 1200 big corporations absorbed more than 6000 independent businesses. By 1929, 200 corporations controlled nearly half of all industry, which limited competition and made it difficult for new, smaller businesses to flourish.

The concentration of wealth among the richest Americans during the 1920s contributed to the persistence of the crisis in the 1930s.

Although the economy looked healthy on the surface, prosperity rested on an unsound foundation. Many people obtained consumer goods on credit, so when people lost their jobs, they could not pay their debts. Throughout the 1920s, the gap between the rich and poor increased. By 1929 the top 1 percent of Americans earned 14.7 percent of the nation's income, while the poorest 40 percent shared 12.5 percent. Nearly 80 percent of the nation's families had no savings at all. Those with high annual incomes of $10,000 or more—2.3 percent of the people—held two-thirds of all savings. As Will Rogers and many other social critics would later point out, the concentration of wealth among the richest Americans during the 1920s contributed to the persistence of the crisis in the 1930s.

International factors also played a role in the economic collapse. American overseas loans soared in the 1920s, reaching $900 million by 1924 and $1.25 billion by 1928. Germany was a large borrower, for example. Following its defeat in World War I, Germany had been required to make large reparation payments to France and other countries. The United States provided loans to Germany to help the country make its payments; Germany then made debt payments to the United States. When the stock market crashed, foreign economies like that of Germany also weakened and could not repay their debts. To make matters worse, American exports fell $1.5 billion between 1929 and 1933. The United States had established high tariffs to keep foreign goods out of the country so that Americans would buy only American-made goods. This, in turn, encouraged other countries to establish their own tariff barriers. Between 1929 and 1933, the Gross National Product (GNP) fell by $12 billion.

"We Are Not Bums"

In human terms the Depression of the 1930s dealt a devastating blow to large numbers of Americans: crushing poverty, hunger, humiliation, and loss of dignity and self-worth. Many felt a profound shame that they could no longer earn a living and support their families. The few jobs available often went to the young, strong, well-fed, and well-groomed. Thousands of citizens poured out their hearts in letters to the president, hoping that the government could provide some assistance. In 1934 an Oklahoma woman lamented, "The unemployed have been so long without food-clothes-shoes-medical care-dental care etc—we look pretty bad—so when we ask for a job we dont' get it. And we look and feel a little worse each day—when we ask for food they call us bums—it isent our fault . . . no we are not bums." Yet, the shabby appearance of the jobless helped neither their self-respect nor their work prospects. An unemployed worker from Oregon explained the difficult choices: "We do not dare to use even a little soap when it will pay for an extra egg [or] a few more carrots for our children."

■ Margaret Bourke-White in this 1937 photograph, "At the time of the Louisville Flood," depicts the painful irony of poverty in the midst of affluence. Here, hungry Americans line up at a breadline in front of a billboard proclaiming American prosperity.

Families provided the first line of defense against disaster, especially in the early days of the crisis. Many families adapted to hard times by abandoning time-honored gender roles. As men lost jobs, women went to work. More than 6 million single women held jobs during the Depression. Married women also took jobs to support their families, often providing the only source of income if husbands were out of work. These women often faced hostility from those who assumed that employed wives with husbands to support them took jobs from unemployed men. But, in fact, working women did not take jobs from men; rather, they held jobs defined as "traditional women's work" as secretaries, nurses, and waitresses. These jobs offered lower wages than most jobs held by men. Still, they provided at least a modicum of much-needed income.

Sons and daughters also went to work. For the younger generation, taking on the responsibilities of adulthood provided a sense of independence and self-respect. Marriage rates plummeted as young people delayed or decided against wedlock. As one daughter of Italian immigrants from Providence, Rhode Island, remarked, "It's not that I didn't want to get married, but when you are working and have your own money," there was no hurry to find a husband. Recalled another, "During all the years I worked, I had a boyfriend, but we both had responsibilities at home. . . . Now they say 'career woman' but at the time you wouldn't call yourself that. It's just because you felt you had a responsibility at home, too."

Songs of the Great Depression

Popular songs expressed the spirit, sorrows, and longings of Depression-era Americans. According to folk music historian Alan Lomax, the 12-year-old daughter of a striking Harlan County, Kentucky, mine worker wrote "Which Side Are You On?" in 1937. The song became a popular anthem for labor militancy.

Woody Guthrie (1912–1967) wrote more than a thousand songs about the struggles of common people and the dispossessed. As a teenager, Guthrie left home to hitchhike, ride the rails, live in hobo camps, and follow migrant workers around the country. His song "Union Maid" expresses the hopes and spirit of union workers, and "So Long, It's Been Good to Know Yuh" captures the sorrows of Dust Bowl migrants.

Bettmann/CORBIS

Woody Guthrie, singer and songwriter, immortalized the spirit of ordinary Americans during the struggles of the Great Depression. His songs became anthems of the era and remain classics of American folk music.

"Which Side Are You On?" by Florence Reece (sung to the tune of an old English song, "Jack Munro")

Come all of you good workers
Good news to you I'll tell

Of how the good old union
Has come in here to dwell.

Chorus:

Which side are you on,
Tell me, which side are you on?
My daddy was a miner,
He's now in the air an' sun,

Stick with him, brother miners,
Until this battle's won.

They say in Harlan County
There are no neutrals there
You'll either be a union man,
Or a thug for J. H. Blair.

Many parents struggled to provide for their families under difficult conditions, sometimes risking their health and safety to do so. Erminia Pablita Ruiz Mercer remembered when her father was injured while working in the beet fields in 1933. "He didn't want to live if he couldn't support his family," so he risked experimental back surgery and died on the operating table. Young Erminia then dropped out of school to work as "a doughnut girl" to support her mother and sisters.

Surviving Hard Times

For many poor families, hard times were nothing new. As one black man noted, "The Negro was born in depression. It only became official when it hit the white man." Throughout the 1930s black Americans suffered the impact of economic hard times disproportionately. By 1932 black unemployment reached 50 percent. As increasing numbers of white workers joined the ranks of the unemployed, they began seeking the jobs that were usually held by black workers, even though they would have shunned such work during prosperous times. With local white

O gentlemen, can you stand it,
O tell me if you can,
Will you be a lousy scab,
Or will you be a man?

Don't scab for the bosses,
Don't listen to their lies,
Us poor folks haven't got
a chance,
Unless we organize.

"Union Maid" by Woody Guthrie (first verse and chorus)

There once was a union maid
Who never was afraid
Of goons and ginks and company
finks
And the deputy sheriffs who made
the raids;
She went to the union hall
When a meeting it was called
And when the company boys
came 'round
She always stood her ground.

Chorus:

Oh, you can't scare me.
I'm sticking to the union, (3 times)
Oh, you can't scare me.
I'm sticking to the union, (2 times)
Till the day I die.

"So Long, It's Been Good to Know Yuh (Dusty Old Dust)" by Woody Guthrie (selected verses and chorus)

I've sung this song, but I'll sing
it again,
Of the place that I lived on the wild,
windy plains,
In the month called April, the county
called Gray
And here's what all of the people
there say:

Chorus:

So long, it's been good to know
you; (3 times)
This dusty old dust is a-getting
my home,
And I've got to be driftin' along.

A dust storm hit, and it hit like thunder;
It dusted us over, and it covered
us under;
Blocked out the traffic and blocked
out the sun.
Straight for home all the people
did run.

The sweethearts sat in the dark and
they sparked,
They hugged and they kissed in that
dusty old dark,
They sighed and cried, hugged and
kissed
Instead of marriage, they talked
like this:
Honey, so long, it's been good to
know you. . .

Now, the telephone rang, and it
jumped off the wall;
That was the preacher a-making
his call.
He said, "Kind friend, this may be
the end;
You've got your last chance of salva-
tion of sin."

The churches was jammed, and the
churches was packed,
And that dusty old dust storm blowed
so black;
The preacher could not read a word of
his text,
And he folded his specs and he took
up collection, said:
So long, it's been good to know
you. . . . .

authorities in charge of relief, impoverished Southern blacks had few places to turn for assistance. African Americans also faced increasing violence; the number of lynchings increased from 8 in 1932 to 20 in 1935.

Many poor people joined the growing ranks of hobos, riding the rails from town to town looking for work. But poverty did not erase racial hierarchies or sexual codes, especially for nine young blacks who came to be known as the "Scottsboro Boys." On March 25, 1931, the youths, ranging in age from 13 to 21, were taken from a train in Paint Rock, Alabama, after a fight with a group of white men. Two white women, also on the train, accused the nine of rape. Narrowly avoiding a lynching, the youths were taken to jail in Scottsboro, where they began a long ordeal. Within two weeks an all-white jury convicted them of rape, and they were sentenced to death. The communist-backed International Labor Defense (ILD) took up the case and appealed it to the Alabama Supreme Court. The ILD also organized protests and rallies across the country, calling for justice for the Scottsboro Boys. The National Association for the Advancement of Colored People (NAACP) also tried to get control of the case but withdrew when the defendants committed themselves to the ILD. In spite of the ILD efforts, the

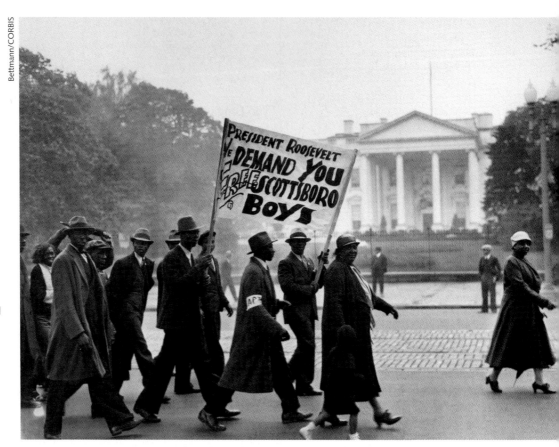

Bettmann/CORBIS

■ In 1933 protesters demonstrated in front of the White House demanding that President Roosevelt release the Scottsboro Boys. The nine black youths were convicted on flimsy evidence of raping a white woman on a hobo train.

Alabama Supreme Court upheld the convictions, but in November 1932 the U.S. Supreme Court ordered a new trial on the grounds that the defendants did not get a fair trial.

The first defendant to be re-tried was quickly convicted again and sentenced to death. At this point, the ILD and the NAACP organized new protests and gained support from across the political spectrum. The case became a major rallying point for civil rights activists, liberals, and radicals throughout the 1930s. Support for the young men came from all over the world, including the British Parliament and the Communist Party. In 1935 the U.S. Supreme Court reversed the second set of convictions on the grounds that excluding blacks from the jury denied the defendants due process. Yet in the next two years, five of the defendants were again tried and found guilty. Although none of the Scottsboro Boys was executed, they all spent long years in prison. The charges against the youngest four were eventually dropped. Although all appeals failed and the five remaining prisoners were never cleared of the crime, several were paroled, and the last of the nine was released from prison in 1950. In 1976 the repentant former segregationist governor of Alabama, George Wallace, pardoned one of the nine, Clarence Norris.

Racial discrimination intensified the suffering of African Americans during the Depression. By 1935, 90 percent of employed black women worked as either domestics or agricultural laborers. As these jobs became scarce, black women's labor-force participation fell from 42 percent to 38 percent over the decade. A white woman working for wages earned, on average, 61 percent of a white man's wages; a black woman earned a mere 23 percent.

Mexican American families could barely survive on the low wages paid to Mexican laborers. According to a 1933 study, working children's earnings constituted more than one-third of their families' total income. The work was often grueling. Julia Luna Mount recalled her first day at a Los Angeles cannery: "I didn't have money for gloves so I peeled chilies all day long

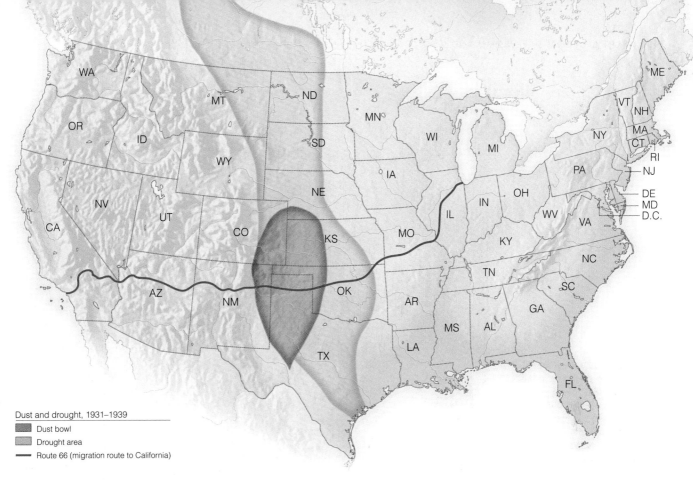

Dust and drought, 1931–1939

- Dust bowl
- Drought area
- Route 66 (migration route to California)

■ **MAP 22.1**

DUST AND DROUGHT, 1931–1939   Drought cut a giant swath across the middle of America during the years of the Great Depression. The hardest hit region was the Dust Bowl area of Oklahoma, Texas, New Mexico, Colorado, and Kansas. Many people fled the afflicted areas, abandoning farms, piling their belongings on their cars, and driving along Route 66 to California.

by hand. After work, my hands were red, swollen, and I was on fire! On the streetcar going home, I could hardly hold on my hands hurt so much." Young Julia was lucky—her father saw her suffering and did not make her return to the cannery. But Carmen Bernal Escobar's father could not afford to be soft-hearted about work: "My father was a busboy and to keep the family going . . . in order to bring in a little more money . . . my mother, my grandmother, my mother's brother, my sister and I all worked together" at the cannery.

Those with cannery work, hard as it was, were among the fortunate. Many more Mexicans were deported. Between 1931 and 1934, more than 500,000 Mexicans and Mexican Americans—approximately one-third of the Mexican population in the United States—were sent to Mexico. Most were children born in the United States. Throughout the century, the United States opened or closed its doors to Mexican immigrants depending on the need for their labor. They were deported during the Depression when unemployment was high, then recruited again during the labor shortage of World War II. In the 1930s Mexicans who applied for relief were offered assistance only if they agreed to return to Mexico. But deportation brought more sorrows. In Ciudad Juarez 2000 repatriates lived in a large open corral without resources or shelter; dozens died from disease.

The Dust Bowl

Severe drought exacerbated the difficulties of farmers across Oklahoma, Texas, Kansas, Colorado, and New Mexico, an area that came to be known as the Dust Bowl. Farmers had used

■ An Oklahoma farmer and his sons try to find shelter from the storm of dust that blew across the plains in 1935. Severe drought after years of excessive plowing created dry loose topsoil that was picked up by high winds. More than half of the residents of the Dust Bowl moved out of the area as a result of the devastation.

Arthur Rothstein, 1936. The Library of Congress

the land mainly for grazing until high grain prices during World War I enticed them to plow under millions of acres of natural grasslands to plant wheat. Plowing removed root systems from the soil, and years of little rainfall caused the land to dry up. By the middle of the decade high winds picked up the loose topsoil, creating dust storms across the open plains, as far as 1000 miles. The worst storm occurred on April 14, 1935, when winds up to 70 miles per hour carried clouds of dust that turned the sky black, suffocated livestock, and lodged in people's homes, clothes, hair, and lungs. The ecological disaster drove 60 percent of the population out of the region.

Migrant farm families fleeing the Dust Bowl came to symbolize the suffering wrought by the Depression. The photographs of Dorothea Lange, the songs of Woody Guthrie, and the writings of John Steinbeck all immortalized their plight. Steinbeck's Pulitzer prize–winning novel *The Grapes of Wrath* and its film version have remained classics of American popular art. Writing in *The Nation* three years before the publication of *The Grapes of Wrath* (1939), Steinbeck described the Dust Bowl migrants streaming into California:

> Poverty-stricken after the destruction of their farms, their last reserves used up in making the trip, they have arrived so beaten and destitute that they have been willing at first to work under any conditions and for any wages offered. . . . They are not drawn from a peon class, but have either owned small farms or been farm hands in the early American sense, in which the "hand" is a member of the employing family. They have one fixed idea, and that is to acquire land and settle on it. . . . They are not easily intimidated. They are courageous, intelligent, and resourceful. Having gone through the horrors of the drought and with immense effort having escaped from it, they cannot be herded, attacked, starved, or frightened.

Thousands of "Okies" piled belongings on their cars and made their way to California in hopes of starting over. There they joined Mexican migrant farm workers, African American laborers, and others down on their luck hoping for work.

Presidential Responses to the Depression

Until the collapse of the economy, President Herbert Hoover's political achievements had earned wide admiration. He seemed the perfect embodiment of the spirit of the prosperous 1920s. But his ideas about politics and economics were ill suited to the crisis of the 1930s. Dissatisfaction with Hoover's response to the Depression gave Franklin Delano Roosevelt a landslide victory in the 1932 presidential election. Promising to take action to ease the nation's suffering, the optimistic Roosevelt seemed to embody hope for an end to the crisis.

Herbert Hoover: Tackling the Crisis

Hoover's first major political achievement came in Europe during World War I, when he headed the Commission for Relief in Belgium. There he organized a massive effort funded by private and government contributions that fed more than 9 million people for nearly five years. Later, he became the U.S. food administrator and headed the American Relief Administration. He earned praise as a visionary progressive for his ability to mobilize volunteer efforts and to find efficient ways to meet people's needs. President Warren Harding then appointed him Secretary of Commerce.

It is no surprise that the popular Republican won the presidency in 1928. But even Hoover worried about "the exaggerated idea the people have conceived of me. They have a conviction that I am a sort of superman, that no problem is beyond my capacity. . . . If some unprecedented calamity should come upon the nation . . . I would be sacrificed to the unreasoning disappointment of a people who expected too much." The unprecedented calamity arrived, and Hoover's predictions were correct.

Had prosperity continued, Hoover might have left a legacy of outstanding leadership. Declaring that "excessive fortunes are a menace to true liberty," he favored steeply graduated inheritance and income taxes on the wealthy, with no tax burden on the poor. He believed that society had a responsibility to care for those in need and that the prosperous should bear much of the burden. After the stock market crash, Hoover increased spending for public works—programs in which the government created jobs for people who needed employment—to the unprecedented sum of $700 million. He established the Reconstruction Finance Corporation to make government credit available to banks and other financial institutions. Seeking to restore confidence in the economy, he strove for a balanced budget by raising taxes and cutting spending—a strategy that underestimated the depth of the Depression and made the situation worse.

As the Depression set in and brought widespread misery, Hoover fully expected that charitable organizations would step in and provide charity to the poor. He believed that government relief to the needy had demoralizing effects on people. In 1931 he pledged that if voluntary and local efforts were unable "to prevent hunger and suffering in my country, I will ask the aid of every resource of the Federal Government." But he had "faith in the American people that such a day [would] never come." Even when it was clear that the crisis was beyond the help of charitable groups, Hoover remained strongly opposed to direct relief for the poor. Private giving did increase to record levels; unfortunately, it was not sufficient.

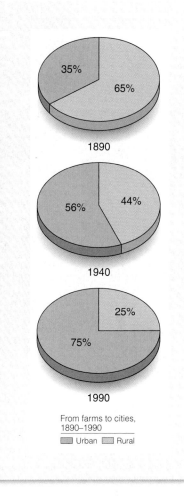

1890

1940

1990

From farms to cities,
1890–1990
■ Urban ■ Rural

■ **FIGURE 22.1**
URBAN AND RURAL POPULATION, 1890–1990
In the nineteenth century the American population was primarily rural. During the twentieth century, the population became predominantly urban.

Franklin D. Roosevelt Library

■ President Franklin Delano Roosevelt and First Lady Eleanor Roosevelt. The two distant cousins were political partners and close friends, but they lived separately during much of their marriage. Eleanor became a major political figure in her own right, remaining active for many years after the death of her husband.

Hoover felt that giving people the means to make a living was better than offering them direct relief. Thus, for example, he approved a grant of $45 million to feed livestock during the 1930 drought but rejected a proposed grant of $25 million to feed farmers and their families. His logic was consistent: Livestock provided farmers with the means to make a living so they could feed their families. But this philosophy offered little comfort to farmers who watched their families starve as their hogs lapped up food provided by the government.

Hoover's popularity reached its lowest ebb in 1932. A group of World War I veterans in Portland, Oregon, organized a march on Washington D.C. called the Bonus March. The veterans were due to receive a bonus of $1000 each in 1945. The group had asked to have their bonuses early, in 1932, to help ease their suffering during the Depression. But Hoover refused. More than 20,000 veterans traveled to Washington to petition Congress. The House passed a bill to pay the bonus immediately, but the Senate refused to follow suit. The determined veterans set up a tent city and settled in with their families. On the last day of the congressional session, when Hoover again refused to meet with the protesters, the veterans began to leave. But some did not depart quickly enough, and a police officer began shooting at the unarmed demonstrators, killing one person.

Army Chief of Staff Douglas MacArthur stepped in and escalated the violence. His troops used tear gas and bayonets to prod the veterans and their families to vacate the area, then set fire to the tent city. The attack injured more than 100 people and killed one baby. The image of federal troops assaulting a group of peaceful veterans horrified the public. Although MacArthur had ordered the brutality, the public directed its outrage against Hoover. As most people saw it, Hoover had heartlessly spurned the veterans' legitimate request. By the time of the 1932 election, Hoover had lost most of his public support.

Franklin Delano Roosevelt: The Pragmatist

In contrast to Hoover, Franklin Delano Roosevelt was born into a family of wealth and privilege whose ancestors included European aristocrats and passengers on the *Mayflower*. Pampered as a child, at age 14 he went to Groton, the nation's most exclusive boarding school; from there he attended Harvard College and Columbia Law School. In 1905, during his first year at Columbia, he married a distant cousin, Eleanor Roosevelt, the niece of former president Theodore Roosevelt. Like Franklin, Eleanor came from a sheltered, upper-class background. But her early life, unlike his, was filled with sadness. Both her parents died when she was a young child, and at age 10 she went to live with her grandmother, who left her in the care of a harsh governess. The young woman began to flourish when she went abroad to study. The rigorous education developed her strengths and confidence, which would serve her well during her marriage to FDR.

Eleanor bore six children in ten years. A reserved woman raised in the Victorian tradition of sexual reticence, she turned to abstinence to avoid additional pregnancies. In 1918 Eleanor discovered that Franklin was having an affair with her social secretary, Lucy Mercer. Eleanor offered him a divorce, but Franklin promised to end the affair, and the two remained married—although they did not live together. The Roosevelts developed a strong bond of friendship and a deep political alliance. FDR's fondness for Mercer did not end, however. When he was on his deathbed, Eleanor was out of town and Mercer was at his side.

Franklin Roosevelt was elected to the New York State Senate in 1911, and in 1913 he became Assistant Secretary of the Navy. He ran unsuccessfully as the Democratic vice presidential nominee in 1920. His political plans derailed suddenly in 1921 when he was stricken with polio. The painful and incapacitating illness threw the normally ebullient young man into despair. He had always assumed that he would control his own destiny. Now he could no longer use his legs. The formerly athletic Roosevelt depended on braces, crutches, and a wheelchair to move around. But his upbringing had given him extraordinary reserves of self-confidence and optimism, and these qualities helped to sustain him in the face of his paralysis.

FDR's bout with polio and subsequent paralysis did nothing to dampen his political ambitions. He became governor of New York in 1928, following in the footsteps of Theodore Roosevelt. But, unlike his Republican cousin, Franklin was a Democrat. In the 1932 presidential campaign, FDR made few specific proposals, but promised the American people a "New Deal." Although Hoover was intensely unpopular, he had supporters within the Republican party who defended his record and supported his efforts to balance the budget. Along with the Republican incumbent, there were other alternatives on the ballot, notably socialist Norman Thomas and communist William Z. Foster. Polls showed that 5 percent of the electorate favored Thomas, but in the end only half of those, fewer than 1 million voters, actually marked their ballots for Thomas, and a much smaller number for Foster. Many voters on the left cast their ballots for Roosevelt, fearing that a vote for Thomas might throw the election to Hoover. FDR won a landslide victory, the largest electoral margin since 1864.

TABLE 22-1			
The Election of 1932			
Candidate	Political Party	Popular Vote	Electoral Vote
Franklin D. Roosevelt	Democratic	22,821,857	472
Herbert Hoover	Republican	15,761,841	59
Norman Thomas	Socialist	881,951	0

"Nothing to Fear but Fear Itself"

Like Theodore Roosevelt before him, FDR was committed to strengthening the federal government. But Franklin was less interested in protecting and preserving old-stock Anglo-Saxon Americans from the cultural and demographic impact of immigration than his Republican cousin had been. Lawmakers in the 1920s closed off immigration, silenced dissenters, deported foreign radicals, and suppressed labor insurgency. In contrast, FDR identified the Depression as the nation's enemy rather than particular groups of Americans. His strategy was one of inclusion rather than exclusion; he welcomed the newcomers into his vision of America and cultivated their allegiance. Immigrants from southern and eastern Europe were among FDR's most ardent supporters. Millions of them became naturalized citizens and voted for the first time in the 1930s, overwhelmingly as Democrats.

In his inaugural address, Roosevelt endeavored to ease the nation's anxieties with reassuring words: "Let me assert my firm belief that the only thing we have to fear is fear itself—nameless, unreasoning, unjustified terror which paralyzes needed efforts to convert retreat into advance." Roosevelt launched his advance immediately. Panic had prompted many Americans to pull out their bank savings, causing many banks to fail. To stop the run on banks, FDR called Congress into a special session and announced a "bank holiday," temporarily closing all the nation's banks. He could have nationalized the banking system, a move toward socialism that would likely have received widespread support. But

Bettmann/CORBIS

■ Across the country a run on banks depleted cash reserves, so that depositors were unable to withdraw their savings. When a crowd gathered in front of Merchants Bank in Passaic, New Jersey, in 1929, the bank closed its doors.

Presidents and the Media

Franklin Delano Roosevelt was one of several American presidents who used the media and the realm of popular culture to communicate effectively with the public and achieve political goals. Roosevelt broke new media ground with his use of the radio, particularly in his "fireside chats," in which he reassured the people during the Great Depression and explained his New Deal programs in order to gain public support. Before the radio, presidents used their oratorical skills in stump speeches and public declarations. Abraham Lincoln was a gifted orator at a time when political rallies were not only important civic events but also major arenas of popular entertainment. Some of Lincoln's major speeches, including his Gettysburg Address and Second Inaugural, have become part of the national democratic canon.

Theodore Roosevelt used the expanding popular press as a "bully pulpit" to gain public support for his

Franklin D. Roosevelt Library

Franklin Delano Roosevelt during a radio broadcast, October 14, 1938. Roosevelt mastered the medium of radio and used it effectively to communicate directly to the people. In what came to be known as "Fireside Chats," Roosevelt addressed his millions of listeners as "my friends."

domestic agenda of progressive reform and "trust busting" of large corporations, as well as for his military exploits abroad. John F. Kennedy took the media presidency to new heights with his effective mastery of television. Kennedy was the first president to inject an element of celebrity stardom into his

media image, projecting an air of charm, grace, and wit. Although some found his media presence arrogant and aggressive, especially in televised debates during the 1960 campaign with his Republican opponent, Richard M. Nixon, he used television effectively throughout his presidency to cast him-

Roosevelt favored government regulation, not government ownership. He proposed the Emergency Banking Bill, providing government support for private banks. Congress passed the bill instantly, to the applause of the bankers who helped draft it.

In the first of his "fireside chats" to millions of radio listeners, whom he addressed as "my friends," Roosevelt assured citizens that the banks that reopened were sound. He used the medium of radio skillfully to explain his policies and to communicate comforting and reassuring messages that reached people in the intimate setting of their homes. The next day, bank deposits exceeded withdrawals as a result of the confidence he inspired.

The New Deal

The New Deal drew on Progressive-era reform impulses to extend the reach of the federal government to solve social problems. It provided assistance to many Americans suffering the effects of the Depression and established the welfare state that would last half a century. Based on pragmatism, experimentation, and shrewd political calculation, FDR's plan began with a flurry of activity in the first 100 days of his administration and developed self as a tough Cold Warrior, a vigorous athlete (despite serious chronic disabilities), and a devoted family man (despite his adulterous behavior). During tense moments of the Cold War, particularly in the midst of confrontations with the Soviet Union over control of Berlin and missiles in Cuba, he appeared on television to warn the Soviet leadership of his resolve and to rally the nation behind him.

Ronald W. Reagan, known as the "great communicator," was the first professional actor elected to the presidency. His ease in front of the camera and his talent as a communicator allowed him to achieve a personal connection with his audience. Reagan's mastery of the media enabled him to convey his conservative political ideology to the nation and maintain broad-based popular support throughout his presidency. In the 1990s, Bill Clinton went one step further, appearing on talk shows, comedy hours, and MTV, where he played his saxophone, talked about his marital troubles, and answered personal questions about such things as the style of underwear he wore. By the time Clinton became president, the private lives and sexual

Taking his cues from media celebrities and attempting to appeal to the nation's youth, President Bill Clinton rouses the crowd at the 1993 MTV Rock 'N Roll Inaugural Ball. Political leaders increasingly used the nation's mass media to promote their campaigns and develop a public persona.

behavior of politicians had become fair game for reporters. FDR and JFK had used the media to cultivate their images as strong leaders, while keeping their physical disabilities and their adulterous affairs far from public view. In those years journalistic ethics and etiquette placed the sexual behavior of presidents out of bounds. But all that had changed by the 1990s. The media exposed Clinton's affair with a White House intern, flooding the nation and the world with massive and detailed coverage. ■

into a more progressive agenda by 1935, often called the "second New Deal." New Deal programs countered the cyclical nature of capitalism and offered a safety net for industrial workers. They legitimized labor unions and established a system of regulation and cooperation between industry and labor. Many New Deal programs failed, but those that succeeded created the foundation of the modern American state. The broad-based reform effort, however, did not end the Depression or eradicate poverty.

The First Hundred Days

FDR understood that the people wanted "action, and action now." Roosevelt acted quickly and pragmatically. As one of his first acts, he encouraged Congress to repeal Prohibition. In 1933 the states quickly ratified the Twenty-First Amendment, repealing the Eighteenth. Repeal of Prohibition helped the economy by providing additional tax revenues from liquor sales, since they were now legal, and a market for farmers' corn and wheat, which were used in the production of liquor. Congress created the Securities and Exchange Commission (SEC) to oversee the stock market and the Federal Deposit Insurance Corporation (FDIC) to reform the banking system and provide insurance for deposits.

TABLE 22-2

Key New Deal Legislation, 1933–1938

Year	Act or Agency	Key Provisions
1933	Emergency Banking Act	Reopened banks under government supervision
	Civilian Conservation Corps (CCC)	Employed young men in reforestation, flood control, road construction, and soil erosion control projects
	Federal Emergency Relief Act (FERA)	Provided federal funds for state and local relief efforts
	Agricultural Adjustment Act (AAA)	Granted farmers direct payments for reducing crop production; funds for payment provided by a processing tax, later declared unconstitutional
	Farm Mortgage Act	Provided funds to refinance farm mortgages
	Tennessee Valley Authority (TVA)	Constructed dams and power projects and developed the economy of a seven-state area in the Tennessee River Valley
	Home Owners' Loan Corporation	Provided funds for refinancing home mortgages of nonfarm homeowners
	National Industrial Recovery Act (NIRA)	Established a series of fair competition codes; created National Recovery Administration (NRA) to write, coordinate, and implement these codes; NIRA's Section 7(a) guaranteed labor's right to organize (act later declared unconstitutional)
	Public Works Administration (PWA)	Sought to increase employment and business activity by funding road construction, building construction, and other projects
	Federal Deposit Insurance Corporation (FDIC)	Insured individual bank deposits
	Civil Works Administration (CWA)	Provided federal jobs for the unemployed
1934	Securities and Exchange Act	Created Securities and Exchange Commission (SEC) to regulate trading practices in stocks and bonds according to federal laws
	Indian Reorganization Act	Restored ownership of tribal lands to Native Americans; provided funds for job training and a system of agricultural and industrial credit
	Federal Housing Administration (FHA)	Insured loans provided by banks for the building and repair of houses
1935	Works Progress Administration (WPA)	Employed more than 8 million people to repair roads, build bridges, and work on other projects
	National Youth Administration (NYA)	WPA program that provided job training for unemployed youths and part-time jobs for students in need
	Federal One	WPA program that provided financial assistance for writers, artists, musicians, and actors
	National Labor Relations Act (Wagner Act)	Recognized the right of employees to join labor unions and to bargain collectively, reinstating the provisions of NIRA's Section 7(a); created the National Labor Relations Board (NLRB) to enforce laws against unfair labor practices
	Social Security Act	Created a system of social insurance that included unemployment compensation and old-age survivors' insurance; paid for by a joint tax on employers and employees
1938	Fair Labor Standards Act	Established a minimum wage of 25 cents an hour and a standard work week of 44 hours for businesses engaged in interstate commerce

Roosevelt appointed a cabinet composed of a number of liberals, including Henry A. Wallace of Iowa as Secretary of Agriculture, Harold L. Ickes of Illinois as Secretary of the Interior, and Frances Perkins of New York as Secretary of Labor—the first woman ever appointed to the Cabinet. In addition to his cabinet, FDR appointed several academics to serve as advisors. Known as the Brain Trust, they included Raymond Moley, Adolfe Berle, and Rexford Tugwell of Columbia University; attorney Basil O'Connor; and Felix Frankfurter of Harvard Law School. They helped shape the New Deal into a program of reform that would preserve American capitalism.

One of FDR's most pressing challenges was to prop up prices for producers while keeping them low enough for consumers. Poverty in the midst of plenty was one of the Depression's cruelest ironies. Because farmers could no longer afford to transport their goods to market, food rotted while millions of people went hungry. FDR took action by developing the Farm Relief Act. Included in the Farm Relief Act was the Farm Mortgage Act, which lowered mortgage rates for farmers to help them keep their farms. Also included was the Agricultural Adjustment Act (AAA). In a highly controversial provision of the AAA, the government sought to prop up farm prices by limiting supply. That is, it paid farmers to destroy livestock and take acreage out of production.

Many Americans recoiled at the systematic slaughter of 6 million piglets and the plowing under of 10 million acres of cotton. This policy boosted profits for larger farms but did little to alleviate the problems of smaller, poorer farmers. Sharecroppers and tenant farmers fared even worse. The desperation and pride of rural Americans came through in countless letters to Eleanor Roosevelt. A woman from Winnsboro, Louisiana, pleaded with the First Lady: "I don't want on the relif if I can help it i want to work for my livin byt the last thing we have is gone. . . . Don't you know its aful to have to get out and no place to have a roof over your sick child and nothing to eat I cant tell all my troubles."

Most Americans in need desperately wanted to work. They considered government relief a signal of failure and

Library of Congress

■ Dorothea Lange took photographs for the Farm Security Administration (FSA) documenting the lives of Depression-era migrants. This 1939 photo, "Mother and Children on the Road, Tulelake, Siskiyou County, California," is one of Lange's many portraits of impoverished families.

a source of deep shame and humiliation. Many citizens searched for ways to preserve their pride. One woman wrote to Eleanor Roosevelt asking to borrow money in order to avoid charity:

> *Please* Mrs. Roosevelt, I do not want charity, only a chance from someone who will trust me. . . . I am sending you two of my dearest possessions to keep as security, a ring my husband gave me before we were married, and a ring my mother used to wear. . . . If you will consider buying the baby clothes, please keep them (rings) until I send you the money you spent. It is very hard to face bearing a baby we cannot afford to have, and the fact that it is due to arrive soon, and still there is no money for the hospital or clothing, does not make it any easier. I have decided to stay home, keeping my 7 year old daughter from school to help with the smaller children when my husband has work. . . . The 7 year old one is a good willing little worker and somehow we must manage—but without charity.

The writer of the letter included a list of items she needed. She concluded with, "If you will get these for me I would rather no one knew about it. I promise to repay the cost . . . as soon as possible."

In March 1933 Congress passed the Federal Emergency Relief Administration (FERA), which provided $500 million in grants to the states for aid to the needy. Roosevelt placed Harry Hopkins in charge. Hopkins, an energetic and brash young reformer, disbursed $2 million during his first two hours on the job. He then persuaded Roosevelt to launch a temporary job program, the Civil Works Administration (CWA). The CWA provided government-sponsored

■ MAP 22.2

AREAS SERVED BY THE TENNESSEE VALLEY AUTHORITY   The Tennessee Valley Authority (TVA) brought electricity to a large area in western Appalachia, one of the poorest regions in the country. The government-owned project strengthened the economy and improved living conditions in the area.

jobs for more than 4 million workers. But the program came under fire from conservatives, and FDR ended it a few months later.

The New Deal included two major programs that addressed conservation and environmental issues. In 1933, Roosevelt combined his interest in conservation with his goal of providing work for unemployed young men. The Civilian Conservation Corps (CCC) operated under the control of the Army. CCC workers lived in camps, wore uniforms, and conformed to military discipline. They planted millions of trees, dug canals and ditches, built more than 30,000 wilderness shelters, stocked rivers and lakes with nearly 1 billion fish, and preserved historic sites. Their work revived depleted forests and provided flood control. By 1935 the CCC had employed more than 500,000 young men and kept them, in FDR's words, "off the city street corners."

Another measure that linked natural resources to the recovery effort was the Tennessee Valley Authority (TVA). On May 18, 1933, Roosevelt signed into law the Tennessee Valley Authority Act, an experiment in government-owned utilities that brought power to rural areas along the Tennessee River in seven states in western Appalachia—among the poorest areas in the nation. This far-reaching government-owned project offered a radical alternative to American capitalism, based on private enterprise. Under the TVA, the government built five dams, improved twenty others, and constructed power plants; it produced and sold electricity to the valley's farmers and facilitated the development of industry in the region. The TVA also boosted local economies by selling fertilizer and electricity, and by providing flood control, and improving river navigation. Business conservatives and Southern Democratic congressmen opposed the plan because it used government money to provide jobs and electricity to rural African Americans in the Tennessee Valley. Nevertheless, the TVA became one of the largest and cheapest suppliers of power in the nation. Although years later, President Dwight D. Eisenhower condemned the TVA as a New Deal example of "creeping socialism," it was one of Roosevelt's most successful and enduring projects.

The National Industrial Recovery Act (NIRA), passed by Congress in 1933, became the centerpiece of the first New Deal. The NIRA established the National Recovery Administration (NRA) to oversee the regulation of the economy. In his second "fireside chat," Roosevelt called the NRA "a partnership in planning" between business and government. The NRA enabled businesses in each sector of the economy to form trade associations and set their own standards for production, prices, and wages. But in return, businesses had to agree to recognize labor unions. Section 7(a) of the NIRA guaranteed collective bargaining rights to workers, sparking new hope for union organizers.

FDR's first 100 days also included the creation of the Home Owners' Loan Corporation, providing refinancing of home mortgages at low rates. Because the plan helped stem the tide of foreclosures and also guaranteed the repayment of loans, it pleased homeowners, banks, and real-estate interests. It also gained for FDR the support of a large segment of the middle class.

One of the boldest New Dealers was John Collier, whom Roosevelt appointed as Commissioner of Indian Affairs. Collier opposed the policy of land allotment that the Dawes Act of 1887 had enacted. Under allotment, Native American land holdings had dwindled from 130 million acres to 49 million acres—much of it desert. Collier also rejected the assumption that Indians' survival depended on their assimilation into white culture. He altered the government boarding schools' curriculum to include bicultural and bilingual education and eliminated military dress and discipline.

Collier's ideas came to fruition in the 1934 Indian Reorganization Act, which recognized the autonomy of Indian tribes, did away with the allotment program, and appropriated funds to help Indians add to their land holdings. It also provided for job and professional training programs as well as a system of agricultural and industrial credit. In keeping with Collier's goal of Indian self-government, each tribe decided whether to accept the terms of the Indian Reorganization Act. In the end, 181 tribes voted to accept the law, while 77 opted out of it.

■ On October 28, 1935, John Collier, Commissioner of Indian Affairs, stands with a group of Flathead Indian chiefs as Secretary of the Interior Harold L. Ickes signs the first constitution providing for Indian self-rule. Franklin Roosevelt appointed Collier to bring the New Deal to Native Americans.

AP/Wide World

The Navajos were among the tribes that rejected the Indian Reorganization Act. Many Navajos perceived Collier as yet another heavy-handed government agent. This tension heightened during an environmental conflict over Navajo herding rights. Convinced that the Navajos were herding far more sheep and goats than the fragile desert ecosystem could support, Collier proposed a plan by which the federal government would purchase 400,000 head of Navajo livestock. Although Collier had been more receptive to Indian concerns than almost any other federal authority who had preceded him, he could not reconcile the conflicting interests of tribal autonomy, environmentalism, and development.

Protest and Pressure from the Left and the Right

Challenges to Roosevelt's New Deal took many forms. In spite of FDR's efforts to help businesses survive and remain profitable during the Depression, many business leaders continued to oppose the New Deal, charging that FDR was a dictator and that his program amounted to socialism. At the same time, FDR faced criticism from the left. Many people believed that Roosevelt's policies did not go far enough to ease the suffering caused by the economic crisis. Some thought that New Deal policies aimed at bolstering capitalism were ill-advised, and that capitalism itself was the problem. Disenchantment with capitalism drew many Americans to the cause of socialism and swelled the ranks of the Communist party.

The Communist party drew its inspiration from the Soviet Union and, during the 1930s, developed a strategy known as the Popular Front to build alliances with sympathetic American liberals. Not all liberals belonged to the Popular Front, but many people with progressive political leanings shared with the socialists and the Communist party a commitment to economic justice, unemployment relief, civil rights, and union organizing. The actual membership of the Communist Party remained small—it peaked at 100,000 during World War II when the United States and the Soviet Union were allies—but its influence increased during the Depression.

By 1934 and 1935 much of the pressure on Roosevelt came from workers, whose hopes that the NIRA would guarantee collective bargaining rights were dashed by the intransigence of employers. The 1920s had taken a toll on labor unions. Membership had declined from a high of 5 million in 1920 to 2 million by 1933. But workers continued to strike for improved wages and working conditions. In 1934 nearly 1.5 million workers participated in 1800 strikes. Often, unemployed laborers joined picket lines, refusing to work as strikebreakers.

> *Many people believed that Roosevelt's policies did not go far enough to ease the suffering caused by the economic crisis.*

Workers all over the country organized for better working conditions. Birmingham, Alabama, provides an apt example. The Depression hit Birmingham early and hard. By 1928, unemployment had reached 18 percent. Many impoverished black steelworkers, along with farm laborers in the surrounding countryside, joined the "invisible army" of the Communist party. Together, they fought for better working conditions and racial justice. One young black coal miner, Angelo Herndon, recalled the dangers of organizing and the need for secrecy: "With our few pennies that we collected we ground out leaflets on an old rickety mimeograph machine, which we kept concealed in the home of one of our workers. We were obliged to work very quietly, like the Abolitionists in the South during the Civil War, behind drawn shades and locked doors." Although most African Americans supported FDR and the Democratic party during the Depression, between 3000 and 4000 members of Birmingham's black community joined the Communist party and related organizations during the 1930s.

Mexican laborers in California launched similar efforts. They faced not only persistent exploitation in fields and factories but also the constant threat of deportation. During the Depression, approximately one-third of the Mexican population in the United States—more than half a million people—was deported to Mexico, even though the majority were native-born citizens. Some of those who remained organized unions and struck for better pay and working conditions. During 1933, agricultural workers mounted 37 major strikes in California alone. They scored a number of successes; more than half of the conflicts led to wage increases.

Dorothy Ray was only 16 years old when she began organizing Mexican workers at the grassroots level in California. She found it particularly rewarding to witness "the diminishing of bigotry . . . watching all those Okies and Arkies . . . all their lives they'd been on a little farm in Oklahoma; probably they had never seen a Black or a Mexicano. And you'd watch in the process of a strike how those white workers soon saw that those white cops were their enemies and that the Black and Chicano workers were their brothers." Another successful effort at biracial organizing occurred in the Arkansas delta in 1934. The Southern Tenant Farmers' Union (STFU) brought together black and white tenants and sharecroppers to fight for better working conditions.

In addition to the communists, socialists, labor unions, and grassroots organizations that sprang up all over the country, a number of individuals proposed alternatives to Roosevelt's program and gained large followings. The most influential of these were Dr. Francis Townsend, Father Charles E. Coughlin, and Senator Huey P. Long. In 1934, Townsend, a retired physician and health commissioner from Long Beach, California, introduced an idea for a pension plan that sparked a nationwide grassroots movement. Townsend proposed a 2 percent national sales tax that would fund a pension of $200 a month for Americans over age 60. The "Townsend Plan" became hugely popular, especially among elderly Americans. In 1936, a national survey indicated that half of all Americans favored the plan. Though the plan was never implemented, the groundswell of support that it generated probably hastened the development and passage of the old age insurance system contained in the 1935 Social Security Act.

Coughlin also inspired a huge following. A Catholic priest from Canada, he served as pastor of a small church outside Detroit, Michigan. He began to broadcast his sermons on the radio, using his magnetic personality to address political as well as religious issues. Soon he became a media phenomenon, broadcasting through 26 radio stations to an audience estimated at 40 million. The "Radio Priest" called for a redistribution of wealth and attacked Wall Street, international bankers, and the evils of capitalism. When a Minnesota radio station polled listeners to see whether they wanted to hear Coughlin's program, 137,000 said yes. Only 400 said no.

Initially, Coughlin strongly supported Franklin Roosevelt and the New Deal. But he soon grew impatient with what he considered the slow pace of New Deal reforms. In 1934, Coughlin launched his own political party, the National Union for Social Justice, which he used to challenge Roosevelt's leadership. The activist priest promoted a populist message that was hostile to both capitalism and communism. He told his radio listeners, "I call upon every one of you who is weary of drinking the bitter vinegar of sordid capitalism and upon everyone who is fearsome of being nailed to the cross of communism to join this Union which, if it is to succeed, must rise above the concept of an audience and become a living, vibrant, united, active organization, superior to politics and politicians in principle, and independent of them in power." Soon, his message turned from social justice populism to right-wing bigotry. His

Herald Examiner Collection/Los Angeles Public Library, (Neg. #HE-000-282 4x5)

■ High rates of unemployment and fierce competition for jobs prompted government officials to deport more than half a million people of Mexican descent. In this 1932 photo Mexicans and Mexican Americans line up in Los Angeles for deportation to Mexico.

virulent anti-Semitism and admiration for the fascist regimes of Adolf Hitler in Germany and Benito Mussolini in Italy drove away many of his followers. By 1940, Coughlin had ceased broadcasting and abandoned all political activities, under orders of the Catholic Church.

Huey P. Long was among the most powerful, and colorful, politicians of the era. He rose from modest origins to become a lawyer and a public service commissioner. In 1928, Long won the governorship of Louisiana. His progressive leadership inspired tremendous loyalty, especially among poor workers and farmers. He did more for the underprivileged people of Louisiana than any other governor. He expanded the state's infrastructure; developed social services; built roads, hospitals, and schools; and changed the tax code to place a greater burden on corporations and the wealthy. He proved unique among Southern politicians in that his public statements were free of racial slurs. But he also trampled the democratic process. His ambition had no bounds, and he used any means to accumulate power. Through his tremendous popular appeal, Long developed a massive power base and eventually gained control of Louisiana's legislature, courts, state bureaucracies, and even local governments.

In 1932 Long resigned the governorship and won election to the U.S. Senate. Soon, he gained a huge national following. Initially he supported FDR, but by 1933 he had broken with the president and forged his own political movement based on his Share-Our-Wealth Plan. Giving voice to the resentments many Americans felt toward "wealthy plutocrats," Long advocated a radical redistribution of the nation's wealth. He called for new taxes on the wealthy and proposed to use the funds to guarantee a minimum annual income of $2500 for all those in need. As he put it, "How many men ever went to a barbecue and would let one man take off the table what was intended for nine-tenths of the people to eat? The only way you'll ever be able to feed the balance of the people is to make that man come back and bring back some of the grub he ain't got no business with." Long's plainspoken radicalism won the hearts of his followers, including Will Rogers, who publicly urged FDR to back Long's proposals. However, many of his congressional colleagues considered him an agitator. Such skepticism did little to limit Long's ambition, and by 1935 he was planning to challenge FDR in the next presidential election. But he never had the chance. In September 1935 the son-in-law of one of his vanquished political opponents assassinated him.

> *Huey P. Long was among the most powerful, and colorful, politicians of the era.*

Other challenges took the form of viable third parties. In Wisconsin, the legacy of Progressive senator Robert M. LaFollette was alive and well, particularly in the political popularity of his two sons, Senator Bob and Governor Phil. In 1934, the brothers formed the Wisconsin Progressive party, which supported the New Deal but pulled it strongly to the left. The state's voters endorsed the radical rhetoric of the LaFollette brothers, reelecting them on the Progressive party ticket with overwhelming victories over their Democratic party rivals.

Meanwhile in neighboring Minnesota, a coalition of workers and farmers formed the Minnesota Farmer–Labor party. In 1930 populist Floyd Olson became the nation's first Farmer–Labor governor. At the party's 1934 convention Olson made his position clear: "I am not a liberal. I enjoy working on a common basis with liberals for their platforms, etc., but I am not a liberal. I am what I want to be—I am a radical. I am a radical in the sense that I want a definite change in the system, I am not satisfied with tinkering, I am not satisfied with patching, I am not satisfied with hanging a laurel wreath upon burglars and thieves and pirates and calling them code authorities or something else." Olson considered the possibility of a third-party bid for the presidency in 1936, but his plans never reached fruition. He contracted cancer and died in August 1936 at age 44.

On the West Coast, discontented voters mounted a similar challenge to party-politics-as-usual. Some Democrats persuaded Upton Sinclair, a veteran socialist and author of the 1906 muckraking novel *The Jungle,* to run for governor on their ticket in 1934. Sinclair ran on his End Poverty in California (EPIC) plan, which would have let the state take over idle land and factories and permit unemployed laborers to use them for their own needs. Sinclair won the

Democratic primary with an overwhelming majority. But Democratic party regulars, including FDR, refused to support his candidacy. Without the support of his own party and facing opposition from wealthy Republicans who spared no expense to defeat him, Sinclair lost the election. Nevertheless, Sinclair's tremendous popularity signaled to Roosevelt that if he hoped to retain the support of his constituents, he would need to move significantly to the left.

Eleanor Roosevelt also pushed FDR to the left, particularly on the issue of civil rights. A political activist in her own right and the most powerful First Lady until Hillary Clinton entered the White House in 1992, Eleanor was among FDR's closest advisors. Although FDR was reluctant to support an anti-lynching bill in Congress for fear of alienating Southern white voters, the First Lady campaigned vigorously against lynching. When the Daughters of the American Revolution (DAR) denied the African American opera star Marian Anderson the right to perform at Constitution Hall in Washington, D.C., Eleanor promptly resigned from the DAR in protest and arranged for Anderson to perform at the Lincoln Memorial on Easter Sunday 1939, where a huge audience stood in the cold to hear her sing.

■ African American contralto Marian Anderson sings on the steps of the Lincoln Memorial on April 9, 1939. Eleanor Roosevelt arranged the concert after the DAR refused to allow Anderson to sing in Constitution Hall. The event attracted an audience of 75,000, and millions listened on the radio.

The Second New Deal

Eleanor Roosevelt's efforts notwithstanding, FDR tread softly on the issue of race. He knew that Southern blacks were disenfranchised, but he depended on Southern white voters to be reelected and to get his New Deal measures through Congress. So he was careful not to alienate Southern Democrats by cultivating African American voters. However, he did reach out to industrial workers. In the spring of 1935, Congress passed the National Labor Relations Act, also known as the Wagner Act, which strengthened and guaranteed collective bargaining and gave a huge boost to labor unions.

Also in 1935, Congress passed the Social Security Act, perhaps the most important and far-reaching of all the New Deal's programs. The Act established a system of old-age pensions, unemployment insurance, and welfare benefits for dependent children and the disabled. The framework of the Social Security Administration shaped the welfare system for the remainder of the century. The welfare state established by the Social Security Act, extensive as it was, did not reach all Americans and left out many of the most needy. It also established a two-track system of welfare. One track provided workers with unemployment insurance and support in their old age. Programs like Social Security, designed primarily for male wage earners, paid retired workers, based on a percentage of the wages they earned while in the workforce. Social Security provided an important safety net for large numbers of workers and the elderly, but it did not cover domestics, seasonal or part-time workers, agricultural laborers, or housewives. The other track made matching funds available to states to provide relief for the needy, mostly dependent women and children with no means of support. Unlike Social Security, which was provided to all retired workers regardless of their circumstances, relief programs, which came to be known as "welfare," were administered according to need.

The architects of this welfare system included top New Deal advisors, many of them women who had been active reformers, such as Eleanor Roosevelt. These advocates hoped to protect women and children from the destitution that almost certainly resulted if a male breadwinner lost his job, deserted his family, or died. The system presumed that a man ordinarily earned a "family wage" that let him support his wife and children and that women were necessarily economically dependent on men. Thus, a deeply entrenched gender system prevailed

■ In this mural on San Francisco's Coit Tower, "Industries of California," Works Projects Administration (WPA) artist Ralph Stackpole depicts the city's diverse workforce. Across the country, government-funded artists created works of public art that portrayed life in local communities.

through the 1930s. As a result, some—though not all—male breadwinners received benefits like Social Security. Impoverished women and children, on the other hand, received public charity. These payments were usually meager, not enough to lift a woman and her children out of poverty. Inadequate welfare payments never helped the needy become self-sufficient and did nothing to eradicate poverty.

Because there were no nationally established guidelines on how to distribute welfare funds, states could determine who received assistance. As a result, the Social Security Act did little to assist African Americans, especially in the South, where black women were deliberately excluded by local authorities who preferred to maintain a pool of cheap African American labor rather than to provide relief for black families. One Southern public assistance field supervisor, explaining the low numbers of African American families on the welfare rolls, articulated the prevailing attitude: "The number of Negro cases is few due to the unanimous feeling on the part of the staff and board that there are more work opportunities for Negro women and to their intense desire not to interfere with local labor conditions. The attitude that they have always gotten along, and that 'all they'll do is have more children' is definite. . . . There is hesitancy on the part of lay boards to advance too rapidly over the thinking of their own communities, which see no reason why the employable Negro mother should not continue her usually sketchy seasonal labor or indefinite domestic service rather than receive a public assistance grant."

In 1935 Congress allocated the huge sum of nearly $5 billion for the Emergency Relief Appropriation. Roosevelt used a significant portion of the money to expand his public works program. By executive order he established the Works Progress Administration (WPA), which provided millions of jobs for the unemployed. The project mandated that WPA jobs would make a contribution to public life and would not compete with private business. The jobs included building streets, highways, bridges, and public buildings; restoring forests; clearing slums; and extending electricity to rural areas. The WPA National Youth Administration gave work to nearly 1 million students.

The wages paid to WPA workers proved pitifully low. And like most other New Deal programs, the WPA left out the most needy. It provided work only to those already on the relief rolls, and just one person per family could hold a WPA job. This policy ruled out most women as well as older children. It also neglected the vast majority of the unemployed who were not on relief. A 1937 letter to Harry Hopkins from the Workers' Council of Colored People in Raleigh, North Carolina, pointed to the failure of the WPA to provide jobs for black women. The writer explained that the wages paid to domestic and farm laborers were so low that, even if they worked 14-hour days, they could not pay their rent. "If we cannot work on WPA Projects & be compel to take these poor paying jobs; [we request] that food, clothes & rent money be provided for us at once because we are suffering. We the Workers Council understood that no colored women [can] be hired this winter on any of the WPA projects. We wish you to tell us why."

The most effective WPA program was Federal One, which provided financial support for writers, musicians, artists, and actors. The Federal Theater Project, under the direction of Hallie Flanagan, former head of Vassar College's Experimental Theater, shaped the project into an arena for experimental community-based theater. Flanagan focused on contemporary issues and developed such innovations as the "Living Newspaper." The Federal Theater Project included 16 black theater units. Their most notable production was an all-black version of *Macbeth* set in Haiti and staged in Harlem.

Federal One supported thousands of artists and brought the arts to a wide public audience through government-funded murals on public buildings, community-theater productions, local orchestras, and the like. By the late 1930s the program came under political attack for supporting artists who expressed leftist sensibilities, and Congress cut off its funding. In 1943 the WPA was dissolved.

The New Deal did not reach everyone. Programs were geared toward full-time industrial workers, most of whom were white men. Domestic workers, Mexican migrant laborers, black and white sharecroppers, Chinese and Japanese truck farmers—all were among those ineligible for Social Security, minimum wages and maximum hours, unemployment insurance, and other New Deal benefits. But the New Deal established the national welfare state and provided assistance and security to millions of working people along with disabled, dependent, and elderly Americans. Such sweeping programs also solidified Roosevelt's popularity among the poor, workers, and much of the middle class.

FDR's Second Term

In the 1936 campaign FDR claimed that the election was a battle between "the millions who never had a chance" and "organized money." He boasted that the "forces of selfishness and of lust for power" had united against him: "They are unanimous in their *hate* for *me—and I welcome their hatred.*" His strategy paid off. Roosevelt won the election by a landslide of more than 60 percent of the popular vote. Six million more voters cast ballots than had done so in 1932, and 5 million of those new votes went to Roosevelt. His strongest support came from the lower ends of the socioeconomic scale. The election also swept Democrats into Congress, giving them a decisive majority in both the House and the Senate.

With such a powerful mandate, Roosevelt was well positioned to promote a new legislative program. As his first major effort, he took on the Supreme Court. Dominated by conservative justices, the court had invalidated some major legislation of Roosevelt's first term, including the AAA and the NIRA. Roosevelt feared that the justices would unravel the New Deal by striking down its progressive elements. To shift the

TABLE 22-3			
The Election of 1936			
Candidate	**Political Party**	**Popular Vote**	**Electoral Vote**
Franklin D. Roosevelt	Democratic	27,751,597	523
Alfred M. Landon	Republican	16,679,583	8
William Lemke	Union	882,479	0

balance of power on the court, he proposed a measure that would let the president appoint one new justice for every one on the court who had at least 10 years of service and who did not retire within six months after turning 70.

Emboldened by his landslide victory, FDR believed that he could persuade Congress and the nation to go along with any plan he put forward, but he was mistaken. Many viewed his "court packing" plan as a threat to the fundamental separation of powers and feared that it would set a dangerous precedent. Some considered it an affront to the more aged justices, such as the respected liberal Lewis Brandeis, a man in his eighties. Powerful Republicans in Congress forged an alliance with conservative Democrats, mostly from the South, to defeat the plan. This informal alliance dominated Congress for the following two decades. The court blunder cost Roosevelt considerable political capital and empowered his opponents. In the end, his plan proved unnecessary anyway. The court did not undercut the New Deal. Within the next few years Roosevelt succeeded in appointing several new justices who tipped the balance in his favor.

A New Political Culture

FDR continued to face strong opposition from conservatives on the right and radicals, communists, and socialists on the left. But his political fortunes benefited from the emergence of a new and more inclusive national culture. This new Americanism emanated from the working class and found expression in the labor movement, the popular culture, and the political coalition that came together in the Democratic party. These nationalizing forces cut across lines of class and region and occasionally challenged hierarchies of gender and race.

The Labor Movement

The labor insurgency that erupted during the early years of the New Deal demonstrated the need for a new national labor movement. The American Federation of Labor (AFL), restricted to skilled workers, left out most of the nation's less skilled industrial laborers. John L. Lewis of the United Mine Workers (UMW) rose to meet these laborers' need for new leadership. Lewis was one of several union leaders from a number of industries—including mining, steel, rubber, and automobile—who left the AFL to form a new and more broad-based labor organization, the Congress of Industrial Organizations (CIO). Lewis played a key role in the organization's growth into a national force, but the impetus came from the workers themselves.

Sidney Hillman, leader of the Amalgamated Clothing Workers of America, was among the labor leaders who organized the CIO. Hillman had a broad vision of labor unions working with management and government to achieve a strong economy and social justice. Under his leadership, the Amalgamated provided its members with education, subsidized housing, health care, and unemployment insurance long before the New Deal incorporated these programs into national policy. His economic ideas were also in keeping with New Deal efforts to pump money into the hands of consumers. Known as Keynesian economics, named after John Maynard Keynes, this strategy promoted increased spending to stimulate economic recovery.

Hillman argued that higher wages were good for the economy because workers would then be able to purchase consumer products, benefiting industry as well as workers. Although Henry Ford also understood that principle (see Chapter 19), Ford was vehemently anti-union. Hillman argued that powerful unions could help to strengthen and regulate the economy and avoid devastating wage wars. Hillman's leadership in the labor movement brought him into the Roosevelt administration, where he served as Associate Director of the Office of Production Management and became a major political force.

The CIO's first major action came in 1936 in Akron, Ohio, where workers in the rubber industry had organized a "sit-down strike," a new strategy whereby laborers stopped work and simply sat down, shutting down production and occupying plants so that strike-breakers could not enter and take their jobs. Sit-down strikes became a prominent labor tactic during 1936 when 48 strikes broke out across the nation. The numbers shot up the following year to about 500 strikes that lasted more than one day. March 1937 alone witnessed 170 sit-down strikes that affected about 170,000 workers. Striking workers expressed their enthusiasm for the tactic in song:

> When they tie the can to a union man,
>   sit down! Sit down!
> When they give him the sack, they'll
>   take him back, sit down! Sit down!
> When the speed up comes, just twiddle
>   your thumbs, sit down! Sit down!
> When the boss won't talk, don't take a
>   walk, sit down! Sit down!

Courtesy, The Wayne State University Archives

■ These sit-down strikers at the Dodge Main plant in Hamtramck, Michigan, slept on their sewing tables while occupying the factory, shutting down production. The sit-down strike became an effective form of labor protest during the 1930s.

The most powerful demonstration of workers' discontent came in the automobile industry, where speed-ups of the assembly line drove workers to rebellion. Charlie Chaplin's poignant film *Modern Times* (1936) expressed workers' frustration at being treated as little more than cogs in machines. "Where you used to be a man," lamented one auto worker, "now you are less than their cheapest tool." In 1936 a spontaneous strike erupted against General Motors in Atlanta; it soon spread to Kansas City, Missouri; Cleveland, Ohio; and the main plants at Flint, Michigan. Two weeks into the strike, workers clashed with police. Frank Murphy, Michigan's prolabor governor, refused to use National Guard troops against the strikers, and Roosevelt declined to send in federal troops. John L. Lewis negotiated on behalf of the workers, who demanded recognition of their union.

Women as well as men participated actively in the Flint strike. Twenty-three-year-old Genora Johnson Dollinger, wife of a striker and mother of two young sons, organized 500 women into the Women's Emergency Brigade, made up primarily of strikers' wives, sisters, and girlfriends. Wearing red berets and armbands, they ran soup kitchens and first-aid stations. They also entered the fray when necessary, as when they broke plant windows so that the company could not use tear gas effectively against the strikers inside. Dollinger arranged a children's picket line as well, in which her two-year-old carried a sign that read, "My daddy strikes for us little tykes." Reflecting on the Women's Emergency Brigade after the strike, Dollinger wrote, "It's a measure of the strength of those women of the Red Berets that they could perform so courageously in an atmosphere that was often hostile to them. We organized on our own without the benefit of professional leadership, and yet, we played a role, second to none, in the birth of a union and in changing working families' lives forever."

The sit-down strike at Flint lasted 44 days and forced General Motors to recognize the United Auto Workers (UAW), which was a CIO union. The strike scored a clear victory for the workers and boosted the CIO's stature as a national union of industrial workers. Membership in the UAW quadrupled in the next year. Bowing to the formidable power of the national union in the wake of the UAW success, U.S. Steel surrendered to the CIO even without a strike, ending its policy of hiring nonunion workers and signing an agreement with the Steel Workers' Organizing Committee. The CIO brought together workers from all over the country. Most of its member unions were open to racial and ethnic minorities and women.

The New Deal Coalition

FDR's support of labor unions brought workers solidly into the Democratic fold. They joined a coalition that included voters who had never before belonged to the same party, particularly Northern blacks and Southern whites. Although African Americans in the South were disenfranchised, blacks in the North had voted Republican for 60 years, loyal to the party of Lincoln. In a dramatic shift, black voters in Northern cities overwhelmingly backed FDR in 1936 and remained in the Democratic party for the rest of the century.

FDR continued to cater to powerful Southern congressmen and Southern white voters. Nevertheless, he made some gestures on behalf of African Americans and put civil rights measures on the liberal agenda for the first time since Reconstruction. In May 1935 FDR issued Executive Order 7046, banning discrimination in WPA projects. By the late 1930s, 15 to 20 percent of those with WPA jobs were black. Although the pay was meager—$12 a week—it was double what many blacks had been able to earn previously. In spite of FDR's lukewarm support for civil rights, African Americans in the North benefited from New Deal programs. As one black preacher exhorted his congregation prior to the 1936 election, "Let Jesus lead you and Roosevelt feed you."

Other racial and ethnic minorities also joined the New Deal coalition. In 1939, Latinos organized their first national civil rights assembly, El Congreso de Pueblos de Habla Española—the Spanish-Speaking People's Congress, which opened with a congratulatory telegram from Eleanor Roosevelt. Immigrants from Europe and their children also became loyal Democratic voters.

In spite of this diverse coalition, many Americans remained bitterly opposed to FDR. Socialists and communists criticized the New Deal for patching up capitalism rather than transforming the economic system. Conservative business leaders despised Roosevelt for the constraints he placed on business and the intrusion of the government into the economy. Critics from the political right considered the New Deal to be akin to communism. In 1938, Congress created the House Un-American Activities Committee (HUAC), chaired by Martin Dies of Texas. Formed ostensibly to investigate American fascists and Nazis in the United States, the Committee instead pursued liberal and leftist groups throughout World War II and the Cold War.

A New Americanism

The New Deal coalition reflected not only Roosevelt's popularity but also a new and more inclusive American identity. An expanding mass culture fostered this sensibility, spread largely through the national media. It is no accident that Franklin Roosevelt found his way into the homes and hearts of Americans through his "fireside chats" over the radio; his mastery of that technology made him the first media-savvy president. During the 1930s, 70 percent of all households owned a radio—more than owned a telephone. The motion-picture industry also expanded into small towns across the country. Many of the ostentatious movie palaces of the 1920s disappeared, replaced by smaller theaters designed in the sleek modern style of the times, often decorated with murals painted by WPA artists that depicted local scenes and histories. Talking films brought vernacular speech and a variety of accents to diverse audiences who gathered in neighborhood theaters.

Movie plots portrayed the triumph of common people over the rich and powerful and celebrated love across class and ethnic lines. Although racial stereotypes persisted in motion pictures throughout the decade, notable exceptions, such as Will Rogers's films, featured strong minority characters. Popular movies also challenged traditional gender and class hierarchies. Female stars, such as Katharine Hepburn, Rosalind Russell, Bette Davis, and Mae West, portrayed feisty, independent women. Even gangsters appeared as sympathetic characters whose illegal activities seemed somehow justified by the corrupt system they tried to thwart.

New sports celebrities also embodied the nation's diversity. Baseball star Joe DiMaggio, son of an Italian immigrant fisherman, became a national hero. African American boxer Joe Louis, the "Brown Bomber" who was born into a sharecropper family in Alabama, became heavyweight champion of the world at age 23. In 1938, when Louis fought German boxer Max Schmeling at Yankee Stadium, the fight attracted 70,000 fans and grossed more than $1 million. When the black fighter knocked out Schmeling in the first round, he seemed to strike a blow for America against Hitler's Nazi Germany.

A number of women also became heroes in the 1930s for their daring exploits, personal courage, and physical prowess. Unlike earlier national heroines, these female celebrities transcended the expected gender role for women. Athletes like tennis champion Helen Wills and Olympic track star and brilliant golfer Babe Didrikson greatly expanded the popularity of women's sports. Renowned aviator Amelia Earhart, the first woman to fly solo across the Atlantic, devoted her life to advancing both feminism and commercial aviation. When her plane disappeared during an attempted 'round-the-world flight in 1937, many of her admirers were so convinced of her invincibility that they refused to believe she had died. Even today, people still speculate about her fate.

Smithsonian Institution

■ Amelia Earhart was the first woman to fly solo across the Atlantic. The legendary aviator gave preliminary flying lessons to her friend Eleanor Roosevelt. FDR convinced his wife not to take up flying, but the First Lady always regretted her decision.

Conclusion

The New Deal set in place a welfare state that established the principle of government responsibility for the well-being of vulnerable citizens. Before the New Deal, people suffered the fluctuations of the market economy with no recourse beyond the assistance of kin, communities, and charities. Older Americans who could no longer work had no government-guaranteed pensions and often faced poverty in old age. Bank failures could wipe away life savings. Unemployment could mean starvation for a worker's family. The New Deal provided Social Security for the elderly, unemployment compensation for workers who had lost their jobs, minimum hours and wages, and economic aid to women and children who had no means of support. It also established national economic regulations, such as the Federal Deposit Insurance Corporation (FDIC) and the Security and Exchange Commission (SEC), as well as the right of workers to unionize and engage in collective bargaining. These government protections offered many Americans an unprecedented level of economic security.

The Roosevelt administration addressed many of the nation's problems and used the federal government in innovative ways to intervene in the economy and to mitigate some of the misfortunes caused by the Depression. Most New Deal policies protected factory workers in large companies. The safety net did not extend to many of the neediest Americans, including Mexican American migrant workers, African American and white sharecroppers, seasonal agricultural laborers, or domestic workers. Although the national government extended its reach considerably, at the local level, many persistent problems remained entrenched. FDR was reluctant to press for anti-lynching legislation for fear of alienating Southern congressmen who still retained enormous power. Efforts to rescue the economy did little to rein in huge corporations like Ford and Standard Oil. Although FDR's conservative opponents accused him of socialist leanings, the New Deal actually rescued and shored up capitalism.

The New Deal was the Roosevelt administration's response to a global economic crisis. With the exception of the communist Soviet Union, which had already abandoned capitalism, almost every industrialized nation responded to the Depression by increasing the role of the state in the economy. Italy, Germany, and Japan moved to fascism and the nearly total state direction of the economy, while Britain and France established welfare states that would become more fully developed after World War II. The United States' system of social welfare was not as extensive and inclusive as those that emerged in some western European democracies. But it was part of a larger trend toward government intervention in the economy and greater protections for citizens. Within the United States, the New Deal neither reached nor satisfied everyone. Some groups thought that it went too far; others believed it did not go far enough. But it eased some of the harshest effects of the Depression and established a national safety net that endured for more than half a century.

Sites to Visit

African American Odyssey: The Depression, New Deal, and World War II
lcweb2.loc.gov/ammem/aaohtml/exhibit/aopart8.html
>This Library of Congress site covers the history of African Americans during the years of the Depression and World War II.

Southern Mosaic: The John and Ruby Lomax 1939 Southern States Recording Trip
memory.loc.gov/ammem/lohtml/lohome.html
>This site from the American Folklife Center, Library of Congress, provides audio, text, and photos of the Lomax collection of America folk songs collected and recorded across the South.

The 1930s Project
xroads.virginia.edu/~1930s/front.html
>This site from the University of Virginia's American Studies program contains materials about the culture and history of the 1930s.

Voices from the Dust Bowl: The Charles L. Todd and Robert Sonkin Migrant Worker Collection, 1940-1941
memory.loc.gov/ammem/afctshtml/tshome.html
>This Library of Congress site includes Farm Security Administration studies of migrant work camps in California in 1940 and 1941, with audio, images, manuscripts, and publications.

The New Deal Network
newdeal.feri.org
>This site includes images, documents, texts, artifacts, and other materials from the New Deal era.

Franklin Delano Roosevelt
www.ipl.org/ref/POTUS/fdroosevelt.html
>This Internet Public Library site contains biographical information about Franklin Delano Roosevelt and his election to the presidency and links to Internet biographies and resources about him.

The Crash of 1929
www.btinternet.com/~dreklind/thecrash.htm
>This site includes a discussion of the causes of the 1929 stock market crash, along with audio clips of songs relating to the crash.

Franklin D. Roosevelt Library and Digital Archives
www.fdrlibrary.marist.edu/
>This site includes documents, images, audio, and other primary source materials from the Franklin D. Roosevelt Library.

A New Deal for the Arts
www.archives.gov/exhibit_hall/new_deal_for_the_arts/
>This site of the National Archives includes artwork, documents, photographs, and information from the New Deal programs that funded artists in the 1930s.

American Life Histories: Manuscripts from the Federal Writers Project, 1936-1940
memory.loc.gov/ammem/wpaintro/wpahome.html
>This site from the Library of Congress includes manuscripts written by Federal Writers Project authors who interviewed Americans all over the country and wrote about them.

For Further Reading

General

Steve Fraser and Gary Gerstle, eds., *The Rise and Fall of the New Deal Order, 1930–1980* (1989).

Robert S. Lynd and Helen Merrell Lynd, *Middletown in Transition: A Study in Cultural Conflicts* (1937).

Robert S. McElvaine, *The Great Depression: America, 1929–1941* (1984, 1993).

James R. McGovern, *And a Time for Hope: Americans in the Great Depression* (2000).

Studs Terkel, *Hard Times: An Oral History of the Great Depression* (1986).

The Great Depression

Glen Elder, Jr., *Children of the Great Depression: Social Change in Life Experience* (1974).

Robert S. McElvaine, ed., *Down and Out in the Great Depression: Letters from the Forgotten Man* (1983).

Vicki L. Ruiz, *From Out of the Shadows: Mexican Women in Twentieth-Century America* (1998).

Judith Smith, *Family Connections: A History of Italian and Jewish Immigrant Lives in Providence, Rhode Island, 1900–1940* (1985).

Presidential Responses to the Depression

Edward D. Berkowitz, *America's Welfare State: From Roosevelt to Reagan* (1991).

Blanche Wiesen Cook, *Eleanor Roosevelt.* (1999)

Frank Friedel, *Franklin D. Roosevelt: A Rendezvous with Destiny* (1990).

William E. Leuchtenberg, *Franklin D. Roosevelt and the New Deal* (1963).

Lawrence W. Levine and Cornelia R. Levine, *The People and the President: America's Conversation with FDR* (2002).

Richard Polenberg, ed., *The Era of Franklin D. Roosevelt, 1933–1945: A Brief History with Documents* (2000).

Arthur M. Schlesinger, Jr., *The Age of Roosevelt*, 3 vols. (1957–1960).

The New Deal

Anthony Badger, *The New Deal* (1988).

Alan Brinkley, *Voices of Protest: Huey Long, Father Coughlin and the Great Depression* (1982).

Sidney Fine, *Sit-Down: The General Motors Strike of 1936–37* (1969).

Steven Fraser, *Labor Will Rule: Sidney Hillman and the Rise of American Labor* (1991).

Linda Gordon, *Pitied but Not Entitled: Single Mothers and the History of Welfare* (1994).

Robin D. G. Kelley, *Hammer and Hoe: Alabama Communists During the Great Depression* (1990).

A New Political Culture

Lizabeth Cohen, *Making a New Deal: Industrial Workers in Chicago, 1919–1939* (1992).

Michael Denning, *Cultural Front: The Laboring of American Culture in the Twentieth Century* (1998).

Gary Gerstle, *Working-Class Americanism: The Politics of Labor in a Textile City, 1914–1960* (1989).

Lary May, *The Big Tomorrow: Hollywood and the Politics of the American Way* (2000).

Online Practice Test

Test your understanding of this chapter with interactive review quizzes at

www.ablongman.com/jonescreatedequal/chapter22

Additional Photo Credits

Page 737: Bettmann/CORBIS
Page 751: Courtesy, Janice L. and David Frent
Page 761: Library of Congress
Page 763: Kobal Collection/United Artists

CHAPTER 23

Global Conflict: World War II, 1937–1945

Tom Lea, *Marines Call It That Two Thousand Yard Stare*, Sept. 16, 1944. U.S. Army Center of Military History, Army Art Collection

■ Tom Lea's haunting painting of a soldier, *Marines Call It That Two Thousand Yard Stare* (1944), evokes the horrors of World War II.

O N DECEMBER 7, 1941, KEITH LITTLE WAS OUT HUNTING RABBITS WITH FRIENDS AT their boarding school on the Navajo reservation of Ganado, Arizona. When they heard the news that the Japanese had attacked the U.S. naval base in Hawaii at Pearl Harbor, the teenage boys pledged to fight for their country. The next morning, Little and his friends showed up with their hunting rifles at the office of the reservation superintendent, ready to enlist. The previous year, the Tribal Council had voted unanimously to defend the United States against invasion. "There exists no purer concentration of Americanism than among the First Americans," the council declared.

The council vote was no idle gesture, especially given the complex status of Indian tribes within the United States. In some respects the tribes were semiautonomous nations within a nation. Several states, including Arizona, denied Indians the basic rights and obligations of citizenship, such as voting. Moreover, the Navajos were still embroiled in disputes with Commissioner of Indian Affairs John Collier and the Roosevelt administration over Collier's request that they destroy their sheep to reduce soil erosion and overgrazing. So it was by no means obvious that the Navajos would, or even should, fight for a nation they had bitterly fought against only 80 years earlier. Although large numbers of Native American soldiers had fought in earlier wars, especially World War I, the boarding-school boys could not have known that they would soon become part of a Navajo unit of "Code Talkers" that helped win the war.

Navajo "Code Talkers" operate a portable radio in the Pacific combat zone in 1943.

Little and about 400 other Navajos became part of a special unit that developed an intricate code, based on the Navajo language, to transmit top-secret information without risk of detection. The Navajo language was particularly well suited to code because very few people besides Navajos knew it. In a process code named "Magic," the all-Navajo 382nd Platoon of the U.S. Marine Corps outperformed the most sophisticated communication technology by encoding and decoding sensitive military information almost instantly and flawlessly. In two days on the Pacific island of Iwo Jima, six "Code Talkers" transmitted more than 800 messages, working around the clock, without a single error. Signal Officer Major Howard Conner recalled, "Without the Navajos the Marines would never have taken Iwo Jima."

The experiences of the Navajo "Code Talkers" echo many larger themes of America's involvement in World War II. Along with numerous other ethnic and racial minorities, the Navajos willingly fought—and many died—for a country that had treated them as second-class citizens. African Americans also joined the war effort, though in segregated units, to fight for the "double V"—victory against fascism abroad and racial discrimination at home. Young Japanese Americans left internment camps where their families had been forcibly detained to join a war against the land from which their parents came.

World War II was a global war, affecting countries and peoples all over the world. The conflict demanded human and technological resources on an unprecedented scale and left massive destruction in its wake. The huge scale of destruction was unlike that of any previous war. At least 55 million people died, including 25 million in the Soviet Union, 10 million in China, and 6 million in Poland. In the Holocaust, Nazi Germany's campaign of genocide, 6 million European Jews perished along with thousands of Romani (Gypsies), Poles, mentally and physically disabled people, homosexuals, and others deemed "racially inferior." The war also had a tremendous impact on countries under colonial rule. France, Holland, Belgium, and Great Britain were major colonial powers, but the war loosened their hold over their colonies. Germany's bombardment of England and occupation of France, Holland, and Belgium weakened all of these countries. Japan's defeat of the American, British, Dutch, and French forces in Southeast Asia from 1940 to 1942 shocked the Western powers and ended white rule in the region, setting in motion a wave of decolonization in Asia and Africa after the war.

The United States was the only major combatant that did not suffer massive destruction on its home territory. It had two powerful advantages: a 3000-mile ocean barrier on its East and West Coasts, plus tremendous natural resources that could provide the materials needed for modern warfare, such as steel and oil. In order to minimize American casualties, President Franklin Delano Roosevelt (FDR) pursued a strategy to make the United States the "arsenal of democracy," providing armaments and supplies to the other Allied powers so that their armies would do most of the fighting. Although the Soviet Union carried the largest burden of fighting the war and suffered the highest losses, millions of Americans also fought, and many died in the conflict. Military service had a leveling effect on social relations, as soldiers came together from all classes and ethnic groups. The vast majority of the troops—more than 85 percent—were white men from a wide variety of backgrounds. Soldiers of color generally fought in segregated units, but their battlefield successes and sacrifices gave them a sense of belonging to the nation and fueled postwar movements for equality and civil rights.

> *The United States was the only major combatant that did not suffer massive destruction on its home territory.*

No bombs dropped on the American mainland, yet the war reached into every aspect of national and personal life. Although wartime brought prosperity, the rationing of essential goods and the scarcity of consumer products brought nearly all Americans into the war effort. As soldiers and war industry workers moved around the country, local and regional sensibilities gave way to a stronger national identity. Factories stopped making consumer items and instead turned out war machines. Scientists developed new weapons of mass destruction. Cities burgeoned as workers flooded into the lucrative war industries. The U.S. military and defense establishment expanded to the formidable scale it would maintain during and after the war, making the United States the most powerful nation in the world.

Most Americans supported the war effort and did their part to stop German and Japanese aggression. Early in 1941, well before the United States entered the war, Roosevelt stressed the need to protect the "Four Freedoms": freedom of speech, freedom of religion, freedom from want, and freedom from fear of armed aggression. For many American GIs, the Four Freedoms translated into intensely personal terms. They fought to stay alive and to return to their sweethearts and families. They fought in hopes of reaping the "good life" that had become the symbol of America. Others, especially soldiers of color, fought not simply to preserve the American way of life, but also to gain access to it.

Mobilizing for War

During the 1930s, the rise of fascism and militarism in Italy, Germany, and Japan created a terrible dilemma for Americans. Disillusioned by World War I and preoccupied with the hardships of the Depression, they disagreed strongly with each other about how to respond to overt aggression in Africa, Europe, and Asia. The ensuing "Great Debate" became a turning point in the nation's relationship with the outside world. Mobilizing for the enormous crusade of World War II gave rise to a unity of purpose that lasted throughout the war and into the postwar era.

The Rise of Fascism

In the 1930s, Depression-era Americans grappled with their problems at home and avoided entanglements abroad. But they found it difficult to ignore events in Europe and Asia. In Italy, Spain, and Germany, where a weak economy and high unemployment created political unrest, fascist leaders rose to power with strong popular support. These new leaders promised economic recovery through strengthening the military and national expansion. They also encouraged intense nationalist sentiments, urging people to identify strongly with the state. Fascist party leader Benito Mussolini had held power in Italy since 1921, suppressing dissident voices and imposing one-party rule. According to Mussolini, "The fascist conception of the state is all-embracing, and outside of the state no human or spiritual values can exist, let alone be desirable." By the early 1930s fascism had gained strength in Germany and Spain. The term *fascist* has since been applied to the various right-wing dictatorships that arose during the period between the two world wars. Fascist governments were antidemocratic, antiparliamentary, and frequently anti-Semitic. Appealing to nationalistic and often racist sentiments, these governments generally ruled by coercion, terrorism, and police surveillance.

Germany emerged as the most powerful fascist state in Europe. After Germany's defeat in World War I and the severe economic depression that Germany experienced in the 1920s, Adolf Hitler's National Socialist (Nazi) party won broad support in the weakened country. On January 30, 1933, five weeks before FDR took the oath as president of the United States, Hitler became chancellor of Germany. Extolling fanatical nationalism and the racial superiority of "Aryan" or "pure" Anglo-Saxon Germans, Hitler blamed Jews for Germany's problems. He began a campaign of terror against Jews, homosexuals, suspected communists, and anyone else he saw as promoting "un-German" ideas. Hitler vowed to unite all German-speaking peoples into a new empire, the "Third Reich."

The fascist governments forged alliances to increase their power and launched campaigns of aggression and expansion. As conflict increased in Europe, hostilities spread into Africa as well. In 1935 Italy invaded Ethiopia, the sole independent African nation. The following year, Nazi troops seized the Rhineland, in the western region of Germany, in violation of the Versailles agreement. Hitler and Mussolini signed the Axis Pact, and Japan forged an alliance with Germany. Soon after that, civil war erupted in Spain. Hitler and Mussolini extended aid to the fascist General Francisco Franco, who was trying to overthrow Spain's republican government.

Although Spanish republicans appealed to antifascist governments for help in the fight against Franco, only the Soviet Union came to their assistance. The United States maintained an official policy of neutrality. Some conservatives believed that the anticommunist Franco would promote social stability. But many on the left, including large numbers of writers and intellectuals, championed the beleaguered Spanish government and denounced the fascists. Cadres of Americans sympathetic to the republican cause, including the "Abraham Lincoln Brigade," joined Soviet-organized international forces to fight against Franco.

In Germany anti-Semitic fervor reached a frenzy on the evening of November 7, 1938. In a spasm of violence known as *Kristallnacht* ("Night of the Broken Glass"), Hitler launched a massive assault against Jews throughout Germany. For three days German mobs attacked synagogues, smashed windows, and vandalized Jewish homes and businesses. Thirty-five Jews were killed, and thousands arrested. The rioters destroyed 7500 shops and 119 synagogues. The Nazi reign of terror against the Jews continued throughout the war, culminating in death camps and genocide.

Aggression in Europe and Asia

In the spring and summer of 1938 Hitler annexed Austria to the Third Reich and then invaded the Sudetenland. In the breakup of the Austro-Hungarian Empire after World War I, this German-speaking area became part of the newly formed Czechoslovakia. The Sudetenland was key to Hitler's goal of uniting all German-speaking Europe into the Third Reich. Josef Stalin, the communist leader of the Soviet Union, offered to join France and Britain to roust Hitler from the Sudetenland and halt his aggression. But the leaders of France and Britain rebuffed Stalin's suggestion. In September they met with Hitler in Munich and agreed to let him keep the Sudetenland in return for his promise that he would seek no more territory. Stalin feared that the anticommunist leaders of France and Britain would try to turn Hitler's aggression toward the Soviet Union. To prevent that possibility, Stalin signed a nonaggression pact with Hitler. Eventually, Hitler broke all his promises. Throughout the war and after, the Munich meeting became the symbol of "appeasement," a warning that compromise with the enemy leads only to disaster.

> *The Nazi reign of terror against the Jews continued throughout the war, culminating in death camps and genocide.*

In the next few years the fascist states expanded their power and territory. In 1939, with the help of the Soviet Union and in violation of the Munich agreement, Germany invaded Poland, which fell quickly, unable to withstand the German *blitzkrieg*, or "lightning war" of land and air strikes. At that point Britain and France declared war on Germany. That same year Madrid finally fell to Franco's forces. Britain, France, and the United States recognized Franco as victor of the Spanish Civil War. The Soviet Union next sent troops into Finland, gaining Finnish territory in 1940.

By 1940 Hitler was sweeping through Europe, invading Denmark, Norway, Holland, Belgium, Luxembourg, and then France. In just six weeks the Nazis had seized most of western Europe. Hitler then turned his forces on Great Britain. In the summer and fall of 1940, German raids on British air bases nearly destroyed the British Royal Air Force (RAF). Hitler then ordered the bombing of London and other English cities, attacking civilians day and night in what came to be called the Battle of Britain.

In the Far East events had taken an equally alarming turn. Nationalistic militarists gained control of the Japanese government in Tokyo and began a course of expansion. In 1931–1932, Japanese troops occupied the large Chinese province of Manchuria, installed a puppet government, and gave the province a Japanese name: Manchukuo. Five years later, the Japanese launched a full-scale war against China. The United States extended aid to China and discontinued trade with Japan. In 1940 Japan joined Germany and Italy in the Axis alliance and invaded the French colony of Indochina. Kazuko Kuramoto remembered the nationalist propaganda she learned as a Japanese child raised in Manchuria:

> I was born into a society of Japanese supremacy and grew up believing in Japan's "divine" mission to save Asia from the "evil" hands of Western imperialism. . . . "You are Japan's only future, a glorious future," adults around us used to say. We believed it with passion. . . . I joined the Red Cross Nurse Corps to help my country win the war. . . . "Asia for the Asians!"

Japan's efforts to rid Asia of white Western imperialism inspired some other Asians who saw Japan as a model of strength. But it was also a cynical ploy of the Japanese leaders, who sought to conquer all of Asia and considered other Asian peoples to be racially inferior to the Japanese. The Japanese treated the people in the countries they occupied with extreme brutality.

The Great Debate: Americans Contemplate War

In the mid–1930s the overwhelming majority of Americans still opposed intervention in foreign conflicts. Congress passed the Neutrality Acts of 1935, 1936, and 1937, outlawing arms sales or loans to nations at war and forbidding Americans from traveling on the ships of belligerent powers. In 1937 a Gallup poll indicated that 70 percent of Americans believed that the United States should have stayed out of World War I. A peace movement spread across university and college campuses. Students marched with banners bearing such slogans as "Scholarships, not Battleships." In a "peace strike" in the spring of 1936, half a million students boycotted classes and attended antiwar events. Nevertheless, President Roosevelt and others believed that the United States would be unable to hold itself aloof from the mounting international crises.

When Japan invaded China in 1937, FDR refused to comply with the provisions of the latest Neutrality Act, on the technicality that neither combatant had officially declared war. By creatively interpreting the law, he was able to offer loans to the embattled Chinese. Roosevelt felt strongly that the United States should actively help to resist the Axis powers. In 1940 he told the nation, "Frankly and definitely there is danger ahead—danger against which we must prepare. But we well know that we cannot escape danger, or the fear of danger, by crawling into bed and pulling the covers over our heads."

U.S. citizens still remained bitterly divided over the question of whether to get involved in the conflict. Those who agreed with Roosevelt believed that the nation should take any action "short of war" to help defeat the aggressors in Europe. By sending supplies, for example, the United States could become the "arsenal of democracy" to fight fascism without sending troops and risking American lives. But opponents to this idea spanned the political spectrum. They included moral or religious pacifists, peace activists of the Communist and Labor parties, and anti-Semites who supported Hitler. The pro-Nazi German American Bund, an organization that supported Germany, complained about Roosevelt's "Jew Deal"—a reference to Jews among FDR's advisors.

The largest organization to resist Roosevelt's effort was the America First Committee. With 450 chapters, the group claimed several hundred thousand members. Centered largely in the Midwest, the America Firsters included some active Nazi supporters. But conservative businesspeople also took part. Committee chair General Robert E. Wood, head of retailer Sears, Roebuck, believed that war would impede American prosperity. Other members had long opposed Roosevelt and the New Deal. They feared that war would give additional power to the already strong federal government. The group's most visible spokesperson was famed aviator Charles Lindbergh, whose anti-Semitism fueled his staunch opposition to any involvement in the conflict. Although Lindbergh's position antagonized many who once admired him, he also attracted followers.

Despite intense nonintervention sentiments, public opinion began to shift. Many Americans were shocked when Hitler swiftly

Norman Rockwell, Four Freedoms, War Bond Poster, printed by permission of the Norman Rockwell Family Trust. ©1943. The Norman Rockwell Museum at Stockbridge

OURS...to fight for

Freedom of Speech

Freedom of Worship

Freedom from Want

Freedom from Fear

■ Norman Rockwell's depiction of the "Four Freedoms" adorned the cover of the *Saturday Evening Post,* inspired the purchase of war bonds, and came to symbolize the democratic values for which the nation was fighting. These four scenes by the popular artist evoked an American ideal of close families and harmonious communities.

conquered much of Europe. Vivid news reports of the German occupation of France, and the intense bombardment of England in the Battle of Britain bolstered FDR's efforts to take action. When Roosevelt made his "Four Freedoms" speech in his annual message to Congress in January 1941, the United States was not yet officially at war. But the president pledged his support for England against the Nazis. A few months later, Congress approved the Lend-Lease agreement to lend rather than sell munitions to the Allied countries.

When Hitler broke his promise to Stalin and attacked the Soviet Union in June 1941, FDR extended Lend-Lease to the Soviets. During the summer, FDR and British Prime Minister Winston Churchill met on a ship off the coast of Newfoundland to develop a joint declaration known as the Atlantic Charter. The two leaders announced that the United States and Britain sought no new territories. Furthermore, they recognized the right of all peoples to choose their own form of government and to approve any territorial changes that might affect them. The charter called for international free trade and navigation as well.

The charter articulated the Allies' war aims, but it also had profound implications for colonial rule around the world. Realizing the possible cost of losing colonies, Churchill retreated from the global implications of the charter. The declaration, he claimed, applied primarily to European nations under Nazi rule. Roosevelt walked a fine line between contradicting Churchill and supporting the idea of empire. However, the words of the charter—along with the Allies' condemnation of racism and territorial expansion by Germany and Japan— emboldened anticolonial activists around the world. Within 15 years after the end of World War II, 800 million previously colonized people won their independence, and 40 new nations would form.

As the United States inched closer to entry into the conflict, FDR still faced political and economic troubles at home. Although Allied munitions orders had already stimulated the economy, as late as 1939, 9.4 million Americans—17.2 percent of the labor force—remained jobless. In the 1940 presidential election Roosevelt defeated Republican challenger Wendell Willkie. FDR began his third term as war loomed and economic hardship at home persisted. But Japan's surprise attack on Pearl Harbor in 1941 ended both the neutrality debate and the Depression.

TABLE 23-1			
The Election of 1940			
Candidate	Political Party	Popular Vote	Electoral Vote
Franklin D. Roosevelt	Democratic	27,244,160	449
Wendell L. Willkie	Republican	22,305,198	82

Pearl Harbor: The United States Enters the War

The Japanese attack on Pearl Harbor shocked the nation and catapulted the United States immediately into World War II. President Roosevelt somberly told millions of Americans gathered around their radios that the day of the attack would "live in infamy." Most former doubters now joined the war effort. The entire nation shifted into high gear to defeat brutal, aggressive regimes intent on conquering much of the world. For some, wartime mobilization offered new opportunities; for others, it brought sacrifice.

December 7, 1941

For nearly a decade, tensions had been mounting between the United States and Japan as American leaders tried to contain Japan's expansion in Asia. Roosevelt assumed that a strong U.S. military presence in the Pacific would persuade Japan's premier, General Hideki Tojo,

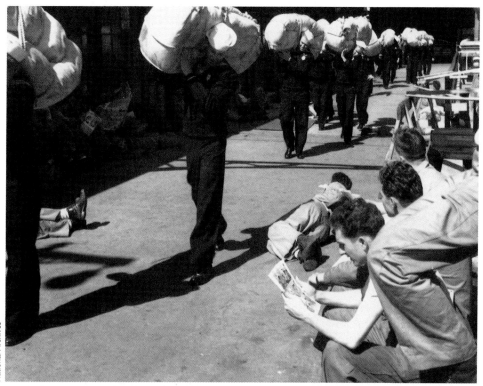

National Archives

■ The attack on Pearl Harbor prompted an immediate mobilization of vast proportions. Within months, thousands of young recruits, such as these sailors boarding ship in San Diego, shouldered their gear and headed overseas. More than 400,000 did not return alive. The government calculated that over four grim years of U.S. involvement, 292,131 Americans died in combat, and there were 115,185 additional service deaths from other causes. Though huge, American losses still proved small in comparison to the destruction suffered in other countries.

to avoid a confrontation with the United States. When Japan continued its aggression in Asia, FDR froze Japanese assets in the United States, putting trade with Japan under presidential control. This move, he hoped, would bring Japan to the bargaining table. Instead, on November 25, the Japanese dispatched aircraft carriers toward Hawaii and sent troops to the border of Malaya in the South Pacific.

Although U.S. intelligence sources had broken the codes with which the Japanese encrypted messages about their war plans, they did not realize that the Japanese intended to strike Hawaii. One memo indicating that the Japanese were heading toward Pearl Harbor lay buried under a pile of intelligence reports. As a result, American military officials failed to warn the U.S. forces stationed in Pearl Harbor. At 7:55 A.M. on December 7, Japanese planes swooped over Pearl Harbor and bombed the naval base. The assault caught the American forces completely off guard and destroyed most of the U.S. Pacific fleet. Only a few aircraft carriers that were out at sea survived. Two hours after the attack on Pearl Harbor, the Japanese also struck the main U.S. base at Clark Field in the Philippines, destroying half of the U.S. Far East Air Force.

At roughly the same time that Keith Little heard the news about Pearl Harbor at his Navajo reservation boarding school, another 16-year-old, John Garcia, watched flames rising at Pearl Harbor from his house four miles away. The young Hawaiian reached the scene in time to witness the second round of bombings. "I spent the rest of the day swimming inside the harbor, along with some other Hawaiians. I brought out I don't know how many bodies, and how many were alive and how many dead. . . . We worked around the clock for three days."

In less than two hours the Japanese had wrecked 188 planes—most of the American aircraft on the island—and sunk 19 ships, including eight battleships, three destroyers, and three cruisers. When the smoke cleared, 2323 American service personnel were dead. Congress immediately declared war against Japan. Representative Jeannette Rankin from Montana cast the only dissenting vote. (The first woman elected to Congress and a lifelong pacifist, Rankin had also voted against the U.S. entry into World War I.) Three days later Germany and Italy declared war against the United States.

Japanese American Relocation

The assault on Pearl Harbor sparked widespread rumors along the U.S. West Coast that Japanese and Japanese Americans living there planned to sabotage the war effort. Although no charges of criminal activity or treason were ever brought against any Japanese Americans, powerful farming interests eager to eradicate Japanese competition pushed for an evacuation. General John L. DeWitt, chief of the Western Defense Command, argued, "The Japanese race is an enemy race, and while many second and third generation Japanese born on United States soil, possessed of United States citizenship, have become 'Americanized,' the racial strains are undiluted. . . . It therefore follows that along the vital Pacific Coast over 112,000 potential enemies, of Japanese extraction, are at large today." People of Japanese descent were the only residents of the United States who were relocated during the war. Although the United States was at war with Germany and Italy, those of German or Italian ancestry were spared internment. Because they were white, nobody claimed that the Germans or Italians belonged to an "enemy race."

Not everyone supported the internment idea. U.S. Attorney General Francis Biddle protested that there was "no reason" for a mass relocation. J. Edgar Hoover, director of the

■ On December 7, 1941, the Japanese launched a surprise attack on the U.S. naval base at Pearl Harbor, Hawaii. The attack brought the United States immediately into World War II and was the only time that the war came to American soil.

AP/Wide World Photos

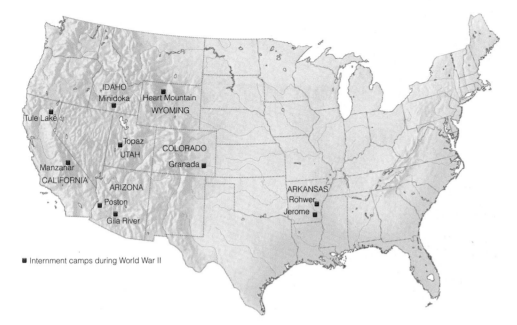

■ **MAP 23.1**
THE INTERNMENT OF JAPANESE AMERICANS DURING WORLD WAR II After the Japanese attack on
Pearl Harbor, President Franklin Delano Roosevelt signed an order authorizing the removal of people of
Japanese descent from the West Coast. These Japanese Americans were relocated to internment camps built
in arid and isolated areas in the West, as well as in two locations in Arkansas.

FBI, also opposed the plan, arguing that DeWitt's suggestion reflected "hysteria and lack of
judgment." Nevertheless, the Roosevelt administration gave in to the pressure, with the support of California Attorney General Earl Warren. In February 1942, Roosevelt signed Executive Order 9066, which suspended the civil rights of American citizens of Japanese
descent. The order authorized the removal of 110,000 Japanese and Japanese Americans from the West Coast. Of those, 70,000 were *Nisei,* native-born American citizens. Families received one week's notice to evacuate their homes and move to
prisonlike camps surrounded by barbed wire and guarded by armed soldiers. There
were 10 such camps in seven states, all of them located in arid, desolate spots in the
West. At the camps internees lived in makeshift wooden barracks, where entire families
crowded into one room.

Not all Japanese Americans were evacuated. General Delos Emmons, the military governor of Hawaii, insisted that removing the Japanese from those islands would cripple the economy, as well as the defense of Oahu. In Hawaii, Japanese and Japanese Americans made up
more than 90 percent of the skilled workers and agricultural laborers needed to rebuild and
sustain the island. In their defense, Emmons proclaimed, "There have been no known acts of
sabotage committed in Hawaii." Business leaders concurred. But the Japanese living on the West
Coast lacked the broad support that those in Hawaii enjoyed.

The experience of internment proved so devastating that, after the war, 5766 *Nisei* renounced
their American citizenship. One of those was World War I veteran Joseph Y. Kurihara, who
recalled, "It was really cruel and harsh. To pack and evacuate in 48 hours was an impossibil-
ity. Seeing mothers completely bewildered with children crying from want and peddlers taking advantage and offering prices next to robbery made me feel like murdering those
responsible." Kurihara emigrated to Japan—a country he had never seen.

While the internment experience alienated some Japanese Americans, fully 33,000 joined
the armed services—including 1200 who enlisted from the internment camps—and proved
their patriotism on the battlefield. In the Pacific, their knowledge of the Japanese language

■ The family pictured here was among thousands of loyal citizens of Japanese ancestry removed from their homes on the West Coast and relocated to internment camps. Here, the Hirano family, George, Hisa, and Yasbei (left to right), pose at the Colorado River Relocation Center in Poston, Arizona. Hisa holds a photo of her son, an American soldier, who is off fighting the war.

proved critical in translating intercepted Japanese military documents. General Charles Willoughby, chief of intelligence in the Pacific, estimated that the Japanese American military contributions shortened the war by two years. The Japanese also served ably in Europe, suffering huge casualties. The Japanese Americans of the 442nd Regiment lost one-fourth of their soldiers in battles in North Africa and Italy. They suffered another 800 casualties rescuing the Texan "Lost Battalion," 211 men surrounded by German troops in the Vosges Mountains of France. As one Texan recalled, "We were never so glad to see anyone as those fighting Japanese Americans." The 442nd Regiment won 18,143 individual decorations for distinguished service. Welcoming them home in 1946, President Harry Truman declared, "You fought not only the enemy, you fought prejudice—and you won."

Nevertheless, the U.S. government would take its time acknowledging that the internment had been a grave injustice. The Supreme Court upheld the constitutionality of the policy, and Roosevelt would not rescind the evacuation order until after his reelection in 1944. The camps finally closed in 1945. All told, Japanese Americans lost property valued at $500 million. Not until 1968 would the government reimburse former internees for some of their losses. And not until 1983 would a Special Commission on Wartime Relocation and Internment of Civilians concede that because of "race prejudice, war hysteria and a failure of political leadership," the U.S. government had committed "a grave injustice" to more than 110,000 people of Japanese ancestry. In 1988 Congress would enact legislation awarding restitution payments of $20,000 each to 60,000 surviving internees—a small gesture for Americans whose only "crime" was their Japanese ancestry.

Wartime Migrations

Even before the United States officially entered World War II, the conflict had begun to change the face of the nation. The sleepy town of Richmond, California, perched near the north end of San Francisco Bay, underwent a profound transformation when the nation stepped up war production. The town's mostly white population of 23,000 ballooned to 120,000 after industrialist Henry Kaiser constructed four shipyards there. The yards employed over 150,000 workers, more than one-fourth of them African American. Most were young, married migrants from the South, and there were slightly more women than men. They came to Richmond attracted by the better pay and benefits, along with the opportunity for greater freedom than they had known in the the Jim Crow South.

Margaret Starks, daughter of southern tenant farmers, moved to Richmond. She established a blues club, edited a black newspaper, and played an active role in the National Association for the Advancement of Colored People (NAACP). Her club became a center for African American cultural and political life. Thus, black migrants not only established their own community institutions but also transformed the life of the city. This same process unfolded all over the country, bringing black culture into cities and creating a diverse urban landscape.

Many cities, however, were ill equipped to handle the influx of migrants. An estimated 60,000 African Americans moved into Chicago, for example, causing an enormous housing crisis. Many newcomers lacked even a modicum of privacy as they crowded into basements and rooms rented from total strangers. Huge numbers of whites also came north, many leaving hardscrabble farms hoping to prosper in booming war industries.

Wartime also saw new migration from abroad and a reversal of earlier immigration policies. Because of the alliance with China in the war against Japan, Congress repealed the Chinese Exclusion Act in 1943, and migrants from China became eligible for citizenship for the first time. Few Chinese actually arrived, however, and most immigration restrictions remained in force. The most significant wartime migration from abroad came from Mexico. In 1942, Mexico joined the Allies and provided an air force squadron trained in the United States that fought in the Pacific. An executive agreement between the United States and Mexico created the *bracero* program, which stipulated that the migrants were to be hired on short-term contracts and treated fairly. Under the *bracero* program, 300,000 Mexican laborers, mostly agricultural workers, came to the United States to labor in rural areas like California's San Joaquin Valley, taking the place of "Okies" who migrated to cities for defense work. By the mid–1960s, nearly 5 million Mexicans had migrated north under the program.

The war also prompted large numbers of émigrés to become American citizens. From 1941 to 1945, more immigrants became naturalized citizens than in any previous five-year period. More than 112,000 were naturalized during their service in the armed forces. But the vast majority of those naturalized—1,539,000—were civilians. For the first time, the majority were women. The largest numbers came from countries that were embroiled in the war: the British Empire, Italy, Germany, Poland, and the Soviet Union. Naturalization was a concrete way for newcomers to clarify their status and their loyalty, especially in the wake of the Smith Act of 1940. This law required all foreign-born residents to be registered and fingerprinted, and broadened the grounds for deportation.

The Home Front

Wartime mobilization brought Americans from all regions and backgrounds together in shared service and sacrifice. Industries as well as citizens dedicated themselves to the war effort. Automobile manufacturers stopped making cars and instead turned out tanks, jeeps, and other military vehicles. Citizens made do with government-rationed basic staples, from food to gasoline. As able-bodied men left their jobs to fight the war, new work opportunities opened up for women as well as for disabled Americans. Cities and centers of war production brought together young women and men who found new opportunities for sexual experimentation, while gay men and lesbians discovered newly visible communities in both military and civilian life. Although class, gender, and racial injustices persisted, the war offered new sources of pride and patriotism for women and minorities and raised expectations that they would achieve full inclusion in the American promise.

Many Americans hoped that the liberal spirit of the New Deal would endure during the war; others were eager for an end to what they perceived as Depression-era class conflict and hostility to business interests. To some extent both sides got their wish. Full employment, the increasing strength of unions, and high taxes on the wealthy pleased New Deal liberals. Profit guarantees, freedom from antitrust actions, no-strike pledges, and cheap imported labor gratified pro-business conservatives. Congress dismantled some of the New Deal's most successful agencies, including the Civilian Conservation Corps (CCC), the Works Projects Administration (WPA), and the National Youth Administration. Republicans opposed continued support for those programs, but full employment during the wartime economy made job programs unnecessary.

Building Morale

The United States, like all other major powers involved in the conflict, mounted a propaganda drive to promote support for the war effort. Roosevelt created the Office of War Information (OWI) in 1942 to coordinate morale-boosting and censorship initiatives. Working in partnership with the motion picture industry and other media outlets, the OWI sponsored

■ Eight American presidents elected consecutively following World War II were veterans of that war. Pictured in wartime service, from top left, are: Dwight D. Eisenhower, John F. Kennedy, Lyndon Johnson, Richard Nixon, Gerald Ford, Jimmy Carter, Ronald Reagan, and George Bush.

movies, radio programs, publications, and posters. These productions portrayed the war as a crusade to preserve the "American way of life" and encouraged American women and men to work in war industries, enlist in the armed forces, and purchase war bonds. Eric Johnston, head of the Motion Picture Producers' Association and FDR's business advisor, insisted that Hollywood remove class conflict from its films: "We'll have no more *Grapes of Wrath,* we'll have no more *Tobacco Roads,* we'll have no more films that deal with the seamy side of American life. We'll have no more films that treat the banker as a villain."

John Ford and Greg Toland heard the message. In the 1930s, they had made movies that carried themes of political dissent. Now they helped to build consensus. In one of their first wartime films, *December 7,* produced for the Navy in 1942, the protagonist is Uncle Sam himself. Visiting Hawaii before the attack on Pearl Harbor, he tolerates labor strikes and lets Japanese Americans speak their own language and practice their Shinto religion. But he learns his lesson when fictional Japanese Americans pass military secrets to the Japanese Imperial Navy, which attacks Pearl Harbor. Uncle Sam then insists that the Japanese shed their distinct traditions, forbids class conflict, and brings all groups together to win the war. Although there was never any evidence of Japanese American sabotage, the film suggested otherwise and warned that ethnic minorities must assimilate into the American mainstream to demonstrate their patriotism.

Maintaining morale of the fighting men was critical to sustaining the war effort. Officials tried to ease the hardships of combat by providing cigarettes and beer, entertainment by and for the troops, and live performances by Hollywood celebrities like Bob Hope and Ginger Rogers. Promises of the good life waiting at home—especially images of cozy houses, warm hearths, and sexual fulfillment—reminded the men overseas why they were fighting. "Pinups"—photos of sexy but wholesome-looking women—adorned the walls of barracks, representing the joys that would follow victory.

Under government sponsorship, all the major radio networks aired a series of programs in 1942 to mobilize support for the war. One highly acclaimed segment, "To the Young," included this conversation:

> YOUNG MALE VOICE: "That's one of the things this war's about."
> YOUNG FEMALE VOICE: "About us?"
> YOUNG MALE VOICE: "About *all* young people like us. About love and gettin' hitched, and havin' a home and some kids, and breathin' fresh air out in the suburbs . . . about livin' an' workin' *decent,* like free people."

The enemy drew on the same images in their efforts to persuade American fighting service personnel to surrender. One lurid piece of propaganda that the Japanese scattered among the American troops in the Pacific pictured a young Caucasian man and woman locked in a passionate kiss under the moonlight. The leaflet read:

> That unforgettable embrace under the beautiful moon with the warmth of HER shapely body nestled against yours; that blood-tingling kiss; that over-powering sense of passion that sweeps over you—these and many other pleasant memories you'll be able to relive again if you'll throw down your arms, surrender and prepare to get out of this hell-hole.

The National Archives

■ Sailors relax in the Aircraft Repair Unit (ARU–145) during their free time at Guadalcanal. The walls above their cots are decorated with "pinups" of young women in alluring poses, reminding the men of the pleasures that await them after the war.

Inside the card was the grim alternative: the same young man's bloody body with the warning: "BUT if you continue to resist—Then, under the beautiful tropical moon, only DEATH awaits you. Bullet-holes in your guts—agonizing death! You have the two alternatives. Take your choice."

Within the United States, government censors made sure that no photographs showing badly wounded soldiers or mutilated bodies reached the public. The censors also removed any images that might elicit sympathy for the enemy, such as pictures of injured or frightened enemy soldiers suffering at the hands of American soldiers. Photographs that appeared in the American media generally sanitized the horror of war, depicting noble American soldiers and a shadowy, faceless enemy. Rarely, if ever, did those on the home front see the true extent of the war's destructiveness and brutality. When men returned home severely traumatized by what they had seen, even their trauma was censored. As just one example, for more than three decades, the army suppressed John Huston's *Let There Be Light*, a film documentary of World War II veterans in a psychiatric hospital suffering from post-traumatic stress disorder.

Home Front Workers, "Rosie the Riveter," and "Victory Girls"

Wartime opened up new possibilities for jobs, income, and labor organizing, for women as well as for men, and for new groups of workers. Disabled workers entered jobs previously considered beyond their abilities, fulfilling their tasks with skill and competence. Norma Krajczar, a visually impaired teenager from North Carolina, served as a volunteer aircraft warden where her sensitive hearing gave her an advantage over sighted wardens in listening for approaching enemy planes. Deaf people streamed into Akron, Ohio, to work in the tire factories that became defense plants, making more money than they ever made before.

Along with new employment opportunities, workers' earnings rose nearly 70 percent. Income doubled for farmers and then doubled again. Labor union membership grew 50 percent, reaching an all-time high by the end of the war. In spite of no-strike pledges, strikes pressured the aircraft industry in Detroit and elsewhere. A major strike of the United Mine Workers Union erupted in 1943. Congress responded with the Smith-Connally Act of 1943, which gave the president power to seize plants or mines wherever strikes interrupted war production.

Women and minorities joined unions in unprecedented numbers. Some organized unions of their own. Energetic labor organizers like Luisa Moreno and Dorothy Ray Healy organized Mexican women working at the California Sanitary Canning Company into a powerful union that achieved wage increases and union recognition. Unions with white male leadership, however, admitted women and minorities reluctantly and tolerated them only during the war emergency. Some unions required women to quit their jobs after the war.

Nevertheless, World War II ushered in dramatic changes for American women. Wartime scarcities led to increased domestic labor as homemakers made do with rationed goods, mended clothing, collected and saved scraps and metals, and planted "victory gardens" to help feed their families. Employment opportunities for women also increased. As a result of the combined incentives of patriotism and good wages, women streamed into the paid labor force. Many of them took "men's jobs" while the men went off to fight.

"Rosie the Riveter" became the heroic symbol of the woman war worker. Pictures of attractive "Rosies" building planes or constructing ships graced magazine covers and posters. Future Hollywood star Marilyn Monroe first gained attention when her photograph appeared in *Yank*,

Library of Congress

■ During World War II, "Rosie the Riveter" became an icon of the working woman doing a "man's job" in the war production industries. The "Rosie" pictured here riveting was one of thousands who enjoyed the excitement and high wages of wartime work.

a magazine for soldiers. The magazine pictured her not as the sex goddess she later became, but as a typical "Rosie the Riveter" clad in overalls, working at her job in a defense plant.

Until 1943, black women were barred from work in defense industries. Poet Maya Angelou recalled that African Americans had to fight for the jobs they wanted. She became the first black streetcar conductor in San Francisco during the war, but not without a struggle. She made herself a promise that "made my veins stand out, and my mouth tighten into a prune: I WOULD HAVE THE JOB. I WOULD BE A CONDUCTORETTE AND SLING A FULL MONEY CHANGER FROM MY BELT. I WOULD." And she did.

For the first time, married women joined the paid labor force in droves and public opinion supported them. During the Depression, 80 percent of Americans had objected to the idea of wives working outside the home; by 1942, only 13 percent still objected. However, mothers of young children found very little help. In 1943 the federal government finally responded to the needs of working mothers by funding day-care centers. More than 3000 centers enrolled 130,000 children. Still, the program served only a small proportion of working mothers. Most women relied on family members to care for their children. A Women's Bureau survey in 1944 found that 16 percent of mothers working in war industries had no child-care arrangements at all. Meager to begin with and conceived as an emergency measure, government funding for child care would end after the war.

> *For the first time, married women joined the paid labor force in droves, and public opinion supported them.*

Before the war, most jobs for women were low-paying, nonunion positions that paid them an average of $24.50 a week. Wartime manufacturing jobs paid almost twice that much—$40.35 a week. During the conflict, 300,000 women worked in the aircraft industry alone. Almira Bondelid recalled that when her husband went overseas, "I decided to stay in San Diego and went to work in a dime store. That was a terrible place to work, and as soon as I could I got a job at Convair [an aircraft manufacturer]. . . . I worked in the tool department as a draftsman, and by the time I left there two years later I was designing long drill jigs for parts of the wing and hull of B–24s."

New opportunities for women also opened up in the armed services. All sectors of the armed forces had dwindled in the years between the two wars and needed to gain size and strength. Along with the 10 million men aged 21 to 35 drafted into the armed services and the 6 million who enlisted, 140,000 women volunteered for the Women's Army Corps (WACs) and 100,000 for the Navy WAVES (Women Accepted for Voluntary Emergency Service).

Most female enlistees and war workers enjoyed their work and wanted to continue after the war. The extra pay, independence, camaraderie, and satisfaction that their jobs provided had opened their eyes to new possibilities. Edith Speert, like many others, was never again content as a full-time housewife and mother. Edith's husband, Victor, was sent overseas in 1944. During the 18 months of their separation, they penned 1300 letters to each other, sometimes two or three times a day. The letters revealed the love and affection they felt for one another, but Edith did not hesitate to tell Victor how she had changed. In a letter from Cleveland, dated November 9, 1945, she wrote:

> Sweetie, I want to make sure I make myself clear about how I've changed. I want you to know *now* that you are not married to a girl that's interested solely in a home—I shall definitely have to work all my life—I get emotional satisfaction out of working; and I don't doubt that many a night you will cook the supper while I'm at a meeting. Also, dearest—I shall never wash and iron—there are laundries for that! Do you think you'll be able to bear living with me?…I love you, Edith

Despite the shifting priorities of women, the war reversed the declining marriage and fertility rates of the 1930s. Between 1941 and 1945 the birthrate climbed from 19.4 to 24.5 per 1000 population. The reversal stemmed, in part, from economic prosperity, as well as the possibility of draft deferments for married men in the early war years. However, the desire to solidify relationships and establish connections to the future during a time of great uncertainty perhaps served as the most powerful motivation. Thus, a curious paradox marked the war years: a widespread disruption of domestic life accompanied by a rush into marriage and parenthood.

At the same time that the war prompted a rush into marriage and parenthood, wartime upheaval sent the sexual order topsy-turvy. For many young women, moving to a new city or taking a wartime job opened up new possibilities for independence, excitement, and sexual adventure. One young worker recalled:

> Chicago was just humming, no matter where I went. The bars were jammed . . . you could pick up anyone you wanted to. . . . There were servicemen of all varieties roaming the streets all the time. There was never, never a shortage of young, healthy bucks. . . . We never thought of getting tired. Two, three hours of sleep was normal. . . . I'd go down to the office every morning half dead, but with a smile on my face, and report for work.

Some young women, known as "victory girls," believed that it was an act of patriotism to have a fling with a man in uniform before he went overseas. The independence of these women raised fears of female sexuality as a dangerous, ungoverned force. The worry extended beyond the traditional concern about prostitutes and "loose women" to include "good girls" whose sexual standards might relax during wartime. Public health campaigns warned enlisted men that "victory girls" would have their fun with a soldier and then leave him with a venereal disease, incapable of fighting for his country.

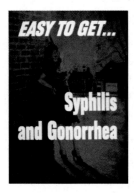

Wartime also intensified concerns about homosexuality. Urban centers and the military provided new opportunities for gay men and lesbians to form relationships and build communities. Although the military officially banned homosexuals from the forces, many served by keeping their orientation secret. If discovered, gay men faced severe punishment, including confinement in cages called "queer stockades" or in psychiatric wards. Lesbians faced similar sanctions, although the women's corps, in an effort to assure the civilian world of their recruits' femininity, often looked the other way.

Antigay crusades and policies sometimes backfired. Nowhere is this more evident than in the 1943 wartime propaganda film *This Is the Army,* starring future U.S. president Ronald Reagan. Sponsored by the Office of War Information and produced by Warner Brothers, the film centers on the romance between a soldier and an army nurse. The two wed just before the hero leaves to fight on foreign shores. The film uses humor to diffuse uneasiness and discomfort with the disrupted gender roles and sexual identities brought about by war. Soldier-comedians joke about their female superior officers. A group of he-men in drag do a clumsy chorus-line routine showing their hairy legs and bulging muscles beneath their skirts. In an ironic twist, *This Is the Army* became a popular wartime cult film among gays and lesbians.

Race and War

The Holocaust, Nazi Germany's campaign to exterminate European Jews, demonstrated the horrors of racial hatred taken to its ultimate extreme. The U.S. government did little to help Jewish refugees or to stem the slaughter of Jews in Europe. Official indifference and widespread anti-Semitism prevailed throughout the war. Nevertheless, Nazi policies against the Jews discredited racial and ethnic prejudice, forcing Americans to confront the reality of racism in their own country. Anthropologist Ruth Benedict, in her 1943 book *The Races of Mankind,* urged the United States to "clean its own house" and "stand unashamed before Nazis and condemn, without confusion, their doctrines of a Master Race." Swedish sociologist Gunnar Myrdal's *American Dilemma: The Negro Problem and Modern Democracy* called on the nation to live up to its democratic promise: "The great reason for hope is that this country has a national experience of uniting racial and cultural diversities and a national theory,

- ■ Concentration camps
- ◻ Extermination camps

■ **MAP 23.2**

NAZI CONCENTRATION AND EXTERMINATION CAMPS Under Hitler, the Nazis established dozens of concentration camps where Jews and others whom the Nazis deemed "undesirable" were imprisoned. In addition to these sites, there were hundreds of slave labor camps attached to factories across Germany where Jews were forced to work for Nazi enterprises. After Hitler began his genocidal "final solution," six camps became sites of systematic mass murder, with efficient killing operations, including gas chambers disguised as shower rooms.

if not a consistent practice, of freedom and equality for all." Americans of color responded to the call for unity and demonstrated their patriotism; in return, they expected full inclusion in the democracy. There would be no return to the old racial order. As black leader W. E. B. DuBois noted, World War II was a "War for Racial Equality" and a struggle for "democracy not only for white folks but for yellow, brown, and black."

The Holocaust

Hitler's war aims included conquering all of Europe and destroying European Jewry. Throughout the war, Nazi anti-Jewish policies escalated from persecution and officially sanctioned violence to imprisonment in concentration camps, slave labor, and ultimately Hitler's "Final Solution," genocide. Nazis developed increasingly efficient means of killing Jews. Some Jewish men, women, and children perished by firing squads in mass executions. Others died of disease and malnutrition in concentration camps or at the hands of Nazi doctors in gruesome medical experiments. In the infamous Nazi death camps, guards herded prisoners into "shower rooms" that were actually gas chambers. Out of a prewar European Jewish population of

10 million, the Holocaust claimed the lives of 6 million Jews, along with homosexuals, the disabled, and Romani (also known as Gypsies).

American officials knew of the Nazi persecution of the Jews but did little about it. Throughout the 1930s, American Jewish groups pressured the Roosevelt administration to ease immigration laws to allow Jewish refugees to enter the country. But the United States raised the legal quota of Jewish immigrants only slightly. In 1938, Roosevelt organized an international conference on the refugee crisis in Evian, Switzerland, with 32 nations attending. But no nation agreed to accept large numbers of refugees, so the conference had little practical impact. In 1939, a pro-Nazi rally in New York City drew 20,000. That same year, congressional leaders defeated the Wagner–Rogers bill, which would have amended immigration quotas to allow the entry of 20,000 Jewish children.

> *The U.S. government turned away boatloads of Jewish refugees, sending them back to Germany to their deaths.*

When the Nazis began their policy of extermination in 1941, they tried to keep it a secret. But Dr. Gerhard Riegner, the World Jewish Congress representative in Geneva, Switzerland, learned about the Holocaust from a German source and informed American diplomats. U.S. State Department officials decided not to pass along the information to Washington. Despite official silence, Rabbi Stephen S. Wise, a prominent American Jewish leader, heard the news and held a press conference in November 1942. But the American press, preoccupied with military events and reluctant to publish stories of atrocities without official verification, gave the Holocaust little coverage. Meanwhile, despite news of Nazi genocide, the U.S. government turned away boatloads of Jewish refugees, sending them back to Germany to their deaths.

Nazi persecution of the Jews raised American sensitivity to the issue of racism but did little to diminish anti-Semitism within the United States. In fact, American hostility toward Jews reached new heights during World War II and exceeded the level of prejudice against any other group. In a 1942 survey of American voters, 51 percent agreed that Jews "have too much power in the United States." At the height of Nazi genocide against the Jews in 1944, when asked to identify the greatest "menace" to the nation, 24 percent of Americans polled listed Jews—more than those who listed Germans, Japanese, radicals, Negroes, and foreigners.

In Europe, American military strategists knew of the existence and location of Nazi death camps, but they refused to destroy them or to bomb the railroad lines leading to the camps. Many Europeans under Nazi domination, however, risked their lives to rescue and shelter Jews. While the United States stood by, smaller nations took action. For example, Denmark defied the Nazis even though occupied by them—taking a far greater risk than anything the United States might have done—and managed to save nearly all Danish Jews. And the tiny Dominican Republic took in more Jewish refugees than any other country in the Western Hemisphere. The United States fought a war against the Nazis but did very little to help their victims.

Racial Tensions at Home

Throughout the war years, racial tensions within the United States persisted. Black workers, who were excluded from the best-paying jobs in the defense industry, mobilized against discrimination on the job. Their most powerful advocate was African American Civil rights leader A. Philip Randolph, who had organized the overwhelmingly black Brotherhood of Sleeping Car Porters and won the union a contract with the railroads in 1937. At the beginning of American involvement in the war in 1941, Randolph pressured FDR to ban discrimination in defense industries. He threatened to organize a massive march on Washington if Roosevelt did not respond. Roosevelt got the message and issued Executive Order 8802, which created the Fair Employment Practices Commission (FEPC) to ensure that blacks and women received the same pay as white men for doing the same job. The FEPC narrowed pay gaps somewhat, but it did not solve the problem. The American Federation of Labor, which included the highest-paid workers, still refused to accept blacks as members and fought with the FEPC over the equal-pay policy.

■ These two political cartoons by Dr. Seuss, known for his whimsical children's books and progressive political ideas, demonstrate that even among liberal activists, racial tolerance during World War II did not include Japanese Americans. Dr. Seuss created dozens of cartoons that criticized anti-Semitic and anti-black prejudices, but he also promoted the idea that Japanese American citizens were disloyal and dangerous. Stereotyped images such as these contributed to anti-Japanese sentiment that ultimately resulted in the relocation of Japanese Americans from the West Coast into internment camps.

Sometimes the presence of racial minorities in previously all-white work settings led to hostilities. White men who labored on the home front resented the women and minorities who were filling "men's jobs," as well as the soldiers who earned praise for their heroic manhood. Many worried about losing their jobs to returning veterans.

For example, Montana's copper workers, concerned about their job security and their masculinity, asked the federal government to issue them special certificates equating their wartime contribution with that of soldiers. The government denied their request and in 1942 sent a regiment of black miners from the South to help fill the labor shortage in Montana's copper mines. White miners—many of whom had immigrant parents and had only just begun to enjoy full inclusion in white America—were now being told that black men were their equals. The white miners refused to work next to black men and walked out of the mines en masse.

In 1943 Detroit, white workers at the Packard auto plant also walked off the job when three black employees were promoted. With increasing numbers of white and black Southerners arriving to work in the city's war industries, overcrowding strained the boundaries of traditionally segregated neighborhoods. Clashes at a new housing complex escalated into several days of rioting, resulting in 34 deaths and 1800 arrests.

In Los Angeles, the death of a Mexican American youth, Jose Diaz, at a gravel pit called Sleepy Lagoon sparked sensational news coverage and whipped up anti-Mexican fervor. Although police never determined the cause of Diaz's injuries, they filed first-degree murder charges against 22 Mexican American boys from the neighborhood. The jury found the young men guilty, but an appeals court overturned the convictions. Nevertheless, hostility continued to mount against Mexican American youths, particularly "pachucos" who sported "zoot suits," distinctive attire with flared pants, long coats, and wide-brimmed hats. Pachucos wore the zoot suit as an expression of ethnic pride and rebelliousness, as well as incipient political consciousness. Both boys and girls flaunted their distinctive clothing and enjoyed the sense of unity it inspired. Some zoot-suiters would later become active in the Chicano Movement of the 1960s—including the future leader of the United Farm Workers, Cesar Chávez. Chávez later remembered that it took "a lot of guts to wear those pants, and we had to be rebellious to do it, because the police and a few of the older people would harass us."

■ African American pilots, known as the Tuskegee Airmen, served in the U.S. army air force. Here members of the Mustang fighter group listen to a mission briefing in Italy in September 1944.

For eight days in June 1943 scores of soldiers hunted zoot-suiters in Los Angeles bars, theaters, dance halls, and even in their homes, pulling off their clothes and beating them. Soon the attacks expanded to all Mexican Americans, and then to African Americans as well, some of whom also wore the zoot-suit style. The Los Angeles police sided with the rioters. They stood by during the beatings and then arrested the naked and bleeding youths and charged them with disturbing the peace. The rioting raged until the War Department made the entire city of Los Angeles off limits to military personnel. Only a handful of soldiers, but more than 600 Mexican Americans, were arrested. President Roosevelt worried that the zoot-suit violence might strain relations with Mexico. He therefore allocated federal funds for job training, educational improvements, and greater access to higher education for Spanish-speaking Americans.

Fighting for the "Double V"

In spite of discrimination at home, members of minority groups responded enthusiastically to the war effort. The numbers of blacks in the Army soared from 5000 in 1940 to 700,000 by 1944, with an additional 187,000 in the Navy, Coast Guard, and Marine Corps. Four thousand black women joined the WACs. Almost all soldiers fought in segregated units, despite protests by the NAACP that "a Jim Crow army cannot fight for a free world." Nearly 1 million blacks also joined the industrial labor force during the war. African Americans fought for the "Double V"—victory over fascism abroad and racial discrimination at home. Wartime experiences and sacrifices would inspire African Americans, along with Mexican Americans and other minority citizens, to mobilize for civil rights after the war.

Like Keith Little and his boarding-school buddies who became Navajo "Code Talkers," American Indians all over the country declared their willingness to fight for the cause. The Iroquois League announced:

> It is the unanimous sentiment among the Indian people that the atrocities of the Axis nations are violently repulsive to all sense of righteousness of our people. This merciless slaughter of mankind upon the part of those enemies of free peoples can no longer be tolerated.

Zelda Webb Anderson, "You Just Met One Who Does Not Know How to Cook"

Zelda Webb Anderson became one of the first black women to enter military service during World War II. She served as an officer in the Women's Army Auxiliary Corps (WAACS), renamed the Women's Army Corps (WACS) in 1942. After the war she earned a doctorate in education at the University of California, Berkeley. Her 42-year career in education included a stint teaching at the University of East Africa in Dar-es-Salaam, Tanzania. She related her wartime experiences to the University of Nevada Oral History Program in 1995.

Zelda Webb Anderson

Courtesy, Zelda Webb Anderson and The University of Nevada Oral History Project

I reported for duty in January 1942. . . . This was so exciting to me. We had black officers, and our basic training was the same as for men. They would simply tell us, "You wanted to be in a man's army, so now you got to do what the men do." We learned military courtesy, history, how to shoot an M–1, go on bivouac, bathe in a teacup of water, eat hardtack rations. . . .

Every evening troops of male soldiers would march by our barracks en route to the mess hall. I told the commanding officer that we would like to have some shades at the windows. "Oh, no. You wanted to be in the man's army. Fine—you have to do what the men do." I told all the girls, "Listen, they won't give us any shades. So I want you to get right in front of the windows buck naked." The next day we had shades at all the windows. . . .

They pulled me out of basic training the third week and sent me to officer training in Des Moines. All of the instructors were white, but white and black officers were being trained in the same facility, in the same classes, and we slept in the same barracks. After OCS I was assigned to a laundry unit.

A black enlisted WAAC could either be in the laundry unit or she could be in the hospital unit. In the laundry unit, if she had a college degree, she could work at the front counter. . . . If she had less than that, then she *did* the laundry— very demeaning. And in the hospital unit they let her wash walls, empty basins, wash windows—all that menial work. . . .

I was assigned to duty at Fort Breckenridge, Kentucky. The post commander's name was Colonel Throckmorton. In a pronounced southern accent he told me, "You're going over to that colored WAC company, and you're going to be the mess officer."

I said, "Sir, I have not had any mess training."

"All you nigras know how to cook."

I said, "You just met one who does *not* know how to cook; but if you send me to Fort Eustis, Virginia, for training I will come back and be the best mess officer you have on this post."

"I ain't sending you to no school, and you're going over there to be a mess officer." When I about-faced, I kept on going. I didn't even salute him. . . .

[Much later, after developing a more cordial relationship with Colonel Throckmorton,] I told him that segregation has not allowed white people to know black people: "We know you very intimately, but you don't know how we think, how we react, and so you just try to push your stuff on us, not giving a damn about how *we* feel about this. And then when we rebel, or you meet somebody like me, who decides that you can't do this to me, then you think I'm cantankerous; you think I'm an agitator. I'm just trying to give you an education. . . ."

I lived out the rest of my days very happy in the Army. If I had succumbed to the treatment that they had given other blacks before, and not spoken up for myself, my morale would have been down. . . . In this life, you've got to speak up for yourself. You can't go around shuffling your feet with your head hung down acting apologetic. If you see something you want, you must go after it. One day somebody will recognize it, and it's a victory for you, especially when it's somebody who has denigrated you because of your race. . . .

Our country has not solved all of its problems. You have to live democracy before you can preach democracy. I've got four granddaughters, and I don't want them put in a position where they don't have equal opportunities, equal chances, and then they have to fight the same old battles that I fought again. ■

The Cheyenne agreed, vowing to defeat an "unholy triangle" determined to "conquer and enslave the bodies, minds and souls of all free people." Fully 25,000 Native Americans, including 800 women, served in the military during the war. By 1945, nearly one-third of all able-bodied Native American men between 18 and 50 had served. Five percent of them were killed or wounded in action. Native Americans enlisted at a higher rate than the general population, prompting the *Saturday Evening Post* to editorialize, "We would not need the Selective Service if all volunteered like the Indians."

In addition to those who enlisted, half of all able-bodied Native American men not in the service and one-fifth of women left reservations for war industry jobs. At the beginning of the war, men on reservations earned a median annual income of $500, less than one-fourth the national average. One-third of all Native American men living off reservations were unemployed. Worse, the average life expectancy for Native Americans in 1940 was just 35 years, compared with 64 years for the population at large. Like others who found new opportunities during the conflict, Native Americans hoped that the economic progress they had made would be permanent. But the boom would end for them when the war ended. Fewer than 10 percent of Native Americans who relocated to cities found long-term employment after the war.

Total War

World War II consisted of two wars, one centered in Europe and the other in the Pacific. Combatants in both conflicts engaged in total war—the bombing of civilian as well as military targets. The advantageous geographic position of the United States enabled it to wage total war without attacks on its own cities.

The war transformed much of the world. By the time it ended, Hitler had killed 6 million Jews and destroyed the Jewish communtties in Europe. Large parts of the Soviet Union, Europe, and Asia lay in ruins. The United States had deployed the most powerful weapon ever used in warfare. Of all the combatants, only the United States escaped physical destruction on its own national soil. Coming out of the war physically unscathed, economically sound, and politically strong, the United States became the most prosperous and powerful nation in the world.

The War in Europe

The attack on Pearl Harbor brought the United States immediately into the war in both Europe and the Pacific. The leaders of the Allied Powers, including the United States, Britain, and the Soviet Union, had to develop a strategy to defeat the Nazis. But the Allies did not always agree on how to conduct the war, and relations between the United States and the Soviet Union remained strained. Unable to fully overcome the hostility and suspicion that had marked their earlier encounters, leaders of both countries fought the war with postwar power considerations in mind.

Like the United States at Pearl Harbor, the Soviet Union suffered a shocking blow when the Nazis launched a surprise invasion in June 1941 in violation of the nonaggression pact Hitler had signed with Stalin in 1938. The Soviets suffered huge losses as 200 German divisions advanced across Eastern Europe and into the Soviet Union toward Moscow. With the full might of the Nazi forces concentrated on the front lines against the Russians in Eastern Europe, Soviet premier Joseph Stalin wanted the United States to open a second front in Western Europe to divert the Nazis toward the west and relieve pressure on the Soviet Union. In May 1942 Roosevelt assured Stalin that the United States would support an Allied invasion across the English Channel into France. But the British prime minister, Winston Churchill, persuaded FDR to delay that dangerous maneuver and instead to launch an invasion of French north Africa, which was controlled by the Nazi occupation forces in Vichy, France.

While the Allies turned their attention to north Africa, the Soviets managed single-handedly to force the German army into retreat at Stalingrad, where fierce fighting lasted from August 1942 to January 1943. The Battle of Stalingrad was a major turning point in the war and stopped Nazi aggression on the eastern front. The north Africa campaign, code-named TORCH, also concluded successfully for the Allies. Axis soldiers in north Africa surrendered in May 1943. The following summer the Allied forces overran the island of Sicily and moved into southern Italy. A fascist Grand Council led by Field Marshall Pietro Badoglio had overthrown Mussolini and opened communication with General Dwight D. Eisenhower, commander of the Allied forces in Europe. By 1944 the Allied forces reached Rome and backed the new Italian regime. Roosevelt and Churchill continued to delay the opening of the second front as the Soviets waited for relief.

The long-awaited Allied invasion across the English Channel, Operation OVERLORD, finally began on June 6, 1944, code named D-Day. On D-Day, the force assembled in England crossed the English Channel to France. At dawn, in the largest amphibious landing in history, more than 4000 Allied ships descended on the beaches at Normandy. As the troops splashed onto shore, they met a barrage of German fire. Many thousands died on the beach that day. Over

■ **MAP 23.3**
WORLD WAR II IN EUROPE   Along the eastern front of the war in Europe, Soviet troops did the bulk of the fighting and sustained the highest casualties. The Battle of Stalingrad, in which Soviet troops finally drove back the Nazis after months of brutal fighting, was a major turning point in the war.

■ A photograph taken on D-Day, June 6, 1944, as U.S. troops waded to shore from their landing craft and faced German artillery fire on Omaha Beach. This is a rare surviving photograph from the initial Normandy invasion because so many of the photographers, along with thousands of soldiers, died at the scene.

the next 10 days, more than 1 million soldiers landed at Normandy, along with 50,000 vehicles and more than 100,000 tons of supplies, opening the way for an advance into Nazi-occupied France.

As the war continued to rage, Roosevelt prepared for the November election. Much of the 1944 campaign swirled around Roosevelt's suitability for reelection: whether he should serve an unprecedented fourth term, and whether his health would hold up—the 62-year-old president suffered from heart disease and high blood pressure. Party regulars persuaded FDR to drop Vice President Henry A. Wallace from the ticket and replace him with Senator Harry S. Truman from Missouri. The Republicans chose Thomas E. Dewey, governor of New York, to run against FDR. Democrats campaigned on the slogan "Don't change horses in midstream," and the electorate apparently agreed. Roosevelt won the election and continued his wartime leadership.

In the months after D-Day, the Allies liberated Paris and went on to defeat the Germans in Belgium at the Battle of the Bulge, sending the Nazis into full retreat. The Allied armies then crossed the Rhine and headed for Berlin. Eisenhower stopped his troops at the Elbe River to let Soviet troops take Berlin. Eisenhower hoped that giving the Soviets the final triumph would ease postwar relations with the Soviet Union—but he also wanted to save American lives. Huge numbers of Soviet troops died in the siege of Berlin, but the war in Europe was nearly over. With the Soviets approaching his bunker in April 1945, Hitler committed suicide. Berlin fell on May 2, and Germany surrendered at Reims, France, on May 7, 1945—V-E (Victory in Europe) Day.

FDR did not live to see the Nazis defeated. On April 12, 1945, he died suddenly of a cerebral hemorrhage. As a stunned nation mourned, Vice President Harry S. Truman took the oath of office as the nation's thirty-third president.

TABLE 23-2			
The Election of 1944			
Candidate	Political Party	Popular Vote	Electoral Vote
Franklin D. Roosevelt	Democratic	25,602,504	432
Thomas E. Dewey	Republican	22,006,285	99

The War in the Pacific

As the conflict in Europe came to an end, the war in the Pacific continued to rage. Following the attack on Pearl Harbor, Japan continued its conquests in the Pacific. In April 1942 General Douglas MacArthur, driven from the Philippines to Australia, left 12,000 American and 64,000 Filipino soldiers to surrender on the Bataan peninsula and the island of Corregidor. On the infamous "Bataan Death March" to the prison at Camp O'Donnell, the Japanese beat, tortured, and shot the sick and starving troops. As many as 10,000 men died on the march.

Now in control of Indochina, Thailand, the Philippines, and the chain of islands from Sumatra to Guadalcanal, Japan's military leaders planned to destroy what remained of the U.S. fleet. But MacArthur marshaled his forces and achieved a major victory in the Battle of the Coral Sea in May 1942. U.S. intelligence sources discovered that the Japanese were planning a massive assault on Midway Island, a naval base key to Hawaii's defense. Under the command of

Admiral Chester Nimitz, the United States launched a surprise air strike on June 4, 1942, sinking four Japanese carriers, destroying 322 planes, preserving the American presence at Midway, and virtually destroying Japanese offensive capabilities. Two months later, Nimitz's forces landed at Guadalcanal in the Solomon Islands, subduing the Japanese in five months of brutal fighting. Having seized the offensive, U.S. troops continued toward Japan. MacArthur's forces took New Guinea, and, by February 1944, Nimitz secured the Marshall Islands and the Marianas.

At about the same time that Allied forces in Europe were landing in Normandy, the United States invaded Saipan, the main island bastion that protected Japan's mainland. In a savage air battle on June 19, the Americans shot down 346 Japanese planes and lost 50 of their own. The attack killed 22,000 Japanese civilians—two-thirds of the island's population. The United States suffered 14,000 casualties. But the grueling battle secured for the United States a strategic base for launching bombing raids on Tokyo. The bloody war in the Pacific continued, with critical Allied victories on the islands of Iwo Jima and Okinawa in the spring of 1945. Crucial to these victories were the sensitive radio communications achieved by the special Marine unit of Navajo "Code Talkers."

In China the struggle against Japanese aggression grew complicated because China was also engaged in a civil war. Initially, the Chinese Nationalists appeared to have the largest military forces to resist the Japanese, so Roosevelt declared support for Jiang Jieshi (Chiang Kai-shek), the corrupt and unpopular Nationalist leader. Jiang continued to demand Allied support as a growing communist movement, led by Mao Zedong (Mao Tse-tung), challenged the Japanese and gained support among Chinese peasants. Although the Nationalists failed to stop the Japanese, Roosevelt continued to back Jiang's ineffective leadership, setting the stage for political tensions that persisted after the war.

The war in the Pacific was particularly vicious. Racism on both sides fueled acts of extreme brutality. Japan's leaders believed that their racial superiority gave them a divine mission to conquer Asia. The Japanese tortured prisoners of war and civilians in their conquered lands. They tested biological weapons and conducted medical experiments on live subjects. Japanese troops forced Chinese and Korean women into sexual slavery, euphemistically calling them "comfort women."

Racial hostility also promoted American battlefield savagery. U.S. troops in the Pacific often killed the enemy instead of taking prisoners and desecrated the enemy dead with disrespect equal to that meted out by the Japanese on the bodies of their foes. On the home front, American cultural images and popular sentiments vilified the Japanese not only as a hated enemy but also as a monstrous race. War correspondent Ernie Pyle explained that "in Europe we felt that our enemies, horrible and deadly as they were, were still people. But . . . the Japanese were looked upon as something subhuman and repulsive, the way some people feel about cockroaches or mice." Respectable magazines such as *Science Digest* ran articles titled "Why Americans Hate Japs More Than Nazis."

As American troops closed in on Japan, Roosevelt approved a plan to firebomb Japanese cities. The Allies had already bombed German cities, destroying much of Hamburg and Dresden and killing thousands of civilians. To persuade Americans to accept the bombing strategy with its inevitable civilian casualties, government censors lifted the ban on stories of Japanese treatment

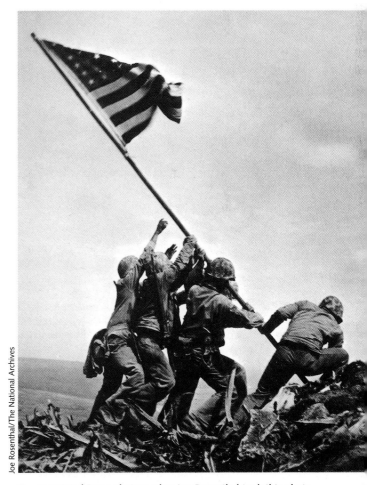

Joe Rosenthal/The National Archives

■ Associated Press photographer Joe Rosenthal took this photo, "Old Glory goes up on Mt. Suribachi, Iwo Jima," and won a Pulitzer Prize for it in 1945. Although controversy surrounded the photo (some witnesses claimed it was staged with a larger flag after the original flag had been planted), it became an icon of American determination and unity in World War II.

■ MAP 23.4
WORLD WAR II IN THE PACIFIC During World War II, the Japanese occupied vast territories in Asia and the Pacific. The Battle of Midway in 1942 was the first major victory for the United States in the Pacific and helped turn the tide of the war in favor of the Allies.

of American war prisoners. Reports of atrocities, as well as virulently racist images of the Japanese, flooded the media. On March 9 and 10, 1945, bombing raids led by General Curtis LeMay leveled 16 square miles of Tokyo—one-fourth of the city—and left 185,000 dead or wounded. LeMay's bombers then turned to other cities. Firebombs reportedly killed a higher number of civilians than Japanese soldiers who died in battle.

The End of the War

Allied leaders met several times to plan for the postwar era. Roosevelt hoped to ensure American dominance and to limit Soviet power. At a conference in Teheran, Iran, in 1943 Roosevelt insisted that the Eastern European states of Poland, Latvia, Lithuania, and Estonia should be independent after the war. As the war wound down, Churchill, Stalin, and Roosevelt met again at Yalta, in Ukraine, in February 1945. They agreed to demand Germany's unconditional surrender and to divide the conquered nation into four zones to be occupied by Britain, the Soviet Union, the United States, and France. It became obvious at Yalta that separate spheres of influence would prevail after the war. Poland was a source of contention. Although Stalin nominally agreed to allow free elections in Eastern Europe, he intended to make sure that the countries bordering the Soviet Union would be under his control. He also pledged to enter the war against Japan and received assurances that the Soviet Union would regain the lands lost to Japan in the 1904–1905 Russo-Japanese War.

In July 1945 the newly sworn-in American president, Harry Truman, joined Stalin and Churchill (replaced by Clement Attlee after Churchill's election loss) at Potsdam, near Berlin. The three leaders issued a statement demanding "unconditional surrender" from Japan while privately agreeing to let Japan retain its emperor. The rest of the conference focused on postwar Europe. At Potsdam Truman learned of the successful test of the atomic bomb. With the new weapon in his hands, he now knew that Soviet assistance would not be needed to end the war in the Pacific.

As the war ended in Europe, Allied troops liberated the Nazi concentration camps. At that moment, the world finally learned the extent of Hitler's "Final Solution." Among the soldiers who first entered the camps were a number of Japanese Americans. Ichiro Imamura described the sight at Dachau: "When the gates swung open, we got our first good look at the prisoners. . . . They were like skeletons—all skin and bones. . . . They were sick, starving and dying." Some of the survivors saw the Japanese American soldiers and feared that they were Japanese allies of the Germans. A *Nisei* soldier reassured them, "I am an American soldier, and you are free."

As the victors carved up Hitler's Third Reich, the war in the Pacific continued. The United States persisted in demanding "unconditional surrender" and vowed to continue to blockade Japan's ports, firebomb its cities, and possibly launch an invasion if the Japanese refused to surrender. Later, critics of this strategy argued that the demand for unconditional surrender strengthened the Japanese will to resist. They noted that the United States did nothing to assure the Japanese that the victorious Americans would not execute the emperor, nor did American leaders respond to Japanese peace overtures.

The atomic bomb offered Truman a new means to end the war. The secret project to develop the bomb had been under way for several years, initially for possible use against Germany. In 1939 scientists in Berlin had achieved atomic fission by splitting the uranium atom, making it possible to release the tremendous energy stored in the atom. Albert Einstein, the German Jewish physicist who came to the United States after Hitler came to power in 1933, had warned Roosevelt that the Germans might be developing an atomic weapon. Einstein urged the United States to establish a small research program to keep pace. In 1942 American scientists reported that with adequate resources, they could develop an atomic bomb in time to affect the course of the war. Impressed, Roosevelt authorized the Manhattan Project, the

The National Archives

■ Slave laborers rest in the Buchenwald concentration camp near Jena, Germany. These inmates were among those who were still alive when troops of the 80th Division entered the camp on April 16, 1945. At labor camps such as this one, and death camps such as Auschwitz, 6 million Jews, along with thousands of Romani (Gypsies), Poles, mentally and physically handicapped people, and homosexuals, died in the Holocaust.

The Atomic Bomb: Political and Cultural Fallout

Since the dawn of the atomic age, the United States has been the only nation that has actually waged nuclear war. The dropping of the atomic bombs on the Japanese cities of Hiroshima and Nagasaki unleashed not only massive death and destruction but also ongoing controversies over the development and use of nuclear weapons and the nature of modern warfare. The level of destruction inflicted on the Japanese civilian population shocked the nation and the world. But well before the nuclear attacks on Japan, hundreds of thousands of civilians had already perished in the war.

During World War II, bombing of civilian targets became commonplace. The Japanese bombed civilians in Nanjing, China; the Germans did the same in Guernica, Spain. Allied bombing raids nearly demolished the German cities of Berlin and Dresden and the Japanese capitol of Tokyo. One night of conventional bombing in Tokyo in March 1945 killed as many civilians as the atomic bomb dropped on Hiroshima. With its huge Air Force, the United States became the greatest bombing power during the war. But the atomic bombs took civilian casualties to a new level, not only because of the enormous death toll wrought by a single bomb but also because of the deadly radioactive fallout that lingered. Conventional bombing raids did not create fallout to harm survivors, their descendants, or the environment.

With the successful 1952 test of the hydrogen (fusion) bomb—1000 times more powerful than the bombs dropped on Japan—scientists warned that the use of such weapons in warfare could create a "nuclear winter" that would destroy life on Earth. Horror at the impact of the bombs discouraged their use throughout the remainder of the twentieth century.

Civilian casualties, however, remained a fact of warfare. Guerrilla warfare increased the likelihood of civilian casualties in Vietnam, where American troops found it nearly impossible to distinguish combatants from noncombatants. American forces made widespread use of napalm, the antipersonnel weapon that set fire to anyone in its path, civilian or military. Massacres of villagers, such as the infamous killings at My Lai, turned many Americans against the war.

Although the United States and the Soviet Union refrained from using atomic weapons during the many hot wars that erupted during the Cold War, the two superpowers developed tens of thousands of nuclear weapons with sophisticated delivery systems to launch

research program to develop nuclear weapons, under the direction of J. Robert Oppenheimer. The project got under way at a top-secret laboratory in Los Alamos, New Mexico. The building of the bomb was the work of 125,000 people and cost nearly $2 billion. The first test of the device took place on July 16, 1945, at Alamagordo, New Mexico.

When Truman learned of the successful test, he wanted to use the bomb immediately. He hoped to avoid an invasion of Japan that would have cost the lives of many American soldiers, and he wanted to send a message to the Soviet Union that the United States would be the dominant power in the postwar world. But Truman's advisors did not all agree about whether or how the new weapon should be deployed. Some of the scientists who had developed the bomb urged a "demonstration" in a remote, unpopulated area that would impress the Japanese but would not cause loss of life. General George C. Marshall and other military leaders argued in favor of dropping the bomb on military or industrial targets, with ample warning ahead of time to enable civilians to leave target areas. But others agreed with Truman that dropping the bomb on a major city, without warning, would be the only way to persuade the Japanese to surrender unconditionally. Given the death and destruction already inflicted on Japanese cities by firebombing, the atomic bomb seemed to some like an escalation of current strategy.

But when the first bomb exploded over Hiroshima on August 6, 1945, and the second on Nagasaki two days later, the horrifying destructiveness of nuclear weapons became apparent. Even though the American public saw few images of the carnage on the ground, the huge mushroom cloud and the descriptions of cities leveled and people instantly incinerated shocked attacks from land, sea, and air. Proponents argued that the nuclear deterrent prevented the outbreak of World War III. But detractors claimed that the arms race increased international tensions and strained the economies of both nations. In 1962 the Cuban Missile Crisis nearly led to nuclear war.

Fifty years after the end of World War II, the controversy over the use of the weapons remained heated. The Smithsonian Institution planned an exhibit to display the *Enola Gay*, the plane that dropped the atomic bomb over Hiroshima, with an explanation of the arguments on both sides on the issue. Fierce opposition to the proposed exhibit forced the Smithsonian to abandon the plan, prompting the institute's director to resign in protest.

At the dawn of the twenty-first century, the arms race continued to generate policy debates. President George W. Bush revived the "Star Wars" plan of President Ronald Reagan to build a satellite shield against

Harry S. Truman Library

This atomic bomb, named "Fat Man," was dropped on Nagasaki, Japan, on August 8, 1945, two days after the first bomb destroyed the city of Hiroshima. The Japanese surrendered soon afterward, bringing World War II to an end. Controversy still surrounds the dropping of these weapons, which killed hundreds of thousands of civilians.

incoming missiles. Advocates of the plan claimed that it would protect the United States from nuclear attack. Critics charged that the system would not work and that it would probably generate a new arms race. As the debate continued, around the world—in missile silos, submarines, and bomber planes—nuclear warheads remained poised to strike. ∎

the nation and the world. In addition to the immediate devastation wreaked by the bomb, deadly radioactive fallout remained in the atmosphere, causing illness and death for months and even years after the attack. The Japanese surrendered on September 2, 1945, V-J (Victory in Japan) Day. Many people breathed a sigh of relief that the war was finally over. But doubts and controversies over the use of the weapon, and the nuclear arms race that it sparked, have continued to this day.

Conclusion

World War II left massive devastation in its wake all across the globe. The United States was the only country involved in the war that emerged from it stronger than before the conflict began. With the exception of Pearl Harbor, no fighting took place on American soil. Although thousands of Americans died in the conflict, American casualties were far below those suffered by other countries. The wartime economy provided full employment and brought the nation out of the Depression. At the end of the war, the United States was the most powerful nation in the world.

The war changed life for Americans in profound ways. Although wartime forged a sense of unity as the nation came together to fight against fascism, it also highlighted fissures within American society. Members of minority groups fought in segregated units, but racial tensions

The National Archives

■ On V-J Day, August 14, 1945, New Yorkers of Italian descent celebrate Japan's surrender. Although the United States fought against the country of their ancestors, these Americans showed their spirited support for the Allied cause.

and conflicts erupted at home, even as the country fought against a racist foe. Women joined the paid labor force and the armed services in unprecedented numbers, while at the same time being bombarded by official and cultural messages reminding them that their ultimate service to the nation was as wives and mothers.

At the end of the war, veterans of color returned to fight for the still unfulfilled side of the Double V: victory against racism at home. Women joined returning veterans to form families and have babies in the most dramatic rush into parenthood in the nation's history, but they did not retreat from the paid labor force. World War II marked the beginning of a steady increase in employment for women that continued for the rest of the century.

While life at home changed dramatically, so did the place of the United States in the world. The war's conclusion did not usher in the era of peace Americans expected. European empires staggered on the brink of collapse. Only the United States and the Soviet Union remained as military forces, shifting the international balance of power from a multipolar to a bipolar system. The victors carved up countries in Europe and Asia according to geopolitical considerations, with little regard for national affinities. Soon American troops would fight again in the artificially divided lands of Korea and Vietnam. For the next half century, the fallout from World War II, as well as the power struggle between the United States and the Soviet Union, would shape political relationships across the globe.

Sites to Visit

Powers of Persuasion—Poster Art of World War II
www.archives.gov/exhibit_hall/powers_of_persuasion/powers_of_persuasion_home.html

This Library of Congress site includes posters created during World War II to encourage support for the war and to build morale.

A-Bomb WWW Museum
www.csi.ad.jp/ABOMB/

This site includes information about the impact of the atomic bombs dropped on Japan during World War II as well as materials and images about the development of nuclear weapons.

A People at War
www.archives.gov/exhibit_hall/a_people_at_war/a_people_at_war.html

This National Archives site includes materials and images about the contributions millions of Americans made to the war effort.

The United States Holocaust Memorial Museum
www.ushmm.org/index.html

This official website of the U.S. Holocaust Memorial Museum in Washington, D.C., covers the history and documents of the Holocaust.

Tuskegee Airmen
www.wpafb.af.mil/museum/history/prewwii/ta.htm

This site of the Air Force Museum at Wright-Patterson Air Force Base includes information and photographs of the African American pilots of World War II.

Abraham Lincoln Brigade Archives
www.alba-valb.org/aboutalb.htm

This site has information and articles about the Spanish Civil War and the unit of American volunteers who fought in it.

The Zoot Suit Riots
www.pbs.org/wgbh/amex/zoot/

This website from the Public Broadcasting Service (PBS) documentary series *The American Experience* covers the World War II Zoot Suit Riots in Los Angeles.

William P. Gottlieb Photographs of the Golden Age of Jazz
memory.loc.gov/ammem/wghtml/wghome.html

This Library of Congress site includes images, audio, and articles from *Down Beat* magazine in the 1940s.

America from the Great Depression to World War II: Photographs from the FSA and OWI, c. 1935–1945
memory.loc.gov/ammem/fsahtml/fahome.html

This site from the Library of Congress includes photographs in the Farm Security Administration–Office of War Information Collection taken during the Depression and World War II years.

For Further Reading

General

Paul Fussell, *Wartime: Understanding and Behavior in the Second World War* (1989).

John Keegan, *The Second World War* (1990).

Richard Polenburg, *War and Society: The United States, 1941–1945* (1972).

Studs Terkel, *"The Good War": An Oral History of World War II* (1984).

Mobilizing for War

Michael E. Birdwell, *Celluloid Soldiers: The Warner Brothers Campaign Against Nazism* (1999).

Justus D. Doenecke, *Storm on the Horizon: The Challenge to American Intervention, 1939–1941* (2000).

Thomas J. Fleming, *The New Dealers' War: Franklin D. Roosevelt and the War Within World War II* (2001).

Cecelia Lynch, *Beyond Appeasement: Interpreting Interwar Peace Movements in World Politics* (1999).

Pearl Harbor: The United States Enters the War

Allan Berube, *Coming Out Under Fire: The History of Gay Men and Women in World War Two* (1990).

Allan M. Brandt, *No Magic Bullet: A Social History of Venereal Disease in the United States* (1987).

Akira Iriye, *Pearl Harbor and the Coming of the Pacific War: A Brief History with Documents and Essays* (1999).

Michael S. Sherry, *The Rise of American Air Power: The Creation of Armageddon* (1987).

The Home Front

John Morton Blum, *V Was for Victory: Politics and American Culture During World War II* (1976).

Lewis A. Erenberg and Susan E. Hirsch, *The War in American Culture* (1996).

Susan Hartmann, *The Home Front and Beyond: American Women in the 1940s* (1982).

Elaine Tyler May, *Pushing the Limits: American Women, 1940–1961* (1994).

Race and War

Beth Bailey and David Farber, *The First Strange Place: The Alchemy of Race and Sex in World War II Hawaii* (1992).

Aaron Berman, *Nazism, the Jews and American Zionism, 1933–1948* (1990).

John W. Dower, *War Without Mercy: Race and Power in the Pacific War* (1987).

Barbara Dianne Savage, *Broadcasting Freedom: Radio, War, and the Politics of Race, 1938–1948* (1999).

Davis S. Wyman, *The Abandonment of the Jews: America and the Holocaust, 1941–1945* (1984).

Total War

Ronald Powaski, *March to Armageddon: The United States and the Nuclear Arms Race, 1939 to the Present* (1987).

George H. Roeder, Jr., *The Censored War: American Visual Experience During World War Two* (1993).

Michael S. Sherry, *In the Shadow of War: The United States Since the 1930s* (1995).

Martin J. Sherwin, *A World Destroyed: Hiroshima and the Origins of the Arms Race* (1987).

Online Practice Test

Test your understanding of this chapter with interactive review quizzes at

www.ablongman.com/jonescreatedequal/chapter23

Cold War and Hot War, 1945–1953

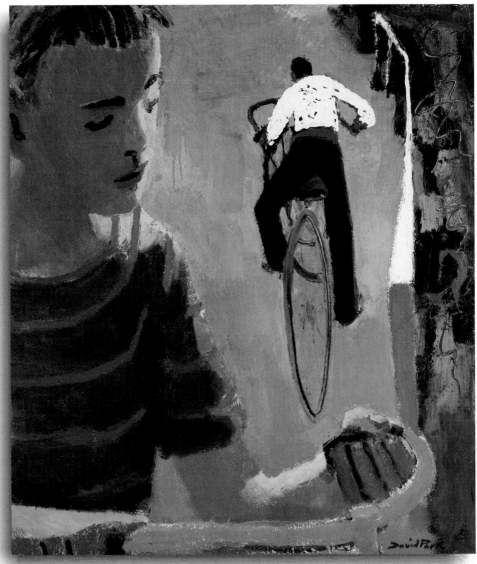

David Parks, "Boys on Bikes," 1950. Curtis Galleries, Minneapolis, MN

■ Robert Park's 1950 painting *Kids on Bikes* reminds viewers that in the midst of the high drama of Cold War international conflicts, most Americans tried to carry on with their normal daily lives. Park himself opted out of the comfortable life of his prominent Boston family, quitting high school and moving to Berkeley, California to work as an artist.

AT 11:30 A.M. ON APRIL 25, 1945, U.S. ARMY PRIVATE JOSEPH POLOWSKY GLIMPSED what looked like the future. The young Chicago native was riding in the lead jeep of an American force along the Elbe River in central Germany when he spotted Russian soldiers on the far side, their medals glistening in the morning sun. Elated, he and five of his comrades found a small boat and paddled across to the eastern bank. Using Polowsky's knowledge of German to communicate, the American soldiers embraced their Soviet allies with laughs and tears. The Russians produced bottles of vodka, and toasts, pledges, singing, and dancing followed. After years of pressing Germany from east and west, the Allies had finally linked up in the heart of Hitler's empire. A reporter wrote of the scene, "You get the feeling of exuberance, a great new world opening up."

Despite his conservative Republican background, Polowsky spent much of his life advocating American–Russian friendship. He could not forget the transforming experience of that April day along the Elbe and the hopes it engendered for a peaceful future. However, what followed the Allied victory turned out not to be a "great new world" of international peace and brotherhood but the Cold War of U.S.–Soviet hostility that lasted for more than four decades. The opposing ideologies—communism and capitalist democracy—joined with conflicting national interests to produce this armed standoff. The American effort to contain the expansion of communist influence entailed a radical reorientation of American involvement abroad in peacetime, including the nation's first peacetime military alliance, the North Atlantic Treaty Organization (NATO). At times the Cold War turned into a hot war of actual shooting, most importantly in the Korean War of 1950–1953.

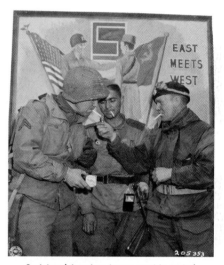

Soviet and American troops meet in central Germany in May 1945.

Soon after the end of World War II, Jim Forman enlisted in the U.S. Air Force. In 1948, he shipped out with his battalion to the huge U.S. base on the island of Okinawa in Japan. There some of the social changes unleashed by World War II caught up with him. President Harry Truman ordered the racial desegregation of the armed forces, and officers chose him to be the first African American to join the 625th Aircraft and Warning Company. Forman reported to his new assignment across the island, expecting trouble from white soldiers: harassment, assaults, and worse. Fearful, he slept only a few hours his first night. When he went to the mess hall for breakfast the next morning, he was stunned. "Fresh eggs. I saw them crack fresh eggs. I did not believe what I saw: fresh eggs. I had been on the Rock [Okinawa] some six months and I had never tasted a fresh egg unless I bought it at the restaurant in town." The white cook asked him how he wanted his eggs cooked and how many. "How many?" Forman asked in amazement. "Do you mean I can have more than two?" It was the same with milk: he could have a whole quart of fresh milk and then come back for more. In his former all-black battalion, he had been served only powdered eggs and powdered milk and only in carefully limited quantities. "I cursed the Air Force for its segregation, but I ate my fresh milk and eggs."

Jim Forman was trying to make sense of the changes and uncertainties that pervaded American society in the late 1940s. Popular support at home was needed for expansive new military commitments abroad, yet Americans had just fought in the largest war in their history, and most were eager to get back to something close to normal peacetime life. For some citizens the war years had provided new opportunities for better work and more independence. Women, workers, and African Americans, for example, did not want to retreat from the advances they had made. Struggles over the place of these groups of citizens helped shape the contours of the immediate postwar years, both in family lives and in the public sphere.

In some ways, the Cold War encouraged efforts at social reform. America's new leading role in world affairs brought its domestic life into the spotlight of world attention. Racial discrimination and violence at home embarrassed American leaders as they spoke of leading the anticommunist "free world" abroad. But in other ways, the Cold War constrained efforts to bring American life more fully into line with its democratic and egalitarian promise. Rising tensions with communist movements and governments overseas stimulated great anxieties about possible subversion within the nation's own borders. Anticommunist fervor put unions on the defensive and encouraged women to shun the workplace in favor of family life and parenting, particularly in the nation's growing suburbs. This second Red Scare—the first had followed World War I in 1919—reached flood tide by 1950 with the rise to prominence of Senator Joseph McCarthy. The young Republican from Wisconsin made a career of blaming supposedly disloyal Americans at home for setbacks to U.S. goals abroad in places such as China and Korea. He left a bitter legacy that long outlasted his political demise in 1954.

The Uncertainties of Victory

It was five in the afternoon when the Senate recessed on April 12, 1945. The Vice President walked through the Capitol building to the private office of his old friend and mentor, Sam Rayburn of Texas, the House majority leader. He had just mixed himself a cocktail when an aide told him that he was to call the White House immediately. Picking up the phone, he was instructed to come to the White House right away. "Jesus Christ and General Jackson," he said as he put down the receiver, his face suddenly pale. Within 15 minutes, Harry Truman was being ushered into the private quarters at 1600 Pennsylvania Avenue. Eleanor Roosevelt greeted him with the somber news: "Harry, the president is dead." Stunned, he finally said, "Is there anything I can do for you?" She replied, "Is there anything *we* can do for *you*? For you are the one in trouble now."

Franklin Roosevelt was dead; it was almost unimaginable. Elected four times to the presidency, he had dominated American politics like no figure before or since. Just as the unprecedented destruction of World War II was finally ending, the leadership of the nation passed into new and less tested hands. Peace brought an array of uncertainties and immediate needs. The victors had to reconstruct a world that had been damaged, physically and psychologically, almost beyond recognition. Spared the destruction visited elsewhere, the United States faced the different challenge of demobilizing its military forces and reconverting to a peacetime economy. Intense conflicts along the color line and in the workplace revealed real differences between Americans about the shape of the democracy they had fought to defend.

Ed Clark/TimePix

■ Franklin D. Roosevelt's death at his vacation home in Warm Springs, Georgia, stunned a nation and a world that had not known another U.S. president since 1932. Navy bandsman Graham Jackson was one of Roosevelt's favorite musicians. As the procession began to transport the president's body north for burial in Hyde Park, New York, Jackson captured the grief of millions of Americans as he played the sweet, slow strains of "Going Home."

Global Destruction

World War II wrought death on a scale that defies comprehension: 60 million human beings lost their lives. From England in the west to the islands of New Guinea in the east, from Scandinavia in the north to the Sahara Desert in the south, much of Europe and Asia was left in ruins. Soviet and American power had finally crushed the Axis, with Berlin now a "city of the dead" and Japan's urban landscape devastated by firebombing and nuclear attacks. Most of the victors were only marginally better off. China lost 10 million of its citizens to Japanese guns and starvation, and the Soviet victory over Germany came at the cost of more than 20 million Russian lives. Poland, the battleground for the Germans and the Soviets, was a wasteland. And the Nazis had murdered 6 million European Jews, primarily Poles and Germans.

Only one of the major combatants emerged from the war in better shape than at the beginning. With no fighting on their soil after the initial Japanese attack on Pearl Harbor, American civilians spent the war years in safety. Orders for war materials ended the Great Depression in the United States and created full employment as factories worked overtime to supply the Allied armies. The American people, one official remarked in 1945, "are in the pleasant predicament of having to learn to live 50 percent better than they have ever lived before." Many Americans suffered terribly in the war, of course; 400,000 died, leaving behind desolate families, and millions of veterans returned with traumas that colored the remainder of their lives. But such casualties paled in comparison to those of other belligerent nations. With just 6 percent of the world's population and 50 percent of its wealth, the United States enjoyed a position of staggering economic advantage in comparison with the rest of the world.

Americans' overriding fear was that the end of the fighting might return the country to the state it had faced when the war began: economic depression. The nation's awesome industrial productivity depended on government spending, which was now to be cut back sharply. International trade might pick up much of the slack, but the war had destroyed most of the purchasing power of U.S. trading partners in Europe and Asia. Rising tensions between the two primary victors—the United States and the Soviet Union—hampered the process of postwar reconstruction. President Truman showed his frustration with the Soviet military occupation of eastern

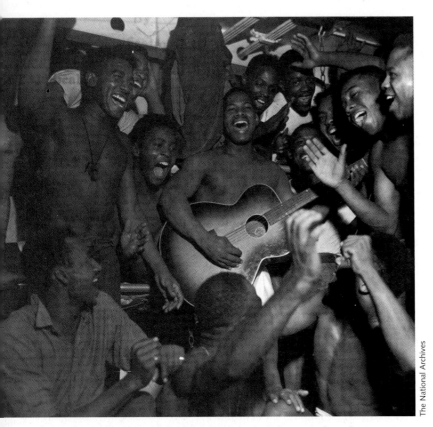

■ American sailors at Pearl Harbor in Hawaii gather around a radio to celebrate the news of Japan's surrender on August 14, 1945. Their lives were suddenly free from the perils of the brutal warfare in the Pacific, where Japanese pilots known as kamikazes had crashed suicide planes into U.S. warships.

The National Archives

Europe by lecturing Soviet diplomats and abruptly cutting off Lend–Lease aid to the USSR. Soviet dictator Joseph Stalin feared America's new global military might, manifest in its monopoly of the atomic bomb, and was determined to secure his European border against future invasion from the West.

Vacuums of Power

World War II altered the world's ideological and physical landscape. Japan and Germany, the centers of prewar power in Asia and continental Europe, were vacuums waiting to be filled and reshaped by their conquerors. In addition to defeating two nations, the Allies had also discredited the ideas on which those governments had been built: fascism and militarism. These were the ideas of the extreme Right: the glorification of the racially defined state and its aggressive military expansion. Fascism's murderous character tarred those who had collaborated with the Axis during the war, primarily conservatives in countries such as France who preferred fascism to socialism. White supremacy and colonialism, two underpinnings of the United States and its western European allies, also lost much of their legitimacy in the war to defend democracy against Hitler's racially genocidal Third Reich.

Into many of the postwar vacuums of power flowed a newly prominent worldwide Left. Socialists, communists, and other radicals espoused communal rather than individualistic values. The Red Army's primary role in defeating the German troops who had overrun Europe evoked admiration for the Soviet Union among antifascists everywhere. The occupying Soviet forces installed communist governments in eastern Europe by force (sometimes called "Red Army socialism"), and Socialist and Communist parties rose sharply in popularity in France, Italy, Belgium, and Scandinavia. The nominally socialist Labor party took power in Great Britain, defeating war leader Winston Churchill and his Conservative party at the polls. Europeans across the continent established welfare states to provide a minimum standard of living for all their citizens.

This turn to the left encompassed most of the globe. Africans began organizing for eventual independence from European rule, and Asians launched the final phase of their anticolonial struggle for liberation. Indonesia fought its way free from the Dutch, and India gained its freedom from Britain. "The sun never sets on the British Empire" had long been a proud colonial refrain, but it was no longer true. In French Indochina, Ho Chi Minh quoted from

Thomas Jefferson's Declaration of Independence as he announced the creation of an independent Vietnam. (Truman ignored Vietnam's appeal for American recognition, just as Wilson had done 26 years earlier at the Versailles peace conference after World War I; see Chapter 20). Masters of much of the world a few years earlier, the European colonial powers fought desperately to hold onto the last pieces of their escaping empires. The Allies created the new United Nations (UN) in San Francisco in April 1945, just days after Truman succeeded FDR. Eventually housed in New York, it embodied hopes for a more peaceful and democratic world. Its General Assembly gave all nations an equal voice and vote in deliberations, and its small Security Council—responsible for guiding any UN military actions—gave a permanent seat and veto power to five nations: the United States, the USSR, Britain, France, and China. The 1948 UN Human Rights Charter helped put practitioners of colonialism and racial discrimination on the defensive by declaring worldwide support for the principles of national self-determination and equal treatment for all peoples.

Postwar Reconversion

The fundamental task for Americans at home was to reconvert from a wartime society back to a peacetime one. They were especially eager to "bring the boys home." The 12 million men in uniform represented nearly two-thirds of all men between 18 and 34 years old. Despite the worries of U.S. commanders and strategists that rapid demobilization would exacerbate vacuums of power abroad, 9 million American troops came home by mid-1946. Eager to return to civilian life, they walked off ships' gangplanks into a country in transition. Factories were trying to convert from producing war materials to making consumer products. Wartime rationing was lifted on goods such as sugar and gasoline, and the 35-mph speed limit was withdrawn, but unemployment and inflation threatened. Orders for war materials dried up, taking jobs with them, but wartime inflation ("too many dollars chasing too few goods") persisted. Housing remained especially scarce. In the richest country in the world, one-third of the citizens still lived in poverty, with neither running water nor flush toilets.

To ease the transition home, Congress had passed the Servicemen's Readjustment Act of 1944 (the GI Bill) to provide crucial financial aid to veterans. It gave low-cost mortgages that helped create an explosion in home ownership. It created Veterans Administration hospitals to provide lifetime medical care. And it paid tuition and stipends for colleges and vocational training, making higher education broadly available for the first time. The 2 percent of veterans who were women also made use of these benefits. In the postwar era, when American politics generally became more conservative—shifting away from the New Deal reform spirit and toward an anticommunist emphasis—the GI Bill was the one area in which the United States expanded its own welfare state. The $14.5 billion spent on veterans over the next decade marked a public investment that helped propel millions of families into an expanding middle class.

The postwar transition presented particular challenges to American women. Millions of them had gone to work outside the home during the war and found economic independence in doing so. Now they faced powerful pressures to leave the workforce and return to a domestic life of old and new families. Employers fired women, and male veterans expecting jobs did not welcome female competition. The federal government abruptly halted funding for wartime daycare facilities, forcing mothers to quit their jobs. Many women accepted this return to the domestic sphere, content to focus on marriage and family life. But millions felt varying degrees of resentment over their loss of hard-earned compensation and self-esteem. "War jobs have uncovered unsuspected abilities in American women," one argued. "Why lose all these abilities?"

■ Japanese American women pack lima beans into boxes for freezing at Seabrook Farms, near Bridgeton, New Jersey, in 1947. Unlike the northern part of the state, which was closely tied to New York City, rural southern New Jersey was a rich fruit- and vegetable-growing region. After their release from the internment camps of World War II, Americans of Japanese descent joined their fellow citizens in finding work where they could in a peacetime economy no longer shrouded by the Great Depression.

Contesting Racial Hierarchies

African Americans faced a similar problem. After finding new opportunities in industrial employment during the war, they were laid off afterward in favor of returning white veterans. Like women, blacks were expected by others to retreat into deference. Black veterans spearheaded

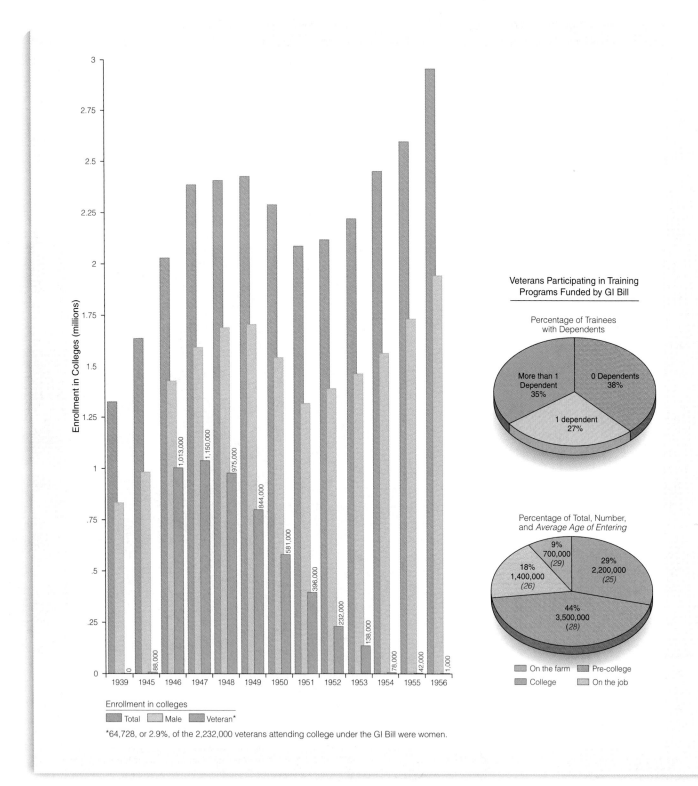

Enrollment in colleges
Total   Male   Veteran*

*64,728, or 2.9%, of the 2,232,000 veterans attending college under the GI Bill were women.

■ **FIGURE 24.1**
OPPORTUNITIES FOR VETERANS   The number of Americans attending college increased sharply after World War II. In the early postwar years, federal government spending through the 1944 GI Bill gave veterans unprecedented opportunities for access to education and other job training programs.

the resistance to this notion. They had fought in disproportionate numbers for their country and for the cause of defeating the world's most murderous racists, the Nazis. They then returned to a nation still deeply segregated, by law in the South and by practice elsewhere. Like Native American, Latino American, and Asian American veterans, they were determined to be full citizens in the country for which they had spilled their blood. "I went into the Army a nigger," one black soldier said about typical white views of him, but "I'm coming out a man."

African American efforts to overcome discrimination met fierce white resistance in 1946 and 1947. In the South, where most black Americans still lived, a wave of beatings and lynchings greeted black veterans in uniform and their attempts to register to vote. White Northerners also used violence to preserve the segregated character of neighborhoods in Chicago, Detroit, and other cities. They destroyed the property and threatened the lives of blacks who dared to move to previously all-white blocks, effectively confining African Americans to impoverished areas. Sometimes local authorities encouraged such extralegal use of force. The police chief of Cicero, Illinois, was indicted for conspiracy to incite a riot in 1951 after several thousand white residents destroyed an all-white apartment building to prevent African American veteran Harvey E. Clark and his family from moving in.

The retreat of European colonialism and American competition with the Soviet Union nonetheless encouraged many white Americans to acknowledge the contradiction between leading the "free world" and limiting the freedoms of Americans of color. A series of Supreme Court decisions validated the long-term strategy of the National Association for the Advancement of Colored People (NAACP) for contesting segregation in the courts. Court rulings outlawed segregation in voting primaries (*Smith v. Allwright,* 1944), interstate transportation (*Morgan v. Virginia,* 1946), contracts for house sales (*Shelley v. Kraemer,* 1948), and graduate schools (*Sweatt v. Painter* and *McLaurin v. Oklahoma,* 1950). The California Supreme Court in 1948 overturned a state law banning interracial marriage, pointing the way toward the elimination two decades later of similar laws in other states in the U.S. Supreme Court's *Loving v. Virginia* decision (1967).

Popular culture moved in the same direction of breaking down racial barriers. *Billboard* magazine in 1949 changed the category of "race music" to "rhythm and blues" as white record producers and radio disc jockeys such as Alan Freed began to bring the early rock 'n' roll of African American musicians to mainstream white audiences. By 1955 young white musicians such as Bill Haley and Elvis Presley joined black stars such as Chuck Berry and Little Richard in creating a wildly popular sound that transcended racial categories. Professional baseball erased its color line when Jackie Robinson, a former four-sport star at the University of California–Los Angeles and lieutenant in the U.S. Army, joined the Brooklyn Dodgers in 1947. In a pretelevision era when professional basketball and football had only minor followings, baseball ruled as the great national pastime. Despite vicious verbal taunting and threats of bodily harm by some fans and players, Robinson refused to lose his temper and remained a model of dignity and excellence as he won the National League's Rookie of the Year honors. Two years later he won the Most Valuable Player award.

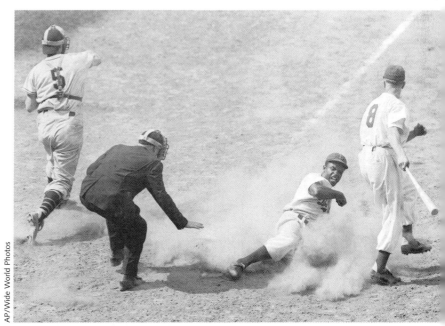

AP/Wide World Photos

■ The first person of color to play major league baseball, Jackie Robinson starred for the Brooklyn Dodgers from 1947 to 1956, helping them win six National League pennants and one world championship. His success opened the way for other black players to follow, eventually bringing the demise of the old professional Negro Leagues. Robinson credited Dodgers general manager Branch Rickey for his willingness to break the color line in what was still the nation's favorite game.

In his ten years with the team, the Dodgers won six National League titles. Millions of white Americans found themselves cheering for their first black hero, and Robinson came in second only to singer Bing Crosby in a national popularity poll.

Native Americans and Mexican Americans faced similar discrimination in the Southwest and elsewhere. With war veterans in the fore, they also organized to contest unfair education and election practices. "If we are good enough to fight, why aren't we good enough to vote?" asked returning Navajo soldiers in New Mexico and Arizona, where the state constitutions prohibited Indian residents from voting until successfully challenged in 1948. When the family of Private Felix Longoria, who died in combat in the Philippines, was denied the right to bury him in the all-white cemetery in Three Rivers, Texas, a new Latino veterans' organization called American GI Forum publicized the injustice. A young Texas senator named Lyndon Johnson, destined for the White House, stepped in and arranged a burial with full military honors in prestigious Arlington National Cemetery instead. The League of United Latin American Citizens (LULAC) followed a strategy similar to that of the NAACP regarding educational discrimination, leading to the Supreme Court's decision in *Mendez v. Westminster* (1946) outlawing segregated schools for Mexican Americans in California. In parallel fashion, indigenous Alaskans organized in the Alaska Native Brotherhood successfully lobbied the territorial legislature in Juneau to pass an antidiscrimination law in 1945.

Class Conflict

In many ways 1946 seemed like 1919. A world war had just ended, in which corporations had made handsome profits. American workers had enjoyed nearly full employment and improving wages and had joined unions in large numbers. In 1946 one-third of the workforce held a union card, the largest portion ever. But the end of war-related orders led to job cuts and the loss of overtime wages. As inflation kicked in, workers felt their marginal economic security slipping away, and by the spring of 1946, 1.8 million of them were out on strike.

Mirroring World War I, the conclusion of hostilities in 1945 revealed rising tensions between the United States and the Soviet Union. The spread of leftist revolutions abroad amplified fears of communist influence in American unions, especially because a few of the most effective Congress of Industrial Organizations (CIO) organizers were Communist party members or at least sympathetic to an emphasis on class conflict between owners and workers. As in 1919, a Red Scare began to develop, egged on by a business community that used the supposed threat of the tiny U.S. Communist party to weaken the much larger and less radical union movement. In contrast to the end of World War I, however, federal law guaranteed the right of workers to bargain collectively, and the strikes of 1946 resulted in some negotiated wage increases.

Organized labor after World War II functioned increasingly as a narrow special interest group rather than as part a broader democratic movement. The tide turned against unions as anticommunism intensified. President Truman, long considered a friend to organized labor, helped crush major strikes by railroad workers and coal miners in 1946 when he saw them as threatening the nation's economy. The CIO's Operation Dixie to organize southern workers of all colors failed, defeated by the skillful appeals of local businesses to white supremacist sentiment in the working class. The Republican party claimed a sweeping victory in the 1946 congressional elections, taking control of both the House and the Senate in a stark rejection of Truman's leadership. Republicans and conservative Democrats then passed the Taft–Hartley Act in 1947 over the president's veto, weakening unions by prohibiting secondary boycotts (against the products of a company whose workers were on strike) and requiring union officials to swear anticommunist oaths. Two years later the increasingly conservative CIO expelled 11 unions that still had leftist and communist leadership. At the same time, the expanding U.S. economy after 1947 pulled many skilled workers up into the middle class and gave them a larger stake in the status quo.

The Quest for Security

On February 21, 1947, a British official in Washington drove to the State Department to inform the U.S. government that Britain could no longer provide financial assistance to the anticommunist governments of Greece and Turkey. This marked a watershed in modern world history. Long the greatest imperial power and the dominant outside force in the Middle East, Britain was beginning a long, slow retreat. Left in its wake were vacuums of power, particularly in the Middle East, South Asia, and Africa. President Truman and his advisers believed that either Soviet or American influence would flow into those regions. In the face of the Soviet Union's eagerness to expand its influence by promoting communist revolutions abroad, American leaders believed they must seize the opportunity for world leadership. The Truman administration formulated a policy to contain communism in the eastern Mediterranean that it quickly expanded to encompass the entire noncommunist world.

Redefining National Security

U.S. policymakers had ended World War II with one primary goal. They were determined to revive the global capitalist economy that had nearly dissolved in the Great Depression of the 1930s and had then been battered by the war. American prosperity and freedom, they believed, depended on a world system of free trade because Americans simply could not consume all the products of their efficient farms and factories. If they could not sell the surplus abroad, the United States would slide back into a depression. The 1930s had shown that closed economic doors led to despair, poverty, and aggression, as in Germany and Japan. "We can't go through the thirties again," President Truman emphasized to his aides. He and other political leaders hoped for a world with greater liberty and more democracy. But Dean Acheson, the powerful undersecretary (1945–1947) and then secretary of state (1949–1953), emphasized that U.S. foreign policy was not primarily concerned with "a lot of abstract notions." Instead, the emphasis with each country was on "what you do—these business transactions."

"National security" was expanding to mean something very different from simply defending the nation's territory against invasion. For the disproportionately powerful United States, national security after 1945 came to be identified with the creation and preservation of a free-trading capitalist world order. American national security was seen to be at stake almost everywhere around the globe—a recipe for riches but also for trouble.

The primary threat to that security came from the Soviet Union. The Red Army's occupation of eastern Europe was part of the problem, as it symbolized the Soviets' military prowess. Even more troubling to the Truman administration was the political influence of the USSR in a world turning leftward. The real danger lay in Soviet encouragement, by example and assistance, of revolutions that rejected market economies and individualist ethics. Demoralized by the war's destruction and by grim postwar economic conditions, western Europeans and others seemed to be considering the paths of socialism and communism. "Hopeless and hungry people," Acheson warned, "often resort to desperate measures."

> *"Hopeless and hungry people,"* Acheson warned, *"often resort to desperate measures."*

Conflict with the Soviet Union

The antifascist alliance of the Soviet Union and the United States dissolved rapidly as their conflicting interests reemerged after the war. Long skeptical of the capitalist world it wanted to replace, the Soviet government viewed expansive U.S. interests as evidence of "striving for world supremacy." Yet Moscow was just as clearly expanding its own sphere of national security, with Soviet troops remaining in areas they had occupied during the war: Manchuria, northern Korea, Iran, and especially eastern and central Europe. These forward military positions, combined with Moscow's rhetoric of encouraging revolution abroad, increased American anxieties about rising communist movements in Asia and Europe. Each side spoke of the other's goal as "world domination."

Contrasting experiences in World War II amplified historical and ideological differences. America and Russia had each entered the war after being attacked by surprise in 1941. But whereas the war brought the United States out of the global capitalist depression (which the Soviets had avoided), it brought the USSR into a depression caused by the invading Germans' destruction of the western portion of the country. With a decimated population, a battered economy, and minimal air and naval forces, the postwar Soviet Union remained a regional power based on its army. The United States was the only truly global power, with a vast naval armada and air force projecting military might on to every continent, undergirded by the most productive economy in world history. The two nations' visions of the postwar world order reflected these relative positions. Americans sought an open world for the free flow of goods and most ideas and proved willing to tolerate and even embrace dictatorial governments as long as they were anticommunist and open to foreign trade and investment. Meanwhile, the Soviets called for a more traditional division into separate spheres of influence for the great powers. The horrific experience of near national extinction at the hands of the Nazis ensured that Stalin would not budge on issues of fundamental Soviet security. At the same time, the exhilarating experience of low-cost victory and unparalleled wealth and might emboldened Truman. The United States "could not, of course, expect to get 100 percent" of what it wanted, he told his advisers, but on important matters "we should be able to get 85 percent."

> *"The reins of world leadership are fast slipping from Britain's . . . hands. These reins will be picked up either by the United States or by Russia."*

Conflicts over specific areas liberated from the Nazis hastened the onset of the Cold War in the first 18 months after the end of World War II. Whereas the Soviets wanted reparations and a deindustrialized Germany that could never threaten it again, the United States considered a rebuilt industrial German state crucial for a healthy, integrated western European economy. Britain and France had gone to war in defense of an independent Poland, and Truman told Stalin bluntly that a free election there, as promised in the Yalta accords, was crucial for 6 million Polish Americans; for Stalin, however, control of Poland was not negotiable because it had been "the corridor for attack on Russia." Moscow and Washington clashed over Iran, on Russia's southern border, where the Soviets briefly encouraged a leftist uprising in the northern part of the oil-rich country to counteract British and American influence in the capital city of Teheran. U.S. policymakers worried about Soviet requests to Turkey for greater control of the Bosporus and Dardanelles, the straits leading out of the Black Sea into the Mediterranean. When the British announced in February 1947 their imminent withdrawal from Greece, where leftists and monarchists were fighting a fierce civil war, the Truman administration believed it was time to respond decisively.

The Policy of Containment

Diplomat George Kennan best articulated the idea of containing Soviet power in an influential telegram sent from his post at the U.S. embassy in Moscow in February 1946. Kennan explained Soviet hostility as a function of traditional Russian insecurity overlaid with newer Marxist justifications. He called for "the adroit and vigilant application of counterforce" against all Soviet efforts at expanding their influence. One month later, on March 5, 1946, former British prime minister Winston Churchill gave a prominent speech in Fulton, Missouri, in which he warned that a Russian "iron curtain" had descended across Europe from the Baltic Sea in the north to the Adriatic Sea in the south, imprisoning all those to the east of it. Kennan and other U.S. policymakers viewed communism as a monolithic movement, directed by Moscow. The metaphor of disease was commonly used, as in references to the Soviets injecting "a hypodermic needle full of Moscow virus" into a vulnerable country. The prominence of local communists, the carriers of that "disease," in the Greek civil war might give Stalin a foothold on the Mediterranean. "The reins of world leadership are fast slipping from Britain's competent but now very weak hands," the State Department argued. "These reins will be picked up either by the United States or by Russia."

Picking up those reins meant a fundamental reorientation for the United States. No longer just the dominant force in the Western Hemisphere, it would have to maintain its wartime projection of military forces around the globe—permanently. To do so would take huge expenditures that Congress had to approve and public support for an unprecedented international role. Critics questioned the virtue of supporting a monarchy in Greece and a dictatorship in Turkey. So Truman and his advisers chose to "scare hell out of the American people," as Senator Arthur Vandenberg put it, to gain their support. In an address to Congress on March 12, 1947, asking for $400 million in aid for Greece and Turkey, the president simplified the world system into two "ways of life," those of "free peoples" and those of "terror and oppression" under communist rule. All nations must choose between them, he declared, and the United States must support "free peoples who are resisting attempted subjugation by armed minorities or outside pressures."

■ **MAP 24.1**
OCCUPATION OF GERMANY AND AUSTRIA, 1946–1949 By the end of World War II, U.S. and British forces had liberated western Europe and Soviet forces controlled eastern Europe. In central Europe, the Allies jointly occupied Germany and Austria.

The Truman Doctrine, as it became known, exaggerated a real problem to win public support for a new international role for the United States. It funded the governments of Turkey and Greece but it framed the new policy broadly, opening the path to supporting anticommunist regimes and opposing revolutions around the world for decades to come. The most important immediate step was the reconstruction of a vibrant, reintegrated western European economy. The United States provided $13 billion between 1948 and 1952 to fund the European Recovery Program, commonly known as the Marshall Plan for its chief architect, Secretary of State George Marshall (1947–1949). His assistant, Dean Acheson, reminded Americans doubtful about such expenditures that western Europe's recovery was "chiefly a matter of national self-interest" for the United States, for European markets were crucial for American economic health.

Ensuring western European security against the Red Army also entailed the first U.S. military alliance in peacetime. The victors of World War II divided a defeated Germany into separate zones of occupation, based on wartime agreements that reflected their respective military positions. The Allies also shared occupation of the capital city of Berlin, although it was deep in the Soviet-controlled eastern sector of the country, in the expectation that a reunified, de-Nazified Germany would be governed from there someday. The British, French, and

> *For the world's nonwhite majority, national independence and racial equality was the great issue of the late 1940s and 1950s.*

American decision in March 1948 to create a unified state out of the western sectors of Germany led a few months later to a year-long Soviet blockade of western access to Berlin and fears of a general war. The joint U.S.–British "Operation Vittles" airlifted tons of food to the isolated residents of West Berlin, preserving that city as a capitalist island in a communist country. The creation of NATO in 1949 made the American military commitment to Europe permanent, a firm rejection of George Washington's warning against "entangling alliances." The United States banded together with Britain, France, and the other western European countries to provide for each other's mutual defense against an attack on any member of the alliance, presumably by the Soviets. Headquartered first in Paris and later in Brussels, Belgium, NATO was the first U.S. military alliance in peacetime. The point of NATO for western Europe, its British first secretary general said, was to "keep the Americans in, the Russians out, and the Germans down."

The onset of the Cold War determined the fate of the defeated powers of World War II. The Truman administration was determined to "push ahead with the reconstruction of those two great workshops of Europe and Asia—Germany and Japan." This agenda replaced initial concerns about rooting out Nazism and punishing war criminals, as at the Nuremberg trials of surviving Nazi leaders in 1945–1946. While the Soviets extracted what reparations they could from their sector of Germany, the Americans and British rebuilt the new nation of West Germany. A similar story unfolded in Japan, where the use of atomic weapons left U.S. forces the sole occupiers. The American occupation under General Douglas MacArthur initially (1945–1947) emphasized democratization of Japanese society, including building labor unions, weakening corporate monopolies, ensuring women's political rights, and punishing war criminals. But rising U.S. tensions with the Soviets and the imminent victory of the Communist forces in China's civil war prompted American officials to shift course by 1948. Henceforth, they focused on rebuilding as quickly as possible Japan's industrial economy as the hub of capitalist Asia and reduced efforts at social reforms that might slow that process.

Colonialism and the Cold War

The world's nonwhite majority still lived under European colonial control, and for them the struggle for national independence and racial equality was the great issue of the late 1940s and 1950s. In this North–South conflict, as opposed to the East–West conflict of the Cold War, the United States held an awkward position. Its primary NATO partners included the

Members of NATO (1949)
Members of Warsaw Pact (1955)
Nonaligned counties
$ Participants in the Marshall Plan, 1947–1952
Year first atomic device was tested by that country

U.S loan of $3.5 billion, 1946

Berlin blockade, 1948–1949

Communist coup, 1948
U.S.S.R. invasion, 1968

Anti-communist revolution failed, 1956

Withdrew forces from NATO, 1966

Joined NATO, 1955

Zones of occupation ended, 1955

Joined NATO, 1982

Tito–Stalin Schism, 1948

Withdrew from Warsaw Pact, 1968

Truman Doctrine, 1947 joined NATO, 1952

■ **MAP 24.2**
EUROPE DIVIDED BY THE COLD WAR For centuries Europe had controlled much of the rest of the world. After 1945, Russians occupied the eastern half of the continent and Americans wielded dominant influence in the western half. This division of Europe into Communist and non-Communist blocs lasted until the end of the Cold War in 1989.

greatest colonial powers: Britain, France, Belgium, Holland, and Portugal. Racial segregation in the United States further undercut American leadership of the "free world," as did U.S. support for the anticommunist apartheid (white supremacist) regime that took power in South Africa in 1948. Anticolonial radicals who pointed out these contradictions found their voices drowned out by the rising din of anticommunism.

With European rule in Asia and Africa on the way out, the Truman administration sought a gradual transfer of colonial rule into the hands of local pro-West elites. Violent revolutions—

The Origins of the Cold War

American and Soviet patriotic symbols predominated in the Cold War era. The Stars and Stripes and the eagle faced off against the hammer and sickle in a global competition for influence.

The earliest American accounts of how the Cold War began were written by officials who had participated in the decisions that cemented U.S.–Russian hostility for two generations (1946–1989). Officials such as the State Department's Herbert Feis and academic historians through the 1950s and early 1960s accepted the U.S. government view that Soviet aggression and subversion made the Cold War unavoidable. They pointed to the absence of political and religious freedom and the severe restrictions on the ownership of private property in communist nations, combined with the expansion of communist control into eastern Europe and China. Stalin and his successors in the Kremlin, they believed, were at fault for trying to take over the world. Arthur Schlesinger, Jr., summarized this view in 1967 when he called early U.S. Cold War policies "the brave and essential response of free men" to totalitarian provocations.

America's deepening involvement in the Vietnam War destroyed the Cold War consensus among historians. Schlesinger's "orthodox" interpretation of the events of the late 1940s seemed increasingly suspect to a group of mostly younger historians who saw their own government as the aggressor in southeast Asia in the mid-1960s. They took their lead in part from the iconoclastic William Appleman Williams of the University of Wisconsin, who in 1959 declared U.S. expansionism to be "the tragedy of American diplomacy." Casting a skeptical eye back a generation, these "revisionists" found evidence indicating a greater American than Soviet responsibility in bringing on the Cold War. Gar Alperovitz identified the use of atomic bombs on Japan as unnecessary for the military defeat of Tokyo but useful as "atomic diplomacy" to intimidate Moscow in regard to the postwar world order. Gabriel Kolko emphasized the structural need of U.S. capitalism to expand abroad in search of new markets and new sources of raw materials. As U.S. actions in Vietnam alienated more and more Americans and as the Watergate scandal (1972–1974) starkly revealed the readiness of top U.S. leaders to deceive the public, the early histories blaming the Soviet Union exclusively for the onset of the Cold War lost much of their credibility.

By the 1980s historians had largely exhausted the debate over responsibility for Soviet–American hostilities. Then the fall of the Berlin Wall in 1989 and the dissolution of the USSR in 1991 (turning back into Russia and independent neighboring nations such as Ukraine) encouraged rethinking of the early Cold War. Even Washington's staunchest defenders could admit that the U.S. government had acted in an often imperial fashion. But was it perhaps a matter primarily of the expansion of American popular culture abroad—a kind of "cultural imperialism" that other peoples often welcomed, from Paris to Beijing? Jazz and later rock 'n' roll music, along with Hollywood movies, American consumer goods, and the English language, proved more powerful agents for spreading the American way of life than U.S. Marines or even democratic political institutions. Though still concerned with the role of national governments, armies, and diplomats, some historians of the Cold War are exploring issues such as race relations and gender relations, which were also frontiers of freedom after 1945. Improved U.S.–Russian relations and the release of once-secret documents added interest to Cold War studies. ■

in the spirit of 1776—were to be avoided. The U.S. grant of official independence to the Philippines in 1946, though masking significant continued American influence, was offered as a model, as was the British departure from India a year later. However, America's European priorities included support even for imperialists who did not leave peacefully, such as the French digging in against Communist-led revolutionaries in Vietnam.

The British withdrawal from Palestine in 1948 created a peculiar dilemma for the United States. Jewish settlers—primarily from Europe and often survivors of the Holocaust—proclaimed the new state of Israel against the wishes of the Arab majority. Secretary of State Marshall and others urged Truman not to recognize Israel to avoid imperiling U.S. relations with the Arab oil-producing states. The president sympathized with the Jewish desire for a homeland, however, and understood the importance of American Jews as constituents of the Democratic party in the 1940s. His decision to recognize Israel, which most Middle Easterners viewed as a new colonial state, set the United States on a course of enduring friendship with that nation and enduring conflict with Israel's Arab neighbors and the Palestinians.

The Impact of Nuclear Weapons

Scientists in the 1940s dramatically increased Americans' sense of personal safety by introducing the use of antibiotics. "Miracle drugs" such as penicillin cured common bacterial infections that had previously been debilitating or fatal. Antibiotics suggested a future of personal health and longevity unimaginable to previous generations. What science gave with one hand it threatened to take away with the other, however. The use of atomic weapons on Japan foreshadowed a future of utter insecurity in which instantaneous destruction of entire nations could occur without warning. The ongoing quest for human control over the natural world—over even microorganisms and the insides of the atom—produced mixed results for the American land and people.

Even without being fired again in war after 1945, nuclear weapons altered the American environment. Weapon tests with such code names as "Dirty Harry" released vast quantities of radiation into the atmosphere. The Atomic Energy Commission assured those near the mushroom clouds, "Fallout does not constitute a serious hazard." But local cancer rates spiked upward for Bikini Islanders in the Pacific, where the first tests occurred, and then for farmers

Bettmann/CORBIS

■ Soldiers watch as "Dog," a 21-kiloton nuclear device, is dropped from a bomber at the Nevada Test Site at Yucca Flat, northwest of Las Vegas, in November 1951. U.S. atomic specialists tested nuclear weapons first in the Marshall Islands of the western Pacific Ocean, especially the Bikini atoll, beginning in 1946, and then in Nevada beginning in January 1951. Residents downwind from the test sites suffered various deleterious health effects from radiation exposure, including high cancer rates.

and ranchers in Utah and Nevada, when tests began 65 miles northwest of Las Vegas in 1953. At St. George, Utah, downwind from the test site, radioactive plutonium dusted the citizens, livestock, and a crew shooting a movie in the desert. Of the 220 people from Hollywood who worked on *The Conqueror,* 91 had contracted cancer by 1980 and 40 had died, including film star John Wayne.

Related dangers stalked other parts of the "nuclear West." Navajo Indians mining uranium in the Four Corners region (where Utah, Colorado, Arizona, and New Mexico meet) paid dearly for their intensive exposure to the poisonous material, as did thousands of workers involved

in nuclear weapon production. Weapon assembly plants in Hanford, Washington, and Rocky Flats, Colorado, leaked radioactivity into the groundwater. In combination with the nuclear power industry, atomic weapon development resulted in an enormous supply of radioactive waste—deadly for 10,000 more years—that the U.S. government still does not know how to dispose of safely. The quest for security produced a whole new kind of insecurity.

The government offered reassurances about the safety of the atom, and the Atomic Energy Commission covered up evidence of radioactivity's ill effects. But many Americans were deeply anxious about this destructive new power that loomed over their lives, especially as the Soviet–American arms race intensified. Science fiction stories painted frightening pictures of a future devastated by nuclear war. Movies such as *The Blob* and *The Attack of the Crab Monsters* portrayed a world haunted by exposure to radiation. *Them!* featured mutant ants the size of buses crawling out of a New Mexico atomic test site. Concerns about a nuclear world escalated with the successful 1952 test of an American hydrogen bomb, a thousand times more powerful than the device that destroyed Hiroshima. Always suspicious of centralized power, Americans worried that one person in the Oval Office or the Kremlin could almost instantaneously obliterate entire continents.

A Cold War Society

Expanding economic opportunities and narrowing political freedoms characterized American society in the first decade of the Cold War. A withering fire of anticommunist repression pushed dissident views to the margins of the nation's political life. Americans largely accepted this new conformity for two reasons: their desire to support their government during international crises, especially the Korean War (1950–1953), and a consumer cornucopia that surrounded them with attractive material goods. A generation that had survived the Great Depression embraced the culture of consumption and convenience that emerged after World War II. Factories that had produced jeeps, tanks, and weaponry turned to manufacturing cars and appliances; men who had learned to build roads and barracks for the military now began to erect suburban housing with equal speed.

Expanding economic opportunities and narrowing political freedoms characterized American society in the first decade of the Cold War.

By 1947 the United States was launching into an era of extraordinary economic expansion that continued for 25 years. Senator McMahon of Connecticut suggested "mailing millions of mail-order catalogues to the Iron Curtain countries" to turn their inhabitants green with envy over "the consumers' wonderland contained within the pages of a Sears–Roebuck or a Montgomery Ward catalogue." Since Ben Franklin's time, Americans had been known for thrift in their pursuit of wealth, but after 1945 the long-cherished principle of delaying gratification declined steeply. "Buy now, pay later," General Motors urged as it offered an installment plan to customers. Diner's Club introduced the first credit card in 1950. In a formulation breathtaking for its distance from Puritan and immigrant traditions of saving for the future, writer William Whyte observed that "thrift is now un-American."

Family Lives

Many white Americans embraced the opportunity to move to the suburbs after World War II. Seeking larger homes and yards and quieter neighborhoods, they flocked to new developments such as Levittown outside New York City on Long Island. In their first three hours of business in 1949, Levittown's developers sold 1400 houses. In 1944 construction had begun on just 114,000 new houses; in 1950, the number jumped to 1.7 million. Suburbs were not for everyone, however. Even as federal courts struck down segregation laws in some spheres of American life, other federal agencies were encouraging residential separation by race. The Veterans Administration and the Federal Housing Administration distributed billions of dollars in low-cost mortgage loans for suburban homes to white applicants while screening out most people of color. Private banks did the same, and the contracts that developers such as Alfred and William Levitt signed with homebuyers prohibited resale to nonwhites. Other government policies, including highway construction and tax benefits for homeowners, promoted the growth of suburbs at the cost of cities. A third epoch in American residential history began by 1970 when more Americans resided in suburbs than cities, parallel to the 1920 shift from a rural majority to an urban one.

Suburban life encouraged a sharpening of gender roles among the growing middle class. Men commuted to work while women were expected to find fulfillment in marriage and motherhood, including a nearly full-time job of unpaid housework. Most women did so while either feeling isolated in their homes or finding community with other women in their neighborhoods and churches. "We married what we wanted to be," one female college graduate said. "If we wanted to be a lawyer or a doctor we married one." An enormous amount depended on a woman's choice of a husband, including class status and lifelong material well-being. Despite this partial retreat from wartime employment, however, fully one-third of American women continued to work for pay outside the home. The economic circumstances of most black women offered them little choice, and most wound up doing double housework: their own and that of families employing them as domestics. Middle-class women tended to view their paid work as a job rather than a career, a way to increase the family income if they did not have small children at home. Quotas in graduate schools and sex-segregated employment limited the number of female professionals.

Children moved even more firmly to the center of American family lives in these years. After a lengthy decline during the 1930s, marriage and birth rates picked up during the war and then accelerated sharply after 1945. After a brief upward spike in 1946, divorce rates declined for the first time in a century. From 1946 to 1964 women giving birth at a younger age to more children created the demographic bulge known as the baby boom. Large families reinforced the domestic focus of most women, putting the work of child-rearing at the center of their lives. Fatherhood became increasingly a badge of masculinity, with Father's Day emerging as a significant holiday for the first time. Family physician Benjamin Spock published *Baby and Child Care* (1946), a runaway best-seller that helped shift the emphasis in American parenting from strictness to greater nurturance.

Strong feelings about pregnancy hinged on the marital status of the expectant mother. Married mothers were celebrated, but unmarried ones were rebuked. Despite the greater freedom of the war years, the sexual double standard remained in place, with women's virtue linked directly to virginity in a way that men's was not. Birth control devices such as the diaphragm were legal only for married women and only in certain states. Women seeking to terminate unwanted pregnancies had to consider illegal abortions, the only kind available before 1970; millions did so, including one-fifth of all married women and a majority of single women who became pregnant. Two studies of American sexual behavior by Dr. Alfred Kinsey of Indiana University revealed that Americans often did not practice what they preached. The Kinsey reports of 1948 and 1953 shocked the public with their revelation of widespread premarital and extramarital sexual intercourse as well as homosexual liaisons. Rates of sex before marriage actually remained stable from the 1920s to the 1960s, but after World War II rates of teenage sex soared because so many teenagers got married. The average age of couples at the altar dropped as social pressures aimed to contain sex within marriage.

The Growth of the South and the West

Before World War II American cultural, industrial, and financial power had always been centered in the urban North, but federal expenditures during the war began to change this. The U.S. Army built most of its training bases in the South, where land close to the coasts was thinly populated and inexpensive. Military bases and defense industries sprang up along the West Coast to project power into the Pacific against Japan. California alone received 10 percent of all federal dollars spent during the war. The San Francisco Bay area sprawled with shipyards and sailors, and southern California became the center of the nation's aircraft industry. U.S. troops built the Alcan (Alaska–Canada) Highway, and millions of GIs passed through Hawaii en route to the Pacific battlefront. Fighting against the Japanese to defend Pearl Harbor and the Aleutian Islands brought the once-distant territories of Hawaii and Alaska more into Americans' consciousness, setting them on the path to statehood in 1959.

The Sunbelt of the South, the Southwest, and California grew rapidly after the war, whereas older Rustbelt cities of the Northeast and Midwest such as Buffalo and Detroit began to lose manufacturing jobs and population. Like the 440,000 people who moved to Los Angeles during the war, postwar migrants to California and Arizona appreciated the weather and the eco-

■ A new cloverleaf intersection on a freeway arches across the northern New Jersey suburbs in 1949. Multilane, limited-access highways became common after World War II. A new word, "smog" (neither smoke nor fog), appeared to describe the urban pollution caused by trucks and commuter vehicles.

Bettmann/CORBIS

nomic opportunities. Military spending underwrote half the jobs in California during the first decade of the Cold War. Migrants from south of the border, meanwhile, found work primarily in California's booming agricultural sector. The U.S. government continued to use the Bracero program as an exception to immigration laws for Mexicans willing to do arduous labor in the hot fields of the Golden State, thus encouraging the large influx of Mexicans into the U.S. Southwest. Agriculture in the arid Southwest depended on water management and irrigation, especially from dams on the lower Colorado River for Arizona and on several rivers flowing down from the Sierra Nevada range into California's fertile central valley.

Two industries particularly stimulated the growth of the Sunbelt: cars and air conditioning. Automobiles helped shape the economies of western states, where new cities were built out of sprawling suburbs, and governments erected highways rather than railroads, subways, or other forms of public transportation. New car sales shot up from 70,000 in 1945 to 7.9 million in 1955. Inexpensive gasoline, refined from the abundant crude oil of Texas and Oklahoma, powered this fleet. Automobile exhaust pipes replaced industrial smokestacks as the primary source of air pollution, which by the 1960s shrouded Los Angeles—the "city of angels"—in smog. Air conditioning also became widely available after World War II and contributed to the breakdown of the South's regional distinctiveness. From Miami and Atlanta to Houston and Washington, D.C., the dramatic economic and demographic expansion of the Sunbelt depended on the indoor comfort brought by controlling summertime heat and humidity.

Harry Truman and the Limits of Liberal Reform

The onset of the Cold War narrowed the range of American political discourse. In seeking to consolidate the New Deal legacy, President Truman found himself boxed in by conservative Republican opponents. Allied governments in western Europe had embraced the idea that access to health care was a right of every citizen in a modern democratic state. But when Truman proposed a system of national health care, conservatives quashed his proposal in Congress, pushed by an American Medical Association lobbying campaign that denounced the idea as a "monstrosity of Bolshevik bureaucracy."

Perhaps the most blatant omission of the New Deal was protection against racial discrimination. Now, as the Cold War intensified, the fact that millions of Americans still lacked basic guarantees for their civil rights was a glaring and embarrassing contradiction amid rhetoric about ensuring rights and liberties throughout the "free world." The President's Committee on Civil Rights called in 1947 for a strong federal commitment to racial equality. Truman campaigned for reelection in 1948 on a platform of support for civil rights that was unprecedented in the White House, including the first presidential address to the NAACP. That summer he ordered the desegregation of the armed forces and the federal civil service. Truman was not a complete egalitarian and did not address underlying structures of segregation in housing and schools. But blatant racial abuses angered him, and he helped set the Democrats on the path to becoming the party of racial equality.

The president's promotion of civil rights also had a political purpose in 1948. Black voters in Chicago, Cleveland, and other northern cities played a key role in swing states; their solid support lifted Truman to a narrow and surprising victory over the heavily favored Republican candidate, New York governor Thomas Dewey. Truman's reelection was all the more impressive because of the fracturing of the Democratic party. Alienated by the civil rights plank, white Southerners walked out of the Democratic convention and ran South Carolina governor Strom Thurmond as an independent candidate. The "Dixiecrats" won four states in

TABLE 24-1			
The Election of 1948			
Candidate	**Political Party**	**Popular Vote**	**Electoral Vote**
Harry S. Truman	Democratic	24,205,695	304
Thomas E. Dewey	Republican	21,969,170	189
J. Strom Thurmond	State-Rights Democratic	1,169,021	38
Henry A. Wallace	Progressive	1,156,103	0

the Deep South, foreshadowing the abandonment by white Southerners of the party of their parents in the 1960s. From the opposite side of the party, many liberals jumped ship for Henry Wallace, Roosevelt's former vice president, running as the Progressive party candidate. Truman won as a man of the moderately liberal center, fierce against communism, usually supportive of the rights of organized labor, and opposed to discrimination.

The Cold War at Home

Anticommunism turned out to be an inadequate shield for liberals and moderates in the partisan warfare pervading American politics in the late 1940s and early 1950s. In a pattern that became known as McCarthyism, mostly Republican conservatives explained communist successes abroad—especially in China and Korea—by "red-baiting" liberal Democrats in the administration, accusing them of sympathizing with and even spying for the Soviet Union. The hunt for domestic subversives to explain international setbacks was grounded in the reality of a handful of actual Soviet spies, most notably Julius Rosenberg (who was executed for treason in 1953 along with his apparently innocent wife, Ethel) and nuclear scientist Klaus Fuchs. But this second Red Scare expressed primarily the frustration of being unable to translate vast U.S. power into greater control of world events. And it served, above all, to cast suspicion on the patriotism of liberals at home. "The fact that a person believes in racial equality doesn't prove he's a Communist," argued the head of one government loyalty board, "but it certainly makes you look twice, doesn't it?"

Despite his general support for civil liberties, Truman helped set the tone for pursuing suspected traitors. In an unsuccessful effort to fortify his right flank against Republican attacks, he established a federal employee loyalty program in March 1947 as the domestic equivalent of the Truman Doctrine. Attorney General Tom Clark drew up a list of supposedly subversive organizations that the FBI and state committees on "un-American activities" then hounded.

The president red-baited the Progressive party in the 1948 campaign, referring to its ticket as "Henry Wallace and his Communists." In a case with sobering implications for free speech, federal courts in 1949 convicted the leaders of the U.S. Communist party of promoting the overthrow of the U.S. government. Words alone, the courts ruled, could be treasonable—the same logic as the wartime Sedition Act of 1918 (see Chapter 20). Conservative congressional Democrats pushed through the Internal Security Act of 1950 to require Communist party members to register with the government and allow emergency incarceration of suspected subversives. Calling it "a long step toward totalitarianism," Truman vetoed the measure, but Congress overrode the veto by a huge margin.

Republicans reaped the benefits of the Red Scare. Most Americans who had sympathized in any way with the Soviet Union in the Depression years were by the late 1940s merely liberal Democrats, but the House Un-American Activities Committee (HUAC) zeroed in on their earlier records. Investigating Hollywood, the television industry, and universities as well as the executive branch of the U.S. government, HUAC destroyed the careers of prominent figures and average Americans. California congressman Richard Nixon made his initial reputation as a young HUAC member by investigating charges that State Department official Alger Hiss had spied for the USSR. Hiss's conviction in 1950

■ Americans later knew Richard M. Nixon as the president who traveled to China in 1972 and brought his administration down in disgrace two years later with the Watergate scandal. Nixon first gained prominence as a young California congressman serving on the House Un-American Activities Committee (HUAC) who led the investigation into accusations that prominent U.S. diplomat Alger Hiss had spied for the USSR in the 1930s.

Bettmann/CORBIS

on charges of perjury (lying under oath) frightened Americans by associating a powerful administration figure with communism.

The era found its name in the previously obscure junior senator from Wisconsin, Republican Joseph McCarthy. With a single speech in Wheeling, West Virginia, on February 9, 1950, this genial but ambitious politician soared to prominence. "I have here in my hand a list of 205" Communist party members working in the State Department, he declared. Over the next four years, the numbers and names changed as McCarthy stayed one step ahead of the evidence while intimidating witnesses before his Senate subcommittee. In reality, one reporter joked, McCarthy "couldn't find a Communist in Red Square" in Moscow. He talked about Communists, but his show was about Democrats. As the war in Korea raged, he mercilessly red-baited the Truman administration. But after the Republican electoral victory in 1952, his excesses lost their partisan utility. With the end of the war in Korea and his ill-advised attacks on the U.S. Army itself as supposedly infiltrated by Communists (the Army–McCarthy hearings), he was at last censured by his Senate colleagues in 1954 and died an early, alcohol-related death in 1957.

Who Is a Loyal American?

The Cold War politics of inclusion and exclusion established a new profile for loyal Americans. Private familial and material concerns were expected to replace public interest in social reform. "No man who owns his own house and lot can be a Communist," real estate developer William Levitt declared. "He has too much to do." He also had a wife, presumably, in an era when anticommunists launched a withering assault on homosexuals as "perverts" and threats to the nation's security. Church membership climbed in tandem with condemnations of "godless Communism," and Congress added the words "under God" to the Pledge of Allegiance. Warning that "God is giving us a desperate choice, a choice of either revival or judgment," revivalist preacher Billy Graham launched his first evangelical crusade in Los Angeles in 1949, en route to becoming the nation's foremost religious figure. Discrimination against Roman Catholics and Jews, though still evident, declined as Catholics such as McCarthy proved intensely anticommunist and as pictures and stories emerged to reveal the horrors of the Nazi Holocaust against the Jews. More inclusive references to the "Judeo-Christian tradition" became common.

American leadership of the global anticommunist cause strengthened the struggle for racial equality at home, within certain limits. The NAACP and most African Americans took an anticommunist position in accord with Truman, in return for his support of civil rights. They downplayed their concern for colonial independence in Africa and Asia to support NATO. The American GI Forum (Latino veterans) and the Japanese American Citizen League also worked within the confines of Cold War politics to end discrimination. More radical black leaders such as scholar W. E. B. Du Bois and actor and singer Paul Robeson refused to make any such accommodation to anticommunism. Offended by the hypocrisy of segregation in the land of liberty, they insisted on full freedom everywhere in the "free world." The government responded by restricting their travel and diminishing their livelihoods. In a move right out of the Soviet playbook, Robeson's name was erased from the list of football All-Americans for 1917 and 1918 (he had starred for Rutgers University), leaving only ten men on those teams.

For impoverished Native Americans, the government seemed to give with one hand and take away with the other. In 1946 Truman established the Indian Claims Commission to consider payment for lands taken and treaties broken. But gestures toward compensation led to policies of termination. Developers seeking access to Indian lands joined reformers troubled by reservation poverty in urging Congress—with limited success—to terminate the special status Indian tribes had held with the federal government since its founding. Dillon S. Myer, who had overseen internment camps for Japanese Americans during World War II, became director of the Bureau of Indian Affairs in 1950. He closed reservation schools, withdrew support for traditional cultural

> *McCarthy talked about Communists, but his show was about Democrats. As the war in Korea raged, he mercilessly red-baited the Truman administration.*

■ From 1951 to 1953 Mexican American miners went on strike against the Empire Zinc Mining Company in Silver City, New Mexico. Women took on major roles in this labor action, which inspired a famous movie, *Salt of the Earth.* Defiant in the face of police and company shotguns and billy clubs, Elvira Molano (center) served as cochair of the union negotiating committee and became known as "the most arrested woman" during the strike.

activities, and launched an urban relocation program, all intended to move Native Americans into the mainstream and get the government "out of the Indian business."

Immigrants also received mixed messages. The McCarran–Walter Act (1952) ended the long-standing ban on allowing people of Asian descent not born in the United States to become U.S. citizens. But it preserved the discriminatory 1924 system of "national origins" for allocating numbers of immigrants from different countries. The bill also strengthened the attorney general's authority to deport aliens who were suspected of subversive intentions. Like Guatemalan-born leftist Luisa Moreno, a successful labor organizer in California deported in 1950, immigrants learned that their welcome depended on their politics.

The United States and Asia

Japan did not conquer independent nations in its sweep southward at the start of World War II. Tokyo's army defeated imperial powers: the French in Indochina, the Dutch in Indonesia, the British in Singapore and Malaya, and the Americans in the Philippines. In a single swoop, Japanese soldiers demonstrated the absurdity of white supremacy and cleared the way for the end of colonialism in Asia. Japan's retreat in 1945 left vacuums of power throughout the region. Into them flowed two contenders: the returning but gravely weakened European imperialists and Asian nationalists such as Ho Chi Minh in Vietnam (part of French Indochina). Americans were not passive observers of this struggle as they sought to establish a new free-trading order in the region. Less than five years after millions of American citizens had served in the war in the Pacific, hundreds of thousands returned to Asia to fight for an anticommunist regime in South Korea. In Asia, as in much of the Third World, the Cold War quickly turned hot.

The Chinese Civil War

Despite frequent discrimination against Chinese immigrants in the United States, Americans had long felt a special connection to China. Half of the thousands of Christian missionaries sent out by American churches in the early 20th century had been posted there. Entrepreneurs eyed the Chinese market, home to one-fifth of the world's potential consumers. Selling cigarettes to the Chinese brought tobacco baron James B. Duke much of his wealth, which he then used to endow the university in North Carolina that bears his name. During World War II Chinese resistance to Japan's invasion occupied millions of Tokyo's soldiers who would otherwise have been shooting at American GIs. The close U.S. alliance with the government of Jiang Jieshi seemed to confirm American hopes that Asia's largest nation would follow a pro-American path. Republican senator Kenneth Wherry of Nebraska declared that the United States would "lift Shanghai up and up, ever up, until it looks just like Kansas City."

However, many Chinese wanted Shanghai to look just like itself—or perhaps like Moscow. The partisans of the Chinese Communist Party (CCP) under Mao Zedong's leadership fought more effectively against the Japanese than Jiang's soldiers did. Japan's withdrawal in 1945 initiated four years of warfare between the Communists and Jiang's anticommunist Nationalists. Younger American diplomats and journalists in China, many of them missionaries' children who had grown up there, argued that the CCP was more popular than the corrupt Nationalist regime and was independent of the USSR. Rejecting the advice of these "China hands," the Truman administration provided $3 billion in aid to Jiang. The logic of the Truman Doctrine required containment of communism everywhere. Nevertheless, it failed in China. Americans watched in frustration as the CCP defeated the Nationalists, who retreated to the island of Taiwan. On October 1, 1949, addressing a vast crowd in Beijing's Tiananmen Square, Mao announced the establishment of the People's Republic of China (PRC).

Americans were appalled. The most populous nation in the world, the key to Asia, was gone—into the communist camp. More ominously, it was the first communist government created without the presence of Soviet troops. Might the rest of Asia also choose communism? Profound suspicions on both sides prevented any Sino-American accommodation. The U.S. government refused to recognize the People's Republic, just as it had done with the USSR in 1917; instead, Washington for the next 23 years pretended that the

Xu Xiaobing/China Stock, Beijing

■ Mao Zedong led the Communist party that took power in China during the civil war of 1945–1949. Although Americans called this "the fall of China," Mao officially introduced the new government in Beijing by declaring that "China has stood up." Mao (left) talks here with his favorite son, Mao Anying, who was killed in Korea on November 25, 1950, apparently in a U.S. bombing raid.

Nationalists on the tiny island of Taiwan were the real government of China. The CCP had come to power on its own, with minimal help from the Soviets. But faced with U.S. hostility and sharing a common ideology with the Soviet Union, Mao papered over historic Chinese–Russian tensions (which reemerged in the 1960s) and signed a mutual defense pact with Moscow in February 1950. The so-called loss of China increased the importance for American policymakers of building capitalist societies in the rest of Asia, particularly Japan and—fatefully—South Korea and Vietnam. China's revolution also became a major issue in American politics. "Who lost China?" Republicans demanded rhetorically and effectively, presuming that it had once been America's to lose.

The Creation of the National Security State

A week before Mao's announcement that China had become a communist country, President Truman shared some equally grim news with the American public: the Soviet Union had detonated its first nuclear device. The United States had lost the atomic monopoly that for four

UNION OF SOVIET SOCIALIST REPUBLICS

ALEUTIAN ISLANDS
(U.S.)

MONGOLIA

AFGHANISTAN

TIBET
(to China 1950)

CHINA

NORTH
KOREA
(1948)

PAKISTAN
(1947)

SOUTH
KOREA
(1948)

JAPAN
(U.S. Administration,
1945–1952)

PACIFIC
OCEAN

INDIA
(1947)

LAOS
(1953)

Okinawa
(U.S. Administration until 1972)

Midway Island

BURMA
(1948)

TAIWAN (1949)

Wake Island

BANGLADESH
(1971)

VIETNAM
(1954)

PHILIPPINE
ISLANDS
(1946)

PACIFIC TRUST
ISLANDS

INDIAN
OCEAN

THAILAND

KAMPUCHEA
(CAMBODIA, 1953)

MALAYSIA
(1957–1963)

SRI LANKA
(1946)

Singapore
(1965)

PAPUA
NEW
GUINEA
(1975)

SOLOMON
ISLANDS
(1978)

INDONESIA
(1949)

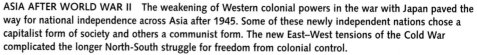 Countries gaining independence after WWII
(date of independence)

Communist bloc

Allied with United States

Countries gaining independence after WWII
that also have bilateral defense treaties with U.S.

Countries gaining independence after WWII
that are also a part of the Communist bloc

AUSTRALIA

■ **MAP 24.3**
ASIA AFTER WORLD WAR II The weakening of Western colonial powers in the war with Japan paved the
way for national independence across Asia after 1945. Some of these newly independent nations chose a
capitalist form of society and others a communist form. The new East–West tensions of the Cold War
complicated the longer North-South struggle for freedom from colonial control.

years had assured Americans of their unique position of military strength. These events in
the fall of 1949 shook the confidence of American political leaders. Truman asked his advisers for a full reevaluation of the nation's foreign policy.

The result was the top-secret National Security Council document 68 (NSC-68), which
articulated the logic of what became the national security state: a government focused on the
imperatives of military power, global involvement, and radically increased defense spending.
NSC-68 argued that there was no longer any such thing as peacetime. The United States had

NSC-68

Concerned about the trend of international events in the wake of the Communist revolution in China and the Soviet Union's acquisition of nuclear weapons, President Truman ordered his National Security Council on January 31, 1950, to conduct "a reexamination of our objectives in peace and war and of the effect of these objectives on our strategic plans." The resulting study, known as NSC-68, called for a military buildup to counter Soviet expansionism. Some specialists on the USSR, such as George Kennan, questioned NSC-68's accuracy regarding Soviet intentions and successes. But the subsequent North Korean invasion of South Korea seemed to confirm the idea of "international communism" on the march.

Bettmann/CORBIS

Workers at the Douglas Aircraft Company's Santa Monica factory assemble Nike guided missiles for the U.S. Army in 1955. Large military contracts proliferated during the Cold War and stimulated the growth of Sunbelt states like California.

From NSC-68: U.S. Objectives and Programs for National Security (April 14, 1950)

The Soviet Union, unlike previous aspirants to hegemony, is animated by a new fanatic faith, antithetical to our own, and seeks to impose its absolute authority over the rest of the world. . . .

Any substantial further extension of the area under the domination of the Kremlin would raise the possibility that no coalition adequate to confront the Kremlin with greater strength could be assembled. It is in this context that this Republic and its citizens in the ascendancy of their strength stand in their deepest peril.

The issues that face us are momentous, involving the fulfillment or destruction not only of this Republic but of civilization itself. . . . The assault on free institutions is world-wide now, and in the context of the present polarization of power a defeat of free institutions anywhere is a defeat everywhere. . . .

Our policy and actions must be such as to foster a fundamental change in the nature of the Soviet system. . . . In a shrinking world, which now faces the threat of atomic warfare, it is not an adequate objective merely to seek to check the Kremlin design, for the absence of order among nations is becoming less and less tolerable. . . .

The integrity of our system will not be jeopardized by any measures, covert or overt, violent or non-violent, which serve the purposes of frustrating the Kremlin design, nor does the necessity for conducting ourselves so as to affirm our values in actions as well as words forbid such measures. . . .

The total economic strength of the U.S.S.R. compares with that of the U.S. as roughly one to four. . . . The military budget of the United States represents 6 to 7 percent of its gross national product (as against 13.8 percent for the Soviet Union). . . . This difference in emphasis between the two economies means that the readiness of the free world to support a war effort is tending to decline relative to that of the Soviet Union.

It is true that the United States armed forces are now stronger than ever before in other times of apparent peace; it is also true that there exists a sharp disparity between our actual military strength and our commitments. . . . It is clear that our military strength is becoming dangerously inadequate. . . .

In summary, we must . . . [engage in] a rapid and sustained build-up of the political, economic, and military strength of the free world. ■

■ Were all Communists conspiring together against the United States and its interests? New Chinese leader Mao Zedong (left) helps Soviet ruler Josef Stalin celebrate his birthday on December 21, 1949. Two months later, the two men signed a mutual defense treaty. But, as their expressions suggest, they shared little personal warmth. Conflicting Chinese and Russian national interests soon strained—and eventually broke—their alliance.

entered an era of permanent crisis because of the expansion of communism and the hostile intentions of the Soviet Union. America's worldwide interests meant that it must oppose revolutions or radical change anywhere on the globe. NSC-68 went beyond the containment policy of the Truman Doctrine to call for fostering "a fundamental change in the nature of the Soviet system." This armed struggle necessitated secrecy and centralization of power in the hands of the federal government.

The National Security Act of 1947 and its 1949 amendments created the institutions of the new national security state. The Central Intelligence Agency (CIA) organized spying and covert operations, the Department of Defense unified the separate branches of the military and the National Security Council (NSC) coordinated foreign policy information for the president. NSC-68 called for permanent military expenditures at a level of war readiness; it argued that this would stimulate rather than bankrupt the U.S. economy. Scores of communities became dependent on military spending—a kind of military welfare state—and many were devastated by its withdrawal at the end of the Cold War in the 1990s. NSC–68's call for secrecy encouraged government deception of the public in the interest of "national security," with a consequent decline in democratic input into the nation's foreign relations.

At War in Korea

Two months after NSC-68 arrived on the president's desk and four months after Senator McCarthy began his attacks on the Democratic administration, troops from Communist North Korea poured across the 38th parallel into South Korea on June 25, 1950. The alarmist recommendations of NSC-68 now seemed fully justified to U.S. policymakers. The origins of the conflict on the Korean peninsula were more complicated than they appeared at first glance, however, and the United States was deeply involved.

Korea had been colonized by Japan since 1910. After Japan's defeat in 1945, Soviet and U.S. forces each occupied half of the peninsula. In the north, the Soviets installed a dictatorial Communist regime under Kim Il-Sung, who had fought with the Chinese Communists in their common struggle against Japan. In the south, the Americans established an authoritarian capitalist regime led by Syngman Rhee, who had taken classes at Princeton University with Woodrow Wilson and had lived in the United States most of the previous four decades. The 38th parallel was an arbitrary dividing line for a nation that had been unified for 1300 years, and both governments sought to reunite Korea under their control. Border skirmishes intensified after the Soviets and Americans withdrew in 1948, and leftist rebellions continued across much of the south. The CIA acknowledged that Rhee was even "unpopular among many—if not a majority—of non-Communist Koreans." Some 100,000 Koreans lost their lives in the fighting between 1945 and 1950, before "the Korean War" officially began with the north's invasion.

U.S. forces arrived in late June 1950, just in time to prevent the South Korean army from being driven off the peninsula, and then slowly pushed the North Koreans backward toward the 38th parallel in hard fighting. Truman received UN approval for this "police action," but he bypassed Congress rather than seek a declaration of war; immediate action, not debate, was needed, and he had support from leaders of both political parties. The precedent of presidential war without public debate facilitated U.S. military involvement in Vietnam a few years later.

Most importantly, Americans believed the North Korean invasion had been orchestrated by Moscow as part of a plan of worldwide communist aggression. The Truman administration considered defense of South Korea crucial to demonstrate the credibility of U.S. power. "Korea is the Greece of the Far East," the president told aides. "If we are tough enough now, if we stand up to them like we did in Greece three years ago, they won't take any next steps." American leaders adhered to the "domino theory," in which a successful communist takeover of one country would supposedly lead to its neighbors falling like dominoes into communist rule. Secretary of State Acheson reminded his colleagues that in Korea "we are fighting the second team, whereas the real enemy is the Soviet Union." The U.S. government took preemptive actions against possible aggression elsewhere. It sent the 7th Fleet to defend Taiwan, which it had previously assumed China would eventually conquer and reabsorb; it increased assistance to anticommunist forces in the Philippines and Vietnam; and it rearmed West Germany as part of NATO. The U.S. annual military budget increased from $13 billion in 1950 before the war to $50 billion in 1953, never to fall again below that level. The United States was fully rearmed.

Sfc. Al Chang/Defense Visual Information Center (Department of Defense), HD-SN-99-03118

■ **Near Haktong-ni, Korea, on August 28, 1950, an Army corpsman fills out casualty tags, while one American soldier comforts another who has just seen his buddy killed in action. Men who fought together on the front lines in Korea, as in other wars, experienced physical and psychological traumas unparalleled in civilian life. They often developed strong friendships with each other but sometimes had difficulty making the transition back to peacetime routines at home.**

General Douglas MacArthur's brilliantly executed landing of fresh U.S. troops at the port of Inchon behind North Korean lines on September 15, 1950, created a turning point in the war. North Korean forces abandoned the South's capital city of Seoul, fleeing northward to avoid being caught between two American armies advancing from different directions. South Korea was retaken; containment had succeeded. Should American commanders now shift to rolling back communism by proceeding north of the 38th parallel? The opportunity was irresistible, despite Truman's determination to keep this a limited war. MacArthur ignored signals that the Chinese would not allow U.S. soldiers to come all the way to their border at the Yalu River—the equivalent for Americans of having the Soviet Army arrive at the Rio Grande. As UN forces—mostly Americans and South Koreans, with a sprinkling of troops from other nations—closed in on the Yalu, 200,000 Chinese soldiers struck hard on November 27. American soldiers were driven all the way south of the 38th parallel again in the longest retreat in U.S. history, some 300 miles.

CHINA

U.S.S.R.

Chongjin

Chinese intervention, Oct. 1950

Hyesanjin

Yalu R.

Chosan

Chosin
Reservoir

Farthest U.S. advance,
Oct.–Nov. 1950

Taedong R.

Hungnam

Wonsan

Sea of
Japan

Tokyo

NORTH
KOREA

Pyongyang

Nan R.

Armistice Line, July 27, 1953

Kaesong

38th Parallel
(Border of North and
South Korea, 1945–1950)

Panmunjom

SOUTH
KOREA

Kangnung

Seoul

Han R.

Chinese and North Korean troops
push UN forces back to here, Jan. 1951

Inchon

U.S. landing,
Sept. 1950

U.S. forces use
occupied Japan
as a base

JAPAN

Yellow
Sea

Naktong R.

Pusan
perimeter

Pusan

PACIFIC
OCEAN

Farthest North Korean
advance, Sept. 1950

North Korea
South Korea
North Korean forces
United States (United Nations) forces
Chinese forces
Capitals

■ **MAP 24.4**
THE KOREAN WAR, 1950–1953
The strategic location of the Korean peninsula enhanced the importance of what had originally been a civil conflict among Koreans. Korea's close proximity to China, the Soviet Union, and U.S.-occupied Japan made the outcome of that conflict very important to all of the great powers. The Americans and Chinese wound up doing the bulk of the fighting against each other in the full-scale war that unfolded in 1950.

MacArthur wanted to take this "entirely new war" directly to the Chinese, using conventional or even nuclear bombing campaigns against the People's Republic. However, Joint Chiefs of Staff chair Omar Bradley called this idea "the wrong war, at the wrong place, at the wrong time, and with the wrong enemy." MacArthur's growing insubordination forced Truman to fire the popular general in April 1951 because the president had no desire to start a larger war

The National Archives

■ Korean refugees carry what they can of their worldly goods through heavy snow near Kangnung, on the east coast just south of the 38th parallel, on January 8, 1951. Wild swings in fortune in the Korean War contributed to the devastation wreaked on the peninsula's civilians who were caught in the fighting, sometimes more than once. First North Korean troops conquered almost all of South Korea, except the Pusan perimeter; then U.S. and UN troops pushed all the way to the Chinese border in the north. At that point, Chinese forces entered the war and hurled the Americans back far south of the 38th parallel. Finally, U.S. and UN troops fought their way back to just north of the 38th, where the ceasefire in 1953 drew the new border between the two Koreas.

that would draw in the USSR. The bloody fighting in Korea stalemated that spring close to the original dividing line, where the front remained as the two sides negotiated for two years before signing a ceasefire in July 1953. All the while, the U.S. Air Force used its supremacy in the skies to rain down extraordinary destruction on the North. "We burned down *every* town in North Korea," boasted General Curtis LeMay. American deaths totaled 37,000, and China lost nearly a million soldiers. Three million Koreans on both sides died—10 percent of the population of the peninsula—and another 5 million were made refugees. Containment succeeded at enormous cost.

Conclusion

The Korean War shaped subsequent American politics and society in critical ways. The stalemate frustrated Americans, who were never very enthusiastic about fighting in a place they knew little about. Having won all previous wars, they agreed with MacArthur that there was "no substitute for victory." But the ominous threat of nuclear weapons meant that wars had to be limited. The fighting in Korea enabled McCarthy and the Red Scare to dominate political life in the United States. The results were sometimes absurd, with the Democratic authors of the containment policy and the national security state being red-baited as "soft on communism." The Republican party rode such charges to electoral victory in November

TABLE 24-2			
The Election of 1952			
Candidate	Political Party	Popular Vote	Electoral Vote
Dwight D. Eisenhower	Republican	33,936,252	442
Adlai E. Stevenson	Democratic	27,314,992	89

1952. (They also benefitted from evidence of petty corruption among some Truman administration officials, such as the president's appointment secretary accepting bribes). Republican presidential nominee General Dwight Eisenhower was perhaps the most popular American alive because of his leadership of the Allied victory in Europe in World War II, and he swept into the White House over Democrat Adlai Stevenson, the governor of Illinois.

The war in Korea ensured a generation of hostility between the United States and China. It tied the People's Republic more closely to the USSR, strengthening the common belief that international communism was a unified movement. The United States committed itself to defending Taiwan from recapture by the Beijing government. The firing of the "China hands" deprived the State Department of the bulk of its Asian expertise, smoothing the path to an ill-informed war in Vietnam. The Korean War also jump-started the moribund Japanese economy as American dollars poured into Japan, where the U.S. war effort was based. Japanese conservatives called it "a gift from the gods."

Frustrations with the course of war in Korea affirmed the inward focus of American society in the 1950s. The American public largely accepted its own diminished role, and even the smaller role of its elected Congress, in decisions made by national security managers. Despite the organizing efforts of political activists such as civil rights workers, most citizens seemed to look increasingly to their personal and familial lives for satisfaction and meaning. From the powerful U.S. economy flowed an unprecedented river of consumer goods, including the new artificial materials—plastic, vinyl, nylon, polyester, styrofoam—that have pervaded and polluted American life ever since. As peace came to Korea and U.S. soldiers returned from across the Pacific, Americans sought the good life at home.

Sites to Visit

The National Security Archive at George Washington University
www.gwu.edu/~nsarchiv/

This extraordinary site includes the most recent declassified documents on the making of U.S. foreign policy.

Cold War International History Project
cwihp.si.edu/default.htm

The Woodrow Wilson International Center for Scholars maintains this excellent site, which offers newly released documents and up-to-date interpretive essays on the American-Soviet struggle.

The Ad*Access Project of Duke University Library
scriptorium.lib.duke.edu/adaccess/

This site presents fascinating images from over 7,000 advertisements in U.S. and Canadian newspapers and magazines between 1911 and 1955, offering insights into popular culture and consumer life.

Truman Presidential Museum and Library
www.trumanlibrary.org/index.html

The Harry Truman Presidential Library maintains this site, which contains an especially useful collection of documents regarding crucial foreign policy decisions in the early Cold War.

The Avalon Project at the Yale Law School: Documents in Law, History, and Diplomacy
www.yale.edu/lawweb/avalon/avalon.htm

Researchers can find here the texts of a large number of the most important primary documents illuminating U.S. relations with other countries.

Korea + 50: No Longer Forgotten
www.trumanlibrary.org/korea/

The Truman Library's site on the Korean War has documents, photos, and interpretive essays by prominent historians.

The Bancroft Library Collections
bancroft.berkeley.edu/collections/

The Bancroft Library of the University of California at Berkeley has extensive collections, exhibits, and links revealing the history of California, the nation's most populous state.

For Further Reading

General

William H. Chafe, *The Unfinished Journey: America Since World War II,* 3rd ed. (1995).

Alonzo Hamby, *Man of the People: A Life of Harry S. Truman* (1995).

Godfrey Hodgson, *America in Our Time* (1976).

Walter LaFeber, *America, Russia, and the Cold War, 1945–1996,* 8th ed. (1997).

James T. Patterson, *Grand Expectations: The United States, 1945–1974* (1996).

The Uncertainties of Victory

Thomas Borstelmann, *The Cold War and the Color Line: American Race Relations in the Global Arena* (2001).

Melvyn P. Leffler, *The Specter of Communism: The United States and the Origins of the Cold War, 1917–1953* (1994).

Harvey A. Levenstein, *Communism, Anti-Communism, and the CIO* (1981).

Richard Polenberg, *One Nation Divisible: Class, Race, and Ethnicity in the United States Since 1938* (1980).

Thomas Sugrue, *The Origins of the Urban Crisis: Race and Inequality in Postwar Detroit* (1996).

The Quest for Security

Carolyn Woods Eisenberg, *Drawing the Line: The American Decision to Divide Germany, 1944–1949* (1996).

Michael J. Hogan, *The Marshall Plan: America, Britain, and the Reconstruction of Western Europe, 1947–1952* (1987).

Walter Isaacson and Evan Thomas, *The Wise Men: Six Friends and the World They Made: Acheson, Bohlen, Harriman, Kennan, Lovett, McCloy* (1986).

Melvyn P. Leffler, *A Preponderance of Power: National Security, the Truman Administration, and the Cold War* (1992).

Thomas G. Paterson, *On Every Front: The Making and Unmaking of the Cold War* (1992).

Stewart L. Udall, *The Myths of August: A Personal Exploration of Our Tragic Cold War Affair with the Atom* (1994).

A Cold War Society

Paul S. Boyer, *By the Bomb's Early Light: American Thought and Culture at the Dawn of the Atomic Age* (1985).

Richard M. Fried, *Nightmare in Red: The McCarthy Era in Perspective* (1990).

Kenneth T. Jackson, *Crabgrass Frontier: The Suburbanization of the United States* (1985).

Elaine Tyler May, *Homeward Bound: American Families in the Cold War Era* (1988).

Ellen Schrecker, *Many Are the Crimes: McCarthyism in America* (1998).

Stephen J. Whitfield, *The Culture of the Cold War* (1991).

The United States and Asia

Warren I. Cohen, *America's Response to China: A History of Sino-American Relations,* 4th ed. (2000).

Bruce Cumings, *The Origins of the Korean War,* 2 vols. (1981, 1990).

Jon Halliday and Bruce Cumings, *Korea: The Unknown War* (1988).

Michael J. Hogan, *A Cross of Iron: Harry S. Truman and the Origins of the National Security State, 1945–1954* (1998).

Walter LaFeber, *The Clash: A History of U.S.–Japan Relations* (1997).

Online Practice Test

Test your understanding of this chapter with interactive review quizzes at

www.ablongman.com/jonescreatedequal/chapter24

P A R T   N I N E

The Cold War at Full Tide, 1953–1979

DURING THE THIRD QUARTER OF THE TWENTIETH CENTURY, THE COLD War cast a long shadow over the United States and the rest of the world. Tensions mounted at home and abroad as the United States and the Soviet Union vied for power among the world's nations. In poor Third World countries, insurgents attempted to throw off the yoke of colonialism and play the two superpowers against each other. The United States used a variety of strategies to counter Soviet influence in Latin America, Africa, the Middle East, and Southeast Asia, including military force in Korea and Vietnam, white-knuckle diplomacy in Cuba, extensive aid to non-aligned countries and covert operations worldwide.

Soviet advances in science and technology spurred the U.S. government to sponsor bold new domestic initiatives in the areas of public education and space exploration. The Cold War even helped to shape a post–World War II domestic ideal: a nuclear family living in a house in the suburbs, with a breadwinner father and a full-time homemaker mother. Many Americans believed that their prosperous, consumer-oriented economy, with its emphasis on individualism and personal choice, was a key weapon in the fight against communism.

In a feverish arms race, both the United States and the USSR rushed to stockpile weapons of mass destruction. Constant innovations in the technology of nuclear weaponry (such as intercontinental ballistic missiles) made the bombers used in World War II obsolete. The hydrogen bomb, tested successfully for the first time in 1953, dwarfed the power of the atomic bomb that had leveled Hiroshima. Nevertheless, citizens who criticized the arms buildup risked being branded unpatriotic. More than ever before, domestic policy was intertwined with foreign policy.

The rise of multinational corporations meant that large, impersonal institutions, whether government or private, were shaping American life. Middle-level managers—men in "grey flannel suits"—represented the corporate ethos of loyalty to the company above all else. At the same time, many Americans sought to work within their local communities for social and political change. In the South, African American men and women launched a dramatic assault on the system of legal segregation known as "Jim Crow." Working at the grassroots level, these activists boycotted buses, marched, sat in at lunch counters, and went to jail. Their efforts provoked the courts and Congress to act, culminating in the Civil Rights Acts of 1964 and 1965. For the first time in American history, the federal government assumed responsibility for eliminating discrimination in the workplace and guaranteeing all its citizens the right to vote.

Other groups also organized and entered the political arena. Indians, disabled Americans, California farm workers, and gay men and lesbians all formed organizations to counter discrimination and advance their civil rights. The women's movement affected all aspects of American society, enabling women to play a fuller role in the political and economic life of the country. A new environmentalist movement secured legislation protecting wilderness areas and endangered species and ensuring that Americans had clean air to breathe and clean water to drink.

Lyndon B. Johnson assumed the presidency after the assassination of John F. Kennedy in 1963. Johnson hoped to revitalize the New Deal legacy by expanding social welfare programs. His program, called the Great Society, sought to address seemingly intractable problems such as poverty, lack of health care for the elderly, and the deterioration of inner-city neighborhoods. But Johnson also expanded the U.S. military presence in Vietnam, an effort that cost an increasing number of American lives. Even constant bombing proved futile to stem the civil war that pitted Americans and anticommunist Vietnamese against the National Liberation Front of South Vietnam and their comrades in the north. Johnson's successor, Richard M. Nixon, also found himself mired in a war that was becoming increasingly unpopular among Americans.

Protests against the war in the late 1960s and early 1970s highlighted an emerging youth culture. The baby boom generation, born in the two decades after World War II, embraced sexual freedom and new forms of music (such as rock 'n' roll) in an apparent attempt to defy their parents and "the Establishment" in general. Many Americans felt betrayed by both Johnson and Nixon, believing that tens of thousands of American soldiers had died in vain in Vietnam. The Watergate break-in at Democratic headquarters, leading eventually to Nixon's resignation, contributed to a growing, widespread disenchantment with government authority.

By the late 1970s, developments abroad had greatly complicated Cold War politics. Middle Eastern oil-producing nations imposed an oil embargo on the United States, highlighting U.S. dependence on fossil fuels. Islamic fundamentalists were beginning to retaliate violently against the spread of American influence and culture in Muslim countries. And at home, a conservative backlash emerged to counter the expansion of the welfare state, the heightened visibility of the feminist movement, and widening civil rights protests.

1968 Martin Luther King, Jr., assassinated.
Robert Kennedy assassinated.
My Lai massacre.
Wild and Scenic Rivers Act.
Tet offensive.

1969 Huge antiwar protests in Washington, D.C.
Indians occupy Alcatraz, San Francisco Bay.
Stonewall raid, New York City.
Astronauts Neil Armstrong and Buzz Aldrin walk on the moon.

1970 U.S. invades Cambodia.
National Guardsmen kill four students, Kent State University.

1971 Pentagon Papers published.
Nixon administration creates "plumbers" for illegal activities.

1972 Watergate break-in.
Nixon visits China.
Founding of *Ms.* magazine.

1973 *Roe v. Wade* legalizes abortion.
American Indian Movement members occupy Wounded Knee.
Endangered Species Act.
OPEC oil embargo.
American troops withdrawn from Vietnam.

1974 Nixon resigns presidency; Gerald R. Ford becomes president.

1975 *Mayaguez* incident.
Vietnam reunified under communist rule.
Congressional investigations of CIA covert operations.

1976 Hyde Amendment prohibits use of Medicaid funds for abortions.
Nation celebrates bicentennial.

1977 Carter issues general amnesty for draft evaders.
Trans-Alaska pipeline system completed.
ABC airs miniseries *Roots,* based on book by Alex Haley.

1978 Bakke Supreme Court decision.
California Proposition 13.

1979 Camp David peace accords.
Partial meltdown of nuclear core at Three Mile Island nuclear plant.
Iranian Revolution.

CHAPTER

25

Domestic Dreams and Atomic Nightmares, 1953–1963

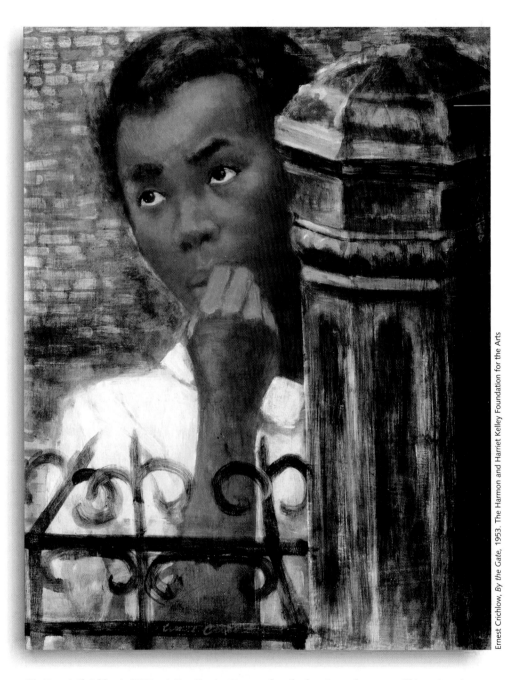

Ernest Crichlow, *By the Gate*, 1953. The Harmon and Harriet Kelley Foundation for the Arts

■ Ernest Chrichlow's 1953 painting *By the Gate* evokes the longings of a young African American.

IN 1959 VICE PRESIDENT RICHARD M. NIXON TRAVELED TO THE SOVIET UNION TO ENGAGE IN what became one of the most noted verbal sparring matches of the century. In a lengthy and often heated debate with Soviet Premier Nikita Khrushchev at the opening of the American National Exhibition in Moscow, Nixon extolled the virtues of the American way of life; his opponent promoted the Communist system. The two leaders did not discuss missiles, bombs, or even modes of government. Rather, they argued over the relative merits of American and Soviet washing machines, televisions, and electric ranges in what came to be known as the "Kitchen Debate."

The Kitchen Debate was a major skirmish on the Cold War's cultural battleground, where the two superpowers struggled for ideological supremacy. For Nixon, American superiority rested on the ability of average Americans to purchase a suburban home, complete with modern appliances. He proclaimed that the home adorned with a wide array of consumer goods represented the essence of American freedom:

> To us, diversity, the right to choose, . . . is the most important thing. We don't have one decision made at the top by one government official. . . . We have many different manufacturers and many different kinds of washing machines so that the housewives have a choice. . . . Would it not be better to compete in the relative merits of washing machines than in the strength of rockets?

Nixon's focus on household appliances was not accidental. After all, arguments over the strength of rockets would only point out the vulnerability of the United States in the event of a nuclear war between the superpowers. Debates over consumer goods provided a reassuring vision of the good life available in the atomic age. So Nixon insisted that American superiority in the Cold War rested not on weapons but on prosperous families living in comfortable suburban homes. Freed by modern appliances from the drudgery of household chores, mothers could spend their time nurturing happy, well-adjusted children. Consumerism provided the means for achieving individuality, leisure, domestic bliss, and upward mobility.

Vice President Richard M. Nixon and Soviet Premier Nikita Khrushchev touring the 1959 American National Exhibition in Moscow.

The American National Exhibition in Moscow was a showcase of American consumer goods and leisure equipment. But the main attraction, which the two leaders toured under international media spotlight, was a full-scale, six-room, ranch-style model house. This model home, filled with labor-saving devices and presumably available to Americans of all classes, offered tangible proof, Nixon claimed, of the superiority of free enterprise over communism.

Nixon called attention to a built-in panel-controlled washing machine. "In America," he said, "these [washing machines] are designed to make things easier for our women." Khrushchev countered Nixon's boast of comfortable American housewives by expressing pride in productive Soviet female workers. The Soviets, he claimed, did not share that "capitalist attitude toward women."

According to American journalists, Nixon's knock-out punch in his verbal bout with the Soviet premier was his articulation of the American postwar domestic dream: successful breadwinners supporting attractive homemakers in well-appointed, comfortable homes. Sharing Nixon's sentiments about politics, consumerism, and gender, most reporters hailed the vice president's trip as a major triumph. The American National Exhibition in Moscow seemed to demonstrate the superiority of the American way of life.

Science and expertise reigned supreme during the Cold War years. Parents turned to Dr. Benjamin Spock's best-selling *Baby and Child Care,* first published in 1946, to guide them in raising their children. Unlike prewar child-rearing experts who encouraged discipline and discouraged coddling, Dr. Spock emphasized nurture and affection. He urged parents to hold and comfort their infants, feed them on demand, and abandon rigid toilet-training routines. Dr. Jonas Salk became a hero for developing a vaccine against polio. Approved for use in 1955 and distributed widely to children in schools and clinics, the Salk vaccine virtually eliminated the dreaded illness within a few years. The oral contraceptive pill, which came on the market in 1960, provided relatively safe and effective birth control. Hailed initially as a boon to family planning, the pill also helped to usher in the sexual revolution of the 1960s.

Scientific discoveries in the 1950s also inaugurated the modern era of exploration beyond the Earth's atmosphere, fueled by the space race between the United States and the Soviet Union. The National Aeronautics and Space Administration (NASA), established in 1958, sent the first American into space in 1961. But science also brought pesticides, smog, and other pollutants. Americans, at the time, rarely considered the environmental effects of consumer goods, cars, petrochemicals, or nuclear power.

The decade from 1953 to 1963 was a time of expansive optimism about the future. The civil rights movement challenged the nation to live up to its promise of democracy for all. The baby boom, generated by young parents from all backgrounds, demonstrated widespread faith in the future for American children. It was also a decade of growth for U.S. influence abroad, the domestic economy, consumer culture, and television. Suburbs, highways, and shopping malls expanded to meet the needs of increasing numbers of families with young children. The nation itself expanded with the addition of Hawaii and Alaska as states.

It was also a decade of anxiety. Americans worried about the perils of the atomic age as the nuclear arsenals of both superpowers continued to grow. The brainwashing of prisoners of war in Korea raised fears about communist propaganda and psychological warfare. Science fiction films about alien invaders reflected concerns about foreign dangers. The Soviet Union's 1957 launching of Sputnik, the first artificial satellite to orbit the earth, alarmed Americans and forced the nation to confront the possibility of Soviet technological superiority. The United States appeared to be at the height of its strength and power, yet, at the same time, more vulnerable than ever before.

Cold War, Warm Hearth

The postwar era was a time of deep divisions in American society, yet in certain ways Americans behaved with remarkable conformity. This is nowhere more evident than in the overwhelming embrace of the nuclear family. The GI Bill, with its provisions for home mortgage loans, enabled veterans of modest means to purchase homes. Although residential segregation prevailed throughout the postwar era, limiting most suburban developments to prosperous white middle- and working-class families, many veterans of color were able to buy their

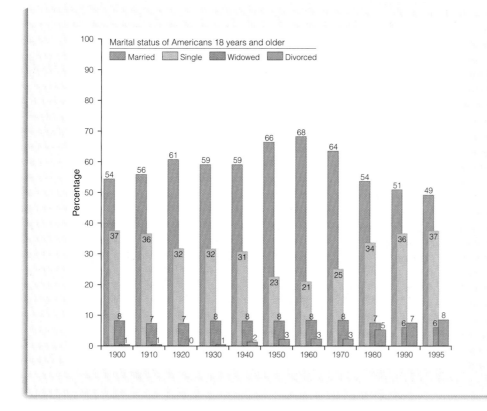

■ **FIGURE 25.1**
**MARITAL STATUS OF THE U.S.
ADULT POPULATION, 1900–1995**
Following World War II, Americans
married in record numbers. The high
rate of marriage corresponded with a
relatively low divorce rate. Beginning
in the 1970s, the marriage rate
plummeted and the divorce rate
rose dramatically.

first homes. Family fever swept the nation and affected all Americans. The trends that began during and immediately after World War II, including the rising rates of marriage and childbirth and the declining age at marriage, continued during the 1950s. Americans of all racial, ethnic, and religious groups, of all socioeconomic classes and educational levels, brought the marriage rate up and the divorce rate down. Popular television shows such as *The Honeymooners,* featuring working-class couples, and *Leave It to Beaver,* depicting middle-class families, placed the consumer-oriented home at the center of attention. So did mainstream *Life* magazine and the African American glossy, *Ebony.* The "American way of life" embodied in the suburban nuclear family, as a cultural ideal if not a universal reality, motivated countless postwar Americans to strive for it, to live by its codes, and—for Americans of color—to demand it.

Consumer Spending and the Suburban Ideal

The postwar years witnessed a huge increase in spending power. Between 1947 and 1961, the number of families rose 28 percent, national income increased more than 60 percent, and the number of Americans with money to spend beyond basic necessities doubled. Rather than putting this money aside for a rainy day, Americans were inclined to spend it. Investing in one's home, along with the trappings that would enhance family life, seemed the best way to plan for a secure future.

Between 1950 and 1970, the suburban population more than doubled, from 36 million to 74 million. Fully 20 percent of the population remained poor during this prosperous time. But most families of ample as well as modest means exhibited a great deal of conformity in their consumer behavior, reflecting widely shared beliefs about the good life. They poured their money into homes, domestic appliances, televisions, automobiles, and family vacations. As prosperity spread throughout the 1950s, expenditures for food and clothing increased modestly, and

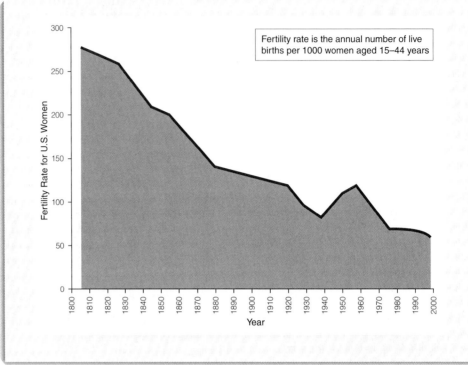

■ FIGURE 25.2
THE BABY BOOM IN HISTORICAL CONTEXT After a decline of nearly a century and a half, the fertility rate of American women surged during and after World War II, producing the baby boom. The boom resulted from the high marriage rate, the lower marriage age, and the rise in the average number of children per couple.

spending on household appliances, recreation, automobiles, and televisions more than doubled. Homeowners moved into more than 1 million new suburban houses each year.

Nuclear families who settled in the suburbs provided the foundation for new types of community life and leisure pursuits, sometimes at the expense of older ones grounded in ethnic neighborhoods and kinship networks. Family-oriented amusement parks such as Disneyland in Anaheim, California, which opened in 1955, catered to middle-class tastes, in contrast to older venues such as Coney Island, known for their thrill rides, class and ethnic mixing, and romantic environments. Religious affiliation rose to an all-time high as Americans built and joined suburban churches and synagogues, complete with youth programs and summer camps. Families piled into the car for outings to local drive-in theaters and weekend excursions or shared leisure time gathered around television sets. In 1949, fewer than 1 million American homes had a television. Within the next four years, the number soared to 20 million.

The house and commodity boom had tremendous propaganda value during the Cold War, as Nixon demonstrated in the Kitchen Debate. Although they may have been unwitting soldiers, consumers who marched off to the nation's shopping centers to equip their new homes joined the ranks of Americans taking part in the Cold War. As early as 1947, newscaster and noted cold warrior George Putnam described shopping centers as "concrete expressions of the practical idealism that built America . . . plenty of free parking for all those cars that we capitalists seem to acquire. Who can help but contrast [them] with what you'd find under communism?"

The Cold War made a profound contribution to suburban sprawl. In 1951 the *Bulletin of Atomic Scientists* devoted an issue to "defense through decentralization" that argued in favor of depopulating the urban core to avoid a concentration of residences or industries in a potential target area for a nuclear attack. Joining this effort was the American Road Builders' Association, a lobbying group second only in power and wealth to the munitions industry. As a result of these pressures, Congress passed the Interstate Highway Act in 1956, which provided $100 billion to cover 90 percent of the cost for 41,000 miles of national highways. When President Dwight D. Eisenhower signed the bill into law, he stated one of the major reasons for the new highway system: "[In] case of atomic attack on our key cities, the road net must permit quick evacuation of target areas." Many people believed that the suburbs also provided protection against labor unrest, which might lead to class warfare.

According to the Cold War ethos of the time, class conflict within the United States would weaken the nation and harm its image abroad, bolstering the Soviet Union and making the United States vulnerable to communism.

The worst-case scenario was communist takeover and the defeat of the United States in the Cold War. Pentagon strategists and foreign policy experts feared that the Soviet Union might gain the military might to allow its territorial expansion and, eventually, world domination. But observers also worried that the real dangers to America were internal: racial strife, emancipated women, class conflict, and familial disruption. To alleviate these fears, Americans turned to the family as a bastion of safety in an insecure world. Most postwar Americans longed for security after years of depression and war and saw family stability as the best bulwark against the new dangers of the Cold War.

■ During the 1950s, churches and synagogues sprang up in suburban communities across the country, helping to strengthen community ties for newcomers to the suburbs. In the same decade, Congress inserted the phrase "under God" to the Pledge of Allegiance and added "In God We Trust" to U.S. currency.

Race, Class, and Domesticity

Many Americans think of the 1950s as a golden era of economic prosperity and happy families nestled in comfortable suburban homes. But this mythical vision obscures the fact that the government subsidized suburban developments and restricted who could live in them. After World War II, the nation faced a severe housing shortage. The federal government gave developers financial subsidies to build affordable single-family homes and offered Federal Housing Authority (FHA) loans and income tax deductions to homebuyers. These benefits enabled white working-class and middle-class families to purchase houses. Second- and third-generation European immigrants moved out of their neighborhoods in the cities and into the suburbs. Postwar prosperity, government subsidies, and the promise of assimilation made it possible for white-skinned Americans of immigrant background to blend into the suburbs.

In many suburbs, contracts for the sale of houses had included restrictions that prevented Jews and racial minorities from purchasing homes in white neighborhoods. Gradually, these restrictions began to lift. But it remained difficult for people of color to move to the suburbs. Despite the expansion of the black and Latino middle class and the increase in home ownership among racial minorities, most suburban developments excluded nonwhites. The FHA and lending banks maintained policies known as "red lining," which designated certain neighborhoods off limits to racial minorities. They refused mortgage loans to people of color wishing to buy houses in redlined areas, even if the prospective buyers could afford the purchase price. Although Americans of color remained concentrated in urban and rural areas, some did move to the suburbs, usually into segregated communities.

For Americans of color, suburban home ownership offered inclusion in the postwar American dream. In her powerful 1959 play *A Raisin In the Sun,* African American playwright Lorraine Hansberry articulated with great eloquence the importance of a home in the suburbs, not to assimilate into white America but to live as a black family with dignity and pride. Asian Americans also had good reason to celebrate home

Betty Engle/Minnesota Historical Society, Neg. #64025

■ **The Women's Council of St. Paul, Minnesota, was one of many service organizations in which black and white women joined in common projects. Volunteer activities enabled women to serve their communities as well as develop important political and leadership skills.**

and family life. With the end of the exclusion of Chinese immigrants during World War II, wives and war brides began to enter the country, helping to build thriving family-oriented communities. After the disruptions and anguish of internment, Japanese Americans were eager to put their families and lives back together. Mexican Americans and Mexican immigrants, including *braceros,* established flourishing communities in the Southwest. Puerto Ricans migrated to New York and other eastern cities, where they could earn four times the average on the island.

Racial segregation did not prevail everywhere. For example, in Shaker Heights, Ohio, a suburb of Cleveland, white residents made a conscious decision, as a community, to integrate their neighborhood. Drawing on postwar liberal ideals of civil rights and racial integration, they welcomed black homeowners. They succeeded in this effort by emphasizing class similarity over racial difference. White residents encouraged other white families to move into Shaker Heights, pointing out that their prosperous black neighbors were "just like us." The city of Claremont, California, established an interracial housing cooperative of Mexican and African American residents along with white married college students at the edge of the Arbol Verde barrio, a Mexican American neighborhood. Desegregation experiments such as these established harmonious racially integrated communities at a time when residential segregation was the norm across the country.

White attitudes toward racial integration began to shift, but only slightly. In the late 1950s, 60 percent of whites outside the South said they would stay in their homes if a black family moved next door, but only 45 percent said they would remain in the neighborhood if large numbers of people of color moved in. In 1964, demonstrating their belief in property rights over civil rights, 89 percent of those polled in the North and 96 percent in the South believed that "an owner of property should not have to sell to a Negro if he doesn't want to." Disapproval of racial integration was strongest in the most intimate realm of life:

the family. During the 1950s, most white Americans—92 percent in the North and 99 percent in the South—approved of laws banning marriage between whites and nonwhites. As late as the mid-1960s, more than half of northern whites and more than three-fourths of southern whites still opposed interracial marriage.

As residents and businesses migrated to the suburbs, slum housing and vacant factories remained in the central cities. With declining tax bases, city governments had few resources to rebuild and revitalize urban neighborhoods. The Housing Acts of 1949 and 1954, promising "a decent home and suitable living environment for every American family," granted funds to municipalities for urban renewal. However, few of those federal dollars provided low-income housing. Mayors, bankers, and real estate interests used the money to bulldoze slums and build gleaming office towers, civic centers, and apartment complexes for affluent citizens, leaving the poor to fend for themselves in the remaining dilapidated corners of the cities.

Although intended to revitalize cities, urban renewal actually accelerated the decay of inner cities and worsened conditions for the urban poor. Federally funded projects often disrupted and destroyed ethnic communities. In St. Paul, Minnesota, the construction of U.S. Highway 94, while enabling suburbanites to commute to the city, obliterated the thriving urban African American neighborhood of Rondo. In Los Angeles, the Dodgers' stadium built in Chávez Ravine offered baseball fans and their families access to the national pastime, but it destroyed the historically rooted Mexican American neighborhood in its path. The $5-million project displaced 7500 people and demolished 900 homes.

Park Forest, Illinois, 1953. Courtesy, Sandra Weiner. Photo by Dan Weiner

■ Commuters, mostly men, left their suburban homes each morning to go to jobs in the cities, returning home at night. Suburbs served as "bedroom communities," inhabited mostly by women and children during the day.

Along with the urban poor, rural Americans reaped few benefits of postwar affluence. Many rural residents had no electricity or running water during the 1950s and therefore had no TV sets or washing machines. Much of rural America, especially in the South, remained poor. The 1950s marked the greatest out-migration from the South as the mechanization of farms reduced the number of workers on the land. More than one-fourth of the population left Kentucky and West Virginia, where unemployment in some areas reached 80 percent. For black migrants, the situation was particularly grim. One-tenth of all southern blacks moved north during the decade as the mechanical cotton picker eliminated the need for 80 percent of the sharecroppers. But life in the North did not offer much improvement. Automation in heavy industries reduced the number of available skilled jobs.

Women: Back to the Future

The nuclear family ideal of the 1950s included a full-time wife and mother and a breadwinner husband. This vision of domesticity marked a giant step backward for women, whose opportunities and experiences had expanded dramatically during World War II. The elevation of the housewife as a major cultural icon contrasted sharply with the reality. The proportion of women who fit the mold of full-time homemaker was rapidly shrinking. Although most American women married, had children, and carried the lion's share of responsibility for housework and child-rearing, increasing numbers of married women also held jobs outside the home. The employment of married women began to rise during World War II and kept rising after the war, even though most of the well-paying and highly skilled jobs returned to men at the war's end.

For the majority of white working-class and middle-class women, the end of the war closed off a number of possibilities for occupational training, professional education, and career opportunities. Often a woman's best chance to secure a decent standard of living was to marry a competent breadwinner. But the pressures on blue-collar as well as white-collar men to earn enough money for the trappings of middle-class affluence strained their ability to provide. Married women took jobs to help pay the bills. College-educated women often worked in clerical positions as secretaries or clerks, but these jobs did not make use of their knowledge and skills. Working-class women found work in the "pink collar" service sector of the economy—such jobs as waitress and hairdresser—with low pay and few chances for advancement. But for most Mexican women, pink-collar work was an improvement over migrant labor or factory work. African American women also found these jobs preferable to domestic work in white middle-class homes.

Many women worked part-time while their children were at school, but they considered their primary occupation to be homemaker. With few other opportunities for creative work, women embraced their domestic roles and turned homemaking into a profession. Many fulfilled their role with pride and satisfaction and extended their energies and talents into their

■ After World War II, women were forced out of most of the high-paying skilled jobs that they had occupied during wartime to make room for the returning men. The jobs available to women were mostly so-called pink-collar jobs in the service industry. Here, women operate rolling food carts that enabled a New Jersey factory to feed its workers lunch in a mere 20 minutes.

The National Archives

communities, where they made important contributions as volunteers in local parent–teacher associations (PTAs) and other civic organizations. Most postwar mothers finished childbearing by the time they were 30 and had many years ahead of them when their child-rearing responsibilities ended. Some expanded part-time employment into full-time occupations when their children left the nest. Others felt bored and frustrated and drowned their sorrow with alcohol or tranquilizers. In 1963 author Betty Friedan described the constraints facing women as the "problem that has no name" in her feminist manifesto, *The Feminine Mystique.*

Despite the powerful cultural expectation that women's primary responsibilities were to care for their homes and families, there were many single and married women who followed alternative paths. Women pursued careers in a wide range of fields, including the arts, business, and politics. Harvard Medical School admitted its first female students in 1945, although the medical profession remained heavily male-dominated. Some women managed to buck the prevailing gender role with ease; others found it difficult. Minnesota Democratic Congresswoman Coya Knudson paid a heavy price for her political ideals. While she was in Washington, D.C., working to pass legislation for such causes as college scholarships and school lunches, her husband told *Life* magazine that his wife had abandoned her domestic responsibilities to dally in the male world of politics. The article, titled "Coya Come Home," cast aspersions on the congresswoman's morals and featured a photo of the family having Thanksgiving dinner in a seedy Washington, D.C., cafeteria. Knudson lost her seat in Congress to a Republican challenger who used "Coya Come Home" as a campaign slogan.

Education was one avenue available to women, as students as well as teachers. But higher education did not open its doors fully to women. Because few women gained access to graduate and professional schools and most well-paying jobs were reserved for men, college degrees for white women did not necessarily open up career opportunities or greatly improve their job and earning prospects. By 1956, one-fourth of white female students married while still in college. Many of these women dropped out of school to take jobs in order to support their husbands through college. But the situation was quite different for black women. Like their mothers and grandmothers, most black women had to work to help support their families. Even in the prosperous postwar years, few black families could survive on the meager earnings of a single breadwinner. Job prospects for black women generally were limited to menial, low-paying occupations. Young black women knew that a college degree could mean the difference between working as a maid for a white family and working as a secretary, teacher, or nurse. Although few in number, more than 90 percent of black women who entered college completed their degrees.

Black women also aspired to the role of homemaker, but for very different reasons than white women. Although poverty still plagued large numbers of black citizens, the black middle class expanded during the 1950s. Postwar prosperity enabled some African Americans, for the first time, to strive for family life in which the earnings of men were adequate to allow women to stay home with their own children rather than tending to the houses and children of white families. Celebrating that possibility in 1947, *Ebony* magazine proclaimed, "Goodbye Mammy, Hello Mom." World War II "took Negro mothers out of white kitchens, put them in factories and shipyards. When it was all over, they went back to kitchens—but this time their own. . . . And so today in thousands of Negro homes, the Negro mother has come home, come

Courtesy, Herb and Dorothy McLaughlin Collection, Arizona State University Libraries

■ Following World War II, hospital nurseries barely had room for all the babies. After a century and a half of steady decline, the birthrate rose dramatically in the 1940s and 1950s. Americans from all backgrounds and socioeconomic levels contributed to the surge in births.

Russell Lee/Library of Congress

■ **At a time when many corporations and professions still excluded African Americans, many black entrepreneurs opened their own establishments to serve their own communities. This black-owned dress shop in Chicago catered to middle-class African American women.**

home perhaps for the first time since 1619 when the first Negro families landed at Jamestown, Virginia." For black women, domesticity meant "freedom and independence in her own home." It is no wonder that in the early 1960s, women of color bristled when white feminists such as Betty Friedan called upon women to break free from the "chains" of domesticity.

The Civil Rights Movement

As the civil rights movement gained momentum in the South, African American activists faced fierce opposition from local white authorities and contempt from national leaders. Persistent racial discrimination proved to be the nation's worst embarrassment throughout the Cold War. Black leaders and federal officials understood that the national government needed to promote civil rights at home to save face abroad. The Soviet Union and other communist countries pointed to American race relations as an indication of the hypocrisy and failure of the American promise of freedom for all. Yet national leaders paid only lip service to racial justice and failed to provide the strong support necessary to defeat the system of racial segregation in the South known as the "Jim Crow" system. Jim Crow was a legal, or *de jure,* set of institutions that prevailed throughout the South. Although the nation's leaders acknowledged the need to address Southern segregation, they did nothing to address the unofficial, or *de facto,* segregation that prevailed throughout the rest of the country. Nevertheless, at the grassroots level racial minorities continued to work for equal rights. For example, Mexican Americans in the Southwest continued to press for desegregation of schools, residential neighborhoods, and public facilities through organizations such as the League of United Latin American Citizens (LULAC) and the Asociación Nacional México-Americana (ANMA), a civil rights organization that emerged out of the labor movement. It was not until 1963 that the power of the civil rights movement—and the violence of southern white opposition—finally compelled the federal government to take action.

Brown v. Board of Education

The first major success in the struggle to dismantle the Jim Crow system in the South came in the 1954 Supreme Court decision *Brown v. Board of Education*. Civil rights strategists decided to pursue their cause in the courts rather than through Congress. They knew that Southern Democrats in Congress, who held disproportionate power through their seniority and control of major committees, would block any civil rights legislation that came before the House or Senate. They believed that they had a better chance of success through the courts.

Initially, civil rights attorneys worked within the system of segregation. The *Plessy v. Ferguson* decision in 1896 justified Jim Crow laws on the principle of providing "separate but equal" facilities. The attorneys argued that southern school systems violated the segregation laws because the separate, racially segregated schools were far from equal. In Clarendon County, South Carolina, for example, public funds provided $179 per white child compared to $43 per black child. Soon the lawyers shifted their strategy to claim that separate was inherently unequal and began the push to overturn *Plessy v. Ferguson*. Leading the charge was Thurgood Marshall, general counsel of the NAACP and a graduate of Howard University Law School.

The NAACP lawyers filed suit against the Topeka, Kansas, Board of Education, on behalf of Linda Brown, a black child in a segregated school. The case reached the U.S. Supreme Court, where Marshall argued that separate facilities, by definition, denied African Americans their equal rights as citizens. A key argument in the case was the psychological effect of the stigma of segregation on black children. Psychologist Kenneth Clark, testifying as an expert witness, gave evidence showing that black children educated in segregated schools developed a negative self-image and responded more positively to white dolls than to black dolls. Although this

Ed Clark/TimePix

■ Children in segregated schools studied in wretched physical conditions but benefited from dedicated African American teachers. The Supreme Court struck down school segregation in the landmark 1954 case *Brown v. Board of Education,* arguing in its unanimous decision that separate facilities were inherently unequal.

argument was persuasive with the Court and helped to bring about school desegregation, some black leaders at the time objected to the use of that psychological argument. Those critics of the strategy argued that black children did not need to interact with white children in order to gain self-esteem and pointed to the positive influence of black teachers who believed in their students' capabilities. They claimed that low self-esteem among black children resulted from widespread discrimination against black Americans, not simply black students' lack of interaction with white students.

In 1953, during the three years that the Supreme Court had the *Brown* case before it, President Eisenhower appointed Earl Warren as chief justice. Warren had been state attorney general and then governor of California during World War II and had approved the internment of Japanese Americans—a decision he later deeply regretted. He now used his political and legal skills to strike a blow for justice. He knew that such a critical case needed a unanimous decision to win broad political support. One by one, he persuaded his Supreme Court colleagues of the importance of striking down segregation. On May 17, 1954, Warren delivered the historic unanimous ruling: "To separate [black children] from others of similar age and qualifications solely because of their race generates a feeling of inferiority as to their status in the community that may affect their hearts and minds in a way unlikely ever to be undone. . . . We conclude that in the field of public education the doctrine of 'separate but equal' has no place. Separate educational facilities are inherently unequal. . . . Any language in *Plessy v. Ferguson* contrary to these findings is rejected."

White Resistance, Black Persistence

Winning the *Brown* case was a great triumph, but it was only the first step. Desegregation would be meaningful only when it was enforced, and that was another matter entirely. At first, there seemed to be some cause for optimism. Although a few white officials in the South protested vehemently, many others seemed resigned to accept the decision. However, none was willing to take action to implement desegregation. Even the Supreme Court delayed its decision on implementation for a full year and then simply called for the process to begin "with all deliberate speed" but specified no timetable. Political leaders did not come forward to work on the task, leaving sympathetic educators and eager black Americans with no support.

The leader who could have done the most but in fact did the least was President Eisenhower. Instead of calling for immediate desegregation, he made it clear that he strongly disagreed with the Court's decision. Expressing neither "approbation nor disapproval," Eisenhower said, "I don't think you can change the hearts of men with laws or decisions." Just before the Court's ruling, he told Chief Justice Warren that southern white segregationists simply wanted to make sure "that their sweet little girls are not required to sit in schools alongside some big overgrown Negroes." After the decision went against his wishes, Eisenhower remarked that his decision to appoint Warren to the court was the "biggest damn fool mistake" he ever made, claiming that "the Supreme Court decisions set back progress in the South at least fifteen years. . . . The fellow who tries to tell me that you can do these things by force is just plain nuts."

In 1955, the year after the *Brown* decision, several white Mississippians murdered 14-year-old Emmett Till for allegedly whistling at a white woman. The boy had come from Chicago to Mississippi, where he was visiting relatives. His mutilated body was found in the Tallahatchie River. Although Till's killers confessed to the murder, an all-white jury found them not guilty. Eisenhower remained silent about Till's murder and the travesty of justice, even when E. Frederick Morrow, his one black adviser, beseeched him to condemn the lynching.

Eisenhower's hands-off policy emboldened southern segregationists to resist the Supreme Court's desegregation decision. When it became clear that the federal government would do nothing to enforce the ruling, white resistance spread across the South. State legislatures passed resolutions vowing to protect segregation, and most southern congressmen signed the "Southern Manifesto" promising to oppose federal desegregation efforts. To avoid suits by the NAACP, southern states transferred authority over schools to local school boards that assigned students to schools according to concern for the "general welfare," thereby maintaining segregation without specifying race as a criterion.

A crisis at Central High School in Little Rock, Arkansas, finally forced Eisenhower to act. Under a federal district court's order to desegregate, school officials were prepared to comply and had carefully mobilized community support. But Arkansas Governor Orville Faubus, facing reelection, decided to play the race card. Using Central High's integration plan as his target, he created a crisis by instructing National Guard troops to maintain "order" by blocking the entry of black students into the school.

Eisenhower initially refused to intervene in the crisis. Hoping for a compromise, he met with Faubus, who agreed to allow the school to integrate peacefully. But Faubus broke his word, withdrew the National Guard troops, and left Little Rock, leaving the black students unprotected. On September 23, 1957, as nine black students attempted to enter Central High, a huge angry crowd of whites surrounded them. With international news cameras broadcasting pictures of the shrieking and menacing mob, Eisenhower took action to stop the embarrassing fracas. Furious at Faubus for his insubordination, Eisenhower denounced the "disgraceful occurrence," federalized the Arkansas National Guard, and sent 1000 paratroopers to Little Rock. Unwilling to "acquiesce in anarchy and the disillusion of the union," Eisenhower acted to maintain federal authority rather than to support integration. Although the Little Rock Nine, as the courageous students came to be called, finally gained entry to Central High, Governor Faubus closed the schools in Little Rock for the entire next year. Out of 712 school districts that had desegregated after the *Brown* decision, only 49 remained desegregated by the end of Eisenhower's term. Most of the others reverted to segregation.

Boycotts and Sit-Ins

Under Jim Crow laws in the South, black passengers were required to sit in the back section of buses, leaving the front of the bus for whites. If the "white" section at the front of the bus filled up, black passengers were required to give up their seats for white passengers. On December 1, 1955, Rosa Parks and the black community of Montgomery, Alabama, were ready to take on the system. Parks, who worked as a seamstress, was a widely respected leader in Montgomery's black community, active in her church, and secretary of the local NAACP. On her way home from work that day, sitting in the first row of the "colored" section of the bus when the front of the bus filled with passengers, she refused to move when a white man demanded her seat. Parks was arrested, and black Montgomery sprang into action.

Eisenhower acted to maintain federal authority rather than to support integration.

Literally overnight, the Montgomery bus boycott was born. E. D. Dixon, president of the Alabama NAACP and the head of the local chapter of the Brotherhood of Sleeping Car Porters, and Jo Ann Robinson, the leader of the local Women's Political Council (a black alternative to the segregated League of Women Voters), mobilized the boycott. They gathered with 50 community representatives that night at the Dexter Avenue Baptist Church to plan strategy. They mobilized other black churches to spread the word to their congregations on Sunday, and black-owned taxi companies geared up to take the place of buses. By Monday, all of black Montgomery had heard the news of the boycott. The buses that day were empty of black riders. For 381 days, more than 90 percent of Montgomery's black citizens sacrificed their comfort and convenience for the sake of their rights and dignity. As one elderly black woman replied when a white reporter offered her a ride as she walked to work, "No, my feets is tired but my soul is rested."

Martin Luther King, Jr., pastor of the Dexter Avenue Baptist Church, was a newcomer to Montgomery when the bus boycott began. He embraced the opportunity to become the leader of the boycott and, eventually, the most powerful spokesperson for the civil rights movement. His stirring and impassioned words inspired thousands of black citizens to join the cause. As he told the 5000 listeners who gathered in his church on the first night of the boycott, "If you will protest courageously and yet with dignity and Christian love, in the history books that are written in future generations, historians will have to pause and say, 'there lived a great people—a black people—who injected a new meaning and dignity into the veins of civilization.' This is our challenge and our overwhelming responsibility."

The bus boycott ended a year later when the Supreme Court ruled that Montgomery's buses must integrate, but the momentum generated by the boycott galvanized the civil rights movement. King and other leaders formed the Southern Christian Leadership Conference (SCLC), which united black ministers across the South in the cause of civil rights. The boycott tactic spread to other southern cities. As boycotts continued, a new strategy emerged: the sit-in.

NEBRASKA

IOWA

In Brown v. the Topeka Board of Education, the U.S. Supreme Court ruled in 1954 that public school segregation was unconstitutional

KANSAS   Topeka

MISSOURI

President Eisenhower ordered troops to enforce the intergration of Central High School in 1957

ARKANSAS   TENNESSEE
Little Rock   Memphis
    Oxford

OKLAHOMA

In 1962, James Meredith integrated the University of Mississippi

    Birmingham
    Greenwood
MISSISSIPPI   Selma
Jackson   ALABAMA
    Montgomery

TEXAS   LOUISIANA

In 1955, the murder of Emmett Till (age 14) by whites drew national attention

New Orleans

ILLINOIS   INDIANA   OHIO

WEST VIRGINIA

KENTUCKY

Nashville   Rock Hill

Anniston   Atlanta

GEORGIA
    Tuskegee
    Albany

Tallahassee   St. Augustine

FLORIDA

Washington, D.C.   *The 1963 March on Washington*

DELAWARE
MARYLAND

VIRGINIA

Sit-ins began in 1960
    Greensboro
NORTH CAROLINA

SOUTH CAROLINA

1961 Freedom Ride met with violence

Bus boycott in 1955–1956 begun by Rosa Parks

Routes of 1961 Freedom Rides

→ CORE (Congress on Racial Equality) route from Washington, D.C., to Birmingham, Alabama

→ SNCC (Student Nonviolent Coordinating Committee) route from Birmingham, Alabama, to Jackson, Mississippi

■ **MAP 25.1**

MAJOR EVENTS OF THE AFRICAN AMERICAN CIVIL RIGHTS MOVEMENT, 1953–1963 Most of the major events of the early stages of the black freedom struggle took place in the South. Black southerners formed the backbone of the movement, but the grass roots protest movement drew participants from all regions of the country, all racial and ethnic groups, cities and rural areas, churches and universities, old and young, lawyers and sharecroppers.

On February 1, 1960, four African American students at North Carolina Agricultural and Technical College in Greensboro, inspired by the example of the bus boycott, entered the local Woolworth store and sat down at the lunch counter. When they were told, "We do not serve Negroes," they refused to leave, forcing the staff at Woolworth's to physically remove the nonviolent protesters. Undaunted, they returned to the lunch counter the next day with 23 classmates. By the end of the week more than a thousand students joined the protest. By this time, white gangs had gathered, waving Confederate flags and menacing the black under-graduates. But the students responded by waving American flags. An expression of their patri-otism as well as their political shrewdness, the flag identified the protesters not as subversives acting against social order but as citizens claiming the values and identity of the nation. Black football players kept the angry whites at bay. Taunted with shouts of "Who do you think you are?" they replied, "We are the union army."

In May 1961 members of the Congress of Racial Equality (CORE) organized the Free-dom Rides, in which black and white civil rights workers attempted to ride two interstate buses from Washington, D.C., to New Orleans in an effort to challenge segregation at facilities used in interstate travel. Their journey began peacefully, but when they reached Rock Hill, South Carolina, a group of whites beat John Lewis, one of the young black riders, for entering a whites-only rest room. In Anniston, Alabama, a mob slashed the tires of one of the buses, threw a fire bomb through a window, and pummeled the riders with fists and pipes. After the brutal beatings, reinforcements from the Student Non-violent Coordinating Committee (SNCC) arrived to continue the Freedom Rides. They persevered, facing beatings along the way until they reached Jackson, Mississippi, where they were immediately arrested and jailed. By August, 300 additional protesters had been locked in the jail, all refusing bail. The spirit and strength of the civil rights workers inspired many others to join them in the movement. They came from all over the South as well as the North, white as well as black, giving up comfort and safety, risk-ing—and sacrificing—their lives.

The Eisenhower Years

Dwight D. Eisenhower, elected president in 1952, squandered his opportunity to provide strong support for the civil rights movement. A respected and widely admired World War II general, Eisenhower could have used his leadership to bolster the cause, but he did just the opposite. Eisenhower's failure to use his presidential power allowed southern segregationists to block implementation of the *Brown* decision and opened the way for violent resistance to the civil rights movement. His presidency was notable largely for moderation and maintaining the status quo, with very few major new initiatives and a style of leadership that rested more on his personal stature than his actions. Ike, as he was known, presided over the nation during a time of great prosperity, and his policies encouraged business expansion. However, the former general did try to stem the defense buildup. In his farewell address at the end of his second term as president, Eisenhower warned the nation against the growing power of the "military–industrial complex," the term he coined to describe the armed forces and the politically powerful defense industries that supplied arms and equipment to them.

The Middle of the Road

Born in Texas, raised in Kansas, and educated at the U.S. Military Academy at West Point, Eisenhower became a career soldier who served as the supreme commander of the Allied forces in western Europe during World War II. Eisenhower planned and carried out the daring Allied invasion at Normandy on D-Day. As early as 1948, both the Democrats and the Republicans courted Eisenhower as a presidential candidate. But he resisted, believing that military leaders should not get involved in politics; indeed, he had never even registered to vote. In 1952, however, when he was president of Columbia University, he changed his mind and accepted the Republican nomination, choosing California Senator Richard M. Nixon—known as a dogged anticommunist crusader—as his running mate. The Democrats nominated Illinois Governor Adlai E. Stevenson. The cerebral Stevenson, dubbed an "egghead" by the press, was no match for the former general whose supporters donned campaign buttons boasting "I Like Ike." The popular Eisenhower won the election with the largest landslide up to that time and was reelected by an even wider margin in 1956.

As president, Eisenhower pursued a path down the middle of the road. His probusiness legislative agenda and appointments pleased conservatives, and he placated liberals by extending many of the policies of the welfare state enacted during the New Deal. He agreed to the expansion of Social Security and unemployment compensation and an increase in the minimum wage. He also made concerted efforts to reduce defense spending, believing that continued massive military expenditures would hinder the nation's economic growth. In December 1953, with Admiral Arthur Radford, chair of the Joint Chiefs of Staff, Eisenhower announced the New Look, a streamlined military that relied less on expensive conventional ground forces and more on air power and advanced nuclear capabilities.

Eisenhower's plans to reduce defense spending derailed on October 4, 1957, when the Soviet Union launched Sputnik, the first artificial Earth satellite. Although Sputnik could not be seen with the naked eye—it was only 22 inches in diameter and weighed only 184 pounds— it emitted a beeping noise that was broadcast by commercial radio stations in the United States,

TABLE 25-1

The Election of 1952

Candidate	Political Party	Popular Vote	Electoral Vote
Dwight D. Eisenhower	Republican	33,936,252	442
Adlai E. Stevenson	Democratic	27,314,992	89

TABLE 25-2

The Election of 1956

Candidate	Political Party	Popular Vote	Electoral Vote
Dwight D. Eisenhower	Republican	35,575,420	457
Adlai E. Stevenson	Democratic	26,033,066	73

making its presence very real and causing near hysteria among the public. The Soviet's launching of Sputnik II a month later seemed to confirm widespread fears that the United States was behind in the space race and, more significantly, in the arms race. Eisenhower's popularity in the polls suddenly dropped 22 points.

Acquiescing to his critics, the president allotted increased funds for military, scientific, and educational spending. The National Aeronautics and Space Administration (NASA), which developed the program of space exploration, was one result of this increase. But Eisenhower believed that "the most critical problem of all" was the lack of American scientists and engineers. He proposed that the federal government subsidize additional science and math training for both teachers and students. He also called for an improvement in overall education so that the next generation would be "equipped to live in the age of intercontinental ballistic missiles." On September 2, 1958, Eisenhower signed Public Law 85-864, also known as the National Defense Education Act (NDEA), which authorized more than $1 billion in education spending.

"What's Good for General Motors . . ."

Eisenhower's Secretary of Defense, former head of General Motors Charles Wilson, made the memorable comment that "what's good for General Motors business is good for America." But not everyone agreed. Eisenhower's probusiness policies had a devastating impact on the nation's environment. He promoted the passage of the Submerged Land Act, which removed from federal jurisdiction more than $40 billion worth of oil-rich offshore lands. Under the control of state governments, oil companies could—and did—gain access to them. The *New York Times* called the act "one of the greatest and surely the most unjustified give-away program" in the nation's history. The administration's willingness to allow businesses to expand with little regulation, and with virtually no concern for the environment, contributed to increasing pollution of the air, water, and land during the 1950s and sparked the environmental movement of the 1960s and 1970s.

Eisenhower also supported the Interstate Highway Act of 1956, inspired in part by Cold War concerns. An interstate highway system could allow the swift movement of military supplies and, presumably, the evacuation of urban centers in the event of a nuclear attack. The Highway Act had its greatest impact on business and transportation, however. As the largest public works project the nation had ever mounted, this centrally planned transportation system was a boon to the auto, trucking, oil, concrete, and tire industries. In addition, it contributed to the national pastime of family road vacations and tourism. Cheap gas also fueled America's car culture. Cars gave Americans increased mobility, and enabled suburban dwellers to drive to work in the cities. But reliance on the automobile doomed the nation's passenger train system and led to the decline of public transportation. Cars also contributed to suburban sprawl, air pollution, and traffic jams.

Eisenhower's Foreign Policy

The New Look, while containing military spending, also shifted American military priorities from reliance on conventional weapons to nuclear deterrence and covert operations. During Eisenhower's presidency, the United States and the Soviet Union both solidified their separate alliances. The North Atlantic Treaty Organization (NATO), formed in 1949, increased American influence in Western Europe. The 12 NATO nations agreed that an attack on any one of them would be considered an attack on all, and they maintained a force to defend the West against a possible Soviet invasion. NATO expanded in 1952 to include Greece and Turkey, and West Germany joined in 1955. The Soviet Union formed a similar alliance, the Warsaw Pact, with the countries of Eastern Europe. Confrontations between the United States and the Soviet Union over the fate of Europe gave way to more subtle maneuvers regarding the Third World—a term originally referring to unaligned nations in the Middle East, Africa, Asia, and Latin America.

When Joseph Stalin died in 1953, Nikita Khrushchev became the new leader of the Soviet Union and called for peaceful coexistence with the United States. To limit military expenditures and improve relations, the superpowers arranged high-level summit meetings. In 1955 delegates from the United States, the Soviet Union, Britain, and France met in Geneva. Although the meeting achieved little of substance, it set a tone of cooperation. In 1959 Khrushchev came to the United States, met with Eisenhower, and toured the country. But a planned Paris summit in May 1960 was canceled when the Soviets shot down an American U-2 spy plane. U.S. officials initially denied that the plane was on a spy mission until the captured American pilot, Gary Powers, confessed. Powers served two years of a ten-year sentence in a Soviet prison before his release in exchange for a suspected Soviet spy incarcerated in the United States. Despite the U-2 incident, the superpowers began to discuss arms limitation. Both countries agreed to limit aboveground testing of nuclear weapons in light of the health and environmental risks such tests posed.

Anticommunism became the guiding principle behind nearly all U.S. foreign policy, taking precedence over other American ideals.

As the United States and the Soviet Union worked toward greater cooperation, they faced challenges from within their separate "spheres of influence" and vied for the loyalty of newly independent states in the Third World. In 1956 the Soviet Union faced armed uprisings in Poland and Hungary, two "satellite" nations chafing under Soviet domination. In Poland, rebels resisting Moscow's control took to the streets, demanding that the Soviet Union recognize Wladyslaw Gomulka, who had been an opponent of Stalin, as the leader of Poland. After three days of fighting, the Soviet Union capitulated to the rebels' demand. In Hungary, maverick communist Imre Nagy took power and pledged to create a multiparty democracy. As revolution spread across Hungary, Soviet troops brutally crushed the rebellion, killing Nagy and thousands of other Hungarians.

While the United States and the Soviet Union competed with each other to gain influence in Third World countries, leaders from those countries came together to discuss ways to achieve self-determination. In April 1955 in Bandung, Indonesia, representatives from 29 nations—primarily from Asia, Africa, and the Middle East—met in what President Sukarno of Indonesia called "the first international conference of colored peoples in the history of mankind." Nearly all the participants came from countries that had previously been colonized by western European countries. Most were former colonies of Britain, France, Belgium, Holland, or Portugal. Although they shared no specific political ideology, the conference carried an implicit condemnation of western powers and a commitment to eliminating the vestiges of colonialism and racial discrimination worldwide. Suspicious of the motives of the participants and worried about the outcome, Eisenhower sent no greeting to the gathering and tried to ignore or sabotage it. However, Adam Clayton Powell, one of three black members of the U.S. Congress, attended the conference as a "journalist," providing an unofficial U.S. presence.

The Eisenhower administration continued to distrust countries that maintained neutrality in the Cold War, fearing that those not aligned with the United States might turn to communism and become allies of the Soviet Union. In 1956 Secretary of State John Foster Dulles declared that neutrality "is an immoral and shortsighted conception." Anticommunism became the guiding principle behind nearly all U.S. foreign policy, taking precedence over other American ideals, such as support for democratically elected governments and national self-determination. Acting on its anticommunist priority, the United States helped overthrow democratically elected leaders and prop up corrupt and often brutal dictatorships.

The Central Intelligence Agency (CIA) was a major player in this drama, with 15,000 agents working around the world by the end of the 1950s. Congress established the CIA in 1947 to gather strategic intelligence from foreign countries and to engage in covert political activity. Through covert operations, the CIA helped to overthrow the elected government in Iran and to restore the dictatorship of Shah Reza Pahlavi, whose unpopular western-leaning regime was finally overthrown by Muslim fundamentalists in 1979. In 1954 the CIA, working closely

■ MAP 25.2

COLD WAR SPHERES OF INFLUENCE, 1953–1963 During the early years of the Cold War, the United States and the Soviet Union developed formal military alliances, most importantly NATO and the Warsaw Pact. The American and Soviet informal spheres of influence also included trading and cultural ties to several other countries. Many independent nations, especially those just emerging from colonialism, remained neutral in the Cold War.

Military alliances in the 1950s

- U.S. allies
- U.S. allies/NATO members
- USSR allies
- USSR allies/Warsaw Pact members

with the United Fruit Company, helped overthrow the elected government of Jacobo Arbenz in Guatemala. U.S. and company officials considered Arbenz a communist because he sought to nationalize and redistribute large tracts of land, including some owned by United Fruit. Eisenhower also supported unpopular anticommunist dictators in Peru and Venezuela. In 1958 Latin Americans expressed their displeasure when Vice President Richard M. Nixon, on a goodwill tour of South America, faced angry protesters wherever he went. Nixon was nearly killed in Caracas, Venezuela, when demonstrators attacked his motorcade.

In 1959 revolutionary leader Fidel Castro overthrew Cuba's U.S.-friendly dictator Fulgencio Batista. Castro established a regime in Cuba based on principles of socialism. His government took control of foreign-owned companies, including many owned by Americans. Castro's socialist policies alarmed U.S. officials and investors in Cuba. Eisenhower's hostility encouraged Castro to forge an alliance with the Soviet Union. The CIA then launched a plot to overthrow Castro, which would culminate in an ill-fated invasion in 1961. In 1960–1961, the CIA also helped orchestrate the overthrow and assassination of the charismatic left-leaning Patrice Lumumba, the first minister of the Republic of the Congo, soon after its independence from Belgium.

U.S. policymakers, with their anticommunist preoccupations, and people in Third World countries, with their campaigns against colonialism and racism, had little interest in each other's priorities. A case in point was Egypt, where in 1952 Gamal Abdul Nasser overthrew the corrupt monarchy of King Farouk and established a government based on neutrality. In 1954 Nasser declared himself prime minister of the new government and accepted aid from both the United States and the Soviet Union. When Nasser engaged in trade with Soviet-bloc countries and extended diplomatic recognition to communist China, the United States canceled loans that were to support the building of the huge Aswan Dam, a major development project for the Egyptian economy. In response, Nasser nationalized the British-controlled Suez Canal in 1956, arguing that canal tolls would provide alternative funding for the dam. The British government, with the help of France and Israel, launched an attack against Egypt to regain control of the canal.

Although he distrusted Nasser, Eisenhower strongly criticized Britain for its effort to retain its imperial position in the Middle East. To avoid further antagonizing Nasser and other Third World leaders, Eisenhower denounced Britain's Suez attack and threatened economic sanctions, forcing the British to back down. Although leaders in Africa and Asia applauded Eisenhower's actions, the episode weakened U.S. relations with Nasser, who forged ties with the Soviet Union. Eisenhower now feared that "Nasserism" might spread throughout the Middle East.

In the spring of 1957, Congress approved the Eisenhower Doctrine, a pledge to defend Middle Eastern countries "against overt armed aggression from any nation controlled by international communism." However, U.S. policymakers rarely distinguished between nationalist movements and designs by "international communism," which they defined as Soviet aggression. Because American leaders believed that struggles for national self-determination in Third World countries were inspired and supported by the Soviet Union, they used the Eisenhower Doctrine to provide justification for U.S. military intervention to support pro-Western governments. When leaders in Lebanon and Jordan appeared friendly to Nasser, Eisenhower stepped in, sending 14,000 U.S. marines to Lebanon and setting up an anti-Nasser government there. Britain intervened in Jordan, restoring King Hussein to the throne.

CORBIS/Sygma

■ Jackson Pollock shocked the art world when he began dripping paint on large canvasses. Abstract expressionist painters like Pollock celebrated their break from conventional forms and representations. National leaders embraced abstract expressionism as symbolic of American artistic freedom, and thousands of Americans hung reproductions of abstract art on the walls of their suburban homes.

Outsiders and Opposition

The 1950s often are remembered as a time of political and cultural complacency among white Americans, with most of the opposition to the nation's institutions emanating from people of color. There is a good deal of truth to this picture. But it obscures the many ways in which white Americans also resisted and rebelled against the status quo. Some young whites, in the South as well as North, joined in the struggle for civil rights; their numbers increased in the 1960s. Others were drawn to the music and dance of black America, especially the fusion of rhythm-and-blues with country-and-western, which took the form of early rock 'n' roll. Distinct forms of protest also emerged from within the white middle class: the rebellion of the Beats who rejected staid conformity, the stirrings of discontent among women, and the antinuclear and environmental movements. The arts also reflected a rejection of mainstream values, as Jackson Pollock and other abstract expressionist painters challenged the artistic conventions of the time and shifted the center of the art world from Paris to New York. Even the sexual revolution of the 1960s had its roots in the widespread defiance of the rigid sexual codes of the 1950s. In many ways, the placid surface of white America hid the smoldering cauldron underneath that would erupt in the years ahead.

Youth, Sex, and Rock 'n' Roll

One clue that all was not tranquil was the widespread panic that the nation's young were out of control. Adult authorities worried about an epidemic of juvenile delinquency, blaming everything from parents to comic books. New celebrities such as Marlon Brando and James

Dean portrayed misunderstood youth in rebellion against a corrupt and uncaring adult world. In the classic youth movie *Rebel Without a Cause,* Dean played a good-hearted but angry young man who suffers from a domineering mother and a wimpish apron-clad father who refuses to stand up to her. When asked, "What are you rebelling against, Johnny?" Brando's tough-guy character in *The Wild One* answers, "I dunno; what've you got?" In these films, and in J. D. Salinger's now-classic novel *Catcher in the Rye,* young women and men strain against the authority and expectations of their parents and the adult world, dreaming of freedom and personal fulfillment.

Sexual mores were rigid in the 1950s—and were widely violated. Single young women who became pregnant faced disgrace and ostracism unless they married quickly, which many did. Abortion, which had been illegal since the late nineteenth century but tacitly accepted until after World War II, became increasingly difficult to obtain, with hospitals placing new restrictions on legal therapeutic abortions. Illegal abortionists who had long practiced without interference faced increasing harassment, forcing the practice underground, where it became much more dangerous. A double standard encouraged men to pursue sexual conquest as a mark of manhood and virility but tarnished the reputation of women who engaged in sexual intercourse prior to marriage.

In many ways, the youth of the 1950s were already undermining the constraints that toppled in the next decade. Nowhere is this development more obvious than in the explosion of rock 'n' roll, with its roots in African American rhythm-and-blues, its raw sexuality, and its jubilant rebelliousness. Chuck Berry's hit "School Days" expressed youthful restlessness, and Little Richard's "Long Tall Sally" and "Rip It Up" exulted in sensual pleasure. Bill Haley and his Comets invited youngsters to "Rock Around the Clock."

Rock 'n' roll emerged out of the fusion of musical traditions. Artists from many ethnic backgrounds experimented with a variety of forms. Jewish songwriters Jerry Leiber and Mike Stoller wrote songs such as "Hound Dog" for black artists such as Willie Mae Thornton that were later recorded by white Southerner Elvis Presley. The first Mexican American rock 'n' roll star, Ritchie Valens, sang such romantic ballads as "Donna" along with jazzed-up versions of Mexican folk songs such as "La Bamba." Rosie and the Originals—an all-girl band led by Mexican American Rosie Mendez—sang rock 'n' roll hits such as "Angel Baby."

Performances as well as lyrics carried erotic power. Chuck Berry pumped his electric guitar and shimmied across stages, Little Richard danced on piano tops and tore off his shirts, and James Brown begged "Please, please, please," while collapsing on the floor. Elvis Presley thrust his hips in his trademark style, sending young audiences into a frenzy. Criticism of his sexually charged gyrations persuaded producers to show him only above the waist during his appearance on Ed Sullivan's TV show. Rock 'n' roll music and dancing added powerful elements of sexuality and rebellion to the youth culture of the 1950s. Many of those impulses found political expression in the 1960s.

Rebellious Men

Men, too, were in revolt. According to widely read sociological tracts of the time, such as William Whyte's *The Organization Man,*

Photofest

■ In *The Wild One* (1954), Marlon Brando portrayed a young man angry at the world. The young actor from Omaha, Nebraska, had already earned acclaim on Broadway. Two decades later he won an Oscar playing the title role in *The Godfather* (1972).

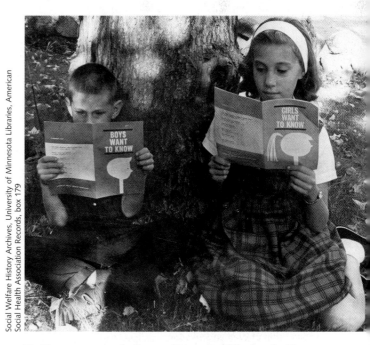

Social Welfare History Archives, University of Minnesota Libraries, American Social Health Association Records, box 179

■ Since sex was rarely discussed in most middle class families, many parents relied on schools to provide elementary sex education, and a generation of suburban children learned the facts of life from nervous teachers and a variety of simplified texts.

C. Wright Mills's *White Collar,* and David Reisman's *The Lonely Crowd,* middle-class men were forced into boring, routinized jobs, groomed to be "outer-directed" at the expense of their inner lives, and saddled with the overwhelming burden of providing for ever-growing families with insatiable consumer desires.

A few highly visible American men provided alternative visions. Hugh Hefner built his Playboy empire by offering men the trappings of the "good life" without its burdensome responsibilities. The Playboy ethic encouraged men to enjoy the sexual pleasures of attractive women without the chains of marriage and to pursue the rewards of consumerism in well-appointed "bachelor flats" rather than appliance-laden homes. *Playboy* magazine celebrated this lifestyle, epitomized in the airbrushed photographs of nearly nude, young, female "bunnies" who seemed to promise sex without commitment.

Beat poets, writers, and artists offered a very different type of escape. In their literary works such as Allen Ginsberg's poem *Howl* and Jack Kerouac's novel *On the Road* and in their highly publicized lives, the Beats celebrated freedom from conformity, eccentric artistic expression, playful obscenity, experimentation with drugs, open homosexuality, and male bonding. While eschewing the sort of luxurious consumerism Hefner extolled, the Beats shared with the Playboy ethic a vision of male rebellion against conformity and responsibility. The mainstream men who indulged in these fantasies were more likely to enjoy them vicariously than to bolt from the breadwinner role. The dads who were honored on the new consumer holiday of Father's Day far outnumbered the freewheeling Beats and bachelors.

Mobilizing for Peace and the Environment

Some women did not wait for the new feminist movement to make their voices heard. Rachel Carson was one such woman. Born in 1907 in Springdale, Pennsylvania, she developed a love of books and nature as a child. She went to college and graduate school during the pre–World War II years before domesticity settled like a fog over women's education. Deeply attached to the sea, she wrote several books and articles about the marine world, most notably her 1951 bestseller, *The Sea Around Us.* Carson became increasingly concerned about the impact of manufactured chemicals on the environment, especially the insecticide DDT, which had been poisoning the earth since World War II. Her last book, *Silent Spring,* published in 1962, brought attention to the worldwide problem of pesticide poisoning. Officially endorsed by President John F. Kennedy's Science Advisory Committee and scorned by the agricultural chemical industry, the book helped launch the environmental movement that has flourished ever since.

Women also led the movement to stop the testing and proliferation of nuclear weapons. On November 1, 1961, 50,000 suburban homemakers in more than 60 communities staged a protest, Women Strike for Peace (WSP). Participants lobbied government officials to "End the Arms Race—Not the Human Race." The strikers were mostly educated, middle-class mothers; 61 percent did not work outside the home. WSP leaders were part of a small group of feminists who had worked on behalf of women's rights throughout the 1940s and 1950s. According to *Newsweek* magazine, the strikers "were perfectly ordinary looking women. . . . They looked like the women you would see driving ranch wagons, or shopping at the village market, or attending PTA meetings. . . . Many [were] wheeling baby buggies or strollers." Within a year their numbers grew to several hundred thousand. The FBI kept the group under surveillance, and in 1962 the leaders were called before the House Un-American Activities Committee (HUAC). Under questioning, these women spoke as mothers, claiming that saving American children from nuclear extinction was the essence of Americanism. They brought their babies to the hearings and refused to be intimidated by their

Washington Post. Reprinted by permission of the D.C. Public Library

■ On November 1, 1961, 50,000 women in communities across the country took to the streets to protest nuclear testing. Under the sponsorship of Women Strike for Peace, these demonstrators used their authority as mothers, and brought along their children, to highlight their stake in the future.

Rachel Carson, *Silent Spring*

In 1962, Silent Spring, *Rachel Carson's eloquent exposé of the chemical industry's deadly impact on the health of the planet, landed on the best-seller list, where it stayed for months. The book, which eventually sold 1.5 million copies and remains in print today, galvanized the environmental movement of the 1960s and 1970s. Carson called the chemical industry "a child of the Second World War" and creator of "elixirs of death." She reported that annual pesticide production increased from 124 million pounds in 1947 to 637 million pounds by 1960. Twenty years later it had reached 2.4 billion pounds. "In the course of developing agents of chemical warfare," she noted, "some of the chemicals created in the laboratory were found to be lethal to insects. The discovery did not come by chance: insects were widely used to test chemicals as agents of death for man."*

Environmentalist Rachel Carson, author of *Silent Spring.*

Alfred Eisenstaedt/TimePix

It took hundreds of millions of years to produce the life that now inhabits the earth—eons of time in which that developing and evolving and diversifying life reached a state of adjustment and balance with its surroundings. The environment, rigorously shaping and directing the life it supported, contained elements that were hostile as well as supporting. Certain rocks gave out dangerous radiation; even within the light of the sun, from which all life draws its energy, there were short-wave radiations with power to injure. Given time—time not in years but in millennia—life adjusts, and a balance has been reached. For time is the essential ingredient; but in the modern world there is no time.

The rapidity of change and the speed with which new situations are created follow the impetuous and heedless pace of man rather than the deliberate pace of nature. Radiation is no longer merely the background radiation of rocks, the bombardment of cosmic rays, the ultraviolet of the sun that have existed before there was any life on earth; radiation is now the unnatural creation of man's tampering with the atom. The chemicals to which life is asked to make its adjustment are no longer merely the calcium and silica and copper and all the rest of the minerals washed out of the rocks and carried in rivers to the sea; they are the synthetic creations of man's inventive mind, brewed in his laboratories, and having no counterparts in nature.

To adjust to these chemicals would require time on the scale that is nature's; it would require not merely the years of a man's life but the life of generations. And even this, were it by some miracle possible, would be futile, for the new chemicals come from our laboratories in an endless stream; almost five hundred annually find their way into actual use in the United States alone. The figure is staggering and its implications are not easily grasped—500 new chemicals to which the bodies of men and animals are required somehow to adapt each year, chemicals totally outside the limits of biologic experience.

Among them are many that are used in man's war against nature. Since the mid-1940s over 200 basic chemicals have been created for use in killing insects, weeds, rodents, and other organisms described in the modern vernacular as "pests"; and they are sold under several thousand different brand names.

These sprays, dusts, and aerosols are now applied almost universally to farms, gardens, forests, and homes—nonselective chemicals that have the power to kill every insect, the "good" and the "bad," to still the song of the birds and the leaping of fish in the streams, to coat the leaves with a deadly film, and to linger on in the soil—all this though the intended target may be only a few weeds or insects. Can anyone believe it is possible to lay down such a barrage of poisons on the surface of the earth without making it unfit for all life? They should not be called "insecticides" but "biocides." ■

congressional inquisitors as supporters cheered and threw flowers from the gallery. These women carried the banner of motherhood into political activism, much as their nineteenth-century predecessors had done. Their ability to make a mockery of the dreaded congressional committee that had broken the spirits and ruined the careers of so many innocent citizens indicated that the consensus supporting the nuclear arms race was losing its grip.

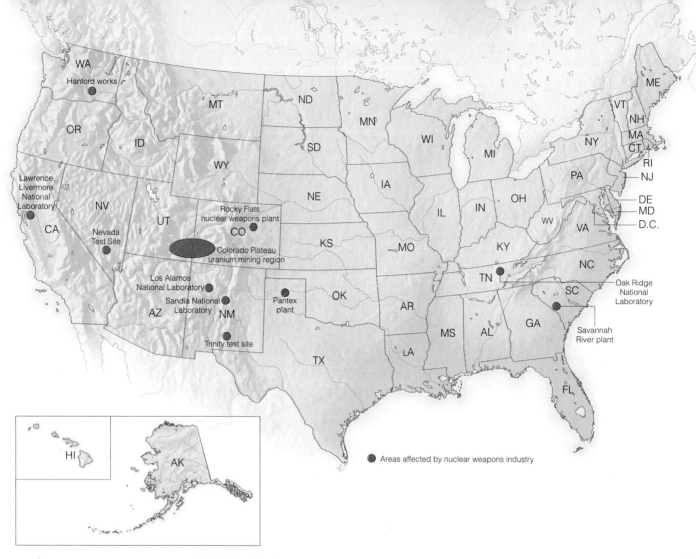

■ MAP 25.3
THE NUCLEAR LANDSCAPE The production and testing of nuclear weapons affected many regions across the country, especially in the West and South. Sites established during World War II remained active during the Cold War, as the nuclear arms race accelerated. The sites included testing grounds, uranium mining areas, laboratories, and plants where weapons were manufactured.

Decades later, the antinuclear protesters were vindicated—unfortunately too late for many people exposed to radiation during the early years of the Cold War. At the time, the real dangers of nuclear testing had not yet come to light. But in the 1980s and 1990s, top-secret documents were declassified, confirming that people living in the path of fallout from nuclear test sites, as well as military personnel working at or near the sites during the 1940s and 1950s, suffered disproportionately from cancer and other illnesses caused by radioactivity.

The Kennedy Era

John Fitzgerald Kennedy was the first American president born in the twentieth century and the first Catholic president. In his inaugural address, he claimed that "the torch has been passed to a new generation." It was a fitting metaphor for a young man who had been reared to compete and to win, whether the contest was athletic, intellectual, or political. But at the time of his election, it was not clear that a new generation had grabbed the torch. The young candidate was largely the creation of his father, Joseph, whose forebears had emigrated from Ireland during the 1840s. Joseph Kennedy rose to power and wealth as a financier, Hollywood executive, and ambassador to England. Ambitious and demanding, the elder Kennedy was known for his ruthlessness in business and politics and for his blatant philandering. He groomed his oldest son, Joseph P. Kennedy, Jr., for greatness, specifically for the presidency. But when young Joe was killed in World War II, the father's ambitions settled on the next in line, John.

John (Jack) Kennedy became a hero during World War II, winning military honors for rescuing his crewmates on his patrol boat, PT-109, when it was rammed by a Japanese destroyer. The rescue left him with a painful back impairment and exacerbated the symptoms of Addison's disease, which plagued him all his life and necessitated daily cortisone injections. His father coached him to bear up under the pain, hide his infirmity, and project an image of health and vitality. "Vigor" was a word Kennedy used often and an aura he projected, inspiring a national craze for physical fitness that survives to this day. Young JFK also emulated his father's brash sexual promiscuity, even after his marriage to Jacqueline Bouvier in 1953.

In 1946 Kennedy won election to the House of Representatives, and in 1952 he defeated the incumbent Republican Henry Cabot Lodge to become the Democratic senator from Massachusetts. JFK's father financed all of his political campaigns, and in 1960 the elderly Kennedy bankrolled and masterminded JFK's run for president. Kennedy selected as his running mate the powerful Senate majority leader, Lyndon B. Johnson of Texas, whom he had battled for the nomination. Concerned that his Catholicism would be a liability in the campaign, Kennedy spoke publicly about his faith, explaining that his religious beliefs would not interfere with his ability to do the job.

TABLE 25-3			
The Election of 1960			
Candidate	Political Party	Popular Vote	Electoral Vote
John F. Kennedy	Democratic	34,227,096	303
Richard M. Nixon	Republican	34,108,546	219

Just before the election, with the help of his brother Robert—whom he later appointed as attorney general—Kennedy arranged to have Martin Luther King, Jr., released from prison in Georgia, where hostile authorities had sentenced him to six months in jail for a minor traffic violation. This intervention secured the African American vote for Kennedy and the support of other minorities: Mexican Americans formed "Viva Kennedy" clubs throughout the Southwest. Voters of color helped Kennedy defeat his Republican foe, Eisenhower's vice president Richard Nixon, by a slim margin.

Domestic Policy

With such a thin margin of victory, Kennedy lacked a popular mandate for change. But he quickly established himself as an eloquent leader. In his inaugural address, the new president inspired the nation with his memorable words, "And so, my fellow Americans, ask not what your country can do for you; ask what you can do for your country." Focusing his address on foreign policy, he declared, "Let every nation know . . . that we shall pay any price, bear any burden, meet any hardship, support any friend, oppose any foe to assure the survival and the success of liberty." In his first two years, he sought mainly to avoid division at home and to wage the Cold War forcefully abroad. He believed that prosperity was the best way to spread the fruits of affluence, rather than government programs that would promote a redistribution of wealth. Accordingly, he supported corporate tax cuts to stimulate the economy, which grew at a rate of 5 percent each year from 1961 to 1966. Kennedy's economic policies continued many of the probusiness initiatives of Eisenhower.

Although Democrats held strong majorities in both houses, powerful southern conservatives often teamed up with Republicans to form a functional majority in Congress to defeat reform legislation. Kennedy knew that it would be futile to champion the cause of civil rights in the face of that alliance. But he did support issues important to his working-class constituents and proposed a number of legislative initiatives, including increasing the minimum wage,

Anticommunism

Throughout the twentieth century, American leaders have felt uneasy about revolutionary movements. On one hand, the United States was the great model of a successful anticolonial rebellion against a European colonial power. But on the other hand, the United States wanted to preserve order and stability in the world. The Russian Revolution of 1917 raised particular concerns because the victorious new communist regime denied Soviet citizens the essential democratic and economic principles that Americans cherished: free speech and elections, freedom of religious expression, private property, and capitalism. The United States officially refused to recognize the Soviet government from 1917 to 1933, as well as the People's Republic of China from 1949 until 1978 and Fidel Castro's Cuba from 1961 until today.

With these national principles and policies providing a foundation, anticommunism tapped widespread political and emotional passions within the United States. At times those passions, whipped up in moments of unsettling international or domestic events, led to extensive domestic repression of the very freedoms Americans have long cherished: free speech and political choice.

The first major wave of anticommunism in the United States came after World War I, in the wake of the founding of the American Communist party. The success of the Bolshevik Revolution and the establishment of the Soviet Union energized a segment of socialists to form a Communist party in the United States in support of Soviet communism. The Red Scare of 1919–1920 was a wave of political repression that targeted not only communists but also left-leaning immigrants, radicals, and labor unions. Immigration officials rounded up thousands of foreign-born radicals and deported many, including the anarchist Emma Goldman. Many employers also used the rallying cry of anticommunism to break strikes and suppress unions. The Red Scare effectively silenced the Communist party and much of the left throughout the 1920s.

During the Great Depression of the 1930s, as fascism emerged in Europe, the Communist party attracted new members as well as thousands of liberal sympathizers. But enthusiasm for communism diminished in 1939 with the Nazi–Soviet pact and the communist opposition to Roosevelt's foreign policy. Anticommunist sentiment declined in 1941, when Hitler invaded Russia and the Soviet Union became an ally. The alliance was tense, however, as the United States vied with the Soviet Union over power in the postwar world.

The Cold War transformed anticommunism from a right-wing to a mainstream ideology and made it central to American politics and domestic

---

health care for the aged and increased Social Security benefits, and the creation of the Department of Housing and Urban Development (HUD).

When the steel industry challenged Kennedy's authority and threatened his economic policy by announcing a major price increase shortly after he had helped to negotiate a new contract with the steel union that would have kept prices stable, he mobilized all the power of his administration to force the steel magnates to back down. Kennedy also demonstrated strong leadership in the space program, presiding over the first manned space flight and declaring that the United States would land a man on the moon by the end of the 1960s.

Foreign Policy

Kennedy was the first U.S. president to understand and recognize the legitimacy of movements for national self-determination in the Third World. In 1957, while still in the Senate, he gave a speech calling on the French to grant independence to Algeria, which was still under French rule. As President, he endeavored to support movements to end colonial rule while at the same time containing the spread of communism. His efforts earned him a great deal of goodwill among Africans and other non-Europeans. But if nationalist movements appeared friendly to the Soviet Union, Kennedy worked against them. Critical of Eisenhower's defense policies but determined to continue his struggle against the spread of communism, Kennedy sharply increased military spending and nuclear arms build-up as a show of strength and preparedness against possible Soviet aggression.

One of Kennedy's most popular initiatives was the creation of the Peace Corps, a program that sent Americans, especially young people, to nations around the world to work on culture. Because the United States vied with the Soviet Union for strategic power and territorial influence, the Communist party, with its links to the USSR, was considered a subversive organization. In 1947, the Truman administration barred from government jobs anyone associated with communists, and in 1949 the Justice Department prosecuted the 11 top leaders of the party for violation of the 1940 Smith Act, which made it illegal "to teach and advocate the overthrow and destruction of the United States government by force and violence." They were all convicted and sentenced to prison terms. Under the Smith Act, several hundred communists went to jail, while the House Un-American Activities Committee (HUAC) investigated suspected communist subversives. Hollywood became a primary target of anticommunism in the late 1940s and early 1950s, leading to the blacklisting of dozens of filmmakers

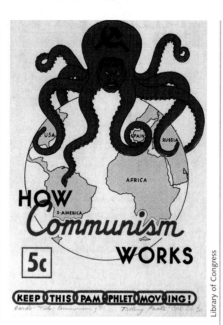

Anticommunist pamphlet published by the Catholic Library Service.

and actors who refused to "name names" before HUAC.

Senator Joseph McCarthy and other zealots used anticommunism to further their own political ambitions at a time when Democrats were on the defensive for being allegedly "soft" on communism. Official anticommunism targeted not only members of left-wing political organizations but also gays, lesbians, and others who allegedly might be vulnerable to blackmail and therefore should not be allowed to work in government offices. The Federal Bureau of Investigation (FBI), under the leadership of J. Edgar Hoover, made anticommunism a high priority. The FBI targeted Martin Luther King, Jr., and other civil rights activists whom Hoover believed were communist agents seeking to destabilize American society. By the late 1950s the anticommunist hysteria had subsided, but it remained part of the political culture throughout the Cold War. During the 1980s, President Ronald W. Reagan revived anticommunist rhetoric when he called the Soviet Union the "evil empire." ■

development projects. In 1961 Kennedy signed the Charter of Punta del Este with several Latin American countries, establishing the Organization of American States (OAS) and the Alliance for Progress, a program designed to prevent the spread of anti-Americanism and communist insurgencies in Latin America. The alliance offered $20 billion in loans to OAS countries for democratic development initiatives.

Kennedy continued the strategies of Truman and Eisenhower to fight communism in South Vietnam by supporting the corrupt regime of Ngo Dingh Diem. But the National Liberation Front (NLF), founded in 1960 and supported by Ho Chi Minh's communist regime in North Vietnam, gained the upper hand in its struggle against Diem. In response, Kennedy increased the number of military advisers there from 800 to 17,000. By 1963 it was obvious that Diem's brutal regime was about to fall to the NLF, and Kennedy allowed U.S. military advisers and diplomats to encourage Diem's dissenting generals to depose and assassinate Diem.

Kennedy also faced a crisis brewing in Cuba. Fidel Castro's revolution initially represented the sort of democratic insurgency that Kennedy wanted to support. But Castro's socialism turned the United States against him, and he established close ties with the Soviet Union. Kennedy now saw the small impoverished island as a major threat where "communist influence . . . festers some 90 miles off the coast of Florida." During the Eisenhower administration, the CIA began planning an invasion of Cuba with the help of Cuban exiles in Florida. Kennedy's national security advisers persuaded Kennedy to allow the invasion to proceed.

On April 17, 1961, U.S.-backed and -trained anticommunist forces, most of them Cuban exiles, landed at the Bahia de Cochinas (Bay of Pigs) on the southern coast of Cuba. Castro expected the invasion—his agents in Florida had infiltrated the Cuban exiles—so his well-prepared troops quickly surrounded and captured the invaders. With no domestic uprising against Castro to support the invasion, Kennedy quickly realized that his only chance of success would be to call in the military with large-scale air support. Unwilling to take that step, Kennedy pulled back in humiliating defeat, telling his adviser Clark Clifford, "I have made a tragic mistake." Nevertheless, Kennedy continued to support covert efforts that tried but failed to destabilize Cuba and assassinate Castro.

Another crisis soon erupted in Berlin. Located 200 miles deep in East Germany, with only two highways connecting it to West Germany, West Berlin was a showcase of western material superiority and an espionage center for the western powers. It was also an important symbolic site, reassuring West Berliners along with western Europeans that the United States would not abandon them. At a summit in Vienna between Kennedy and Khrushchev in June 1961, Khrushchev threatened to end the western presence in Berlin and unite the city with the rest of East Germany. His plan was motivated in part to stop the steady stream of East Germans into West Berlin. Kennedy refused to relinquish West Berlin. On August 13, 1961, the East German government constructed a wall to separate East and West Berlin. Guards patrolled the wall with orders to shoot anyone who tried to cross, and many who tried lost their lives. Two years later, Kennedy stood in front of the wall and pledged to defend the West Berliners, making his memorable statement of solidarity, "*Ich bin ein Berliner*" ("I am a Berliner").

> *Kennedy put the Strategic Air Command on full alert for possible nuclear war.*

The most serious foreign policy crisis of Kennedy's presidency came in 1962, when the Soviet Union, at Castro's invitation, began to install intermediate-range nuclear missiles in Cuba. Kennedy's close advisers presented a series of options for actions that could be taken in response. The most dramatic and dangerous would be a full-scale military invasion of the island, which would topple Castro but would surely have prompted military retaliation by the Soviet Union. Another option was a more limited military intervention, an air strike to destroy the missiles before they became operational. Others proposed a blockade of Cuban ports to prevent the missiles from entering. Another possibility was to negotiate secretly with Castro, Soviet leaders, or both. Kennedy decided against behind-the-scenes negotiations as well as the drastic move of military intervention and instead established a "quarantine" around the island to block Soviet ships from reaching Cuba, hoping that the Soviet Union would back down and withdraw the missiles. A quarantine, unlike a blockade, was not considered an act of war; nevertheless, Kennedy put the Strategic Air Command on full alert for possible nuclear war.

It was a risky move. On national television, Kennedy warned the Soviet Union to remove the missiles or face the military might of the United States: "We will not prematurely or unnecessarily risk the costs of worldwide nuclear war in which even the fruits of victory would be ashes in our mouth, but neither will we shrink from that risk at any time it must be faced." Khrushchev accused Kennedy of bringing the two nations to the brink of nuclear war. For the next five days, tensions mounted as Russian ships hovered in the water beyond the quarantine zone. Finally Khrushchev proposed an agreement, offering to remove the missiles if the United States would agree not to invade Cuba. In secret negotiations, Kennedy also privately promised to remove the Jupiter missiles in Turkey as soon as the crisis was over. The two leaders managed to diffuse the crisis, but they were both sobered by the experience of having come to the brink of nuclear war. They soon established a telephone "hotline" linking the White House and the Kremlin for quicker communication in any future crisis. In 1963 the two leaders signed a nuclear test ban treaty.

A Year of Turning Points

In 1963 the President's Commission on the Status of Women, which Kennedy had appointed under the leadership of Eleanor Roosevelt, published a report that documented widespread discrimination against women in jobs, pay, education, and the professions. In response to the findings, Kennedy issued a presidential order requiring the civil service to hire people "without regard to sex" and supported passage of the Equal Pay Act of 1963. The commission's report, along with the publication the same year of Betty Friedan's call to arms, *The Feminine Mystique,* provided fuel for the feminist movement that burst across the nation in the next few years.

In the spring of that same year, in Birmingham, Alabama, Martin Luther King, Jr., led a silent and peaceful march through the city. Chief of Police Bull Connor unleashed the police, who blasted the demonstrators with fire hoses and attacked them with vicious police dogs. Four black children were later killed when segregationists bombed an African American church.

The Kennedy administration responded by bringing the full force of its authority to bear on the officials in Birmingham. But the crisis intensified. Alabama's segregationist governor, George Wallace, refused to admit two black students to the University of Alabama, threatening to stand in the doorway to block their entrance.

Finally, on June 10, 1963, Kennedy federalized the Alabama National Guard and for the first time went before the American people to declare himself forcefully on the side of the civil rights protesters and to propose a civil rights bill. The violence in the South had raised "a moral issue," he declared, "as old as Scriptures and . . . as clear as the Constitution." A few months later, on August 28, more than 250,000 people gathered at the nation's capitol in front of the Lincoln Memorial for the culmination of the March on Washington, a huge demonstration for jobs as well as freedom, where Martin Luther King, Jr., delivered his inspiring "I Have a Dream" speech, which included these memorable words:

> I say to you today, my friends, that in spite of the difficulties and frustrations of the moment, I still have a dream. It is a dream deeply rooted in the American dream.
>
> I have a dream that one day this nation will rise up and live out the true meaning of its creed: "We hold these truths to be self-evident: that all men are created equal."
>
> I have a dream that one day on the red hills of Georgia the sons of former slaves and the sons of former slave owners will be able to sit down together at a table of brotherhood. I have a dream that one day even the state of Mississippi, a desert state, sweltering with the heat of injustice and oppression, will be transformed into an oasis of freedom and justice. I have a dream that my four children will one day live in a nation where they will not be judged by the color of their skin but by the content of their character. . . . Let freedom ring from every hill and every molehill of Mississippi. From every mountainside, let freedom ring. When we let freedom ring, when we let it ring from every village and every hamlet, from every state and every city, we will be able to speed up that day when all of God's children, black men and white men, Jews and Gentiles, Protestants and Catholics, will be able to join hands and sing in the words of the old Negro spiritual, "Free at last! Free at last! Thank God Almighty, we are free at last!"

In the fall of 1963, a confident Kennedy began planning his reelection campaign for the next year. To mobilize support he visited Texas. "Here we are in Dallas," he said on November 22, 1963, "and it looks like everything in Texas is going to be fine for us." Within an hour of uttering those optimistic words, the president lay dying of an assassin's bullet.

As shock and grief spread across the nation, a bizarre series of events confounded efforts to bring the assassin to justice. Police arrested Lee Harvey Oswald, who had previously lived in the Soviet Union and who had loose ties to organized crime and to political groups interested in Cuba. Oswald claimed that he was innocent. But before he could be brought to trial, Oswald himself was murdered. Jack Ruby, a nightclub owner who also had links to organized crime, shot Oswald while he was in the custody of the Dallas police—an event witnessed by millions on live television. Ruby later died in prison. The newly sworn-in president, Lyndon B. Johnson, appointed a commission to investigate the assassination under the leadership of Supreme Court Chief Justice Earl Warren. The Warren Commission eventually issued a report concluding that Oswald and Ruby had both acted alone. The commission findings created a heated controversy. Many people at the time and since believed that there was evidence of a conspiracy. In 1978 a panel of the House of Representatives suggested that Kennedy may have been the victim of a plot, possibly involving the Mafia. Conspiracy theories continue to circulate to this day, finding expression in dozens of books, articles, and motion pictures.

Conclusion

During the years between the election of Dwight D. Eisenhower and the assassination of John F. Kennedy, the nation experienced unprecedented prosperity as increasing numbers of Americans moved into middle-class suburbs and enjoyed the fruits of a rapidly expanding consumer economy. Men and women rushed into marriage and childbearing, creating the baby boom and a powerful domestic ideology resting on distinct gender roles for women and men. At the same time, fears of nuclear war, intense anticommunism, and pressures to conform to mainstream political and cultural values contributed to anxieties and discontent.

Beneath the apparently tranquil surface, some Americans began to resist the limitations and exclusions of the widely touted "American way of life." African Americans in the South demanded their rightful place as full citizens, challenging the Jim Crow system and accelerating the civil rights movement through nonviolent protests, boycotts, and sit-ins. Young people created a vibrant youth culture to the pulsating rhythms of rock 'n' roll. Beatniks, peace activists, and environmentalists expressed incipient political and cultural dissent. The rumblings of vast social change had already begun and would explode in the years ahead.

Sites to Visit

We Shall Overcome: Historic Places of the Civil Rights Movement
www.cr.nps.gov/NR/travel/civilrights/index.htm

This site of the National Register of Historic Places provides maps and information about the historic locations of the civil rights movement.

Dwight David Eisenhower
www.ipl.org/ref/POTUS/ddeisenhower.html

This site contains basic information about Eisenhower's election and presidency, and online biography.

The Literature & Culture of the American 1950s
dept.english.upenn.edu/~afilreis/50s/home.html

This site by University of Pennsylvania Professor Al Filreis contains a large array of 1950s documents, literature, and images.

Levittown: Documents of an Ideal American Suburb
tigger.uic.edu/~pbhales/Levittown/

Peter Bacon Hales of the Art History Department at the University of Illinois at Chicago developed this website, which includes images, articles, and information about the post-World War II Levittown suburb.

Hollywood and the Movies during the 1950s
lib.berkeley.edu/MRC/50sbib.html

This site from the University of California at Berkeley libraries includes information about Hollywood during the 1950s, and links to related sites, such as the Hollywood blacklist and film noir.

Rock and Roll
www.rockhall.com/home/default.asp

This website of the Rock and Roll Hall of Fame and Museum includes information about the history and major artists of rock and roll.

Little Rock 1959: Pages from History—The Central High Crisis
www.ardemgaz.com/prev/central/

This site documents the events surrounding the effort to desegregate Central High in Little Rock, Arkansas, in 1959.

From *Plessy v. Ferguson* to *Brown v. Board of Education*: The Supreme Court Rules on School Desegregation
www.yale.edu/ynhti/curriculum/units/1982/3/82.03.06.x.html

This site includes information about the landmark Supreme Court decision compiled by the Yale-New Haven Teachers Institute.

The Civil Rights Era
lcweb2.loc.gov/ammem/aaohtml/exhibit/aopart9.html

This Library of Congress site includes information about the people, events, and developments of the civil rights movement.

John F. Kennedy
www.ipl.org/ref/POTUS/jfkennedy.html

This site contains basic information about Kennedy's election and presidency, and online biography.

For Further Reading

General

Taylor Branch, *Parting the Waters: America in the King Years, 1954–1963* (1988).

William H. Chafe, *The Unfinished Journey: America Since World War II* (1986).

Pete Daniel, *Lost Revolutions: The South in the 1950s* (2000).

Eric Foner, *The Story of American Freedom* (1998).

Godfrey Hodgson, *America in Our Time* (1976).

Cold War, Warm Hearth

Stephanie Coontz, *The Way We Never Were: American Families and the Nostalgia Trap* (1992).

Barbara Ehrenreich, *The Hearts of Men: American Dreams and the Flight from Commitment* (1984).

Ruth Feldstein, *Motherhood in Black and White: Race and Sex in American Liberalism, 1930–1965* (2000).

Kenneth T. Jackson, *Crabgrass Frontier: The Suburbanization of the United States* (1985).

George Katona, *The Mass Consumption Society* (1964).

Elaine Tyler May, *Homeward Bound: American Families in the Cold War Era* (1999).

The Civil Rights Movement

Clayborne Carson, *In Struggle: SNCC and the Black Awakening of the 1960s* (1981).

Mary Dudziak, *Cold War Civil Rights: Equality as Cold War Policy, 1946–1968* (2000).

Hugh Davis Graham, *The Civil Rights Era: Origins and Development of National Policy* (1990).

Steven F. Lawson, *Running for Freedom: Civil Rights and Black Politics in America Since 1941* (1990).

Harvard Sitkoff, *The Struggle for Black Equality, 1954–1992* (1993).

The Eisenhower Years

Stephen E. Ambrose, *Eisenhower* (1983–84).

Thomas Borstelmann, *The Cold War and the Color Line: Race Relations and American Foreign Policy Since 1945* (2001).

Robert F. Burk, *The Eisenhower Administration and Black Civil Rights* (1984).

Robert A. Divine, *The Sputnik Challenge* (1993).

Peter B. Dow, *Schoolhouse Politics: Lessons from the Sputnik Era* (1991).

Dwight D. Eisenhower, *The White House Years: Waging Peace, 1956–1961* (1965).

Fred I. Greenstein, *The Hidden-Hand Presidency: Eisenhower as Leader* (1994).

Outsiders and Opposition

Winifred Breines, *Young, White, and Miserable: Growing Up Female in the Fifties* (1994).

Paul Brooks, *The House of Life: Rachel Carson at Work* (1972).

Rachel Carson, *Silent Spring* (1963).

Betty Friedan, *The Feminine Mystique* (1963).

James Gilbert, *A Cycle of Outrage: America's Reaction to the Juvenile Delinquent in the 1950s* (1986).

Charlie Gillett, *Sound of the City: The Rise of Rock and Roll* (1983).

Serge Guilbaut, *How New York Stole the Idea of Modern Art* (1985).

Joyce Johnson, *Minor Characters: A Young Woman's Coming-of-Age in the Beat Orbit of Jack Kerouac* (1999).

Joanne Meyerowitz, ed., *Not June Cleaver: Women and Gender in Postwar America, 1945–1960* (1994).

Leslie Reagan, *When Abortion Was a Crime: Women, Medicine, and the Law in the United States, 1867–1973* (1997).

Rickie Solinger, *Wake Up Little Susie: Single Pregnancy and Race Before Roe v. Wade* (1992).

The Kennedy Era

Roger Hilsman, *To Move a Nation: The Politics of Foreign Policy in the Administration of John F. Kennedy* (1967).

Elizabeth Cobbs Hoffman, *All You Need Is Love: The Peace Corps and the Spirit of the 1960s* (1998).

Herbert S. Parmet, *J.F.K.: The Presidency of John F. Kennedy* (1983).

Arthur M. Schlesinger, Jr., *A Thousand Days: John F. Kennedy in the White House* (1965).

Online Practice Test

Test your understanding of this chapter with interactive review quizzes at

www.ablongman.com/jonescreatedequal/chapter25

Additional Photo Credits

Page 835: AP/Wide World Photos
Page 836: Library of Congress
Page 839: Photofest
Page 849: Courtesy, Janice L. and David Frent
Page 851: Roger Ressmeyer/CORBIS
Page 863: Fair Street Pictures

The Nation Divides: The Vietnam War and Social Conflict, 1964–1971

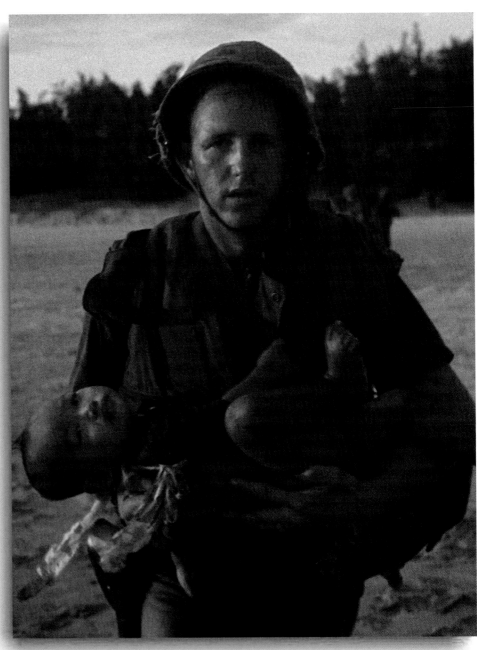

Paul Schutzer/TimePix

■ The deployment of hundreds of thousands of American soldiers in Vietnam intimately affected life there, sometimes in terrible ways and sometimes in helpful ways.

THE SOFT-SPOKEN BLACK MAN WITH THE STRANGE ACCENT FIRST SHOWED UP IN THE small town of McComb, Mississippi, in the summer of 1961. Robert Parris Moses had come on a mission of democracy: he was there to encourage impoverished African Americans to register to vote. He had grown up in Harlem, attended Hamilton College in upstate New York on a scholarship, and was doing graduate work in philosophy at Harvard when his mother's death brought him back to Manhattan to help care for his father. Moses was teaching math at an elite private school when the student sit-in movement against segregation spread across the upper South in the spring of 1960. Deeply impressed by the courage and leadership of those young black southerners, he went south that summer to work with Martin Luther King, Jr.'s Southern Christian Leadership Conference. The following spring, Moses returned to the South as a full-time organizer for the new Student Nonviolent Coordinating Committee (SNCC).

A leading spokesman for the Black Muslims, Malcolm X converted to orthodox Islam and softened his antiwhite rhetoric in the 2 years before his murder in 1965. Like SNCC's Bob Moses, Malcolm increasingly identified with the Third World. Here he is shown in Egypt on a 1964 pilgrimage to Mecca, Saudi Arabia.

Encouraging citizens to vote in the leading nation of the "free world" was a subversive act in 1961, at least when the citizens had dark skin and lived in the southeastern states of the former Confederacy. Over the next 4 years in the Deep South, Bob Moses paid a price for his commitments. Local police imprisoned him, white supremacists beat him severely, and they murdered dozens of his fellow activists in the black freedom movement. But Moses remained committed to nonviolence and racial integration. His quiet courage became legendary in the movement. One summer night in 1962, he returned to a deserted SNCC office in Greenwood, Mississippi, that had just been ransacked by a white mob; three other SNCC workers had barely escaped with their lives. Moses looked around, made up a bed in the corner of the devastated main room, and went to sleep. He refused to be intimidated.

For all his distinctiveness, Moses did not promote himself as a charismatic leader. Like his comrades in SNCC, he did not believe in traditional, top-down leadership. The women and men in SNCC worked instead to get local black communities to organize themselves and to find their leadership among their own members. When others became too dependent on his guidance, Moses even dropped his biblical surname and became simply "Bob Parris" to reduce his public profile. Such rejection of hierarchy put SNCC at odds with other civil rights organizations and with the national Democratic party, which sought black support. By 1964 Moses and other freedom workers grew disillusioned with white liberal leadership, especially after the Democratic convention that August, where President Lyndon Johnson crushed the integrated Mississippi Freedom Democratic party's bid to replace the all-white regular Mississippi delegation. Two trips to Africa expanded Moses' sense of connection to the Third World, and he became increasingly involved with the growing movement against the U.S. war in Vietnam. The federal government responded by drafting him. Moses moved to Canada to avoid being inducted to fight a war he opposed, and then went to east Africa, where he and his wife taught school and raised a family in Tanzania for almost a decade. He returned to the United States only after President Jimmy Carter's general amnesty for draft resisters in 1977.

The trajectory of Bob Moses' life across these years suggests much about the 1960s. An extraordinary number of idealistic young people became involved in public life in an effort to make real their nation's abstract promises of freedom and justice. The civil rights movement inspired the social movements that followed: for ending the war, for preserving the environment, and for liberating women, Latinos, Indians, and gay men and lesbians. But organizing for change inevitably brought activists up against fierce resistance from what they called "the establishment." Disillusionment and radicalization often followed. Whereas Moses went to Africa, other young African Americans moved toward black nationalism at home, a proud cultural identity at odds with the pursuit of integration. Public life became deeply contentious by 1968 as young radicals challenged more conservative citizens on issues of race, war, and gender.

The escalating American war in Southeast Asia loomed over all. Lyndon Johnson brought the nation to its apex of liberal reform with his extensive Great Society legislation. His purpose was to complete and surpass the New Deal promise of his hero, Franklin Roosevelt. However, the high-flying hopes of Democratic liberals crashed to earth with the destructive war that the Johnson administration waged against seasoned communist revolutionaries in far-off Vietnam. Out of the wreckage of 1968 emerged a Republican president, Richard Nixon, and a growing conservative backlash against the social changes advocated by people of color, the counterculture, the antiwar movement, and the rising tide of women's liberation. By the beginning of the 1970s, American politics turned to the right, even as American culture generally remained more tolerant of different lifestyles and values than it had been before the 1960s. This libertarian combination of distrusting government while accepting greater cultural diversity has predominated in American life ever since.

Lyndon Johnson and the Apex of Liberalism

Wealth provided the foundation on which the Great Society was built. American economic expansion since World War II had created history's richest nation by 1960. From 1961 to 1966, the economy accelerated at an annual growth rate of more than 5 percent with very low inflation, stimulated by large tax cuts and extensive military spending. The 41 percent increase in per capita income during the 1960s was not evenly distributed, however. Economist Paul Samuelson explained in 1970, "If we made an income pyramid out of a child's blocks, with each layer portraying $1000 of income, the peak would be far higher than the Eiffel Tower, but almost all of us would be within a yard of the ground." And the distribution of wealth (stocks and real estate) was far more skewed than that of income. U.S. policymakers believed that economic expansion would continue indefinitely and the nation could therefore afford government policies to improve the welfare of less affluent Americans.

The New President

Lyndon Baines Johnson was one of the most remarkable American characters of the twentieth century. Journalist David Halberstam called him "a man of stunning force, drive and intelligence, and of equally stunning insecurity"—both a giant among political leaders and a bully with those who worked for him. Johnson grew up in a family struggling to stay out of

■ Lyndon Johnson took the presidential oath of office on board Air Force One, returning to Washington from Dallas, where John Kennedy had just been assassinated on November 22, 1963. His wife, Lady Bird, is on his right, and Jacqueline Kennedy, still in blood-stained clothes, stands on his left. Johnson adroitly channeled the public outpouring of grief for the murdered young president into support for their shared legislative goals.

poverty in the Texas hill country west of Austin. He entered Democratic politics early as an avid supporter of Franklin Roosevelt and the New Deal, aided by the business savvy and loyalty of his wife, Lady Bird Johnson, who grew wealthy through ownership of TV and radio stations. As First Lady, she became widely known for her leadership in highway beautification. Lyndon Johnson rose like a rocket through Congress to become perhaps the most powerful Senate majority leader ever (1954–1960) and then vice president (1961–1963). Kennedy's assassination catapulted him into the Oval Office as the nation's first Texan president.

Like his home state, Johnson was physically big and at times intimidating. His earthy humor and homely style contrasted sharply with Kennedy's telegenic sophistication. Eastern elites cringed at the idea of Johnson as Kennedy's successor in the White House; the fact that Kennedy was killed in Texas did not help. But Johnson retained Kennedy's cabinet and advisers and used the memory of the fallen young president to rally support for his administration. Johnson turned out to be the more liberal of the two men in part because his early years in Texas had given him a visceral understanding of poverty and discrimination that his predecessor lacked. Johnson's focus was different, too. He retained Kennedy's anticommunist commitments abroad, but his heart remained at home. "I don't want to be the President who built empires, or sought grandeur, or extended dominion," he told the nation. He wanted to perfect American society: to enhance American security by refashioning the central nation of the "free world" into a model for all others.

First he had to win reelection because less than a year remained until voters went to the polls in 1964. The Republicans nominated right-wing Senator Barry Goldwater of Arizona, a sign of the party's sharp swing away from its moderate eastern elements toward its fiercely conservative western and southern constituencies. Conservative organizers such as the Young Americans for Freedom considered such Republican leaders as Dwight Eisenhower and Richard Nixon too much like Democrats. Goldwater instead believed in unrestricted markets and a minimal role for the federal government in every aspect of American life except the

TABLE 26-1
The Election of 1964

Candidate	Political Party	Popular Vote	Electoral Vote
Lyndon B. Johnson	Democratic	43,126,506	486
Barry M. Goldwater	Republican	27,176,799	52

military. He spoke casually about using nuclear weapons against communists abroad. "In your heart you know he's right" his campaign slogan promised. "In your guts you know he's nuts," retorted the Democrats. Goldwater declared that "extremism in the defense of liberty is no vice," but Johnson zeroed in on that extremism and swept to the largest electoral majority of any president (61 percent). Voters also chose the most liberal Congress since the Great Depression. Few realized then that Goldwater, not Johnson, was the better indicator of where American politics would soon be heading.

The Great Society: Fighting Poverty and Discrimination

In pursuit of what he called the Great Society, Johnson first declared a "War on Poverty." No citizen in the richest nation on earth should live in squalor, he believed. The president's sen-

sitivity to this issue, despite his personal rise to wealth, fit with a growing national concern, stimulated in part by political activist Michael Harrington's widely read book *The Other Americans* (1962). The poor were everywhere, from decaying inner cities to rural areas such as Appalachia. More than one out of five Americans lived below the conservatively estimated official poverty line ($3022 for a nonfarm family of four in 1960), and 70 percent of them were white.

The president and a large congressional majority passed several measures to alleviate poverty. They sharply increased the availability of money and food stamps through the Aid to Families with Dependent Children ("welfare") program, and they raised Social Security payments to older Americans. Several programs focused on improving educational opportunities as an avenue out of poverty: Head Start offered preschool education and meals for youngsters, the Elementary and Secondary Education Act sent federal funds to the least affluent school districts, and an expanded system of student loans facilitated access to college. The Job Corps provided employment training, and Volunteers in Service to America (VISTA) served as a domestic Peace Corps, funneling people with education and skills into poor communities to serve as teachers and providers of other social services.

How well did these programs work? Americans have argued vigorously over this question ever since. Some defended the programs as reducing the number of people living in poverty and giving educational and employment opportunities to many previously deprived of such chances. Critics on the right believed that the programs instead encouraged dependence on government and thus actually worsened the problem. Critics on the left noted that the programs did not go far enough in attacking the root causes of poverty. Three conclusions seem clear about the War on Poverty. First, it did not eliminate poverty. Second, it did help reduce the number of poor people by one-third between 1960 and 1969 (22 percent to 14 percent). Third, the elderly benefited most from the higher payment schedules put into place by the War on Poverty, as the share of Americans over age 65 in the poor population dropped from 40 percent in 1959 to 16 percent by 1974.

No barrier to opportunity in the early 1960s was higher than the color bar. Both opportunist and idealist, Johnson as president shed his segregationist voting record (necessary for election in Texas before 1960) and became the most vocal proponent of racial equality ever to occupy the Oval Office. Two factors facilitated his change in position. Blatant inequalities for American citizens weakened the United States in its competition with the Soviets and Chinese for the loyalty of the nonwhite Third World majority. Moreover, the African American freedom struggle in the South had reached a boiling point. Black frustration was mounting over white brutality and the seeming indifference or even hostility of the national government. "The Negroes are tired of this patient stuff and tired of this piecemeal stuff," the president acknowledged privately. The persistence of local organizers across the South, such as Bob Moses, forced the U.S. government to move.

The Civil Rights Act of 1964 fulfilled the implicit promise of the *Brown v. Board of Education* decision a decade earlier. The 1964 act made desegregation the law of the land as it

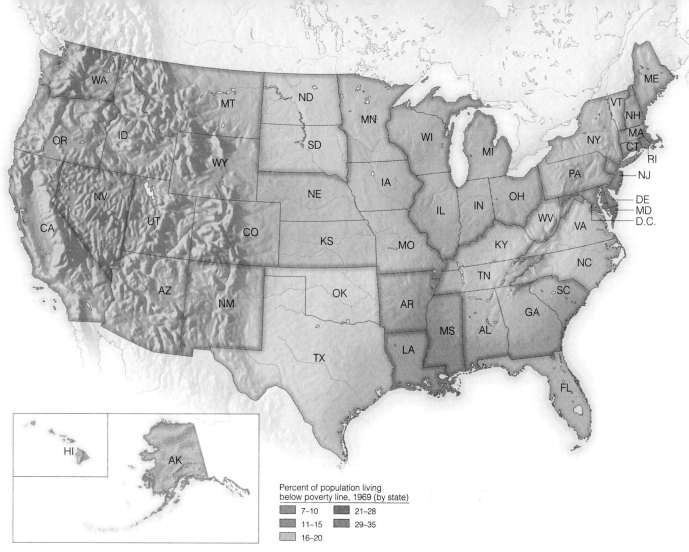

■ **MAP 26.1**

PERCENTAGE OF POPULATION LIVING BELOW THE POVERTY LINE, 1969 (BY STATE)　The United States in the 1960s was a nation of unprecedented wealth and comfort. Yet millions of Americans still lived in poverty. Prodded by other reformers, President Johnson sought to reduce the number of impoverished citizens through the Great Society programs. The southeastern and south central states had the highest poverty rates, a legacy of slavery and limited industrialization.

outlawed discrimination in employment and in public facilities such as restaurants, theaters, and hotels. When Alabama police beat peaceful marchers on the Edmund Pettis Bridge outside Selma on March 7, 1965, horrifying most national television viewers, Johnson seized the opportunity to push through Congress the Voting Rights Act. This legislation outlawed poll taxes and provided federal voting registrars in states that refused the ballot to African Americans. The single most important legislation of the twentieth century for bringing political democracy to the South, the Voting Rights Act increased the percentage of blacks voting in Mississippi from 7 percent to 60 percent in 2 years. Black electoral power began to bring unprecedented change to Dixie's political and racial landscape.

The Great Society: Improving the Quality of Life

Johnson's vision of the Great Society extended to the broader quality of life in the United States. Health care was perhaps the most fundamental issue for citizens' sense of personal security. After 1965, the new Medicare system paid for the medical needs of Americans over 65, and Medicaid underwrote health care services for the indigent. Rising concern about the quality of corporate products led to new federal efforts to protect citizens as consumers. In 1964, when more than half of adults smoked tobacco, the surgeon-general issued the first government report linking smoking to cancer. A year later, consumer advocate Ralph Nader used research studies to show that Chevrolet's sporty new Corvair was "unsafe at any speed." Despite industry resistance, higher federal standards for automotive safety followed. Public pressures also led to the establishment of new requirements for publishing the nutritional values of packaged food. The federally funded Public Broadcasting System (PBS) was established to provide television programs that were more educational than the fare tied to advertising on the three corporate networks (NBC, CBS, and ABC). In fact, most Great Society measures targeted all Americans rather than just the disadvantaged.

Nothing more directly threatened the quality of American life than the degradation of the natural environment. The costs of the unrestrained and much-heralded economic growth since World War II showed up in the nation's air, water, and land. The leaded gasoline that fueled products of the booming auto industry created smog, industrial effluents polluted lakes and rivers, and petrochemical wastes poisoned the ground. Biologist Garrett Hardin called these developments "the tragedy of the commons," wherein the pursuit of narrow individual self-interest leads to the despoiling of the common environment. For example, the very low price of gasoline in the United States compared with that of other industrialized nations did not (and still does not) recoup any of the vast environmental costs of its use. Millions of Americans read Rachel Carson's indictment of chemical pesticides in *Silent Spring* (1962). The products of science that had contributed so much to the production of wealth were turning out to have hidden costs, and a new wave of citizen action to protect the environment began to build.

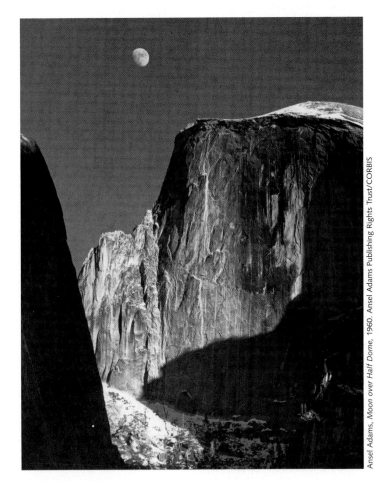

Ansel Adams, *Moon over Half Dome*, 1960. Ansel Adams Publishing Rights Trust/CORBIS

■ The moon rises over Half Dome in Yosemite Valley, Yosemite National Park, California, 1960. With this and other spectacular shots, renowned photographer Ansel Adams contributed to a growing national appreciation for wilderness in the years after World War II.

Growing public awareness prompted the Clean Air Act (1963) and the Clean Waters Act (1966), which set federal guidelines for reducing smog and preserving public drinking sources from bacterial pollution. Even the long dam-building tradition in the American West faced new questions. A quarter century after Hoover Dam blocked the Colorado River, engineers completed the Glen Canyon Dam (1963) upstream at the Arizona–Utah border, drowning one of the nation's most spectacular canyons under the new Lake Powell. Demands for the dam's removal began immediately (they continue to this day) and helped spur passage of the Wild and Scenic Rivers Act in 1968. Meanwhile, Congress passed the Wilderness Act in 1964, setting aside 9 million acres of undeveloped public lands as a place "where man is a visitor who does not remain." No longer were wild lands (almost all west of the Mississippi River) targeted solely for economic development and settlement. In a nation growing more urban and more crowded, most Americans began to accept the idea that what little wilderness remained should be preserved. By the year 2000, the wilderness system incorporated 95 million acres of roadless areas.

The Liberal Warren Court

Just as the government's executive branch responded to pressures for reform, so did the judicial branch. Dwight Eisenhower did not expect liberal leadership from Earl Warren when he named him Chief Justice of the U.S. Supreme Court in 1953. As California's secretary of state, Warren had helped implement the internment of Japanese Americans during World War II, but he later came to regret that policy. The Warren Court produced the unanimous 1954 school desegregation case, *Brown v. Board of* Education (see Chapter 25), and steadily expanded the constitutional definition of individual rights. This shift in interpreting the law reached even those deemed to have lost many of their rights: prisoners. *Gideon v. Wainwright* (1963) established the right of indigent prisoners to legal counsel, and *Escobedo v. Illinois* (1964) confirmed the right to counsel during interrogation, a critical hindrance to the use of torture. After *Miranda v. Arizona* (1966), police were required to inform anyone they arrested of their rights to remain silent and to speak to a lawyer. Reading suspects their "Miranda rights" became a touchstone scene for a whole generation of television police shows.

The Warren Court bolstered other rights of individuals against potentially coercive community pressures. Decisions in 1962 and 1963 strictly limited the practice of requiring prayers in public schools. In 1963 the Court narrowed standards for the definition of "obscenity," allowing freer expression in the arts but also in pornography. *Griswold v. Connecticut* (1965) established the use of contraceptive devices as a matter of private choice protected by the Constitution. In 1967 the Court heard the case of Mildred Jeter, a black woman, and Richard Loving, a white man, Virginians who had evaded their state's ban on interracial marriage by traveling to Washington, D.C., for their wedding and then returned to Caroline County to live. In the aptly titled *Loving v. Virginia,* the Court declared marriage one of the "basic civil rights of men" and overturned the laws of the last 16 states restricting interracial unions. Also in 1967 President Johnson appointed the esteemed chief National Association for the Advancement of Colored People (NAACP) legal counsel, Thurgood Marshall—who had mounted the successful argument in *Brown v. Board of Education* 13 years earlier—to the bench, making him the first black Supreme Court justice.

The Supreme Court's interpreting of the Constitution to expand individual rights disturbed many conservative Americans. They saw the Court as another arm of an intrusive national government that was extending its control over matters previously left to local communities. For them, the goal of integration did not justify the busing of school children. Rising crime rates troubled them more than police brutality. Many Roman Catholics were disturbed by the legalization of contraceptives. Incensed by the ban on requiring school prayer, Protestant fundamentalists sought redress through political involvement, which they had previously shunned, initiating a grassroots religious conservative movement that helped bring Ronald Reagan to power in 1980. The Warren Court served as a lightning rod for traditionalists' distress at changes in Americans' private behavior. In the contest between local and national authorities ongoing since the Articles of Confederation of the 1780s, the 1960s represented a high-water mark of Washington's influence in the lives of individual citizens.

Into War in Vietnam

The 1960s also marked the culmination of the U.S. government's efforts to control revolutionary political and social change abroad. The Truman Doctrine's logic of containing communism spanned the entire globe, but few imagined that the United States would overreach itself, tragically, in Vietnam. Johnson's accomplishments at home was forever overshadowed by the war he sent Americans to fight in the quiet rice paddies and beautiful highland forests of Southeast Asia. Putting U.S. combat troops into Vietnam in 1965, where they remained until 1973, drained funds and political will that could have been used to implement the Great Society more fully. The Vietnam War of these years might be better named the "American War": it reflected the beliefs and commitments of Cold Warriors in Washington more than the realities of life on the ground in Southeast Asia. An aggressive U.S. anticommunist policy abroad collided with leftist revolutionaries throughout the Third World, and it was ill fortune for the Vietnamese that this collision struck them hardest of all. "They were just in the intersection when our convertible rolled up," former Stanford University student body president and draft resistance organizer David Harris recalled.

The Vietnamese Revolution and the United States

Americans viewed the conflict in Vietnam as part of a broader struggle between communist and noncommunist nations. It did not start out that way, however. It began as one of many efforts to end European colonialism. Vietnamese nationalists, varying in ideologies but led by Ho Chi Minh and the Indochinese Communist party, sought since the 1930s to liberate their country from French colonial rule. Japanese advances during World War II put the Vietminh (Vietnamese nationalists) on the same side as the Americans, and Ho worked closely with the U.S. Office of Strategic Services (OSS), precursor to the Central Intelligence Agency (CIA). Ho declared the creation of an independent state of Vietnam on September 2, 1945, quoting at length from the American Declaration of Independence with OSS officers looking on.

Independent Vietnam did not last. After the defeat of Germany and Japan, the French wanted to regain control of their colonies in Africa and Asia, including Vietnam. Their British friends provided troop transport ships for French soldiers, and the United States provided most of the funds to support France in its war against the Vietminh (1946–1954). Cold War priorities won out: a weakened France had to be bolstered as the linchpin of a reintegrated, anticommunist western Europe, while the Vietminh were led by Communist party members. Unfortunately for Washington, the Vietnamese defeated the much more heavily armed French, capped by the climactic victory at the battle of Dien Bien Phu in May 1954, which surprised most Western observers. Two months later, the Geneva Accords divided the country temporarily at the seventeenth parallel until national elections could be held within 2 years to reunify Vietnam. Like the thirty-eighth parallel in Korea, the seventeenth parallel was an arbitrary latitude on the map used to divide peoples who did not want to be separated. Ho's forces solidified their control of the north, the French pulled out entirely, and the Eisenhower administration made a fateful decision to intervene directly to preserve the southern part of Vietnam from communism. The United States created a new government led by the Roman Catholic, anticommunist Ngo Dinh Diem in a new country called "South Vietnam." "This is our offspring," Senator John Kennedy observed of the rulers in the capital city of Saigon, but most Americans still knew nothing about South Vietnam.

The Vietnamese Revolution was only half over, however. The French colonialists withdrew, but the Saigon regime ignored the Geneva Accords and the promise of elections to reunify the country. In the north, the internal revolution for the creation of a socialist society proceeded with an extensive program of land redistribution. In the south, Diem ruled for 8 years with increasing repression of communists and other dissenters. U.S. funding kept him in power. One reporter noted that "Diem could not have survived a week without foreign aid." Desperate in the face of Diem's secret police, southern members of the old Vietminh began a sabotage campaign against the Saigon government and formed the National Liberation Front (NLF) in 1960, with the support of the government of North Vietnam in Hanoi. Diem and his American supporters called them Viet Cong or VC, roughly equivalent to the derogatory American term *Commies*. As the struggle to overthrow Diem intensified in the early 1960s, President Kennedy increased the number of U.S. military personnel from the 800 under Eisenhower to 16,000. They made little difference, however, as the unpopular Saigon government continued to lose ground to the NLF guerrillas. Just 3 weeks before Kennedy's murder, several of Diem's own generals assassinated him with the tacit support of U.S. officials in South Vietnam and Washington.

> *As the struggle to overthrow Diem intensified in the early 1960s, President Kennedy increased the number of U.S. military personnel from the 800 under Eisenhower to 16,000.*

Johnson's War

Lyndon Johnson inherited his predecessors' commitment to preserving a noncommunist South Vietnam. Bolstered by Kennedy's hawkish advisers, especially Secretary of Defense Robert McNamara (1961–1968), he believed that American credibility was at stake. But Johnson faced a swiftly deteriorating military situation. The NLF, which the administration portrayed as

Wars and Social Reform in the Twentieth Century

Lyndon Johnson knew that in going to war in Vietnam, he risked losing public support and congressional funding for his Great Society programs. Yet he felt he had little choice. Facing the growing success of the communist-led insurgency in South Vietnam, the president believed that he had to escalate U.S. involvement there to continue preserving a noncommunist part of Vietnam. That policy had been a commitment of every American president since late in World War II: Franklin Roosevelt, Harry Truman, Dwight Eisenhower, and John Kennedy. Johnson also feared the conservative Republican domestic backlash that he believed would follow a U.S. withdrawal from Southeast Asia and the "fall" of another Asian nation to communist rule. "That bitch of a war" in Vietnam, he said, was forcing him to leave "the woman I really loved—the Great Society."

Johnson's was not the first presidential administration in the twentieth century to find that military conflicts abroad constrained and even derailed domestic efforts at social and political reform. Three other Democratic presidents had encountered similar situations. Woodrow Wilson's Progressive reform agenda was waylaid by the onset of World War I in 1914 and his decision to lead the nation into that conflict 3 years later. Franklin Roosevelt's extensive New Deal programs to restart the ailing economy and improve an array of social ills tapered off as the United States entered World

An elderly woman thanks President Johnson for signing the Medicare bill, which provided health care benefits for Americans over age 65 through the Social Security program. The bill, which became effective in July 1966, incorporated parts of the program of national health care proposed by President Truman in 1949.

War II in 1941, as he acknowledged by announcing that "Dr. Win the War" was replacing "Dr. New Deal." Harry Truman's "Fair Deal" reform hopes were more modest than those of Roosevelt, but they included a program of national health care and civil rights legislation. A hostile Congress effectively blocked such initiatives, but Truman's own efforts to promote them declined after he took the nation into the undeclared war in Korea in 1950.

The huge scale of mobilization to fight a major war took a single-mindedness of purpose that left little time for other concerns. Social reformers such as Martin Luther King, Jr., feared military engagements abroad for just this reason (see "Interpreting History" in this chapter). Going to war did sometimes encourage policies that increased social justice if those policies contributed to the war effort. One

example was the War Industries Board in World War I that helped mediate labor disputes and improve workplace conditions; another was the desegregation of the armed forces that happened soon after World War II (in part because of that war's rhetoric about defeating Nazi racism) and was implemented during the Korean War. But having citizens dying in battle abroad more often increased intolerance at home for dissent or diversity. The Alien and Sedition Acts in World War I, the incarceration of Japanese Americans in World War II, and the anticommunist purges led by Joseph McCarthy during the Korean War all undercut civil liberties and discouraged efforts at social reform. Johnson's diminished attention to building the Great Society after he escalated the war in Vietnam in 1965 fit in this broader pattern. ■

CORBIS

merely a tool of North Vietnam, was winning the political war for the south, taking control of the countryside from the demoralized Army of the Republic of Vietnam (ARVN). Faced with the choice of escalating U.S. involvement to prevent an NLF victory or withdrawing entirely from the country, Johnson escalated.

How he did so was crucially important. There was neither a national debate nor a congressional vote to declare war. Johnson did not want to distract Congress from his Great Society agenda, nor did he want to provoke the Soviet Union or China. But he believed he had to preserve a noncommunist South Vietnam or else face a debilitating backlash from Republicans, who would skewer him as McCarthy had done to Truman over the "loss" of China 15 years earlier. So the president used deception, describing offensive American actions as defensive and opening up a credibility gap between a committed government and a skeptical public. This gap widened steadily until it finally drove Johnson not to run for reelection in 1968.

In 1963–1965, while St. Louis was building its famous arch commemorating the city's history as the Gateway to the West, where so many U.S.–Indian wars had been fought, Johnson took the nation through the gateway of the Pacific into a new war in the farther west of Asia. In August 1964, North Vietnamese ships in the Gulf of Tonkin fired on the U.S. destroyer *Maddox,* which was aiding South Vietnamese sabotage operations against the North. The president portrayed the incident as one of unprovoked communist aggression, and Congress expressed almost unanimous support through its Gulf of Tonkin Resolution. With this substitute for a declaration of war, Johnson ordered American planes to begin bombing North Vietnam, and the first American combat troops splashed ashore at Da Nang in South Vietnam on March 8, 1965. In July the administration made the key decision to add 100,000 more soldiers, with more to follow as necessary.

The president also offered a piece of the Great Society to his opponents in Vietnam if they would halt their struggle. He promised a vast economic development program for the Mekong River delta "on a scale even to dwarf our" Tennessee Valley Authority. Like most of his compatriots, the president assumed that foreign peoples fundamentally wanted to be like Americans. Johnson and his advisers tended to believe that, in the words of a U.S. officer in the film *Full Metal Jacket,* "Inside every [Vietcong] there is an American trying to get out."

The carrot of American-style economic development was accompanied by the stick of U.S. military force. American strategy had two goals: to limit the war so as not to draw in neighboring China (to avoid a repeat of the Korean War) and to force the NLF and North Vietnam to give up their struggle to reunify the country under Hanoi's control. The problem was the political nature of the guerrilla war in the South: a contest for the loyalty of the population, in which NLF operatives mingled easily with the citizenry. This kind of war made the enemy difficult to find, as was often true for the British in fighting the American revolutionaries in the 1770s. Because guerrillas were like fish swimming in the sea of citizens who supported them, in Chinese leader Mao Zedong's formulation, U.S. commanders decided to drain the sea. The "strategic hamlet" program uprooted rural peasants and concentrated them in fortified towns, creating "free fire zones" in their wake where anything that moved was a target. The U.S. Air Force pounded the south as well as the north, dropping more bombs on this ancient land (smaller than either Germany or Japan) than had been used in all theaters on all sides in World War II. Under Operation Ranch Hand, American planes used defoliants such as Agent Orange to remove ground cover, rendering one-seventh of the south's land uninhabitable. Their informal slogan was "Only We Can Prevent Forests."

These tactics destabilized and traumatized society in South Vietnam as one-fourth of the population became refugees. The American war urbanized the south by force: from 85 percent rural in 1965, it became 65 percent urban by 1974. The strategy of attrition wielded by General William Westmoreland, the commander of U.S. forces in Vietnam, also alienated the citizenry of the South. Lacking a clear military front in a guerrilla conflict, U.S. commanders used body counts of enemy dead as a primary method of demonstrating progress in the war. This strategy created great pressure on officers to produce bodies. In a war where Americans had difficulty distinguishing the enemy from noncombatants, a new rule became increasingly standard: "If it's dead and Vietnamese, it's VC."

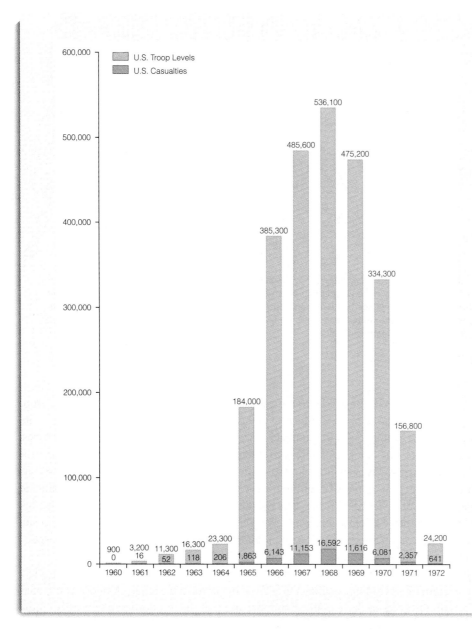

■ **FIGURE 26.1**
U.S. TROOP AND CASUALTY LEVELS IN VIETNAM (AS OF DECEMBER 31 OF EACH YEAR)

Americans in Southeast Asia

Given America's wealth, size, and superior weaponry, most U.S. soldiers who went to Vietnam in 1965–1966 had no doubt they would win the war. Their confidence reflected generations of American successes on battlefields across Europe and the Pacific Ocean. As emissaries from a culture that valued material wealth and technological sophistication, they tended to dismiss Vietnamese people as primitive and weak. They typically looked down on Asians. Very few knew anything about Vietnamese history or culture, and almost none spoke the Vietnamese language. This war, unlike World War II of their parents' generation, had no D-Day on the beaches of France as in 1944, with a staging across the narrow channel in familiar England. Although a small number of Americans worked closely with their South Vietnamese allies, most GIs encountered Vietnamese in subservient roles as laundry workers, prostitutes, waitresses, and bartenders. Blinkered by anticommunism and far removed from their own revolutionary roots, Americans from the top brass to the lowest "grunts" marched into a country they did not understand but assumed they could control.

Universal Press Syndicate

■ Cartoonist Jules Fieffer suggested in 1966 some of the ongoing confusion of many Americans about Asia and its many nations and peoples, and why the United States was involved in a war in Vietnam. Anti-Asian prejudice had long contributed to problems in U.S.–Asian relations. President Johnson claimed that the United States was protecting the lives and interests of South Vietnamese against both North Vietnam and China.

The immense problems of counterinsurgent warfare quickly put an end to this optimism. President Johnson spoke of the conflict in Vietnam as a case of one sovereign nation—the North—invading another one—the South. However, few Vietnamese saw the war in those terms. The United States, dismissing the failure of the French before them, had intervened not so much in an international war as in an ongoing revolution that aimed to reunify the country. Few Vietnamese, whatever their opinions of communism, viewed the corrupt Saigon regime as legitimate or democratic. After all, it was kept in place by foreigners, whereas the North was ruled by people who had expelled the French foreigners. Even the U.S. Embassy admitted privately that "if any elected assembly sits in Saigon, it will be on the phone negotiating with Hanoi within one week." One U.S. sergeant concluded that "anticommunism is a lousy substitute for democracy."

Initial U.S. optimism reflected a grave underestimation of the NLF and the North Vietnamese. From President Johnson down to soldiers on patrol in the jungle, Americans assumed that communists did not have popular support and that the inferior weaponry of communist forces could not withstand the firepower of the world's strongest military, which dominated the air and the surrounding sea. These assumptions were fatal miscalculations. Ho Chi Minh was an extremely popular leader, and intervention from the other side of the world only strengthened his position. As the war expanded, NLF recruiting in the south snowballed, and the people of North Vietnam remained loyal to their authoritarian government.

Communist forces proved willing to endure fantastic hardship and sacrifices to prevail, some even living underground in the labyrinthine tunnels of Cu Chi to avoid U.S. bombs. Their morale was much higher than that of the ARVN. Superior organization and commitment enabled them to overcome their technological deficit, and small victories hardened their resolve. The NLF in the south had long armed itself with U.S. weapons captured from the ARVN, declaring that "Ngo Dinh Diem will be our supply sergeant." After Diem's death, American weapons poured into the country at an increasing rate, but the tenacity of the NLF prompted the Soviets and the Chinese to provide antiaircraft guns and other vital military assistance to the north.

Who were the 3 million Americans who went to Vietnam? The initial forces contained experienced soldiers, but as the war escalated this professional army was diluted with hundreds of thousands of young draftees. Student deferments protected more comfortable Americans, so GIs were predominantly those who lacked money and education. Although 70 percent

Bettmann/CORBIS

■ Vietnamese villagers flee from an accidental U.S. napalm raid 26 miles southwest of Saigon in the Mekong River delta. U.S. Air Force planes dominated the skies above Vietnam, dropping conventional bombs and antipersonnel weapons such as napalm over both the North and the South. At least 2 million Vietnamese died, many of them civilians caught in the crossfire of a guerrilla war, but sheer destructiveness was unable to win the war for the United States.

were white men, black, Hispanic, and Native American enlistees shipped out in disproportionate numbers. It became a teenaged army, filled with 18-year-olds whose main aim, one ABC correspondent reported, "was to become 19." In sharp contrast to the motives of the NLF and the North Vietnamese army, these young men (along with 10,000 women who volunteered as nurses) were not in Vietnam to win the war regardless of the cost or duration. They had only to survive 12 months before returning home to the safety of a peacetime society. There could hardly have been a sharper contrast between this undeclared war and the total mobilization of the United States in a declared war such as World War II.

Only a small fraction of the American personnel in Southeast Asia experienced actual combat. Most worked in the extensive support systems on bases in rear areas, where daily life was safer and more comfortable. Those who fought in the jungles and rice paddies lived in extreme peril. North Vietnamese regular army units came south to match the growing number of U.S. forces, and they occasionally engaged the Americans in large set battles, as at Ia Drang valley in the fall of 1965. U.S. troops fought well in such firefights, making devastating use of their superior weapons and air power. However, the bulk of the fighting consisted of smaller engagements with deceptive enemies on their home turf who faded in and out of the civilian population with ease. Ambushes and unexpected death haunted Americans on patrol, and relentless heat and humidity wore them down.

American soldiers felt mounting frustration and rage over the nature of the war that they were ordered to fight. Lacking a clear battlefront and an understandable strategy for winning the war, they were commanded simply to kill the often mysterious enemy. Yet distinguishing civilians from combatants in a popular guerrilla war was not always easy, especially when so many civilians evidently supported the NLF and so few Americans spoke Vietnamese. "How can you tell the enemy?" one GI asked. "They all look the same." The U.S. ally, the ARVN, was riddled with NLF infiltrators and rarely fought effectively. Realizing that few of the people they were supposed to be defending actually wanted them there but under orders to produce enemy bodies, U.S. troops on the ground began to slide toward a racial war against

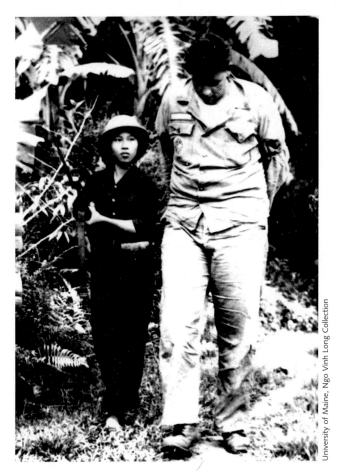

University of Maine, Ngo Vinh Long Collection

■ A North Vietnamese militia fighter named Kim Lai escorts an American pilot whom she captured after his plane crashed over the North. American GIs often were struck by the diminutive size of the average Vietnamese in comparison to the average American. Bigger, better equipped, and much more well armed than their opponents, most U.S. soldiers and officers before 1968 went into the field in Vietnam certain that they would be victorious.

all Vietnamese. "You can't have a feeling of remorse for these people," said one Marine. "I mean, like I say, they are an enemy until proven innocent."

Many GIs resisted this logic, sometimes showing real kindness to Vietnamese civilians. But atrocities on both sides inevitably followed from this kind of war. The worst came in the village of My Lai on March 16, 1968, where 105 soldiers from Charlie Company—enraged by the recent deaths of several comrades in ambushes—slaughtered, often after torturing or raping, more than 400 Vietnamese women, children, and old men. The Army covered up the massacre for a year and a half, and eventually found only Lieutenant William Calley, the leader of Charlie Company's First Platoon, guilty of murdering Vietnamese civilians. Public sympathy for him as a scapegoat for the failings of U.S. military strategy encouraged President Nixon to reduce Calley's sentence of life imprisonment to 3 years. Americans at home were horrified when grim photographs appeared in *Life* magazine, but those who knew the war up close were not surprised. "The people back in the world don't understand this war," one GI in Vietnam bitterly told a reporter. "We are here to kill dinks. How can they convict Calley for killing dinks? That's our job."

1968: The Turning Point

In late 1967 the public face of the war effort remained upbeat, as General Westmoreland declared that he could now see "some light at the end of the tunnel." But other prominent members of the administration, including Secretary of Defense McNamara, were beginning to express doubts privately to the president. Any remaining hopes of an imminent victory were crushed by the startling Tet Offensive (named for the Vietnamese New Year) that began on January 30, 1968. NLF insurgents and North Vietnamese troops attacked U.S. strongholds throughout South Vietnam, even occupying the courtyard of the U.S. Embassy for 6 hours. This risky tactic paid off for the communists with enormous political gains, despite military losses. U.S. troops killed thousands of their enemy as they ended and then reversed the advances of Tet. But the blow to American public confidence in Johnson and his military commanders proved irreversible. Far from being on the verge of defeat, as the administration had been claiming, the communists had shown that they could mount simultaneous attacks around the country. Revered television newscaster Walter Cronkite announced that "we are mired in stalemate" in Vietnam.

The Tet Offensive coincided with two other crises in early 1968 to convince American political and business elites that U.S. international commitments had become larger than the nation could afford. First, a week before Tet began, the North Korean navy seized the U.S. intelligence ship *Pueblo* in the Sea of Japan and temporarily imprisoned its crew. U.S. commanders were left scrambling to find enough forces to respond effectively without weakening American commitments in Europe and elsewhere. Second, a British financial collapse devalued the pound and caused the London government to announce its imminent withdrawal from its historic positions east of the Suez Canal, placing new military burdens on the United States in the Middle East. These events reduced international confidence in the U.S. economy, causing a currency crisis in March 1968 as holders of dollars traded them in for gold. The chairman of the Federal

CHINA

NORTH VIETNAM

U.S. air raids
1966–1968, 1972
Haiphong
Hanoi — harbor mined 1972

Gulf of Tonkin

LAOS
(Communist Pathet
Lao victory, 1975)

Gulf of Tonkin
incident
Aug. 4, 1964

Hainan
Island

U.S. Seventh Fleet
operations during the war

Vientiane

THAILAND

Demilitarized Zone
(DMZ)

Invasion of Laos
Feb. 6–Mar., 1971

Khe Sanh
Quang Tri
Hue: Tet offensive Jan. 30–Feb., 1968
Da Nang
Hoian

Lang Vei
A Chau

Kham Dua

Quang Ngai
Dak To

Kontum
Pleiku
Qui Niun

(Communist Khmer
Rouge victory, 1975)

SOUTH
VIETNAM

CAMBODIA

Tuy Hoi
Ban Me Thuoi

Invasion of Cambodia
Apr. 29–June 29, 1970

Nha Trang
Dalat

South
China Sea

Cam Ranh Bay

Phnom Penh

Bien Hoa
Cholon
Saigon: Tet offensive Jan. 30–Feb., 1968

Chau Dua
Vinh Long

Gulf of
Thailand

Saigon

My Tho

Ben Tie
Can Tho
Ca Mau

Vietnam
Major battles or actions
Major North Vietnamese supply
routes into South Vietnam
NLF-North Vietnamese victory
and U.S. withdrawal, April 30, 1975

Capitals
U.S. and South Vietnamese
troop movements
"Boat People" refugees after 1975

■ **MAP 26.2**

THE AMERICAN WAR IN VIETNAM   Before U.S. combat troops entered Vietnam in 1965, few Americans
knew where this Southeast Asian country was. Vietnam's geography and place names quickly became
familiar in the United States as hundreds of thousands of young Americans served there and some 58,000
died there. Vietnam's elongated shape, its borders with Cambodia and Laos, and its proximity to China all
affected the course of the fighting for Americans between 1965 and 1973.

Reserve Board warned Wall Street leaders of "either an uncontrollable recession or an uncontrollable inflation" as fears rose of another 1929. Financial leaders added their powerful voices
to those of other dismayed Americans demanding a deescalation of the war.

The political career of Lyndon Johnson was a final casualty of these events. His support
on the left withered as the antiwar and black power movements expanded. Meanwhile, his more
centrist supporters were joining the backlash against civil rights, urban violence, and antiwar
protesters, peeling off to the Republican party. On March 12 antiwar challenger Senator Eugene
McCarthy of Minnesota nearly defeated the incumbent president in the New Hampshire Democratic primary. Johnson's vulnerability was obvious. Senator Robert Kennedy of New York joined
the race 2 weeks later. In a televised speech on March 31 that caught the divided nation by
surprise, Johnson announced an end to U.S. escalations in the war, the start of negotiations in

Martin Luther King, Jr., and the Vietnam War

Most Americans approved of the war in Vietnam until at least 1968. Appreciative of Lyndon Johnson's commitment to reduce poverty and end racial discrimination at home, African Americans generally supported the president's policies in Southeast Asia. However, younger, more radical civil rights workers were among those who opposed the first insertion of U.S. combat troops in 1965. Within 2 years, the nation's most prominent black leader, Martin Luther King, Jr., decided that he could no longer keep quiet about his growing unease with the American war effort. A storm of criticism greeted his public denunciation of the war, most of it suggesting that he should limit himself to domestic civil rights work. But King no longer believed that events at home and abroad could be separated. The following excerpt is from his speech at Riverside Church, New York City, April 4, 1967:

Lyndon B. Johnson and American Liberalism

A few years ago there was a shining moment in that struggle [against poverty and discrimination]. It seemed as if there was a real promise of hope for the poor—both black and white—through the Poverty Program. There were experiments, hopes, new beginnings. Then came the build-up in Vietnam and I watched the program broken and eviscerated as if it were some idle political plaything of a society gone mad on war. . . . I was increasingly compelled to see the war as an enemy of the poor and to attack it as such . . . .

We were taking the black young men who had been crippled by our society and sending them 8,000 miles away to guarantee liberties in Southeast Asia which they had not found in Southwest Georgia and East Harlem. So we have been repeatedly faced with the cruel irony of watching Negro and white boys on TV screens as they kill and die together for a nation that has been unable to seat them together in the same schools . . . .

As I have walked among the desperate, rejected and angry young men [in the ghettos of the North the last three summers] I have told them that Molotov cocktails and rifles would not solve their problems. I have tried to offer them my deepest compassion while maintaining my convictions that social change comes most meaningfully through non-violent action. But they asked—and rightly so—what about Vietnam? They asked if our own nation wasn't using massive doses of violence to solve its problems, to bring about the changes it wanted. Their questions hit home, and I knew that I would never again raise my voice against the violence of the oppressed in the ghettos without having first spoken clearly to the greatest purveyor of violence in the world today—my own government . . . .

His birthday now a national holiday, Martin Luther King, Jr., has become widely accepted as a heroic figure in the American past. But in the last few years of his life, King's increasingly sharp criticisms of injustice in American society disturbed many fellow citizens.

[Our troops in Vietnam] must know after a short period there that none of the things we claim to be fighting for [such as freedom, justice, and peace] are really involved. Before long they must know that their government has sent them into a struggle among Vietnamese, and the more sophisticated surely realize that we are on the side of the wealthy and the secure while we create a hell for the poor. ■

Source: Bruce J. Schulman, *Lyndon B. Johnson and American Liberalism* (Boston: Bedford, 1995), 208–212.

Paris with North Vietnam, and an end to his own career: "I shall not seek, and I will not accept, the nomination of my party for another term as your President."

The Movement

While national leaders were defending what they called the "frontiers of freedom" abroad, young Americans in the mid- and late 1960s organized to expand what they considered to be the frontiers of freedom at home. Television for the first time tied

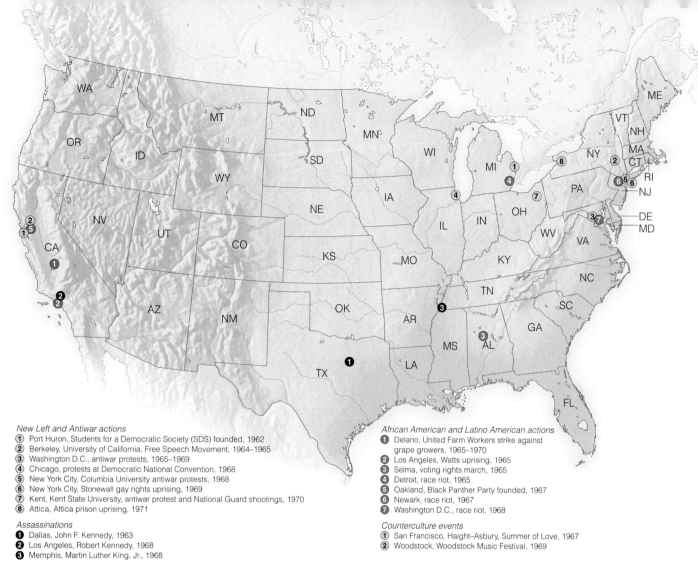

New Left and Antiwar actions
1. Port Huron, Students for a Democratic Society (SDS) founded, 1962
2. Berkeley, University of California, Free Speech Movement, 1964–1965
3. Washington D.C., antiwar protests, 1965–1969
4. Chicago, protests at Democratic National Convention, 1968
5. New York City, Columbia University antiwar protests, 1968
6. New York City, Stonewall gay rights uprising, 1969
7. Kent, Kent State University, antiwar protest and National Guard shootings, 1970
8. Attica, Attica prison uprising, 1971

Assassinations
1. Dallas, John F. Kennedy, 1963
2. Los Angeles, Robert Kennedy, 1968
3. Memphis, Martin Luther King, Jr., 1968

African American and Latino American actions
1. Delano, United Farm Workers strike against grape growers, 1965–1970
2. Los Angeles, Watts uprising, 1965
3. Selma, voting rights march, 1965
4. Detroit, race riot, 1965
5. Oakland, Black Panther Party founded, 1967
6. Newark, race riot, 1967
7. Washington D.C., race riot, 1968

Counterculture events
1. San Francisco, Haight–Asbury, Summer of Love, 1967
2. Woodstock, Woodstock Music Festival, 1969

■ **MAP 26.3**
MAJOR SOCIAL AND POLITICAL PROTESTS, 1962–1971 While not the first decade to witness dramatic public protests, the 1960s did become synonymous with large groups of citizens—especially young ones—demanding changes in public policies that they perceived as unjust. Foremost among these groups were civil rights workers, antiwar activists, women's rights supporters, and countercultural youth. Students emerged as important agents of change in the 1960s.

the country together in a common culture whose shared images were transmitted simultaneously around the nation. Over all of the protest movements of the 1960s loomed the expanding war in Vietnam, which radicalized people who had initially been optimistic about reforming American society. Black power, the New Left, the counterculture, women's liberation, and other liberation movements often had quite divergent goals. But participants overlapped extensively and activists spoke of "the Movement" as if it were a unified phenomenon. At the heart of the youth movements of the decade lay a common quest for authenticity—a rejection of hypocrisy and a distrust of traditional authorities—that fused cultural and political protest. Few American households remained untouched.

From Civil Rights to Black Power

The black freedom struggle in the South that broke into the national consciousness so dramatically in the early 1960s inspired other activists. By 1966, however, the civil rights movement fractured as it confronted the limits of its success. It had achieved the goals of ending legal discrimination and putting southern African Americans in the voting booth, but it had not brought about a colorblind society. Racial prejudice among white conservatives remained virulent, and white liberals, such as those in the Kennedy and Johnson administrations, revealed themselves as not always trustworthy allies. Expecting only hostility from conservatives, civil rights workers were more disillusioned with what they saw as liberal betrayals.

The Justice Department and the Federal Bureau of Investigation (FBI) did little to restrain the violence of the Ku Klux Klan until the murders of white organizers Michael Schwerner and Andrew Goodman in the summer of 1964—along with black co-worker James Chaney. Two months later, at the national Democratic party convention in Atlantic City, New Jersey, Johnson crushed the effort of the biracial Mississippi Freedom Democratic party to replace the state's regular, all-white Democratic delegates. The president was determined to avoid further alienating white southern voters as he pursued a huge victory in the November elections. Even the thousand white volunteers from northern and western colleges who courageously came to Mississippi for the 1964 "Freedom Summer" wound up unintentionally alienating many younger black organizers. The confident style and skills of volunteers from Yale, Stanford, and other elite universities highlighted anew the tendency of even well-intentioned whites to try to take over and manage African Americans' lives.

The black freedom struggle for centuries had woven together elements of racial separatism with elements of integration into the larger American culture. For many younger African Americans the pendulum swung toward a need for greater independence from the white majority. They took inspiration from Malcolm X, the fiery and eloquent minister of the Nation of Islam (Black Muslims), who until his murder in 1965 captivated listeners with denunciations of white perfidy and demands for black self-respect. The day after he won the heavyweight boxing title in 1964, Cassius Clay announced that he was a Black Muslim and was changing his name to Muhammad Ali. After fielding hostile questions from journalists at the news conference, Ali declared, "I don't have to be what you want me to be." In 1966 SNCC members began to speak of the need for "black power" rather than for the integrated "beloved community" they had initially sought in 1960.

> *The day after he won the heavyweight boxing title in 1964, Cassius Clay announced that he was a Black Muslim and was changing his name to Muhammad Ali.*

The issue of violence loomed large in the shift from civil rights to black power. Militant spokesmen Stokely Carmichael and H. Rap Brown called for African Americans to stop turning the other cheek when confronted with white violence—to "stop singing and start swinging," as Malcolm X had put it. The Black Panther party formed in Oakland, California, in response to police brutality. The heavily armed Panthers engaged in several shootouts with police and were eventually decimated by an FBI campaign against them. White Americans were shocked by the uprisings and riots that swept through black urban communities during the summers of 1964–1968. Triggered by the actions of white police, the riots expressed the fierce frustrations of impoverished people whose lives remained largely untouched by the achievements of the civil rights struggle. The most destructive outbreaks occurred in the Watts district of Los Angeles in 1965 and in Detroit and Newark in 1967. The violence in Watts killed 34 people, wounded 1000, and destroyed $45 million of property. Ninety people died, and 4000 were injured across the country in the 1967 riots, most of them African Americans killed by police as fires and looting spread through African American neighborhoods. "Our nation is moving toward two societies, one black, one white—separate and unequal," the National Advisory Commission on Civil Disorders announced in its 1968 report.

The greatest significance of black power turned out to be neither its use of mostly rhetorical violence nor its unclear political agenda of black separatism. Rather, black power thrived as a cultural movement that promoted pride in African American and African history and life. The slogan "black is beautiful" captured this spirit: long degraded by their white compatriots as inferior, black Americans in the late 1960s and 1970s reversed this equation to celebrate their cultural heritage. This could be as basic as a hairstyle, the natural Afro replacing hair straightened to look like Caucasian hair. At universities new departments of African

American studies fostered the exploration of black history. Unlearning habits of public deference to whites, most African Americans began referring to themselves as "black" rather than "Negro."

Cultural black power mixed with a different kind of political black power by the late 1960s: the election of black officials. Although militant black power advocates garnered the most media attention, most African Americans supported Lyndon Johnson and used the Voting Rights Act to pursue their goals in the realm of electoral politics. In 1966, Carl Stokes of Cleveland was elected the first black mayor of a major American city. African Americans won local offices across the South, and in 1972 Andrew Young of Georgia and Barbara Jordan of Texas became the first black U.S. representatives elected from the South since Reconstruction. African American public life has blended elements of cultural nationalism with the pursuit of political integration ever since, just as a similar combination has helped define the public engagement of other Americans of color: Latinos, Asians, and Indians.

The New Left and the Struggle Against the War

In the summer of 1962 a group of young liberal college activists met at a labor union summer camp in Michigan. The Students for a Democratic Society (SDS) wrote a charter that became known as the Port Huron Statement, which called for a rejuvenation of American politics and society to replace the complacency that they saw pervading the country. Racial bigotry and poverty particularly troubled these optimistic young reformers, along with the overarching threat of nuclear destruction (highlighted anew by the missile crisis in Cuba a few months later). They hoped to become a kind of "white SNCC," promoting participatory democracy to redeem the promise of Cold War America.

SDS served as the central organization of the New Left. In contrast to the Old Left of the 1940s and 1950s, which had been obsessed with distinguishing itself from communism and the Soviet Union, the New Left considered the Cold War a mask for preserving inequalities in the United States. Communism was simply not important to these activists, nor was conservatism, which was then at its nadir. They focused instead on the behavior of the liberals who ran the U.S. government from 1961 to 1968. They developed a critique of "corporate liberalism" as promoting the interests of the wealthy and the business community far more than providing for the needs of the disadvantaged. From this perspective, communism was a red herring and anticommunism a distraction from the real problems of the nation, especially as the war in Vietnam expanded. New Leftists became, above all, anti-anticommunists.

After 1965, SDS's initially broad reform agenda narrowed to stopping the Vietnam War. Protests about other issues also disrupted college campuses, such as the Free Speech Movement at Berkeley in 1964–1965; this successful effort to eliminate restrictions on students' lives set a precedent for campus activists elsewhere. But the escalation of the war moved draft-age opponents to focus on ending it. "Hell no, we won't go!" became their slogan. SDS members organized the first major antiwar protest outside the White House on April 17, 1965, bringing their organization into alliance with the small group of religious and secular pacifists already working against the war. Most importantly, mainstream Democrats began abandoning Johnson over the war as it grew. The president had alienated the powerful chair of the Senate Foreign Relations Committee, J. William Fulbright of Arkansas, with his misleading reports during the brief U.S. military intervention in the Dominican Republic in April 1965 to defeat a left-leaning but not communist coup attempt. Fulbright then held televised hearings on the American war in Southeast Asia in January 1966, raising grave doubts about its wisdom. Within a year prominent African Americans such as Martin Luther King, Jr., and Muhammad Ali joined the growing opposition to the war. Draft resistance increased as young men moved to Canada like SNCC's Bob Moses

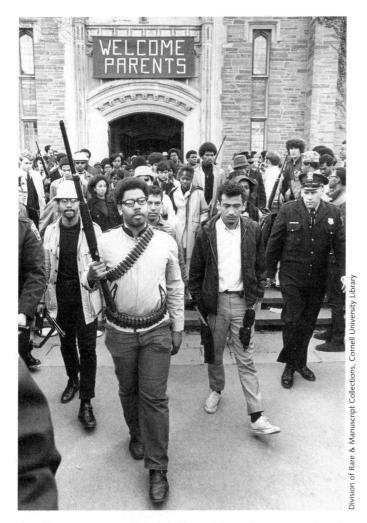

Division of Rare & Manuscript Collections, Cornell University Library

■ African American students march out of the student union at Cornell University in April 1969 after occupying the building during the annual Parents' Weekend on campus. With the support of radical white students such as those in SDS and some faculty, the black Ivy Leaguers were protesting racial discrimination, racial threats, and a recent cross-burning on campus, and they demanded the creation of a black studies program. The weapons in the picture went unused, but their presence on university grounds symbolized the extreme divisiveness and anger in American society between 1968 and 1970.

or went to jail like Ali. "Man, I ain't got no quarrel with the Vietcong," the boxer explained.

Antiwar protesters followed the same trajectory of radicalization as black power advocates. Their dismay turned to rage as the Johnson administration continued to expand a war that was destroying much of Vietnam while killing tens of thousands of American soldiers for no reason its opponents considered legitimate. Protesters refused to be what they called "good Germans": those who had watched silently as the Nazis killed millions of Jews. Having long admired Castro's revolution in Cuba, SDS began cheering for Ho Chi Minh and imagining itself as "the NLF behind Lyndon Johnson's lines." In combination with or in support of black militants, white radicals took over buildings on university campuses in 1968–1969: Columbia, Cornell, Harvard, San Francisco State, and many others. SDS ultimately broke apart in the confusion and exhilaration of its growing demand for revolution against the larger systemic enemies, imperialism and capitalism, not just corporate liberalism. Such fantasies of violence, as well as real bombings by a splinter group called the Weather Underground, alienated most Americans, including most peaceful antiwar protesters. But radical rage could not be understood apart from the ongoing destruction of Vietnam by a government acting in the name of all Americans.

Cultural Rebellion and the Counterculture

While the New Left moved from wanting to reform American society to wanting to overthrow it, the counterculture sought to create an alternative society. Called "hippies" by those who disliked them, these young people were alienated by the materialism, competition, and conformity of American life in the Cold War. Like utopian idealists in previous centuries, they envisioned an America free from hypocrisy and artificiality. They tried to live out alternative values of gentleness, tolerance, and inclusivity. Sporting headbands, long hair, and beads, many identified with traditional Native Americans, who had repeatedly challenged the greed and deceptions of white culture from the time of Metacom and Popé in the seventeenth century. In place of junk foods, they promoted health foods; in place of profit-seeking businesses, they established co-ops. Referring to themselves as "freaks" for not fitting into "straight" society, they pursued what they saw as an authentic life. "Do your own thing" was the common slogan.

In reaction against the conformity of mainstream society, members of the counterculture explored the limitations of consciousness to expand their self-knowledge. They went beyond the nicotine and alcohol that were the common stimulants of their parents' culture to experiment with such mind-altering drugs as marijuana, peyote, hashish, LSD, cocaine, and even heroin. Spirituality was an important path into consciousness for many in the counterculture. Religious traditions associated with Asia, particularly Buddhism, gained numerous adherents, as did spiritual customs and practices of traditional Native Americans. Others rediscovered the "authentic" Jesus obscured by the institutional structures of the formal Christian church (earning themselves the nickname "Jesus freaks"); Campus Crusade for Christ, Inter-

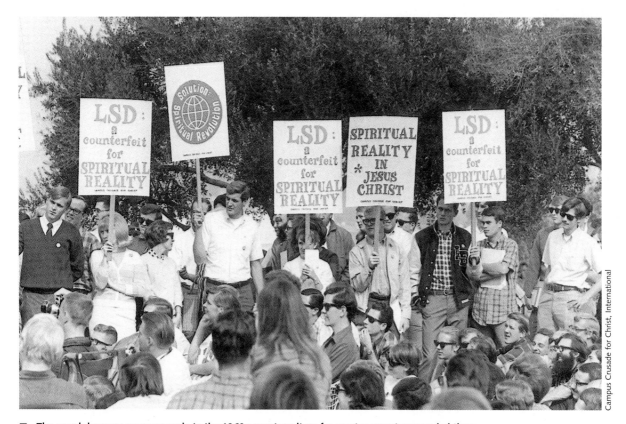

Campus Crusade for Christ, International

■ The search by many young people in the 1960s counterculture for greater consciousness led them to a spiritual path. These young evangelists held a Campus Crusade for Christ rally at the University of Texas at Austin in 1969. The emphasis of evangelical Christians on the person of Jesus rather than on a particular denominational tradition attracted many converts. The sandals, long hair, and gentleness associated with Jesus made a particularly good fit with the style and values of the "hippies," although most evangelicals appeared traditionally clean-cut and held conservative political views.

Varsity, and other evangelical college groups spread across the country. Music served as the most common coin of the countercultural realm, from the political folk sound of Joan Baez and Bob Dylan to the broadly popular Beatles and the more distinctly countercultural rock 'n' roll of the Grateful Dead and Jefferson Airplane.

By its nature the counterculture had no clear membership. Millions of American youth dabbled in it to varying extents, smoking marijuana and listening to rock 'n' roll. A much smaller, more committed group pursued the building of communities—communes—that might coexist with the quest for unrestrained individual expression. These young people were centered in the Haight–Asbury neighborhood of San Francisco until the 1967 Summer of Love, they gathered at the Woodstock music festival in upstate New York in August 1969, and they established 3500 rural communes from Vermont to New Mexico by 1970. With the nation at war against communists in Southeast Asia, critics pointed to communes at home as subversive of the nuclear family and of American capitalist values.

Older Americans experienced the counterculture largely as spectacle. The mainstream media emphasized the alternative aspects of the hippie lifestyle in its coverage. Viewers were varyingly disgusted by, attracted to, and titillated by the hair, clothing, nudity, and blurred gender distinctions. Celebrating the counterculture and its rock 'n' roll sound, the musical show *Hair* took Broadway by storm in 1968. Meanwhile, entrepreneurs realized that they could market the antimaterialist counterculture profitably. Young Americans eagerly bought up records, clothing, jewelry, and natural foods—a revealing demonstration of how consumer values pervaded American life.

■ MAP 26.4

THE SAN FRANCISCO BAY AREA   In the 1960s California was still a bit exotic for Americans from the East and Mideast. But continuing immigration to the Golden State and the emergence of air travel in this decade as a common means of transportation tied the nation more closely together. San Francisco, or "The City" to locals, became a hub of the counterculture and rock 'n' roll music and a place known for its tolerance and celebration of diversity.

One of the most visible changes of the 1960s was often called the sexual revolution. It had earlier roots, evident in the Kinsey Reports of 1948 and 1953 and in the emergence of *Play-boy* magazine's "swinger" style of the 1950s. Changes in Americans' sexual behavior in the 1960s reflected in part the counterculture's goal of living an authentic, honest life in which words matched actions. The sexual revolution removed some of the penalties for the premarital and extramarital sex that had previously been fairly common but unacknowledged. The appearance of the birth control pill in 1960 underpinned the shift to more open sexual relationships by freeing women from the fear of pregnancy. Attitudes toward abortion also became more tolerant. New York passed the first state law legalizing some abortions in 1970, and 3 years later the Supreme Court established a woman's constitutional right to abortion in the landmark case of *Roe v. Wade*. For American women the sexual revolution proved a double-edged sword. It legitimated female sexuality and helped remove the old stereotyping of women as either "madonna" (virginal until married) or "whore" (lustful and degraded). But it also created pressures from men, especially within the counterculture, for women to have sex with many partners lest they be cast as "uptight" and unliberated.

Women's Liberation

The movement for women's liberation arose in the late 1960s as a way to resist these kinds of limitations and expectations. Women's liberation built on developments earlier in the decade. In 1963 writer Betty Friedan, a former labor journalist and then homemaker, published *The Feminine Mystique,* a widely read book that captured the frustrations of many women who had accepted the role of suburban homemaker after World War II. Friedan condemned the middle-class home as a "comfortable concentration camp" for women that limited their growth as individuals with the often monotonous routines of housework and child-rearing. Friedan and other liberal feminists founded the National Organization for Women (NOW) in 1966 to lobby against sexual discrimination in the public sphere in such areas as employment, wages, education, and jury duty. These challenges had radical implications for women's and men's earnings and thus for responsibilities within families, but NOW did not yet focus on issues inside the private sphere of the home.

The shift to the view that "the personal is political" came from younger, mostly white women who had been active in the civil rights and antiwar struggles. Inspired by the courage and successes of the protest movements in which they figured prominently, these female activists had also learned that traditional gender roles restricted them even in organizations dedicated to participatory democracy. Ironically, radical men could be as patronizing and disrespectful of women's abilities as mainstream men. Younger feminists in 1967 and 1968 began to organize themselves to promote their own liberation from the shackles of traditional gender roles. They agreed with NOW's challenge to discrimination in the public sphere, but they focused even more on the personal politics of women's daily lives, on critical issues such as parenting, child care, housework, and abortion. Feminism should liberate men as well as women, they believed, for men also had the contours of their lives unnecessarily constrained by gendered expectations. The women's liberation movement gained visibility at the 1968 Miss America contest in Atlantic City, where feminists denounced the parading of women to be "appraised and judged like animals at a county fair."

The new wave of feminism that washed through American culture at the end of the 1960s triggered fierce debates about the nature of gender. Was there a uniquely feminine way of knowing, seeing, and acting, or were women in essence the same as men, distinguishable ultimately by their individuality? Was womanhood biologically or only culturally constructed? Feminists disagreed sharply in their answers. Other differences inevitably divided a broad movement that addressed the lives of 51 percent of the entire American people. For example, NOW did not support gay rights until 1973, whereas many radical feminists believed lesbianism to be critical for women's full independence and autonomy. Women of color often found hierarchies of race and class more significant than those of sex; to them, as to many white working-class women, Friedan's statement that she wanted "something more than my husband and my children and my house" seemed the distant complaint of a woman of the leisure class. One's sex alone did not define one's entire identity.

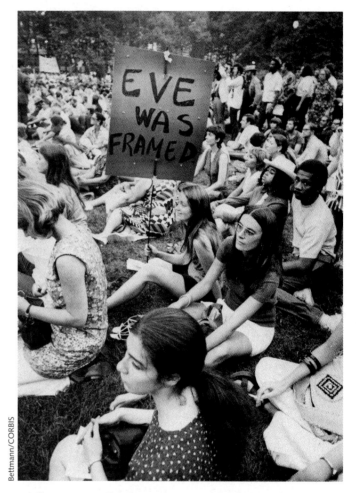

Bettmann/CORBIS

■ The new wave of organizing for women's rights that emerged in the late 1960s had many faces. Some protests against sex discrimination and disrespect for women were angry and others were gentle, as in this 1970 scene. "Raising consciousness" was a central strategy of the movement, as women and men became more aware of the gendered assumptions that had long governed—and channeled—their lives and their thoughts.

However, diversity within the feminist movement did not hide a common commitment to expanding women's possibilities. One critical aspect was the need to unlearn niceness and passivity, just as black power advocates sought to unlearn deference. White men would no longer be the sole proprietors of assertiveness; grown women would no longer be "girls" nor grown black men "boys." The women's movement that emerged out of the 1960s permanently transformed women's lives and gender relations in American society, in areas ranging from job and educational opportunities, sexual harassment, and gender-neutral language to family roles, sexual relations, reproductive rights, and athletic facilities.

The Many Fronts of Liberation

Like the women's movement, the Chicano, pan-Indian, and gay liberation movements of the late 1960s were grounded in older organizing efforts within those communities. The struggles for "brown power," "red power," and "gay power" also reflected the newer influence of black power and its determination to take pride in what the dominant American society had denigrated for so long. Activists on college campuses successfully pressured administrations to establish interdisciplinary ethnic studies programs, such as the first Chicano studies program at California State University at Los Angeles in 1968. Ethnic cultural identity went hand in hand with the pursuit of political and economic integration into mainstream American life.

The most prominent push to organize Latinos was the effort led by Cesar Chávez to build a farm workers' union in California and the Southwest. These primarily Mexican American migrant workers harvested most of the hand-picked produce that Americans ate, but their hard work under severe conditions failed to lift them out of poverty. National consumer support for boycotts of table grapes and iceberg lettuce helped win recognition for the United Farm Workers (UFW) union and better pay by 1970, despite efforts by Republicans such as President Richard Nixon and California governor Ronald Reagan to encourage grape consumption in support of large growers. Younger Mexican Americans organized to oppose the discrimination against them that remained common across the Southwest, especially in schools. They looked with pride on their Mexican heritage, even appropriating the formerly pejorative term *Chicano*. In March 1968, 10,000 youngsters walked out of their East Los Angeles schools to demand curriculum revisions that would include Latino history, recruitment of more Mexican American teachers, and an end to tracking Chicanos into vocational education classes. Two years later 20,000 people attended the Chicano Moratorium in East Los Angeles to protest the U.S. war in Vietnam.

Puerto Ricans, the largest Spanish-speaking ethnic group located primarily on the East Coast, experienced a similar growth in militancy and nationalist sentiment during the late 1960s. Since the United States annexed Puerto Rico after the end of the Spanish–American War in 1898, the Caribbean island had the unusual status of being ruled as a commonwealth of the United States while its residents were U.S. citizens who could not vote in national elections. By the 1960s more than a million islanders had moved to the East Coast, most to the New York City area. The majority came after World War II, and 47,000 served in the Vietnam War. Despite being the only Latino immigrants already holding American citizenship when they arrived, Puerto Ricans experienced similar patterns of both discrimination and opportunity as Mexican Americans. Younger Puerto Ricans formed the Young Lords in 1969 as a more militant and nationalist alternative to established Puerto Rican community organizations, one that combined pride in Puerto Rican identity and the Spanish language with leftist politics and opposition to the Vietnam War.

The most destitute of Americans, Indians also sought to reinvigorate their communities. On the Northwest coast they staged "fish-ins" in the mid-1960s to assert treaty rights, and in 1968 urban activists in Minneapolis formed the American Indian Movement (AIM). On November 20, 1969, just days after the largest antiwar march in Washington, 78 Native Americans seized the island of Alcatraz in San Francisco Bay "in the name of all American

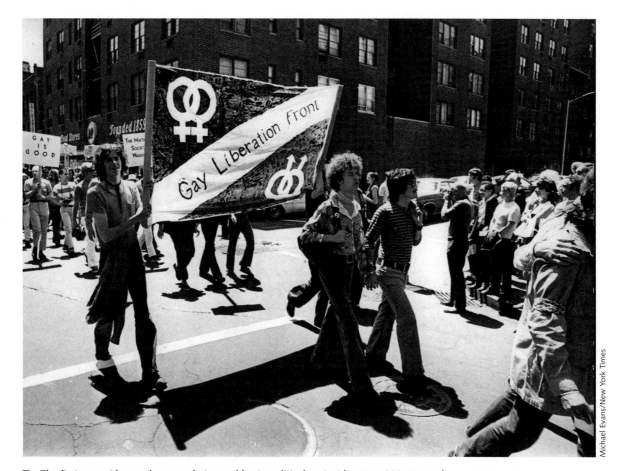

Michael Evans/New York Times

■ The first gay pride parade was a daring and hasty political protest by some 200 men and women, who walked for an hour up the Avenue of the Americas in New York City in 1970. They were taking a public stand against widespread discrimination and violence against homosexuals. Such discrimination and violence did not disappear over the next three decades, but the movement for gay rights dramatically altered the visibility and mainstream acceptance of gays and lesbians in the United States. By 1999 the gay pride parade had become a 6-hour party sponsored by the likes of Budweiser beer and United Airlines and attended by the Democratic first lady of the United States, Hillary Rodham Clinton, and the Republican mayor of New York, Rudolph Giuliani.

Indians by right of discovery." For a year and a half they used their occupation of the former federal prison site to publicize grievances about anti-Indian prejudice and to promote a new pan-Indian identity that reached across traditional tribal divisions. In 1973 armed members of AIM occupied buildings for two months at Wounded Knee near Pine Ridge, South Dakota, site of the infamous 1890 U.S. Army massacre of unarmed Sioux. AIM sought to bring down the conservative tribal government of the Oglala reservation, but the failure of that effort led to internal dissent and FBI harassment that eventually dissolved the organization. Tribal governments sought "red power" in their own quieter way. They asserted greater tribal control of reservation schools across the country. They also regained sovereignty over some lands previously lost, such as Blue Lake in northern New Mexico, which the Taos Indians reacquired.

Although they lacked a unifying ethnic identity, gay men and lesbians also found opportunities to construct coalitions in the more open atmosphere of the late 1960s. Building on the earlier but quieter community organizing of older homosexuals in New York, San Francisco, and Los Angeles, more militant youth began to express openly their anger at the homophobic prejudice and violence prevalent in American society. The demand for tolerance and respect reached the headlines when gay patrons of the Stonewall Bar in New York fought back fiercely against a typically forceful police raid on June 27, 1969. Activists of the new Gay Liberation Front emphasized the importance of "coming out of the closet": proudly acknowledging one's sexual orientation as legitimate and decent. Like "black is beautiful," this tactic represented an effort to recast the terms of one's identity apart from an ongoing tradition of prejudice. The American Psychiatric Association still listed homosexuality as a mental disorder until 1973.

The Conservative Response

The majority of Americans had mixed feelings about the protests that roiled the nation. They were impressed by the courage of many who stood up against discrimination, and by 1968 they wanted to find a way out of the war in Southeast Asia. But they were alienated by the style and values of others who loudly demanded change in American society. Moderate and conservative citizens and generations of recent European immigrants resented what they saw as a lack of appreciation for the nation's virtues and successes. Powerful backlashes developed against the counterculture, antiwar radicals, and changes in race and gender relations. The political and social upheavals of 1968 opened the door to a Republican return to the White House, and Richard Nixon slipped through.

Backlashes

The backlash first developed in response to the increasing assertiveness of people of color. European Americans in every part of the United States had long been accustomed to deference from nonwhites and racial segregation, either by law in the South or by custom elsewhere. Conservatives resented what they considered to be black ingratitude at the civil rights measures enacted by the federal government, including black power's condemnation of whites as "crackers" and "honkies." Urban riots and escalating rates of violent crime, along with the Supreme Court's expansion of the rights of the accused, deepened their anger. They associated crime with urban African Americans, for although whites were still the majority of criminals, blacks (like any other population with less money) were disproportionately represented in prisons. Many in the white working class feared that desegregating schools and neighborhoods would lead to a decline in their property values. While keeping darker-skinned Americans economically and socially subordinated, most whites still expected them to want to emulate mainstream white American society. Leaders such as Cesar Chávez and Martin Luther King, Jr., were devout Christians who emphasized equality and nonviolence, and many whites admired them. But the rise of often angry nonwhite nationalism dismayed most European Americans. They were troubled by the militancy of Chicanos in the Southwest, Puerto Ricans in the Northeast, Indians on reservations and in cities, and African Americans almost everywhere.

The backlash was not only about race. It also represented a defense of traditional hierarchies against the cultural rebellions of the 1960s. Proud of their lives and values, conservatives rejected a whole array of challenges to American society. Raised to believe in respecting one's elders, they resented the disrespect of many youth, who warned, "Don't trust anyone over 30." A generation that had fought and sacrificed in the "good war" against the Nazis found the absence of patriotism among many protesters unfathomable. The United States remained one of the most religious of industrialized societies, and conservative churchgoers emphasized obedience to authorities. They feared the effects of illegal drugs on their children. They resented being told that their assumptions about the roles and behavior of men and women, on which they had built their daily lives, were wrong. They did not want to argue about the behavior of the U.S. government; "America: Love It Or Leave It" became a favorite bumper sticker.

The backlash against the social changes of the 1960s contained elements of class antagonism as well. Working-class whites resented both the often affluent campus rebels and the black

Jules Fieffer

■ Cartoonist Jules Fieffer portrayed the generation gap that separated many younger Americans from many older ones by the early 1970s. Movements for black and Native American civil rights and against the U.S. war in Vietnam led to a profound shift in how many citizens, especially younger ones, understood their nation and its politics. A new generation of historians began to cast serious doubts on many long-accepted truisms about the American past.

and Latino poor targeted by some Great Society programs. They believed that their values of hard work, restraint, and respectability were increasingly unappreciated and even mocked. The counterculture's disdain for material comfort and economic security offended many older Americans of all colors who had experienced great deprivation in the 1930s. Politicians seized on these feelings of working-class alienation for political gain. Republican leaders from Goldwater to Nixon to Reagan gave voice to these resentments and drew votes away from Democratic blue-collar strongholds. Democratic governor George Wallace of Alabama also became a spokesperson for the anger of many "forgotten" whites on both sides of the Mason–Dixon line. Even television gave voice to the backlash in the likable character of Archie Bunker on *All in the Family,* a wildly popular program from its first airing in January 1971.

The Turmoil of 1968 at Home

The traumas of 1968 brought the conservative backlash to the critical stage. First came the Tet Offensive in Vietnam, creating fears that the war might become an interminable quagmire. Conservatives, like most other Americans, found it incredible that the mighty United States could not vanquish so small an enemy. Then, on April 4, just 5 days after President Johnson announced his retirement plans, a gunman named James Earl Ray assassinated Martin Luther King, Jr., in Memphis, where he had gone to support a strike by sanitation workers. King had become more openly radical in his final years, opposing the war and working on class-based organizing of poor people. But he remained the nation's leading apostle of nonviolence, and his murder evoked despair among millions of citizens, especially African Americans. Police battled rioters and arsonists in black neighborhoods of 130 cities across the nation, with 46 people dying in the clashes. National Guard troops ringed the White House as smoke from hundreds of fires rose over Washington, D.C.; large parts of the nation's capital looked like a war zone.

Summer brought more shocking news. Robert Kennedy's entry into the presidential campaign inspired renewed hopes among Democratic liberals. The charismatic senator turned against the war in Vietnam, and, unlike Eugene McCarthy, he seemed like a candidate who could attract support from a wide array of Americans, white and nonwhite, young and old. On the night of his victory in the June 5 California primary,

Kennedy was shot by a deranged gunman and died the next morning. Americans were stunned by this second murder of a Kennedy. Vice President Hubert Humphrey seemed assured of the nomination at the Democratic convention in Chicago in August, despite his association with Johnson's war policies. Some 10,000 antiwar activists, including hundreds of FBI *agents provocateurs* (spies seeking to provoke violence), showed up to engage in protests outside the convention. Chicago's Democratic mayor Richard Daley warned that "as long as I am Mayor, there will be law and order in the streets." Instead, he unleashed thousands of police on protesters, bystanders, and photographers in an orgy of beatings that subsequent investigations called a police riot. Ninety million Americans watched on television as a deeply divided Democratic party appeared helpless before the violence.

Into the vacuum of public anger and alienation that accompanied the liberals' self-destruction in Chicago stepped two men. George Wallace had long spoken for white Southerners resentful of the federal government and its growing support for racial equality. The spread of the conservative backlash from 1964 to 1968 gave him a wider constituency for his right-wing populist message of hostility to liberals, blacks, and federal officials. With the national Democratic party committed to racial integration, Wallace ran for president as an independent candidate and won 13.5 percent of the popular vote in November. Republican candidate Richard Nixon, fresh from a unified convention in Miami, campaigned as the candidate of "law and order" and promised that he had a secret plan to end the war in Vietnam. His contacts with the South Vietnamese government helped ensure that no last-minute breakthrough in the Paris peace talks would boost Humphrey's popularity, and the former vice president squeezed past the current one by less than 1 percent of the popular vote.

TABLE 26-2			
The Election of 1968			
Candidate	Political Party	Popular Vote	Electoral Vote
Richard M. Nixon	Republican	31,770,237	301
Hubert H. Humphrey	Democratic	31,270,533	191
George Wallace	American Independent	9,906,141	46

The Nixon Administration

A lonely, aloof man of great tenacity and ambition, Richard Nixon had worked hard to remake his public image for 1968. Widely viewed as a somewhat unscrupulous partisan since his early career in Congress, he had refashioned himself as a statesman with a broad vision for reducing international tensions between the great powers. Foreign policy fascinated him, and, unlike Johnson, he found domestic governance utterly dull—a matter of "building outhouses in Peoria." He won the Republican presidential nomination primarily because he bridged the gap between the party's conservative Sunbelt wing and its moderate eastern wing. He sounded like a conservative in the campaign against Humphrey, but once in the White House he governed as the most liberal Republican since Theodore Roosevelt, pressed by a Congress still controlled by Democrats.

Nowhere was this clearer than on issues related to natural resources. Much had happened to the environment since the Republican Roosevelt's conservation efforts, none of it for the better. A powerful movement was building to protect natural resources and human health from the effects of air and water pollution. Biologist Paul Ehrlich's best-selling *The Population Bomb* (1968) warned of the dire consequences of the globe's runaway growth in human population. In 1969, the government banned the carcinogenic pesticide DDT, its original usefulness against mosquito-born malaria in World War II now almost forgotten in light of its broadly toxic effects on wildlife and aquatic ecosystems. That same year a huge oil spill off Santa Barbara fouled 200 miles of pristine California beaches, and the Cuyahoga River in Cleveland, its surface coated with waste and oil, caught fire and burned for days. *Apollo 8* astronauts brought home unprecedented pictures of the earth that seemed to dramatize the vulnerability of the small blue-green planet as it hung alone in space. Environmentalists around the country proclaimed April 22, 1970, as "Earth Day."

Congress responded with legislation that mandated the careful management of the nation's natural resources. The Environmental Protection Agency was established in 1970. Amendments to the Clean Air (1970) and Clean Water (1972) acts tightened restrictions on harmful emissions from cars and factories. The Endangered Species Act (1973) created for the first time the legal right of nonhuman animals to survive, a major step toward viewing the quality of human life as inextricable from the earth's broader ecology. Nixon did not take the lead in promoting environmental laws, about which he personally cared little, telling business supporters that "in a flat choice between smoke and jobs, we're for jobs." But the president recognized the bipartisan popularity of actions to limit ecological damage, and he followed Congress's lead.

What Nixon did care deeply about at home was politics, not policy. Antiwar demonstrations reached their height during Nixon's first 2 years in the White House (1969–1970). He and Vice President Spiro Agnew loathed the protesters, whom they saw as weakening the nation. The two men pursued what Agnew called "positive polarization": campaigning to further divide the respectable "silent majority," as the president labeled his supporters, from voluble liberal Democrats in Congress and radical activists on the streets, whom they associated with permissiveness and lawlessness. In this broad cultural battle for political supremacy, the president appealed to conservative white southern and northern ethnic Democrats. His "Southern strategy" centered on opposing the use of court-ordered busing to desegregate public schools. He nominated two very conservative Southerners to the Supreme Court, only to see the Senate vote both of them down.

Antiwar demonstrations reached their height during Nixon's first 2 years in the White House (1969–1970).

Early in his administration Nixon began wielding the power of the federal government to harass his political opponents. Johnson had used the FBI, the CIA, and military intelligence agencies to infiltrate and thin the ranks of antiwar demonstrators and nonwhite nationalists. Nixon continued those illegal operations, agreeing with his predecessor that radical activists constituted a threat to national security. Nixon even suggested that the nation's worst enemies were at home: "North Vietnam cannot defeat or humiliate the United States. Only Americans can do that." He went beyond other presidents in assembling an "Enemies List" that included prominent elements of the political mainstream, especially liberals, the press, and his Democratic opponents. The president was particularly concerned about controlling secret information. The Pentagon Papers were a classified Defense Department history of U.S. actions in Vietnam revealing that the government had been deceiving the American public about the course of the war. When disillusioned former Pentagon official Daniel Ellsberg leaked the study to the *New York Times* for publication in 1971, Nixon was enraged. The White House created a team of covert operatives nicknamed the Plumbers to "plug leaks" by whatever means necessary, including breaking into the office of Ellsberg's psychiatrist in search of information they might use to discredit him publicly.

Escalating and Deescalating in Vietnam

Nixon recognized that in Vietnam the Truman Doctrine (see Chapter 24) had been stretched to the breaking point. The United States simply could not afford to send its troops everywhere abroad to contain the expansion of communism. The president and his national security adviser, Henry Kissinger, had ambitious plans for shifting the relationships of the great powers to America's advantage. To deal with China and the Soviet Union, they first had to reduce the vast U.S. engagement in the small country of Vietnam, which had grown wildly out of proportion to actual U.S. interests there. Their vision became known as the Nixon

Doctrine, in which the United States would provide military hardware rather than U.S. soldiers to allied governments, which would have to do their own fighting against leftist insurgencies. In South Vietnam this doctrine required "Vietnamization," or withdrawing American troops so ARVN could shoulder the bulk of the war.

The key to a successful withdrawal from Vietnam for Nixon was to preserve U.S. "credibility." The perception of power could be as important as its actual exercise, and the president wanted other nations, both friend and foe, to continue to respect and fear American military might. There was no immediate pullout but a gradual process that lasted for 4 years (1969–1973), during which almost half of the total U.S. casualties in Vietnam occurred. To avoid a humiliating collapse of the Saigon regime as soon as Americans left, Nixon did his utmost to weaken the communist forces during the slow withdrawal. The administration escalated in order to deescalate. The president ordered the secret bombing and invasion of neighboring Cambodia and Laos, an intensified aerial assault on North Vietnam, and the mining of Haiphong Harbor near Hanoi. Enormous protests rocked the country after the announcement of the Cambodian invasion on April 30, 1970, including a strike by hundreds of thousands of students that disrupted classes on more than 700 college campuses. National Guard troops killed four students at a demonstration at Kent State University in Ohio and two at Jackson State College in Mississippi, deepening the sense of national division. The hit song "Four Dead in Ohio" by the popular group Crosby, Stills, Nash, and Young quickly became an antiwar anthem.

A majority of Americans now opposed the nation's war effort, a level of dissent unprecedented in U.S. history. Most telling of all was the criticism of some veterans returning from Vietnam. Although most stayed quiet about their traumatic experiences, some organized the Vietnam Veterans Against the War and even held public hearings into atrocities—war crimes—they and others had committed. These dissenters were extremely hard for prowar Americans to discredit. The morale of American soldiers still in Vietnam plummeted as the steady withdrawal of their comrades made clear that they were no longer expected to win the war. Drug abuse and racial conflict increased sharply among GIs. Even "fragging" (killing one's own officers) escalated before the peace accords were signed in Paris and the U.S. evacuated its last combat troops in 1973.

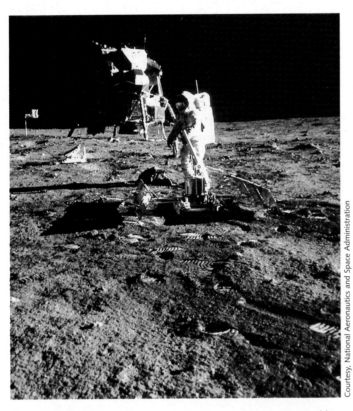

Courtesy, National Aeronautics and Space Administration

■ On July 20, 1969, astronauts Neil Armstrong and Edwin "Buzz" Aldrin put the first footprints on the moon. The U.S. flag they planted epitomized the sense of national accomplishment in space, even as divisions wracked American society at home. The actual flag here was made of rigid material because no lunar breeze existed to make the flag wave.

Conclusion

Between 1964 and 1971 changes shook the foundations of society and altered how Americans understood themselves. Many long-standing hierarchies of age, race, and gender began to break up as young, non-white, and female Americans laid claim to greater equality. The ratification of the Twenty-Sixth Amendment in 1971 reduced the voting age from 21 to 18, in acknowledgment of the sacrifices of young people sent to fight in Vietnam. In large numbers, women challenged and overcame traditional limits on their personal and work lives. Racial discrimination and segregation were outlawed. Immigration law for the first time welcomed new Americans equally regardless of nation of origin or color of skin.

©1976 George Ballis/Take Stock

■ Cesar Chávez led a march during the United Farm Workers strike—*huelga*—against large grape growers in Delano, in California's central valley, in 1966. The UFW effort, in which women such as UFW vice-president Dolores Huerta (a mother of 11) figured prominently, included not only union organizing but also building a broader network of community institutions to improve the lives of Mexican American laborers. The Roman Catholic faith and pacifism of Chávez and others in the movement deeply impressed many non-Chicanos who supported the strike, such as Senator Robert F. Kennedy.

These years also witnessed striking disjunctures. The nation accomplished humanity's age-old dream of walking on the surface of the moon when Neil Armstrong stepped out of the *Apollo 11* spacecraft on July 20, 1969, while at home the country sometimes appeared to be coming apart at the seams. Poverty rates dropped to their lowest point ever, yet violence seemed to pervade the land. The slaughter of 43 people (mostly African Americans) by white state police retaking the Attica prison in upstate New York after an inmate insurrection in 1971 was one of the single most deadly confrontations between Americans since the Civil War.

The Vietnam War ended the Cold War consensus about the nation's duty to oppose communism abroad. The loss of this cornerstone of public purpose disoriented many citizens. The deceptive manner in which Johnson and Nixon waged the war eroded Americans' faith in their public officials, a process that the Watergate scandal accelerated between 1972 and 1974. American life also grew more informal as the egalitarian style of the various social movements of the 1960s spread into the broader culture. But the removal of some of the most blatant distinctions of race and gender did not extend to differences of class. In the watershed cases of *San Antonio*

Independent School District v. Rodriguez (1973) and *Milliken v. Bradley* (1974), the Supreme Court, led by Chief Justice Warren Burger, affirmed the autonomy of local school districts. Wealthier districts did not have to share financing with poorer ones, nor did they have to share students by means of busing. The Court ruled that there was no constitutional right to an education of equal quality. The ladder of social mobility remained slippery in a nation whose neighborhoods were still stratified between the affluent and the poor.

Sites to Visit

The Sixties Project
lists.village.virginia.edu/sixties/

This University of Virginia site has extensive exhibits, primary documents, and personal narratives from the 1960s.

Lyndon B. Johnson Library and Museum
www.lbjlib.utexas.edu/

This presidential library site has images and online exhibits.

Vietnam War Internet Project
www.vwip.org/vwiphome.html

This site offers one of the most extensive collections on the Web of useful information on various aspects of the war.

My Lai Court Martial (1970)
www.law.umkc.edu/faculty/projects/ftrials/mylai/mylai.htm

This site contains images, chronology, and court and official documents maintained by Dr. Doug Linder at the University of Missouri–Kansas City Law School.

The Digger Archives
www.diggers.org

This site provides information about the San Francisco Diggers, a prominent countercultural group in the Haight–Asbury scene of 1966–1968.

U.S. Latino History and Culture (Smithsonian Institution)
www.si.edu/resource/faq/nmah/latino.htm

This site offers exhibits, photos, resources, and links to other useful sites on the lives of Latino Americans.

Gay Rights Movement
www.columbia.edu/cu/libraries/events/sw25/casel.html

This site includes articles from the New York City press as well as first-hand accounts of the 1969 Greenwich Village riots that are commemorated throughout the country during Gay Pride celebrations.

For Further Reading

General

Chafe, William H. *The Unfinished Journey: America Since World War II.* 3rd ed. 1995.

Farber, David. *The Age of Great Dreams: America in the 1960s.* 1994.

Farber, David, ed. *The Sixties: From Memory to History.* 1994.

Isserman, Maurice and Michael Kazin. *America Divided: The Civil War of the 1960s.* 2000.

Patterson, James T. *Grand Expectations: The United States, 1945–1974.* 1996.

Lyndon Johnson and the Apex of Liberalism

Dallek, Robert. *Flawed Giant: Lyndon Johnson and His Times, 1961–1973.* 1998.

Matusow, Allen J. *The Unravelling of America: A History of Liberalism in the 1960s.* 1984.

Powe, Lucas A., Jr. *The Warren Court and American Politics.* 2000.

Schulman, Bruce J. *Lyndon B. Johnson and American Liberalism.* 1995.

The Autobiography of Malcolm X. 1965.

Into War in Vietnam

Gardner, Lloyd C. *Pay Any Price: Lyndon Johnson and the Wars for Vietnam.* 1995.

Herr, Michael. *Dispatches.* 1977.

Herring, George C. *America's Longest War: The United States and Vietnam, 1950–1975.* 3rd ed. 1996.

Rotter, Andrew J., ed. *Light at the End of the Tunnel: A Vietnam War Anthology.* Revised ed. 1999.

Schulzinger, Robert D. *A Time for War: The United States and Vietnam, 1941–1975.* 1997.

Young, Marilyn B. *The Vietnam Wars, 1945–1990.* 1991.

The Movement

Anderson, Terry H. *The Movement and the Sixties: Protest in America from Greensboro to Wounded Knee.* 1995.

Echols, Alice. *Daring to Be Bad: Radical Feminism in America, 1967–1975.* 1989.

Evans, Sara. *Personal Politics: The Roots of Women's Liberation in the Civil Rights Movement and the New Left.* 1979.

Gitlin, Todd. *The Sixties: Years of Hope, Days of Rage.* 1987.

Miller, Timothy. *The '60s Communes: Hippies and Beyond.* 1999.

Van Deburg, William L. *New Day in Babylon: The Black Power Movement and American Culture, 1965–1975.* 1992.

Wells, Tom. *The War Within: America's Battle over Vietnam.* 1994.

The Conservative Response

Carter, Dan T. *The Politics of Rage: George Wallace, the Origins of the New Conservatism, and the Transformation of American Politics.* 2nd ed. 2000.

Kimball, Jeffrey. *Nixon's Vietnam War.* 1998.

McGirr, Lisa. *Suburban Warriors: The Origins of the New American Right.* 2001.

Rothman, Hal K. *The Greening of a Nation? Environmentalism in the United States since 1945.* 1998.

Small, Melvin. *The Presidency of Richard Nixon.* 1999.

Online Practice Test

Test your understanding of this chapter with interactive review quizzes at

www.ablongman.com/jonescreatedequal/chapter26

Additional Photo Credits

Page 867: John Launois/Black Star
Page 870: Courtesy, Janice L. and David Frent
Page 884: Courtesy, Janice L. and David Frent
Page 885: Library of Congress
Page 893: Courtesy, Janice L. and David Frent
Page 895: Courtesy, Janice L. and David Frent

Reconsidering National Priorities, 1972–1979

■ This 1976 sculpture by George Segal hinted at the uncertainties that pervaded American society in the mid-1970s.

KAREN SILKWOOD GREW UP IN AN UNASSUMING MIDDLE-CLASS FAMILY IN NEDERLAND, Texas, near the Gulf Coast. She baby-sat at her church nursery, earned straight A's through high school, and went to Lamar College on a full scholarship to study medical technology. Marriage, three children, and a divorce intervened, and in 1972 she began working as a laboratory analyst at Kerr–McGee's plutonium processing plant in Crescent, Oklahoma. There the highly poisonous radioactive material was made into fuel rods for nuclear power plants.

In the summer of 1974, at age 28, Silkwood was elected a local official of the union that represented many Kerr–McGee workers and began organizing for greater worker safety. She learned of numerous incidents of radioactive contamination at the plant. She also uncovered evidence of significant quantities of missing plutonium and of doctored quality assurance records for defective fuel rods. On November 5, she was mysteriously contaminated with potentially lethal levels of plutonium. On November 13 Silkwood set out for Oklahoma City to meet a national representative of her union and a *New York Times* reporter, intending to give them documents proving that Kerr–McGee was knowingly manufacturing defective nuclear products. She never made it. Her car was forced off the road and she died instantly when it crashed into a concrete culvert.

Karen Silkwood became a symbol of courage to many.

Karen Silkwood challenged the power of one of the nation's largest energy corporations and paid with her life. Her brief career as a whistleblower brought together major issues of the 1970s: labor organizing, environmental damage, the safety record of nuclear energy, and the power of corporations over individual citizens. Her dismissive treatment by some fellow workers, her employers, and the media also suggested the lack of respect that women had long endured, especially when they moved out of the traditional homemaker role. ABC television news anchor Howard K. Smith began his coverage of a women's rights march in New York City in 1970 by quoting with approval the words of Vice President Spiro Agnew: "Three things have been difficult to tame. The ocean, fools, and women. We may soon be able to tame the ocean, but fools and women will take a little longer."

Condescension toward women still pervaded American society, and few men even noticed it. The political upheavals of the 1960s had barely touched the relationships between most women and men by the start of the new decade. But all this changed as the 1970s unfolded. The spread of ideas about women's liberation in the 1970s transformed the personal lives of almost every American, female and male alike. Feminism challenged the most basic and intimate assumptions about relationships, family, work, and power. It also sharply expanded women's opportunities. At the end of the decade, Dr. Martha Hurley of Kansas City recalled, "In the middle of an operation today, I looked around the room—to the first assistant, my scrub nurse, and circulating nurse, the anesthesia doctor, nurse anesthetist, and the patient—and suddenly realized that we were performing major surgery and there was not a man in the room!"

Who were the feminists? They were mothers and wives, college students, professional women, and working-class women. Their growing awareness of gender discrimination had made them angry but also optimistic about change. And some feminists were men who realized that the movement could liberate them from their own narrowly defined masculine roles. Feminists of all stripes could be both deadly serious and disarmingly funny. Journalist Gloria Steinem, who founded *Ms.* magazine in 1972, became one of the prominent faces of the movement. Steinem's appearance enabled her to finagle a job as a cocktail waitress at the New York Playboy Club in 1963. Her goal: to write an exposé of the decidedly unsexy working conditions of the famous Playboy "bunnies." Steinem later lampooned men's common sense of entitlement and privilege and their often competitive attitudes toward their bodies in an essay called "If Men Could Menstruate": "Clearly, menstruation would become an enviable, boastworthy, masculine event: Men would brag about how much and how long. Young boys would talk about it as the envied beginning of manhood. Gifts, religious ceremonies, family dinners, and stag parties would mark the day."

Not all Americans were amused by challenges to long-standing beliefs about men's and women's proper roles. J. Edgar Hoover, director of the Federal Bureau of Investigation (FBI), exemplified the resistance that could catalyze against demands for fair treatment of women. Well known for his dislike of leftists, African Americans, homosexuals, and anyone else who questioned the existing social order—including labor organizers such as Karen Silkwood—Hoover ordered his agents to infiltrate the women's liberation movement. (Ironically, Hoover was a crossdresser in private and perhaps also gay, an apparent case of self-loathing.) Feminists, he warned FBI regional directors, "should be viewed as part of the enemy, a challenge to American values." At one point, the director instructed an FBI field office to "identify the officers and aims and objectives of this organization." But despite determined digging for information, a paid informant could report only that "this movement has no leaders, dues or organizations." Women's liberation was both nowhere and everywhere. No one could trace it to a specific group of conspirators.

> *The feminist wave called traditional values and hierarchies into question as it washed over the United States in the 1970s.*

In a certain sense, Hoover was right: the feminist wave did call traditional values and hierarchies into question as it washed over the United States in the 1970s. It joined with other developments of the decade to force Americans to reexamine much that they had taken for granted. Elected on the promise to end the war in Southeast Asia "with honor," President Nixon escalated the fighting before eventually withdrawing U.S. forces from Vietnam. At the same time, he repaired relations with both China and the Soviet Union as those two communist powers drew apart. Americans thus suffered their first clear defeat in war while also seeing the Cold War splinter. Scandal in the White House then forced the first resignation of a U.S. president and deepened public distrust of political authorities. American economic growth—the foundation of the country's power—stumbled because of spending on the Vietnam War and oil shortages. High-paying manufacturing jobs declined as factories began to move overseas in pursuit of cheaper labor, and skilled blue-collar workers saw their status as middle-class Americans start to slip. Unemployment grew sharply. And a growing environmental movement raised disturbing questions about whether an expanding economy and exploitation of natural resources should continue to top the country's list of priorities.

The nation celebrated its two-hundredth birthday in 1976 amid these uncertainties. That year, one-term Georgia governor Jimmy Carter won election to the White House by promising to restore honesty and trust to the federal government. In his first two years in office, Carter shifted the nation's foreign policy focus away from fighting communism toward building warmer relations with the Third World. He saw Americans' dependence on imported oil as a primary national security problem and implored citizens to scale back their lavish consumption of fossil fuels. But his presidency eventually foundered on persistent economic stagnation and inflation at home, upheavals abroad, and Carter's own limitations as chief executive.

Journalist Tom Wolfe dubbed the 1970s the "Me Decade," a phrase that proved even more appropriate for the 1980s. The label did have some merit: many Americans turned away from the public sphere after the exhilarating but divisive politics of the 1960s and pursued self-exploration and self-fulfillment instead. Crime, divorce, premarital and extramarital sex, and drug use all increased while the nation's economic health and international status declined. But the 1970s also witnessed a rethinking of long-standing assumptions: about how democracy should work at home, what role the nation should play in international affairs, how people ought to treat the environment, and how men and women should relate to each other. The decade offered a window of opportunity for Americans to reimagine their values and priorities for the future.

Twin Shocks: Détente and Watergate

Richard Nixon had long been the nation's leading anticommunist. No one had more fiercely opposed leftists at home and communists in China and the Soviet Union. However, the president was more a savvy political opportunist than an ideologue. He and his national security adviser, Henry Kissinger, saw a chance to use mounting Chinese–Soviet tensions to the advantage of the United States as they withdrew American armed forces from Vietnam. Nixon and Kissinger recognized that the United States had entered an era of new limits to its power. They cleverly tapped into the rivalry dividing the communist world to preserve U.S. influence overseas. Their efforts ultimately eased Cold War tensions.

At the same time that Nixon manipulated the Cold War abroad, the Republican president initiated a campaign of illegal actions at home to destroy his political opponents in the Democratic party. This strategy backfired in a scandal that drove him from office in 1974. Having undercut the logic of anticommunism abroad by warming relations with communist leaders in Beijing and Moscow, Nixon eroded the bipartisan consensus at home that had long supported the Cold War. Wearied by the deceptions and debates of Vietnam, Americans found themselves questioning anew their political assumptions and the trustworthiness of their leaders.

Triangular Diplomacy

Nixon and Kissinger prided themselves on their "realpolitik" approach to foreign policy: their pragmatic assessment of other powers' security needs, regardless of ideology, and their collaboration with those powers on issues of common concern. In 1969, China and the USSR gave Nixon and Kissinger an ideal opportunity to exercise their realpolitik skills. That year, tensions that had

The National Archives

■ **President Nixon met the premier of the People's Republic of China, Mao Zedong, in Beijing on February 29, 1972. The U.S. government had shunned China since its communist revolution in 1949. Richard Nixon's amiable visit there stunned observers and altered the dynamics of the Cold War.**

■ **MAP 27.1**

NUCLEAR WEAPONS BEFORE DÉTENTE The massive nuclear arsenals of the United States and the Soviet Union utterly surpassed those of the other nuclear powers. During the 1970s the Soviets achieved rough parity with the Americans in total nuclear warheads. The numbers for both sides were sufficient to destroy the entire populated world many times over.

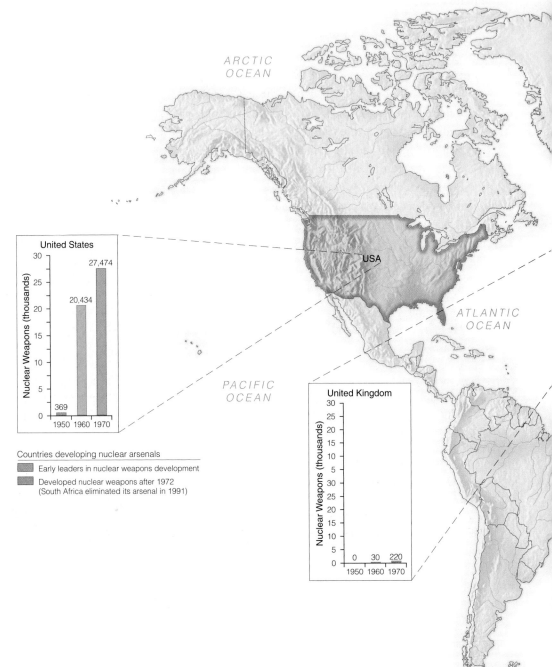

been building between the two communist states erupted in brief skirmishing between Chinese and Soviet troops on their shared border. For two decades, Americans had seen the Communist bloc as impenetrable. Nixon realized he could play China and the USSR against each other, and he seized the chance. That is, he saw a way to make both Soviet leader Leonid Brezhnev and Chinese leader Mao Zedong into another "Tito," an independent communist with ties to the West, like Premier Josef Tito of Yugoslavia. He thus envisioned a "triangular diplomacy" that he hoped would divide the communist world.

The president and Kissinger, a former Harvard professor with an intriguing German accent, also shared a commitment to secrecy. Any fundamental revision of the nation's for-

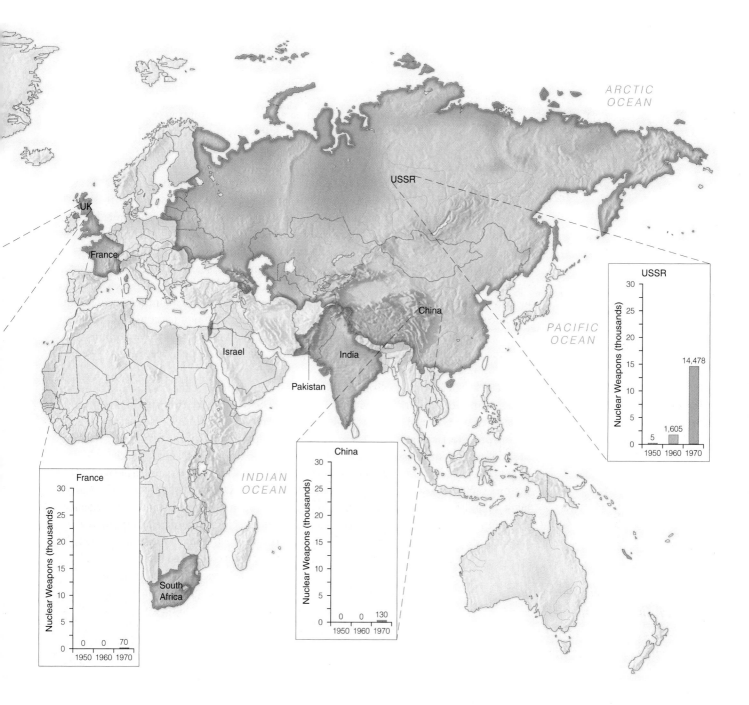

eign policy, they believed, could happen only if they concentrated all decision-making in the White House. They set out to keep Congress, the press, and even their own State Department in the dark. Diplomatic innovation thus went hand in hand with an unprecedented extension of the secretive national security state.

In February 1972, after a secret foray by Kissinger to Beijing, Nixon stunned Americans and the world by announcing that he would be the first U.S. president to visit China. The Soviets and the Vietnamese expressed dismay at the news, and liberal Democrats at home could only gape, speechless, at their opponent's diplomatic coup: how could Nixon, a dyed-in-the-wool anticommunist, go to China? But that was precisely the point: as Democratic party insider

Clark Clifford explained, Nixon was "the first president since the [Second World] War who didn't have to worry about Richard Nixon" attacking him for being "soft" on communism.

As it turned out, Nixon's visit brought a host of benefits. Live television coverage showed Nixon toasting Mao while a Chinese military band played "America the Beautiful" and "Home on the Range." Americans' impression of the People's Republic as a grim, forbidding land began to give way to a renewed interest in China as an exotic but intriguing place. Cultural exchanges soon proliferated: first ping-pong teams, eventually legions of students. U.S. businesses also cast a covetous eye at the immense China market. Trade between the two nations rose dramatically over the next three decades.

Nixon and Kissinger now constructed the other leg of their diplomatic triangle. As they anticipated, the Soviets had taken alarm at the warming of relations between their two greatest rivals. They signaled their concern to Washington and suggested that the United States include them in the new arrangements. Nixon and Kissinger understood that behind Moscow's veneer of revolutionary dogma stood a powerful nation increasingly committed to the international status quo. Moreover, the Russians and the Americans shared similar concerns. Both wanted to reduce the costliness of maintaining enormous nuclear arsenals, and each side saw lucrative trading possibilities with the other. Nixon flew to Moscow for a summit meeting with Brezhnev in May 1972 that initiated a policy of détente (relaxation of tensions). A trade pact quickly followed. The two superpowers also agreed to limit offensive nuclear weapons (the Strategic Arms Limitations Treaty, or SALT I) and to ban antiballistic missile defense systems (the ABM treaty).

Like the Soviet leaders, Nixon and Kissinger sought to preserve the existing international balance of power. Deal-making with China and the USSR constituted one step in this process. In another, the two men sought to stifle socialist revolutions in Third World nations by bolstering pro-American allies there. For instance, the duo feared that the democratic election of socialist Salvador Allende in Chile in 1970 would lead to "another Cuba." A socialist leader might nationalize the investments of U.S. corporations in Chile and perhaps challenge Washington's capitalist hegemony in the Western Hemisphere. Determined to block these possibilities, the CIA secretly funded a right-wing military coup in Chile in September 1973. Allende died in the assault on the presidential palace, and the rebel forces murdered thousands of his supporters and established a brutal military dictatorship under General Augusto Pinochet. "I don't see why we need to stand by and watch a country go Communist because of the irresponsibility of its own people," Kissinger explained privately.

After the bungled Watergate break-in, the president directed the cover-up from the beginning, then lied about it to the public.

There was little danger of such voter "irresponsibility" in South Africa, a nation that would not see democratic elections for another two decades. Still, the Nixon administration backed the white minority regime there, despite worldwide criticism of the government's policies of total racial segregation, or apartheid. Nixon's "southern strategy" of appealing to segregationist whites at home during the 1968 election campaign thus had an international parallel. In South Africa, "the whites are here to stay," a key National Security Council study declared. The study affirmed the president's goal of preserving a pro-American order in South Africa, the southern tip of a continent rife with political instability.

Nixon and Kissinger reached beyond Latin America and Africa. They also bolstered the autocratic regime of Shah Reza Pahlavi of Iran. They sold him unlimited arms in return for Iranian oil shipments and political support in the strategic Middle East, where the United States had few allies. The president could not know it at the time, but preserving the Shah's oppressive rule carried a high price—one that the United States would pay later.

Scandal in the White House

On June 17, 1972, Washington police caught agents of Nixon's reelection campaign breaking into the Democratic National Committee headquarters in the Watergate hotel and office complex. The burglars' goal was to put in place secretive listening devices, or "bugs." Later, the White House tried to cover up its connections to the caper. Ironically, the Republicans hardly needed to resort to illegal actions to hold onto the White House in 1972. The New Deal coalition that had kept the Democrats as the majority party since the 1930s was fast unraveling. White Southerners and many ethnic European Northerners were abandoning the party amid its increasing identification with black civil rights, feminism, and cultural liberalism. Middle- and upper-middle-class liberal activists had helped nominate South Dakota senator George McGovern, a former World War II pilot and college professor, as the Democratic presidential candidate, primarily on the basis of his principled and long-standing opposition to the war in Vietnam. Playing upon voter anxiety about cultural changes, the Republicans tarred McGovern's supporters with favoring "the 3 A's": acid (the drug LSD), abortion, and amnesty for draft evaders. McGovern's campaign never overcame that image of radicalism, and in November Nixon won 61 percent of the popular vote. He also swept the electoral votes of every state but one. Bumper stickers reading "Don't blame me, I'm from Massachusetts" proliferated as the Watergate scandal deepened.

TABLE 27-1			
The Election of 1972			
Candidate	Political Party	Popular Vote	Electoral Vote
Richard M. Nixon	Republican	47,169,911	520
George S. McGovern	Democratic	29,170,383	17

But the Watergate break-in was only one step in Nixon's broader campaign of illegal warfare against his political opponents. An insecure and unhappy loner, Nixon harbored an almost paranoid suspicion when he took office in early 1969. The conflict still raging in Vietnam had polarized Americans more than at any time since the Civil War, and the president compiled a lengthy and secret "enemies list." "This is a war. . . . They are asking for it and they are going to get it," he told aides. The president continued his predecessor's harassment of antiwar dissidents. He also agreed with Johnson's advice that "leaks can kill you" and sought tighter control over all executive agencies of the federal government.

Nixon and Kissinger took things one step further in May 1969, when they established the first in a long series of wiretaps without court warrants on their own staffs and reporters. They were determined to discover the source of a newspaper story that had mentioned secret American bombing of neutral Cambodia. Several wartime presidents in the past had successfully silenced dissenters, but Nixon overreached still further. The president ultimately poisoned the very heart of American politics by his clandestine use of the government's powerful executive branch to undermine the mainstream opposition party and others who seemed to challenge his policies.

The president and his aides regularly discussed "how we can use the available federal machinery to screw our political enemies," in the words of White House counsel John Dean. They persuaded the FBI and the CIA to monitor and harass antiwar activists and pushed the Internal Revenue Service to investigate prominent Democrats. They extorted large contributions to the Republican party from corporate executives by making it clear that federal agencies would otherwise impede the pursuit of their business interests. The *New York Times*'s publication of the classified Pentagon Papers in 1971 stiffened the resolve of the Committee to Reelect the President (CREEP) to stop any further leaks. The committee assembled a group of undercover operatives (the "plumbers") to engineer "dirty tricks" against the Democrats. Their activities included smearing the reputation of one leading presidential candidate, Senator Edmund Muskie of Maine, and sowing dissent and distrust among Democratic voters. For example, during the New Hampshire primary, Democrats in that nearly all-white state received late-night phone calls from a mysterious "Harlem for Muskie" committee. Callers urged them to vote for the senator because of his supposed support for African Americans' interests—a devious ploy to arouse potential racism.

After the bungled Watergate break-in, the president directed the cover-up from the beginning, then lied about it to the public. He also used the CIA to hinder the FBI's investigation

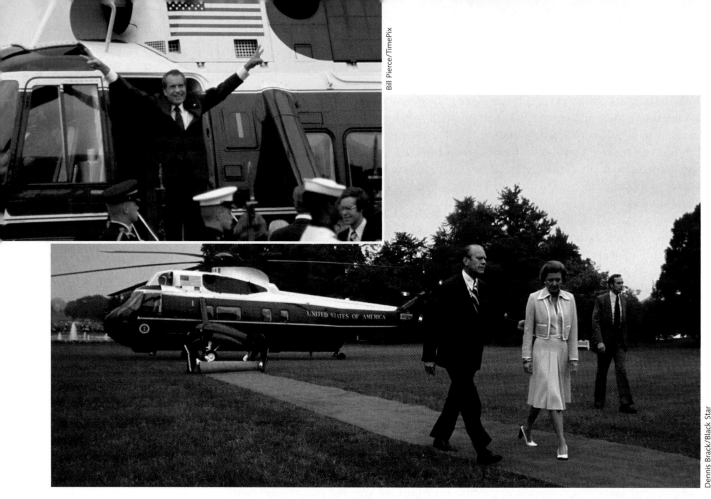

■ On August 9, 1974, Richard Nixon became the only U.S. president to resign from office. As he left by helicopter one last time from the South Lawn of the White House, he offered a defiant victory gesture rather than a presidential salute (inset). Vice President Gerald Ford and his wife, Betty, then walked back to the White House for him to be sworn in as the nation's 38th president.

into the matter. He approved payments of hush money to the burglars to keep them quiet about their ties to the White House. Nixon's abuse of power escalated as he pressured his subordinates to perjure themselves in court. For most of a year the cover-up held, and Nixon won reelection in 1972.

But the persistent investigations by *Washington Post* journalists Bob Woodward and Carl Bernstein kept the heat on. In early 1973, the administration began to crack due to a grand jury probe in the federal court of Judge John Sirica. The president's men lost confidence that the cover-up would hold and began looking for ways to save their own skins. Convicted Watergate burglar James McCord wrote Judge Sirica that the White House had indeed been involved in the break-in. White House counsel Dean and former Attorney General John Mitchell refused Nixon's requests to absorb full blame and become scapegoats. Congress initiated its own televised investigations that mesmerized a national audience. The Senate Watergate committee, chaired by eloquent conservative North Carolina Democrat Sam Ervin, methodically exposed the criminal actions in the White House with growing bipartisan support. The key issue, as framed by Republican committee member Howard Baker of Tennessee becam, "What did the president know, and when did he know it?"

On July 16, 1973, White House aide Alexander Butterfield told the Ervin Committee that a built-in recorder taped all conversations in the Oval Office. Almost certainly, these tapes would provide answers to questions about the president's role. Both Congress and Justice Department special prosecutor Archibald Cox subpoenaed the White House tapes, but Nixon refused to hand them over. Instead, he fired Cox on October 20 in what became known as the Saturday Night Massacre. Outraged, Congress initiated impeachment proceedings against the president.

In the spring of 1974, the House of Representatives passed bills of impeachment for his specific abuses of power. Before the Senate could vote on whether to find Nixon guilty of the House charges, the Supreme Court ruled that the White House had to turn over the subpoenaed tapes. The content of the tapes revealed the extent of the president's involvement in the cover-up and his personal crudeness, vindictiveness, and ethnic and racial prejudices. Facing a certain guilty verdict, Nixon resigned on August 9, 1974, less than halfway through his second term.

A President Laid Low

Never before had a U.S. president been driven from office. Many citizens celebrated the outcome of the Watergate investigations as evidence of democracy's resilience and power to uncover criminal activity in the White House and bring down a corrupt president. But the affair also discredited political institutions Americans had long respected. If you can't trust the president, U.S. citizens lamented, whom *can* you trust? Indeed, the Nixon administration proved quite corrupt. A whole raft of senior officials, including the president's closest aides, H. R. Haldeman and John Ehrlichman, went to prison. Even Vice President Spiro Agnew was forced to resign amid the Watergate investigations when a Maryland jury found him guilty of tax evasion dating back to his years as governor there. The actions of Nixon and those who served him permanently tarnished the reputation of politicians, and citizens responded by disengaging from the political process. The percentage of eligible voters actually casting ballots sank from 61 percent in 1968 to 53 percent in 1980, diminishing the practice of democracy: rule by the people.

Unlike the impeachment of President Bill Clinton 26 years later, which centered on executive lying about a sexual affair in the Oval Office, the Watergate scandal involved larger issues of presidential power in the public realm. It also raised questions about the balance of power throughout the U.S. political system. Since 1945, the executive branch had grown increasingly powerful during the international crises of the Cold War, but Nixon's fall crippled the "imperial presidency." After Watergate, Congress began to reclaim its constitutional responsibilities in international affairs. As the bicentennial of American independence approached, citizens' suspicion of corruption in high places recalled the Whiggish attitudes of the country's revolutionary leaders two centuries before. Most immediately, Congress swung strongly to the Democrats in the 1974 elections, slowing the Republicans' rise to the status of majority party.

> *As the bicentennial approached, suspicion of corruption in high places recalled the attitudes of the country's revolutionary leaders two centuries before.*

The man who replaced Nixon in the White House faced a daunting situation. Gerald Ford, longtime Republican congressman and House minority leader from Grand Rapids, Michigan, had been tapped by Nixon to replace Agnew as vice president. Well liked by members of both parties, Ford seemed to embody the antidote to the extreme styles of both Nixon and Agnew. To restore decency and trust in the government, Ford saw his role as healing what he called "the wounds of the past." Within a month, he granted a "full, free, and absolute pardon" to Nixon for any crimes he may have committed as president, precluding any trial and punishment within a court of law. However, most Americans believed that Nixon should have faced justice for his actions, just as the people did who carried out his orders. Ford's popularity plummeted overnight from 72 percent to 49 percent and never fully recovered.

If Ford inherited the fallout from Watergate at home, abroad he inherited the pending defeat in Vietnam. Few Americans wanted to dwell on the meaning of the disastrous U.S. involvement in Southeast Asia. Military veterans returned to a nation determined to ignore or demean their sacrifices, and they quickly learned to keep their combat-induced traumas to themselves (and sometimes even from their families). When Saigon finally fell to the combined invasion of National Liberation Front and North Vietnamese fighters on April 30, 1975, Americans watched the televised images with both bitterness and relief. Two weeks later, Cambodian communist forces briefly seized the U.S. container ship *Mayaguez*, provoking Ford to demonstrate

■ The last U.S. combat troops left Vietnam in 1973. Forces of the National Liberation Front and North Vietnam swept into the capital of South Vietnam, Saigon, on April 30, 1975. Here, one day earlier, a Marine helicopter on the roof of the U.S. embassy loads Americans and a few Vietnamese allies onto one of the last flights out.

that the United States was still ready and willing to flex its military muscle. But 41 U.S. soldiers died in the rescue mission to save 39 sailors whom, it turned out, Cambodia had already released. Ford and Kissinger, serving as the new president's secretary of state, continued to pursue détente with the Soviets at summit meetings in Vladivostock (1974) and Helsinki (1975). At the same time, they supported anticommunist forces in various Third World conflicts, such as the civil war that erupted in Angola after that country achieved its independence in 1975.

Discovering the Limits of the U.S. Economy

If money makes the world go around, the United States began to lose some of its ability to spin the globe in the early 1970s. Generation after generation of Americans had watched their incomes rise, and most children expected to be wealthier than their parents had been. Since World War II had pulled the U.S. economy out of the Great Depression, median family income had doubled. Most Americans saw themselves as citizens of the world's richest country and prized the status that came with this privilege. But by 1973, the famous American standard of living began to decline. The three pillars of postwar prosperity—cheap energy, rising wages, and low inflation—simultaneously crumbled. The costs of the Vietnam War struck home at the same time that an oil embargo spawned by conflict in the Middle East gripped the country. Moreover, a widening environmental movement raised questions about the pursuit of endless economic growth on a planet that more and more people realized had limited natural resources. For the first time since the 1930s, Americans started to doubt what the economic future had in store for them.

The End of the Long Boom

Stagnation and inflation typically do not strike an economy at the same time. With stagnation, prices and wages stay level or even decline; with inflation, prices rise and jobs grow. During the 1970s, however, a terrible new economic scourge dubbed "stagflation" hit the United States. For the first time, employment and wages stagnated while prices climbed. What explained this phenomenon? Spending on the Vietnam War had pulled prices upward. The government had never raised enough taxes to cover the expense of the war, so it paid the bills by simply printing more dollars—a sure-fire way to create inflation. In 1971, annual inflation stood at 4.5 percent, more than twice the pre-Vietnam rate; two years later it reached 10 percent, and by 1980 it topped out at 18 percent.

These figures devastated Americans' sense of economic security. Average real wages (income adjusted for inflation) dropped by 2 percent a year from 1973 to the 1990s. Unemployment rose to 9 percent in 1975, driven in part by continued automation of the workplace. Only the continued flow of women into the workforce, seen by most families as an economic necessity, kept the majority of U.S. families afloat financially. The number of citizens living in poverty, which had dropped sharply through the 1960s to 11 percent in 1973, rose again, hitting 15 percent by 1982. The gap between rich and poor began widening, a process that persisted into the next millennium.

So ended the long boom of economic growth that had buoyed American life since 1945. But perhaps the most important evidence of the weakening economy came with the drop in the growth of productivity: output per worker-hour had risen at an annual average of more than 3 percent during the boom. From 1974 to 1992, it rose at less than half that rate.

This decline stemmed in part from competition from abroad, particularly West Germany and Japan. With U.S. assistance (and without the military expenditures that so burdened the United States), those countries had finally rebuilt their economies after World War II and boasted new, more efficient industrial facilities. Imported cars, for example, grew from just 8 percent of the U.S. market in 1970 to 22 percent in 1979 as Hondas, Toyotas, Volkswagens, and Mercedes streamed onto American highways. And the trade surplus that had long symbolized global U.S. economic superiority evaporated in 1971. That year, U.S. imports overtook exports for the first time in the twentieth century. Worried international investors traded in dollars for gold, forcing Nixon to end the 27-year-old Bretton Woods monetary system that had linked all other currencies to the dollar at fixed exchange rates. Freed from the fixed rate of $35 per ounce of gold, the dollar dropped like a stone; by the end of the decade, it took $800 to buy an ounce of gold.

> *Only the continued flow of women into the workforce, seen by most families as an economic necessity, kept the majority of U.S. families afloat financially.*

In this competitive environment, the *Wall Street Journal* reported, American companies "seek places where labor, land, electricity, and taxes are cheap." Corporations found those places in the American South and Southwest, regions characterized by scarce unions, low wage rates, minimal taxes, and negligible local government regulations. Many more such places were in neighboring Mexico. The long-term decline of the Rustbelt—the series of urban industrial centers strung across the Northeast and Midwest—accelerated in the 1970s. As one example, RCA (the Radio Corporation of America) moved its production facilities from Camden, New Jersey, to Bloomington, Indiana, in the 1940s, and eventually to Ciudad Juarez, just over the border from El Paso, Texas, in the 1970s.

Workers lost positions on assembly lines and found jobs at lower wages in the expanding and less unionized service sector. There were exceptions. For instance, when the mostly female Mexican workers at the Farah slacks company in El Paso and other Southwestern cities went on strike from 1972 to 1974, they won the sympathy of a national consumer boycott. Eventually they received some concessions from the company. But the logic of what would soon be called globalization kept most workers at a disadvantage as owners of capital moved production lines to wherever costs were lowest.

Increasingly, U.S. companies shifted their manufacturing to Mexico, where they established *maquiladoras* as early as 1965. These assembly plants, often just a few hundred yards across

■ Many South Vietnamese fled the communist victory in their country in 1975, including this woman and her children crossing the Mekong River. Most of the refugees undertook extremely perilous journeys by boat to other Southeast Asian nations, and hundreds of thousands eventually made their way to the United States.

the Mexican–U.S. border, gave corporations an opportunity to hire primarily female workers at low wages and avoid strict U.S. environmental, labor, and safety laws. "The worst drawback of maquiladora work is all the damage we do to our health" by working with toxic chemicals and solvents, one employee reported. The wages, cheap by U.S. standards, were nonetheless higher than elsewhere in Mexico and drew laborers from central Mexico north to the border region. And few Americans noticed the damage that the factories south of the border were causing to the environment and to the health of workers.

High unemployment and shrinking real wages contributed to rising anti-immigrant sentiment. Two white autoworkers in Detroit in 1982 got into an altercation in a bar with Vincent Chin, a Chinese American (and son of a World War II veteran) whom they called a "Jap." Angered that Japanese auto sales were undercutting jobs in Detroit, they made Chin a scapegoat for their rage, chasing him down the street and beating him to death with a baseball bat. At the same time, Vietnamese refugees who had fled the communist victory in their homeland in 1975 to make a life as shrimp fishers on the Gulf Coast of Texas found their equipment sabotaged by some white competitors.

From Texas to California, Latinos also suffered violence at the hands of both officials and private citizens. For example, three members of the Ku Klux Klan abducted a Latino hitchhiker outside San Diego and delivered him to the U.S. Immigration Service for deportation to Mexico even though he was an American citizen. A wave of police brutality against Latinos alarmed even the White House by 1978, thanks to the lobbying of outraged Latino citizen organizations.

Black Americans also faced an increasing backlash against hard-won civil rights gains. While court-ordered busing to integrate schools in segregated neighborhoods proceeded slowly but peacefully in the South, northern urban whites dug in their heels. In Boston, violence erupted in the school hallways and the streets from 1975 to 1978 as economically vulnerable working-class whites harassed African Americans attending schools in white ethnic neighborhoods of South Boston, and blacks defended themselves.

The Oil Embargo

Nothing revealed Americans' newfound economic vulnerability more than the 1973–1974 boycott initiated by the Oil Producing and Exporting Countries (OPEC). The United States and the Soviet Union, along with Mexico and Venezuela, retained large oil reserves. But the largest producers were the Arab countries around the Persian Gulf, especially Saudi Arabia. These nations had resented the creation of Israel in 1948 and the resulting displacement of the Palestinians. Hostility intensified with the events of 1967. That year, Israel seized control of the West Bank of the Jordan River and the Gaza Strip. Six years later, Egypt and Syria struck back, attacking jointly on Yom Kippur, the holiest day of the Jewish year. The Arab armies threatened to overrun Israel until the United States gave the Israeli army a critical resupply of weapons, which helped turn the tide of battle.

Henry Kissinger then shuttled between Tel Aviv and Cairo to negotiate a ceasefire. His diplomatic skills won him the Nobel peace prize and laid the groundwork for a warming of U.S. relations with Egypt (the most populous Arab nation but not an oil producer). However, the other Arab states expressed outrage at this demonstration of America's close links with the

Stanley J. Forman, *The Soiling of Old Glory*, Pulitzer Prize 1976

■ White resistance to school busing in Boston sometimes turned violent in the mid–1970s. On April 5, 1976, white high school students from South Boston and Charlestown met with a city councilwoman who supported their boycott of classes. Outside City Hall, they chanced upon lawyer Theodore Landsmark and assaulted him. Photographer Stanley J. Forman won the Pulitzer Prize for this photo.

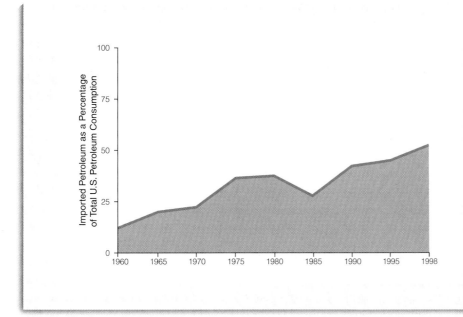

■ **FIGURE 27.1**
IIMPORTED PETROLEUM AS SHARE OF U.S. CONSUMPTION
Abundant natural resources, especially coal and oil, encouraged Americans' long-standing feeling of national strength and autonomy. After World War II, however, the United States switched from exporting oil to importing oil. Conservation measures in the 1970s temporarily reversed America's growing dependence on oil from abroad.

Energy Use in the United States

Most Americans who lived through the 1970s remember gasoline shortages and price hikes as one of the decade's most distinctive features. No previous generation had experienced so steep a decline in the availability of a primary source of energy that was the key to its transportation system. In World War II the government had rationed gasoline to conserve it for military use. But never before had international market forces confronted Americans with their growing dependence on imported petroleum.

The Arab oil embargo of 1973–1974 and the decline in oil supplies after the Iranian revolution of 1979 battered a U.S. economy already weakened by spending on the Vietnam War. The oil shocks drove inflation sharply upward. They raised fundamental questions—not asked since the Great Depression of the 1930s—about whether the world's largest economy could continue to grow. And the oil price rise suggested that energy independence might be a crucial component of real national security.

Rich natural resources had long satisfied Americans' needs for energy sources. During the colonial period, wood from abundant forests and coal deposits provided heat. Whale oil powered lamps. Transportation came from the work of domesticated animals as well as sailing vessels that captured the force of the wind. In the era of the American Revolution, manufacturers built the first factories on riverbanks next to falls, where waterwheels produced the power to drive mechanical equipment.

In the 1800s, the spread of the Industrial Revolution increased the demand for energy, particularly coal. By the 1830s, coal fired the steam engines that pushed ships across the Atlantic Ocean and the railroads that would one day tie the growing nation together.

In 1859, on the eve of the Civil War, drillers near Titusville in northwestern Pennsylvania made a momentous discovery: oil. Refined into kerosene, oil lighted many American homes and city streets for more than a generation. Then Thomas Edison designed the first electricity-generating station in New York City in 1892, beginning the era of coal-fired electric utilities that spread rapidly over the next two decades.

Oil's real significance emerged in the twentieth century. Refined into gasoline, oil powered the new internal combustion engines that revolutionized transportation. Gasoline allowed the Wright brothers' airplane to leave the ground in 1903 and fueled the automobiles that began to pour off Henry Ford's assembly line with the first Model T in 1908. Inexpensive gasoline enabled cars to become Americans' foremost means of transportation. U.S. military forces depended on oil in all their wars of the twentieth century. Indeed, the United States fought in the Persian Gulf

Israelis, and Kissinger's being Jewish only underlined the point. The U.S. commitment to Israel had never been clearer, and Arabs of all political persuasions were determined to voice their displeasure.

In October 1973, the OPEC nations initiated an embargo on selling oil to the United States and to western European nations that had supported Israel in the war. Never before in peacetime had foreign policy affected Americans so directly. Oil supplies dwindled, and prices at gas pumps skyrocketed to four times their previous levels. Even when OPEC lifted the embargo afer five months, it kept prices high by limiting production.

Steeper energy costs powerfully accelerated inflation. Decades of easy access to cheap gasoline came to a sudden halt. As American drivers formed long lines at the pump, President Ford urged them to drive at lower speeds to conserve gas. The independence provided by a well-fueled automobile had come to define daily life for many U.S. citizens. But Americans confronted new and sobering limits on their mobility, just when their country encountered other limits in the form of Nixon's failed presidency and defeat in Vietnam.

The Environmental Movement

The oil embargo encouraged many U.S. citizens to rethink the nation's cavalier use of natural resources. Indeed, environmental consciousness spread rapidly in the 1970s as evidence revealed the impact of industrial growth on the quality of life in the United States. Environ-

War of 1991 primarily to preserve western access to oil from the Gulf region.

In the 1970s, the oil shocks and the growing environmental movement encouraged both energy conservation and the development of alternative, renewable sources. Many citizens paid increasing attention to solar, wind, water, and geothermal power. But corporations, encouraged by the federal government, paid far more attention to another alternative: nuclear energy. (The first American nuclear power plant had been built at Shippingport, Pennsylvania, in 1957.) Despite creating radioactive waste, nuclear power generated one-fifth of the nation's electricity by the twenty-first century.

In 2001, fossil fuels continued to provide 85 percent of the total energy used in the United States: oil, 40 percent; natural gas, 25 percent; and coal, 20 percent. Coal-burning plants created just over half the nation's electricity, and the United States had one-fourth of the world's coal supplies. However, unlike renewable energy sources, fossil fuels are a finite resource that eventually will be used up. Burning them also contributes to air pollution, atmospheric ozone depletion, and global warming.

Nonetheless, at the turn of the century fossil fuels remained the cheapest source of power, a temptation too strong to resist. ■

Oil derricks cover a hillside near Titusville, Pennsylvania in the era of the Civil War. Unlike renewable energy sources such as falling water or the sun, fossil fuels like oil and coal have to be burned and create serious air pollution in the process. The extraction of fossil fuels—so basic to the modern American economy—often involves damaging natural landscapes as well.

Library of Congress

mental organizations such as the Sierra Club, the National Wildlife Federation, and the Audubon Society saw their memberships soar. And for the first time, the media began to examine the daunting range of environmental problems plaguing the United States and the rest of the world: acid rain, groundwater contamination, smog, rainforest destruction, oil spills, nuclear waste disposal, species extinction, ozone depletion, and global warming. A growing interest in ecology—human interaction with the wider web of life—expanded the efforts of conservationists to preserve parklands. Residents of an urbanized mass society began to contemplate the wider consequences of small private acts such as watering the lawn, flushing the toilet, or leaving the lights on.

Environmentalism had perhaps even more radical implications than women's liberation or the counterculture had. "*Indefinite* growth of whatever kind cannot be sustained by *finite* resources," a prominent group of ecologists pointed out in 1972. Yet indefinite economic growth had been Americans' credo since the earliest days of European colonization. "Growth is the ideology of the cancer cell," writer Edward Abbey declared, helping to inspire the formation of the radical environmental group *Earth First!* in 1979. Yet even the nation's fiercest ideological opponents abroad agreed that the creation of wealth entailed the exploitation of natural resources. "Growth of industrial and agricultural production," Soviet leader Nikita Khrushchev had announced a decade earlier, "is the battering ram with which we shall smash the capitalist system." Now environmentalists were questioning an idea that even Communists had taken for granted.

A new generation of Americans, unable to remember Depression scarcities and wartime rationing, was wasteful, sometimes extravagantly so. U.S. soldiers had expressed surprise when displaced Vietnamese civilians built shelters out of the aluminum cans the troops threw away so casually. Home to only 6 percent of the global population, the United States consumed as much as a third of the world's energy from nonrenewable fossil fuels such as oil and coal. Polluted air hung over the largest U.S. cities. The first evidence of global warming began to appear in the 1970s. Scientists also noticed the rapid thinning of the ozone layer in the earth's atmosphere in 1973. They attributed the problem in part to the widespread use of aerosol spray cans—especially by Americans, the world's wealthiest people. The production of inexpensive plastics from oil had also soared since World War II. Styrofoam cups and plastic containers littered the roadsides. Disposable diapers and other nonbiodegradable products accumulated in landfills in what became known as the throwaway culture.

Environmentalists argued that the idea of unlimited consumption of natural resources was fundamentally irresponsible, both to future human generations and to other species. They urged Congress and the Environmental Protection Agency (EPA) to require fuel-efficient engines from carmakers and to promote renewable energy sources such as water, solar, and wind power. Citizen groups such as the Clamshell Alliance in New England and the Abalone Alliance in California protested the construction of new nuclear power plants. These operations, they pointed out, had no reliable method in place for disposing of nuclear waste. What if the public were exposed to radiation? Their warnings had merit: cancer rates began to rise in populations that had close contact with radioactive materials from the early Cold War years forward, such as communities near the Hanford nuclear facility in south central Washington state and towns downwind from the Atomic Test Site in Nevada. One Utah mother who lost a daughter to cancer felt "disappointed and hurt" by the "horrific neglect and indifference" of a government that would permit such contamination and then deny that there was any danger. "We were used. We were conned," another woman testified to Congress about government secrecy regarding the impact of radiation. "They knew and they didn't tell us."

A broad critique of the chemical industry's impact on public health also emerged in the 1970s. As it turned out, pesticides worked their way up the food chain into people's bodies. Some artificial sweeteners proved carcinogenic, and the lead that manufacturers had added to gasoline and house paint for generations caused brain damage. Long-standing industrial dumping of toxic chemicals made headlines. In 1975, for example, investigations revealed that tons of cancer-causing polychlorinated biphenyls (PCBs) from General Electric plants lined the bottom of the Hudson River north of New York City. Four years later, the EPA announced that the nation had 32,000 to 50,000 major sites containing hazardous waste.

Environmentalists argued that the idea of unlimited consumption of natural resources was fundamentally irresponsible, both to future human generations and to other species.

But it was the crisis at Love Canal in New York that helped bring the issue of toxic waste home to Americans. The Hooker Chemical Company had buried tons of poisonous waste in a dry canal in the town of Niagara Falls between 1947 and 1952 and then covered it over with dirt. The company gave the land to the town, which promptly built a school on it. A middle-class neighborhood soon grew up around the site. But the ground smelled odd and oozed mysterious substances. Sometimes it even caught on fire for no apparent reason. By the 1970s local rates of cancer and other severe illnesses had soared. The chemical and industrial plant workers who lived in the neighborhood began to suspect that their quiet loyalty to their employers was no longer worth the risk to the health of their families. Persistent activism by community members, led by Lois Gibbs and publicized by reporter Michael Brown, finally overcame local, state, and company officials' efforts to keep the contents of the buried canal secret. In August 1978, New York governor Hugh Carey at last agreed to buy out the entire neighborhood, seal it off, and move residents elsewhere. An early public revelation of the cost of industrial progress, the Love Canal debacle accelerated American workers' loss of faith in the

Peter Menzel/StockBoston

■ Thousands of runners surge up the Hayes Street hill in San Francisco in the annual 7-mile Bay-to-Breakers race across the city. In the 1970s regular exercise began to become a common part of daily life for many Americans. At the same time, fast food and higher-fat diets contributed to a growing pattern of Americans being overweight and even obese.

corporations and governments they had once trusted. "There are ticking time bombs all over," an EPA official concluded. "We just don't know how many potential Love Canals there are."

Discovering the limits of the U.S. economy so soon after the Vietnam War and the Watergate scandal spawned a crisis of confidence throughout the United States. Some Americans resented the idea of limits: on how much gas they could buy, how much the economy could grow, how much influence the United States could have abroad. At the same time, others began to embrace the idea of creating a healthier lifestyle that focused less on material consumption. Cigarette smoking started to decline. Organic food sales picked up. Exercise, especially running, began to become an increasingly common activity for middle-class adults. The wildly successful Nike athletic shoe company was founded in 1972, and entrants in the New York City Marathon ballooned from 126 in 1970 to 10,000 by 1978. Interest in outdoor recreation—hiking, camping, and bicycling—grew exponentially. Recycling also started its climb from a fringe activity to common practice in a few parts of the country. The government began to get the message, too. Federal agencies banned the use of hazardous products such as the pesticide DDT and the artificial sweetener sodium cyclamate in the original Gatorade formula. And in January 1974, Congress reduced the national speed limit to 55 miles per hour to conserve fuel.

Reshuffling Politics

The skepticism toward authority and tradition spawned by the counterculture, the Vietnam War, and the Watergate scandal spread through American culture in the 1970s. The use of illegal drugs, especially marijuana, was widespread. Casual sexual relationships proliferated in a decade when contraceptive pills had become widely available and the AIDS virus had not yet been identified. Popular and critically acclaimed films featured tales of

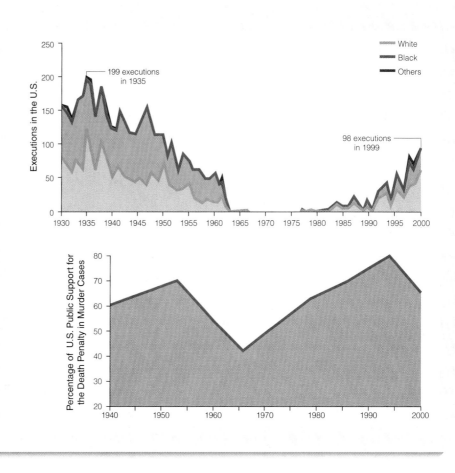

■ FIGURE 27.2

THE DEATH PENALTY: PRACTICES AND OPINIONS The use of the death penalty distinguished the United States from most other industrialized nations, which had banned it. In 1972, The Supreme Court struck down existing capital punishment statutes as "arbitrary and capricious." Four years later, the Court upheld rewritten state and federal laws that provided clearer guidance for the imposition of the death penalty.

malfeasance in high places. *All the President's Men* (1976) told the story of the Nixon administration's Watergate crimes. *Apocalypse Now* (1975) revealed the madness of the American war in Vietnam. *Three Days of the Condor* (1975) portrayed the CIA as a rogue agency beyond democratic control. *Chinatown* (1975) suggested the vast corruption marring the early-twentieth-century growth of Los Angeles. *Blazing Saddles* (1974) hilariously spoofed the heroic Westerns that had long served as the staple of American moviegoers' diet. And *One Flew over the Cuckoo's Nest* (1975) used novelist Ken Kesey's story of an insane asylum to imply that those in charge were more dangerous than the inmates. In this atmosphere Congress began to reassert its authority against the "imperial presidency," and in 1976 voters put an obscure, devout Georgia peanut farmer and former one-term governor in the White House.

Congressional Power Reasserted

Before the twentieth century, the U.S. legislative branch had been the most powerful wing of the federal government. This emphasis on the authority of Congress as the closest representatives of the people had a long history. In the 1770s, Americans had fought their way free from a British empire whose powerful sovereign inspired deep and abiding distrust of executive authority. But the U.S. acquisition of its own overseas empire beginning in 1898 and its growing international prominence had slowly assuaged such anxieties. Many Americans came to believe that the country needed a strong president to direct the assertion of U.S. power abroad. World War II and the Cold War had dramatically accelerated this process. The balance of terror that came with the nuclear age seemed to demand secrecy and centralized decision-making. Americans had rejected this leadership style in their own revolution two centuries before. Yet the tide had turned, and the national security state and imperial presidency from Truman to Nixon emerged as the result.

The double shock of defeat in Vietnam and the Watergate scandal reawakened a Congress that had grown accustomed to deferring to the White House in foreign affairs. Tellingly, Congress had never formally declared war on North Korea or North Vietnam, although such declaration is its constitutional duty. Angered by the illegalities and deception in both the Johnson and Nixon administrations, Congress passed the War Powers Act in 1973 to limit the president's capacity to wage undeclared wars. The bill required the chief executive to obtain explicit congressional approval for keeping U.S. troops in an overseas conflict longer than 90 days. In 1976 Congress reinforced the message. It passed the Clark Amendment to cut off U.S. aid to anticommunist forces in the civil war in newly independent Angola, on the southwest coast of Africa. The House and Senate had resolved not to get drawn into "another Vietnam."

Congress did not limit its muscle-flexing to keeping Americans out of conflicts with Third World leftists. It also promoted human rights within the Communist bloc, cutting against the grain of Secretary of State Kissinger's realpolitik approach to Moscow. The Jackson–Vanik Amendment of 1974 sought to make the Soviet Union pay for its repression of Jewish dissidents by linking détente directly to human rights, much to Kissinger's dismay. To acquire most-favored-nation trading status with the United States, Moscow would have to let Jews emigrate.

With encouragement from voters and journalists, Congress also uncovered its eyes and began to investigate the covert side of American foreign policy that had gathered momentum since 1945. After Watergate popped the cork on the bottled-up secret abuses of the executive branch, other troubling news spilled out about the nation's intelligence agencies. Dissident former CIA agents such as Philip Agee began revealing "dirty tricks" that the agency had long used. And investigative reporter Seymour Hersh, author of the My Lai massacre exposé a few years earlier, uncovered the CIA's Operation Chaos. This program of illegal domestic espionage against antiwar dissidents paralleled FBI abuses such as the COINTELPRO campaigns to defame Martin Luther King, Jr., and destroy the Black Panthers and the American Indian Movement. Congressional committees led by Otis Pike of New York in the House and Frank Church of Idaho in the Senate initiated their own investigations of the national security state's tactics. Their documentation of CIA involvement in assassination attempts against foreign leaders such as Fidel Castro of Cuba and Patrice Lumumba of the Congo suggested that United States government agencies would secretly go to any lengths to prevail in the Cold War.

> *Defeat in Vietnam and the Watergate scandal reawakened a Congress that had grown accustomed to deferring to the White House in foreign affairs.*

These revelations stirred fierce controversy among those who took an interest in national and international politics. The United States apparently had been almost as devious in its covert actions abroad as the reviled Soviet Union had been. Many citizens decried what their government had done in their names and without their knowledge. However, officials claimed that the extreme conditions of the Cold War and the duplicity of the Soviets necessitated secrecy. Convinced that information gathered by the Church and Pike committees threatened to undermine public trust in U.S. foreign policy officials, congressional leaders stopped official publication of the Pike report (although the *Village Voice* published a leaked copy). Nonetheless, in combination with the Freedom of Information Act of 1974—which forced the public release of most federal documents after 25 years—these congressional reports created a paper trail that altered Americans' perceptions of what their government did abroad.

At the core of this controversy were two burning questions. How transparent could a democratic society and its government afford to be when they also had global interests to protect? And when democratic openness and imperial self-interest conflicted, which should win out?

The Church Committee and CIA Covert Operations

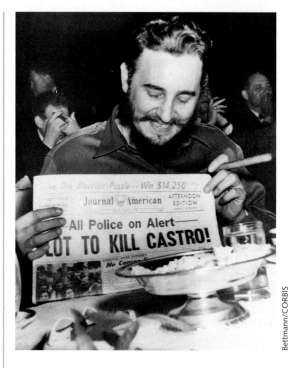

A star baseball pitcher who once turned down an offer to sign with the New York Yankees, Fidel Castro led a leftist, anti-American revolution in Cuba in 1959. U.S. hostility and Castro's evolving politics led him to declare Cuba a Communist state in 1961. The CIA tried unsuccessfully to arrange for Castro's assassination.

In 1975–1976 the U.S. Senate Select Committee to Study Governmental Operations with Respect to Intelligence Activities engaged in the first comprehensive review by Congress of the actions of the Central Intelligence Agency. Under the leadership of Frank Church (D-Idaho), the committee investigated both intelligence gathering ("spying") and covert operations, the secret side of American foreign policy during the Cold War. One of the most controversial issues that the Church Committee examined was evidence of the CIA's attempted use of assassination as a means of dealing with key figures in Cuba, the Congo, the Dominican Republic, South Vietnam, and Chile.

Alleged Assassination Plots Involving Foreign Leaders (Interim Report, November 20, 1975)

The Committee has received evidence that ranking Government officials discussed, and may have authorized, the establishment with the CIA of a generalized assassination capability. . . .

The evidence establishes that the United States was implicated in several assassination plots. . . . Our inquiry also reveals serious problems with respect to United States involvement in coups directed against foreign governments. . . .

Once methods of coercion and violence are chosen, the probability of loss of life is always present. There is, however, a significant difference between a coldblooded, targeted, intentional killing of an individual foreign leader and other forms of intervening in the affairs of foreign nations. . . .

Non-attribution to the United States for covert operations was the original and principal purpose of the so-called doctrine of "plausible denial."

Evidence before the Committee clearly demonstrates that this concept, designed to protect the United States and its operatives from the consequences of disclosures, has been expanded to mask decisions of the President and his senior staff members. . . .

"Plausible denial" can also lead to the use of euphemism and circumlocution, which are designed to allow the President and other senior officials to deny knowledge of an operation should it be disclosed. . . .

It is possible that there was a failure of communication between policymakers and the agency personnel who were experienced in secret, and often violent, action. Although policymakers testified that assassination was not intended by such words as "get rid of Castro," some of their subordinates in the Agency testified that they perceived that assassination was desired and that they should proceed without troubling their superiors. . . .

Running throughout the cases considered in this report was the expectation of American officials that they could control the actions of dissident groups which they were supporting in foreign countries. Events demonstrated that the United States had no such power. This point is graphically demonstrated by cables exchanged shortly before the coup in Vietnam. Ambassador Lodge cabled Washington on October 30, 1963, that he was unable to halt a coup; a cable from William Bundy in response stated that "we cannot accept conclusion that we have no power to delay or discourage a coup." The coup took place three days later. . . .

Officials of the CIA made use of persons associated with the criminal underworld in attempting to achieve the assassination of Fidel Castro. These underworld figures were relied upon because it was believed that they had expertise and contacts that were not available to law-abiding citizens. . . .

It may well be ourselves that we injure most if we adopt tactics "more ruthless than the enemy." ■

"I Will Never Lie to You"

These same questions underlay the presidential election in the bicentennial year of 1976. As the nation celebrated the two-hundredth anniversary of its Declaration of Independence, some commentators could not help noting that the U.S. withdrawal from Vietnam in some ways echoed the British surrender at Yorktown in 1781. In each case, a determined nationalist army seeking freedom from foreign control had forced the world's strongest military power to withdraw in defeat.

In the backwash of Watergate, two presidential candidates—both outsiders to national politics—became advocates for opposing sides in the power and openness debate. Former California governor Ronald Reagan made a strong run at the Republican nomination, falling just short at the Kansas City convention as incumbent Gerald Ford held on to head the GOP ticket. Reagan articulated conservative Americans' anger at seeing U.S. autonomy and power abroad hemmed in. He opposed détente with the Soviets, supported anticommunists everywhere, and warned against a treaty that would return control of the Panama Canal to the Panamanians. Ford found himself burdened by the faltering economy, weakened by Reagan's criticisms from the right, and hampered by widespread resentment of his pardon for Nixon. He struggled back from a 33-point deficit in opinion polls to fall just short with 49 percent of the votes in the general election. The hopes of moderate Republicans faded as the party moved to the right after 1976.

TABLE 27-2			
The Election of 1976			
Candidate	Political Party	Popular Vote	Electoral Vote
Jimmy Carter	Democratic	40,828,587	297
Gerald R. Ford	Republican	39,147,613	241

Jimmy Carter was the winner. The former Georgia governor had worked relentlessly to gain the Democratic nomination after starting out as the choice of just 4 percent of primary voters. He based his candidacy on moral uplift. Contrasting himself to the Nixon administration, he told audiences, "I will never lie to you." Instead, Carter promised openness, accountability, and a government "as good and decent as the American people." He pledged to heal a nation exhausted by conflict. The emphasis on morality came naturally to the born-again Christian who taught Sunday school. His campaign manager admitted wryly that Carter's religious bent was a "weirdo factor" in national politics. The Georgian was also the first president to hail from the Deep South in more than a century. His open faith and cultural conservatism won him support from less liberal Democrats whom the McGovern campaign had alienated in 1972.

Carter was also a Naval Academy graduate, a former nuclear engineer, and a successful peanut farmer and businessperson. Yet the unusual green color of his campaign buttons and posters conveyed a subtle conservationist message, and liberals appreciated his attention to issues of poverty. Moreover, his support for civil rights during his governorship in Georgia had made him a symbol for a pragmatic new generation of white and black southerners. Americans were not sure who their new president really was. Carter kept his diminutive first name: Jimmy, not James or even Jim. He wore denim, and he carried his own bags. At his inaugural parade, he and his wife Rosalynn chose to walk down Pennsylvania Avenue rather than ride in a limousine.

The new president entered the White House at a time of unusual resistance to executive authority. He encountered an assertive and suspicious Congress. He served an alienated and isolationist public that had given him a slim victory with no clear mandate. He had to grapple with an alert and skeptical media that had dropped most vestiges of its traditional deference to the Oval Office. And he faced an economy still mired in stagflation as unemployment and prices kept rising and interest rates reached 21 percent.

Politics and ideology also hamstrung the new president, limiting his ability to lead his own party in governing the nation. The New Deal coalition of the working class,

Jimmy Carter Library

■ After his inauguration as president, Jimmy Carter got down to work in the Oval Office. Serious, conscientious, and extremely hard-working, Carter immersed himself in many of the details of his administration's policies. The image of him sequestered and industrious at his desk came to symbolize, for many, both the strengths and weaknesses of his presidency.

people of color, and liberals had been unraveling for more than a decade. Carter had campaigned almost as an independent and developed few ties to the main Democratic constituencies. Thus he enjoyed little loyalty from his own party. The Georgian was also the first Democratic president since the 1930s who did not fully subscribe to the New Deal principle of government regulation of the economy. As a social moderate but an economic conservative, Carter had a strong desire to balance the federal budget. This vision placed him closer to the Republicans than to many in his own party. A businessperson, he also considered fiscal responsibility a primary virtue. Powerful liberal Democrats in Congress, by contrast, remained committed to government spending on programs such as Social Security and welfare, which Carter supported with less enthusiasm.

Carter's tendency to take moralistic stands did not mesh well with the horse-trading style of compromise that characterized Congress. In this sense, he was the opposite of Lyndon Johnson. Carter relied on a small circle of advisers from his days as governor in Atlanta. The northeastern-based media dubbed them the "Georgia Mafia." The president and his aides tried to govern as outsiders to the federal government. They viewed insiders as selfish and narrow-minded. They failed to cultivate relationships with Democratic leaders in Congress such as powerful House Speaker Thomas ("Tip") O'Neill of Massachusetts. Meanwhile, seasoned legislators of both parties looked down on the new administration as inexperienced and naive. With suspicion and condescension flowing in both directions between the White House and Capitol Hill, one senior Democratic congressman complained that Carter's popularity with the legislature was so low that he "couldn't get the Pledge of Allegiance through Congress" if he needed to.

Rise of a Peacemaker

Carter's idealism proved more effective, at least during his first two years, in refashioning U.S. foreign policy. The president started the national healing process with his first official act in office: he granted a "full, complete, and unconditional pardon" to those who had evaded the draft during the Vietnam War. He also tried to replace indiscriminate anticommunism with the promotion of human rights as the main theme in international affairs. "We are now free of that inordinate fear of Communism which once led us to embrace any dictator who joined us in that fear," he told an audience at Notre Dame University.

All presidents since 1945 had loudly supported human rights in the Soviet bloc. Carter defended dissidents in authoritarian countries friendly to the United States as well. His commitment to ending racial discrimination at home and his promotion of human rights abroad led to his administration's strong support for an end to white minority rule in southern Africa, including the establishment of Zimbabwe out of the old white-ruled Rhodesia in 1980. In a highly symbolic move, Carter appointed black civil rights leader and fellow Georgian Andrew Young as UN ambassador and point man on Africa policy.

Upon taking office, Carter fired the director of the CIA, George H. W. Bush. In the wake of the congressional investigations of the CIA, he reined in the agency's covert operations. Carter wanted to shift Americans' attention away from East–West Cold War tensions. Instead, he encouraged the public to acknowledge the burgeoning problems between industrialized nations of the North and mostly poor countries of the Southern Hemisphere. The president made control over the Panama Canal a test case for this reorientation. The huge canal sym-

■ MAP 27.2
THE GRADUAL LIBERATION OF SOUTHERN AFRICA FROM WHITE MINORITY RULE The Carter administration supported the ending of white minority rule in Southern Africa. The last redoubts of "white supremacy" included Rhodesia, which became Zimbabwe in 1980, and South Africa, which granted independence to Namibia in 1990 and ended apartheid in 1994.

bolized U.S. dominance of the hemisphere and served as a focus of resentment among many Latin Americans. Since 1903, the United States had ruled the 10-mile-wide Canal Zone as its own colony. Acknowledging this colonialist past, Carter signed treaties on September 7, 1977, to return sovereignty of the canal to Panama.

Defenders of U.S. control of the canal, led by prominent Republican Ronald Reagan, fought the treaties fiercely. They saw them as irresponsibly giving away an American asset. "We built it, we paid for it, and we're going to keep it," Reagan insisted. But other prominent conservatives, including Henry Kissinger and movie star John Wayne, acknowledged the symbolic importance of the canal for strengthening U.S. relations with Latin America. They supported the president. Carter threw all his political weight into the campaign, and the Senate approved the treaties by a thin margin in the spring of 1978.

The Carter administration's other great diplomatic achievement came with the Camp David accord, an agreement between Egypt's president Anwar Sadat and Israel's prime minister Menachem Begin. The Arab–Israeli conflict had remained one of the most intractable problems in modern diplomacy, yet Carter had unusual credibility in tackling the issue. His concern as a Christian for the "Holy Land" claimed by both Jewish Israelis and mostly Muslim Palestinians gave him sympathy for both sides. Sadat himself created an opening for diplomacy in 1977 by becoming the first Arab leader to visit Israel. But as the leading outside power in the region and Israel's closest ally, only the United States could move the peace process further along.

Carter took action. He invited Sadat and Begin to Camp David, the presidential retreat in rural western Maryland. There his persistence, plus promises of American aid to all parties, kept the marathon negotiations on track. In March 1979, the Egyptian and Israeli leaders signed two accords: Egypt became the first Arab state to grant official recognition to Israel. In turn, Israel agreed to withdraw its troops from the Sinai peninsula and apparently to stop building additional settlements on the Palestinian West Bank of the Jordan River. The framework for peace implied eventual autonomy for the Palestinians in the West Bank and the Gaza strip.

Though promising, the Camp David accords failed to bring peace to the Middle East. Israeli settlements in the West Bank continued to proliferate, and anti-Israeli terrorism by Palestinians persisted. But Carter had persuaded two major players in the region to take a big step back from open hostility. The world rightly proclaimed him a peacemaker.

The War on Waste

Within three months of taking office, Carter called for the "moral equivalent of war" to meet the deepening national energy crisis. The OPEC oil embargo of 1973 and his own thought-

■ Mt. McKinley in Alaska's Denali National Park rises to 20,320 feet above sea level, the tallest peak in North America. Its scale and beauty inspired many supporters of the Alaska National Interest Lands Conservation Act of 1980, which dramatically expanded the nation's parklands and wilderness areas. The Alaska Lands Act and the new trans-Alaska oil pipeline, completed three years earlier, helped many residents of the lower 48 learn more about the nation's largest and most remote state.

Danny Lehman/CORBIS

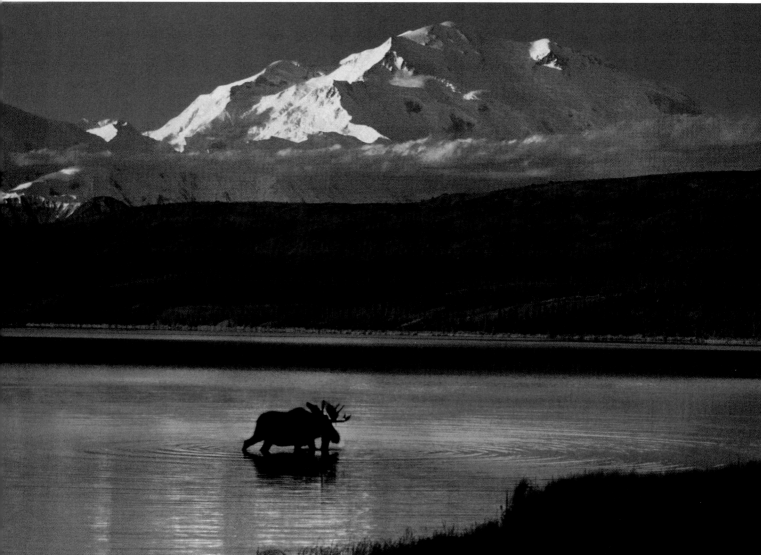

fulness allowed the president to understand better than his immediate predecessors that the country's addiction to imported oil put Americans at the mercy of other oil-producing nations. He exhorted his fellow citizens to stop being "the most wasteful nation on Earth." Conserve energy, he implored them. Switch off lights and turn down thermostats.

The administration created the Department of Energy and granted tax incentives to promote development of alternative sources such as solar energy. The EPA required U.S. automakers to meet stricter fuel efficiency standards for their engines. High prices encouraged a renewed search for domestic sources of oil. In 1977 workers completed the 800-mile-long, 48-inch-wide Trans-Alaska Pipeline System. The system linked the state's northern oil fields at Prudhoe Bay on the Arctic Ocean with a tanker terminal in Valdez, on Alaska's southern coast on the Pacific Ocean. With new oil now flowing freely, Carter worked with Congress to pass the 1980 Alaska National Interest Lands Conservation Act. This legislation created the single largest addition ever to the nation's wilderness system, 47 million acres, and the new Wrangell–St. Elias National Park.

The most controversial power alternative came in the form of nuclear energy. Obtained by harnessing the force of splitting atoms, nuclear energy seemed to promise unlimited pollution-free power. But it entailed the use of a deadly radioactive fuel, uranium. Was it the clean solution to the nation's energy needs or a lethal nightmare waiting to overtake an unsuspecting public? *The China Syndrome,* a popular 1978 film, suggested the latter. A few months later, life imitated art. In March 1979, a partial meltdown of the nuclear core of the Three Mile Island reactor near Harrisburg, Pennsylvania, leaked radiation and forced a major evacuation. Government officials tried to reassure a panicked public. However, in July, a dam burst near Church Rock, New Mexico, flooding the Rio Puerco valley with radioactive wastewater.

Despite these obstacles, existing nuclear power plants continued to generate 11 percent of the nation's electricity in 1979, a figure that climbed to 22 percent by 1992 as other plants under construction came on line. Nonetheless, because of negative public opinion and the high cost per unit of nuclear power, no new plants ordered by utility companies after 1974 were ever completed.

In 1979, a revolution in Iran cut off the United States from the world's second-largest oil producer. The event initiated a new round of energy price increases, escalated inflation, and further intensified public anxieties. In an unusual display of frankness for a country's leader, President Carter acknowledged that the nation seemed adrift. He gathered an array of advisers at Camp David for extended reflection on how the nation might set a new direction for itself. He emerged to give a major speech on July 15, 1979. In it, he linked America's energy problems to a broader national "crisis of confidence." "In a nation that was proud of hard work, strong families, close knit communities and our faith in God," he explained, "too many of us now tend to worship self-indulgence and consumption."

John S. Zeedick/AP/Wide World

■ The cooling towers of the Three Mile Island nuclear power plant loom over the Susquehanna River just south of Harrisburg, Pennsylvania. Nuclear energy epitomized the centralization of power: citizens benefited from the electricity produced but had little knowledge or control of a technology that could go astray more easily than authorities liked to admit.

■ **MAP 27.3**
BUILDING NUCLEAR POWER PLANTS Between 1969 and 1980, all of the nation's 103 commercial nuclear power reactors either came on line (56) or were in the process of being planned or built (47). The United States has roughly one-quarter of the 434 commercial nuclear power reactors in the world. Despite nuclear energy's important role in U.S. electricity production, there is still no system in place for the permanent disposal of radioactive waste.

But Carter proved more effective at identifying the problem of America's insatiable appetite for energy than he was at offering a remedy. His call for sacrifice and unity made for courageous but ultimately self-defeating politics in a society accustomed to unrestrained consumption. Other politicians, such as Ronald Reagan, moved swiftly to smooth Americans' ruffled feathers with a cheerful message: U.S. citizens were fine just as they were. As one supporter of the oil and gas industry claimed, "This country did not conserve its way to greatness. It produced its way to greatness."

Diffusing the Women's Movement

"Good morning, boys and girls!" This standard classroom greeting reveals the central place of gender in how Americans identify people from a young age. Few people consider the phrase offensive, even though they probably would protest if a teacher addressed class members as "blacks and whites" or "tall people and short people." Should one's sex (a biological characteristic) or gender (the social assumptions associated with sex) constitute the fundamental dividing line among human beings? The spread of feminism through U.S. society from the 1970s onward raised this question.

The Meanings of Women's Liberation

In a decade marked by hard rethinking of major issues, feminists provided one of the most profound challenges of all. Few American households avoided at least some reconsideration of the

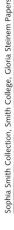

■ Gloria Steinem, on her knees, speaks at a meeting of a women's consciousness-raising group in the early 1970s. Similar groups gathered informally in homes around the country and helped women articulate their common struggles against discrimination.

roles of men and women. Just as the nation reimagined its foreign policy in less assertive terms and with greater concern for human rights, feminists called for equality between the sexes while honoring their differences. This call resonated with a growing number of Americans. The women's movement cast a spotlight on the need for justice in both the private sphere of personal relationships and the public sphere of the workplace and the law.

Between 1968 and 1973 some 500 new feminist publications cropped up in the United States. Gloria Steinem's *Ms.* magazine became the most prominent, selling out the 250,000 copies of its first issue in January 1972 within eight days. Its then-revolutionary name symbolized women's desire not to have their marital status revealed through the title of "Miss" or "Mrs." After all, the title "Mr." said nothing about a man's marital status, so why should not a woman's title be similarly neutral? Thousands of consciousness-raising meetings also made women aware that their own experiences with discrimination were part of a broader pattern of injustice toward women.

The millions of American women who found their lives changing in the 1970s did not agree on all issues. African American and Latino American women balanced identities as women with identities as people of color, which aligned them closely with men of their communities. Like Karen Silkwood, working-class women of all colors often focused on issues common to all workers, including wages, workplace conditions, and union representation. Community organizers such as Lois Gibbs of Love Canal zeroed in on neighborhoods and families. The educated white women who tended to form the most visible part of the movement for equality differed among themselves on such issues as pornography: some found it inherently exploitive of women, while others considered it primarily a matter of free expression.

However, all women shared certain concerns. Even as many female Americans remained wary of the label *feminist*—fearing associations with anger, militancy, and dislike of men—they nonetheless tended to side with feminist positions on issues from equal pay for equal work, to abortion rights, to more egalitarian distribution of household chores within families. Even women who still chose to wear makeup and dress in traditionally feminine fashion shared a desire for men to take women more seriously for their ideas and beliefs than for their appearance. The women's movement also sought to unmask the violence constraining all women's lives: sexual harassment, domestic abuse, and rape. Whereas some men joked about rape, women called it what it was: a form of torture that kept many reluctant to venture out of their homes alone. And even a woman's home was not safe at times. Until the mid-1970s, a husband could force himself sexually on his wife and not be considered a rapist by the law.

New Opportunities in Education, the Workplace, and Family Life

In the 1970s, educated women gained access to a host of new opportunities in the workplace. Young women in college, unlike their mothers, expected to choose and develop a career after graduation even more than they anticipated getting married. The number of women entering graduate and professional schools soared. The percentage of female students in law school shot up from 5 percent to 40 percent between 1970 and 1980. In addition, most single-sex private colleges and universities, such as Yale and Vassar, went coeducational. Many dormitories housed both men and women, allowing young people from the middle and upper classes to live in close physical proximity for the first time.

A similar process unfolded in the workplace. Employment in the United States, formerly divided into "men's" and "women's" work, saw a blurring of those lines. Help-wanted advertisements stopped categorizing jobs as male and female, and women joined the ranks of police officers and construction workers. The post-1950 pattern of women flocking into the paid workforce passed a milestone in 1980. That year, more than half of women with children under six years old had paying jobs outside the home. However, most of these jobs were lower-wage service positions that offered neither union support nor much upward mobility. Women fared better in the professions; the percentage of female lawyers and Ph.D.s tripled in the 1970s, and that of female physicians doubled.

Despite these gains, professional women still averaged only 73 percent of the pay of their male colleagues. They also encountered stubborn traditional gender expectations. Late in the decade, one New York City judge ordered a female attorney—dressed in a tailored designer pantsuit and silk blouse—to leave his courtroom and not return unless she showed up in a skirted suit that demonstrated "proper respect" for the court.

Not surprisingly, family life also changed shape in these years. In the 1950s more than 70 percent of American families with children had had a father who worked outside the home and a mother who stayed at home. In 1980, only 15 percent of families were configured that way. Yet society's growing acceptance of mothers in the workforce did not necessarily mean that these women enjoyed a lighter domestic load. Most working mothers still had primary responsibility for parenting. For example, President Nixon vetoed a 1970 bill to establish a federally funded daycare system. Such a program, he declared, "would lead to the Sovietization of American children." Although many fathers accommodated their wives' work lives, working mothers continued to bear the brunt of the "second shift": child-rearing and housework in addition to a full-time paid job.

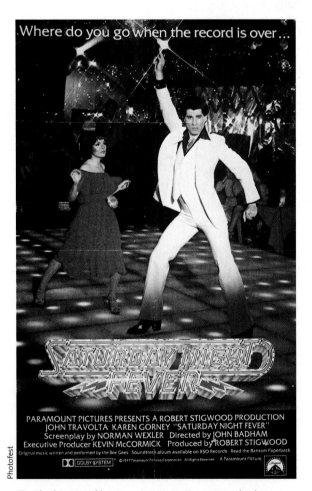

Photofest

■ The hit 1977 film *Saturday Night Fever* starred John Travolta, Karen Gorney, and the popular disco music of the late 1970s. Disco's many critics granted its success as dance music but condemned it as banal and uncreative. Punk was an angrier and edgier musical style that evolved in the same years out of the rock 'n' roll of the late 1960s and early 1970s.

Changing roles brought new marital stresses, and divorce rates climbed in this decade. In 1970, one-third as many divorces as marriages occurred annually; in 1980, the figure was one-half. No-fault divorce laws, beginning with California's in 1970, eased the process and the stigma attached to divorce, although its emotional impact on adults and children remained hard to measure. Men benefited financially when marriages split up. Their average living standard rose sharply, whereas that of women and their children plummeted. Children living with both parents had a 1-in-19 chance of growing up poor. The likelihood rose to 1 in 10 for kids living with just a father; for those living with just a mother, the odds reached 1 in 3.

Equality Under the Law

Paralleling the logic of the black civil rights movement, the modern women's movement pressured lawmakers to eliminate the legal underpinnings of sex-based discrimination. Title IX of the Educational Amendments of 1972 required schools to spend comparable amounts on women's and men's sports programs. This critical step symbolized women's shift away from spectatorship and cheerleading to the female athleticism that helped define American popular culture by the end of the twentieth century. Mia Hamm and her teammates—members of the wildly popular U.S. women's soccer team that won the world championship in 1999—represented the first generation of women to grow up with strong institutional support for girls' sports.

After languishing for decades among failed proposals in Congress, the proposed Equal Rights Amendment to the Constitution finally rode to an overwhelming victory among senators and representatives in 1972. The legislature then sent it to the states for possible ratification by 1980. Simple in its language, the ERA declared, "Equality of rights under law shall not be denied or abridged by the United States or by any State on account of sex." On January 22, 1973, in the landmark case of *Roe v. Wade,* the Supreme Court ruled (by a 7–2 vote) that constitutional privacy rights were "broad enough to encompass a woman's decision whether or not to terminate her pregnancy" in its first six months. This decision established women's constitutional right to determine the course of their own pregnancies. Feminists had pointed out that the question was never *whether* women would have abortions but *how:* they would have them at the hands of illegal and often dangerous practitioners or in the offices of skilled physicians.

Finally, women's battle for equality under the law raised questions about military service. The Selective Service Act of 1980 still required only men to register for the draft on their eighteenth birthdays. But women's exemption from one of the highest duties of national citizenship was slipping fast. Within ten years, some 35,000 American women in the volunteer armed forces served in the 1991 Persian Gulf War, mostly in rear support positions but also as pilots flying reconnaissance and search-and-rescue missions. Fifteen died, and enemy forces captured two others. Even though many of these female service personnel in the war had small children, their assignments close to the line of fire generated little public outcry. American women could now be warriors.

Backlash

Even as the majority of Americans accepted the fundamental tenets of feminism, some fiercely defended existing gender roles. The mainstream media often painted women's rights activists as angry man-haters. Indeed, the media seized the opportunity to associate feminism with "bra-burning," a titillating way to blend women's rights with the sexual revolution and thus avoid the serious issues that women were raising. One Chicana worker involved in the strike against the Farah slacks company in Texas responded, "I don't believe in burning your bra, but I do believe in having our rights."

The women's movement posed a daunting challenge to traditional ideas about masculinity. "We have new men as well as a new society to build," feminist Kathie Amatniek (who later changed her surname to Sarachild) wrote in 1968. Men wondered what equality for women really meant and how it might change their intimate and professional relationships with them. Should men still open doors for women? Should they begin to do half (or more) of housework and parenting? Should they not comment on a female colleague's appearance?

To be sure, women's growing economic independence and educational opportunities often altered the dynamics of power in male–female relationships. Many men from all classes and ethnicities, feeling defensive about assumptions and behaviors that were increasingly labeled sexist, resisted these changes. One Latino graduate student at Stanford University resolved never to date "college girls." "When I want a real woman, I go to the barrio in East San Jose and pick up a high school girl." Many men also found the increasingly open acknowledgment of lesbianism threatening because it implied their potential irrelevance to women. The challenge to machismo took the form of public spectacle in 1973. That year, women's tennis champion Billie Jean King agreed to play 55-year-old former Wimbledon champion Bobby Riggs in a nationally televised "Battle of the Sexes" in the Houston Astrodome. More than 45 million Americans watched King crush her self-proclaimed "male chauvinist pig" opponent in straight sets.

> *Should men still open doors for women? Should they begin to do half (or more) of housework and parenting?*

That men would have mixed feelings about women's liberation surprised no one. But some of the stiffest resistance came from certain women. Those who had built their identities on motherhood and homemaking fiercely defended that tradition. Led by Illinois lawyer Phyllis Schlafly, antifeminists sought to uphold an established family structure that they believed divorce, gay rights, abortion, and daycare would destroy. In their view, femininity meant service to one's family. "Feminists praise self-centeredness," Schlafly declared, "and call it liberation." In addition to defending their own choices, female antifeminists also worried about the impact of dual-career families on children.

Opponents of women's liberation made two major legislative gains in the late 1970s. First, Congress passed the Hyde Amendment in 1976, which forbade the use of Medicaid funds for abortions. In practice, the amendment limited access to abortion to those women who could afford to pay for it themselves. Second, Schlafly's Stop-ERA campaign helped defeat the Equal Rights Amendment by limiting its ratification to only 35 of the required 38 states. Schlafly claimed that the amendment would "destroy the family, foster homosexuality, and hurt women." ERA opponents condemned "unisex toilets" and the drafting of women into combat that they believed the amendment would bring. In these women's views, the ERA would also draw out the worst in men, letting husbands opt out of supporting their wives and freeing divorced men from paying alimony. Antifeminists resented the disrespect for motherhood that they felt from some feminists. Still, they agreed with feminists that tens of millions of American women were just one man removed from welfare. At the heart of the controversy, the two sides differed on the best way to protect women's interests. Should their economic independence be enhanced, or should men be tied more tightly to their families?

Though discouraging for some, the narrow defeat of the ERA could not mask feminism's growing influence throughout American culture. The "first woman" stories that began showing up in the media during the 1970s marked the entrance of women into previously all-male roles. Like physicians, lawyers, and other figures of cultural authority, religious leaders now increasingly consisted of women, including the first Lutheran pastor (1970), the first Jewish rabbi (1972), and the first Episcopal priest (1974). In 1981 Sandra Day O'Connor became the first female Supreme Court justice. And mainstream organizations such as churches and municipalities ran feminist-created community institutions, including rape crisis centers, women's health clinics, and battered women's shelters. In 1978 the National Weather Service began using male as well as female names for hurricanes. By the 1980s, the movement had made major inroads into gender discrimination, although subtle forms of it remained. Younger women, confident that their fair treatment under the law was secure, began shying away from the term *feminism* and its lingering associations with rejection of men.

Conclusion

In 1978 a divided U.S. Supreme Court handed down a ruling on the contentious policy of affirmative action. The justices decided by a 5–4 vote in the *Bakke* case that strict racial quotas were unconstitutional but that universities could consider race as one of several factors in determining a candidate's qualifications for admission. The Court, like the American public, was wrestling with the broader 1970s problem of how to reform American society in ways that would preserve its historic strengths while removing the ills that the previous decade's political activism had laid bare. Traditional hierarchies of gender, race, and even presidential privilege were fraying badly, even as differences in wealth and income between citizens remained dramatic.

A central problem was the tension between the ideal of colorblind integration and new expressions of pride in distinctive racial and ethnic identities. In 1973 the armed American Indian Movement activists who for two months occupied buildings in Wounded Knee, South Dakota—site of the infamous 1890 U.S. Army massacre of defenseless Sioux—promoted a pan-Indian nationalist consciousness. In 1977 ABC's enormously popular eight-part television miniseries, *Roots*, dramatized the human pathos contained in the long saga of African American slavery. Many white ethnic Americans in these years leavened their long-standing cultural assimilation with renewed attention to their own roots in particular European countries, especially Ireland and Italy. The debates over the roles of women and men likewise reflected reconsideration of some fundamental matters of identity in the United States.

Americans' self-confidence and pride as a nation had been deeply shaken by the combination of the Vietnam War, the Watergate scandal, and the economic downturn after 1973. Disillusioned by the corruptions of public life, many citizens turned inward and heeded the advice of Robert J. Ringer in his 1977 bestseller, *Looking Out for Number One*. But others found motivation in the decade's events—especially the revelation that presidents, corporate executives, and other authorities had lied to them. They learned what earlier Americans had discovered in the 1760s about imperious British officials and the corrupting effects of managing a global empire. Like the revolutionaries of George Washington's generation, they sought to strengthen democracy. They pressed Congress to investigate the executive branch, and they elected an unusual outsider as president in 1976. Historians in this decade began to write more skeptically about those in power and more sympathetically about average Americans whom the history books had long ignored. The resurgence of conservatism in the 1980s recast many public policies, but it could not erase the vision of gender equality, environmental responsibility, and egalitarian governance that had taken hold among many citizens.

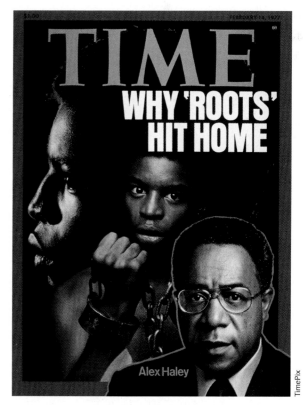

■ The 1977 miniseries version of Alex Haley's *Roots* captured the largest television audience ever to that time. The powerful drama about Haley's ancestors offered tens of millions of Americans an intimate and sympathetic understanding of the horrific story of black slavery and survival. *Roots* also represented the post-1960s emphasis on preserving and respecting group histories and identities rather than emphasizing only individual success and assimilation into the mainstream.

Sites to Visit

Divining America: Religion and the National Culture
www.nhc.rtp.nc.us:8080/tserve/divam.htm

This site has essays by prominent historians on diverse aspects of the religious history of the United States.

Documents from the Women's Liberation Movement
scriptorium.lib.duke.edu/wlm/

Provocative and fascinating articles from feminists of the late 1960s and 1970s make this site worthy of a visit.

The National Security Archive at George Washington University
www.gwu.edu/~nsarchiv/

This extraordinary site includes the most recent declassified documents on the making of U.S. foreign policy.

The Natural Resources Defense Council
www.nrdc.org/

This site contains considerable information and links about environmental issues, particularly those that emerged into public consciousness in the 1970s.

The Oyez Project of Northwestern University
oyez.nwu.edu/

Arguments from important Supreme Court cases plus information about Supreme Court justices make this a most useful site for legal history.

Gerald R. Ford Library and Museum
www.ford.utexas.edu/

The Ford presidential library maintains this site, with documents and photographs from the mid-1970s.

Watergate 25
www.washingtonpost.com/wp-srv/national/longterm/watergate/front.htm

The *Washington Post* created this informative site about the Watergate scandal 25 years after the events took place.

For Further Reading

General

William C. Berman, *America's Right Turn: From Nixon to Bush* (1994).

Peter N. Carroll, *It Seemed Like Nothing Happened: America in the 1970s* (1990).

William H. Chafe, *The Unfinished Journey: America Since World War II,* 3rd ed. (1995).

E. J. Dionne, Jr., *Why Americans Hate Politics* (1991).

Bruce J. Schulman, *The Seventies: The Great Shift in American Culture, Society, and Politics* (2001).

Twin Shocks: Détente and Watergate

Stephen E. Ambrose, *Nixon,* 3 vols. (1987, 1989, 1991).

Walter Isaacson, *Kissinger* (1992).

Jeffrey Kimball, *Nixon's Vietnam War* (1998).

Stanley I. Kutler, *The Wars of Watergate: The Last Crisis of Richard Nixon* (1992).

Melvin Small, *The Presidency of Richard M. Nixon* (1999).

Discovering the Limits of the U.S. Economy

J. Anthony Lukas, *Common Ground: A Turbulent Decade in the Lives of Three American Families* (1985).

Allen J. Matusow, *Nixon's Economy: Booms, Busts, Dollars, and Votes* (1998).

Thomas J. McCormick, *America's Half-Century: United States Foreign Policy in the Cold War and After,* 2nd ed. (1995).

Hal K. Rothman, *The Greening of a Nation? Environmentalism in the United States Since 1945* (1998).

Daniel Yergin, *The Prize: The Epic Quest for Oil, Money, and Power* (1991).

Susan Zakin, *Coyotes and Town Dogs: Earth First! and the Environmental Movement* (1993).

Reshuffling Politics

Samuel P. Hays, *Beauty, Health, and Permanence: Environmental Politics in the United States, 1955–1985* (1987).

Burton I. Kaufman, *The Presidency of James Earl Carter, Jr.* (1993).

John Ranelagh, *The Agency: The Rise and Decline of the CIA* (1986).

Gaddis Smith, *Morality, Reason, and Power: American Diplomacy in the Carter Years* (1986).

U.S. Congress, Church Committee, *Alleged Assassination Plots Involving Foreign Leaders: Interim Report of the Select Committee to Study Governmental Operations with Respect to Intelligence Activities* (1976).

Diffusing the Women's Movement

Susan J. Douglas, *Where the Girls Are: Growing Up Female with the Mass Media* (1994).

Alice Echols, *Daring to Be Bad: Radical Feminism in America, 1967–75* (1989).

Arlie Russell Hochschild, *The Second Shift: Working Parents and the Revolution at Home* (1997).

Ruth Rosen, *The World Split Open: How the Modern Women's Movement Changed America* (2000).

Gloria Steinem, *Outrageous Acts and Everyday Rebellions* (1983).

Online Practice Test

Test your understanding of this chapter with interactive review quizzes at

www.ablongman.com/jonescreatedequal/chapter27

Additional Photo Credits

Page 901: Sean Sweeney
Page 906: Courtesy, Janice L. and David Frent
Page 916: Courtesy, Sharp Electronics Corporation
Page 921: Courtesy, Janice L. and David Frent
Page 929: Courtesy, Inkworks Publishers

PART TEN

A Nation of Immigrants, a Global Economy, 1979–2001

SOON AFTER THE BEGINNING OF THE TWENTY-FIRST CENTURY, AMERICANS confronted a frightening paradox: the defeat of old enemies gave rise to new ones. The Cold War had ended with the demise of the Soviet Union. And yet the post–Cold War world continued to be a violent, and in certain respects even more terrifying, place. As colonial and totalitarian political systems collapsed around the globe, local ethnic and religious conflicts rose to the surface. To some extent, those conflicts remained confined within regions: the Balkans, Indonesia, the former Soviet Union, and parts of Africa. However, the spread of worldwide terrorist networks threatened all parts of the globe. Instances of mass murder on American soil, especially the attacks on the World Trade Center and the Pentagon in 2001, proved that the United States was vulnerable to horrific acts of violence initiated from home and abroad.

In the 1980s, President Ronald Reagan left his imprint on both domestic and foreign affairs. Reagan gave voice to conservatives, including those who favored a federal retreat from social welfare programs. Bolstered by the Moral Majority and other fundamentalist Christian groups, conservatives engaged in the so-called culture wars with liberals. Conservatives disapproved of feminists, black power advocates, gay rights activists, and environmentalists. Reagan and Congress implemented policies that shrank the federal government's commitment to social welfare programs. Reagan also reinvigorated Cold War rhetoric—he denounced the Soviet Union as an "evil empire"—and pushed military spending to unprecedented levels. Yet Reagan welcomed the initiatives of Soviet leader Mikhail Gorbachev, who sought to ease tensions with the West.

Unable to meet the basic needs of its own people and bogged down in an unwinnable war in Afghanistan, the Soviet Union disintegrated in 1991. Simultaneously, the United States embarked on a remarkable period of economic growth and expansion. President Bill Clinton favored free trade policies, such as the North American Free Trade Agreement (NAFTA), which he and others hoped would knit the world's nations together in pursuit of political and economic progress.

Nevertheless, domestic and foreign conflicts thwarted much of this hopeful vision. At home, the AIDS epidemic and drug addiction claimed many lives. Clashes among African Americans, Latinos, and Koreans in Los Angeles in 1992; the bombing of an Oklahoma City federal building by domestic antigovernment terrorists in 1995; attacks on abortion clinics; and a series of shootings by high school students revealed persistent faultlines in American society. Backed by the Supreme Court, a number of state and local governments passed anti-immigrant and anti–affirmative action laws. The culture wars were hot and, in some cases, deadly.

The most violent assault on the United States came from forces outside as well as within it. The Middle East had become a tinderbox of fears and resentments. In Iran, Islamic militants overthrew the U.S.-backed Shah in 1979. Throughout the region, many Islamic fundamentalists expressed their resentment over the military and political presence of the United States in Israel and Saudi Arabia. During the 1991 Gulf War, the United States successfully reversed Iraq's seizure of oil fields in Kuwait. Yet U.S. attempts to protect its economic and political interests in the Middle East continued to outrage Islamic militants.

By the end of the 1990s, some Americans were able to focus inward and enjoy prosperity. The stock market was booming. Cheap gas prices encouraged affluent Americans to purchase huge sport utility vehicles with little regard for their environmental impact. However, ten years of high employment masked the hidden effects of a transformed economy, one characterized by a decline in labor union membership and the rise of an ill-paid service sector. A substantial proportion of Americans lived from paycheck to paycheck.

On September 11, 2001, Americans were forced to confront their own vulnerabilities. Anti-U.S. terrorists hijacked commercial airliners and flew them into the Twin Towers of the World Trade Center in New York City and into the Pentagon outside Washington, D.C. Some 3000 people were killed. Within a month, anthrax-laced letters caused death and havoc in the offices where they were delivered and the postal centers that processed them, heightening pervasive fear and insecurity among Americans.

The events of September 11 highlighted a grim reality: certain foreign groups despised such cherished American values as democracy, liberalism, and consumerism. Moreover, U.S. foreign policies in the Middle East fanned the fires of anti-western extremism. Terrorists were becoming more successful in enlisting people who were willing to die in attacks on the United States and more resourceful in using modern technology in those attacks. These terrorists were stateless, freed from the political tasks of protecting their own citizens, monitoring national borders, or dealing with internal dissidents. In contrast to the cold warriors, fighters against terrorism faced an elusive, dispersed, and, in some cases, suicidal enemy.

1991	Clarence Thomas–Anita Hill congressional hearings.
	Persian Gulf War against Iraq.
	Los Angeles police beat, arrest Rodney King.
	Soviet Union dissolves into Russia and other component states.
1992	South Central Los Angeles riots follow acquittal of police in King case.
	FBI shootout at Ruby Ridge, Idaho.
1993	FBI storms compound of the Branch Davidian cult in Waco, Texas.
	Congress approves North American Free Trade Agreement (NAFTA).
	Arab–Israeli peace talks.
	18 American soldiers die in Somalia; U.S. withdraws.
1994	House leadership announces "Contract with America."
	Republicans win majority in House of Representatives.
	O. J. Simpson murder trial.
	Freedom of Access to Clinic Entrances Act.
1995	Truck bomb destroys federal building in Oklahoma City.
	Congress revokes 55-mph speed limit.
	U.S. intervenes against Serbs in war in Bosnia.
	Dayton peace accords signed.
1996	Welfare Reform Act.
1997	Dow Jones average passes 8000.
1998	Lewinsky–Clinton affair revealed.
	Clinton impeached by House of Representatives.
1999	Senate acquits Clinton.
	Dow Jones passes 10,000.
	U.S. bombing campaign frees province of Kosovo from Serbian rule.
	Preparations for "Y2K."
	Elian Gonzales affair.
2000	Supreme Court decides contested election; George W. Bush (R) becomes president.
	Scientists map human genome.
2001	Democrats regain control of Senate after Sen. James Jeffords leaves Republican party.
	Terrorists attack World Trade Center and Pentagon.
	Anthrax in letters causes illness and death in Florida, Washington, D.C., and New York City.

CHAPTER
28

The Cold War Returns— and Ends, 1979–1991

©1999 Peter Menzel

■ After the economic and international uncertainties of the 1970s, the 1980s brought a renewed sense of patriotism and a concentration on material acquisitions for many Americans.

O N JULY 16, 1979, JUST WEST OF ALBUQUERQUE, NEW MEXICO, A DAM HOLDING wastewater and residue from a uranium mine broke. Some 94 million gallons of radioactive water flooded into the Rio Puerco, giving it what one resident called "a terrible odor and a dark chocolatey color" as it flowed toward the Rio Grande. One of the worst nuclear accidents in U.S. history, the flooding proved far graver than the well-publicized meltdown of the Three Mile Island reactor in Pennsylvania a few months earlier. Yet few Americans heard about it for it affected mostly Navajo and Laguna Indians.

Nearby, the Anaconda Copper Company operated the nation's largest uranium mine, which closed in the early 1980s. At public hearings in 1986 concerning the future of the mine and its small mountain of poisonous tailings, Anaconda's scientists argued that the mine did not threaten human health in the area. Thus, they said, the tailing piles and the polluted ponds did not need to be cleaned up. Herman Garcia, a Laguna Indian who lived in the adjoining village of Paguate, listened carefully but remained unconvinced. "We lost five people from cancer" last year in tiny Paguate alone, he explained. "I'm no expert," he concluded, but "I'd like for some of these experts to go out there and swim in those ponds. Then when I see them swim, then maybe I feel more secure."

Uranium fuels nuclear power. The largest deposits of the element in the United States lie underground in the Four Corners region, where New Mexico, Arizona, Colorado, and Utah meet. Known on American Automobile Association maps as "Indian Country," this region is also home to the vast Navajo, Hopi, Laguna, and other Native American reservations.

The Native American West and the nuclear West have overlapped to a remarkable extent ever since participants in the Manhattan Project began building the first atomic bomb in 1942. Repeatedly, the U.S. government constructed major nuclear sites in the West on lands surrounded by Indian settlements. These included the laboratories of Los Alamos, New Mexico; bomb factories and nuclear waste dumps of Hanford, Washington; the Nevada Test Site for atomic weapons north of Las Vegas; and uranium mines in the Black Hills of South Dakota. Some of this overlap resulted from geological coincidence: almost 90 percent of the nation's uranium lay on or adjacent to Indian lands. Some of it stemmed from politics. The sparse populations of Pueblos, Western Shoshones, and Yakimas lacked the political clout to prevent their lands from becoming what the National Academy of Science called "national sacrifice areas." Raymond Yowell, chief of the Western Shoshones living immediately downwind from the Nevada Test Site, observed, "We are now the most bombed nation in the world."

Ronald Reagan loved spending time at his ranch near Santa Barbara, California.

In the 1980s, nuclear weapons and waste once again sparked controversy in the United States. President Ronald Reagan expanded the nation's nuclear arsenal, and his administration publicly discussed fighting and winning a nuclear war against the Soviet Union. An accident in 1986 at the Chernobyl nuclear power plant outside the Soviet city of Kiev only heightened public concerns. The disaster killed more than 100 people and irradiated hundreds of thousands more. Frightened by rising U.S.–Soviet tensions, citizens in western Europe and the United States organized an international movement to freeze further development of nuclear weapons.

In these same years, non-Indians grew more aware of Native Americans, in part because of economic growth in the southwestern Sunbelt. Indians made up a larger percentage of the population there than in the rest of the country. White emigration from urban California to the Rocky Mountain states also contributed to this process. So did the growing popularity of "New Age" spiritualism, with its appropriation of many Indian religious symbols. And writer Tony Hillerman achieved great commercial success with his crime novels set on the Navajo reservation in Arizona and New Mexico and populated by interesting Indian characters.

Native Americans themselves responded to the renewed focus on nuclear weaponry with a combination of resistance and accommodation. Along with their non-Indian supporters, some protested at the Nevada Test Site. At the same time, former Navajo uranium miners—many of them now stricken with cancer—sued the government for failing to inform them of the risks in handling radioactive materials. Other Indians, such as the Mescalero Apaches in New Mexico and the Goshutes in Utah, allowed nuclear waste storage facilities on their land. In their view, this move would gain them both money and control over radioactive materials that were within their borders anyway. In 1990, the U.S. Congress finally passed the Radiation Exposure Act. The law designated funds to provide some compensation for those damaged by the nation's quest for nuclear supremacy during the Cold War.

> *At its root, what did the Iranian challenge mean for American power? Khomeini and his followers despised the values they associated with modern U.S. culture.*

The controversies over nuclear power, weapons, and radioactive waste revealed several key themes characterizing the 1980s, especially U.S. military standing, government deregulation, and renewed anticommunism. In 1979, two international incidents raised questions about U.S. military effectiveness. That year, a revolution in Iran led to the taking of American hostages and a dramatic rejection of American cultural values, and the Soviet Union sent troops into Afghanistan to prop up a Soviet-allied but weakening government. Humiliated, Americans put tough-talking Republicans in the White House for 12 years. These leaders' emphasis on military might challenged the Soviet leadership, while changes in eastern Europe and the USSR brought an end to the Cold War and the breakup of the Soviet Union.

The Reagan administration also avidly promoted free markets. Its policies produced astounding wealth at the top of the socioeconomic ladder, increasing the distance between the daily experiences of the rich and the poor. And these policies catalyzed bitter struggles over natural resources, particularly those on western public lands.

Finally, the newly organized religious right clashed with liberal opponents over such issues as abortion and homosexuality. In these years, Christian fundamentalists and their allies sought to reverse cultural liberties that had emerged since the late 1960s. This conservatism paralleled a political shift to the right. After nearly half a century, the New Deal order that had relied on Washington to get things done gave way to a diminished faith in government. The turning tide renewed the hopes of some Americans—disillusioned by the persistence of poverty and crime—that a self-governed marketplace might solve the nation's most pressing social problems.

Anticommunism Revived

"We're going down!" cried U.S. political officer Elizabeth Swift on the phone to the State Department. These were her last words as a crowd of young Iranians poured into the U.S. embassy in Teheran on the morning of November 4, 1979, and cut telephone lines. In a move that shocked Americans, Islamic militants next seized 52 embassy personnel. They held the hostages for over a year.

In the late 1970s, revolutionaries of a different political bent—that of socialism and the left—took the offensive against authoritarian regimes in Central America. Indeed, the Third World seemed to be turning away from U.S. leadership in the wake of the American defeat in Vietnam. To make matters worse, the Soviet Union stepped up its support for leftists abroad. In December 1979, the Red Army invaded Afghanistan. Fed up with these humiliating events overseas and with relentless inflation at home, American voters elected Ronald Reagan as president—the most conservative chief executive since Calvin Coolidge. Reagan promised to resurrect the Cold War, and he delivered.

Iran and Afghanistan

In January 1979, the Iranian people overthrew the longtime authoritarian government of Shah Reza Pahlavi. Under the Shah's rule, the nation's enormous oil wealth had flowed into the hands of a small elite. Meanwhile, the impoverished majority of devout Shi'ite Muslims grew increasingly resentful of the Shah's closeness with his American allies. His secret police had detained 50,000 political prisoners; in the Shah's time, his critics said, "only the cemeteries prospered." The revolution found its leader in the austere religious figure Ruhollah Khomeini, who shouldered aside more moderate opposition groups. Returning from exile in Iraq and then Paris, Ayatollah Khomeini created a popular theocratic state grounded in a strict interpretation of Islamic law.

For the United States, connections with both Iran and Saudi Arabia since the 1940s had formed the two pillars of American policy toward the oil-rich Persian Gulf. Indeed, the CIA had engineered the 1953 coup that overthrew the short-lived Iranian nationalist government of Muhammad Mussadiq and restored the young Shah to power. American officials maintained close ties with the Shah thereafter.

The drop in Iran's oil production that accompanied the 1979 revolution unleashed the United States' second oil shock of the 1970s. By that time, the nation depended on imports for as much as 42 percent of its oil. American gas prices soared by 60 percent amid shortages, sending another wave of inflation rolling through the U.S. economy.

Hunted by the rebels, the Shah took his money and fled Iran. Several months later, the Carter administration let him fly to New York to seek treatment for cancer. Enraged that the United States harbored their nation's most wanted criminal, Iranians demanded the Shah's extradition to Teheran to stand trial. Washington refused. Within a month, militants stormed the U.S. Embassy—"that nest of spies," Khomeini called it, referring to the CIA's presence in Iran.

The hostages' captors paraded them before television cameras to force Washington to return the Shah. Carter refused to give in, but he focused the rest of his presidency on engineering the hostages' release. He thus had little energy and few resources to devote to his campaign for reelection. ABC television created the news show *Nightline* to provide daily reports on the crisis. In April 1980, Carter finally approved a military rescue effort. But mechanical failures forced the mission to abort, and the collision of two helicopters during the attempt killed several U.S. soldiers. Secretary of State Cyrus Vance resigned in protest against the attempted use of force. He was the first State Department head to quit over a matter of principle since William Jennings Bryan resigned in 1915 to express his desire to stay out of World War I. Americans' frustration deepened, and their resentment of anti-American radicals in the Third World intensified. Not until after the Shah's death in 1980 did the two governments finally negotiate the hostages' release. Even then, the Iranian leaders delayed the Americans' departure until moments after Carter left office in January 1981.

At its root, what did the Iranian challenge mean for American power? Khomeini and his followers despised the values they associated with modern U.S. culture: secularism,

■ Ruhollah Khomeini led the 1979 revolution in Iran that established the modern world's first Islamic theocratic state. The events in Iran encouraged Islamic revolutionaries across the Middle East, Asia, and North Africa. For Americans, the closest analogy was the Bolshevik revolution of 1917 in Russia, which provided a model for other Communist revolutions abroad.

Bettmann/CORBIS

■ MAP 28.1

TROUBLE SPOTS IN THE MIDDLE EAST, 1979–1993 Oil production around the Persian Gulf and the close American relationship with Israel made political instability in the Middle East a central concern of the U.S. government. American leaders particularly feared the spread of either Soviet influence or Islamic revolution, both of which opposed American cultural values and U.S. strategic interests.

materialism, gender equality, alcohol consumption, and sexual titillation. Back in the 1630s, John Winthrop and other members of the new Massachusetts Bay colony might well have understood this perspective. But the modern Iranian radicals sought to export the cleansing power of a puritanical Islamic faith throughout the Middle East and beyond. Indeed, the revolutionaries condemned the atheistic Soviets just as fiercely as they did the materialistic Americans. Khomeini applauded all movements that sought "to gain liberation from the superpowers of the left and the right." U.S. policymakers had feared that instability in Iran might lead to a communist takeover of that country. Instead, the creation of the world's first revolutionary Islamic state in 1979 presented an entirely different challenge to American interests overseas.

Just seven weeks after the outbreak of the hostage crisis in Teheran, the first of 110,000 Russian troops rolled south across the USSR's border into neighboring Afghanistan. Their goal: To stabilize the pro-Soviet government there against anticommunist Islamic guerrilla fighters. Moscow had resolved to prevent the spread of Islamic revolution into the heavily Muslim southern regions of the USSR.

But few Americans saw this invasion as a defensive operation. Rather, they feared a push toward vulnerable Iran as Red Army troops marched beyond eastern Europe for the first time in more than 30 years. The Carter administration halted most trade with the Soviets and withdrew the Strategic Arms Limitation Treaty (SALT II) nuclear arms control treaty from Senate consideration. In addition, the president organized a western boycott of the 1980 Olympics in Moscow and increased military spending. The "Carter Doctrine" proclaimed the U.S. commitment to preserve the status quo in the Persian Gulf region, even if it meant the use of military force. And the CIA began funding the Afghan guerrillas. Détente was dead; containment was back. Next came efforts to roll back the Soviets.

The Conservative Victory of 1980

By mid–1980, Carter's public approval rating had dropped to the lowest level of any modern president. Interest rates surpassed 20 percent, and inflation reached 17 percent. Even the president acknowledged a "crisis stage." With their dollars no longer buying what they used to, Americans wondered what the future would bring. For many voters, Carter's inability to free the hostages in Teheran or reverse the Soviet occupation of Afghanistan symbolized the limitations of his presidency. Even his own party threatened to abandon him, as the vigorous challenge in the Democratic primaries by liberal Senator Edward Kennedy of Massachusetts revealed. Many moderate Democrats and unaffiliated voters backed the independent candidacy of John Anderson. The moderate Republican congressman from Illinois managed to win 7 percent of the popular vote that November.

Onto this stage strode Ronald Reagan. Long considered too conservative to win the presidency, the former California governor projected the confidence and strength that many Americans wanted, even if they did not share all of his views. The 69-year-old one-time actor sailed through the Republican primaries. For his main tactic, he appealed to nostalgia, particularly among white men, for a rosier past—a time of rising wages and U.S. military might. While Carter spoke of learning to live within limits, Reagan insisted that "we are too great a nation to limit ourselves to small dreams." He painted a compelling picture of military pride and power abroad, of unlimited consumption of energy, and of infinite economic growth. Reagan located Carter's "crisis of confidence" in the U.S. government, not in the American people. The "truth is," he

contended, "there are simple answers—just not easy ones." Still, his answers looked both simpler and easier than Carter's, and Reagan crushed the incumbent in the November election.

Reagan's victory symbolized the meshing of politics and entertainment. An actor on the ultimate stage, he understood the presidency as a matter of public performance more than substantive policies. With little interest in the actual process of governing, he gave his advisers minimal guidance. He focused his own efforts on selling an idealized version of America to the public. He deeply believed in this version, even when his stories about it derived from film plots. For example, he claimed to have filmed the liberation of Nazi death camps in Europe in World War II, when in fact he did not leave the United States during the war. Nevertheless, with his sunny disposition and ease before the camera, Reagan projected the image of an attractive, competent leader.

TABLE 28-1			
The Election of 1980			
Candidate	**Political Party**	**Popular Vote**	**Electoral Vote**
Ronald Reagan	Republican	43,901,812	489
Jimmy Carter	Democratic	35,483,820	49
John B. Anderson	Independent	5,719,722	0

The media loved Reagan. Indeed, his presidency fit with the new emphasis on constant entertainment, as cable television, VCRs (1976), MTV (1981), and CDs (1983) swept the culture. Daily newspaper readership plummeted from 73 percent to 50 percent during the 1980s. Equally telling, the average length of an uninterrupted "sound bite" on the evening news dropped from 42 seconds in 1968 to fewer than 10 seconds in 1988. Anything longer, the networks believed, would bore viewers. And no one projected simplicity with greater warmth or sincerity than Reagan. Even his fiercest opponents admired his irrepressible humor when, after being shot by would-be assassin John Hinkley in 1981, the president surveyed the surgeons standing around his operating table and announced, "I hope you're all Republicans."

Yet the 1980 election was about more than just Reagan's likable personality. It revealed the nation's renewed infatuation with conservative ideas. Republicans won control of the Senate for the first time since 1952. They managed to defeat several of the chamber's most respected liberal Democratic members, such as Frank Church of Idaho, who had led the investigation of CIA spying practices. The Grand Old Party had repositioned itself to be more ideologically consistent. It now had fewer traditionally moderate northeastern members and millions of new conservative white southern members.

Several basic values united the party: an unhindered private sector and entrepreneurial initiative to create affluence plus free markets and individual responsibility to solve the nation's social problems. Republicans, like most Democrats, also believed that the United States had a moral obligation to preserve world order and halt further expansion of communist influence. Reagan proclaimed that "government was the problem, not the solution." For conservatives, government had two specific roles: to prevent disorder—crime at home, revolution abroad—and to support the business community. The United States' key European allies also moved to the right in the 1980s, especially Great Britain under the leadership of Margaret Thatcher.

Renewing the Cold War

"Sometimes in our administration," Reagan once joked, "the right hand doesn't know what the far-right hand is doing." But all hands in the White House agreed on the importance of restoring confidence in the nation's engagements abroad, particularly in the Third World. In the 1970s, leftist insurgencies in Asia, Africa, and Latin America—especially Vietnam, Cambodia, Angola, Ethiopia, El Salvador, and Nicaragua—had suggested the retreat of U.S. power. Equally troubling to many, when the U.S. government did assert its power, it often seemed to support anti-democratic or racist governments—as long as they were anticommunist and open to foreign investment. Never much concerned with foreign affairs in the best of times, most Americans now felt disillusioned.

Reagan set out to heal the public's bruised pride, using the logic of his new UN ambassador, Jeane Kirkpatrick. A former Georgetown University professor, Kirkpatrick distinguished between nondemocratic nations on the right ("authoritarian") and the left ("totalitarian"). They were not morally equivalent, she argued. In her view, "authoritarian" regimes were friendly to the United States and could be reformed, but "totalitarian" communist governments had close ties to the Soviet Union and could be changed only by force. The peaceful fall of the Berlin Wall in 1989 disproved her theory.

Reagan blamed the Soviet Union for "all the unrest that is going on." He rejected the 1970s policy of détente that had emerged during the Nixon administration and had taken further shape under Ford and Carter. Often, Reagan spoke as though the Chinese–Soviet split had never happened. His was "a kind of 1952 world," one aide recalled. "He sees the world in black and white terms." Pointing to the Soviet occupation of Afghanistan and its 1983 shoot-down of a Korean Air Lines civilian jet that had strayed into Soviet airspace, the president denounced the USSR as "an evil empire." His pronouncement echoed the language of the wildly popular film *Star Wars* (1977) and its two sequels. The three movies cast the plucky heroes—like Americans and their allies—as righteous rebels against a malignant imperial power. The Vietnam War, Reagan insisted, was not a destructive imperial cause but a "noble effort" on the part of dedicated American patriots. Indeed, as governor of California in the late 1960s, Reagan had declared that the United States should "level Vietnam, pave it, paint stripes on it, and make a parking lot of it." Americans, Reagan vowed, must overcome their post–1973 "Vietnam syndrome" and stand ready once again to use force abroad.

The Reagan administration backed up the president's words by launching the largest peacetime military build-up in American history. The Pentagon's budget ballooned 40 percent between 1980 and 1984. The new president also revived covert operations. He gave CIA director William Casey the green light to provide secret assistance to anticommunist governments and insurgencies throughout the Third World, despite their often gruesome human rights records.

However, the administration's aggressive rhetoric about rolling back communism masked an unwillingness to put U.S. soldiers in harm's way abroad. The one exception came during the civil war in Lebanon in 1983. U.S. forces initially deployed as peacekeepers there began siding with the Israeli-backed Christian government troops against Syrian-supported Muslim rebels. Within weeks, a Muslim suicide bomber—one of the first of many to come in the Middle East—drove a truck full of explosives into the American barracks at the Beirut airport, killing 241 marines. The administration quietly backed off from mediating further Middle East conflicts. It covered its retreat with an invasion two days later of the tiny Caribbean island of Grenada. There, thousands of U.S. troops quickly overthrew a Marxist government and a small contingent of Cuban supporters.

Reagan was the only Cold War president to take almost no interest in the details of foreign policy. International issues "weren't terribly important to the president," national security adviser Robert McFarlane explained. Reagan delegated most foreign policy planning to his advisers—except for the rising tide of leftist revolution in Central America. In that region, extreme inequalities between landowning elites and vast peasant majorities had fueled insurgencies against the authoritarian governments of El Salvador, Guatemala, and Nicaragua. Moreover, some small assistance from Cuba and the Soviet Union had found its way to the rebels. Reagan passionately opposed these insurgents. He authorized the CIA to work hand in hand with the regimes, even though they used death squads to torture and murder dissidents and slaughtered whole villages and towns to wipe out possible resistance.

In Nicaragua, the Sandinista rebels had managed to overthrow the pro-American dictatorship of Antonio Somoza in 1979. Their name reflected loyalty to a long-standing left-leaning effort in Nicaragua to eliminate U.S. dominance of the country; in the 1920s and early 1930s, General Augusto Sandino had led rebel troops against the U.S.-supported dictatorial regime of Somoza's father. Forty years later, the Sandinistas set about building a more egalitarian and socialistic state while still preserving 60 percent of the nation's wealth in private hands. Carter had adopted a wait-and-see attitude. But after Reagan took office in 1981, the CIA created the counterrevolutionary "Contras," recruited primarily from Somoza's murderous former National Guard. The Contras waged an undeclared war on the new government in the Nicaraguan capital of Managua. By 1987, 40,000 Nicaraguans had died in the fighting, most of them civilians. Reagan called the Contras "freedom fighters" and declared them "the moral equal of our Founding Fathers."

Nevertheless, several European and Latin American allies considered the Contras an illegitimate force of terrorists. A large coalition of church and university groups in the United States agreed. They organized fact-finding visits to Nicaragua and lobbying trips to Washington. Christian activists formed the "Sanctuary" movement to aid refugees from the right-wing dictatorships in Central America that sympathized with the Contras. The Pentagon, for its part, had no interest in sending troops to fight a popular government abroad. The opposition finally prevailed; Congress passed the Boland Amendments of 1982 and 1984 to restrict U.S. assistance to the Contras.

■ **Critics of Reagan's policies toward Central America** believed that he ignored the indigenous problems encouraging revolutions there, blaming instead the USSR and Cuba. The cartoon suggests that the Democratic party took a different view than the president. Many Democrats in the Congress did, and they were responsible for limiting Reagan's promotion of the Nicaraguan Contras. But many others went along with the popular president in defending the Contras and supporting right-wing regimes in the region.

The plight of refugees fleeing the civil wars in Central America exposed the politicized thinking that had influenced U.S. immigration policies for decades. Officials distinguished between "political" refugees and "economic" refugees. The former, they felt, had a well-founded fear of persecution. The latter were supposedly looking only for better economic opportunities. The Reagan administration used this distinction to justify supporting certain foreign governments while opposing others. For example, the U.S. government had warmly welcomed and financially assisted people fleeing communist regimes, such as Hungary in the 1950s and Cuba since the 1960s. Likewise, Nicaraguan immigrants were treated well because their choice to leave Nicaragua provided ammunition in the propaganda war against the Sandinistas. However, Salvadorans and Guatemalans, deemed "economic" refugees, were turned away. In 1984, U.S. officials admitted only 328 Salvadorans into the country while refusing 13,045—a ratio opposite that for Nicaraguans.

These policies encouraged the emergence of militantly anticommunist expatriate communities in the United States. These groups then lobbied to sustain U.S. hostility toward leftist regimes in their homelands. The anti-Castro Cuban community in Miami offered the most dramatic example. Immigrants who left Vietnam and Cambodia after the communist victories there in 1975 brought a similar perspective.

Republican Rule at Home

Lori was what the president called a "welfare cheat." Writer Barbara Ehrenreich told the story of a young neighbor in New York City representative of welfare recipients: a single white mother with one child. Lori had been married for two years to a man who beat her and once chased her around the house with a gun. Welfare had made it possible for her to leave him, a move she described as like being born again, "as a human being this time." Lori sometimes earned close to $100 a week from cleaning houses and waiting tables—not enough to support herself and her daughter, but a useful supplement to the small government payments. She chose not to report this to the welfare office, spending it instead on little things deemed inessential by welfare regulations: deodorant, hand lotion, and an occasional commercial haircut.

Lori's story helps illuminate some of the major trends of the 1980s. Just as its commitment to expanding U.S. economic opportunities abroad helped renew the Cold War early in the decade, the Reagan administration's beliefs in free markets and scant government regulation of the private sector shaped politics at home during this decade. In some ways, the economy's behavior seemed to affirm the wisdom of these beliefs: inflation finally eased and the stock market perked up. Congress and the White House slashed taxes. However, annual budget deficits and the national debt (the accumulation of previous deficits) soon soared as tax revenues decreased and military spending increased. The administration shrank government programs for the poor and portrayed welfare recipients like Lori as lazy and irresponsible. Washington turned a cold shoulder to concerns over the environment and opened public lands in the West to new commercial uses. By the 1990s, the gap between rich and poor widened so much that the vaunted American middle class threatened to shrink beyond recognition.

"Reaganomics" and the Assault on Welfare

Taxes played a crucial role in the Reagan administration's efforts to reduce government involvement in the economy. Compared with America's closest allies in Europe, U.S. tax rates were already low because of the country's smaller welfare provisions. But a tax revolt had begun brewing in the 1970s, exemplified by California's Proposition 13 (1978), which cut property taxes by more than half. In 1981, Reagan proposed a new tax law to lower federal income tax rates by 25 percent over three years. Congress passed the legislation, and the top individual rate—paid only by the wealthiest Americans—dropped from 70 percent to 28 percent. Congress also slashed taxes on corporations, capital gains, and inheritances, further benefiting the most affluent Americans.

As taxes shrank, federal spending on the military soared. The Pentagon bolstered its conventional and nuclear arsenals and gave service personnel a morale-boosting salary increase. After 1983, billions of dollars poured from the U.S. Treasury into the president's proposed Strategic Defense Initiative (SDI). An immense project, SDI sought to create a national missile defense system involving lasers that could shoot down incoming nuclear missiles. Most scientists considered the concept technically unfeasible, and critics dubbed it "Star Wars" for its resemblance to some of the fantasy weapons in the popular science fiction film of the same name. Still, the jump in military spending created new jobs, just as earlier boosts had done under Truman and Kennedy.

With less money coming in from taxes but more money flowing out to the military, the government did not seem to be on the path to fiscal responsibility touted by the Republican party. The funds for the weapons build-up could come from only one source: social programs at home. However, most domestic spending went to popular programs, such as Social Security and Medicare, which primarily benefited the middle class. Leaving those in place, Reagan instead reduced funding for welfare programs, including food stamps, school lunches, job training, and low-income housing. His administration derided impoverished single mothers as "welfare queens." The welfare state, the administration contended, was only encouraging dependence and stifling individual responsibility. Frustrated by the persistence of poverty, many well-off Americans found this view persuasive. Numerous people, such as conservative writer George Gilder, found it much easier to assume that the poor "are refusing to work hard" than to examine the more complicated roots of poverty.

Congress slashed taxes on corporations, capital gains, and inheritances, further benefiting the most affluent Americans.

The assault on welfare had links to racial issues as well. Reagan portrayed welfare recipients—most of whom were white and lived in rural areas—as primarily urban and African American. The president had made a blunt appeal to white southern voters in 1980. He had campaigned in Philadelphia, Mississippi, a tiny town but a national symbol of antiblack violence since three civil rights workers had been murdered nearby in 1964. There, Reagan spoke of his support for "states' rights"—the same language that those who supported the killers had used.

The Republican desire to transfer the responsibility for citizens' well-being from the national government to the states resonated with opponents of the civil rights movement. In 1978, the Supreme Court's *Bakke* decision had supported this goal by banning the use of actual racial quotas in college admissions, although the Court did allow the affirmative action principle of considering race as merely one of many factors in admission decisions. The Reagan administration opposed any form of affirmative action, calling instead for the "colorblind" application of law. The president and his supporters argued that prejudice no longer had any effect on the decisions that employers and others made. Ironically, Reagan's own Justice Department demonstrated the opposite: it sought unsuccessfully to win tax-free status for Bob Jones University in Greenville, South Carolina, and other schools and colleges that discriminated against people of color.

Reducing welfare spending did not close the budgetary gaps that lower taxes and higher military outlays had opened. "Supply-side" economists had promised that tax cuts would encourage investment and thereby generate wealth and eventually more tax revenues, even with lowered rates. But Reagan's own vice president and former challenger in the Republican primaries, George H.W. Bush, had dismissed these assumptions as "voodoo economics." Bush's perspective had merit. To close the budget gaps, the government resorted to borrowing money. Formerly the world's largest creditor nation, the United States became its largest debtor nation. Between 1981 and 1989, the national debt ballooned to almost $3 trillion. Moreover, during 12 years of Republican rule, annual budget deficits jumped from $59 billion to $300 billion. Paying the interest on the new debt pushed interest rates higher and siphoned off funds that could have been used for any number of productive purposes.

Despite these problems, "Reaganomics" helped the national economy recover somewhat from the traumas of the 1970s. The tight money policies of the Federal Reserve Board after 1979 eventually tamed inflation, which dropped from 14 percent in 1980 to less than 2 percent in 1983. The Fed's high interest rates also choked off the nation's cash flow and provoked a severe recession in 1981–1982, with unemployment reaching above 10 percent. However, the economy revived again in 1983 and was growing at a robust annual rate of 6.8 percent by 1984.

In that year, rising confidence in the economy helped Reagan crush his opponent, Carter's former Vice President Walter Mondale. Even the novelty of placing a woman, Geraldine Ferraro, on a major ticket as the vice presidential candidate could not bolster the Democratic challenge. Reagan, now 73 and limiting his campaign appearances to well-orchestrated photo oportunities, won re-election handily and continued his economic course. After several years of excellent returns on Wall Street, the stock market crash of October 1987 caught investors by surprise. Nevertheless, it did not provoke a broader economic downturn, as the 1929 crash had done.

TABLE 28-2

The Election of 1984

Candidate	Political Party	Popular Vote	Electoral Vote
Ronald Reagan	Republican	54,455,075	525
Walter Mondale	Democratic	37,577,185	13

An Embattled Environment

The 1980 election marked the sharpest turn ever in American environmental politics. The new administration reversed two decades of growing bipartisan consensus on the need for greater protection of the environment. Reagan instead supported corporations' demands for fewer environmental regulations and easier access to natural resources on public lands. The president ridiculed the idea of preserving wilderness for its own sake. Noting that plants emit carbon dioxide, he even claimed that "trees cause more pollution than automobiles do." A

■ James Watt, Reagan's first Secretary of the Interior, became one of the most polarizing figures in a polarized decade. He made clear that he considered environmentalists to be his opponents as he worked to promote the interests of mining and timbering companies as well as ranchers. The Department of the Interior manages the national parks, monuments, and wildlife refuges, as well as the Bureau of Land Management's extensive lands (national forests fall under the Department of Agriculture's jurisdiction).

'SURELY,' SAYS I, 'NOT THE JAMES WATT, FOLK-HERO AND FAMOUS WILDERNESS RAPIST!' 'THAT'S ME,' SAYS HE. AND I SAYS, 'NOT THE RENOWNED DESPOILER OF OUR PRECIOUS NATIONAL HERITAGE!' 'RIGHT,' SAYS HE. SO I ATE HIM.'

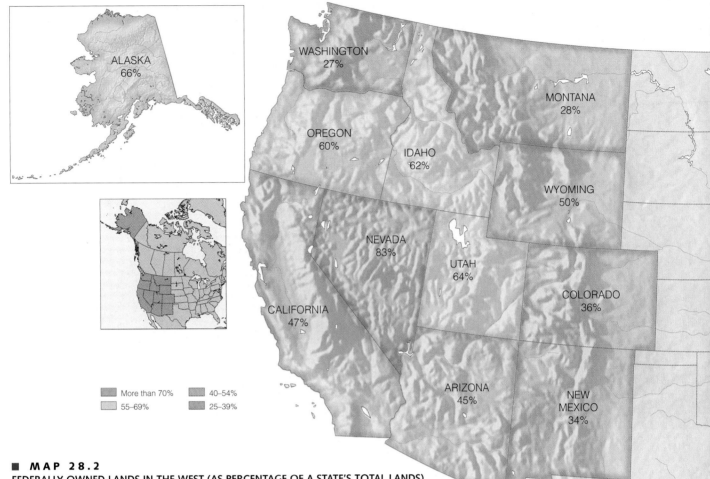

■ MAP 28.2
FEDERALLY OWNED LANDS IN THE WEST (AS PERCENTAGE OF A STATE'S TOTAL LANDS)
The vast majority of public lands lie in the states west of the Mississippi River, managed by agencies
of the U.S. government. In the 1980s those lands were at the center of a dispute between citizens who saw
them as national treasures and others, mostly local businessmen and ranchers, who wanted the lands sold
to individuals or transferred to states that would open them to easier exploitation.

coalition of powerful western land users and politicians known as the "Sagebrush Rebellion" had an ally in the White House. Emboldened, they launched a quest to turn federal lands
over to the states and open them to commercial use. These lands, most of them in the West,
were administered by the U.S. Forest Service and the Bureau of Land Management (BLM).
They had ended up in federal hands primarily because successive waves of settlers had deemed
them undesirable. They included snowy mountains in the Rockies and Sierras and vast deserts
in the Great Basin of Nevada and Utah. By the 1980s, different groups desired them for two
mutually exclusive purposes: corporations and ranchers wanted to harvest timber and minerals from them and use them for grazing, and environmentalists and outdoor enthusiasts
sought to designate them for recreational and scenic use.

The officials Reagan appointed to oversee these lands and assume responsibility for protecting them had little respect for the agencies they ran. Critics described the situation as "foxes
guarding the chicken house." The officials openly disdained environmentalists, including those
in the moderate wing of the Republican party. Anne Gorsuch at the Environmental Protection Agency (EPA), Robert Burford at the BLM, and John Crowell in charge of the Forest
Service explicitly rewrote regulations to favor private enterprise. They sold grazing, logging,
and mining rights on public lands at prices far below market value, despite their stated commitment to market economics.

(Left) Roger Worth/Woodfin Camp; (right) Elaine Thompson/AP/Wide World

■ On May 18, 1980, a spectacular volcanic eruption blew the top off of Mt. St. Helens in Washington's Cascade Range. The hot ash and lava flows killed 57 people and created an ash-covered landscape out of a previously lush forest. The eruption reminded Americans of all political persuasions of the power and unpredictability of nature, just months before the Reagan administration initiated new environmental policies opening up natural resources to easier exploitation.

Gorsuch, Burford, and Crowell were moderates in comparison to James Watt, the new Secretary of the Interior who controlled national parks and wildlife refuges. A native of Wheatland, Wyoming, Watt had worked as a lawyer in Denver for a private foundation dedicated to businesses seeking access to public lands. An ideologue, he declared that only two kinds of people lived in the United States: "liberals and Americans." Watt was also a Christian fundamentalist who believed that the end of time was very near. In his Senate confirmation hearings, he suggested that the nation had little need for long-term public land management because Christ would soon be returning and the known world would pass away—an interpretation of stewardship that not even all fundamentalists shared, much less the broader American public. Watt's abrasive personal style eventually alienated even the White House, and he resigned in 1983.

The administration's reversal of federal environmental policies alarmed a wide range of citizens and stimulated a powerful backlash. In particular, Watt's smug extremism made him a lighting rod for criticism. Membership in environmental organizations soared, in such traditional groups as the Sierra Club and the Audubon Society, as well as in more radical ones, such as Greenpeace. Most Americans wanted to breathe cleaner air, drink safe water, and make recreational use of national forests, national parks, and BLM lands. Even Americans sympathetic to extractive industries such as timbering lamented the scars that clearcutting and strip mining left. In much of the rural West, jobs in the recreation industry

outnumbered those in the logging, mining, and ranching businesses. The public also took alarm at the 1986 Chernobyl nuclear accident in the USSR. Three years later, concerns intensified when the oil tanker *Exxon Valdez* ran aground in Prince William Sound in Alaska, coating 1000 miles of pristine coastline with crude oil. Reagan's Republican successor in the White House, George Bush, caught on and tried to portray himself as an environmentalist.

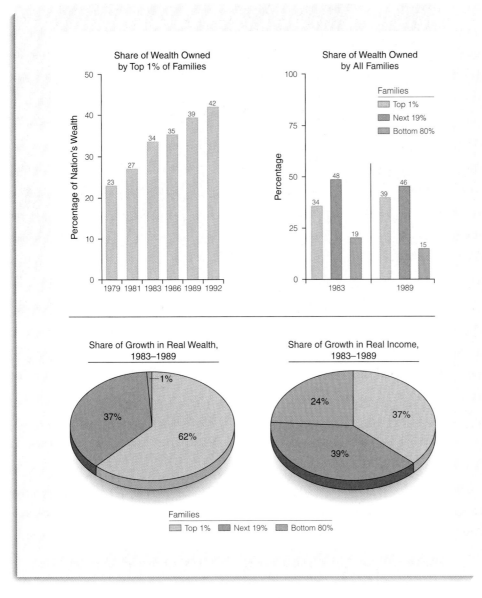

■ **FIGURE 28.1**
DISTRIBUTION OF WEALTH AND INCOME   The 1980s were excellent years for wealthy Americans. The "trickle-down" effect touted by some Reagan administration officials—predicting that greater wealth accumulation among the rich would trickle down to the less affluent—had little impact.

A Society Divided

As the Reagan administration eased corporate access to the nation's natural resources, the disparity between rich and poor expanded further. This gap was already more prominent than that of other industrialized democracies, including Japan and West Germany. But the distribution of income became even more skewed, and wealth flowed increasingly to already affluent Americans.

Whereas most Americans' real wages (wages after inflation is factored in) declined, the professional classes fared well, and the wealthiest citizens gained enormously. For example, the salary of an average corporate chief executive officer was 40 times greater than that of a typical factory worker in 1980; by 1989, it was 93 times greater. The net worth of the 400 richest Americans tripled. The wealthiest 1 percent of citizens received 60 percent of the after-tax income gain during the decade. By 1989, the top 1 percent of American families possessed more assets than the bottom 90 percent—a ratio typical of Third World nations.

A series of corporate mergers and consolidations further enriched well-off Americans, as did financial speculation and manipulation on Wall Street. *Business Week* wrote of a "Casino

Is Material Success Corrupting?

"Will you tell me," former president John Adams asked former president Thomas Jefferson in 1819, "how to prevent riches from becoming the effects of temperance and industry? Will you tell me how to prevent riches from producing luxury? Will you tell me how to prevent luxury from producing effeminacy, intoxication, extravagance, vice and folly?"

Adams had his finger on one of the enduring dilemmas in American life. Discipline and hard work—"temperance and industry"—tended to lead to material success. But acquiring riches tended to change people. It made them more self-indulgent and less virtuous as citizens of a republic, Adams feared.

Adams's concerns mirrored those of his Puritan ancestors who had arrived in Massachusetts almost two centuries earlier. So strongly had the Puritans rejected what they saw as the spiritual and material corruptions of life in England that they left to start anew across the

Wealthy Americans have had varying attitudes about how to deal with their good fortune. The newly rich of the 1980s seemed eager to display their wealth publicly. Here New York real estate tycoon Donald Trump and his wife Ivana pose with part of the domestic staff that catered to their daily needs.

Ted Thai/CORBIS/Sygma

Atlantic Ocean, a profoundly dangerous enterprise. Once they had survived the terrible first winters and established secure colonies in what they called New England, they began to face a new problem. Building a godly society meant "doing good": following the model of Jesus. But their disciplined lives led many Puritans also to "do well": make money.

Were these two compatible? After all, Jesus himself had warned, "It is easier for a camel to go through the eye of a needle than for a rich man to enter into the kingdom of God" (*Matthew* 19:24). Puritans and their descendants wrestled with this problem for generations.

Waves of immigration since the 1600s replenished American society

Economy" in which insider trading and leveraged buyouts (business takeovers financed by debt) created paper wealth rather than actual products. Defenders of the aggressive new tactics on Wall Street argued that those taking great risks deserved great rewards and that new wealth trickled down to the broader American citizenry. "Greed is all right," fabulously wealthy financier and corporate takeover specialist Ivan Boesky assured the 1986 graduating class of the business school of the University of California at Berkeley. "I want you to know that. I think greed is healthy. You can be greedy and still feel good about yourself." Six months later, however, Boesky began a three-year prison term for illegal insider trading.

The explosion of wealth at the top fueled an emerging culture of extravagance, reminiscent of similar trends in the late nineteenth century and the 1920s. Newly identified "yuppies" (young urban professionals) embodied the drive for material acquisition, in contrast to the anticonsumerist inclinations of the late 1960s and early 1970s. Jerry Rubin had made a reputation as a member of the anarchist "yippies" in the 1960s. He and comrade Abbie Hoffman once dropped dollar bills onto the floor of the New York Stock Exchange—which traders

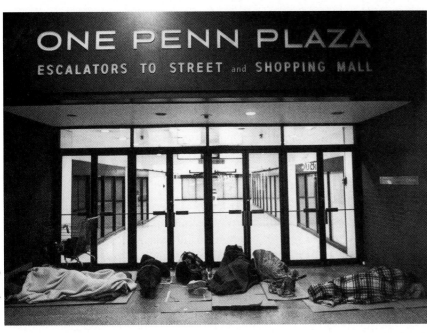

Neither homelessness nor poverty in general was new in American society in the 1980s. But the numbers of Americans living on the streets increased sharply. They were especially visible in the centers of large cities, such as these sleeping in New York City's Pennsylvania station in January 1990.

with people seeking opportunity. The hardships that attend moving to a new country ensured that new Americans tended to be strivers and risk-takers. Some came for religious and political freedom, but many others were drawn by the possibility of "doing well" economically. With effort, most fared much better than they had previously. The United States remained, in the old words of nineteenth-century Chinese immigrants, "the Golden Mountain."

Despite their enthusiasm for pursuing private material success, Americans in the twentieth century at times indicated public ambivalence about great wealth. During the trauma of the Great Depression and the national unity of World War II, displays of extravagance drew scorn, and government policies became somewhat more redistributive of the national wealth. The communes of the 1960s, like earlier utopian communities, sought to create a life free from what their members saw as the corruptions of materialism. In the Cold War competition for influence abroad, U.S. officials sent diplomats and aid workers to Africa but worried that Soviet and especially Chinese personnel, accustomed to fewer material comforts at home than Americans, were fitting much better into poor African societies and making more positive impressions on their hosts.

In other periods of modern American history, however, public life celebrated the success of the nation's richest citizens. During the Gilded Age of the late 1800s and the Jazz Age of the 1920s, political and cultural leaders admired and shared the affluence associated with names such as Rockefeller, Carnegie, and Ford. The 1980s became another era for ostentatious displays of wealth. "If you've got it, flaunt it," became a familiar expression. The proliferation of stretch limousines epitomized a decade marked by "conspicuous consumption." ■

scurried madly to grab—to dramatize the stock market's pursuit of profit. By the 1980s, however, Rubin was working as an investment banker. Ronald and Nancy Reagan were older but shared similar values. They relished lavish amenities like those made popular on the television shows *Dynasty, Dallas,* and *Lifestyles of the Rich and Famous.* The contrast to the austere Jimmy Carter could hardly have been more stark.

As the affluence gap widened, the broad middle class watched its job security slip. Early in the decade, the recession had prompted factory shutdowns and mass layoffs. More than a million industrial jobs disappeared in 1982 alone. Manufacturers' decisions to keep moving plants abroad for cheaper labor only worsened the situation. Although the 1980s saw the creation of 20 million new jobs, most of these were in the nonunionized service sector. Thus they offered low pay and few benefits. By 1990, 8 million Americans had tried the unskilled work available at McDonald's fast-food restaurants. "To work at McDonald's you don't need a face, you don't need a brain," one of them recalled. "You need to have two hands and two legs and move 'em as fast as you can. That's the whole system. I wouldn't go back there for anything."

Organized labor suffered during these years as well, losing 3 million members as the manufacturing sector of the economy shrank and the government encouraged corporate opposition to unions. In his first year in office, Reagan broke a strike by the nation's 12,000 air traffic controllers by firing the protesting public employees and hiring permanent replacements. Worried about the disappearance of high-wage industrial jobs, American families tried to preserve their living standards by putting more of their members in the workforce, especially women and teenagers. They also put off paying for their lifestyles by charging more purchases to credit cards, taking out larger home mortgages, and signing on for longer car loans. As their government carried more debt, so did private citizens.

The poorest Americans fared badly in the 1980s. The bottom tenth saw their already meager incomes decline by another 10 percent. In 1986, a full-time worker at minimum wage earned $6700 per year—almost $4000 short of the poverty level for a family of four. Homelessness worsened in the cities as the government cut funding for welfare and institutional care for the mentally ill while housing costs rose. More than 1 million people lived on the streets, one-fifth of them still employed. One out of eight children went hungry, and 20 percent lived in poverty, including 50 percent of black children.

These Americans received minimal sympathy from the nation's political leaders. By contrast, Congress and the White House provided huge federal subsidies to "needy" businesses such as the Chrysler Corporation. The collapse of the savings and loan (S&L) industry provides the most striking example. Deregulation in the late 1970s had reduced oversight of the formerly sedate financial practices of S&Ls by federal regulators. But S&Ls remained insured by the U.S. government. As a result, some S&L executives, such as Charles Keating, engaged in rampant speculation and fraud. A decline in real estate prices bankrupted 600 shaky S&Ls by 1991, leaving taxpayers with a bill for nearly $500 billion. Federal Deposit Insurance Corporation chairman William Seidman described the U.S. government as "a full partner in a nationwide casino."

Despite Reagan's record, many working-class and middle-class Americans voted for him twice. Forty percent of union household members and 50 percent of all blue-collar workers cast their ballots for this staunch opponent of unions. Why? Part of the explanation lies in the decline of working-class voting during the 1970s. Disillusioned with a political process they saw as corrupt, numerous workers neglected to go to the polls on voting day. Many of those who did vote decided that the Democratic party had become increasingly co-opted by cultural liberalism and no longer spoke for the working class. They cast their ballots for the Republicans for the first time. Reagan had great personal charisma, and his staff brilliantly managed his image in the media. The former actor's effective appeal to patriotism also attracted many citizens who might once have voted for their economic interests instead. Finally, white Americans increasingly defined their political loyalties on the basis of social and cultural issues—such as opposition to abortion, homosexuality, and affirmative action—rather than economic interests. Conservative Christians, in particular, strongly supported the Republican cause.

Cultural Conflict

One of the nation's foremost religious figures, Reverend Pat Robertson controlled the Christian Broadcasting Network and ran unsuccessfully for the 1988 Republican presidential nomination. Like other social conservatives of this era, he promoted "family values" and traditional gender roles. Robertson went so far as to declare that feminism "encourages women to leave their husbands, kill their children [and] practice witchcraft." In contrast, author Susan Faludi wrote the 1991 best-seller *Backlash* about opposition to the women's movement. She became an important critic of gender roles in American society and how they limit people's life experiences and possibilities. In completely opposite fashion from Robertson, Faludi concluded, "All women are feminists. It's just a matter of time and encouragement."

Throughout the 1980s, Americans embroiled themselves in a contentious debate about values. Their society had changed in the previous generation in ways that some citizens disdained but others applauded. Americans argued primarily about issues that had come to the fore during the social movements of the 1960s and 1970s: sexuality, gender roles, the place of religion in public life, and multiculturalism. These often bitter "culture wars" dominated talk shows and newspaper editorial pages throughout much of the last two decades of the twentieth century.

The Rise of the Religious Right

Some of the Americans most troubled by the state of American society were conservative white Protestants. Disproportionately from the South, they had long avoided political involvement and sought to keep church and state separate. They had particularly distrusted Roman Catholicism and state aid for religious education that would include parochial schools. But anti-Catholicism declined sharply among these conservative Christians after the Supreme Court banned organized school prayer in 1962 and legalized abortion in 1973. Increasingly, conservative white Protestants saw secularism as their real enemy and conservative Catholics as allies.

Together these groups bemoaned the post–1960s shift in mainstream values away from respect for traditional authorities—the church, political leaders, and the military—and toward freer sexual expression and general self-indulgence. What the nation needed, they believed, was a return to reverence for God. The growth of this Christian fundamentalism also paralleled rising religious fundamentalism around the globe, whether among Jews in Israel, Hindus in India, or Muslims in Iran and the Arab Middle East. For all their differences, religious people in these cultures shared a common quest: preserving spiritual purity and cultural traditions in an increasingly secular, integrated world.

Conservative Protestants were not a fringe group. As many as 45 million Americans—20 percent of the population—considered themselves fundamentalist Christians in 1980. In combination with a similar number of Catholics, they represented a vast potential force in American politics. And their ranks were growing. While membership in the more liberal mainline Protestant denominations, such as the Presbyterians and Episcopalians, declined steadily after the 1960s, the fundamentalist Assemblies of God grew 37 percent and the Southern Baptists 18 percent between 1965 and 1975. Rather than emphasizing theological doctrine, these groups focused on individuals' emotional connection with a forgiving God. They built church schools, Bible colleges, and publishing houses to reinforce their message. Evangelism on secular college campuses expanded through such organizations as Intervarsity and Campus Crusade for Christ. Hal Lindsey's apocalyptic story about the second coming of Christ, *The Late Great Planet Earth*, sold more than 10 million copies in the 1970s.

Americans argued primarily about issues that had come to the fore during the social movements of the 1960s and 1970s.

Conservative Christians mobilized in the 1980 campaign to support Reagan's candidacy. Critics noted that Reagan himself attended church only occasionally and seemed an indifferent father. They contrasted the divorced candidate with his born-again, Sunday-school–teaching opponent, Jimmy Carter. But Reagan's conservative views on abortion and gay rights and his support for school prayer resonated with fundamentalists. They flocked to the Republican party and to new right-wing religious organizations, such as the Moral Majority, founded in 1979 in Lynchburg, Virginia, by Reverend Jerry Falwell. More than 60 million people each week watched—and many sent money to—"televangelists," including Falwell, Robertson, and Jim Bakker.

Suffusing the GOP with a distinctly southern, grassroots flavor, the religious right also highlighted a major faultline in the modern Republican party: the tension between social conservatives, who emphasized community and tradition, and free marketeers, who promoted

Religion and Politics in the 1980s

In 1979, Baptist minister Jerry Falwell founded the Moral Majority in Lynchburg, Virginia. The organization represented the growing engagement of conservative evangelical Christians in American politics, and Falwell emerged as the most prominent figure of the new religious right. However, not all Christians were conservative. Robert McAfee Brown, a Presbyterian minister and theologian, represented more liberal elements of the church that understood both the Bible and the problems of American society differently than Falwell.

The Goals of the Moral Majority (1980) by Jerry Falwell

We must reverse the trend America finds herself in today. Young people . . . have learned to disrespect the family as God established

William E. Savro/The New York Times, Nov. 11, 1980

Before he became involved in politics, Jerry Falwell had already made a name for himself as a prominent preacher in his hometown of Lynchburg, Virginia, as the senior minister of the large Thomas Road Baptist Church and the founder of Liberty University. His organization, the Moral Majority, became the most well-known conservative evangelical Christian organization of the 1980s.

it. They have been educated in a public-school system that is permeated with secular humanism.

They have been taught that the Bible is just another book of literature. They have been taught that

entrepreneurial capitalism. In its quest for profits, unrestrained capitalism had no inherent respect for tradition. Indeed, it could bring unwelcome changes, as Rustbelt industrial workers had discovered when their employers moved south and overseas. Marrying Jesus to the market proved difficult: should the state play a minimal role in the economy and society, as free-market libertarians believed, or should it monitor personal behavior, as social conservatives implied?

Reagan managed to keep the two wings of the party together, often referring to his "11th Commandment" to "speak no ill of another Republican." But tensions persisted. When Falwell called on "all good Christians" to oppose the 1981 Supreme Court nomination of Arizona's conservative Sandra Day O'Connor on the grounds that she was insufficiently hostile to abortion, Arizona senator and party elder Barry Goldwater—a staunch proponent of small government and personal privacy—retorted that "every good Christian ought to kick Jerry Falwell right in the ass."

Gender and sexuality issues particularly aroused the ire of religious conservatives. They blamed feminism for weakening male authority in the family and for increasing divorce rates. A growing anti-abortion movement gained national visibility by 1980; "Operation Rescue" even borrowed the tactics of civil disobedience from the civil rights movement. During the 1970s, 22 states repealed their sodomy laws, reflecting a slowly increasing acceptance of gays and lesbians. But the religious right, which viewed homosexuality as an abomination, fiercely resisted this trend. Dismayed by the prevalence of casual sexual relationships in the 1970s, church conservatives urged abstinence on young Americans.

there are no absolutes in our world today. . . . These same young people have been reared under the influence of a government that has taught them socialism and welfarism. . . .

I personally feel that the home and the family are still held in reverence by the vast majority of the American public. I believe there is still a vast number of Americans who love their country, are patriotic, and are willing to sacrifice for her. I remember that time when it was positive to be patriotic. . . . I remember as a boy . . . when the band struck up "The Stars and Stripes Forever," we stood and goose pimples would run all over me. . . .

It is now time to take a stand on certain moral issues. . . . We must stand against the Equal Rights Amendment, the feminist revolution, and the homosexual revolution. . . .

Americans have been silent much too long. We have stood by and watched as American power and influence have been systematically weakened in every sphere of the world. . . .

The hope of reversing the trends of decay in our republic now lies with the Christian public in America. We cannot expect help from the liberals. They certainly are not going to call our nation back to righteousness and neither are the pornographers, the smut peddlers, and those who are corrupting our youth.

The Politics of the Bible (1982) by Robert McAfee Brown

In Christian terms, and I think in terms with which all Jews could also agree, my real complaint about the Moral Majority's intrusion of the Bible into American politics, is that they are not biblical enough. . . .

The Moral Majority's biblically inspired political agenda involves a very selective, very partial, and therefore very distorted use of the Bible. They have isolated a set of concerns that they say get to the heart of what is wrong with America—homosexuality, abortion, and pornography. . . .

Take the issue of homosexuality. If one turns to the scriptures as a whole, to try to come up with their central concerns, homosexuality is going to be very low on such a list even if indeed it makes the list at all. There are perhaps seven very ambiguous verses in the whole biblical canon that even allude to it. . . . [But there are] hundreds and hundreds of places where the scriptures are dealing over and over again with question of social justice, the tendency of the rich to exploit the poor, the need for all of us to have a commitment to the hungry, . . . [and] the dangers of national idolatry, that is to say, making the nation into God, accepting uncritically whatever we have to do as a nation against other nations. . . .

When one looks over the agenda of the Moral Majority there is absolutely no mention of such things. . . . We seem to be living in two different worlds, reading two different books. ■

Source: Irwin Unger and Robert R. Tomes, *American Issues,* 2nd edition (Prentice-Hall, 1999), vol. 2, pp. 362–364, 375–377.

The heyday of the sexual revolution ended in 1983, when researchers identified the human immunodeficiency virus (HIV), which causes acquired immunodeficiency syndrome (AIDS). The deadly epidemic spread swiftly through the gay male communities of San Francisco and New York as a result of unprotected sex. Many fundamentalists viewed AIDS as a divine punishment for homosexual activity. "The poor homosexuals," Reagan aide Pat Buchanan wrote. "They have declared war on nature and now nature is exacting an awful retribution." The Reagan administration refused to help mobilize a campaign against the new plague. AIDS continued to spread during the 1990s and beyond, among gays and heterosexuals, both in the United States and abroad—especially in such places as China, southern Africa, and Russia. New drugs slowed the onset of actual AIDS in many HIV-infected Americans while scientists continued the frustrating quest for a cure for the disease.

Yet another epidemic swept through the United States during the 1980s, striking impoverished urban neighborhoods especially hard. The culprit was crack cocaine. Powerfully addictive, it contributed to gang violence and record homicide rates in several cities. Drug-related convictions skyrocketed, stimulating a boom in prison building and a doubling of the nation's inmate population. Conservatives strongly supported the "war on drugs" touted by the White House, and police departments created special weapons and tactics (SWAT) teams to deal with heavily armed drug operators.

This effort tended to ignore the real forces behind drug dealing, which included persistent poverty and a consumer culture obsessed with immediate gratification. Dealing crack offered a rare avenue to wealth to the poorest communities. On the wall of one Detroit crack house, a dealer posted this notice for employees: "[With] hard work and dedication we will all be rich within 12 months." Yet for all the mayhem they caused, crack and other illicit drugs killed less than 1 percent as many Americans per year as the 500,000 felled by tobacco and alcohol. Clearly, addiction to legal as well as illegal substances remained a pervasive problem.

Dissenters Push Back

The liberal and radical reform energies that had percolated in the late 1960s and early 1970s did not evaporate entirely in the conservative 1980s. To be sure, some former activists converted to Republican orthodoxies, investing on Wall Street and enjoying the material comforts of affluence. However, many activists continued to work for social justice in their communities. Numerous activists focused on environmental issues. In combination with younger organizers, many from college campuses, they kept alive a national resistance to conservative politics. Some coined the term "politically correct" or "PC" as an inside joke about fellow leftists who were overly concerned with ideological purity in an era of pervasive conservatism. Right-wingers soon turned "PC" into a derogatory term for those deemed too supportive of multiculturalism or egalitarian causes.

Nuclear threats engaged activists from both the peace and environmental movements. The accidents at Three Mile Island (1979) and Chernobyl (1986) intensified public anxieties about the dangers of nuclear energy. Nuclear weapons were even deadlier: after all, their very purpose was to wreak destruction on a scale that would create what scientists called "nuclear winter," a depopulated planet shrouded in radioactivity. The sharp increases in both Soviet and U.S. nuclear arsenals alarmed residents in those countries and across Europe, where many of the missiles were located. Americans and others who remembered Hiroshima expressed shock when Reagan administration officials spoke of winning a nuclear war and the president wrongly claimed that commanders could recall submarine-based missiles after firing them. The broad-based nuclear freeze movement that emerged in the United States and western Europe in the early 1980s instead encouraged arms control negotiations that would bear fruit a few years later.

Gays and lesbians remained the only Americans against whom tens of millions of their fellow citizens openly believed it acceptable to discriminate

Racial justice remained a primary concern for Americans of color and liberal and leftist activists, particularly in light of the Republican administration's opposition to affirmative action. Determined to honor the foremost leader of the civil rights movement, antiracists convinced Congress in 1983 to designate Martin Luther King, Jr.'s birthday a national holiday. By 1985, a robust antiapartheid movement—inspired by South African church leader and Nobel peace prize winner Desmond Tutu—successfully campaigned to reduce U.S. investments in racially segregated South Africa. A year later, Congress passed the Comprehensive Anti-Apartheid Act over the president's veto, enacting economic sanctions against South Africa—despite opposition from conservatives, such as Congressman Dick Cheney of Wyoming and Senator Jesse Helms of North Carolina. Such international pressure played a central role in the South African government's decision four years later to end apartheid and release African National Congress leader Nelson Mandela from jail. The long era of explicit white supremacy, embodied in international colonialism and American segregation as well as South African apartheid, finally ended.

Perhaps the most prominent face of left-leaning politics in the decade was that of Reverend Jesse Jackson, a former aide to Martin Luther King, Jr. Jackson sought the Democratic nomination for president in 1984 and 1988, winning a handful of primaries in 1988 with his multiracial Rainbow Coalition. Jackson's candidacy encouraged several million African Americans to register to vote for the first time. They, in turn, helped pressure southern Democratic senators to provide the crucial votes in 1987 to reject Robert Bork, a right-wing ideologue (and former Solicitor General in the Nixon administration) nominated by Reagan for a seat on the Supreme Court.

Gay rights advocates also raised their voices in the 1980s. Faced with the twin scourge of AIDS and homophobic violence, homosexuals and their heterosexual supporters lobbied for the inclusion of sexual orientation as a category of discrimination in civil rights laws. Others took to the streets, organized by the militant organization AIDS Coalition to Unleash Power (ACT-UP). In October 1987, nearly half a million Americans marched in Washington in support of gay rights. A few widely admired figures, such as tennis champion Martina Navratilova, publicly acknowledged their homosexuality, helping others to view this sexual orientation as acceptable rather than deviant. By the end of the 1980s, the record was mixed. Gays and lesbians remained the only Americans against whom tens of millions of their fellow citizens openly believed it acceptable to discriminate, but the rights of homosexuals, nonetheless, had much wider support than ever before.

The New Immigration

For two decades after the restrictive immigration law of 1924, the flow of newcomers from abroad had slowed to a trickle. The trickle became a stream again after World War II, and then legislation in 1965 opened the gates even wider. As a result, a wave of new immigrants, 3.5 million in the 1960s and 4.5 million in the 1970s, hit the United States. The 1980s set the record as 6 million people entered the country legally, along with a similar number without documentation.

These newcomers brought an unprecedented cultural and ethnic diversity. Communist rule in eastern Europe and prosperity in western Europe had reduced the emigration from that continent; only 10 percent of the most recent arrivals in the United States were Europeans. Forty percent came instead from Asia—particularly China, the Philippines, and South Korea—and 50 percent from Latin America and the Caribbean, particularly Mexico. From 1965 to 1995, 7 million Latinos and 5 million Asians moved to the United States. Mexicans had been journeying north in smaller numbers since that country's 1910 revolution. But between 1970 and 1990, the Mexican American population of the southwestern states tripled, and the Asian American population of the western states increased sixfold.

The new immigrants came for the same reasons their predecessors had. Many were fleeing political and religious persecution in their home countries, but most sought new economic opportunity. A small number, primarily from South Korea and Hong Kong, arrived with some assets that helped them get started in business. However, most came with few resources and took what work they could find. Although Canada and Australia attracted them as well, no country matched the United States in its reputation for the sheer creation of wealth. The immense difficulties facing new immigrants often induced homesickness. Maria Salas told of crossing the U.S.–Mexican border with her children to join her husband, who was working as a migrant farm laborer in North Carolina: "We walked six days. We suffered a lot. And there were so many snakes. . . . Now that we are here, I ask the girls if they want to go back to Mexico. They say they wish to return, but not if they have to walk back."

Like other new arrivals of earlier eras, the most recent immigrants were more willing than U.S. residents to work for low wages in poor conditions. An employer's dream, they quickly

Eric Draper/AP /Wide World

■ While immigrants brought their own distinctive cultures to the United States, American popular culture spread abroad. The broadcast of National Basketball Association (NBA) games in dozens of other countries helped basketball climb to being the world's second most popular game (after soccer). Personable stars like Earvin "Magic" Johnson of the Los Angeles Lakers and particularly Michael Jordan of the Chicago Bulls became popular icons around the world.

found work in garment sweatshops, on farms, as domestic servants and janitors, and as gardeners. Hailing from countries with dramatically lower standards of living than in the United States, they willingly endured profound hardship to build better lives for their families. They also rekindled the nation's long-standing cultural diversity, especially in Sunbelt cities from Miami, Florida, to San Diego, California. The historic Mexican majority in El Paso, Texas, grew larger. In 1981, citizens of San Antonio elected Henry Cisneros as the first Mexican American mayor of a major city. In Los Angeles, one-third of residents were foreign born by 1990, and the city had more Spanish speakers than anywhere else in North America besides Mexico City.

Most Americans had foreign-born ancestors who had come to the United States with the same dreams that motivated the newest arrivals. Still, the non-European origins of the latest immigrants troubled some white citizens. Conservatives, in particular, worried about the growing diversity of American society and feared a decline of the Eurocentric culture they had grown up with. They were also anxious that poor immigrants might drain taxpayers' dollars by winding up on welfare. The Immigration and Naturalization Service (INS) stepped up patrols of the 2000-mile U.S. border with Mexico to limit the rising number of undocumented Mexican workers heading north. By the early 1990s, the INS was apprehending and expelling 1.7 million undocumented workers every year. The desperate efforts of migrants to elude Border Patrol officers and cross into the United States led to deaths from thirst and exposure in the deserts that stretched across much of the region. A sign on one California freeway near the border showed the silhouette of a fleeing family as a warning to drivers to watch for pedestrians.

Despite the distaste that some Americans of European heritage felt for the new immigrants, the Latin American and especially Asian origins of the recent arrivals mirrored the rising economic significance of the Pacific Rim countries to the United States. In 1979, U.S. trade across the Pacific surpassed trade across the Atlantic for the first time. By 1996, the value of American trade with Asia was more than twice that with Europe. And Latin Americans, particularly Mexicans, provided a convenient supply of workers for the U.S. economy. They were available when companies needed them, and they could be shut out when that need evaporated.

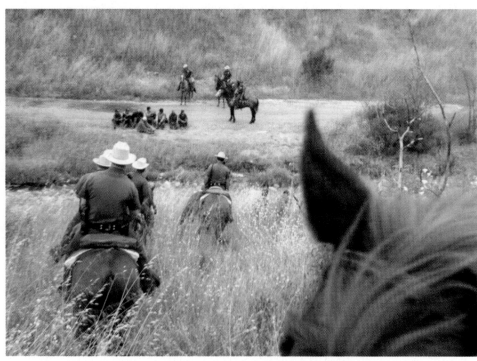

■ U.S. Border Patrol agents on horseback surround a group of Mexicans arrested after crossing into the United States near San Diego, California, without documentation. The growing number of Latino immigrants working in the United States illegally—but to the satisfaction of the American businesses, farmers, and families who employed them—caused a rise in anti-immigrant sentiments by the 1990s. For many Mexicans working in "El Norte" but maintaining families and commitments at home, the border at the Rio Grande became almost as familiar as state lines within the United States for interstate travelers.

U.S. Border Patrol, San Diego HQ, Public Information Office

The End of the Cold War

"My fellow Americans, I'm pleased to tell you today that I've signed legislation that will outlaw Russia forever. We begin bombing in five minutes." Ronald Reagan, in 1984, thought he was telling a joke at a microphone that was not turned on. He was wrong. Indeed, after three years of the president's military build-up and confrontational rhetoric toward the Soviet Union ("the focus of evil in the world")—including talk of fighting and winning a nuclear war—many Americans found his attempted humor appalling. However, by the end of his presidency four years later, a stunning reversal had occurred. Reagan had traveled to Moscow, embraced Soviet leader Mikhail Gorbachev in front of Lenin's tomb, and announced that the Soviets had changed.

For Americans, the greatest surprise of the 1980s came with this warming of U.S.–Soviet relations after 1985. Few had imagined such a scenario during Reagan's first two years in office. During that period, his administration became the first in four decades not to collaborate on nuclear arms control with the USSR. In the Soviet Union, the rise to power of Communist Party reformer Gorbachev permanently changed the face of international politics. The American president finally agreed to work toward the common goal of reducing tensions between the two superpowers.

At the same time, the Reagan administration stumbled badly at home when a scandal involving Iran and the Nicaraguan Contras came to light in 1986. The disaster revealed a secret foreign policy apparatus and a president out of touch with the daily governance process. Dramatic events in Europe then unfolded with little input from the administrations of either Reagan or George H.W. Bush, his successor in the White House. In 1989, Eastern Europeans tore down the Berlin Wall and ended Soviet rule in their countries. Two years later, the Soviet Union itself unraveled into its separate components, Russia being the largest. The end of the Cold War enabled Bush to focus on the Middle East, where an international force drove Iraq out of occupied Kuwait and reestablished the status quo in that oil-rich region.

From Cold War to Détente

In the 1980s, internal Soviet politics finally ended the Cold War. Gorbachev was the key figure. He and other reformers had grown up during the post–1956 campaign to reinterpret the leadership of former General Secretary Josef Stalin. Like Americans in the 1960s, Gorbachev's generation boldly questioned orthodox thinking. They could see that the vast military expenditures of the 1960s and 1970s, along with efforts after 1980 to keep up with skyrocketing U.S. military spending, had devastated the Soviet economy. By the 1980s, the USSR's state-run economy was creaking to a halt. It simply could not provide the consumer products that Soviet citizens had learned about from the world outside their borders. Gorbachev warned of the danger of Russia becoming merely "an Upper Volta with missiles"—an impoverished nation that had sqaundered its wealth to build a nuclear arsenal.

As the 1980s unfolded, events further weakened the authority of the Soviet government. The USSR's occupation of Afghanistan became a quagmire resembling the United States' disastrous involvement in Vietnam. The brutality and illegitimacy of the occupation disillusioned Red Army soldiers on the front lines and their families at home. Moreover, the Afghan resistance proved tougher than the USSR expected. The last Soviet troops finally withdrew in 1989. Initial government efforts to cover up the nuclear accident at Chernobyl only worsened matters, revealing the costs of corrupt communist rule. And nationalist movements for independence in the Baltic states, the Caucasus region, and central Asia gathered momentum. In his six years in power (1985–1991), Gorbachev tried to preserve the Soviet system by reforming it through *glasnost* (greater political liberty) and *perestroika* (economic restructuring

East News/Sipa Press

■ Workers in Prague, Czechoslovakia, haul away a bust of Josef Stalin after the peaceful "Velvet Revolution" that overthrew communist rule there in 1989. Similar scenes unfolded across eastern Europe as Czechs, Poles, Hungarians, and others removed symbols of four and a half decades of Soviet domination. Accustomed to often extravagant accounts of the strength of the Soviet Union, Americans were stunned by the swiftness with which the Soviet empire and then the USSR itself unraveled.

allowing some private enterprise). However, his government proved unable to control the forces for change that it had helped unleash.

Reagan's primary role in ending the Cold War was to support Gorbachev's quest for change within the Soviet Union. To that end, Reagan moved from confrontational rhetoric to pursuing a policy of détente. His trajectory contrasted directly with that of Jimmy Carter, who had shifted from an initial period of détente to helping renew U.S.–Soviet tensions.

Reagan's timing was now crucial. Gorbachev became head of the Soviet Communist party in 1985, at the start of Reagan's second term. The American president had already built up the U.S. military and was now thinking about his place in history. He wanted to leave office having earned a reputation as a peacemaker. His influential wife, Nancy, helped promote this idea, and the two received additional support from the less hawkish members of the administration, particularly Secretary of State George Schultz.

Beneath Reagan's strident rhetoric about national military strength ran a streak of radical idealism, including a desire to eliminate the threat of nuclear warfare. This desire prompted him to launch the Strategic Defense Initiative. He expected the United States to eventually share the technology with the Soviets. Despite his Cold War posturing during his first term, the U.S. president had been troubled by the 1983 television drama *The Day After*. The movie conveyed sobering images of the aftermath of a nuclear war on American soil. The Soviet downing of a

Korean Air Lines civilian jet that fall reminded him and others of the tragic costs of making mistakes with weapons.

Once he felt convinced of Gorbachev's seriousness about internal reform and rapprochement with the United States, Reagan took action. At a summit conference in Reykjavik, Iceland, in 1986, the two leaders came within a whisker of agreeing to eliminate nearly all of their nations' nuclear arsenals. The next year, they signed the more limited but still symbolically important Intermediate Nuclear Force (INF) treaty. The agreement removed short-range and intermediate-range missiles from Europe and enabled each side to conduct on-site verification of the other side's compliance. INF marked the first actual reduction in the total number of nuclear weapons stored in the two nations' arsenals.

The Iran–Contra Scandal

Failures elsewhere offset Reagan's success with the Russians. His administration suffered its worst damage when it tried through illegal means to solve two foreign policy challenges with one stroke. Its main strategy consisted of linking a problem in the Middle East with one in Central America. Since the 1940s, the U.S. government had struggled to balance three often conflicting goals in the Middle East: maintaining access to the region's oil, preserving a strong Israel, and excluding communist influence. But a new problem emerged when the pro-Iranian, anti-American, and anti-Israeli Islamic revolution began to spread after the 1979 overthrow of the Shah.

As revolutionary fervor intensified in the region, hostage taking and terrorism—the "poor man's nuclear bomb"—proliferated. In 1981, U.S. warplanes shot down two Libyan fighter jets when the jets tried to restrict American pilots' movements over the Mediterranean Sea. In 1986, Americans bombed the Libyan capital of Tripoli in retaliation for apparent Libyan involvement in the killing of two U.S. soldiers in Germany. In 1988, things took an even nastier turn when an American warship in the Persian Gulf killed 290 civilians by shooting down an Iranian airliner, apparently by mistake. In revenge, pro-Iranian agents exploded a bomb on Pan Am Flight 109 over Lockerbie, Scotland, before the end of the year, killing 11 on the ground and 259 aboard the plane, including 35 students from Syracuse University.

Bettmann/CORBIS

■ **U.S. Lieutenant Woody Lee guards the briefcase (known as "the football") containing the codes to be used by President Reagan if he were to decide to launch nuclear weapons. Lee's job was to remain close to the president at all times and to protect "the football" with his life. Ironically, Lee stands here in Moscow's Red Square in 1988, where Reagan was holding a summit meeting with Soviet leader Mikhail Gorbachev, so many of those U.S. nuclear missiles, presumably, were aimed at them.**

Islamic revolutionaries also threatened moderate Arab leaders and assassinated Egyptian president Anwar Sadat in 1981. Lebanon became the center of a radical anti-Israeli campaign to seize Americans as hostages, especially after the United States' 1983 engagement against Muslim forces in the civil war there. Despite his 1980 campaign promise never to negotiate with terrorists, Reagan approved the illegal sale of U.S. arms to Iran in return for the freeing of a handful of hostages held by pro-Iranian radicals in Lebanon.

Events were heating up in Central America as well. The CIA-created Contras failed to overturn the new Sandinista government in Nicaragua. Even though the Contras lacked public support in Nicaragua and the United States, the president and his advisers were determined to keep them afloat. But they had a problem: how to fund the effort. Most Americans did not share Reagan's enthusiasm for the Contras and feared greater U.S. military involvement in Central America. Beginning in 1982, Congress passed the Boland Amendments, restricting aid to the

Nicaraguan counterrevolutionaries. These restrictions culminated in a 1984 ban on helping them "directly or indirectly" beyond a token dose of humanitarian assistance. Faced with their chief's expressed desire to shore up the Contra cause, the president's men found an alternative solution.

The National Security Council (NSC) established a secret operation run by staff member Lieutenant Colonel Oliver North. Free from public or congressional oversight, North worked closely with CIA director William Casey. North and his colleagues solicited funds for the Contras from wealthy, conservative Americans and from sympathetic foreign governments, including Saudi Arabia and Taiwan. Then North hit on what he called the "neat idea" of "using the Ayatollah Khomeini's money to support the Nicaraguan freedom fighters." Iran desperately needed weapons for its war against neighboring Iraq (1980–1988), so North and his colleagues started diverting profits to the Contras from new sales of U.S. Army property to Teheran. One operative joked about the "Contra-bution," although some of the funds wound up in the private accounts of North and others involved in the diversion.

The NSC's action was illegal: it sold U.S. government property without authorization from the Pentagon, and it broke U.S. laws banning aid to the Contras. When news of the operation finally leaked out in November 1986, it shocked the nation. Details emerged from separate investigations by a presidential commission, a Justice Department independent prosecutor, and a congressional committee.

North's televised testimony before Congress made him a hero to some. He indicted Congress for its failure to support the president's policies in Central America, and he painted his own actions as patriotic. Others thought him a scoundrel. After all, he had run a private foreign policy that subverted the legislature's constitutional responsibilities and then had shredded documents that detailed his role. He later admitted, "I tried to avoid telling outright lies [before Congress], but I certainly wasn't telling the truth." His celebrity status among conservatives almost won him a victory as the Republican candidate for the U.S. Senate from Virginia in 1992.

What did the president know, and when did he know it? The old Watergate question about Richard Nixon came to the fore again. Reagan called North a "national hero" but claimed ignorance of any illegal activities, including the diversion of funds from Iranian arms sales to the Nicaraguan rebels. When some of Reagan's aides testified that he had approved negotiating with terrorists for the release of hostages, the president denied it. Questioned by investigators, the president said he could not remember details about his decisions and policies. This possibility gained credence a few years later when the public learned of his affliction with Alzheimer's disease.

But in early 1987, 90 percent of Americans did not believe Reagan was telling all he knew. His reputation for candor suffered permanent damage. People could not decide which scenario was worse: that Reagan knew about the Iran–Contra deal and approved it or that he did not know what his own administration was doing in his name. It was hard even to imagine the latter situation occurring under any other president.

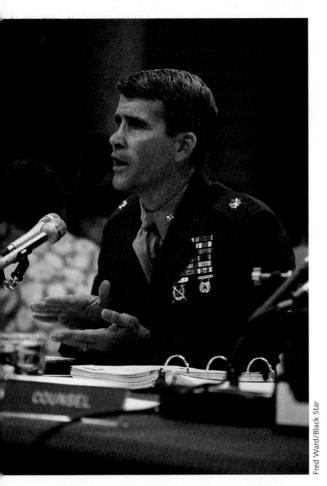

Fred Ward/Black Star

■ Lieutenant Colonel Oliver North of the National Security Council became the public face of the Iran-Contra scandal. North displayed his medals from the Vietnam War in testimony before Congress, but his smug version of patriotism and his deceitfulness alienated many senators and congressmen.

Reagan's job approval ratings dropped from 67 percent to 46 percent within a month as the Iran–Contra revelations came on the heels of the failed Reykjavik summit and the Democrats' victory in the 1986 congressional elections. The first round of memoirs by former aides also appeared in the final years of his administration. These books revealed an isolated president out of touch with the government he nominally headed. For example, the former actor breezily admitted that he was happiest when "each morning I get a piece of paper that tells me what I do all day long." The leaking of news that an astrologer—hired by First Lady Nancy Reagan—had helped set the president's schedule for years did not help either. Nonetheless, Reagan held onto much of his personal popularity to the end of his term. In the phrase of Representative Pat Schroeder of Colorado, he was the "Teflon president" to whom no bad news could stick.

A Global Policeman?

Although George H. W. Bush had made his career in the Texas oil business and then in that state's Republican party, his roots lay in the party's moderate northeastern elite. His father, Prescott Bush, had been a U.S. senator from Connecticut, and he himself ran the CIA in 1975–1976. After losing in the 1980 party primaries, Bush agreed to run as Reagan's vice-presidential candidate. He then moved to the political right throughout the 1980s.

When Bush's turn at the presidency finally came in 1988, he ran a bruising campaign that made a caricature of his Democratic opponent, Governor Michael Dukakis of Massachusetts. Even more than previous presidential campaigns, this one turned on symbols rather than issues. Three proved particularly important. First, Bush repeatedly led audiences in reciting the Pledge of Allegiance in response to a wave of flag-burning demonstrations. (A year later, the Supreme Court affirmed the act as a form of free speech guaranteed by the Constitution.)

Second, Bush skewered his opponent as a liberal and a "card-carrying member" of the American Civil Liberties Union, an organization dedicated to defending the Bill of Rights. Senator Joseph McCarthy had used precisely this phrase to describe members of the American Communist party four decades earlier. Thus, Bush implied that liberals were subversives.

Third, Bush accused Dukakis of coddling criminals. His campaign ads focused on Willie Horton, a black man convicted of murder. While on parole from a Massachusetts prison during Dukakis's governorship, Horton raped a white woman and killed her husband. Republicans appealed to whites' anxieties about race, sex, and safety. "If I can make Willie Horton a household name," Bush's campaign strategist Lee Atwater promised, "we'll win the election." He succeeded on both fronts.

As president, however, Bush proved cautious. Hemmed in by a Democrat-controlled Congress, he had what his chief of staff called a "limited agenda" at home. His most enduring domestic action came with his 1991 appointment of archconservative Clarence Thomas, an African American lawyer from Georgia, to fill the seat of retiring Supreme Court justice Thurgood Marshall. Only 43 years old and with little experience as a judge, Thomas was chosen because of his conservative views and his race. The Senate narrowly confirmed him, 52–48, after contentious hearings in which a former aide, Anita Hill, accused Thomas of sexual harassment.

"I much prefer foreign affairs," the president once confided in his diary. Yet he proceeded just as carefully in this realm as he did with domestic policy. Some of the most dramatic events of the twentieth century unfolded during his presidency. Poles, Czechs, and Hungarians—encouraged by Gorbachev's promise not to intervene militarily in other Warsaw Pact nations—peacefully overthrew their communist rulers in 1989. East Germans did the same. The Berlin Wall—the 28-year-old symbol of Cold War tensions—finally toppled on November 8. Three months later, Nelson Mandela walked out of the South African prison where he had been held for 27 years. The white supremacist government there agreed to hold the first elections in which all South Africans could vote. The Baltic states of Lithuania, Latvia,

TABLE 28-3

The Election of 1988

Candidate	Political Party	Popular Vote	Electoral Vote
George H. W. Bush	Republican	48,886,000	426
Michael S. Dukakis	Democratic	41,809,000	111

and Estonia also seceded from the USSR in 1990 and 1991. Rather than rejoicing at the shrinking of Soviet power, Bush urged Soviet citizens to move cautiously. The president feared that too much change too fast might create unrest across Russia and eastern Europe. But after a failed coup attempt by Communist hard-liners in August 1991, the Soviet Union broke into its 16 constituent states. Russian president Boris Yeltsin replaced Gorbachev as the major figure in Moscow.

The Bush administration acted more boldly in its own hemisphere. In Panama, under the brutal leadership of Manuel Noriega, tensions grew between the Panamanian Defense Forces (PDF) and U.S. soldiers based in the Canal Zone. Bush and Noriega had known each other since the mid–1970s, when each had headed his country's intelligence agency. They had worked together in the early 1980s when Noriega provided logistical support for the Contras' war in nearby Nicaragua. But the Panamanian strongman had since parted ways with the Americans and had deepened his lucrative role as an intermediary in smuggling Colombian cocaine into the United States. Meanwhile, the crack cocaine epidemic tightened its grip in

■ **MAP 28.3**
THE SOVIET BLOC DISSOLVES   No change in world politics since World War II was greater than the collapse of the Soviet Union and its satellite states in eastern Europe. Eastern European countries soon sought membership in NATO and post-Communist Russia built closer relations with the United States and western Europe. The transition from socialist to capitalist economies was difficult, however, and many poorer citizens found daily life little easier than it had been before.

poor American neighborhoods. Rising popular concern about crack-related violence increased Americans' willingness to take action against Noriega. When the dictator overturned Panamanian election results that went against him and further confrontations erupted between American and Panamanian soldiers, Bush decided to step in.

In December 1989, 24,000 U.S. troops invaded the small Central American nation. They crushed the PDF, and thousands of civilians died in the crossfire. Noriega took refuge in the home of the Vatican emissary in Panama City. U.S. commanders applied psychological pressure. Knowing Noriega's distaste for rock 'n' roll music, they set up enormous speakers and floodlights outside the residence. At a deafening volume, they blared such songs as Linda Ronstadt's "You're No Good" and Sonny Curtis's "I Fought the Law (and the Law Won)." Noriega eventually surrendered and was brought to Miami, where he was convicted of drug trafficking and imprisoned.

Developments in the Middle East provoked the most important move of the Bush administration: the initiation of the Gulf War of 1991. After the Iranian revolution, Iraq and Iran had clashed over disputed border territories. The Reagan administration had provided weapons to both sides at different points. The president wanted neither combatant to win a decisive victory that would destabilize the area. With two-thirds of the world's known oil reserves in the states surrounding the Persian Gulf, the U.S. government especially dreaded seeing control of the region's oil prices and supplies shift from Saudi Arabia to revolutionary Iran.

Iraq ended the war in a strong position in 1988, and two years later, it invaded tiny, neighboring oil-rich Kuwait, annexing it as Iraq's "19th province." With Americans and their Japanese and European allies dependent on Middle Eastern oil, Bush declared the invasion unacceptable. He rushed more than 200,000 troops to Saudi Arabia in "Operation Desert Shield" to discourage further aggression by Iraqi leader Saddam Hussein. At the same time, the United Nations slapped economic sanctions on Iraq.

Three months later, Bush shifted his attention to liberating Kuwait. He doubled the number of U.S. troops in the region to 430,000. He also gained the support of the UN, which demanded Iraqi withdrawal by January 15, 1991. The U.S. Congress backed him as well, voting to support any actions necessary to drive Iraq out of Kuwait. Bush went on the offensive because he faced a shrinking window of opportunity. He had wide international support, including troops from several Arab nations, but growing clashes in Jerusalem between Israelis and Palestinians threatened to break up this alliance by rekindling Arab anger at Israel. Meanwhile, Saddam Hussein loudly supported the Palestinians and denounced the Americans as Israeli allies.

> *Bush believed that the brief war helped Americans to finally "kick the Vietnam syndrome": no longer would they hesitate to use force abroad.*

On January 16, 1991, Allied planes began five and a half weeks of bombing against Iraq. Then, on February 25, Allied forces poured across the border from Saudi Arabia in "Operation Desert Storm." The offensive freed Kuwait and sent Iraqi troops in headlong retreat toward Baghdad. The Iraqis burned oil wells as they fell back, blanketing the battlefield in smoke. Four days later, Bush halted the U.S. advance, having restored Kuwaiti sovereignty. Saddam Hussein remained in power and later crushed uprisings by Iraqi dissidents. The politics of coalition warfare helped prohibit further U.S. action, for no Arabs wanted Americans ruling Iraq.

What did the Gulf War reveal? It showed Bush at his most successful, managing an international coalition few would have thought possible a few years earlier. The withdrawal of Soviet power from the region had played a crucial role, after decades of Moscow's support for Iraq. In its first major post–Cold War engagement, the United States demonstrated its military supremacy. Still, the opposition had proven surprisingly weak. One U.S. soldier later described himself as participating in "the biggest firing squad in history." Bush nonetheless believed that the brief war helped Americans to finally "kick the Vietnam syndrome": no longer would they hesitate to use force abroad.

Legend:
- Allied troops
- Iraqi troops
- Allied air bases
- Iraqi air bases
- U.S. Naval forces
- Allied air attacks
- Allied ground attack February 24–28, 1991
- Iraqi retreat
- Iraqi scud attacks

■ **MAP 28.4**

THE GULF WAR, 1990–1991   Rarely had U.S. strategic and economic interests been so openly the motivation for war. Oil brought American soldiers to defend Saudi Arabia and drive Iraqi troops out of Kuwait. But many Arab states supported the U.S.-led coalition because they opposed Iraqi President Saddam Hussein's occupation of Kuwait.

The war's outcome seemed to validate two strategic lessons that U.S. commanders had learned during the Vietnam War. The first was the importance of preserving absolute control of the media. During the Persian Gulf conflict, the Pentagon kept journalists away from most of the action to control the images that Americans saw of the fighting. The public viewed endless videos of "smart" bombs hitting their targets in Baghdad but none of the tens of thousands of Iraqi soldiers being slaughtered during their retreat from Kuwait. Second, General Colin Powell, the African American chair of the Joint Chiefs of Staff who emerged from the war as a national hero, insisted on marshaling overwhelmingly superior forces before going into battle, thus ensuring the success of the operation.

The Gulf War raised the question of whether the U.S. military had become a mercenary force, with allies chipping in more than seven times what Washington spent to fund U.S. soldiers. "Why should I fight?" one wealthy Kuwaiti sitting out the war in comfort in Cairo asked. "We can pay other countries to fight for us." The conflict seemed to demonstrate a

Robert Trippett/Sipa Press

■ In the 1970s anti-feminists defeated the Equal Rights Amendment in part by opposing the idea of American women in combat. Attitudes about women had changed enough by 1991 that thousands of female service personnel participated in the Gulf War—including a few being captured and killed—with no public outcry. In Bethesda, Maryland, one soldier says goodbye to her family before shipping out to the Persian Gulf in September 1990.

U.S. willingness to act as a global police force in the post–Cold War era. But the war also stimulated the further growth of anti-Americanism among Islamic revolutionaries, including Saudi-born Osama bin Laden; they considered it sacrilege for non-Muslim American soldiers to operate bases in Saudi Arabia, home to Mecca, Islam's holiest site. Finally, the war foreshadowed Bush's defiant claim at a 1992 international environmental conference that, when it came to oil, "the American lifestyle is not negotiable."

Conclusion

The Republican era of Ronald Reagan and George H.W. Bush reshaped American relations with the rest of the world, as well as politics and economics in the United States. Both sets of changes hinged on the elevation of individualism and market forces above communal values and government planning. At home, the Republican ascendancy successfully challenged five decades of New Deal assumptions about government's role in economic regulation and its responsibilities toward the poor. A booming stock market underwrote a culture increasingly focused on the individual acquisition of wealth. Popular television shows of the

1980s, such as *Dynasty* and *Lifestyles of the Rich and Famous,* reflected a widespread admiration for affluence and conspicuous consumption.

The collective dreams represented by the Soviet experiment evaporated into history in these years, leaving capitalism unchallenged as a system of economic organization across most of the globe. U.S. military power stepped into the vacuum left by the Soviet demise, most visibly in the Gulf War. But that military revival came at the cost of vast deficit spending and a sharp recession in 1991–1992, which paved the way for Bill Clinton's victory over Bush in the 1992 presidential campaign. The assertion of military strength also demonstrated anew America's overriding Middle Eastern priorities of preserving access to the region's oil and defending Israel. This combination helped motivate the eventual attack on the United States by Islamic extremists on September 11, 2001.

Sites to Visit

Digital Atlas of the United States, 1990
130.166.124.2/USpage1.html

This site offers an overview of the geography and demography of the U.S. population in 1990.

Immigrant Fact Sheet, 1996
www.ins.usdoj.gov/graphics/aboutins/statistics/110.htm

The U.S. Immigration and Naturalization Service posted this site with historical statistics about immigration into the United States, especially from 1981 to 1996.

Divining America: Religion and the National Culture
www.nhc.rtp.nc.us:8080/tserve/divam.htm

This site has essays by prominent historians on diverse aspects of the religious history of the United States.

Ronald Wilson Reagan
www.ipl.org/ref/POTUS/rwreagan.html

The Internet Public Library maintains this site, which has essential information about Reagan and his presidential administrations as well as his most important speeches.

The National Security Archive at George Washington University
www.gwu.edu/~nsarchiv/

This extraordinary site includes the most recent declassified documents on the making of U.S. foreign policy.

Cold War International History Project
cwihp.si.edu/default.htm

The Woodrow Wilson International Center for Scholars maintains this excellent site, which offers newly released documents and up-to-date interpretive essays on the American-Soviet struggle.

The Gulf War
www.pbs.org/wgbh/pages/frontline/gulf/

The Public Broadcasting System's "Frontline" series created this site with information about the Persian Gulf War, including oral histories of U.S. commanders and of Americans taken as prisoners of war.

For Further Reading

General

E. J. Dionne, Jr. *Why Americans Hate Politics* (1991).

Frances FitzGerald, *Way Out There in the Blue: Reagan, Star Wars, and the End of the Cold War* (2000).

Neil Postman, *Amusing Ourselves to Death: Public Discourse in the Age of Show Business* (1985).

Michael Schaller, *Reckoning with Reagan: America and Its President in the 1980s* (1992).

Anticommunism Revived

James A. Bill, *The Eagle and the Lion: The Tragedy of American–Iranian Relations* (1988).

Thomas Ferguson and Joel Rogers, eds., *The Hidden Election: Politics and Economics in the 1980 Presidential Campaign* (1981).

Michael T. Klare and Peter Kornbluh, *Low-Intensity Warfare: Counterinsurgency, Proinsurgency, and Antiterrorism in the Eighties* (1988).

Walter LaFeber, *Inevitable Revolutions: The United States in Central America*, 2nd ed. (1993).

William E. Pemberton, *Exit with Honor: The Life and Presidency of Ronald Reagan* (1998).

Republican Rule at Home

Thomas Byrne Edsall and Mary D. Edsall, *Chain Reaction: The Impact of Race, Rights and Taxes on American Politics* (1991).

Barbara Ehrenreich, *The Worst Years of Our Lives: Irreverent Notes from a Decade of Greed* (1990).

J. R. McNeill, *Something New Under the Sun: An Environmental History of the Twentieth-Century World* (2000).

Kevin Phillips, *The Politics of Rich and Poor: Wealth and the American Electorate in the Reagan Aftermath* (1990).

Mark Robert Rank, *Living on the Edge: The Realities of Welfare in America* (1994).

Cultural Conflict

Susan J. Douglas, *Where the Girls Are: Growing Up Female with the Mass Media* (1994).

Todd Gitlin, *The Twilight of Common Dreams: Why America Is Wracked by Culture Wars* (1995).

Martin E. Marty and R. Scott Appleby, *The Glory and the Power: The Fundamentalist Challenge to the Modern World* (1992).

Nicolaus Mills, ed., *Culture in an Age of Money: The Legacy of the 1980s in America* (1990).

David M. Reimers, *Still the Golden Door: The Third World Comes to America*, 2nd ed. (1992).

Randy Shilts, *And the Band Played On: Politics, People and the AIDS Epidemic* (1987).

The End of the Cold War

Theodore Draper, *A Very Thin Line: The Iran–Contra Affairs* (1991).

John Robert Greene, *The Presidency of George Bush* (2000).

Dilip Hiro, *Desert Shield to Desert Storm: The Second Gulf War* (1992).

Michael J. Hogan, ed., *The End of the Cold War: Its Meanings and Implications* (1992).

Jane Mayer and Doyle McManus, *Landslide: The Unmaking of the President, 1984–1988* (1989).

David Remnick, *Lenin's Tomb: The Last Days of the Soviet Empire* (1993).

Online Practice Test

Test your understanding of this chapter with interactive review quizzes at

www.ablongman.com/jonescreatedequal/chapter28

Post–Cold War America, 1991–2000

©1990 Peter Menzel

■ Underwater explorers examine shells at the manufactured beach in Biosphere 2, an artificially created ecosystem in the Arizona desert inhabited by eight "biospherians" from 1991 to 1993. The attempt to create a self-sustaining "mini-earth" failed within two years.

ON A COLD DECEMBER NIGHT IN 1997, 23-YEAR-OLD JULIA BUTTERFLY HILL CLIMBED onto a small platform that had been constructed 180 feet above ground in a giant redwood tree in a forest in Humboldt County, California. She remained there for two years, trespassing in an act of civil disobedience on the property of the Pacific Lumber Company, which was threatening to cut down the 1000-year-old tree as part of its logging operations. Julia Hill had not planned to become an internationally famous environmental activist. She grew up in Arkansas, the daughter of an itinerant preacher. When friends invited the restless young woman to join them on a drive to California, she eagerly went along. "I had been on a journey, searching for my purpose in life," she recalled, "I ended up finding it in the redwoods." When she first saw the giant redwoods, "Gripped by the spirit of the forest, I dropped to my knees and began to sob. . . . I could feel my whole being bursting forth into new life in this majestic cathedral."

Julia "Butterfly" Hill in the giant redwood tree she named "Luna."

Hill's spiritual connection to the forest drew her to political activism, and she joined Earth First!, an environmental group that was working to save the redwoods from the logging industry. She discovered that 97 percent of the old-growth redwoods had already been destroyed and that the rest were threatened by clearcutting, toxins, and diesel fuel. Tree sitting was a strategy the Earth First! activists developed to protest the destruction of the trees. They had named this particular tree Luna, after the goddess of the moon, because they had built the small platform in it by moonlight. Julia Hill took a forest name—Butterfly—and settled in for her turn at tree sitting. Although the strategy usually involved tree-sitting for a week at a time, Butterfly Hill decided that to have an impact the protest needed to be taken to "a different level." "I realized I had to give more. I needed to give my word that my feet would not touch the ground" until the tree was safe from destruction.

Those two years were rough. The young woman survived rain and hail storms, 90-mile-per-hour winds that tossed the tiny platform into the air, and bone-chilling cold that turned her feet black. Friends and supporters provided her with food and other supplies using a rope pulley. She ate mostly raw fruits and vegetables, slept in a hammock, took sponge baths, and used a bucket for a toilet. She faced harassment from the logging company and derision from some skeptics. But she also had a powerful network of supporters and celebrities who raised money, brought her food, and publicized her protest.

Hill's effort to save an ancient tree as old as the last millennium was conducted using the global technology of the new millennium. Critical to the success of her protest was her ability to communicate with the entire world from her treetop perch. She set up a Web site on the Internet visited by people from all across the globe. Schoolchildren in Germany sent her pictures of themselves in front of their favorite trees. People responded to her from as far away as Turkey and Australia. She used a solar-powered cell phone to speak with radio stations, schools, rallies, religious groups, reporters, and talk show hosts.

The lumber company also used state-of-the-art technology in its efforts to stymie her protest, cutting down trees to make them fall in her direction, flying helicopters to hover noisily over her head, and using air horns to keep her awake at night.

The president of Pacific Lumber, John Campbell, eventually came to the tree to negotiate with Hill, and they made a deal. The company agreed never to cut down the tree or other trees in a 2.9-acre buffer zone. Hill agreed to come down. For her civil disobedience, she paid a $50,000 fine, contributed by supporters, which the court designated to Humboldt State University for forestry research. Although her success was modest in terms of saving endangered forests, her actions raised environmental awareness across the globe.

Activists such as Julia Butterfly Hill addressed political concerns through personal beliefs and direct action as part of social movements that evolved out of a century of such protests. But the issues had reached a global scale. Internationally, Cold War power struggles gave way to other issues: regional and civil wars, ethnic strife, the environment and global warming, trade and labor relations, and terrorism. Domestically, concerns of environmentalists ranged from the protection of a single tree to climate change affecting the entire planet. The labor movement turned much of its attention to service workers and the global economy, with problems ranging from the export of jobs to the existence of sweatshops at home and abroad.

Throughout most of the 1990s, one party controlled the White House while the other controlled the Congress.

In the United States the economy expanded throughout the 1990s. Increasing numbers of Americans invested in the soaring stock market, many for the first time. The crime rate declined. Yet the strong economy also emboldened consumers to buy and use products and resources, such as huge gas-guzzling sport utility vehicles, with little concern for the environmental impact. Moreover, as the economy grew, so did the gap between the wealthy and the poor. As the new millennium dawned, the economy began to falter. The stock market fell, and there were signs of an impending recession.

The 2000 U.S. Census revealed a number of striking changes in the nation's population during the 1990s. Among the most dramatic was the 60 percent growth in the Latino population, from 22.4 million to 35.3 million, making the number of Latinos—most of them Mexican American—nearly equal to that of African Americans. In certain states the increase was even larger. The Latino population in California grew 35 percent during the decade and became a powerful economic and political force in the state. In Nevada the Latino population doubled, to become 20 percent of the state's residents. Immigrants from Asia and Latin America also added increasing linguistic diversity, fueling controversies over bilingual education and "English-only" political initiatives.

In national politics the rifts between liberals and conservatives that had opened up in the 1960s persisted. Struggles over cultural issues such as abortion and gay rights polarized the political climate. Throughout most of the 1990s, one party controlled the White House while the other controlled the Congress. A Democratic Congress during the Republican administration of George H. W. Bush passed the 1990 Americans with Disabilities Act, requiring reasonable accommodation for disabled persons in employment and access to public places. The Clean Air Act, passed in the same year, reduced smokestack and auto emissions. New legislation also increased funding for Head Start and boosted the minimum wage.

After a number of scandals in Congress over misuse of congressional bank accounts and votes to raise their own pay, the 27th Amendment to the Constitution, ratified in 1992, prohibited midterm congressional pay raises. In 1992 Democrats took back the White House, but in 1994 Republicans swept into control of Congress with a conservative agenda, hemming in President Bill Clinton, a Democrat of liberal social inclinations who, nonetheless, presided over the final destruction of the Aid to Families with Dependent Children (AFDC) program, which had been the central feature of the national welfare system since the New Deal of the 1930s.

Throughout the decade, racial hostilities flared, intensified by such events as the beating of motorist Rodney King and the murder trial of media celebrity O. J. Simpson. Anti-immigrant sentiments increased in response to recent immigration from Asia, Latin America, and especially Mexico. Nevertheless, studies showed that Americans had become more accepting of people whose racial or national backgrounds were different from their own. Americans' faith in political leadership, at a low ebb since Watergate, sank even farther as Republicans doggedly pursued Clinton's unseemly sexual behavior, leading to his impeachment by the House of Representatives, although he remained in office.

Money continued to pour into politics, even as voters called for campaign finance reform. New third-party candidates tapped widespread eagerness for a new type of politics. A Supreme Court dominated by conservatives nevertheless upheld liberal decisions, including abortion rights in *Planned Parenthood of Southeastern Pennsylvania v. Casey* (1992), gender equality in *U.S. v. Virginia* (1996) stating that the Virginia Military Institute could not exclude women, and the rights of gays and lesbians in *Romer v. Evans* (1996), which declared unconstitutional a Colorado amendment that nullified civil rights protections for homosexuals. In 2000, however, the Supreme Court decided one of the closest and most divisive elections in the nation's history, handing the White House to the Republican candidate, George W. Bush, son of the former president.

With the end of the Cold War, American foreign and domestic politics no longer revolved around the old, familiar enemies. Global power relations shifted with the dissolution of the Soviet Union, reviving long-dormant ethnic conflicts. Violence erupted in the Balkan countries of central Europe. In the Middle East, conflict between Israelis and Palestinians escalated, even as efforts at a peace process continued. Military confrontations flared elsewhere in the region as well. The post–Cold War era raised new questions about the role of the United States in the world. Americans no longer looked to Russia as a threat but to new international foes, especially terrorist networks operating outside the authority of particular countries. Within the nation, episodes of domestic terrorism, such as the bombing of a federal building in Oklahoma City and a series of school shootings by children made Americans feel that dangers lurked within their previously safe havens.

The Economy: Global and Domestic

After the sharp recession of 1991–1992, by nearly all measures, the economy expanded in the 1990s. The stock market boomed, unemployment declined, and most Americans appeared to be better off financially at the end of the decade than at the beginning. But the overall growth of the economy did not benefit everyone, and many actually lost ground—especially those who lost jobs to mechanization, nonunionized workers who toiled for low wages under grim working conditions, and the nation's most vulnerable workers: poor single mothers, new immigrants, and unskilled people of color.

The Post–Cold War Economy

The end of the Cold War had a profound effect on the nation's economy. The demise of the Soviet Union put a final end to the arms race against a superpower foe and made cutting the defense budget politically acceptable. But the closing of defense-related plants in southern

California, once the center of the nation's Cold War defense contracts that absorbed nearly a fifth of all federal defense dollars, devastated the regional economy. By the mid-1990s, half the workers in the southern California aerospace industry had been laid off, part of a national trend that resulted in the loss of more than half a million jobs, half of them in the manufacturing sector. Many workers lost not only their jobs but also their homes, their economic security, and their sense of community. Louis Rodriguez, president of the International Federation of Professional and Technical Engineers Local 174, explained how he felt when his Long Beach, California, shipyard closed: "The shipyard has been a second family to me. When I get out of here, I'm really going to be lost as a whole. I will have lost my family."

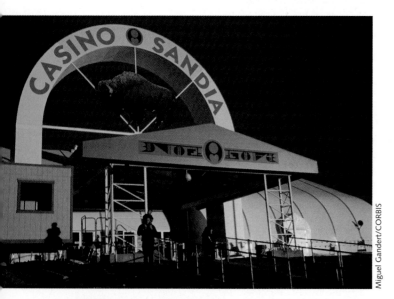

While defense industries shrank, the technology sector of the economy expanded, opening up new opportunities for young computer experts and entrepreneurs and generating fortunes for corporate executives. At the same time, mergers of giant multinational companies concentrated wealth and power in an ever-smaller number of ever-larger corporations. In the last three years of the decade, mergers totaled $5 trillion. Media giants America Online and Time–Warner merged in 2000. In 2001 Nestlé bought Ralston–Purina for $10 billion. Many of the largest mergers crossed national boundaries, such as German automobile maker Daimler–Benz and U.S. Chrysler. American companies were the largest target of global buyouts. In 1999 alone, foreigners paid $233 billion to buy American companies.

While corporations expanded, so did efforts to control their power. Microsoft initially lost an antitrust suit that ordered the computer software giant to be split into two companies. Microsoft appealed the ruling in 2001, and ultimately the Justice Department settled the suit with minor sanctions against the company. The controversial settlement generated opposition. Nine states that participated in the original suit refused to endorse the agreement, and calls for tougher penalties continued. In several states, civil suits against huge tobacco companies limited cigarette advertising and marketing and levied fines on tobacco companies totaling in the billions. Although the publicity surrounding these cases exposed the tobacco companies' efforts to deceive the public about the health risks of cigarettes, the lawsuits did not lead to a decline in cigarette smoking, and tobacco companies continued to advertise and market their product at home as well as abroad.

The nation's elite were not the only ones to capitalize on new entrepreneurial opportunities. The 1988 Indian Gaming Regulatory Act enabled Native Americans to build lucrative Las Vegas–style casinos on tribal lands, bringing new jobs and an estimated $4 billion a year to formerly impoverished communities. The Mashantucket Pequots east of Hartford, Connecticut, opened Foxwoods in 1992, and it quickly became the largest casino in the Western Hemisphere. The Oneidas followed suit a few years later with the Turning Stone casino near Utica, New York. In Arizona casinos brought in $830 million a year. Some Indian casinos failed, however, and gambling always took a largely hidden toll in the losses of already poor local residents. Native Americans remained divided about the wisdom of trying to profit from America's growing inclination to take risks in hopes of winning big. Jose Lucero of New Mexico's Santa Clara tribe near Santa Fe feared that rebuilding Indian life around gambling was "like a leisure virus—we're trading our souls for money (when) we are supposed to be stewards of this land."

However, the advantages for the tribes were substantial. The Oneida tribe of Wisconsin, for example, used the profits from its 2000-slot-machine complex outside Green Bay for an electronic component factory, an industrial park, a printing firm, a bank, a hotel, and four convenience stores. Tribal

■ Casino Sandia on the Sandia Pueblo in New Mexico. Many Native American communities across the country built gambling facilities on tribal lands. Although casinos brought needed income, they remained controversial.

Miguel Gandert/CORBIS

Distribution of the Nation's Wealth

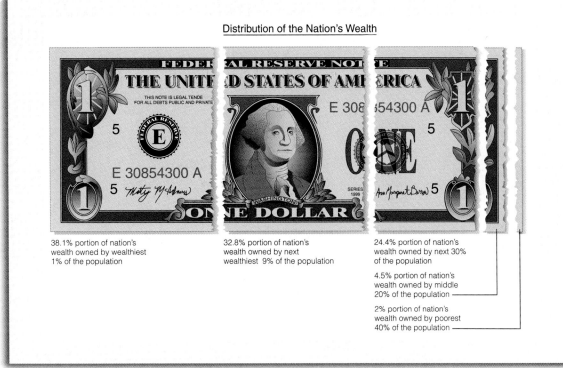

38.1% portion of nation's wealth owned by wealthiest 1% of the population

32.8% portion of nation's wealth owned by next wealthiest 9% of the population

24.4% portion of nation's wealth owned by next 30% of the population

4.5% portion of nation's wealth owned by middle 20% of the population

2% portion of nation's wealth owned by poorest 40% of the population

■ **FIGURE 29.1**

CONCENTRATION OF WEALTH, 1990s During the final decades of the twentieth century, the gap between the wealthy and the poor increased as the nation's wealth became concentrated in the hands of a small number of very wealthy people. By the end of the century, the richest 1 percent of Americans owned 38 percent of all the nation's wealth while the poorest 40 percent shared a mere 0.2 percent of the nation's wealth. The figure also demonstrates that more than 70 percent of the nation's total wealth was in the hands of the most affluent 10 percent of the population, while the majority of Americans—60 percent— was left sharing a mere 5 percent of the nation's wealth.

government outlays increased from $40 million to $250 million over the decade, providing subsidized housing, health care, student counseling, a new daycare center, and a new elementary school built in the shape of a turtle, a sacred creature in Oneida mythology. The money also helped to revive the Oneida language, with a new written form and a CD of ancestral tales told by tribal elders. The tribe also spent $11 million in 1995 recovering property it once owned, bringing it into the tax-free zone of the reservation. In addition to this communal spending, the tribe paid out $225 a year to all its members. By comparison, the tiny band of Minnesota Shakopees, just south of Minneapolis and St. Paul, used much of the profits from its bustling casino to provide annual bonuses of $400,000 to each of its members.

The Widening Gap Between Rich and Poor

Commenting on the state of the economy in the mid–1990s, two economists noted, "The tide of economic growth no longer lifts all boats. We see the recent period as one in which the large yachts, moored in the safe harbors, rose with the tide, while the small boats ran aground. The notion that we can 'grow our way out' of the economic problems facing so many families is now obsolete." In the last decade of the century, the bottom 60 percent of the population saw their income decline, even as the economy boomed. Accumulated wealth—property and investments—was an even better measure of security and influence, and the top 1 percent of Americans owned more wealth than the bottom 90 percent combined. Microsoft chair Bill Gates alone

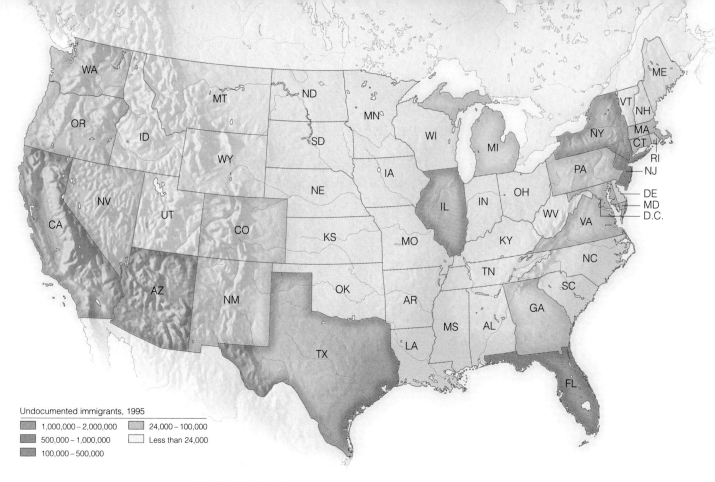

Undocumented immigrants, 1995

- 1,000,000 – 2,000,000
- 500,000 – 1,000,000
- 100,000 – 500,000
- 24,000 – 100,000
- Less than 24,000

■ **MAP 29.1**

STATES WITH LARGE NUMBERS OF UNDOCUMENTED IMMIGRANTS, 1995 Fully 77 percent of all undocumented immigrants entered the country legally, with visas in hand. During the 1990s, the total proportion of the foreign born in the United States, including those with and without legal status, was about half what it had been in 1900 (8 percent compared to 15 percent). Immigrants payed $133 billion dollars annually in local, state, and federal taxes, and generated an annual contribution to the American economy in the range of $25 to $30 billion.

was wealthier than the bottom 45 percent of all U.S. households together. Famed capitalist J. P. Morgan maintained a century earlier that no corporate chieftain should earn more than 20 times what his workers were paid, but by 1980 a typical chief executive of a large U.S. company took home 40 times the earnings of an average factory worker; by 1990 the ratio had grown to 85 times, and by 1998 it reached 419 times.

Although one-third of the nation's African Americans were part of the middle class, black families had fewer assets and resources, making their hold on middle-class status more precarious than that of their white peers. The poorest African Americans were concentrated in low-paying jobs, lacking the quality health care and education that would make social and economic mobility possible. Full-time employment did not necessarily mean an escape from poverty. Among fully employed black heads of households without a high school education, 40 percent of the women and 25 percent of the men did not earn enough to achieve economic self-sufficiency. Almost 50 percent of all black children lived in households below the poverty line, compared to 16 percent of white children. The rate of unemployment was more than twice as high for blacks as for whites.

Recent immigrants from Asia, Africa, and Latin America joined African Americans in jobs at the bottom of the economy. Despite the controversy over illegal immigration, a quarter of a million undocumented workers toiled in the fields of agribusiness. At the same time, 2 percent of able-bodied citizens were in jail, nearly half of them black, because of the arrest and incarceration policies of the "war on drugs" that hit minority communities particularly hard. Prisoners were often required to work while incarcerated. Convicts provided data entry, packed

■ Sweatshops like this one in the 1990s resemble those of a century earlier. Immigrant women labor in garment factories, working long hours in miserable conditions for meager wages.

golf balls, and filled a wide array of jobs for less than minimum wage, and most of their earnings went back to the government. These and other workers at the bottom of the labor force gained little or nothing from the economic boom of the 1990s.

Labor Unions

Low-wage workers in the service industries had one advantage over laborers working for multinational corporations: their jobs could not be exported. Many service workers organized successfully for better wages and working conditions. In April 2000, for example, striking janitors of Service Employees International Union (SEIU) Local 1877 in Los Angeles marched 8 miles past cheering crowds to the upscale business center of Century City. A few weeks later, the janitors had achieved a wage increase of 26 percent, raising their hourly pay from less than $8 to more than $10. This was a tremendous triumph for a union whose membership was 98 percent immigrant: 80 percent Central Americans, more than half women, and all of them poor.

Other service workers also won improved contracts. Unionized hotel workers in San Francisco negotiated a five-year contract that increased pay for the lowest-paid workers, room cleaners and dishwashers, by 25 percent, from $12 to $15 an hour. In Las Vegas, African American hotel worker Hattie Canty, who helped organized 40,000 employees of large casino hotels, said of her efforts, "It has not been a picnic for me, but I don't think I'd like to go on a picnic every day. I have enjoyed the struggle. I'm not the only Hattie. There's lots of Hatties out there." Yatta Staples went out on the picket line in front of the Minneapolis hotel where she worked as a waitress, telling reporters, "I'll stay here as long as it takes." In the summer of 1997, 185,000 Teamsters went on strike against the United Parcel Service and won an improved contract with higher wages and benefits for part-time as well as full-time workers.

Strikes did little to benefit nonunionized workers, especially undocumented immigrants, and sweatshop laborers both inside and outside the United States. There were some attempts to improve working conditions for those most exploited by the global economy. In April 1997 representatives from clothing manufacturers, human rights groups, and labor organizations drafted an agreement that tried to improve conditions for garment workers around the world. Companies that agreed to the voluntary pact would limit work weeks to 60 hours, with a maximum of 12 hours of overtime. The companies had to pay "at least the minimum wage required by local law or the prevailing industry wage, whichever is higher." The pact forbade children under 15 to work and contained policies protecting workers from harassment and unsafe working environments. Even full compliance with such minimal standards would leave workers in the global garment industry subject to much longer hours, lower wages, and worse working conditions than legally permitted in the United States. Critics also raised questions about how enforceable such voluntary standards would be. Nevertheless, the pact was a small step in the right direction that at least called attention to widespread exploitation in the global economy.

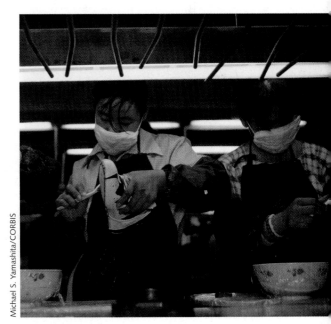

■ U.S.-owned multinational corporations exported jobs to take advantage of cheap labor in developing countries. Here, workers in a Reebok factory in China wear masks as they apply glue to sport shoes.

Tolerance and Its Limits

Racial discrimination had eased over the course of the twentieth century, but persistent inequalities of power and economic opportunity continued to disadvantage Americans of color, who remained disproportionately poor, in prison, and on welfare. The economic downturn of the early 1990s widened the chasm between affluent white and poor non-white Americans. Highly publicized incidents of police brutality directed against Americans of color generated protests and, occasionally, violence. Nevertheless, there were signs that Americans were becoming more tolerant of one another and more willing to accept and even appreciate their diversity.

"We Can All Get Along"

Shortly after midnight on March 3, 1991, police pulled over Rodney King, an African American motorist, after a high-speed chase on a Los Angeles freeway. The four officers dragged the unarmed black man from his car and kicked and beat him with their batons for 15 minutes. The beating left King with a fractured cheekbone, broken bones at the base of his skull, and a broken leg. A bystander recorded the beating on videotape, which was broadcast repeatedly on national television, sparking outrage among Americans of all races. A year later, in April 1992, the four police officers went on trial for use of excessive force.

At the highly publicized trial, defense lawyers for the police officers argued that King, who was clearly cowering on the videotape, was resisting arrest and that the police responded appropriately. The jury of ten whites, one Asian, and one Latino acquitted the officers. The acquittal ignited five days of rioting in the African American community of South Central Los Angeles, leaving 58 people dead and $1 billion in property destroyed. Community leaders called for calm; even Rodney King spoke publicly: "I mean, please, we can get along here," he implored, "We can all get along. We've just got to." Months later, a federal court in Los Angeles convicted two of the officers involved in the beating of violating King's civil rights–too late to avert the violence that erupted after the initial verdict.

Of the 58 people who died in the violence, 18 were Latino, 26 were black, 10 were white, and 2 were Asian. Of the 4000 businesses that were destroyed, most belonged to Latinos and Koreans. Perpetrators of the violence, as well as the victims, came from all racial groups. Antonia Hernandez, president of the Mexican American Legal Defense and Educational Fund, noted, "The hardest part is rebuilding the spirit of the city—what holds us together as Angelinos. It's the rebuilding of trust. . . . It's connecting communities that have never been connected." Several community groups came together in an effort to ease tensions. The Japanese American Citizens League, Chinese for Affirmative Action, and the Asian Pacific Legal Center released statements denouncing the verdict and calling for a federal investigation. "I think that much of the cause of the race relations problem comes down to economics—who has jobs, who has businesses, where is the money going," said Los Angeles City Council member Michael Woo. Jimmy Franco, director of the League of United Latin American Citizens, concurred: "These areas are the poorest areas of the city. If it weren't Rodney King, it would have been something else. It just took something like this to set off the anger."

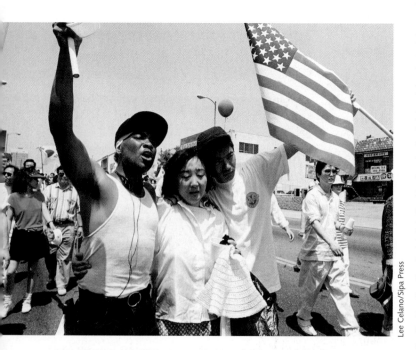

■ In the aftermath of the violent uprising that followed the acquittal of police officers in the beating of motorist Rodney King, Koreans and African Americans in Los Angeles express their solidarity, hoping to heal the wounds and divisions that had torn apart their city.

Lee Celano/Sipa Press

Values in Conflict

In 1991 former University of Colorado football coach Bill McCartney formed the Promise Keepers, a fundamentalist Christian group dedicated to restoring the traditional privileges and responsibilities of husbands and fathers in the home. The Promise Keepers held evangelical revivals that drew tens of thousands of mostly working-class white and some black men to rallies across the country. They believed that men should be good providers for their families, strong role models for their children, and committed spouses. The Promise Keepers were not alone in their concern for what they perceived to be the declining status of fathers. New groups and initiatives appeared that appealed to men across the political spectrum: the National Fatherhood Initiative, Father to Father (launched by Vice President Al Gore in 1995), the Fatherhood Project, the Institute for Responsible Fatherhood and Family Revitalization, and Fathers' Education Network.

Although white men continued to control nearly all the major economic and political institutions in the nation, a 1993 poll found that a majority of white men believed that their advantage in terms of jobs and income, along with their influence over American culture, was declining. African American men also felt the need to bolster manhood and fatherhood. Efforts geared specifically toward African American men included M.A.D. D.A.D.S. (Men Against Destruction—Defending Against Drugs and Social Disorder) and the 1995 Million Man March, organized by Nation of Islam Reverend Louis Farrakhan, which drew hundreds of thousands of black men to demonstrate their solidarity at a rally in Washington, D.C.

At the same time, gay men and lesbians mobilized to gain acceptance and legitimacy for the families that they formed. Many gay and lesbian activists pushed for legalization of same-sex marriage. Although a 1994 poll showed that 52 percent of respondents "claimed to consider gay lifestyle acceptable," 64 percent were opposed to legalizing gay marriage or allowing gay couples to adopt children. Vermont became the first state to grant legal status to civil unions between same-sex couples, although a fierce backlash threatened to overturn the legislation.

Values also collided around the rights and traditions of Native Americans as tribal communities came into conflict with non-Native environmentalists, sports enthusiasts, and

The San Francisco Chronicle. Reprinted with Permission

■ **New reproductive technologies confounded definitions of mothers, fathers, and family members. It was now possible to create embryos in laboratories, and to have children with as many as five "real" parents: genetic mother, genetic father, gestational mother, social mother, and social father. This 1986 cartoon is by Tom Meyer of the *San Francisco Chronicle*.**

Vermont Civil Union Law

On April 26, 2000, Vermont became the first state to grant legal recognition to same-sex couples, affording them all the legal protections, privileges, and responsibilities of married couples. The law unleashed a storm of controversy and raised questions about the legal status in other states of civil unions contracted in Vermont. Nevertheless, in the first year after its enactment, 2479 same-sex couples forged civil unions in Vermont, 478 of them among Vermonters, and the rest from other states. Two-thirds were lesbian unions. Several states began to consider similar bills, but others moved to prohibit such unions. Nebraska amended its state constitution to outlaw same-sex marriage and civil unions. On the national level, conservative lawmakers endeavored to introduce a constitutional amendment that would ban civil unions and restrict marriage to heterosexual couples. Among other provisions, the Vermont Civil Union Law stipulated that

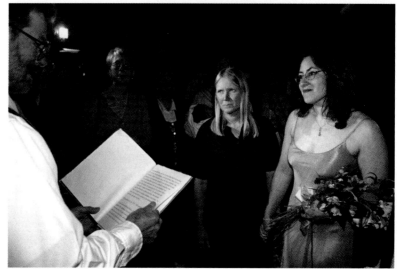

Kathleen Peterson and Carolyn Conrad exchange vows in front of Justice of the Peace T. Hunter Wilson. The ceremony in Brattleboro, Vermont, on July 1, 2000, marked the first legal union under Vermont's Civil Union law. Vermont was the first state to provide recognition and legal status to gay and lesbian couples.

Jim Bourg/Reuters/TimePix

(1) Civil marriage under Vermont's marriage statutes consists of a union between a man and a woman. . . .

(2) Vermont's history as an independent republic and as a state is one of equal treatment and respect for all Vermonters. . . .

(3) The state's interest in civil marriage is to encourage close and caring families, and to protect all family members from the economic and social consequences of abandonment and divorce, focusing on those who have been especially at risk.

(4) Legal recognition of civil marriage by the state is the primary and, in a number of instances, the exclusive source of numerous benefits, responsibilities and protections under the laws of the state for married persons and their children.

(5) Based on the state's tradition of equality under the law and strong families, for at least 25 years, Vermont Probate Courts have qualified gay and lesbian individuals as adoptive parents.

(6) Vermont was one of the first states to adopt comprehensive legislation prohibiting discrimination on the basis of sexual orientation. . . .

(7) The state has a strong interest in promoting stable and lasting families, including families based upon a same-sex couple.

(8) Without the legal protections, benefits and responsibilities associated with civil marriage, same-sex couples suffer numerous obstacles and hardships.

(9) Despite longstanding social and economic discrimination, many gay and lesbian Vermonters have formed lasting, committed, caring and faithful relationships with persons of their same sex. These couples live together, participate in their communities together, and some raise children and care for family members together, just as do couples who are married under Vermont law.

(10) While a system of civil unions does not bestow the status of civil marriage, it does satisfy the requirements of the Common Bene-fits Clause. Changes in the way significant legal relationships are established under the constitution should be approached carefully, combining respect for the community and cultural institutions most affected with a commitment to the constitutional rights involved. Granting benefits and protections to same-sex couples through a system of civil unions will provide due respect for tradition and long-standing social institutions, and will permit adjustment as unanticipated consequences or unmet needs arise.

(11) The constitutional principle of equality embodied in the Common Benefits Clause is compatible with the freedom of religious belief and worship guaranteed in Chapter I, Article 3rd of the state constitution. Extending the benefits and protections of marriage to same-sex couples through a system of civil unions preserves the fundamental constitutional right of each of the multitude of religious faiths in Vermont to choose freely and without state interference to whom to grant the religious status, sacrament or blessing of marriage under the rules, practices or traditions of such faith. ■

scientists. In the upper Midwest, treaties with the government in 1837 and 1842 granted the Chippewa hunting, fishing, and gathering rights in the territories ceded to the United States. Federal courts have consistently upheld these treaties, which include rights to take up to half of the fish and game allowed by state conservation requirements and to use methods such as spear fishing that are illegal for non-Indians. In the 1980s and 1990s, non-Indians challenged these policies and accosted Native Americans in fishing boats with rocks and insults.

REMEMBER
WOUNDED
KNEE

Native American cultural practices also clashed with environmentalist sensibilities over religious practices involving the gathering and sacrificing of golden eaglets. The Department of the Interior, weighing laws protecting Indian religious freedoms against those protecting national parks and wildlife, allowed the Hopis to gather up to 40 young eagles a year. The Hopi usually took about 15 birds for a ceremony that culminated in their sacrifice. The Interior Department's policy is consistent with long-standing treaties as well as recent law, including the American Indian Religious Freedom Act of 1978. But many environmentalists agreed with the news columnist who wrote, "When native peoples, no matter how badly abused by us in the past, seek to perpetrate equally senseless barbarities on helpless creatures, we should stand on principle and use our awesome power to stop, not to enable them." Animal rights activists raised similar arguments against mainstream institutions, including scientific laboratories that used animals for research, and the meat industry, which engaged in inhumane practices.

Courtroom Dramas

Two of the most controversial legal spectacles of the decade centered on accusations against successful black men and exposed deep chasms along class and gender as well as racial lines. The first of these episodes was the Senate hearing of October 1991 to confirm the appointment of Judge Clarence Thomas to the U.S. Supreme Court. President George H. W. Bush nominated the conservative Clarence Thomas to replace retiring liberal Justice Thurgood Marshall. Both jurists were black but otherwise had little in common; they occupied opposite ends of the political and judicial spectrum. Although Bush claimed that Thomas was the "best man for the job," the American Bar Association gave him the lowest rating of any justice confirmed in the previous three decades. Many people became skeptical during the confirmation hearings when Thomas claimed that he had not formed any opinion on the highly charged issue of abortion. Support for Thomas among the Senators on the Senate Judiciary Committee fell largely along party lines. But when University of Oklahoma law professor Anita Hill accused Thomas of sexual harassment when she worked for him at the Equal Opportunity Employment Commission in the early 1980s, the question of Thomas's professional qualifications faded to the background and the hearings focused exclusively on Hill's accusations.

In live televised hearings, the African American law professor testified that Thomas had made crude and lurid remarks to her as well as unwanted sexual overtures. Several of the all-white-male panel of senators questioned Hill's credibility, wondering why she continued to work for Thomas after the alleged harassment. Thomas drew on the long history of black men being falsely accused of sexual aggression to counter the charge of sexual harassment, accusing his Democratic opponents of conducting a "high-tech lynching." In the end Thomas was confirmed. But Hill's testimony, and what appeared to her supporters as the insensitive behavior of the senators, brought the issue of sexual harassment to a high level of national consciousness. The hearings also highlighted the fact that Congress was overwhelmingly white and male, motivating female candidates and their supporters to alter that reality the following year. As a result of the 1992 elections, the number of female senators tripled from two to six, including the first black female senator, Carol Moseley Braun, Democrat from Illinois. The number of congresswomen rose from 28 to 47.

In 1994 television viewers were again riveted by a media spectacle, this time a sensational murder case. On the night of June 12, Nicole Brown Simpson and her friend Ronald Goldman were stabbed to death outside Simpson's West Los Angeles apartment. The murdered white woman was the ex-wife of black celebrity O. J. Simpson, former football star and film actor. O. J. Simpson's blood was found at the scene, hair and other forensic and DNA evidence linked him to the crime, he had no reliable alibi, and a motive was evident in his pattern of jealous rage and brutality against the murdered woman. No other suspects in the case were ever identified. But Simpson's team of lawyers unearthed evidence that before the Simpson case, white police detective Mark Fuhrman had boasted of planting evidence and had made racist comments. The mostly black and female jury was sympathetic to the possibility that Fuhrman had framed Simpson. In Los Angeles, in the wake of the Rodney King beatings, African Americans had good reason to distrust the police.

Finally, in early October 1996, after a trial that lasted nearly a year, it took the jury only two hours to acquit Simpson of all charges. Pundits focused on the racial divide: blacks were more inclined to believe Simpson was innocent, and whites more likely to consider him guilty. The families of Ronald Goldman and Nicole Brown Simpson filed a wrongful death civil suit, in which the standards for conviction require merely a preponderance of evidence rather than guilt beyond a reasonable doubt. Simpson was convicted in the civil suit, which found him responsible for the deaths, and ordered to pay damages.

The Changing Face of Diversity

These highly charged events illuminated racial tensions, but there was also evidence that Americans were starting to accept the nation's diversity and adopt a more inclusive vision. The number of immigrants living in the United States tripled in three decades, to nearly 27 million, representing 10 percent of the population—the highest proportion of foreign-born residents since the 1930s. The numbers of Asians and Pacific Islanders increased by 45.9 percent, with those of Chinese ancestry comprising the largest group, followed by those with origins in the Philippines. The Latino population grew by 39.7 percent. Among the nation's Latinos, nearly two-thirds were of Mexican ancestry.

Not everyone celebrated these developments. In California, with one-third of the nation's Latino population, voters responded with Proposition 187 to deny public education and most other public social services to undocumented immigrants, and Proposition 227 to end bilingual education. Large numbers of Latino voters opposed these measures. In subsequent elections many young Latinos and new citizens marshaled their political power and voted for the first time. Evidence of the growing political power of Latinos was the mounting support in California for a bill that would require the U.S. government to return back pay that was taken from the wages of Mexican agricultural workers who came to the United States during World War II under the *Bracero* program. In Los Angeles during the 1990s, Latinos became the largest single ethnic group. By 2000 whites no longer constituted a majority of California's multiethnic population, dropping from 57 percent in 1990 to 47 percent in 2000.

At the same time, politics and ideas based on distinct and rigid racial lines gave way to a growing recognition of intermixing. Artists actively explored this hybridity. Dramatist Anna Deveare

■ Golf superstar Tiger Woods celebrates his triumph at the U.S. Amateur Championships in North Plains, Oregon, August 25, 1996. Woods, the son of an African American father and a Thai mother, was one of several mixed-race celebrities in the 1990s.

Jack Smith/AP/Wide World

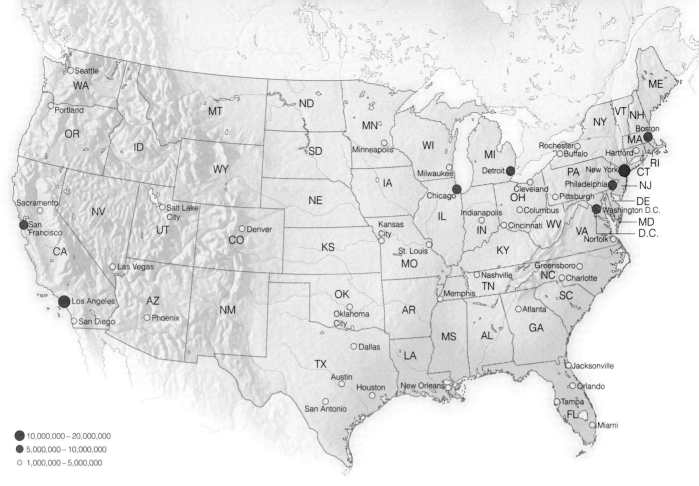

■ **MAP 29.2**

POPULATION OF MAJOR METROPOLITAN AREAS, 1990   By 1990 the nation's population was concentrated in large metropolitan areas, most of them along the East and West coasts, the Sun Belt, and the Upper Midwest. One hundred and twenty million Americans, about half of the population, lived in suburbs.

Smith, for example, wrote and performed a theatrical production in which she interviewed and studied many people involved in the uprising in South Central Los Angeles, from the white chief of police to a Korean woman whose family business was destroyed in the riots. In her widely acclaimed one-woman play *Twilight, Los Angeles,* the mixed-race Smith took on the many identities of the white, black, Asian, Latino, male, female, young, and old people she represented. By transforming herself on stage into each of those people, she suggested that we, as a society, were all of those people as well. In his 1996 film *Lone Star,* John Sayles examined a Texas border town where white, black, Latino, and Indian peoples were all interwoven and connected in their lives, communities, and families. From cross-racial love to debates over the local school's history curriculum, the film explored in microcosm the challenges and rewards of an inclusive American identity.

Racial intermixing was evident in other areas as well. In the world of sports, young golfer Tiger Woods, son of a black Vietnam veteran father and a Thai mother, became the reigning superstar of the sport most closely identified with the world of the white elite. Pop star Prince was one of many artists who crafted a persona that highlighted both racial and gender ambiguity. On job and college application forms, a growing number of mixed-race Americans refused to be identified as belonging to one particular racial group. Reflecting this development, the U.S. Census of 2000 allowed people to check more than one box to indicate their racial identity. In California, where nearly 5 percent of the population checked more than one box, nearly all of those who checked white and another box were Latinos.

Violence and Danger

Violence was nothing new in American society, but new types of mayhem in the 1990s—including domestic terrorism and school shootings–sparked national soul-searching and wide-ranging debate over the causes of violence and what to do about them. Meanwhile, ordinary Americans inflicted various harms on themselves, often in class-distinct ways. Eating disorders and obesity reached epidemic proportions, and Americans continued to turn to drugs, most of them legal, to make them feel better.

Domestic Terrorism

On the morning of April 19, 1995, a 2-ton homemade bomb exploded at the Alfred P. Murrah Federal Building in Oklahoma City. The huge building crumbled, killing 168 people, including 19 children. The attack was the worst act of terrorism in the nation's history to that date. Initial news reports speculated that the terrorists were Arabs, but it turned out that the attack was carried out by American citizens with a hatred for the government. Timothy McVeigh, a Persian Gulf War veteran turned antigovernment terrorist, and his accomplice, Terry Nichols, were found guilty of the bombing.

Antigovernment individuals and groups had long operated within the United States, and during the 1990s, their activities—as well as FBI efforts to curtail them—intensified. Investigations throughout the decade uncovered networks of antigovernment militias, tax resisters, and white supremacist groups, many of them heavily armed and isolated in remote rural areas. Some antigovernment extremists acted alone, like former mathematics professor Theodore Kaczynski, known as the "Unabomber," who for two decades sent bombs through the mail, killing 3 people and injuring 29. His demand to have his antigovernment manifesto published in major national newspapers led to his identification and arrest.

The FBI tried to prevent these extremists from causing harm, but some of their efforts went awry. In 1992 an FBI agent shot and killed the wife and son of Randall Weaver, a former Green Beret and antigovernment militia supporter who had failed to appear for trial on weapons charges, in a shootout at their Idaho home. The following year in Waco, Texas, the FBI stormed the heavily armed compound of an antigovernment religious sect known as the Branch Davidians. The leader of the group, David Koresh, had barricaded the compound. The FBI, acting on reports of abuse of members, particularly women and children, tried to force Koresh and his group out of the building. But a fire broke out, killing 80 men, women, and children inside. The FBI came under intense criticism for its aggressive tactics in these cases. For antigovernment extremists, these actions prompted revenge. The Oklahoma City bombing, apparently, was intended in part as retaliation for the FBI assault against the Branch Davidians precisely two years earlier.

Timothy McVeigh was sentenced to death for the Oklahoma City bombing. But shortly before the scheduled execution in May 2001, more than 4000 pages of FBI documents relating to the case that had not been seen by McVeigh's attorneys suddenly surfaced. The discovery raised new questions about the competence of the FBI and delayed McVeigh's execution for a month. The execution by lethal injection took place on June 11. The case revived a debate about the death penalty, particularly in light of recent evidence of many botched legal defenses in capital cases. Opponents pointed to the preponderance of convicts of color on death row, representation by incompetent attorneys, and the execution of mentally retarded offenders to argue that the death penalty should be abolished. The governor of Illinois declared a moratorium on executions when a study revealed that many death row inmates were cleared of charges as a result of new DNA evidence. Public opinion began to shift, but the majority—including the U.S. presidents from both parties throughout the decade—continued to support the death penalty.

The Oklahoma City bombing was the worst but not the only example of domestic terrorist attacks. After the Supreme Court's 1973 decision in *Roe* v. *Wade* legalized abortion, antiabortion activists worked to have the decision reversed. Most antiabortion protesters were peaceful and law-abiding. But a small militant fringe of antiabortion crusaders switched their targets of protest from elected officials to abortion providers and turned to violence. In 1993 half of all abortion clinics reported hostile actions, including death threats, fires, bombs, invasions, blockades, and shootings. In 1993 and 1994 vigilantes shot and killed one abortion provider, tried to kill another, and shot employees at two clinics in Brookline, Massachusetts.

The violence spurred Congress to pass the Freedom of Access to Clinic Entrances Act in 1994, making it a federal crime to block access to clinics. But ultimately, the intimidation and violence were effective. Although abortion remained legal, the procedure became increasing difficult to obtain. Few medical residency programs in obstetrics and gynecology routinely taught the procedure, and considering the dangers posed by antiabortion terrorists, few physicians were willing to perform abortions. By the end of the decade, there were no abortion providers in 86 percent of largely rural counties in the country. Abortions continued to be available in cities, mostly in specialized abortion clinics. Between 1990 and 1997, the number of abortions declined by 17.4 percent. But the political battles continued. After years of controversy and debate, the French abortion pill RU–486 received FDA approval for use in the United States, making it possible for individual doctors to prescribe the pill and for women to avoid surgery.

Joe Marquette/AP/Wide World

■ Abortion remained one of the most controversial political issues throughout the 1990s. Here abortion rights advocate Inga Coulter of Harrisburg, Pennsylvania, and antiabortion crusader Elizabeth McGee of Washington, D.C., take opposing sides in a demonstration outside the Supreme Court building on December 8, 1993.

Kids Who Kill

Although violent crime declined throughout the decade, especially crimes committed by youths, a spate of school shootings in which children murdered other children sparked national soul searching and finger pointing as Americans wondered whom and what to blame. The murderers were mostly white middle-class boys who appeared to be "normal kids." The worst of these shootings occurred on April 20, 1999, at Columbine High School in a suburb of Denver, Colorado, where two boys opened fire and killed 12 of their schoolmates and a teacher before killing themselves.

These shootings happened in middle-class suburbs where families believed they were safe from the perceived dangers of the inner cities. But such havens could not keep dangerous elements out if the dangers came from within. Some commentators blamed inattentive parents; others pointed to the violence-saturated popular culture. A few noted that when youth of color were victims or perpetrators of violence, the media devoted little attention to the tragedies, suggesting that such crimes were shocking only if committed by white middle-class youths.

The common factors in all of these killings were that the children used guns and that they got the weapons easily, often from their own homes. Gun control advocates noted that the easy access to firearms in the United States was unique among western industrial nations. In 1992, 367 people were killed by handguns in Great Britain, Sweden, Switzerland, Japan, Australia, and Canada combined. The total population of those countries equaled that of the United States, where in that same year, handguns killed 13,220 people. Public opinion polls showed that most Americans favored gun control, but the powerful gun lobby and the National Rifle Association argued that the Second Amendment to the Constitution guaranteed individuals

Getty Images

■ Childhood obesity reached epidemic proportions in the 1990s. Too little exercise, too much TV, and the proliferation of fast food outlets, especially in low-income areas, contributed to the problem.

the right to bear arms. Congress enacted the Brady Bill, a gun control measure named for James Brady, the White House press secretary who was gravely wounded in the 1981 assassination attempt on President Ronald W. Reagan. The bill required a waiting period for handgun purchases and banned assault rifles. Nevertheless, access to firearms remained easy. In the 2000 election, only two states, Oregon and Colorado—where two of the worst school shootings occurred—voted to establish some controls on the purchase of guns.

A Healthy Nation?

Despite the nation's near obsession with fitness, both the wealthy and the poor suffered from a number of afflictions. Eating disorders plagued millions of Americans. Among the affluent, anorexia nervosa (self-starvation) and bulimia (frequent binging and purging) affected an estimated 5 million Americans, especially young women, fed in part by a fashion fad that glamorized emaciated bodies. Men also strove for the fashionable body, sometimes with the aid of drugs to enhance athletic performance or muscle build-up. In 2000 the Mayo Clinic reported a 30 percent increase in eating disorders per year, mostly among young women, but in a growing number of men as well. The opposite problem plagued the lower end of the class ladder, where obesity increased dramatically, especially among children. Fast-food chains targeted low-income areas with franchises and promotions offering "supersized" high-fat meals. Childhood obesity jumped from 5 percent in 1964 to 20 percent in 2000.

Illegal drugs, including marijuana, cocaine, and heroin, remained popular in spite of official efforts to curb the trade. However, illegal drugs represented only one dimension of Americans' desire to solve their problems through the use of substances. Some mind-altering drugs were legal and available by prescription, such as Prozac and other antidepressants. These psychopharmaceuticals saturated the prescription drug market. Some mental health experts worried that these drugs were being overprescribed, especially for children, as life's normal ups and downs were increasingly diagnosed as maladies such as depression and attention deficit disorder. Aging baby boomers also boosted the profits of pharmaceutical companies. Women turned to hormone replacement therapies to offset the effects of menopause. Skyrocketing sales of Viagra, a drug for treating male impotence, reflected middle-aged men's concerns about waning sexual potency.

Medical developments brought new worries in the wake of new cures. Antibiotics were so widely prescribed that forms of drug-resistant bacteria began to proliferate. Tuberculosis appeared in new deadly forms that did not respond to treatment with available antibiotics. In 1997 researchers in Scotland cloned a sheep, raising hopes that cloning could lead to new medical breakthroughs and fears that human cloning might be next. In 2000 scientists charted the entire human genome, or genetic code, offering the hope of finding causes and cures for genetically linked diseases. Advances in reproductive medicine provoked controversies over the benefits and dangers of such procedures as embryo selection, in vitro fertilization for postmenopausal women, and the long-term implications of egg and sperm donation. In one 1999 case that sparked a debate among medical ethicists, a couple advertised for an egg donor in the student newspapers of prestigious colleges, offering $50,000 to a donor who was athletic and tall, had no major family medical problems, and had scored at least 1400 on the Scholastic Achievement Test. Like the eugenic campaigns of earlier decades, these sorts of cases raised concerns about efforts to create "superior" children.

■ **FIGURE 29.2**
CHILDHOOD OBESITY RATES FOR BOYS AND GIRLS AGED 6–17, 1960s AND 1990s   During the last half century, obesity rates among children rose dramatically, especially in the 1990s. Childhood obesity is associated with a wide range of medical problems that can affect the health of overweight children throughout their lives. In the 1960s, boys and girls were equally likely to be overweight. But by the 1990s, obesity had become more prevalent among boys.

The Clinton Presidency

William Jefferson Clinton was the first American president born after World War II. Raised in Arkansas in a working-class family, Clinton attended Georgetown University and studied at Oxford University in England as a Rhodes Scholar. Like many college students of his generation, he opposed the Vietnam War and avoided the draft. He attended Yale Law School, where he met Hillary Rodham from Illinois, whom he married in 1975. In 1978, at the young age of 33, he was elected governor of Arkansas. After one term he was defeated in his bid for reelection. He made a comeback by defining himself as a New Democrat with centrist political inclinations and reclaimed his job as governor. When he ran for president in 1992, Clinton received the support of the Democratic Leadership Council, a group of New Democrats who shifted the national party to the right of its previous New Deal liberal position.

Clinton was a brilliant campaigner and a charismatic leader with a disarming personal style that contributed to his victory over the incumbent George H. W. Bush. The sluggish economy also helped Clinton win the election. Throughout his presidency, despite political failures and scandals, Clinton achieved consistently high presidential job performance ratings in national polls. He also benefited from the recovery of the economy during his administration. But accusations of corruption and sexual impropriety plagued him throughout his two terms. Ultimately, during his second term as president, an affair with a young White House intern led to his impeachment by the House of Representatives. Although he was not removed from office, the incident cast a cloud over his presidency.

Clinton: The New Democrat

In 1992 the incumbent president, George H. W. Bush, faced an uphill battle. The recession of 1991–1992 hit white-collar as well as blue-collar workers as unemployment climbed above

8 percent. During the 12 years of Republican rule, the national debt had more than quadrupled to $4.4 trillion. The Republican party platform, reflecting pressures from the right wing of the party, attacked permissiveness in American society, opposed abortion and gay rights, and called for a smaller government. The Democrats nominated 46-year-old Bill Clinton, who selected as his running mate Al Gore, senator from Tennessee, known as a strong environmentalist and author of *Earth in the Balance: Ecology and the Human Spirit.* A wildcard in the election was the Reform party candidacy of H. Ross Perot, a Texas billionaire who financed his own campaign and used the national media to tap into voter discontent with the two major parties.

Much of the campaign reflected the culture wars, pitting what many saw as the socially permissive legacy of the 1960s against conservative efforts to restore traditional "family values" to American public life. Many Americans worried that the prevalence of single-parent families, the high rate of divorce, and the pervasiveness of sex and violence in the popular culture all reflected a decline in moral standards and an erosion of American society. In May 1992 Vice President Dan Quayle delivered a speech criticizing the popular television show *Murphy Brown,* whose unmarried title character had given birth to a child. Quayle's attack on *Murphy Brown* may have backfired; a poll taken after the Republican national convention showed that 57 percent of respondents had an unfavorable view of him. But Republicans were not the only critics of popular culture. Al Gore's wife, Tipper, for example, had long been an advocate of parental advisories and ratings of popular music. Despite their criticisms, all the candidates made full use of the media in their campaigns.

Clinton won the election by a comfortable margin, but Perot garnered 19 percent of the popular vote, the largest showing for a third-party candidate since Theodore Roosevelt ran on the Progressive party ticket in 1912. Clinton began his term with a solid Democratic House and Senate, which included a new infusion of women, along with the nation's first senator of American Indian descent, Ben Nighthorse Campbell of Colorado. Saying that he wanted his cabinet to "look like America," Clinton appointed two Latinos, three blacks, and three women to the 14-member cabinet. Among his first executive orders were lifting Bush's restrictions on abortion counseling, allowing fetal tissue research, and permitting a review of the prohibited French abortion pill RU-486, which finally gained FDA approval in 2000.

TABLE 29-1			
The Election of 1992			
Candidate	Political Party	Popular Vote	Electoral Vote
William J. Clinton	Democratic	43,728,375	370
George H. W. Bush	Republican	38,167,416	168
H. Ross Perot	Independent	19,237,247	0

Clinton's Domestic Agenda and the "Republican Revolution"

Clinton ran into trouble early in his administration when he tried to fulfill his campaign promise to allow gays and lesbians to serve openly in the military, reversing a policy that dated back half a century. Top military officials, already unhappy with having a new commander-in-chief who had avoided military service during the Vietnam War, vehemently opposed lifting the ban against gays. Ultimately, Clinton compromised and established a new policy of "don't ask, don't tell," which allowed homosexuals to serve as long as they did not make their sexual orientation known. The compromise proved to be unworkable and left many gays and lesbians feeling betrayed.

Clinton's effort to reform the health care system was equally unsuccessful. With rising health care costs and millions of uninsured citizens, Clinton's campaign promises to provide national health insurance and reduce the cost of health care had wide public support but fierce opposition from the medical establishment and the pharmaceutical industry. Clinton appointed his wife, Hillary Rodham Clinton, an attorney and longtime advocate on behalf of children and families, to head a task force to develop a plan. But the task force, deliberating behind closed doors, failed to come up with a workable strategy acceptable to all sides. After a year of hearings and no action in Congress on the complicated task force proposal, the Clintons abandoned the effort.

Clinton achieved a major success when he pushed through Congress a budget that raised taxes on the wealthiest Americans, cut spending to reduce the deficit, and expanded tax credits for low-income families. Vice President Gore cast the tie-breaking vote in the Senate, with no Republican voting in favor. In the next three years the economy markedly improved. Other legislative successes included passage of the "motor voter" act, which allowed eligible voters to register when applying for drivers' licenses, and the Family and Medical Leave Act, which required employers to grant unpaid medical leave for up to 12 weeks. Clinton appointed two new Supreme Court Justices, Ruth Bader Ginsburg in 1993 and Stephen Breyer in 1994, whose liberal perspectives contrasted with the largely conservative bent of the court.

The 1994 congressional elections dealt a devastating blow to Clinton's legislative agenda. In the midst of the campaign, about 300 Republican congressional candidates, under the leadership of Speaker of the House Newt Gingrich, stood on the Capitol steps and endorsed a "Contract with America," calling for welfare reform, a balanced budget, more prisons and longer sentences, increased defense spending, an end to legal abortion, and other conservative measures. Only 39 percent of the electorate voted, and a whisker-thin majority of those voted Republican. Nevertheless, the Republicans declared a "Republican Revolution" as they took control of both the House and Senate for the first time in 40 years and pushed Congress to the right of center.

The new Congress passed a large tax cut and a tough anticrime bill, increased military spending, and reduced federal regulatory power over the environment. Clinton used his veto power to limit the Republican agenda, but he also undercut the conservative momentum by taking on some of their issues as his own, such as free trade and welfare reform. The "Republican

John Duricka/AP/Wide World

■ On September 27, 1994, Congressman Newt Gingrich, a Republican from Georgia, stood on Capitol Hill with Republican congressional candidates and pledged a "Contract with America." Republicans took control of both houses of Congress and declared a "Republican Revolution."

Revolution" did not last long. In 1995 and again in 1996, Congress forced a shutdown of the federal government rather than agreeing to Clinton's proposed budget, leading to widespread frustration and anger as Democrats and Republicans blamed each other for the stalemate. Support for the "Contract with America" wore thin, and the public was quickly disenchanted with the gridlock in Washington. In his 1996 State of the Union address, Clinton announced that the "era of big government is over." In August of that year, after vetoing two earlier versions, Clinton finally agreed to a compromise measure and signed the Welfare Reform Act, abolishing the 60-year-old program Aid to Families with Dependent Children (AFDC).

TABLE 29-2			
The Election of 1996			
Candidate	Political Party	Popular Vote	Electoral Vote
William J. Clinton	Democratic	45,590,703	379
Robert Dole	Republican	37,816,307	159
H. Ross Perot	Reform	7,866,284	0

Clinton won reelection easily in 1996, defeating the 73-year-old Senate Majority Leader, Republican Bob Dole of Kansas. Republicans lost some seats but stayed in control of both houses of Congress. The 1996 campaign was the most expensive in history, with Democrats spending $250 million and Republicans $400 million. Billionaire H. Ross Perot ran again, although his showing at the polls was much weaker than in 1992. Public opinion polls showed a growing concern over the vast amounts of money poured into elections, but campaign finance reform remained a difficult issue for lawmakers, whose own success at the polls depended on large financial contributions.

The Impeachment Crisis

Clinton's personal behavior left him vulnerable to political enemies, who took full advantage of every opportunity to discredit him. In 1993 the Clintons were investigated for possible complicity in a failed Arkansas investment scheme known as Whitewater. Although a few of the Clintons' close associates were found guilty of conspiracy, tax evasion, and mail fraud in the deal, four years of persistent investigation cleared the Clintons of any wrongdoing. Nevertheless, the Whitewater scandal activated the Office of the Independent Counsel, an independent investigative unit put into place during the Nixon administration to investigate the Watergate break-in. The independent counsel, former judge Kenneth Starr, with the help of the congressional Republicans, pursued Clinton throughout his two terms and nearly brought down his presidency. In the end, however, it was not Clinton's financial dealings but rather his sexual behavior that led to his impeachment.

Clinton's sexual behavior became an issue well before he entered the White House. During the 1992 campaign, Gennifer Flowers, a former nightclub singer, told a tabloid that she and Clinton had an affair when he was governor. Early in his presidency, Paula Jones, a former Arkansas state employee, filed a sexual harassment suit against Clinton, claiming that he had propositioned her when he was governor of Arkansas. Eventually, the case was dismissed, but it came back to haunt him later.

In 1998, Kenneth Starr reported to the House Judiciary Committee that he had evidence that Clinton had an extramarital affair with a young White House intern, Monica Lewinsky. Starr claimed that Clinton had broken the law in an effort to cover up the affair. Lewinsky and Clinton had both been called to testify in the Paula Jones case, and both denied having had a sexual relationship. Starr claimed that Clinton had lied under oath and had instructed his close advisor and friend, Vernon Jordan, to find Lewinsky a job to keep her quiet. Starr charged Clinton with perjury, witness tampering, and obstruction of justice. As proof of the affair, Starr produced 20 hours of taped phone conversations recorded by Lewinsky's co-worker and confidante, Linda Tripp. Clinton vehemently denied the charges, but Lewinsky had saved a dress with a stain containing the president's DNA, providing the investigation with the "smoking gun" it needed.

As Starr and congressional Republicans pressed the investigation with relentless determination, the media saturated the nation and the world with sordid and graphic details of the president's sexual encounters with the young intern. Polls showed that Americans disapproved of Clinton's personal behavior, but they did not want him removed from office. With the economy booming and the country running smoothly, Clinton garnered high job performance ratings, rising to 79 percent at the height of the scandal. Negative sentiment against Kenneth Starr and congressional Republicans mounted as the investigation dragged on for four years at a cost to taxpayers of $40 million.

Public opinion notwithstanding, the House of Representatives impeached Clinton on December 19, 1998, charging him with perjury and obstruction of justice, based on Clinton's false testimony in the Paula Jones case. Removal from office requires two steps: the House of Representatives brings formal charges known as "articles of impeachment," and the Senate tries the impeached official on these articles. A two-thirds vote of the Senate is required for conviction. The vote in the House of Representatives fell strictly along party lines. The Bill of Impeachment was then sent to the Senate, where the majority of senators determined that Clinton's misdeeds did not meet the standard for "high crimes and misdemeanors" required to remove a president from office.

The Nation and the World

Clinton tried to prevent the scandals that plagued him at home from interfering with his foreign policy. He hoped to maintain a focus on peacekeeping and peacemaking while expanding trade and diplomatic relations, especially to countries that had been considered unfriendly during the Cold War. Clinton took on the role of peace broker by facilitating negotiations in long-standing conflicts in Northern Ireland and the Middle East. But hostilities in those areas proved too deep to be fully resolved. Military interventions in Somalia, Haiti, and Kosovo yielded mixed results, and trade agreements generated heated controversy. Episodes of international terrorism against U.S. embassies and military personnel killed hundreds of people and highlighted the strength of extremist groups whose members were deeply hostile to the United States and its interventions around the world.

Trade Agreements

In 1993, with President Clinton's strong encouragement, Congress approved the North American Free Trade Agreement (NAFTA), eliminating tariffs and trade barriers among the United States, Mexico, and Canada and thus creating the largest free trade zone in the world. In 1994 Congress approved the General Agreement on Tariffs and Trade (GATT), which reduced tariffs on thousands of goods and phased out import quotas imposed by the United States and other industrialized nations. Supporters argued that these measures would increase global competition and improve the U.S. economy. Businesses would benefit from the easing of trade barriers, and consumers would have access to lower-priced goods.

Reuters NewMedia Inc./CORBIS

■ Activists protest at the opening of the meeting of the World Trade Organization (WTO) in Seattle, Washington, on November 1, 1999. During the four days of the meeting, hundreds of demonstrators took to the streets in opposition to the organization's environmental and labor policies.

But NAFTA and GATT barely passed Congress. Clinton faced strong opposition from liberal Democrats in industrial areas and from labor unions, who feared that these measures would result in jobs going abroad, declining American wages, and a relaxation of environmental controls over companies moving outside the U.S. borders. In the first few years of NAFTA and GATT, these fears seemed justified. Some jobs went abroad, and threats of moving gave employers a negotiating edge over workers. In Mexico the impact of NAFTA was even worse. The peso collapsed as money and goods flowed across the border, and the average wages for workers fell from $1.45 to $.78 per hour.

Equally controversial were Clinton's efforts to grant China most-favored-nation status, which would designate China as a full trading partner with the United States. Human rights activists argued that China's dismal record of violent suppression and imprisonment of political dissenters should preclude such favorable trading terms. But with an eye to China's huge potential market for American goods and favorable site for U.S.-owned factories, Congress approved Clinton's proposal.

Despite this new alliance with a former foe, Cold War politics did not entirely disappear from foreign policy. The tiny communist nation of Cuba, suffering severe economic hardship since the collapse of its benefactor, the Soviet Union, remained off limits to U.S. trade and tourism. Cuban Americans in southern Florida, who had fled Cuba after Fidel Castro's successful revolution, blocked any efforts to ease relations between the two countries. Democrats as well as Republicans were reluctant to alienate these voters; their numbers and political clout in the most populous part of the nation's fourth largest state gave them power.

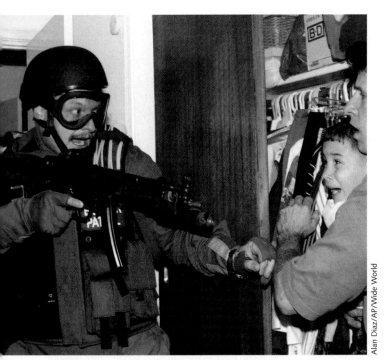

Alan Diaz/AP/Wide World

Cuban–American relations were strained anew in November 1999 when a small boat carrying a group of Cubans trying to escape to Florida capsized, drowning everyone aboard except a six-year-old boy, Elian Gonzales, who was found floating on an inner tube off the coast of Florida. Elian's relatives in Miami argued that Elian should stay in the United States, where he could grow up in a democratic society—a goal his mother died trying to achieve. However, his father wanted him back in Cuba, and the Clinton administration determined that the boy should be returned to his remaining parent. After months of intense media coverage in both countries and futile efforts at negotiation, in April 2000 U.S. government agents stormed the small house where Elian was staying and seized the boy, who eventually returned to Cuba with his father.

■ On the morning of April 22, 2000, federal agents stormed the house where relatives were holding 6-year-old Elian Gonzales. The boy was the sole survivor of a boat carrying a group of Cubans escaping to the United States. His mother was among those who perished. Elian was eventually reunited with his father and returned to Cuba.

Efforts at Peacemaking

Less controversial than relations with China and Cuba were Clinton's peacemaking efforts. Northern Ireland had been fraught with violent conflict for 30 years. Irish Catholic nationalists wanted to break ties with England and join the Republic of Ireland; Protestants loyal to Great Britain wanted to remain part of the United Kingdom. The United States, with political and diplomatic connections to London as well as strong ties to the Irish, wanted to help resolve the crisis. Clinton made several trips to Ireland to promote peace. He appointed former Senator George Mitchell of Maine as negotiator, who spent months working on a settlement. Despite dissent and violence by extremists on both sides, by the time Clinton left office, an agreement had been reached that established a shared coalition government.

In the Middle East, Clinton brought Yasser Arafat, leader of the Palestinian Liberation Organization (PLO), and Yitzak Rabin, Israeli Prime Minister, to Washington for talks that led to a historic 1993 handshake and pledges to pursue a peace agreement. As in Northern Ireland, those efforts were hampered by violent extremists on both sides. Rabin was assassinated by a fanatical right-wing Israeli, leading to the election of a hawkish new prime minister, Benjamin Netanyahu. The peace process fell apart for several years until negotiations finally resumed in the late 1990s. But just when an agreement seemed to be within reach, large-scale violence between Palestinians and Israelis erupted again in the summer of 2000. Clinton left office with no agreement in sight.

In the final weeks of Clinton's presidency in 2000, he made a historic visit to Vietnam—the first by an American president since the war. Because Clinton had protested against the war decades earlier, his visit held great symbolic power. Although the United States lost the war, westernization had taken hold in Vietnam, with investment beginning to flow in from Europe, the United States, and Japan, as well as American popular culture and technology. Cheering crowds welcomed the president of the superpower that had been vanquished 25 years earlier.

Military Interventions and International Terrorism

The end of the Cold War raised new questions about how and when to use American military force. Most of the overseas crises stemmed from problems of national disintegration, ethnic conflict, and humanitarian disasters resulting from political chaos and civil wars. These sorts of problems would have challenged even the most internationally focused president, but Clinton was concerned mainly with domestic matters. Aside from his interest in expanding U.S. trade, he had few guiding principles in foreign policy other than his desire to broker peace agreements in tenacious hot spots.

On the Caribbean island of Haiti, a military coup in 1991 had ousted the democratically elected President Jean Bertrand Aristide. In a striking departure from former Cold War policies, Clinton backed the black populist Aristide against the coup leaders, who had strong ties to the CIA. In 1994, the United States received UN support for an invasion to restore Aristide to power. To avert a large-scale military conflict, Clinton sent former President Jimmy Carter to Haiti to negotiate a settlement. The resulting agreement allowed the coup members to leave the country, and Aristide returned. Six years later, however, the United States criticized Aristide for corruption and fraud in his 2000 reelection.

In 1992 President Bush had sent U.S. marines to Somalia in east Africa as part of a UN effort to provide famine relief and to restore peace in the war-torn nation. After Clinton took office, Somali warlord Mohammed Farah Aidid killed 50 Pakistani UN peacekeepers. The UN forces then mobilized against Aidid, shifting the peacekeeping mission to military engagement. As part of the effort to hunt down Aidid, U.S. soldiers killed hundreds of Somali citizens, creating intense anti-American sentiment among the population. Amid that hostile atmosphere, in September 1993, Aidid's forces killed 18 American soldiers under the UN command in a firefight and dragged one of their bodies through the streets. The outraged American public viewed the grim spectacle on TV, and the experience left Clinton with no clear guidelines on humanitarian intervention abroad. Largely as a result of the disaster in Somalia, when ethnic conflict led to genocide in Rwanda in central Africa in 1994, the United States and other western nations refused to intervene.

Ethnic conflict was also the cause of trouble in the Balkans. From 1945 to 1980 Marshal Josip Broz Tito ruled over a unified communist Yugoslavia, maintaining stability by suppressing ethnic rivalries. But after Tito's death in 1980, ethnic nationalism pulled Yugoslavia apart, with Slovenia and Croatia breaking away, and then Bosnia and Serbia. The region erupted in bloody conflicts, escalating into full-scale war after the breakup of Yugoslavia in 1991. After sustained

Serbian attacks on Muslims in Bosnia between 1992 and 1995, Clinton reluctantly agreed to air strikes against the Serbs, leading to the 1995 Dayton Accords, which brought an end to the war. But Serbian president Slobodan Milosevic continued to foment anti-Muslim and anti-Croat fervor. Soon the Serbs embarked on a murderous campaign to drive the Muslim ethnic Albanians out of Serbia's southern province of Kosovo. The United States was reluctant to intervene despite the brutality, but the situation reached such drastic proportions that Clinton finally decided to send troops to Kosovo in 1999. The action had the unintended effect of weakening the Serbian opposition against Milosevic as Serbs closed ranks against the foreign troops. Eventually, a tenuous peace was restored, and Milosevic was voted out of office in 2000. The following year, Serbian authorities arrested Milosevic and turned him over to the War Crimes Tribunal in The Hague, which had indicted Milosevic for crimes against humanity.

U.S. interventions around the world failed to quell ethnic tensions or eradicate poverty. Although some military actions achieved their immediate goals, the presence of the United States abroad also fueled anti-American sentiment. In some regions of the world, resentment against the United States found expression in violence and terrorism. In June 1996 a truck bomb killed 19 U.S. airmen in Dhahran, Saudi Arabia. Two years later, bombs exploded at two U.S. embassies in east Africa, killing 224 people in Nairobi, Kenya, and Dar es Salaam, Tanzania.

■ **MAP 29.3**

THE BREAKUP OF THE FORMER YUGOSLAVIA   Created in 1919 as a multiethnic nation, Yugoslavia split apart in 1991–1992. After Slovenia and Croatia gained their independence swiftly, Bosnia deteriorated into fierce ethnic fighting dominated by Serb atrocities and encouraged by the Serbian government of Slobodan Milosevic. A brief U.S. bombing campaign in 1995 finally brought the Serbs to peace negotiations. Similar ethnic fighting in the province of Kosovo in 1999 led to another U.S. bombing campaign and Kosovo's current quasi-independence under NATO guidance.

Four men were convicted of conspiracy in the terrorist attacks. They were identified as followers of Islamic militant Osama bin Laden, who was also indicted in connection with the embassy bombings. Bin Laden, originally from Saudi Arabia, was living in Afghanistan under the protection of the fundamentalist Taliban regime and remained a fugitive. He was known to be the leader of the al Qaeda terrorist network operating in several countries throughout the Middle East. On October 12, 2000, a small boat pulled up next to the destroyer USS *Cole* in Yemen's port of Aden. A bomb exploded and ripped a hole in the destroyer, killing 17 Americans and wounding 39 others. Two suicide bombers carried out the attack. U.S. officials believed that they, too, were associated with Osama bin Laden.

On February 26, 1993, a bomb exploded in the parking garage underneath the World Trade Center, the skyscrapers dominating the New York skyline in Lower Manhattan. Five people were killed and more than a thousand were injured. The *New York Times* reported that the explosion "destroyed a multistoried parking garage under the trade center, knocked out power to the center and touched off fires that sent smoke billowing up through its 110-story twin towers and forced 50,000 people into a nightmarish evacuation that took all day and half the night." President Clinton tried to quell the fears of the nation in the face of what appeared to be an act of international terrorism. "Working together, we'll find out who was involved and why this happened," the president declared. "Americans should know we'll do everything in our power to keep them safe in their streets, their offices and their homes." However, international terrorists proved difficult to identify and bring to justice. Eight years later the same twin towers were attacked again, with far more devastating consequences.

The Contested Election of 2000

The first presidential election of the new millennium was the most bitterly contested in more than a century. The Democratic candidate won the national popular vote, but with ballot counts incomplete in the key state of Florida, the Supreme Court ultimately declared the Republican candidate the victor. The election exposed defects in the election process, from faulty ballots and voting machines to the role of the media, and raised serious questions about the value of the Electoral College. The election also revealed that flaws in the system disfranchised large numbers of poor and minority voters. But in the end, the transfer of power took place smoothly, and the nation accepted the outcome.

The Campaign, the Vote, and the Courts

The 2000 campaign was fairly lackluster. The Democrats nominated Vice President Al Gore, who hoped to benefit from Clinton's high approval rating and the healthy economy. The Republicans nominated George W. Bush, governor of Texas and son of the former president. Bush chose as his running mate Dick Cheney, who had been the elder Bush's secretary of state. Gore chose Senator Joe Lieberman from Connecticut as his running mate, the first Jew to run on a presidential ticket. Gore's popularity peaked after the Democratic National Convention, where he delivered a rousing speech filled with populist themes and gave a passionate kiss to his wife, Tipper, which garnered more media attention than the speech itself. But he distanced himself from the popular master campaigner Clinton. Bush gained the upper hand during the televised debates, where he portrayed himself as a "compassionate conservative" and promised to restore "dignity to the White House." As the election neared, Gore's lead in the polls narrowed.

Only half of the nation's eligible voters turned out to vote. But African Americans went to the polls in unusually high numbers and voted overwhelmingly for Gore, largely out of loyalty to Clinton. Even before all the polls had closed, the national media began to report

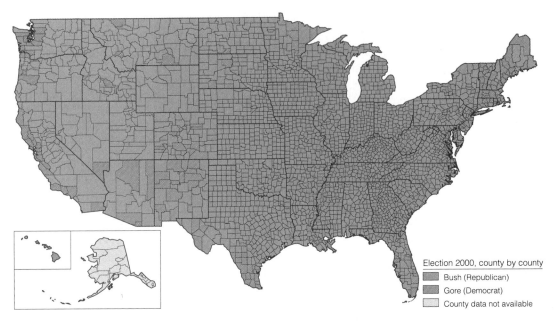

■ **MAP 29.4**

THE CONTESTED ELECTION OF 2000 The 2000 election was so close, and so fraught with problems, that it was ultimately decided by a 5–4 vote of the Supreme Court. As this map shows, Democratic votes were concentrated in the densely populated urban areas and Republican votes in the sparsely populated rural areas.

the results. Early in the evening, they declared that Florida, a key state with 25 electoral votes, had gone to Gore. But soon after that announcement, they changed their projection and put Florida back into the "undecided" group of states. As the hours dragged on, it became clear that whoever took Florida, where Bush's brother Jeb Bush was governor, would win the election. By the next day, Gore had won the national popular vote by half a million votes, but Bush was ahead in Florida. Bush's lead was so narrow that it triggered an automatic recount.

With all eyes on Florida, a number of serious irregularities surfaced. Voters in Palm Beach County were given a confusing "butterfly" ballot, resulting in more than 20,000 mismarked ballots. In other counties, registered voters were turned away at the polls because of inaccurate and incomplete voter registration lists. Some voter lists inaccurately listed eligible voters as felons. Most of these disfranchised voters were African American. In several largely minority counties, old voting machines that used a punched-ballot system failed to count thousands of ballots.

For weeks after the election, the outcome was still unknown. Democrats insisted that because Bush's lead had narrowed to a few hundred votes, tallied by inaccurate voting machines, ballots in four Florida counties should be recounted by hand. Republicans pointed out that it would be unfair to recount votes in only four heavily Democratic counties, especially with no standard way of determining voter intent on punch-card ballots with ambiguous marks on them. Florida's secretary of state, Katherine Harris, a Republican who headed Florida's campaign for George W. Bush, refused to extend the deadline to allow the recounts to take place and declared Bush the winner by 537 votes out of 6 million cast statewide.

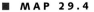

TABLE 29-3

The Election of 2000

Candidate	Political Party	Popular Vote	Electoral Vote
George W. Bush	Republican	50,456,167	271
Al Gore	Democratic	50,996,064	266*
Ralph Nader	Green	2,864,810	0

*One District of Columbia Gore elector abstained.

Gore contested the results, and the Florida Supreme Court ordered that the recount proceed. Bush then appealed to the U.S. Supreme Court to reverse the decision of the Florida Supreme Court. After 36 days of partial vote counting and court battles, the U.S. Supreme Court declared Bush the winner in a sharply divided 5–4 decision. The four dissenting judges issued a stinging rebuke of their five colleagues responsible for the decision. In his dissenting opinion, Justice Stephen Breyer wrote that the majority ruling "can only lend confidence to the most cynical appraisal of the work of judges throughout the land."

The Aftermath

After the election, reporters continued the hand-counting process in Florida in an effort to discover who would have won if all the votes had been counted. The results can never be absolutely conclusive, given the many irregularities in the process. What did become clear in the months after the election were the widespread flaws in the election system in Florida and elsewhere. Across the country outdated voting machines yielded inaccurate vote counts, and long lines at polling places prevented voters from casting ballots. Low-income and minority voters were more likely to be disfranchised because they lived in precincts with faulty voting machines or overcrowded polling places. The U.S. Civil Rights Commission estimated that in Florida black voters were nine times more likely than white voters to have had their votes rejected.

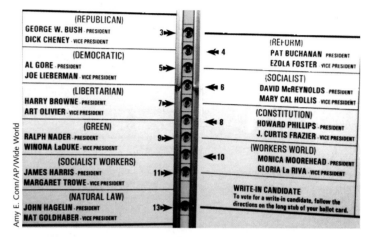

■ In Palm Beach, Florida, voters received this confusing "butterfly ballot." Thousands of voters in this predominantly Democratic county accidentally voted for Reform candidate Pat Buchanan instead of Democrat Al Gore. With only a few hundred votes separating Bush and Gore in Florida, it is quite possible that the butterfly ballot may have cost Gore the election.

In addition to those whose votes did not count, many others were prevented from voting altogether. In Florida, "suspected felons" were removed from voter registration lists without being informed and without the opportunity to demonstrate that they were law-abiding citizens eligible to vote. An estimated 15 percent of the list was inaccurate, and more than half of those voters were African American. According to the U.S. Civil Rights Commission, "Perhaps the most dramatic undercount in Florida's election was the nonexistent ballots of countless unknown eligible voters, who were turned away, or wrongfully purged from the voter registration rolls . . . and were prevented from exercising the franchise." As a result, hundreds of African American citizens with no criminal record arrived at the polls, only to discover that they had been disfranchised. An investigation by scholars of constitutional law concluded that the disfranchisement of African American voters in Florida constituted a violation of the 1965 Voting Rights Act. They determined that if those African American voters had been able to cast ballots, they would have provided more than the 537 votes Gore needed to win.

The election also renewed a national debate over the value of the Electoral College. Opponents argued that Gore was the rightful winner because he won a majority of the popular vote. Advocates claimed that the Electoral College protected the interests of less populous states and that Bush was fairly elected because he won the majority of states. Congress and state legislatures began discussions of various forms of electoral reform, but abolishing the Electoral College was not among them. Representatives of small states probably would block any such measures.

Policymakers and media moguls also debated the role of the media in reporting election returns. Some argued for a blackout on early returns until all polls across the country were closed to avoid the possibility that early results might influence voters who had not yet voted. Others proposed that only official results be announced to avoid the problem of erroneous reporting that occurred on election night 2000. But media representatives countered that a free press should be able to report the news as it happens, although they agreed on the need to ensure accuracy.

Voting

One of the most troubling revelations to surface in the wake of the 2000 election was the news that millions of citizens, in Florida and elsewhere, were thwarted in their effort to vote or to have their votes count. Studies conducted after the election showed that 4 to 6 million Americans were disfranchised as a result of faulty equipment, confusing ballots, erroneous voter registration lists, long lines at polling places, and problems with absentee ballots. Voters in low-income precincts with a large percentage of citizens of color were much more likely to have their votes discarded, or to be turned away at the polls, than voters in more affluent and whiter districts. These revelations sparked outrage among Americans who believe that voting is one of the fundamental rights of democratic citizenship. But the disfranchisement of potential voters has a long history in the United States, beginning with the founding of the nation.

The Constitution does not guarantee anyone the right to vote. After the American Revolution, the majority of Americans—including women, slaves, most free black men, propertyless white men, apprentices, indentured laborers, felons, and those considered mentally incompetent—were denied the right to vote. New Jersey was the only state to allow women the vote.

Debates over who should vote, and efforts both to expand and to restrict suffrage, continued for most of the nation's history. During the first half of the nineteenth century, Democrats viewed the vote as a right of all white men, whereas Whigs argued that voting was a privilege to be reserved for the elite. Although the United States was the first western nation to expand the electorate by lowering economic

The 2000 election exposed many problems in the voting process. This political cartoon suggests that the controversial Florida ballots and methods of counting them were only the final symptoms of an electoral system that was flawed at many levels.

barriers to voting, for a long time after that, the laws governing the right to vote actually limited rather than broadened access to the polls.

Between the Revolution and the Civil War, race and gender replaced property as the primary criteria for voting. Nearly every state disfranchised free blacks while dropping the property requirements for white men. States in the West tended toward more inclusive voting rolls. Several gave the vote to aliens who had established permanent residence and to Native Americans who had relinquished tribal citizenship. Some politicians were eager to expand suffrage to portray themselves as champions of the common people and win the votes of the newly enfranchised.

But several states restricted voting well into the twentieth century. Rhode Island required foreign-born citizens to meet a property requirement to vote, and California prevented Asians from voting. In 1921 New York adopted Eng-

lish literacy tests to prevent immigrants from voting, disfranchising hundreds of thousands of citizens as late as the 1960s. As a result of these restrictions, voter turnout began to decline in the late nineteenth century. This shrinking of the electorate was not accidental. In 1907 the voter registration board of Pittsburgh boasted that in only two years the Pennsylvania registration law had cut the number of registered voters in half. Women achieved the right to vote in 1920, but most women of color and many immigrant women remained disfranchised for decades.

African Americans officially gained the right to vote in 1870 with the ratification of the Fifteenth Amendment. But by 1900, almost all blacks as well as poor whites in the South had been disfranchised through poll taxes and literacy and property requirements. Not until passage of the 1965 Voting Rights Act were African Americans in the South able to vote. Suffrage expanded again in 1971 when the Twenty-Sixth Amendment lowered the voting age from 21 to 18. The Vietnam War revived claims made since the Revolution that citizens old enough to fight and die for their country were old enough to vote.

By the time of the 2000 election, universal suffrage was the law of the land. Although only half of all eligible voters went to the polls that year, the number of voters had increased tenfold since 1888. Still, questions remained about the fairness of the process, whether intentional or not. When the winner of the popular vote lost the election to a candidate without a clear victory in the Electoral College, critics of the system called for direct election of the president. In the end, however, it was neither the voters nor the Electoral College, but the justices of the U.S. Supreme Court, who elected the president by a vote of 5–4. ■

Legacies of Election 2000

In addition to the unprecedented Supreme Court decision, the 2000 election was remarkable in other ways. For the first time, a First Lady was elected to public office: Hillary Rodham Clinton became a Democratic senator from New York. In another Senate race, a deceased candidate was elected. Mel Carnahan, Democratic governor of Missouri, had run against Republican incumbent John Ashcroft. But Carnahan died in a plane crash a few weeks before the election, too late to have his name removed from the ballot. The acting governor pledged to appoint Carnahan's widow if he won the election, and she picked up the campaign. Carnahan was elected and his widow went to the Senate. (The defeated candidate, John Ashcroft, became George W. Bush's attorney general.)

Third-party politics also influenced the outcome of the election. Several third-party candidates had achieved national visibility during the 1990s and won elections at the state and local levels, including professional wrestler Jesse Ventura, elected governor of Minnesota in 1998 on the Reform party ticket. In 2000 Ralph Nader wreaked havoc for the Democrats with his Green party candidacy for president. Although Nader gained fewer than 3 percent of the votes, his candidacy drew off some of the left-leaning elements of the Democratic party—enough votes to cost Al Gore the election.

The election results left the Congress almost evenly divided, with a thin Republican majority in the House and a 50–50 split in the Senate. But within a year, Senator James M. Jeffords from Vermont bolted the Republican party and became an Independent, giving the Democrats a majority in the Senate. The closely divided Congress began to take up issues raised by the contested election, including various measures to improve the voting process, and campaign finance reform.

President George W. Bush immediately began to reverse several Clinton-era policies, including a number of environmental protections. His first major legislative success was the passage of a major tax cut. During his first year in office, the economy went from boom to bust and headed into a recession. The robust stock market of the 1990s wilted in early 2001. Nevertheless, as the new millennium dawned, the United States remained the wealthiest and most powerful nation in the world. Bush retreated from international treaties on issues ranging from global warming to nuclear test ban agreements, and revived the Reagan-era proposal for a nuclear missile shield. But the place of the nation in the global community was yet to be defined. Soon, monumental events shattered the nation's sense of security and forced Bush to abandon his retreat from international alliances and to engage in the world in unprecedented ways.

Conclusion

In the 1990s the role of the nation in the world shifted and a half-century of political certainties evaporated. The end of the Cold War meant that the United States had to develop a new international mission. The struggle against the Soviet Union and the communist foe had come to an end. Russia was our friend; China was our trading partner. Conflicts around the globe, many of them grounded in ancient ethnic hostilities, posed challenges for the world's most powerful nation. The United States had new international concerns, including desires for markets and trade, the nation's supply of oil, the need for political order to maintain international stability, and the danger of "rogue nations" developing nuclear arms. President Clinton tried to be a peacemaker in hot spots around the world while attempting to respond to violent episodes of international terrorism.

At home, Americans demonstrated increasing tolerance for people who looked and acted differently from themselves. Polls showed declining levels of racial, ethnic, and religious hostility and greater acceptance of homosexuality, single parenthood, and family arrangements that deviated from the nuclear family model. But episodes of racial discrimination—by police, courts, and voting officials—continued. Politics remained an arena in which culture wars flared over abortion, gun control, and welfare reform. A Democratic president faced impeachment by his Republican foes in Congress while maintaining high approval ratings from the public.

At the dawn of the new century, several crises challenged Americans' sense of security. A deeply flawed presidential election revealed profound problems in the nation's voting system. A sharp and sudden downturn in the economy shattered the optimism many middle-class people felt during the booming Clinton years and forced many of the working poor into desperate circumstances. Already reeling from these disturbing developments, the nation was soon shaken to its core by a terrorist attack that forced a new reckoning at home and abroad.

Sites to Visit

William Jefferson Clinton
www.ipl.org/ref/POTUS/wjclinton.html

This site contains basic information about Clinton's election and presidency and an online biography.

Distribution of Wealth and Income
www.inequality.org/factsfr.html

This site provides facts and figures about the distribution of wealth and income in the 1990s.

American Identities
xroads.virginia.edu/~YP/ethnic.html

This site of the American Studies program at the University of Virginia includes information and resources for studying America's multiple ethnic identities.

The O.J. Simpson Trial
www.cnn.com/US/OJ/index.html

This CNN site provides basic facts and interpretive essays, plus additional links about the O. J. Simpson trial.

Investigating the President: The Trial
www.cnn.com/ALLPOLITICS/resources/1998/lewinsky/

This CNN site provides information and documents about the scandals surrounding President Clinton's impeachment.

Focus on Kosovo
www.cnn.com/SPECIALS/1998/10/kosovo/

This in-depth CNN interactive site looks at the development and current resolution to the turmoil in Kosovo.

Oklahoma City Bombing
www.cnn.com/US/9703/okc.trial/

This CNN interactive site has information about the domestic terrorist bombing in Oklahoma City and the trial that followed.

Why Do Campaign Polls Zigzag So Much?
www.psych.purdue.edu/%7Ecodelab/Invalid.Polls.html

This site, created by Gerald S. Wasserman of the Psychological Sciences Department at Purdue University, examines polling data from the 1996 presidential campaign.

For Further Reading

General

Stephanie Coontz, *The Way We Really Are: Coming to Terms with America's Changing Families* (1997).

Thomas L. Friedman, *The Lexus and the Olive Tree: Understanding Globalization* (2000).

Clara E. Rodriguez, *Changing Race: Latinos, the Census and the History of Ethnicity in the United States* (2000).

Leland T. Saito and Roger Daniels, *Race and Politics: Asian Americans, Latinos, and Whites in a Los Angeles Suburb* (1998).

The Economy: Global and Domestic

Sheldon Danziger and Peter Gottschalk, *America Unequal* (1995).

Julia Butterfly Hill, *The Legacy of Luna: The Story of a Tree, A Woman, and the Struggle to Save the Redwoods* (2000).

Jacqueline Jones, *American Work: Four Centuries of Black and White Labor* (1998).

William A. Orme, *Understanding NAFTA: Mexico, Free Trade, and the New North America* (1996).

Tolerance and Its Limits

Jeffrey Abramson, ed., *Postmortem: The O. J. Simpson Case: Justice Confronts Race, Domestic Violence, Lawyers, Money, and the Media* (1996).

Robin D. G. Kelley, *Yo' Mama's Disfunktional!: Fighting the Culture Wars in Urban America* (1998).

Jane Mayer and Jill Abramson, *Strange Justice: The Selling of Clarence Thomas* (1994).

Michael Omi and Howard Winant, *Racial Formation in the United States: From the 1960s to the 1990s* (1994).

Alan Wolfe, *One Nation, After All: What Americans Really Think About God, Country, Family, Racism, Welfare, Immigration, Homosexuality, Work, the Right, the Left and Each Other* (1998).

Violence and Danger

Joan Jacobs Brumberg, *The Body Project: An Intimate History of American Girls* (2000).

Joan Jacobs Brumberg, *Fasting Girls: The History of Anorexia Nervosa* (2000).

Susan Faludi, *Stiffed: The Betrayal of the American Man* (1999).

Peter D. Kramer, *Listening to Prozac* (1997).

Rickie Solinger, ed., *Abortion Wars: A Half Century of Struggle, 1950–2000* (1998).

Judith Stacey, *In the Name of the Family: Rethinking Family Values in the Postmodern Age* (1996).

Steven Wisotsky and Thomas Szasz, *Beyond the War on Drugs: Overcoming a Failed Public Policy* (1999).

The Clinton Presidency

William C. Berman, *From the Center to the Edge: The Politics and Policies of the Clinton Presidency* (2001).

James MacGregor Burns and Georgia J. Sorenson, *Dead Center: Clinton–Gore Leadership and the Perils of Moderation* (1999).

Steven E. Schier, ed., *The Postmodern Presidency: Bill Clinton's Legacy in U.S. Politics* (2000).

The Nation and the World

John Dumbrell and David M. Barrett, *The Making of U.S. Foreign Policy* (1998).

Thomas H. Henriksen, *Clinton's Foreign Policy in Somalia, Bosnia, Haiti, and North Korea* (1996).

Richard A. Melanson, *American Foreign Policy Since the Vietnam War: The Search for Consensus from Nixon to Clinton* (2001).

The Contested Election of 2000

Alan M. Dershowitz, *Supreme Injustice: How the High Court Hijacked Election 2000* (2001).

E. J. Dionne and William Kristol, eds., *Bush v. Gore: The Court Cases and the Commentary* (2001).

Samuel Issacharoff, Pamela Karlan, and Richard H. Pildes, *When Elections Go Bad: The Law of Democracy and the Presidential Election of 2000* (2001).

Alexander Keyssar, *The Right to Vote: The Contested History of Democracy in the United States* (2000).

Charles Lewis, *The Buying of the President 2000* (2001).

Richard A. Posner, *Breaking the Deadlock: The 2000 Election, the Constitution, and the Courts* (2001).

Bill Sammon, *At Any Cost: How Al Gore Tried to Steal the Election* (2001).

Jeffrey Toobin, *Too Close to Call: The Thirty-Six-Day Battle to Decide the 2000 Election* (2001).

Online Practice Test

Test your understanding of this chapter with interactive review quizzes at

www.ablongman.com/jonescreatedequal/chapter29

CHAPTER

30

A Global Nation for the New Millennium

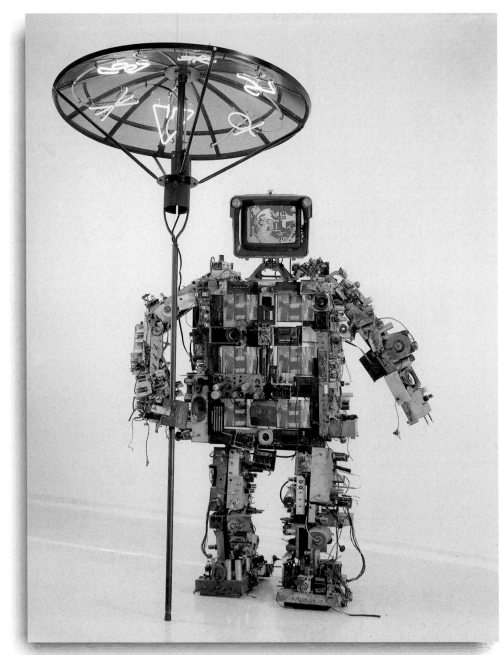

Nam June Paik, *Global Encoder*, 1994. Courtesy of Nam June Paik and Carl Solway Gallery, Cincinnati, Ohio. Photo by Tom Allison and Chris Gomien

■ At the beginning of the new millennium, computer technology and the Internet linked Americans closely to each other and to events around the globe. Electronic circuitry enabled information to flow at a pace unimaginable to previous generations.

"THOSE MEXICAN GUYS WORK, THEY REALLY WORK," THE FORMER OWNER OF A carpet-cleaning business in Las Vegas observed in a sentiment widely shared among employers in southern Nevada's booming desert city. Mostly young Latinos, along with a smattering of whites and blacks, workers lined up on D Street in North Las Vegas every morning waiting for employers to drive up. "Drive past the white guys; they're all derelicts," explained a young white tree-cutter just out of drug rehabilitation and looking for help at the day labor market. He bluntly stereotyped native-born workers of any color in comparison to immigrants. "Drive past the black guys, too. Get the Mexicans. They work." For $8 an hour, he hired a man to work with him trimming palm trees, hard, nasty work made tougher by desert temperatures of more than 100 degrees. At the end of the day, $64 changed hands, and the Latino went his own way, leaving the tree-cutter satisfied. In Las Vegas and across the country, immigrant labor is prized: undocumented immigrants work hard for low wages and cause few problems for those who hire them.

Latinos were not always easily distinguished from other workers in southern Nevada. In 1991, the Frontier Hotel and Casino on the famous Las Vegas Strip slashed employees' wages and benefits, prompting hundreds of unionized workers to walk out and begin the longest strike of the decade in the United States. For more than six years, union members of different races and ethnicities walked the picket line together outside the Frontier. Twelve of them even walked the 300 miles across the Mojave Desert to Los Angeles to promote public awareness of their cause. Gloria Hernandez was a Mexican-born mother of two, a restaurant hostess, and a union activist who stayed out on strike until the Frontier was sold in 1998, and the new owner reinstated wages and benefits similar to those at the other large casinos. In the final year of the strike, Hernandez qualified for naturalization and became an American citizen, just in time to return to her old job.

This was an old story in America, of determined newcomers often making great sacrifices to create a life of better opportunities and greater freedoms for themselves and their families. But like most old stories, it was

Vast power plants allow Las Vegas to glitter at night.

also more complicated than it first appeared. Latino or Hispanic Americans did not form a single, coherent community, despite the prominence of people of Mexican extraction. Their roots ranged from the southern tip of Chile in South America to the Rio Grande, from the Caribbean islands to the Pacific coast. They were not all in the working class: the first Spanish-speaking people drawn to modern Las Vegas for its economic opportunities were middle-class Cuban refugees from Fidel Castro's 1959 revolution, which eliminated Havana's gambling palaces and put skilled casino operators out of work. Nor were they all immigrants. The area that is now southern Nevada was part of Mexico for more than two centuries after the Pilgrims sailed into Massachusetts Bay in 1620, and many of its current

Latino residents were born in the United States. Latinos represented a large part of the future of Las Vegas, where their numbers more than doubled in the 1990s to constitute 18 percent of the population, and they made up the fastest-growing ethnic group in the United States. Las Vegas was on track to join Miami and Los Angeles as major American cities where Spanish was spoken as commonly as English.

For most of the twentieth century, Nevada seemed to outsiders a distant desert state where the rules that governed most American lives could be bent. Prostitution was legal, as was gambling— "gaming," as industry spokespeople called it—and divorce could be easily obtained. A reputation as a mecca for pleasure tourism drew visitors to Las Vegas, especially with the advent of jet airline service in the 1960s and an expansion of the city's McCarran Airport. With its population more than quadrupling since 1970, the fastest-growing metropolitan area in the nation had one and a half million residents in 2000. Even as the city drew migrants to it, its values seemed to spread outward: a nation that had long condemned gambling as a vice now embraced the gaming business as a partial replacement for declining industrial employment. By 2000, most states had lotteries or some other form of legalized betting, and casinos spread from Atlantic City, New Jersey, to riverboats on the Mississippi River and Indian reservations across the country. The early nickname for Las Vegas—"Sin City"—no longer fit a place that had become a model of the new service economy and the American demographic shift to the Sunbelt of the West and South.

Las Vegas resident and historian Hal Rothman has called his city "the last Detroit." Like the famous hub of the auto industry for earlier generations, Las Vegas offered unskilled but industrious workers an opportunity for real upward mobility. Inexpensive housing and a low cost of living were important, and a mostly unionized work force provided the linchpin, just as it had in Detroit's auto plants. The organized housekeepers and other service employees in the city's vast hotels and casinos, whose large Culinary Workers Union was led in 2000 by an African American woman, Hattie Canty, earned decent wages and crucial benefits, such as health insurance and pension plans that could pull them into the middle class. The traditional American dream of improving one's socioeconomic status through sheer hard work was a more viable option here than in most places in the United States, after three decades of declining real wages for those without a college education and two generations of shrinking union membership.

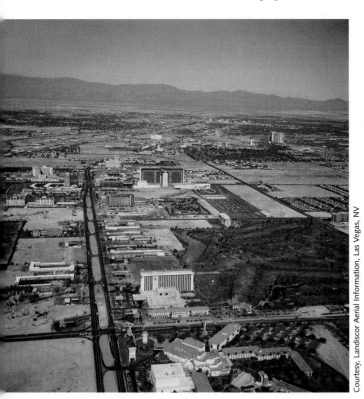

■ Aerial view of Las Vegas, c. 1970.

Courtesy, Landiscor Aerial Information, Las Vegas, NV

These economic dreams and successes were built on a slim and imperiled natural resource base, however. Unplanned and largely unregulated urban sprawl spread like an environmental cancer across Las Vegas and surrounding Clark County as roads, housing developments, and shopping malls swallowed thousands of acres of fragile desert landscape, bringing congestion, smog, and other pollutants to a harsh but once pristine climate. Like its spectacular casinos built to resemble New York City or the Egyptian pyramids, Las Vegas was in many ways an artificial city. Everything was imported from elsewhere: people, food, capital, grass, and especially water. Annual rainfall was less than 5 inches, yet vast fountains and swimming pools graced the grounds of the large casinos. Limited in the share of water it could divert from the nearby Colorado River, the city pumped groundwater to quench its growing thirst—the same process that was drying up underground aquifers across much of the arid West. "There is no lack of water here," essayist Edward Abbey warned about the parched Great Basin country of Nevada and Utah, "unless you try to establish a city where no city should be."

In southern Nevada, the four primary themes of this story of the American past come into focus in the present. It remains a story about the distribution of wealth and power, the identities Americans construct for themselves in a multicultural society, the international ties that help shape American life, and the natural environment in which the United States builds its future.

The American Place in a Global Economy

Mollie Brown grew up in the small Virginia town of Cartersville, 45 miles west of Richmond. In 1950, at age 19, she moved to Paterson, New Jersey, joining the broad river of black Southerners who sought better economic opportunities and greater personal freedom in the North. There she married Sam James, another migrant from Virginia who worked at a foundry in Paterson, and together they raised four children. An employed mother like most African American women, Mollie James took a job in 1955 with the Universal Manufacturing Company in Paterson with wages and decent treatment unlike what had been available to her in Virginia. She stayed with Universal for 34 years, becoming its first female union steward and one of its first black union stewards. With union-negotiated wages, overtime work, and company-paid health insurance, she helped pull her family into the middle-class world of owning their own home and car and saving for retirement. But the peace of mind that came from a secure job vanished in 1989 when Universal closed the Paterson plant and moved its manufacturing operations to Matamoros, Mexico, just across the Rio Grande River from Brownsville, Texas.

James's job did not disappear. It moved and was inherited by 20-year-old Balbina Duque Granados. She, too, had grown up in a small town located in an agricultural area, in the Mexican province of San Luis Potosí, and she, too, had moved 400 miles north to find better-paying work in a booming manufacturing city. She was thrilled to land the difficult, repetitive job—her "answered prayer"—at a *maquiladora*, one of the foreign-owned assembly plants along Mexico's border with the United States that wed First World engineering with Third World working conditions. Her employer was also satisfied, paying her $.65/hour to do what James had been paid $7.91/hour for. But Granados's job was no more secure than James's had been. The beginnings of successful worker organizing in Matamoros encouraged the company to shift many of its operations 60 miles upriver to Reynosa, where the union movement was weaker. A journalist asked whether she would move there if her job did. "And what if they were to move again?" she replied. "Maybe to Juarez or Tijuana? What then? Do I have to chase my job all over the world?"

The Logic and Technology of Globalization

Like many other workers in the United States and abroad, Mollie James and Balbina Duque Granados learned first-hand the relentlessly international logic of the economic system known as capitalism. Those who had capital—extra money—invested it in corporations, whose purpose

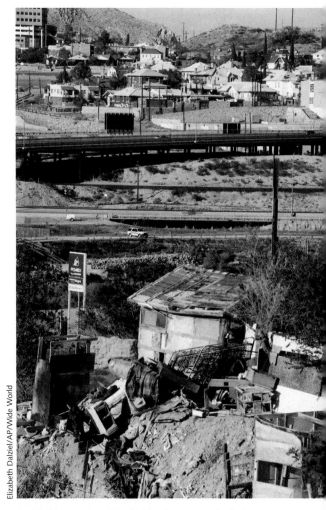

Elizabeth Dalziel/AP/Wide World

■ The U.S.–Mexico border divides a great deal of wealth from stark poverty. Here a shack in Ciudad Juarez contrasts with El Paso in the background. But the border region from Texas to California is also a vibrant economy where the languages and cultures of the two countries mix in fascinating ways.

The Internet and the World Wide Web

For students entering college after the mid-1990s, the Internet and the World Wide Web were an integral part of daily life. Electronic mail (e-mail) made communicating with friends and relatives easy and nearly instantaneous, whether they were on the same college campus or on the other side of the world. The Web transformed the availability of information about nearly all subjects. The foremost symbol of the process of globalization, it linked people everywhere who had access to computers, reducing the importance of a person's geographic location.

The Web had limitations: Internet access remained disproportionately available to people with higher incomes, and there were no controls on the accuracy or usefulness of the information it carried. Risks accompanied the Web as well, including the dissemination of pornography to children, the emergence of sexual predators via e-mail, and the rise in the theft of personal information. But the Web did connect students and other researchers to vast resources for knowledge that seemed destined to grow indefinitely. For a society and an economy increasingly centered on the management of information, the establishment of the Internet and the Web appeared to mark the beginning of a new era.

Yet the Internet and the Web were only the most recent in a long line of developments in telecommunications linking distant parts of the globe more closely together. In the 1830s, the telegraph first enabled instantaneous communication on the same continent. The first undersea cable laid across the floor of the Atlantic Ocean in 1866 enabled Americans to get news directly from Europe. Ten years later, Alexander Graham Bell added the human voice to the technology of the telegraph by creating the telephone. In 1895, Italian inventor Guglielmo Marconi freed long-distance communications from the earthly constraints of copper wires by sending the first radio ("wireless") transmission; in 1901, he established the first radio link from North America to Europe. By 1940 the ability to transmit images enabled television broadcasts in the United States and England, and in the 1950s TV became widely popular and available.

The ENIAC computer, built at the University of Pennsylvania in 1945, and its successors were vast machines that filled entire rooms. Altair offered the first microcomputer, or personal computer (PC), as a kit in 1975. Apple followed with the fully assembled Apple I in 1977 and the Macintosh in 1984, the latter initiating the use of a mouse to point and click at items on a screen. The entry of powerful International Business Machines (IBM) into the PC market in 1981 marked the movement of computers into the mainstream of American society.

The search by the U.S. Department of Defense for a communication net-

was to produce a profit for their shareholders. A corporation's profitability depended on keeping costs—labor and materials—down and expanding into new markets. Those markets were not limited by nationality; a manufacturer tried to sell not just to Americans but to customers wherever they might be found. The technological innovations facilitating the integration of the U.S. economy into the world economy in the late 1900s were not so much a new force as an acceleration of an older trend. Just as the telegraph and telephone had helped create a nation unified by rapid communication, the spread of personal computers and the Internet linked Americans even more closely to other nations. In the 1920s, the head of General Electric, Owen Young, spoke of his ambition to "obliterate the eastern, western, northern and southern boundaries of the United States," for "the sphere of our activities is the world." Capitalists were rarely nationalists but rather internationalists.

At the close of the twentieth century, engineering breakthroughs sped up the process of globalization. Bill Gates of Seattle became the world's wealthiest person in the 1990s, with assets at one point worth $100 billion as the company he headed, Microsoft, provided the software for operating most personal computers. At just 34 years old, Michael Dell of Austin leapt to fifth place on the list of wealthiest Americans in 1999 by selling computers through a mail-order business, Dell Computers. The integration of computers into every aspect of commerce and private life increased the efficiency with which businesses could operate. Retailers, for example, could monitor their inventory much more closely and eliminate unnecessary expenses. The dependence of the entire infrastructure of modern American life on computers generated fears

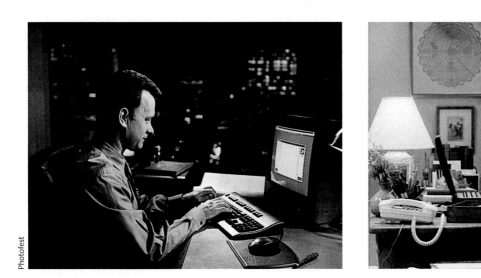

The popular 1998 film *You've Got Mail* starred Tom Hanks and Meg Ryan as bitter New York business rivals by day who unknowingly fall in love through an anonymous computer chat room. Since the mid-1990s, e-mail provided a quick and convenient form of communication that fell somewhere between a telephone call and a traditional letter. Many American workers found that the efficiency of e-mail was somewhat offset by the need to spend more time reading and sending it.

work invulnerable to nuclear attack led to the creation of ARPANET in 1969, a forerunner of the Internet, which began to function in 1983. These systems transmitted only text—words—between computers that were connected to each other by telephone links. In 1990, software researchers created the World Wide Web, which used the Internet to send graphic and multimedia information as well as text. Audio and visual capacity now joined words on the growing web of connected networks. In 1993, the White House joined the rush of users establishing sites on the Web, and by 1995, public access to the World Wide Web was widely available in the United States. ■

that aging software might be unable to handle the "Y2K" (year 2000) problem of changing more than two digits from 1999 to 2000, but the first hours of the new year came and went without incident. Computers boosted American productivity (the amount of work performed by a person in a given time period), which had declined between 1973 and 1996, and the U.S. economy enjoyed its longest-ever expansion during the presidency of Bill Clinton. Americans were plugged in: since the 1980s the spread of cable television and videocassette recorders (VCRs) provided constant entertainment, and Cable News Network (CNN) offered a standardized package of world news available 24 hours a day around the globe. Atlanta-based CNN was so international in its aims that its founder, Ted Turner, banned the word *foreign* from its broadcasts.

Americans were also speeding up their daily routines as the new millennium approached. The desire for immediate gratification and efficiency that had nurtured fast food and microwave ovens encouraged the spread of cell phones, beepers, fax machines, overnight package delivery, and constant news headlines scrolling across TV screens. Computers processed more information faster on ever-smaller silicon chips. Cell phones proliferated among businesspeople, students, and drivers. As prices dropped, they even reached into poorer areas, such as the vast Navajo nation on the Arizona–New Mexico border, where traditional phones were scarce. International air travel for business and pleasure quadrupled between 1980 and 1998, and international tourism vied with oil as the world's largest industry. The spread of the Internet and the use of electronic mail (e-mail) after the early 1990s best represented the shift toward

"On the Internet, nobody knows you're a dog."

■ **The Internet provided both immediate connections with other people around the world and the safety of personal anonymity. Internet users could not be judged by their appearance or material possessions, only by the words they typed. Americans debated whether the popularity of the Internet represented a new kind of virtual community that would strengthen their connections to each other or merely another way for citizens to remain isolated in their own homes rather than engaged with each other in civic organizations.**

instant global communication. Though still in its infancy, the Internet was already shaping patterns of personal and commercial interactions, even as access to the Internet remained disproportionately available to those with greater wealth and education. Just as the Berlin Wall had long symbolized the divided world of the Cold War, the Internet became the emblem of the post–Cold War era of an increasingly unified global economy.

Free Trade and the Global Assembly Line

The ideology of free trade underpinned the tighter meshing of Americans' lives with the world economy. Free trade meant the reduction of tariffs, or taxes on imported and exported goods. Nations that supported free trade had industries that were eager to expand and were strong enough to compete successfully in a global market; nations with less competitive industries used tariffs to protect those industries from less expensive and higher-quality imports. As a new nation in the late 1700s and 1800s, the United States had enacted high tariffs to protect its domestic producers, but England, the world's leading economic power at the time, had sought to reduce tariffs and increase trade with America. When the United States emerged after World War II as the new leading economic nation and U.S. manufacturers and farmers looked increasingly to foreign markets, U.S. tariff rates plummeted. From averages of 30–50 percent before 1945, they dropped to 5 percent by 1990. The minimal tariffs associated with most-favored-nation status became standard for almost all U.S. trading partners. In 1965, the sum of all exports and imports amounted to 10 percent of the U.S. gross national product (GNP); by 1990, it had surpassed 25 percent and continued to climb.

Advocates of free trade argued that global markets unhindered by national tariffs benefited consumers everywhere by giving them access to the best goods at the lowest prices. America's NAFTA treaty with Canada and Mexico reflected this belief (see Chapter 29), as did the European Union with its newly unified currency, the Euro. In the United States, by the start of the new millennium most leaders of both major political parties, corporate executives, bankers, and most other elites supported free trade. But others objected to this internationalist economic ideology. Post-1945 British leaders, sensitive to their country's decline relative to American power, called the U.S. promotion of free trade "freedom of American trade" to emphasize that greater international exchanges of goods disproportionately benefit the more powerful of the trading partners. Larger, more efficient manufacturers could undersell smaller, more labor-intensive local producers. By 2000, environmentalists and labor unions led the forces opposing unregulated globalization of the U.S. economy. Environmentalists warned of the pollution costs to the world's environment of U.S. factories relocating to poorer and less regulated nations, such as Mexico and China. Labor organizers decried the flight of American jobs as manufacturers sought less expensive and more compliant—often desperate—workers abroad. Human rights activists spotlighted the grim working conditions in many overseas plants, including the prevalence of child labor. In 1999, in Seattle, and in 2001, in Genoa, Italy, thousands of antiglobalization protesters disrupted meetings of the World Trade Organization and the leaders of the largest industrialized nations.

A "race to the bottom" for labor and environmental standards resulted from the development of a global assembly line. With capital able to move swiftly around the world and take its factories with it, nations and localities felt that they had little choice but to compete in offering multinational corporations the most advantageous terms possible. Such terms meant minimal government regulation, little protection for workers, nonexistent pollution standards, and even local subsidies in place of corporate taxes. Just as in the 1890s, industries had formed national trusts to evade state regulations on commerce, a century later, multinational corporations escaped the reach of national governments. This trend also represented an extension of the same logic that created the American Sunbelt over the previous half-century: businesses from the Northeast and Midwest relocating to states (that happened to be warmer) with lower wage rates, fewer unions, weaker environmental standards, and minimal taxes. Corporate income taxes, which had been dropping since the 1950s, shrank by another third between 1986 and 2000. The *maquiladoras* on the Mexican border were part of a broader pattern of the corporate search for efficiency and profit, as companies, like Mollie James's Universal Manufacturing Company and RCA, took their production lines first to the American South and then abroad.

As a result, corporations and their products became less identifiable by nationality. Boeing Aircraft had long been the largest employer in the Seattle area, but was its new Boeing 777, manufactured piece by piece in 12 different countries, an "American" airplane? Japanese companies also moved many manufacturing plants overseas, including to the United States, to be closer to important markets. Was a Toyota made by American workers in Georgetown, Kentucky, a "foreign" car? A worker sewing the "American" company label on a trendy piece of clothing might be in Malaysia or Taiwan. Or she might be a Mexican American working in a southern California garment factory—and have a sister across the border in Mexico sewing for the same company at still lower wages. In an age of globalization and international commerce, insistence on purity of product lineage—"Buy American" campaigns—seemed to make little more sense than discredited notions of "racial purity."

> *Was a Toyota made by American workers in Georgetown, Kentucky, a "foreign" car?*

Who Benefits from Globalization?

The increasing globalization of the U.S. economy at the end of the twentieth century created enormous wealth while sharpening class inequalities. The stock market skyrocketed. The Dow Jones average of the value of 30 top companies' stocks rose steadily from 500 in 1956, to 1000 in 1972, and to 3000 in 1991. Then it more than tripled in value in just eight years, surpassing 10,000 in 1999. Wealthy Americans who owned the bulk of corporate stock reaped the most gain, but middle- and even working-class Americans with retirement funds invested in the market also benefited handsomely. However, the process of globalization and the steady expansion of the U.S. economy after 1992 also encouraged a growing belief among Americans, especially affluent ones, that markets alone offered the best solution to social problems. For example, more Americans believed that welfare recipients should be forced to find work in the job market to regain independence and pride. Only the unfettered laws of supply and demand could sustain prosperity, many believed, and government regulation—already gravely weakened by capital's ability to move across national borders—should be kept to a bare minimum. But markets and their strict dependence on the profit motive proved unable to preserve the quality of the environment, to pull the 36 million officially poor Americans above the poverty line ($17,000 for a family of four in 1999), or to preserve the security of the vast middle class that had stabilized American politics since World War II. Inequalities within the United States reflected growing global inequality as 20 percent of the world's people (mostly in Europe and North America) consumed 86 percent of its goods and services. The $8 billion Americans spent annually on cosmetics, for example, could instead provide running water and sanitation for almost all of the 2 billion people worldwide who lack these basic amenities.

■ **MAP 30.1**
TOP TEN U.S. TRADING PARTNERS (RANKED, WITH TOTAL VALUE OF IMPORTS AND EXPORTS COMBINED FOR JANUARY–FEBRUARY 2001) Americans do the most business with Canada and Mexico, followed by east Asia and then western Europe. U.S. economic vitality has always depended to some extent on foreign trade, but that dependence grew steadily in the past generation.

American consumers enjoyed many of the fruits of the more integrated world economy. At least in industries not dominated by monopolies, the corporate quest for lower production costs, along with fierce international competition and technological innovation, reduced prices of many goods and services. Computers, airline travel, and gasoline were all significantly less expensive in real dollars (adjusted for inflation) than they had been a generation earlier. Competition abounded in the robust retail sector of the U.S. economy, including catalog and Internet shopping. Wal-Mart represented the epitome of how the globalized economy could benefit consumers. By 2000, the discount store that Sam Walton had opened in Arkansas in 1962 surpassed General Motors as the largest American company, responsible for 6 percent of all U.S. retail sales. It sold 20,000 pairs of shoes an hour. Wal-Mart's success resulted from relentlessly cutting costs through sharp management, using cheaper imported goods and employing a nonunion workforce, and passing its savings along to customers in the form of lower prices. In towns across the United States, Wal-Mart put smaller local competitors out of business, and its efficiency became the standard to which other retailers aspired.

The benefits that the working-class majority of Americans experienced as consumers in the global economy were offset by their declining status as workers. As manufacturers moved to the Sunbelt and then overseas, high-wage, unionized jobs providing health insurance and pension benefits disappeared. Average real wages declined steadily after 1973, and union membership slid from one-third of the workforce in the early 1950s to one-tenth in 2000. Family incomes were maintained only by the addition of second and third wage earners, especially women. Americans spent more than they earned. The average household had 11 credit cards and carried $7000 in debt on them, in addition to owing car and home mortgage payments. In a nation of debtors, more than 1 million citizens filed for bankruptcy each year. A growing divide separated the experiences of well-educated Americans, who were able to seize

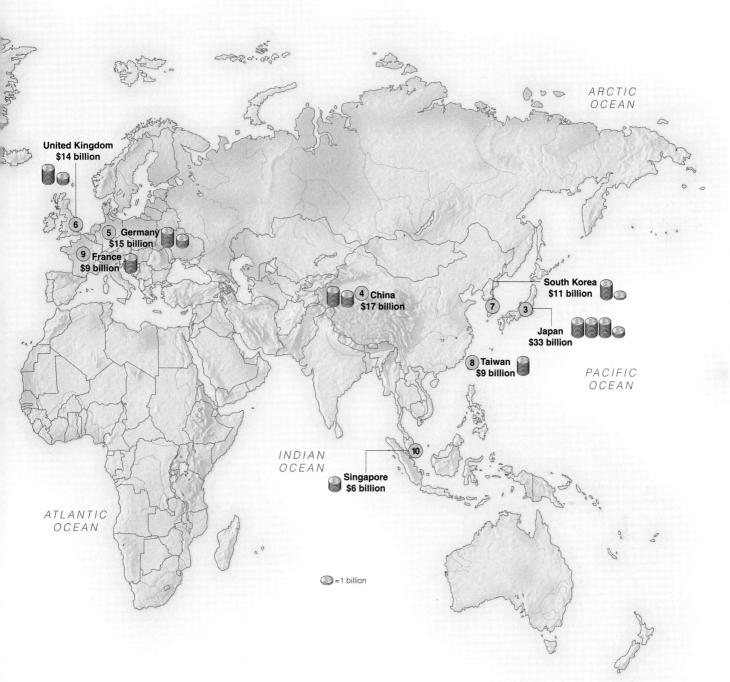

opportunities in the new economy involving high technology and information management, and their fellow citizens with at most a high school education.

Already wider in the United States than in any other industrialized nation, the distance between rich and poor continued to grow, whittling away at Americans' self-image as a middle-class society. The share of the national income going to the richest 1 percent nearly doubled in the last quarter of the twentieth century, while the share going to the bottom 80 percent shrank. Three million Americans lived in gated communities in extremely affluent suburbs, but one of five American children grew up in poverty and 21 million citizens sought emergency food assistance each year. One of the nation's leading newspapers unknowingly captured this disparity with two articles a few pages apart, headlined "As Closets Bulge, Americans' Taste in Gifts Often Turns Toward the Taste Buds" and "Food Drives Find Cupboard Is Nearly Bare."

The political system, which helps determine how wealth and opportunity are distributed in a society, seemed to offer little respite from the widening gap between haves and

"Meritocracy worked for my grandfather, it worked for my father, and it's working for me."

■ An important tension in American history was the conflict between the ideal of equal opportunity for all and the reality of inherited wealth and privilege. The efforts of the George W. Bush administration to eliminate the federal estate tax, which affected the inheritances of less than 1 percent of U.S. citizens, represented the latest round in the debate about the relationship between political democracy and inherited economic inequality. In a pure meritocracy, all citizens would be rewarded for their personal achievements rather than those of their parents or ancestors.

have-nots. The fraction of eligible citizens who make the effort to vote in presidential elections declined to just half in 2000 and in off-year congressional elections to a mere third, with the likelihood of voting closely correlated to a person's affluence. The hardships of daily survival deterred some potential voters, especially among the poor. The fierce partisanship, personal attacks, and culture of scandal that came to dominate American politics in the past two decades alienated others. Some saw little difference between the two major parties during the Clinton presidency, as many Democrats moved closer to Republicans on such issues as welfare, crime, and the budget.

Many citizens were also disillusioned by the blatant manner in which money came to dominate the political process. In the 1990s, President Bill Clinton regularly invited large contributors to the Democratic party to spend a night in the Lincoln Bedroom of the White House. Able to raise millions of dollars, George W. Bush declined federal funding for his 2000 presidential campaign to avoid the spending limits that accompanied such aid. With the average cost of a successful Senate campaign at $5 million and a House campaign approaching $1 million, few but the wealthy could campaign for Congress, and elected members spent inordinate amounts of time raising money from wealthy donors. Democratic Senator Richard Durbin of Illinois admitted that the system of fund-raising is corrupting: "It forces you into compromising yourself." Republican Senator John McCain of Arizona called campaign financing "an elaborate influence-peddling scheme in which both parties conspire to stay in office by selling the country to the highest bidder." For average Americans, exclusive fundraising dinners that sometimes reaped more than $30 million signaled a kind of political access they could not hope to match. The ability of business to outspend labor 15 to 1 in contributing to campaigns helped ensure minimal publicity to any discussions of the gulf between rich and poor.

The Stewardship of Natural Resources

No issue was more global than the environment. Winds and waters did not respect political boundaries, nor did the materials borne on them. The condition of the natural environment affected all living creatures, yet the prevailing calculus of the market and private ownership did not apportion responsibility for its care. The free market system had no mechanism for offsetting, or even measuring, the costs of depleted natural resources. A generation ago, biologist Garrett Hardin had warned of the tragedy of the commons: that individuals' incentives to preserve the quality of their own property did not carry over to resources held in common. The pursuit of narrow self-interest too often resulted in the spoiling of common grounds, such as parks and national forests. Litter was an obvious example, and air, water, and ground pollution were the more serious cases. American culture had long celebrated human domination of the natural world and the benefits it brought, especially the growth in productivity that permitted living standards to rise dramatically across decades and centuries. At the same time, the rise of environmentalism and ecological understanding since 1960 offered a different way of imagining people's place on the earth. A tension existed between exploiting finite natural resources to create wealth and managing them for long-term sustainability. This dilema reached an acute stage by the turn of the new millennium.

Ecological Transformation in the Twentieth Century

Ecosystems are always dynamic, and changes in weather and Native American land use had reshaped the North American environment long before the followers of Christopher Columbus arrived on the continent. But European settlement and industrialization altered the face of the land in ways that would dumbfound a time traveler from the 1500s. Even a visitor from 1900 would be astonished by the intensity of human development of the land: vast cities with their sprawling suburbs and roads and highways everywhere. The key factor was population growth. Just as the number of people in the world quadrupled from 1.5 billion to 6 billion during the twentieth century, the population of the United States almost quadrupled from 75 million to 281 million, with the largest increase for a single decade (33 million) coming in the 1990s. Immigration and natural reproduction accounted for much of this, but so did the much-longer average lifespan ushered in by antibiotics and antiviral vaccines, which sharply diminished the often fatal impact of infectious diseases and allowed noncommunicable maladies, such as cancer and heart disease, to become leading causes of death instead. The various drug-resistant bacteria that began to develop by the 1970s and the emergence of HIV infection and AIDS in the United States by 1980 brought an end to the brief post-1945 golden age of disease containment, locking researchers into a seemingly permanent arms race against virulent microbes. HIV's apparent origins in central Africa suggested the problems of easy introduction of exotic species in an age of frequent international travel.

The most dramatic changes in the land in the twentieth century resulted from the exploitation of wood, minerals, and water, particularly in the majority of the country lying west of the Mississippi River. Commercial logging destroyed all but 3 percent of the old-growth forests of the 50 states, both on private lands and on lands managed by the U.S. Forest Service, which as part of the Department of Agriculture traditionally emphasized the harvesting of wood products. The clearcuts scarring the mountainsides and hillsides of the Pacific Northwest and Alaska told the tale, as did the erosion caused by the overgrazing by cattle of public lands managed by the Interior Department's Bureau of Land Management in Utah, New Mexico, and other western states. The Mining Act of 1872 still granted to private corporations the rights to such valuable minerals as gold and copper on public land for the remarkable nineteenth-century price of $2.50 per acre. Mining companies took full advantage of the opportunity, and resulting rock and chemical wastes piled in vast slagheaps and dumped in toxic holding ponds from Arizona to Montana. In the arid but increasingly populated western states, water was the most critical resource for population growth. The U.S. Army Corps of Engineers and the Bureau of Reclamation built huge dams from the 1930s to the 1980s, providing irrigation, flood control, and hydropower but also destroying wild rivers and causing silt to begin filling up the reservoirs. Increasing diversions of the Rio Grande left that now misnamed river so dry that, by 2001, it failed to reach the Gulf of Mexico, trickling to a halt 50 feet short. Groundwater pumping for agricultural irrigation in the plains

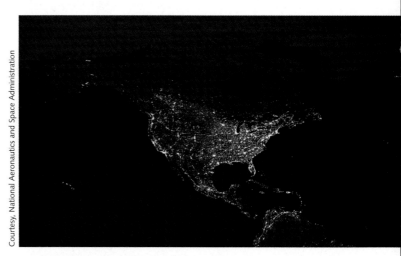

Courtesy, National Aeronautics and Space Administration

■ A nighttime photograph taken from a satellite above the south Pacific Ocean reveals the use of electricity in North America. Only Alaska and some parts of the inland western states (Nevada, Idaho, eastern Oregon) appear mostly unlit. The growth of the Sunbelt states of the South and West after 1970 was dramatic, but the bulk of the U.S. population remained east of the Mississippi River, especially in the Northeast and Midwest. The demand for electrical power even with most citizens in bed was enormous.

■ Clearcutting scars mountainsides on both private and public lands, especially in the Pacific Northwest and here on Kupreanof Island in the Tongass National Forest of southeastern Alaska. Clearcutting is a more efficient method of timber harvesting than selective tree thinning, but it encourages soil erosion, mudslides, and flooding.

states and on the eastern slope of the Rocky Mountains was draining the vast underground Ogallala Aquifer at a rate that will empty it within a few more decades.

American prosperity came at a price. The prodigious growth of the U.S. economy in the twentieth century depended on the consumption of ever-increasing amounts of energy. Some came from renewable sources, such as hydropower and nuclear power and smaller amounts from solar and wind power, but the bulk of the nation's energy was derived from coal, oil, and natural gas. Though making up less than 5 percent of the world's population, Americans accounted for a quarter of the globe's energy consumption. They depended on other countries to provide much of it for them: the United States imported 22 percent of its total energy needs and 69 percent of its oil, primarily from Saudi Arabia, Venezuela, Canada, and Mexico. Fossil fuels, such as coal and oil, could not be renewed; once burned, they were gone, and the world had a finite supply of such fuels. Americans' unquenchable thirst for gasoline and electricity helped them build history's largest and richest industrial economy, but they did so by constructing a lifestyle that was unsustainable in the long run. The energy crisis that began in California in early 2001 after the state ended its regulation of electricity production, and the rolling blackouts it caused, suggested that the long run might come sooner than expected.

Pollution

The world's growing population was consuming five times as much fossil fuel in 2000 as in 1950, helping to stimulate a steady rise in the earth's average temperatures. Americans caused 36 percent of such carbon-based emissions, the largest contribution to the foremost environmental problem, global warming. The release of large amounts of carbon dioxide from burning coal, oil, and other fossil fuels helped trap extra heat within the earth's atmosphere—the greenhouse effect—and melt ice in high-altitude and polar regions. In the summer of 2000, startled scientists found open water at the North Pole, a sight humans had never before seen. Greenhouse gases also contributed to a thinning of the ozone layer of the atmosphere, which

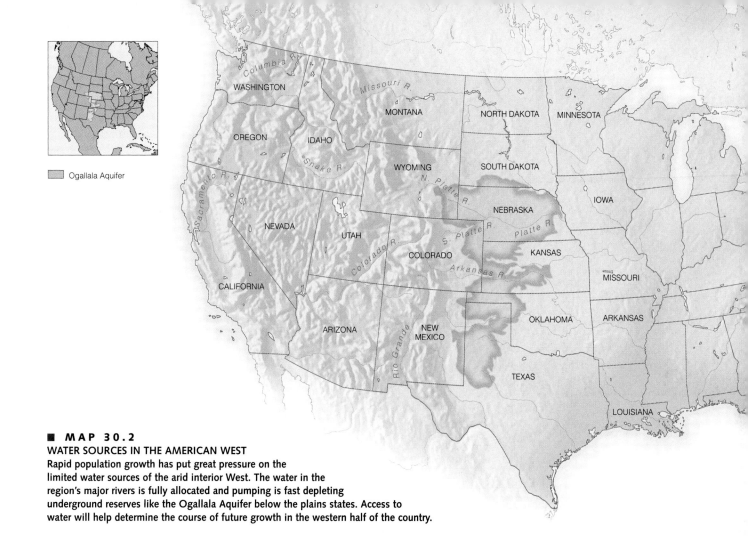

■ **MAP 30.2**

WATER SOURCES IN THE AMERICAN WEST
Rapid population growth has put great pressure on the
limited water sources of the arid interior West. The water in the
region's major rivers is fully allocated and pumping is fast depleting
underground reserves like the Ogallala Aquifer below the plains states. Access to
water will help determine the course of future growth in the western half of the country.

enabled more of the sun's ultraviolet rays to reach the earth's surface. As a result, skin cancer rates soared, particularly in the Southern Hemisphere, where the ozone hole was largest.

Industrial manufacturing still figured importantly in the human assault on the air and the atmosphere, but the internal combustion engine had long since surpassed coal burning as the leading cause of pollution. The United States produced and used more cars and trucks than any other nation. The automobile and its symbolism of convenience and personal freedom defined much of American culture, and citizens who could not drive or did not have access to a car were at a real disadvantage in a nation of freeways, shopping malls, and suburban housing. With minimal public transportation outside a handful of major cities, Americans were deeply committed to a car-dependent lifestyle. As a price, they quietly accepted an annual death toll of more than 40,000 people from accidents on the road, two-thirds the number each year of all U.S. deaths in the Vietnam War. The highway infrastructure strained under the pressure of a 60 percent rise in the number of licensed drivers from 1970 to 2000 but only a 6 percent growth in total miles of roads. Negotiating traffic jams became a standard part of the daily lives of the majority of Americans who lived in the suburbs created by urban sprawl, especially around such cities as Los Angeles and Atlanta. Citizens spent three times as many hours stalled in traffic in 1999 as they did in 1982. Smog increasingly obscured the once-sublime vistas of Arizona's Grand Canyon. Yosemite National Park in the Sierra Nevada mountains of California, a spectacular natural wonder drawing millions of visitors each year in the nation's most populous state, embodied the problems of an automotive society. Thousands of cars jammed Yosemite Valley every day, making it an almost urban setting with air quality on the verge of violating federal standards. Yet park managers' efforts to limit car access to the valley were repeatedly defeated by popular opposition.

Daily life in the United States came to depend in countless ways on the use of synthetic chemicals, production of which was 350 times greater in 1982 than in 1940. Only 3 percent of the 75,000 new chemicals had been tested for safety, but 40 of those examined proved to be human carcinogens. More than 50,000 known toxic waste dumps in the United States leached poisonous chemicals and heavy metals into the soil and water, such as the polychlorinated biphenyls that lined the bottom of the Hudson River north of Albany and the arsenic and cadmium that clogged the Milltown Dam on Montana's scenic Clark Fork River 6 miles upstream from Missoula. Cancer rates among Americans grew sharply in the twentieth century, partly because people lived significantly longer lives (giving more time for cancers to appear) and partly because they were exposed to a much larger array of carcinogenic materials in the environment.

No one knew yet how to dispose safely of millions of tons of materials impregnated with plutonium and other human-made radioactive elements.

No synthetic product was more pervasive in the United States than plastic, a post-1945 product made from petroleum. Its prevalence and extraordinary durability helped it become a major factor in loading up the nation's landfills. But the most deadly and durable pollutants remained the radioactive wastes created by five decades of nuclear development. No one knew yet how to dispose safely of millions of tons of materials impregnated with plutonium and other human-made radioactive elements, 30 percent of it casually poured into dirt or stored in flimsy containers prone to leakage. The chain of nuclear poison arched across the American West—from the bomb factory at Hanford in south central Washington through the weapon testing site in southwestern Nevada—then eastward to the uranium-processing plants in Paducah, Kentucky, and Barnwell, South Carolina.

The U.S. nuclear weapon complex of some 3000 sites put its often fatal touch on the lives of millions of Americans: uranium miners, military workers, soldiers used to observe test explosions at close range, and citizens living downwind from the Nevada Test Site in Nevada and Utah. The National Academy of Sciences concluded in 2000 that many of these sites would be permanent national sacrifice zones, toxic to humans for at least tens of thousands of years. The dissolution of the Soviet Union in 1991 relaxed some of the secrecy surrounding nuclear weapons on both sides. In 1993, the U.S. Department of Energy admitted that it had conducted radiation experiments for years on largely unsuspecting populations, both in the United States and on remote Pacific islands where some early nuclear bombs were tested. Russian sources revealed that Soviet leaders had been even more cavalier in their handling of nuclear wastes, simply dumping many of them in the Arctic Ocean. The environmental costs to Americans and others of the Cold War are yet to be fully calculated.

Environmentalism and Its Limitations

The ideas of most Americans about how to manage natural resources changed in the twentieth century. Environmental consciousness blossomed since the 1960s, rediscovering a tradition that linked eighteenth-century naturalist William Bartram with nineteenth-century transcendentalist Henry David Thoreau and twentieth-century conservationists of both major political parties. Awareness of humans' connections with their broader ecological context led to significant reforms, such as the banning of carcinogenic pesticides and leaded gasoline, the cleaning up of polluted water in the Great Lakes, and the introduction of catalytic converters to reduce harmful emissions from automobile exhaust pipes and factory smokestacks. Recycling became common, and some dams were destroyed, freeing long-constricted rivers, such as the Penobscot in Maine. Yet issues of public land management and pollution control remained among the most controversial problems in American public life. Since 1980, the Republican party has supported the exploitation of natural resources to produce wealth and raise standards of living, departing at least in tone from the party's earlier conservationist bent.

Meanwhile, the Democratic party became associated with environmental protection. This contrast was dramatically displayed in January 2001 when President Clinton rushed to provide new protections to a swath of federal lands in the West before his term ended, while president-elect George W. Bush was appointing as secretary of the interior Colorado attorney Gale Norton, who strongly opposed such protections. Both Bush and his vice president, Dick Cheney, had personal ties to the energy industry, and their administration promoted new oil and gas drilling in wilderness locations that included Alaska's Arctic National Wildlife Refuge.

Beyond partisan differences and the broad tendency of even the most well-known corporate polluters to pose as friendly to the environment, the relationship of Americans to their natural environment continued to be paradoxical. By large majorities in public opinion polls, they supported strong antipollution laws and the preservation of public lands from economic development. They flocked to such films as *Erin Brockovich* and *A Civil Action,* in which average citizens and lawyers won court cases against large corporate polluters. And they no longer agreed with the slogan common in Houston in the 1960s about the odoriferous smog created by the booming city's petrochemical industries and cars: "Smell that—that's prosperity."

But in their daily lives, Americans consumed natural resources, especially gasoline, electricity, and water, at a rate unmatched by other societies. Measures that had reduced some of the nation's energy consumption since the 1970s were reversed by 2000: Congress revoked the national 55-mph speed limit in 1995, and ever-larger cars, trucks, and especially sport utility vehicles steadily reduced the average gas mileage of passenger vehicles. While scientists and some utilities urged a reduction in the nation's expanding use of fossil fuels, Vice President Cheney dismissed conservation as merely "a sign of personal virtue" rather than a basis for a sound energy policy. Many residents across the arid Southwest, most of them newcomers, remained determined to recreate the green lawns they had left behind in the East and Midwest. When an investigator for the Las Vegas city water district confronted one resident about his wasteful sprinkler, the man responded, "Man, with all these new rules, you people are trying to turn this place into a desert."

Justin Sullivan/AP/Wide World

■ The oil crises of the 1970s led automobile manufacturers to improve the efficiency of gas mileage in their cars. By the 1990s, however, gasoline was once again inexpensive and growing numbers of Americans were buying large new sport utility vehicles (SUVs) such as the Chevrolet Suburban, despite their low gas mileage. A few environmentalists placed bumper stickers on other people's SUVs to highlight the key role of auto emissions in the accelerating process of global warming.

The Expansion of American Popular Culture Abroad

Just as the U.S. economy and American environmental problems could not be separated from the outside world, the nation's cultural life grew more closely tied to that of other nations at the dawn of the new millennium. During the Cold War, from the 1940s through the 1980s, American foreign relations hinged on problems of national security and the projection of military might abroad. The dissolution of the Soviet Union in 1991 and the retreat of communism ended the bipolar division of the world and left the United States the sole remaining superpower. But by 2000, American popular culture rather than armed strength had emerged as the leading edge of U.S. influence around the world.

Over the first half of the twentieth century, the United States slowly replaced Great Britain as the dominant force in international affairs. The economic and military aspects of this shift of influence were clear by the end of World War II, and its cultural elements soon followed. American power extended the preeminence of English as the global language of commerce and diplomacy, and ambitious and privileged youth from beyond Europe aimed no longer for an education at England's Oxford and Cambridge but rather at prestigious U.S. universities. American culture had become less regionally distinctive and more nationally homogeneous in the twentieth century because of improvements in transportation and communication. By the end of the century, this same process of homogenization of popular consumer culture was at work on a worldwide scale. American themes and products stood out in an increasingly global popular culture, although they were resisted by some abroad who preferred more local identities and traditions, often rooted in ethnicity or religious conviction.

A Culture of Diversity and Entertainment

Known for its informality and diversity, American culture proved powerfully attractive to peoples all over the world, partly because racial and ethnic diversity was more pronounced in the United States than in any other major power. African Americans, Latino Americans, and Asian Americans all figured prominently in the popular realms of sports, music, and films. Television was the leading medium for this culture of entertainment, beaming CNN, MTV, and "reality" shows, such as *Survivor,* around the world. From jazz to rock 'n' roll to rap, American popular music spread across the globe, as did such clothing of American youth as jeans and sneakers, symbols of informality and comfort. Hollywood's movies dominated cinemas and VCRs everywhere, providing 85 percent of films screened in Europe and projecting the alluring entertainment values of sexuality, violence, and wealth. Overseas markets grew so large that producers edited different versions of popular films for specific cultures, just as American magazines tailored separate editions to expand sales in diverse countries.

From jazz to rock 'n' roll to rap, American popular music spread across the globe, as did such clothing of American youth as jeans and sneakers.

The idea of individual choice pervaded American culture, backed by constitutional guarantees of freedom of expression. Freedom to choose included matters of religion, politics, and other weighty areas, which had long made the United States a beacon of liberty to people oppressed for their beliefs. But freedom of choice came increasingly by the end of the twentieth century to refer to options for consumption in the marketplace. The United States was the largest market in the world, and its affluent citizens had unparalleled choices of what to buy. In 1960, Americans already had 3000 shopping centers and 4 square feet of retail space per person. By 2000, those numbers had soared to 40,000 and 19, respectively, for their children and grandchildren. The premium placed on acquiring material goods seemed to many foreign observers the primary American value, visible anew in the rapid rise of legalized gambling in the last generation and the nation's declining savings rate. Indeed, *saving* had been largely redefined to mean buying at a discount rather than putting money away for the future.

Advertising grew in prominence as the central link between popular culture and the selling of products, and sports became steadily more commercialized. Postseason college football games began in 1985 to include the names of their corporate sponsors, creating such events as the Chick-Fil-A Peach Bowl and the Weed Eater Independence Bowl. By 2000, newspapers ranked bowl games—once hallowed for their own traditions—by the simple criterion of how much money sponsors paid to participating teams. In the 1990s "hoops" joined baseball as a popular U.S. export. Led by such talented and flashy stars as Michael Jordan, an American "Dream Team" won the Olympic basketball competition in Spain amid worldwide fanfare.

■ Perhaps no other element of American popular culture spread abroad as quickly as rock 'n' roll music. Like jazz after the 1920s, rock 'n' roll after the 1950s captured a vast listening audience overseas. Most Russian leaders during the Soviet era before 1991 appeared publicly as stiff, serious figures, but by 1996, Russian president Boris Yeltsin joined Russian rock 'n' rollers on stage in an event during his successful campaign for reelection.

Swiftly, the National Basketball Association (NBA) made the leap from an American league to a global phenomenon, its games telecast to more than 190 countries in 41 languages. Sports also brought foreigners to the United States as professional baseball and basketball teams began recruiting Latin American, European, African, and Asian athletes.

U.S. Influence Abroad Since the Cold War

Cultural influences flowed both ways for Americans, with immigrants in particular bringing with them traditions and perspectives that refreshed the cultural mix of life in the United States. Japanese Pokémon trading cards, Thai cuisine, and Cuban salsa music pervaded daily routines for many Americans. The rapidly growing popularity of American-style pizza outside the United States suggested the complexity of cultural exchange, as fast-food chains Domino's and Pizza Hut sold from Hong Kong to the Congo a food originally brought to New York by Italian immigrants. But increased trade and communication since the end of the Cold War above all enabled the further spread of American popular culture. American-accented English straddled the globe, the language of international commerce and of 80 percent of listings on the World Wide Web. The informality and individualism of the Internet made it feel quintessentially American in style. The U.S. dollar remained the world's primary trading currency and became the de facto and even the de jure currency of many other nations. Mickey Mouse's empire expanded to EuroDisney outside Paris and Tokyo Disneyland; Kodak even sold film in Antarctica. American studies became a major field of scholarship at universities around the world.

THE FINAL MERGER

■ By 2000, the process of globalization tied the world more closely together than ever before. Increasing trade, tourism, and communication encouraged the mixing of different cultures. American popular culture was a powerful influence around the globe, including American music, fast food, television, clothing, and movies. Mickey Mouse's ears famously symbolized the Disney Company, American television and films, and their worldwide prominence in popular entertainment.

America's most popular eatery served 20 million customers a day at its 23,000 franchises across the globe. McDonald's Golden Arches appeared everywhere, from Japan and France to Russia and China. Even Mecca in Saudi Arabia, the holiest site in Islam and the destination of millions of Muslim pilgrims, had a McDonald's. The company generated half of its revenues from non-U.S. operations.

Nor did only U.S. material interests spread abroad swiftly in recent years. American religious missionaries worked in poor countries around the world, combining their spiritual mission with a commitment to improving daily life in concrete ways involving health care, education, and agriculture. Pentecostalists gained millions of converts in Latin America since the 1970s, and mainstream denominations, such as the Lutherans, Episcopalians, and Roman Catholics, saw their numbers rise sharply in Africa. The most fully home-grown American religion was especially active in proselytizing abroad. As a result, the Church of Jesus Christ of Latter Day Saints (Mormons), headquartered in Salt Lake City, had 5 million members in the United States and another 5 million worldwide. Such international growth and Utah's hosting of the 2002 Winter Olympics symbolized how fully integrated into the outside world even America's most remote parts and once-reclusive peoples had become. (Salt Lake City's rapid growth made its population half non-Mormon by 2000.)

The United States retained its military superiority, with a defense budget larger than that of the next ten biggest military powers combined. The country's size, technological sophistication, and bipartisan commitment to a vast armed force ensured that its power on the battlefield was unlikely to diminish any time soon. But the difficulties of unconventional warfare, from Vietnam in the 1960s to Somalia in 1993, combined with the apparent disappearance of a major threat to the nation's security after the demise of the Soviet Union, made U.S. policymakers and citizens reluctant to put American troops in harm's way abroad, at least until after the terrorist attacks of September 11, 2001. Instead, the expansion of American culture abroad seemed a safer and more effective way to influence other nations. A generation earlier, Soviet leader Nikita Khrushchev had threatened to "bury the West," but in 1999 his son Sergei became an American citizen. His decision epitomized the continued allure of life in the United States.

Resistance to American Popular Culture

In the 1920s, Hasan al-Banna, founder of the Muslim Brotherhood, railed against "the wave of atheism and lewdness" engulfing Egypt, a wave that "started the devastation of religion and morality on the pretext of individual and intellectual freedom." Freer western and especially American standards of behavior offended the sensibilities of traditionalists across the Muslim world throughout the twentieth century, especially in matters of gender roles. Referring to tourists and their swimsuits, al-Banna blamed Westerners for importing "their half-naked women into these regions, together with their liquors" and other vices. The Iranian revolution of 1979 gave such complaints a new force by producing a theocratic government in one of the largest Muslim nations.

Like Christian, Jewish, and Hindu fundamentalists, all of whom grew prominent in the final decades of the twentieth century, Muslim fundamentalists rejected the radical egalitarianism and the unbridled pursuit of pleasure—especially the sexual titillation—so prevalent in American popular culture. The relative equality of women and the lack of respect for traditional social and religious hierarchies seemed to them emblems of American decadence, as the Islamic rulers of Afghanistan (known as the Taliban) demonstrated in the 1990s in their brutal repression of women's rights. Osama bin Laden and his followers resented U.S. policies of supporting Israel and certain oil-producing Arab nations, but they also fiercely condemned the secular, egalitarian character of American society, which they considered anti-Islamic. During the 1991 Gulf War, Saudi Arabian officials tried to isolate U.S. troops from Saudi citizens, fearing the effects of contact with such diverse forces as female soldiers, bawdiness, Christianity, and American music and television. An Indian official reflected his government's anxiety about the new availability of MTV in India: "Our own social ethos, our cultural values—we would not like them to be subverted."

■ By the start of the new century, the hopes of nine U.S. presidents that the communist leader of Cuba would be swept out of power had been dashed. Four decades after leading the leftist revolution of 1959 and ten years after the collapse of communism in Russia and eastern Europe, Castro remained defiant toward the United States. He continued to denounce free market capitalism, whose price, he claimed, was paid in human misery, child labor, prostitution, and vast social inequalities.

The demise of Communist regimes in Russia and eastern Europe opened the gates to a flood of western influences and brought the opportunities and inequalities of a suddenly privatized economy. State-provided safety nets disappeared, class differences widened, women's economic status declined, and the old Communist parties regained some popularity among voters scared by the instabilities of American-style capitalism. Western Europeans also remained ambivalent about the spread of American values and lifestyles. Although many of them, especially among the young, found American culture attractive and learned English in record numbers, traditionalists who were proud of their own national culture took a dim view of such innovations as fast food. A "slow food" movement emerged in France, celebrating traditional home and café meals, and protesters against McDonald's became national celebrities.

Other nations sometimes found the U.S. government overbearing and resented its unparalleled military power. Bin Laden and many other Middle Easterners blamed American arms for bolstering the governments of Israel and the Arab states whose moderate stance toward the West they abhorred. Rapidly modernizing China, the world's most populous country, seemed a growing rival to the United States in Asia, even as the two nations became major trading partners. In April 2001, a U.S. surveillance plane collided over the South China Sea with a Chinese fighter jet that had been following it. The Chinese pilot died, but the American plane managed to crash-land safely at a Chinese military airport on Hainan Island. China detained the crew of 24 men and women for ten days. Public and congressional anger in the United States paralleled the outrage in China, but the two governments, mindful of their growing economic interdependence, resolved the crisis after a brief standoff. Americans who had assumed that China's greater political openness of recent years, including widening access to the Internet, would reveal a people eager to be like Americans were surprised by the intensity of anti-American nationalism within Chinese society.

Two opposing trends characterized world affairs. One consisted of the unifying forces of economic internationalism and globalization, carrying with them a tide of American-dominated

The Slow Food Movement

For many people in countries other than the United States, as for many Americans, McDonald's and other U.S.-based fast food restaurants offered an attractive dining experience. Customers everywhere appreciated the efficient and friendly service, clean surroundings, and the consistent quality of the food. Their enthusiasm explained the extraordinary international growth and profitability of such chains as Burger King and Kentucky Fried Chicken at the end of the twentieth century.

For other people, the rapid spread of fast-food franchises around the globe threatened cherished values and lifestyles. The Slow Food Movement emerged in western Europe in the late 1980s as a loose-knit organization, headquartered in the northern Italian town of Bra. The movement sought to preserve and celebrate traditional cuisines and methods of food production in Europe and around the world. Slow Food's 60,000 members objected not only to the specific taste of fast food, but also to broader cultural changes symbolized by McDonald's and its competitors: the speeding up of daily life, including the loss of sociability around more leisurely meals; the gradual replacement of family farming and food production by corporate agriculture; and the erosion of distinctive local cooking and dining traditions.

The spread of American fast food chains around the globe suggested that American culture may be a more powerful influence abroad than U.S. military might. The end of the Cold War led to McDonald's restaurants proliferating in downtown Moscow and Beijing, the capital cities of America's greatest opponents since World War II. The Golden Arches even invaded Mecca, Saudi Arabia, the holiest city of Islam.

The Slow Food Manifesto (November 9, 1989)

Our century, which began and has developed under the insignia of industrial civilization, first invented the machine and then took it as its life model.

We are enslaved by speed and have all succumbed to the same insidious virus: *Fast Life,* which disrupts our habits, pervades the privacy of our homes and forces us to eat *Fast Foods.*

To be worthy of the name, *Homo sapiens* should rid himself of speed before it reduces him to a species in danger of extinction.

A firm defense of quiet material pleasure is the only way to oppose the universal folly of *Fast Life.*

May suitable doses of guaranteed sensual pleasure and slow, long-lasting enjoyment preserve us from the contagion of the multitude who mistake frenzy for efficiency.

Our defense should begin at the table with *Slow Food.* Let us rediscover the flavors and savors of regional cooking and banish the degrading effects of *Fast Food.*

In the name of productivity, *Fast Life* has changed our way of being and threatens our environment and our landscapes. So *Slow Food* is now the only truly progressive answer.

That is what real culture is all about: developing taste rather than demeaning it. And what better way to set about this than an international exchange of experiences, knowledge, projects?

Slow Food guarantees a better future.

Slow Food is an idea that needs plenty of qualified supporters who can help turn this (slow) motion into an international movement, with the little snail as its symbol.

Slow Food operates to protect the right to pleasure, the respect of the rhythms of life and a harmonious relationship with nature. It also seeks to explore, describe and improve the culture of food, to develop a proper education of taste and smell from childhood and to safeguard and defend the agroindustrial heritage while respecting the cuisines of each single country.

The Slow food Manifesto *was ratified in Paris at the Founding Congress of the International Slow Food Movement on December 9, 1989.*

Source: http://www.slowfood.com.

■ MAP 30.3

ASIA AS A FOCUS OF U.S. FOREIGN POLICY Early in 2001, President Bush faced his first diplomatic crisis when a Chinese fighter jet collided with a U.S. spy plane near Hainan Island. Tensions rose between the United States and China, suggesting that their renewed rivalry might dominate international politics in the new millenium. But the September 11 terrorist attacks from the Afghanistan-based Al Qaeda network shifted diplomatic attention to a different part of Asia. The United States and China, along with Russia, worked to oppose radical Islamic revolutionaries and to prevent a nuclear war between India and Pakistan over the disputed region of Kashmir.

cultural styles. The other was made up of the resisting forces of political and ethnic nationalism. A world more tightly integrated in economic ways was at the same time divided by ethnic conflicts, revealed in wars in the Balkans in southeastern Europe, the Caucasus region on Russia's southern border, and central Africa. As people around the world felt themselves increasingly sucked into the vortex of a powerful global economy that they could not control, many of them responded by renewing their allegiances to older, more local traditions. Ethnic, religious, and national identities often offered more meaningful alternatives to a purely economic identity as consumers. "I don't find foreign countries foreign," Gillette Corporation chair Alfred M. Zeien said, and many people in other nations felt the same way about the United States. But for others, as the terrorist attacks of 2001 made all too clear, American life seemed fundamentally alien and increasingly threatening.

Identity in Contemporary America

The 2000 U.S. census revealed a society in the midst of change. Americans have long been known as a particularly restless and mobile people, and one out of five changed residences every year. The post-1965 wave of immigrants continued to rise (and foreign adoptions rose dramatically), bringing in millions of new Americans of Asian heritage. Latino Americans came to equal African Americans as the nation's two largest minorities with 35 million people each. This latest surge in immigration boosted the number of Roman Catholics and Buddhists as American society remained the most openly religious—still primarily Protestant—of the industrialized nations. Geographically, Americans lived farther south and west than earlier generations. Of the ten largest cities 100 years ago, only New York, Chicago, and Philadelphia remained on the list, while cities such as Atlanta, Houston, and San Diego replaced Boston, Cleveland, and St. Louis. None of the 20 fastest-growing states were in the Northeast or Midwest. The West Coast housed the country's two largest philanthropic foundations: the Gates Foundation of Seattle and the Packard Foundation of Los Altos, California. Rooted in the new money of the computer and high-technology sectors, these institutions surpassed the older foundations in the Northeast built on the wealth of heavy industries, such as Rockefeller (oil), Carnegie (steel), and Ford (automobiles).

Americans were older than they used to be: life expectancy rose to 77 from 45 years in 1900. More than half lived in suburbs. Average household size dropped by 50 percent over the twentieth century, as only one in four consisted of a married couple with children. Whereas in 1900, just 6 percent of married women worked outside the home, 61 percent did so by 2000, including 64 percent of those with children under age 6. The "family wage" that so many men earned in the mid-twentieth century was disappearing, helping bring in its wake changes in gender roles as women became crucial breadwinners, as well as homemakers and child-raisers.

Photograph by Michael O'Brien

■ One aspect of American identity that continued to distinguish the United States from the industrialized countries of western Europe was enthusiastic support for the death penalty. Most surviving victims and relatives of victims of the 1995 Oklahoma City federal building bombing were eager for the execution of the confessed and unrepentant perpetrator, Timothy McVeigh, in 2001. However, a few overcame their grief and rage to oppose having the government kill the killer, including Bud Welch, Kathy Wilburn, Patrick Reeder, and Rosemary Koelsch (L to R), each of whom lost loved ones in the mass murder.

Negotiating Multiple Identities

Americans derived their sense of identity from myriad sources, including nationality, work, socioeconomic status, religion, race, ethnicity, family, gender, region, and sexual orientation. Since the struggles for equality that emerged dramatically in the 1960s, individual identities and group identities have often been in tension. The black civil rights movement, along with the struggles of women, Latinos, Native Americans, and homosexuals, sought an end to unequal treatment and full inclusion in American life for all individual citizens, regardless of race, sex, sexual orientation, or disability. However, the achievement of legal equality and the outlawing of

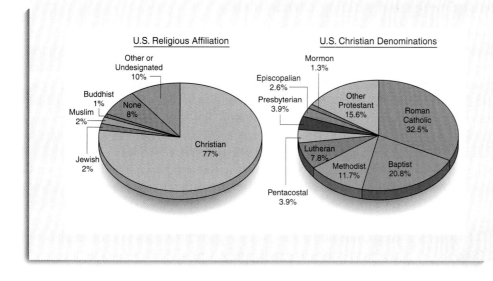

■ **FIGURE 30.1**
SELF-DESCRIBED RELIGIOUS AFFILIATION IN THE UNITED STATES, 2000   The most noticeable change of the last 30 years in American religious life has been the growth of evangelical and fundamentalist Protestant congregations (shown here as Pentacostals and "Other Protestants") and the shrinking of mainline Protestant denominations.

explicit discrimination did not immediately change deeply embedded patterns of exclusionary behavior. The policy of affirmative action had developed as a preference in hiring or admission for members of an underrepresented group who were roughly comparable to others in qualifications. It aimed to balance some of the effects of existing but little-noticed habits of "affirmative action" for white Americans and men, as when colleges used lower admission standards for children of alumni or powerful white men tended to hire other white men. Opponents of affirmative action called it "reverse discrimination" and argued that race and sex should no longer be criteria for success in a colorblind society that promoted individual achievement. By 2000, these opponents had succeeded in eliminating affirmative action from the admission process of the large state university systems of Texas and California. Supporters of the policy, including President Bill Clinton, observed that employers and others were certainly not colorblind yet, so that a group remedy, such as affirmative action, remained essential for the advancement of more than a token few from groups that had faced discrimination in the past.

Ideas about racial identity remained at the heart of controversy over affirmative action. Those who used the term *race* to group people according to skin color and other visible features, such as eye shape, commonly assumed that race had an important biological meaning as a way of distinguishing one human population from another. However, biologists noted that the genetic differences between races are miniscule compared with differences between individuals of the same race; they suggested that categorizing people by skin color made as much sense as organizing library books by the size and color of their covers rather than their internal contents. The mapping of the entire human genome by 2001 further clarified the biological insignificance of race. Indeed, the racial category "white" had changed over time to encompass such formerly excluded groups as Irish Americans and Jewish Americans. Despite its lack of scientific basis, the use of race as a primary marker of identity long served to preserve a higher status for Americans of European heritage. One could be mostly white yet still be "black," thanks to the one-drop tradition regarding African heritage (that any observable percentage of African "blood" defined a person as black). Thus, a white woman could have a black child in the United States, for example, but a black woman could not have a white child. The U.S. government's decision in the 2000 census to allow citizens to identify themselves as belonging to more than one racial group reflected the complications and occasional absurdities of racial categorization.

Social Change and Abiding Discrimination

One of the most striking changes in American society over the past five decades has been the desegregation of public life. Latinos and Asians became much more numerous in the United States, and African Americans emerged from the enforced separation of Jim Crow into greater prominence. Roughly one-third of blacks were middle-class and thousands won election to local, state, and national political offices, and black Americans became central in the nation's cultural life in music, literature, theater, and sports. By 2001, even a new president from the Republican party—known since 1964 for its lack of support from black voters—appointed two African Americans to run the nation's foreign relations: Secretary of State Colin Powell and National Security Adviser Condoleezza Rice. Workplaces were racially integrated to an extent that would have been hard to imagine in 1950, and interacial marriages rose steeply in the final

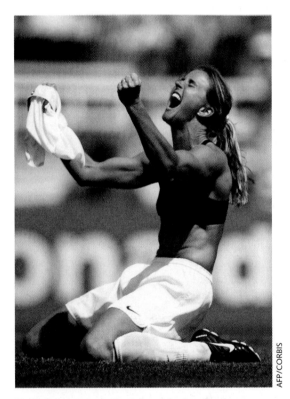

AFP/CORBIS

■ Defender Brandi Chastain celebrates after her decisive penalty kick against China gave the U.S. women's soccer team the 1999 World Cup title. Ripping off her shirt just as male soccer players often did (to reveal a not very revealing sports bra), Chastain shocked some viewers but impressed others who saw muscular athleticism rather than the sexual suggestiveness of bikini swimsuits.

decades of the twentieth century. In the 2000 presidential campaign, George W. Bush received sharp criticism for giving a speech at Christian fundamentalist Bob Jones University in South Carolina, which retained a campus ban on interracial dating. One of the most revealing aspects of the controversy was the response of conservative and even reactionary religious and political leaders: none supported the ban. "The fact is you have an indefensible policy," declared U.S. Representative and Bob Jones alumnus Asa Hutchinson of Arkansas. The sexual fears that had so long underpinned white racial violence in the past had dramatically receded in the nation's public life.

The lives of women in the United States also changed dramatically during the last half of the twentieth century. Most worked outside the home, from jobs in the service and manufacturing sectors to careers in the professions and politics. In 2000, women made up a third of the students in the nation's medical schools and a half in law schools. Their presence in leading political positions ranged from local officials to more than a dozen U.S. senators, two U.S. Supreme Court justices, a U.S. attorney general, and a U.S. secretary of state. The passage of Title IX in 1972, prohibiting gender discrimination in school programs that received federal money, created a tidal wave of social change for American girls. In 1971, 1 in 27 girls played high school sports; by 1998, the ratio was 1 in 3. Sports programs and teams for girls comparable to those for boys nourished a new generation of American women for whom athletic competition and achievement were the norm rather than the exception. The U.S. national women's soccer team won the World Cup in 1999 and became a popular sensation, with players like Mia Hamm emerging as household names. Anti-homosexual attitudes persisted as one of the nation's fiercest prejudices but nonetheless declined in mainstream American society during the 1980s and 1990s. Gay men and lesbians became more open and prominent in such public venues as television and politics, helping millions of other Americans to shed some of the homophobia they had unknowingly learned during childhood.

These improvements for the majority of Americans who were not heterosexual white men jostled against abiding forms of discrimination and inequality. Violence and the threat of violence against homosexuals, people of color, and particularly women (primarily domestic violence at the hands of husbands and lovers) remained very real, but most prejudices found more subtle avenues of expression. Working women continued to average less than three-quarters the wages of working men. Many employers, police officers, store owners, bank loan officers, and others in positions of authority treated African Americans and Latino Americans with greater suspicion than they did other citizens, a practice that became known as racial profiling. Poverty and unemployment disproportionately affected black communities and families. Given the powerful legacy of the past, white individuals on average possessed ten times more real wealth (much of it inherited) than their African American counterparts. Residential neighborhoods and public schools remained largely segregated by race, and the deeply symbolic Confederate flag still occupied a place of public honor in several southern states. Popular black comedian Chris Rock reminded mostly white audiences of the enduring but unstated advantage of being white in the United States: "Ain't no white man here willing to trade places with me—and I'm rich!"

Native Americans shared this combination of improving status and continuing discrimination. Their numbers were reviving, from a mere 250,000 in 1900 to 2 million in 2000, and a new National Museum of the American Indian arose on the mall in the nation's capital. A series of federal court decisions in the 1970s and 1980s strengthened Indians' "unique and limited" sovereignty over the tribal reservations, which constituted 2 percent of U.S. land. Starting with the Iroquois of upstate New York in 1970, several eastern Indian nations sued state and federal governments for the return of parts of lands that had been illegally seized from them in the past. From Florida to Maine, these nations won a combination of small portions of public land and millions of dollars in compensation in cases from the 1970s through the 1990s. Casino revenues in the 1990s brought much-needed resources to a number of Indian nations. At the same time, the process of assimilation continued as a majority of Indians lived in urban areas and were married to non-Indians. Reservations suffered from severe unemployment rates and remained some of the poorest communities in the country, dependent on federal assistance for food and other basic necessities. Anti-Indian sentiments occasionally surfaced in states as diverse as Montana, Wisconsin, Arizona, and New York.

> *Chris Rock reminded mostly white audiences of the enduring but unstated advantage of being white in the United States.*

Still an Immigrant Society

Economic opportunity and individual liberty continued to lure millions of people from other nations to the United States at the start of the new millennium. From its peak in the first decade of the twentieth century, the annual number of immigrants declined steadily after the restrictive immigration laws of the early 1920s, the Great Depression of the 1930s, and World War II in the 1940s. After the war, the number began to rise slowly again until the 1965 reforms encouraged a new period of immigration as large, by the 1990s, as that of a century earlier. Some 800,000 now came legally each year, and another 300,000 entered without official papers. For the first time since the 1930s, 1 in 10 Americans had been born abroad; in New York City the ratio was 1 in 4. Fifteen percent came from Europe, 26 percent arrived from Asia, and 51 percent moved north from Latin America and the Caribbean. Like Italy in 1900, Mexico in 2000 became the most important single source of new Americans, highlighting the importance of the nation's 2000-mile southern border as a conduit. The cultural exchange from Europe to the American East and Midwest 100 years earlier was replaced by a new exchange from Asia and Latin America centered in the Sunbelt states from Florida to California. The demographic transition of California in 2000 from a white majority to a more diverse ethnic and racial mix like that of Hawaii symbolized the nation's turn to the South and West, even as the motives and work habits of the newcomers remained very much the same as those of their European predecessors.

Only the hardiest and most motivated people made the difficult, emotionally wrenching, and often dangerous move to the United States. Many fled political persecution in countries like Guatemala, Haiti, Vietnam, and Cuba. In contrast to the left-leaning and often socialist

States whose population grew more than 20%

States that gained more than one million new residents

States whose population grew more than 20% and gained more than one million new residents

Four largest states, ranked by population

❶ California
❷ Texas
❸ New York
❹ Florida

■ **MAP 30.4**
STATE POPULATION GROWTH, 1990–2000   The population of the United States continued to shift slowly out of the long-urbanized Northeast to the Sunbelt of the South and West. Los Angeles replaced Chicago as the nation's second largest city, after New York. Retirees and workers alike seemed to prefer sunnier, warmer climates.

attitudes of immigrants in 1900, political refugees in 2000 were sometimes fierce anticommunists who helped pressure the U.S. government to take an even harder line toward regimes in Havana and Hanoi. Most newcomers sought greater economic security, like the 80 percent of young men of the village of Ting Jiang in China's Fujian province who made the perilous voyage by sea to find work in American restaurants or construction. "Sure, work is hard" in the United States, one of their wives at home in China explained, "but with tips you can make more than $2000 a month," compared with $40 a month at home in Ting Jiang. "So now no one in the village works before they go to America. There's no point." Most immigrants came to stay, but some worked to save money and return home to their families, carrying with them not only money, but also bits of American culture. Other people flowed outward too, as American students and tourists traveled all over the globe. Some Americans worked abroad, usually for U.S.-based multinationals such as oil companies, to earn better wages and then return home. Others served in the military, worked for aid agencies and church groups, or joined in the resurgence of the Peace Corps.

Despite increasing contacts overseas, Americans responded to the wave of newcomers with an ambivalence common in previous periods of high immigration. For a society made up of people from elsewhere and their descendants, there was no obvious answer to the question of when to close the door to new arrivals. Many in the working class feared competition from highly motivated laborers accustomed to much lower wages. Many elites worried whether cultural diversity might weaken national unity. Conservative political leaders promoted new restrictions and stronger border patrols. One Arizona resident wrote to *The Arizona Republic* to defend controversial police harassment of Latinos in the Phoenix suburb of Chandler in 1997: "If your skin is brown, this is a probable cause [for arrest as an illegal alien] and a police officer may assume you are breaking the law until proved differently." Some U.S. Congressmen ridiculed the idea of there being value in traveling abroad by boasting that they did not even have passports. In 1998, Republican House majority leader Dick Armey of Texas announced, "I've been to Europe once; I don't have to go again." Such disdain for other cultures among some American political leaders dismayed U.S. allies overseas.

Most Americans got used to having more immigrants around. Americans cheered for the one in four major league baseball players who were born in Latin America or had parents from there, and they became accustomed to the high number of Asian Americans in college classrooms. Many churches worked to help new arrivals adjust to life in the United States. Above all, American employers depended on immigrant workers to keep the nation's powerful economy afloat—to pick its fruits and vegetables, tend its young children, and work in its factories. Nearly all-white Iowa even began an immigrant recruitment drive to sustain a vibrant state economy that lacked sufficient workers. If the estimated 6 million mostly Latino undocumented workers in the United States were expelled, thousands of hotels, restaurants, meatpacking plants, landscaping companies, and garment manufacturers would be forced to close.

Conclusion

What held Americans together as they set off into the twenty-first century was a common loyalty to a set of ideas about economic opportunities and individual liberties. Unlike such nations as Germany and Israel, where citizenship was extended automatically to people of a certain ethnicity, the United States awarded citizenship to those who were born within its borders, regardless of ethnicity or race. Those born elsewhere became citizens on the basis not of their past lineage but of their future commitments—of their newly sworn loyalty to the U.S. Constitution, with its guarantees of freedom and its responsibilities of citizenship. In a vast society of multiple political and cultural beliefs, the scope of specific freedoms and the nature of individual responsibilities inevitably remained matters of ongoing tension and conflict. Nonetheless, the United States continued to address most of its problems through an orderly legal system, in contrast to the ethnic and religious strife marking so many of the world's nations.

That strife from abroad impinged on Americans in a shocking new way on September 11, 2001. On a sunny Tuesday morning, 19 hijackers—four of them trained as pilots—seized control simultaneously of four large commercial jets and turned them into suicidal missiles. At 8:48 A.M., one flew into the 110-story north tower of New York City's World Trade Center, igniting an enormous fireball. Fifteen minutes later, the second plane flew into the south tower. In less than two hours, both towers collapsed, trapping hundreds of firefighters, police officers, and other rescue workers who had raced into the building to evacuate the thousands of occupants. The third plane flew into the Pentagon. The fourth was also being directed towards Washington, apparently to destroy the White House or the Capital Building, when the passengers rushed the hijackers in the cockpit. In the ensuing struggle, the plane crashed in a field 75 miles southeast of Pittsburgh.

The carefully coordinated assaults killed some 3000 people, destroyed the two tallest buildings in the country's largest city, and left a gaping hole in the headquarters of the nation's military command. Not since the Japanese assault on Pearl Harbor 60 years earlier had the United States experienced such a devastating attack on its soil. During the intervening half-century of the Cold War, the Soviet Union and other Communist forces had never attempted direct aggression against the American homeland. Who was responsible for the most horrific act of terrorism against civilians in U.S. history?

The 19 perpetrators were self-styled holy warriors of a secretive, extremist Islamic organization known as Al Qaeda, organized by wealthy, charismatic Saudi Arabian expatriate Osama bin Laden. The rage of bin Laden and other Islamic terrorists against the United States had been building throughout the 1990s, fueled by the presence of "infidel" American troops in Saudi Arabia since the Gulf War, by American support for Israel, and by the rapid spread of secular American popular culture around the globe. At odds with moderate Islamic mainstream thought throughout the world, bin Laden announced in 1998, "To kill Americans and their allies, is an individual duty of every Muslim who is able."

Al Qaeda worked out of Afghanistan. It was hosted by the most repressive Islamic government on Earth, the Taliban, which came to power in 1996 out of the chaos that followed the withdrawal of the Soviet army in 1989. U.S. aid had helped in the anti-Soviet struggle, but the American government had ignored Afghanistan after the Soviets left. Four weeks after the attacks on New York City and Washington in 2001, U.S. planes began bombing Taliban and Al Qaeda positions in Afghanistan. Meanwhile, U.S. special operations forces worked on the ground with anti-Taliban Afghan forces. By December, the Taliban had been driven from power throughout the country, and U.S. forces had captured hundreds of Taliban and Al Qaeda fighters. President Bush warned of a long struggle still ahead against remaining forces of anti-American terrorism, regardless of bin Laden's fate.

The terrorist attacks of September 11, 2001 tested—and often strengthened—ties across religious and ethnic lines as Americans shared a renewed sense of national unity and pride. Anti-government sentiments dropped sharply and flag sales soared. Traditional social divisions ebbed at least temporarily as citizens contemplated the assault on their nation. New Yorker Louis Johnson, the son of immigrants from Trinidad, said that previously, "I just thought of myself as black. But now I feel like I'm an American, more than ever." The Bush administration's subsequent restrictions on the civil liberties of young Arab men, part of an effort to prevent further attacks while the United States was at war in Afghanistan, riled defenders of American constitutional freedoms on both the left and the right, as well as such influential mainstream leaders as Democratic Senate Judiciary Committee chair Patrick Leahy from Vermont. But the president and his attorney general, John Ashcroft, maintained broad public support for their actions a year after 9-11.

Following September 11, national unity was threatened by sporadic hostility and vengeful assaults against Muslims and others of Middle Eastern appearance. A handful of deaths and hundreds of incidents of harassment and vandalism revealed the difficulty some citizens had in distinguishing between a few Islamic terrorists and several million Muslim Americans. But Muslims also encountered a powerful trend of support for them and curiosity about their faith. President Bush set the tone in highly publicized meetings with Muslim leaders in which he emphasized that "this is not a war against Islam" but only against terrorists, a point underlined by the close U.S. cooperation with the Islamic Republic of Pakistan and with Muslim anti-Taliban fighters in the war in Afghanistan. Within a few hours of the September 11 attacks, the leadership of the Ford Motor Company reached out to Detroit's large Arab American community (including several hundred of its own workers) and began a series of interfaith meetings to promote dialogue and tolerance. And the Coca-Cola Company hired Muhammad Ali, one of most famous figures on the planet, to do publicity work. "I am a Muslim," declared the former Olympic and world boxing champion from Louisville, Kentucky. "I am an American."

Average Americans also sought to improve communication and understanding between Muslims and non-Muslims. Fearful of possible vandalism, the handful of Muslims in Laramie,

Wyoming, stayed home after September 11. "And then our neighbors called up," homemaker Zubaida Husain said, and promised to help protect homes and property. "That made me feel very good." The unfortunately named "Osama's Place," a restaurant owned by a Jordanian American right near the entrance to Fort Bragg in Spring Lake, North Carolina, did not change its name and experienced little loss of business. Indeed, several thousand Muslims served in the U.S. armed forces, where the number of Islamic chaplains was increasing rapidly. In Cary, North Carolina, conservative Christian Yvonne Young-Capece and Muslim immigrant Mona el-Ramly were neighbors who had become so close that Young-Capece traveled to Egypt for the wedding of Ramly's son. After the terrorist attacks, Young-Capece hosted a get-together for 16 of her friends along with Ramly and a few other Muslim friends to combat prejudice.

At the heart of American society remained a common assumption that this was a democratic country. The events on United Airlines Flight 93, one of the four doomed planes on September 11, 2001, revealed the tenacity of the belief in majority rule. After the hijackers seized control and herded the passengers into the rear of the cabin, a few passengers were able to communicate by cell phone with loved ones on the ground. They learned that two other planes had already crashed into the World Trade Center towers in New York City, and they realized that

Val McClatchey

■ Smoke rises from the crash of United Airlines Flight 93 near Shanksville, Pennsylvania. For almost all Americans, the hijackings and destruction of September 11, 2001 came indeed out of a clear blue sky. Anti-American actions of the previous decade by Islamic terrorists had created little anxiety in a powerful nation that had imagined itself safe from major attack.

these hijackers—unlike previous ones who sought concrete gains and an escape—planned only destruction for them all. Face-to-face with imminent death and the certainty that many others would perish if they failed to act, the passengers discussed what to do. They made a plan to rush the hijackers, led by several large, athletic passengers, including Mark Bingham, a prominent gay businessperson and rugby player from San Francisco. Should they proceed? Quintessential Americans, they took a vote. GTE Airfone operator Lisa Jefferson heard the rest: "Are you guys ready?" asked Todd Beamer, a tall father of two from Cranbury, New Jersey. Pause. "Let's roll." Screams and a scuffle followed before the line went dead. The plane, headed for the heart of Washington, crashed minutes later in an unpopulated part of western Pennsylvania with no casualties on the ground.

Sites to Visit

Smithsonian Center for Latino Initiatives

latino.si.edu/

This site offers an array of links to information on Latino culture and history.

How Race Is Lived in America

www.nytimes.com/library/national/race/most-recent.html

This is a collection of revealing articles from the *New York Times* in 2000 on race relations and racial identities in contemporary America.

Islam in the United States

usinfo.state.gov/usa/islam/

Here, researchers can find information on Muslims in modern America and links to other sources for research.

History Link: The History of Seattle and King County

www.historylink.org/welcome.htm

This site provides an array of historical information about one of the fastest growing areas in the country.

The September 11 Digital Archive

911digitalarchive.org/stories/

Created by the Center for History and New Media and George Mason University and the American Social History

Project at City University of New York Graduate Center, this site offers a large collection of stories and images from September 11, 2001, when terrorists attacked New York City and Washington, D.C.

Native Americans

www.americanwest.com/pages/indians.htm

This site contains information about American Indian history and culture, along with links to the home pages of many Indian nations.

The National Security Archive at George Washington University

www.gwu.edu/~nsarchiv/

This extraordinary site includes the most recent declassified documents on the making of U.S. foreign policy.

The Natural Resources Defense Council

www.nrdc.org/

This site contains considerable information and links about an array of current environmental issues.

For Further Reading

General

Harvard Sitkoff, ed., *Perspectives on Modern America: Making Sense of the Twentieth Century* (2001).

The American Place in a Global Economy

William M. Adler, *Mollie's Job: A Story of Life and Work on the Global Assembly Line* (2000).

Richard J. Barnet and John Cavanagh, *Global Dreams: Imperial Corporations and the New World Order* (1994).

Jefferson Cowie, *Capital Moves: RCA's Seventy-Year Quest for Cheap Labor* (1999).

Thomas L. Friedman, *The Lexus and the Olive Tree: Understanding Globalization* (1999).

William Greider, *One World, Ready or Not: The Manic Logic of Global Capitalism* (1997).

Robert Kuttner, *Everything for Sale: The Virtues and Limits of Markets* (1996).

The Stewardship of Natural Resources

Lester R. Brown, Michael Renner, and Brian Halweil, *Vital Signs 2000: The Environmental Trends That Are Shaping Our Future* (2000).

J. R. McNeill, *Something New Under the Sun: An Environmental History of the Twentieth-Century World* (2000).

David Quammen, *The Song of the Dodo: Island Biogeography in an Age of Extinction* (1996).

Hal K. Rothman, *Saving the Planet: The American Response to the Environment in the Twentieth Century* (2000).

The Expansion of American Popular Culture Abroad

Benjamin R. Barber, *Jihad vs. McWorld: How the Planet Is Both Falling Apart and Coming Together and What This Means for Democracy* (1995).

Chalmers Johnson, *Blowback: The Costs and Consequences of American Empire* (2000).

Richard F. Kuisel, *Seducing the French: The Dilemma of Americanization* (1993).

Richard Pells, *Not Like Us: How Europeans Have Loved, Hated, and Transformed American Culture Since World War II* (1997).

Ronald Steel, *Temptations of a Superpower* (1995).

Reinhold Wagnleitner and Elaine Tyler May, eds., *"Here, There and Everywhere": The Foreign Politics of American Popular Culture* (2000).

Identity in Contemporary America

Gary Gerstle, *American Crucible: Race and Nation in the Twentieth Century* (2001).

Charles Hirshman and Philip Kasinitz, eds., *The Handbook of International Migration: The American Experience* (1999).

David A. Hollinger, *Postethnic America: Beyond Multiculturalism*, rev. ed. (2000).

Gary Y. Okihiro, *Common Ground: Reimagining American History* (2001).

Robert D. Putnam, *Bowling Alone: The Collapse and Revival of American Community* (2000).

Ruth Rosen, *The World Split Open: How the Modern Women's Movement Changed America* (2000).

Alan Wolfe, *One Nation After All: What Americans Really Think About God, Country, Family, Racism, Welfare, Immigration, Homosexuality, Work, the Right, the Left and Each Other* (1998).

Online Practice Test

Test your understanding of this chapter with interactive review quizzes at

www.ablongman.com/jonescreatedequal/chapter30

Additional Photo Credits

Page 1003: PhotoDisc
Page 1004: W. Cody/CORBIS
Page 1007: Courtesy, Samsung Corporation
Page 1018: Photofest
Page 1019: Courtesy, Newstream.com
Page 1022: Permission to reproduce logo provided courtesy of Slow Food U.S.A.

Appendix

The Declaration of Independence

The Articles of Confederation

The Constitution of the United States
of America

Amendments to the Constitution

Presidential Elections

Present Day United States

Present Day World

For additional reference material, go to
www.ablongman.com/jonescreatedequal/appendix
The online appendix includes the following:

The Declaration of Independence

In Congress, July 4, 1776

The Unanimous Declaration
of the Thirteen United States of America

When, in the course of human events, it becomes necessary for one people to dissolve the political bonds which have connected them with another, and to assume, among the powers of the earth, the separate and equal station to which the laws of nature and of nature's God entitle them, a decent respect to the opinions of mankind requires that they should declare the causes which impel them to the separation.

We hold these truths to be self-evident: That all men are created equal; that they are endowed by their Creator with certain unalienable rights; that among these are life, liberty, and the pursuit of happiness; that, to secure these rights, governments are instituted among men, deriving their just powers from the consent of the governed; that whenever any form of government becomes destructive of these ends, it is the right of the people to alter or to abolish it, and to institute new government, laying its foundation on such principles, and organizing its powers in such form, as to them shall seem most likely to effect their safety and happiness. Prudence, indeed, will dictate that governments long established should not be changed for light and transient causes; and accordingly all experience hath shown that mankind are more disposed to suffer, while evils are sufferable, than to right themselves by abolishing the forms to which they are accustomed. But when a long train of abuses and usurpations, pursuing invariably the same object, evinces a design to reduce them under absolute despotism, it is their right, it is their duty, to throw off such government, and to provide new guards for their future security. Such has been the patient sufferance of these colonies; and such is now the necessity which constrains them to alter their former systems of government. The history of the present King of Great Britain is a history of repeated injuries and usurpations, all having in direct object the establishment of an absolute tyranny over these states. To prove this, let facts be submitted to a candid world.

He has refused his assent to laws, the most wholesome and necessary for the public good.

He has forbidden his governors to pass laws of immediate and pressing importance, unless suspended in their operation till his assent should be obtained; and, when so suspended, he has utterly neglected to attend to them.

He has refused to pass other laws for the accommodation of large districts of people, unless those people would relinquish the right of representation in the legislature, a right inestimable to them, and formidable to tyrants only.

He has called together legislative bodies at places unusual, uncomfortable, and distant from the depository of their public records, for the sole purpose of fatiguing them into compliance with his measures.

He has dissolved representative houses repeatedly, for opposing, with manly firmness, his invasions on the rights of the people.

He has refused for a long time, after such dissolutions, to cause others to be elected; whereby the legislative powers, incapable of annihilation, have returned to the people at large for their exercise; the state remaining, in the mean time, exposed to all the dangers of invasions from without and convulsions within.

He has endeavored to prevent the population of these states; for that purpose obstructing the laws for naturalization of foreigners; refusing to pass others to encourage their migration hither, and raising the conditions of new appropriations of lands.

He has obstructed the administration of justice, by refusing his assent to laws for establishing judiciary powers.

He has made judges dependent on his will alone, for the tenure of their offices, and the amount and payment of their salaries.

He has erected a multitude of new offices, and sent hither swarms of officers to harass our people and eat out their substance.

He has kept among us, in times of peace, standing armies, without the consent of our legislatures.

He has affected to render the military independent of, and superior to, the civil power.

He has combined with others to subject us to a jurisdiction foreign to our constitution, and unacknowledged by our laws, giving his assent to their acts of pretended legislation:

For quartering large bodies of armed troops among us;

For protecting them, by a mock trial, from punishment for any murder which they should commit on the inhabitants of these states;

For cutting off our trade with all parts of the world;

For imposing taxes on us without our consent;

For depriving us, in many cases, of the benefits of trial by jury;

For transporting us beyond seas, to be tried for pretended offenses;

For abolishing the free system of English laws in a neighboring province, establishing therein an arbitrary government, and enlarging its boundaries, so as to render it at once an example and fit instrument for introducing the same absolute rule into these colonies;

For taking away our charters, abolishing our most valuable laws, and altering fundamentally the forms of our governments;

For suspending our own legislatures, and declaring themselves invested with power to legislate for us in all cases whatsoever.

He has abdicated government here, by declaring us out of his protection and waging war against us.

He has plundered our seas, ravaged our coasts, burned our towns, and destroyed the lives of our people.

He is at this time transporting large armies of foreign mercenaries to complete the works of death, desolation, and tyranny already begun with circumstances of cruelty and perfidy scarcely paralleled in the most barbarous ages, and totally unworthy the head of a civilized nation.

He has constrained our fellow-citizens, taken captive on the high seas, to bear arms against their country, to become the executioners of their friends and brethren, or to fall themselves by their hands.

He has excited domestic insurrection among us, and has endeavored to bring on the inhabitants of our frontiers the merciless Indian savages, whose known rule of warfare is an undistinguished destruction of all ages, sexes, and conditions.

In every stage of these oppressions we have petitioned for redress in the most humble terms; our repeated petitions have been answered only by repeated injury. A prince, whose character is thus marked by every act which may define a tyrant, is unfit to be the ruler of a free people.

Nor have we been wanting in our attentions to our British brethren. We have warned them, from time to time, of attempts by their legislature to extend an unwarrantable jurisdiction over us. We have reminded them of the circumstances of our emigration and settlement here. We have appealed to their native justice and magnanimity; and we have conjured them, by the ties of our common kindred, to disavow these usurpations, which would inevitably interrupt our connections and correspondence. They,

too, have been deaf to the voice of justice and of consanguinity. We must, therefore, acquiesce in the necessity which denounces our separation, and hold them, as we hold the rest of mankind, enemies in war, in peace friends.

We, therefore, the representatives of the United States of America, in General Congress assembled, appealing to the Supreme Judge of the world for the rectitude of our intentions, do, in the name and by the authority of the good people of these colonies, solemnly publish and declare, that these United Colonies are, and of right ought to be, FREE AND INDEPENDENT STATES; that they are absolved from all allegiance to the British crown, and that all political connection between them and the state of Great Britain is, and ought to be, totally dissolved; and that, as free and independent states, they have full power to levy war, conclude peace, contract alliances, establish commerce, and do all other acts and things which independent states may of right do. And for the support of this declaration, with a firm reliance on the protection of Divine Providence, we mutually pledge to each other our lives, our fortunes, and our sacred honor.

JOHN HANCOCK

New Hampshire
Josiah Bartlett
William Whipple
Matthew Thornton

Massachusetts
John Adams
Samuel Adams
Robert Treat Paine
Elbridge Gerry

New York
William Floyd
Philip Livingston
Francis Lewis
Lewis Morris

Rhode Island
Stephen Hopkins
William Ellery

New Jersey
Richard Stockton
John Witherspoon
Francis Hopkinson
John Hart
Abraham Clark

Pennsylvania
Robert Morris
Benjamin Rush
Benjamin Franklin
John Morton
George Clymer
James Smith
George Taylor
James Wilson
George Ross

Delaware
Caeser Rodney
George Read
Thomas McKean

Maryland
Samuel Chase
William Paca
Thomas Stone
Charles Carroll of Carrollton

North Carolina
William Hooper
Joseph Hewes
John Penn

Virginia
George Wythe
Richard Henry Lee
Thomas Jefferson
Benjamin Harrison
Thomas Nelson, Jr.
Francis Lightfoot Lee
Carter Braxton

South Carolina
Edward Rutledge
Thomas Heyward, Jr.
Thomas Lynch, Jr.
Arthur Middleton

Connecticut
Roger Sherman
Samuel Huntington
William Williams
Oliver Wolcott

Georgia
Button Gwinnett
Lyman Hall
George Walton

The Articles of Confederation

Between the States of New Hampshire, Massachusetts Bay, Rhode Island and Providence Plantations, Connecticut, New York, New Jersey, Pennsylvania, Delaware, Maryland, Virginia, North Carolina, South Carolina, Georgia

Article 1

The stile of this confederacy shall be "The United States of America."

Article 2

Each State retains its sovereignty, freedom and independence, and every power, jurisdiction, and right, which is not by this confederation expressly delegated to the United States, in Congress assembled.

Article 3

The said states hereby severally enter into a firm league of friendship with each other for their common defence, the security of their liberties and their mutual and general welfare; binding themselves to assist each other against all force offered to, or attacks made upon them, or any of them, on account of religion, sovereignty, trade, or any other pretence whatever.

Article 4

The better to secure and perpetuate mutual friendship and intercourse among the people of the different states in this union, the free inhabitants of each of these states, paupers, vagabonds, and fugitives from justice excepted, shall be entitled to all privileges and immunities of free citizens in the several states; and the people of each State shall have free ingress and regress to and from any other State, and shall enjoy therein all the privileges of trade and commerce, subject to the same duties, impositions, and restrictions, as the inhabitants thereof respectively; provided, that such restrictions shall not extend so far as to prevent the removal of property, imported into any State, to any other State of which the owner is an inhabitant; provided also, that no imposition, duties, or restriction, shall be laid by any State on the property of the United States, or either of them.

If any person guilty of, or charged with treason, felony, or other high misdemeanor in any State, shall flee from justice and be found in any of the United States, he shall, upon demand of the governor or executive power of the State from which he fled, be delivered up and removed to the State having jurisdiction of his offence.

Full faith and credit shall be given in each of these states to the records, acts, and judicial proceedings of the courts and magistrates of every other State.

Article 5

For the more convenient management of the general interests of the United States, delegates shall be annually appointed, in such manner as the legislature of each State shall direct, to meet in Congress, on the 1st Monday in November in every year, with a power reserved to each State to recall its delegates, or any of them, at any time within the year, and to send others in their stead for the remainder of the year.

No State shall be represented in Congress by less than two, nor by more than seven members; and no person shall be capable of being a delegate for more than three years in any term of six years; nor shall any person, being a delegate, be capable of holding any office under the United States, for which he, or any other for his benefit, receives any salary, fees, or emolument of any kind.

Each State shall maintain its own delegates in a meeting of the states, and while they act as members of the committee of the states.

In determining questions in the United States, in Congress assembled, each State shall have one vote.

Freedom of speech and debate in Congress shall not be impeached or questioned in any court or place out of Congress: and the members of Congress shall be protected in their persons from arrests and imprisonments, during the time of their going to and from, and attendance on Congress, except for treason, felony, or breach of the peace.

Article 6

No State, without the consent of the United States, in Congress assembled, shall send any embassy to, or receive any embassy from, or enter into any conference, agreement, alliance, or treaty with any king, prince, or state; nor shall any person, holding any office of profit or trust under the United States, or any of them, accept of any present, emolument, office or title, of any kind whatever, from any king, prince, or foreign state; nor shall the United States, in Congress assembled, or any of them, grant any title of nobility.

No two or more states shall enter into any treaty, confederation, or alliance, whatever, between them, without the consent of the United States, in Congress assembled, specifying accurately the purposes for which the same is to be entered into, and how long it shall continue.

No State shall lay any imposts or duties which may interfere with any stipulations in treaties entered into by the United States, in Congress assembled, with any king, prince, or state, in pursuance of any treaties already proposed by Congress to the courts of France and Spain.

No vessels of war shall be kept up in time of peace by any State, except such number only as shall be deemed necessary by the United States, in Congress assembled, for the defence of such State or its trade; nor shall any body of forces be kept up by any State, in time of peace, except such number only as, in the judgment of the United States, in Congress assembled, shall be deemed requisite to garrison the forts necessary for the defence of such State; but every State shall always keep up a well regulated and disciplined militia, sufficiently armed and accoutred, and shall provide, and constantly have ready for use, in public stores, a due number of field pieces and tents, and a proper quantity of arms, ammunition and camp equipage.

No State shall engage in any war without the consent of the United States, in Congress assembled, unless such State be actually invaded by enemies, or shall have received certain advice of a resolution being formed by some nation of Indians to invade such State, and the danger is so imminent as not to admit of a delay till the United States, in Congress assembled, can be consulted; nor shall any State grant commissions to any ships or vessels of war, nor letters of marque or reprisal, except it be after a declaration of war by the United States, in Congress assembled, and then only against the kingdom or state, and the subjects thereof, against which war has been so declared, and under such regulations as shall be established by the United States, in Congress assembled, unless such States be infested by pirates, in which case vessels of war may be fitted out for that occasion, and kept so long as the danger shall continue, or until the United States, in Congress assembled, shall determine otherwise.

Article 7

When land forces are raised by any State for the common defence, all officers of or under the rank of colonel, shall be appointed by the legislature of each State respectively, by whom such forces shall be raised, or in such manner as such State shall direct; and all vacancies shall be filled up by the State which first made the appointment.

Article 8

All charges of war and all other expences, that shall be incurred for the common defence or general welfare, and allowed by the United States, in Congress assembled, shall be defrayed out of a common treasury, which shall be supplied by the several states, in proportion to the value of all land within each State, granted to or surveyed for any person, as such land and the buildings and improvements thereon shall be estimated according to such mode as the United States, in Congress assembled, shall, from time to time, direct and appoint.

The taxes for paying that proportion shall be laid and levied by the authority and direction of the legislatures of the several states, within the time agreed upon by the United States, in Congress assembled.

Article 9

The United States, in Congress assembled, shall have the sole and exclusive right and power of determining on peace and war, except in the cases mentioned in the 6th article; of sending and receiving ambassadors; entering into treaties and alliances, provided that no treaty of commerce shall be made, whereby the legislative power of the respective states shall be restrained from imposing such imposts and duties on foreigners as their own people are subjected to, or from prohibiting the exportation or importation of any species of goods or commodities whatsoever; of establishing rules for deciding, in all cases, what captures on land or water shall be legal, and in what manner prizes, taken by land or naval forces in the service of the United States, shall be divided or appropriated; of granting letters of marque and reprisal in times of peace; appointing courts for the trial of piracies and felonies committed on the high seas, and establishing

courts for receiving and determining, finally, appeals in all cases of captures; provided, that no member of Congress shall be appointed a judge of any of the said courts.

The United States, in Congress assembled, shall also be the last resort on appeal in all disputes and differences now subsisting, or that hereafter may arise between two or more states concerning boundary, jurisdiction or any other cause whatever; which authority shall always be exercised in the manner following: whenever the legislative or executive authority, or lawful agent of any State, in controversy with another, shall present a petition to Congress, stating the matter in question, and praying for a hearing, notice thereof shall be given, by order of Congress, to the legislative or executive authority of the other State in controversy, and a day assigned for the appearance of the parties by their lawful agents, who shall then be directed to appoint, by joint consent, commissioners or judges to constitute a court for hearing and determining the matter in question; but, if they cannot agree, Congress shall name three persons out of each of the United States, and from the list of such persons each party shall alternately strike out one, in the petitioners beginning, until the number shall be reduced to thirteen; and from that number not less than seven, nor more than nine names, as Congress shall direct, shall, in the presence of Congress, be drawn out by lot; and the persons whose names shall be drawn, or any five of them, shall be commissioners or judges to hear and finally determine the controversy, so always as a major part of the judges who shall hear the cause shall agree in the determination; and if either party shall neglect to attend at the day appointed, without shewing reasons which Congress shall judge sufficient, or, being present, shall refuse to strike, the Congress shall proceed to nominate three persons out of each State, and the secretary of Congress shall strike in behalf of such party absent or refusing; and the judgment and sentence of the court to be appointed, in the manner before prescribed, shall be final and conclusive; and if any of the parties shall refuse to submit to the authority of such court, or to appear or defend their claim or cause, the court shall nevertheless proceed to pronounce sentence or judgment, which shall, in like manner, be final and decisive, the judgment or sentence and other proceedings being, in either case, transmitted to Congress, and lodged among the acts of Congress for the security of the parties concerned: provided, that every commissioner, before he sits in judgment, shall take an oath, to be administered by one of the judges of the supreme or superior court of the State where the cause shall be tried, "well and truly to hear and determine the matter in question, according to the best of his judgment, without favour, affection, or hope of reward": provided, also, that no State shall be deprived of territory for the benefit of the United States.

All controversies concerning the private right of soil, claimed under different grants of two or more states, whose jurisdictions, as they may respect such lands and the states which passed such grants, are adjusted, the said grants, or either of them, being at the same time claimed to have originated antecedent to such settlement of jurisdiction, shall, on the petition of either party to the Congress of the United States, be finally determined, as near as may be, in the same manner as is before prescribed for deciding disputes respecting territorial jurisdiction between different states.

The United States, in Congress assembled, shall also have the sole and exclusive right and power of regulating the alloy and value of coin struck by their own authority, or by that of the respective states; fixing the standard of weights and measures throughout the United States; regulating the trade and managing all affairs with the Indians not members of any of the states; provided that the legislative right of any State within its own limits be not infringed or violated; establishing and regulating post offices from one State to another throughout all the United States, and exacting such postage on the papers passing through the same as may be requisite to defray the expences of the said office; appointing all officers of the land forces in the service of the United States, excepting regimental officers; appointing all the officers of the naval forces, and commissioning all officers whatever in the service of the United States; making rules for the government and regulation of the said land and naval forces, and directing their operations.

The United States, in Congress assembled, shall have authority to appoint a committee to sit in the recess of Congress, to be denominated "a Committee of the States," and to consist of one delegate from each State, and to appoint such other committees and civil officers as may be necessary for managing the general affairs of the United States, under their direction; to appoint one of their number to preside; provided that no person be allowed to serve in the office of president more than one year in any term of three years; to ascertain the necessary sums of money to be raised for the service of the United States, and to appropriate and apply the same for defraying the public expences; to borrow money or emit bills on the credit of the United States, transmitting, every half year, to the respective states, an account of the sums of money so borrowed or emitted; to build and equip a navy; to agree upon the number of land forces, and to make requisitions from each State for its quota, in proportion to the number of white inhabitants in such State; which requisitions shall be binding; and, thereupon, the legislature of each State shall appoint the regimental officers, raise the men, and cloathe, arm, and equip them in a soldier-like manner, at the expence of the United States; and the officers and men so cloathed, armed, and equipped, shall march to the place appointed and within the time agreed on by the United States, in Congress assembled; but if the United States, in Congress assembled, shall, on consideration of circumstances, judge proper that any State should not raise men, or should raise a smaller number than its quota, and that any other State should raise a greater number of men than the quota thereof, such extra number shall be raised, officered, cloathed, armed, and equipped in the same manner as the quota of such State, unless the legislature of such State shall judge that such extra number cannot be safely spared out of the same, in which case they shall raise, officer, cloathe, arm, and equip as many of such extra number as they judge can be safely spared. And the officers and men so cloathed, armed, and equipped, shall march to the place appointed and within the time agreed on by the United States, in Congress assembled.

The United States, in Congress assembled, shall never engage in a war, nor grant letters of marque and reprisal in time of peace, nor enter into any treaties or alliances, nor coin money, nor regulate the value thereof, nor ascertain the sums and expences necessary for the defence and welfare of the United States, or any of them: nor emit bills, nor borrow money on the credit of the United States, nor appropriate money, nor agree upon the number of vessels of war to be built or purchased, or the number of land or sea forces to be raised, nor appoint a commander in chief of the army or navy, unless nine states assent to the same; nor shall a question on any other point, except for adjourning from day to day, be determined, unless by the votes of a majority of the United States, in Congress assembled.

The Congress of the United States shall have power to adjourn to any time within the year, and to any place within the United States, so that no period of adjournment be for a longer duration than the space of six months, and shall publish the journal of their proceedings monthly, except such parts thereof, relating to treaties, alliances or military operations, as, in their judgment, require secrecy; and the yeas and nays of the delegates of each State on any question shall be entered on the journal, when it is desired by any delegate; and the delegates of a State, or any of them, at his, or their request, shall be furnished with a transcript of the said journal, except such parts as are above excepted, to lay before the legislatures of the several states.

Article 10

The committee of the states, or any nine of them, shall be authorized to execute, in the recess of Congress, such of the powers of Congress as the United States, in Congress assembled, by the consent of nine states, shall, from time to time, think expedient to vest them with; provided, that no power be delegated to the said committee for the exercise of which, by the articles of confederation, the voice of nine states, in the Congress of the United States assembled, is requisite.

Article 11

Canada acceding to this confederation, and joining in the measures of the United States, shall be admitted into and entitled to all the advantages of this union; but no other colony shall be admitted into the same, unless such admission be agreed to by nine states.

Article 12

All bills of credit emitted, monies borrowed and debts contracted by, or under the authority of Congress before the assembling of the United States, in pursuance of the present confederation, shall be deemed and considered as a charge against the United States, for payment and satisfaction whereof the said United States and the public faith are hereby solemnly pledged.

Article 13

Every State shall abide by the determinations of the United States, in Congress assembled, on all questions which, by this confederation, are submitted to them. And the articles of this confederation shall be inviolably observed by every State, and the union shall be perpetual; nor shall any alteration at any time hereafter be made in any of them; unless such alteration be agreed to in a Congress of the United States, and be afterwards confirmed by the legislatures of every State.

These articles shall be proposed to the legislatures of all the United States, to be considered, and if approved of by them, they are advised to authorize their delegates to ratify the same in the Congress of the United States; which being done, the same shall become conclusive.

The Constitution of the United States of America

Preamble

We the People of the United States, in Order to form a more perfect Union, establish Justice, insure domestic Tranquility, provide for the common defence, promote the general Welfare, and secure the Blessings of Liberty to ourselves and our Posterity, do ordain and establish this Constitution for the United States of America.

Article I

Section 1

All legislative Powers herein granted shall be vested in a Congress of the United States, which shall consist of a Senate and House of Representatives.

Section 2

The House of Representatives shall be composed of Members chosen every second Year by the People of the several States, and the Electors in each State shall have the Qualifications requisite for Electors of the most numerous Branch of the State Legislature.

No Person shall be a Representative who shall not have attained to the Age of twenty five Years, and been seven Years a Citizen of the United States, and who shall not, when elected, be an inhabitant of that State in which he shall be chosen.

Representatives and direct Taxes shall be apportioned among the several States which may be included within this Union, according to their respective Numbers, *which shall be determined by adding to the whole Number of free Persons, including those bound to Service for a Term of Years, and excluding Indians not taxed, three fifths of all other Persons.** The actual Enumeration shall be made within three Years after the first Meeting of the Congress of the United States, and within every subsequent Term of ten Years, in such Manner as they shall by Law direct. The Number of Representatives shall not exceed one for every thirty Thousand, but each State shall have at Least one Representative; *and until such enumeration shall be made, the State of New Hampshire shall be entitled to chuse three, Massachusetts eight, Rhode-Island and Providence Plantations one, Connecticut five, New York six, New Jersey four, Pennsylvania eight, Delaware one, Maryland six, Virginia ten, North Carolina five, South Carolina five, and Georgia three.*

When vacancies happen in the Representation from any State, the Executive Authority thereof shall issue Writs of Election to fill such Vacancies.

The House of Representatives shall chuse their Speaker and other Officers; and shall have the sole Power of Impeachment.

---

*Passages no longer in effect are printed in italic type.

Section 3

The Senate of the United States shall be composed of two Senators from each State, *chosen by the Legislature thereof,* for six Years; and each Senator shall have one Vote.

Immediately after they shall be assembled in Consequence of the first Election, they shall be divided as equally as may be into three Classes. The Seats of the Senators of the first Class shall be vacated at the Expiration of the second Year, of the second Class at the Expiration of the fourth Year, and of the third Class at the Expiration of the sixth Year so that one third may be chosen every second Year; and if Vacancies happen by Resignation, or otherwise, during the Recess of the Legislature of any state, the Executive thereof may make temporary Appointments until the next Meeting of the Legislature, which shall then fill such Vacancies.

No Person shall be a Senator who shall not have attained to the Age of thirty Years, and been nine Years a Citizen of the United States, and who shall not, when elected, be an Inhabitant of that State for which he shall be chosen.

The Vice President of the United States shall be President of the Senate, but shall have no Vote, unless they be equally divided.

The Senate shall chuse their other Officers, and also a President *pro tempore,* in the Absence of the Vice President, or when he shall exercise the Office of President of the United States.

The Senate shall have the sole Power to try all Impeachments. When sitting for that Purpose, they shall be on Oath or Affirmation. When the President of the United States is tried the Chief Justice shall preside: And no Person shall be convicted without the Concurrence of two thirds of the Members present.

Judgment in Cases of Impeachment shall not extend further than to removal from Office, and disqualification to hold and enjoy any Office of honor, Trust or Profit under the United States: but the Party convicted shall nevertheless be liable and subject to Indictment, Trial, Judgment and Punishment, according to Law.

Section 4

The Times, Places and Manner of holding Elections for Senators and Representatives, shall be prescribed in each State by the Legislature thereof; but the Congress may at any time by Law make or alter such Regulations, except as to the Places of chusing Senators.

The Congress shall assemble at least once in every Year, *and such Meeting shall be on the first Monday in December, unless they shall by Law appoint a different Day.*

Section 5

Each House shall be the Judge of the Elections, Returns and Qualifications of its own Members, and a Majority of each shall constitute a Quorum to do Business; but a smaller Number may adjourn from day to day, and may be authorized to compel the Attendance of absent Members, in such Manner, and under such Penalties as each House may provide.

Each House may determine the Rules of its Proceedings, punish its Members for disorderly Behaviour, and, with the Concurrence of two thirds, expel a Member.

Each House shall keep a Journal of its Proceedings, and from time to time publish the same, excepting such Parts as may in their Judgment require Secrecy; and the Yeas and Nays of the Members of either House on any question shall, at the Desire of one fifth of those Present, be entered on the Journal.

Neither House, during the Session of Congress, shall, without the Consent of the other, adjourn for more than three days, nor to any other Place than that in which the two Houses shall be sitting.

Section 6

The Senators and Representatives shall receive a Compensation for their Services, to be ascertained by Law, and paid out of the Treasury of the United States. They shall in all Cases, except Treason, Felony and Breach of the Peace, be privileged from Arrest during their Attendance at the Session of their respective Houses, and in going to and returning from the same; and for any Speech or Debate in either House, they shall not be questioned in any other Place.

No Senator or Representative shall, during the Time for which he was elected, be appointed to any civil Office under the Authority of the United States, which shall have been created, or the Emoluments whereof shall have been encreased during such time, and no Person holding any Office under the United States, shall be a Member of either House during his Continuance in Office.

Section 7

All Bills for raising Revenue shall originate in the House of Representatives; but the Senate may propose or concur with Amendments as on other Bills.

Every Bill which shall have passed the House of Representatives and the Senate, shall, before it become a Law, be presented to the President of the United States; If he approve he shall sign it, but if not he shall return it, with his Objections to the House in which it shall have originated, who shall enter the Objections at large on their Journal, and proceed to reconsider it. If after such Reconsideration two thirds of that House shall agree to pass the Bill, it shall be sent, together with the Objections, to the other House, by which it shall likewise be reconsidered, and if approved by two thirds of that House, it shall become a Law. But in all such Cases the Votes of both Houses shall be determined by yeas and Nays, and the Names of the Persons voting for and against the Bill shall be entered on the Journal of each House respectively. If any Bill shall not be returned by the President within ten Days (Sundays excepted) after it shall have been presented to him, the Same shall be a Law, in like Manner as if he had signed it, unless the Congress by their Adjournment prevent its Return, in which Case it shall not be a Law.

Every Order, Resolution, or Vote to which the Concurrence of the Senate and House of Representatives may be necessary (except on a question of Adjournment) shall be presented to the President of the United States; and before the Same shall take Effect, shall be approved by him, or being disapproved by him, shall be repassed by two thirds of the Senate and House of Representatives, according to the Rules and Limitations prescribed in the Case of a Bill.

Section 8

The Congress shall have Power To lay and collect Taxes, Duties, Imposts and Excises, to pay the Debts and provide for the common Defence and general Welfare of the United States; but all Duties, Imposts and Excises shall be uniform throughout the United States;

To borrow Money on the credit of the United States;

To regulate Commerce with foreign Nations, and among the several States, and with the Indian Tribes;

To establish an uniform Rule of Naturalization, and uniform Laws on the subject of Bankruptcies throughout the United States;

To coin Money, regulate the Value thereof, and of foreign Coin, and fix the Standard of Weights and Measures;

To provide for the Punishment of counterfeiting the Securities and current Coin of the United States;

To establish Post Offices and post Roads;

To promote the Progress of Science and useful Arts, by securing for limited Times to Authors and Inventors the exclusive Right to their respective Writings and Discoveries;

To constitute Tribunals inferior to the supreme Court;

To define and punish Piracies and Felonies committed on the high Seas, and Offences against the Law of Nations;

To declare War, grant Letters of Marque and Reprisal, and make Rules concerning Captures on Land and Water;

To raise and support Armies, but no Appropriation of Money to that Use shall be for a longer Term than two Years;

To provide and maintain a Navy;

To make Rules for the Government and Regulation of the land and naval Forces;

To provide for calling forth the Militia to execute the Laws of the Union, suppress Insurrections and repel Invasions;

To provide for organizing, arming, and disciplining, the Militia, and for governing such Part of them as may be employed in the Service of the United States, reserving to the States respectively, the Appointment of the Officers, and the Authority of training the Militia according to the discipline prescribed by Congress;

To exercise exclusive Legislation in all Cases whatsoever, over such District (not exceeding ten Miles square) as may, by Cession of particular States, and the Acceptance of Congress, become the Seat of the Government of the United States, and to exercise like Authority over all Places purchased by the Consent of the Legislature of the State in which the Same shall be, for the Erection of Forts, Magazines, Arsenals, dock-Yards, and other needful Buildings;—And

To make all Laws which shall be necessary and proper for carrying into Execution the foregoing Powers, and all other Powers vested by this Constitution in the Government of the United States, or in any Department of Officer thereof.

Section 9

The Migration or Importation of such Persons as any of the States now existing shall think proper to admit, shall not be prohibited by the Congress prior to the Year one thousand eight hundred and

eight, but a Tax or duty may be imposed on such Importation, not exceeding ten dollars for each Person.

The Privilege of the Writ of Habeas Corpus shall not be suspended, unless when in Cases of Rebellion or Invasion the public Safety may require it.

No Bill of Attainder or ex post facto Law shall be passed.

No Capitation, or other direct, Tax shall be laid, unless in Proportion to the Census or Enumeration herein before directed to be taken.

No Tax or Duty shall be laid on Articles exported from any State.

No Preference shall be given by any Regulation of Commerce or Revenue to the Ports of one State over those of another: nor shall Vessels bound to, or from, one State, be obliged to enter, clear, or pay Duties in another.

No Money shall be drawn from the Treasury, but in Consequence of Appropriations made by Law; and a regular Statement and Account of the Receipts and Expenditures of all public Money shall be published from time to time.

No Title of Nobility shall be granted by the United States: And no Person holding any Office of Profit or Trust under them, shall, without the Consent of the Congress, accept of any present, Emolument, Office, or Title, of any kind whatever, from any King, Prince, or foreign State.

Section 10

No State shall enter into any Treaty, Alliance, or Confederation; grant Letters of Marque and Reprisal; coin Money; emit Bills of Credit; make any Thing but gold and silver Coin a Tender in Payment of Debts; pass any Bill of Attainder, ex post facto Law, or Law impairing the obligation of Contracts, or grant any Title of Nobility.

No State shall, without the Consent of the Congress, lay any Imposts or Duties on Imports or Exports, except what may be absolutely necessary for executing its inspection Laws: and the net Produce of all Duties and Imposts, laid by any State on Imports or Exports, shall be for the Use of the Treasury of the United States; and all such Laws shall be subject to the Revision and Controul of the Congress.

No State shall, without the Consent of Congress, lay any Duty of Tonnage, keep Troops, or Ships of War in time of Peace, enter into any Agreement or Compact with another State, or with a foreign Power, or engage in War, unless actually invaded, or in such imminent Danger as will not admit of delay.

Article II

Section 1

The executive Power shall be vested in a President of the United States of America. He shall hold his Office during the Term of four Years, and, together with the Vice President, chosen for the same Term, be elected, as follows:

Each State shall appoint, in such Manner as the Legislature thereof may direct, a Number of Electors, equal to the whole Number of Senators and Representatives to which the State may be entitled in the Congress: but no Senator or Representative, or Person holding an Office of Trust or Profit under the United States, shall be appointed an Elector.

The Electors shall meet in their respective States, and vote by Ballot for two Persons, of whom one at least shall not be an Inhabitant of the same State with themselves. And they shall make a List of all the Persons voted for, and of the Number of Votes for each; which List they shall sign and certify, and transmit sealed to the Seat of the Government of the United States, directed to the President of the Senate. The President of the Senate shall, in the Presence of the Senate and House of Representatives, open all the Certificates, and the Votes shall then be counted. The Person having the greatest Number of Votes shall be the President, if such Number be a Majority of the whole number of Electors appointed; and if there be more than one who have such Majority, and have an equal Number of Votes, then the House of Representatives shall immediately chuse by Ballot one of them for President; and if no Person have a Majority, then from the five highest on the List the said House shall in like Manner chuse the President. But in chusing the President, the Votes shall be taken by States, the Representation from each State having one Vote; A quorum for this Purpose shall consist of a Member or Members from two thirds of the States, and a Majority of all the States shall be necessary to a Choice. In every Case, after the Choice of the President, the Person having the greatest Number of Votes of the Electors shall be the Vice President. But if there should remain two or more who have equal Votes, the Senate shall chuse from them by Ballot the Vice President.

The Congress may determine the time of chusing the Electors, and the Day on which they shall give their Votes; which Day shall be the same throughout the United States.

No person except a natural born Citizen, *or a Citizen of the United States, at the time of the Adoption of this Constitution,* shall be eligible to the Office of President; neither shall any Person be eligible to that Office who shall not have attained to the Age of thirty five Years, and been fourteen Years a Resident within the United States.

In Case of the Removal of the President from Office, or of his Death, Resignation, or Inability to discharge the Powers and Duties of the said Office, the Same shall devolve on the Vice President, and the Congress may by Law provide for the Case of Removal, Death, Resignation or Inability, both of the President and Vice President, declaring what Officer shall then act as President, and such Officer shall act accordingly, until the Disability be removed, or a President shall be elected.

The President shall, at stated Times, receive for his Services, a Compensation, which shall neither be increased nor diminished during the Period for which he shall have been elected, and he shall not receive within that period any other Emolument from the United States, or any of them.

Before he enter on the Execution of his Office, he shall take the following Oath or Affirmation:—"I do solemnly swear (or affirm) that I will faithfully execute the Office of President of the United States, and will to the best of my Ability, preserve, protect and defend the Constitution of the United States."

Section 2

The President shall be Commander in Chief of the Army and Navy of the United States, and of the Militia of the several States, when called into the actual Service of the United States; he may require the Opinion, in writing, of the principal Officer in each of the executive Departments, upon any Subject relating to the Duties of their respective Offices, and he shall have

Power to grant Reprieves and Pardons for Offences against the United States, except in Cases of Impeachment.

He shall have Power, by and with the Advice and Consent of the Senate, to make Treaties, provided two thirds of the Senators present concur; and he shall nominate, and by and with the Advice and Consent of the Senate, shall appoint Ambassadors, other public Ministers and Consuls, Judges of the supreme Court, and all other Officers of the United States, whose Appointments are not herein otherwise provided for, and which shall be established by Law: but the Congress may by Law vest the Appointment of such inferior Officers, as they think proper in the President alone, in the Courts of Law, or in the Heads of Departments.

The President shall have Power to fill up all Vacancies that may happen during the Recess of the Senate, by granting Commissions which shall expire at the End of their next Session.

Section 3

He shall from time to time give to the Congress Information of the State of the Union, and recommend to their Consideration such Measures as he shall judge necessary and expedient; he may, on extraordinary Occasions, convene both Houses, or either of them, and in Case of disagreement between them, with Respect to the Time of Adjournment, he may adjourn them to such Time as he shall think proper; he shall receive Ambassadors and other public Ministers; he shall take Care that the Laws be faithfully executed, and shall Commission all the officers of the United States.

Section 4

The President, Vice President and all civil Officers of the United States, shall be removed from Office on Impeachment for, and Conviction of, Treason, Bribery or other high Crimes and Misdemeanors.

Article III

Section 1

The judicial Power of the United States, shall be vested in one supreme Court, and in such inferior Courts as the Congress may from time to time ordain and establish. The Judges, both of the supreme and inferior Courts, shall hold their offices during good Behaviour, and shall, at stated Times, receive for their Services, a Compensation, which shall not be diminished during their Continuance in Office.

Section 2

The judicial Power shall extend to all Cases, in Law and Equity, arising under this Constitution, the Laws of the United States, and Treaties made, or which shall be made, under their Authority;—to all Cases affecting Ambassadors, other public Ministers and Consuls;—to all Cases of admiralty and maritime Jurisdiction;—to Controversies to which the United States shall be a Party;—to Controversies between two or more States;— *between a State and Citizens of another State;*—between Citizens of different States;—between Citizens of the same State claiming Lands under Grants of different States, and between a State, or the Citizens thereof, and foreign States, Citizens or Subjects.

In all Cases affecting Ambassadors, other public Ministers and Consuls, and those in which a State shall be Party, the supreme Court shall have original Jurisdiction. In all the other Cases before mentioned, the supreme Court shall have appellate Jurisdiction, both as to Law and Fact, with such Exceptions, and under such Regulations as the Congress shall make.

The Trial of all Crimes, except in Cases of Impeachment, shall be by Jury; and such Trial shall be held in the State where the said Crimes shall have been committed, but when not committed within any State, the Trial shall be at such Place or Places as the Congress may by Law have directed.

Section 3

Treason against the United States, shall consist only in levying War against them, or in adhering to their Enemies, giving them Aid and Comfort. No person shall be convicted of Treason unless on the Testimony of two Witnesses to the same overt Act, or on Confession in open Court.

The Congress shall have Power to declare the Punishment of Treason, but no Attainder of Treason shall work Corruption of Blood, or Forfeiture except during the Life of the Person attainted.

Article IV

Section 1

Full Faith and Credit shall be given in each State to the public Acts, Records, and judicial Proceedings of every other State. And the Congress may by general Laws prescribe the Manner in which such Acts, Records and Proceedings shall be proved, and the Effect thereof.

Section 2

The Citizens of each State shall be entitled to all Privileges and Immunities of Citizens in the several States.

A Person charged in any State with Treason, Felony, or other Crime, who shall flee from Justice, and be found in another State, shall on Demand of the executive Authority of the State from which he fled, be delivered up, to be removed to the State having Jurisdiction of the Crime.

No Person held to Service or Labour in one State, under the Laws thereof, escaping into another, shall, in Consequence of any Law or Regulation therein, be discharged from such Service or Labour, but shall be delivered up on Claim of the Party to whom such Service or Labour may be due.

Section 3

New States may be admitted by the Congress into this Union; but no new State shall be formed or erected within the Jurisdiction of any other State; nor any State be formed by the Junction of two or more States, or Parts of States, without the Consent of the Legislatures of the States concerned as well as of the Congress.

The Congress shall have Power to dispose of and make all needful Rules and Regulations respecting the Territory or other Property belonging to the United States; and nothing in this Constitution shall be so construed as to Prejudice any Claims of the United States, or of any particular States.

Section 4

The United States shall guarantee to every State in this Union a Republican Form of Government, and shall protect each of them against Invasion; and on Application of the Legislature, or of the Executive (when the Legislature cannot be convened) against domestic violence.

Article V

The Congress, whenever two thirds of both Houses shall deem it necessary, shall propose Amendments to this Constitution, or, on the Application of the Legislatures of two thirds of the several States, shall call a Convention for proposing Amendments, which, in either Case, shall be valid to all Intents and Purposes, as Part of this Constitution, when ratified by the Legislatures of three fourths of the several States, or by Conventions in three fourths thereof, as the one or the other Mode of Ratification may be proposed by the Congress; Provided *that no Amendment which may be made prior to the Year One thousand eight hundred and eight shall in any Manner affect the first and fourth Clauses in the Ninth Section of the first Article;* and that no State, without its Consent, shall be deprived of its equal Suffrage in the Senate.

Article VI

All Debts contracted and Engagements entered into, before the Adoption of this Constitution, shall be as valid against the United States under this Constitution, as under the Confederation.

This Constitution, and Laws of the United States which shall be made in Pursuance thereof; and all Treaties made, or which shall be made, under the Authority of the United States, shall be the supreme Law of the Land; and the Judges in every State shall be bound thereby, any Thing in the Constitution or Laws of any State to the Contrary notwithstanding.

The Senators and Representatives before mentioned, and the Members of the several State Legislatures, and all executive and Judicial Officers, both of the United States and of the several States, shall be bound by Oath or Affirmation, to support this Constitution; but no religious Test shall ever be required as a Qualification to any Office of public Trust under the United States.

Article VII

The Ratification of the Conventions of nine States, shall be sufficient for the Establishment of this Constitution between the States so ratifying the Same.

Done in Convention by the Unanimous Consent of the States present the Seventeenth Day of September in the Year of our Lord one thousand seven hundred and Eighty seven and of the Independence of the United States of America the Twelfth* IN WITNESS whereof We have hereunto subscribed our Names,

George Washington
President and Deputy from Virginia

Delaware	*South Carolina*	*New York*
George Read	John Rutledge	Alexander Hamilton
Gunning Bedford, Jr.	Charles Cotesworth Pinckney	
John Dickinson	Charles Pinckney	*New Jersey*
Richard Bassett	Pierce Butler	William Livingston
Jacob Broom		David Brearley
	Georgia	William Paterson
Maryland	William Few	Jonathan Dayton
James McHenry	Abraham Baldwin	
Daniel of St. Thomas Jenifer		*Pennsylvania*
Daniel Carroll	*New Hampshire*	Benjamin Franklin
	John Langdon	Thomas Mifflin
Virginia	Nicholas Gilman	Robert Morris
John Blair		George Clymer
James Madison, Jr.	*Massachusetts*	Thomas FitzSimons
	Nathaniel Gorham	Jared Ingersoll
North Carolina	Rufus King	James Wilson
William Blount		Gouverneur Morris
Richard Dobbs Spraight	*Connecticut*	
Hugh Williamson	William Samuel Johnson	
	Roger Sherman	

*The Constitution was submitted on September 17, 1787, by the Constitutional Convention, was ratified by conventions of the several states at various dates up to May 29, 1790, and became effective on March 4, 1789.

Amendments to the Constitution

Amendment I

Congress shall make no law respecting an establishment of religion, or prohibiting the free exercise thereof; or abridging the freedom of speech, or of the press; or the right of the people peaceably to assemble, and to petition the Government for a redress of grievances.

Amendment II

A well regulated Militia being necessary to the security of a free State, the right of the people to keep and bear Arms, shall not be infringed.

Amendment III

No Soldier shall, in time of peace be quartered in any house, without the consent of the Owner, nor in time of war, but in a manner to be prescribed by law.

Amendment IV

The right of the people to be secure in their persons, houses, papers, and effects, against unreasonable searches and seizures, shall not be violated, and no Warrants shall issue, but upon probable cause, supported by Oath or affirmation, and particularly describing the place to be searched, and the persons or things to be seized.

Amendment V

No person shall be held to answer for a capital, or otherwise infamous crime, unless on a presentment or indictment of a Grand Jury, except in cases arising in the land or naval forces, or in the Militia, when in actual service in time of War or public danger; nor shall any person be subject for the same offense to be twice put in jeopardy of life or limb; nor shall be compelled in any criminal case to be a witness against himself, nor be deprived of life, liberty, or property, without due process of law; nor shall private property be taken for public use, without just compensation.

Amendment VI

In all criminal prosecutions, the accused shall enjoy the right to a speedy and public trial, by an impartial jury of the State and district wherein the crime shall have been committed, which district shall have been previously ascertained by law, and to be informed of the nature and cause of the accusation; to be confronted with the witnesses against him; to have compulsory process for obtaining witnesses in his favor, and to have the Assistance of Counsel for his defence.

Amendment VII

In Suits at common law, where the value in controversy shall exceed twenty dollars, the right of trial by jury shall be preserved, and no fact tried by a jury, shall be otherwise re-examined in any Court of the United States, than according to the rules of the common law.

Amendment VIII

Excessive bail shall not be required, nor excessive fines imposed, nor cruel and unusual punishments inflicted.

Amendment IX

The enumeration in the Constitution, of certain rights, shall not be construed to deny or disparage others retained by the people.

Amendment X*

The powers not delegated to the United States by the Constitution, nor prohibited by it to the States, are reserved to the States respectively, or to the people.

Amendment XI
[Adopted 1798]

The Judicial power of the United States shall not be construed to extend to any suit in law or equity, commenced or prosecuted against one of the United States by Citizens of another State, or by Citizens or Subjects of any Foreign State.

Amendment XII
[Adopted 1804]

The Electors shall meet in their respective states, and vote by ballot for President and Vice President, one of whom, at least, shall not be an inhabitant of the same state with themselves; they shall name in their ballots the person voted for as President, and in distinct ballots the person voted for as Vice President, and they shall make distinct lists of all persons voted for as President, and of all persons voted for as Vice President, and of the number of votes for each, which lists they shall sign and certify, and transmit sealed to the seat of the government of the United States, directed to the President of the Senate;—The President of the Senate shall, in the presence of the Senate and House of Representatives, open all the certificates and the votes shall then be counted;—The person having the greatest number of votes for President, shall be the President, if such number be a majority of the whole number of Electors appointed; and if no person have such majority, then from the persons having the highest numbers not exceeding three on the list of those voted for as President, the House of Representatives shall choose immediately, by ballot, the President. But in choosing the President, the votes shall be taken by states, the representation from each state having one vote; a quorum for this purpose shall consist of a

---

*The first ten amendments (the Bill of Rights) were ratified and their adoption was certified on December 15, 1791.

member or members from two-thirds of the states, and a majority of all the states shall be necessary to a choice. And if the House of Representatives shall not choose a President whenever the right of choice shall devolve upon them, before *the fourth day of March* next following, then the Vice President shall act as President, as in the case of the death or other constitutional disability of the President.—The person having the greatest number of votes as Vice President, shall be the Vice President, if such number be a majority of the whole number of Electors appointed, and if no person have a majority, then from the two highest numbers on the list, the Senate shall choose the Vice President; a quorum for the purpose shall consist of two-thirds of the whole number of Senators, and a majority of the whole number shall be necessary to a choice. But no person constitutionally ineligible to the office of President shall be eligible to that of Vice President of the United States.

Amendment XIII
[Adopted 1865]

Section 1

Neither slavery nor involuntary servitude, except as a punishment for crime whereof the party shall have been duly convicted, shall exist within the United States, or any place subject to their jurisdiction.

Section 2

Congress shall have power to enforce this article by appropriate legislation.

Amendment XIV
[Adopted 1868]

Section 1

All persons born or naturalized in the United States, and subject to the jurisdiction thereof, are citizens of the United States and of the State wherein they reside. No State shall make or enforce any law which shall abridge the privileges or immunities of citizens of the United States; nor shall any State deprive any person of life, liberty, or property, without due process of law; nor deny to any person within its jurisdiction the equal protection of the laws.

Section 2

Representatives shall be apportioned among the several States according to their respective numbers, counting the whole number of persons in each State, excluding Indians not taxed. But when the right to vote at any election for the choice of electors for President and Vice President of the United States, Representatives in Congress, the Executive and Judicial officers of a State, or the members of the Legislature thereof, is denied to any of the male inhabitants of such State, being twenty-one years of age, and citizens of the United States, or in any way abridged, except for participation in rebellion, or other crime, the basis of representation therein shall be reduced in the proportion which the number of such male citizens shall bear to the whole number of male citizens twenty-one years of age in such State.

Section 3

No person shall be a Senator or Representative in Congress, or elector of President and Vice President, or hold any office, civil or military, under the United States, or under any State, who, having previously taken an oath, as a member of Congress, or as an officer of the United States, or as a member of any State legislature, or as an executive or judicial officer of any State, to support the Constitution of the United States, shall have engaged in insurrection or rebellion against the same, or given aid or comfort to the enemies thereof. But Congress may by a vote of two-thirds of each House, remove such disability.

Section 4

The validity of the public debt of the United States, authorized by law, including debts incurred for payment of pensions and bounties for services in suppressing insurrection or rebellion, shall not be questioned. But neither the United States nor any State shall assume or pay any debt or obligation incurred in aid of insurrection or rebellion against the United States, or any claim for the loss or emancipation of any slave; but all such debts, obligations and claims shall be held illegal and void.

Section 5

The Congress shall have power to enforce, by appropriate legislation, the provisions of this article.

Amendment XV
[Adopted 1870]

Section 1

The right of citizens of the United States to vote shall not be denied or abridged by the United States or by any State on account of race, color, or previous condition of servitude.

Section 2

The Congress shall have power to enforce this article by appropriate legislation.

Amendment XVI
[Adopted 1913]

The Congress shall have power to lay and collect taxes on incomes, from whatever source derived, without apportionment among the several States, and without regard to any census or enumeration.

Amendment XVII
[Adopted 1913]

The Senate of the United States shall be composed of two Senators from each State, elected by the people thereof, for six years; and each Senator shall have one vote. The electors in each State shall have the qualifications requisite for electors of the most numerous branch of the State legislatures.

When vacancies happen in the representation of any State in the Senate, the executive authority of such State shall issue writs of election to fill such vacancies: *Provided,* That the legislature of any State may empower the executive thereof to make temporary appointments until the people fill the vacancies by election as the legislature may direct.

This amendment shall not be so construed as to affect the election or term of any Senator chosen before it becomes valid as part of the Constitution.

Amendment XVIII
[Adopted 1919, repealed 1933]

Section 1

After one year from the ratification of this article the manufacture, sale, or transportation of intoxicating liquors within, the importation thereof into, or the exportation thereof from the United States and all territory subject to the jurisdiction thereof for beverage purposes is hereby prohibited.

Section 2

The Congress and the several States shall have concurrent power to enforce this article by appropriate legislation.

Section 3

This article shall be inoperative unless it shall have been ratified as an amendment to the Constitution by the legislatures of the several States, as provided in the Constitution, within seven years from the date of the submission hereof to the States by the Congress.

Amendment XIX
[Adopted 1920]

The right of citizens of the United States to vote shall not be denied or abridged by the United States or by any State on account of sex.

Congress shall have power to enforce this article by appropriate legislation.

Amendment XX
[Adopted 1933]

Section 1

The terms of the President and Vice President shall end at noon on the 20th day of January, and the terms of Senators and Representatives at noon on the 3d day of January, of the years in which such terms would have ended if this article had not been ratified and the terms of their successors shall then begin.

Section 2

The Congress shall assemble at least once in every year, and such meeting shall begin at noon on the 3d day of January, unless they shall by law appoint a different day.

Section 3

If, at the time fixed for the beginning of the term of the President, the President elect shall have died, the Vice President elect shall become President. If a President shall not have been chosen before the time fixed for the beginning of his term, or if the President elect shall have failed to qualify, then the Vice President elect shall act as President until a President shall have qualified; and the Congress may by law provide for the case wherein neither a President elect nor a Vice President elect shall have qualified, declaring who shall then act as President, or the manner in which one who is to act shall be selected, and such person shall act accordingly until a President or Vice President shall have qualified.

Section 4

The Congress may by law provide for the case of the death of any of the persons from whom the House of Representatives may choose a President whenever the right of choice shall have devolved upon them, and for the case of the death of any of the persons from whom the Senate may choose a Vice President whenever the right of choice shall have devolved upon them.

Section 5

Sections 1 and 2 shall take effect on the 15th day of October following the ratification of this article.

Section 6

This article shall be inoperative unless it shall have been ratified as an amendment to the Constitution by the legislatures of three fourths of the several States within seven years from the date of its submission.

Amendment XXI
[Adopted 1933]

Section 1

The eighteenth article of amendment to the Constitution of the United States is hereby repealed.

Section 2

The transportation or importation into any State, Territory, or possession of the United States for delivery or use therein of intoxicating liquors in violation of the laws thereof, is hereby prohibited.

Section 3

This article shall be inoperative unless it shall have been ratified as an amendment to the Constitution by conventions in the several States, as provided in the Constitution, within seven years from the date of the submission hereof to the States by the Congress.

Amendment XXII
[Adopted 1951]

Section 1

No person shall be elected to the office of the President more than twice, and no person who has held the office of President, or acted as President, for more than two years of a term to which some other person was elected President shall be elected to the office of the President more than once. But this Article shall not apply to any person holding the office of President when this Article was proposed by the Congress, and shall not prevent any person who may be holding the office of President, or acting as President, during the term within which this Article becomes operative from holding the office of President or acting as President during the remainder of such term.

Section 2

This article shall be inoperative unless it shall have been ratified as an amendment to the Constitution by the legislatures of three-fourths of the several States within seven years from the date of its submission to the States by the Congress.

Amendment XXIII
[Adopted 1961]

Section 1

The District constituting the seat of Government of the United States shall appoint in such manner as the Congress shall direct:

A number of electors of President and Vice President equal to the whole number of Senators and Representatives in Congress to which the District would be entitled if it were a State, but in no event more than the least populous State; they shall be in addition to those appointed by the States, but they shall be considered, for the purposes of the election of President and Vice President, to be electors appointed by a State; and they shall meet in the District and perform such duties as provided by the twelfth article of amendment.

Section 2

The Congress shall have power to enforce this article by appropriate legislation.

Amendment XXIV
[Adopted 1964]

Section 1

The right of citizens of the United States to vote in any primary or other election for President or Vice President, for electors for President or Vice President, or for Senator or Representative in Congress, shall not be denied or abridged by the United States or any state by reason of failure to pay any poll tax or other tax.

Section 2

The Congress shall have the power to enforce this article by appropriate legislation.

Amendment XXV
[Adopted 1967]

Section 1

In case of the removal of the President from office or his death or resignation, the Vice President shall become President.

Section 2

Whenever there is a vacancy in the office of the Vice President, the President shall nominate a Vice President who shall take the office upon confirmation by a majority vote of both houses of Congress.

Section 3

Whenever the President transmits to the President pro tempore of the Senate and the Speaker of the House of Representatives his written declaration that he is unable to discharge the powers and duties of his office, and until he transmits to them a written declaration to the contrary, such powers and duties shall be discharged by the Vice President as Acting President.

Section 4

Whenever the Vice President and a majority of either the principal officers of the executive departments or of such other body as Congress may by law provide, transmit to the President pro tempore of the Senate and the Speaker of the House of Representatives their written declaration that the President is unable to discharge the powers and duties of his office, the Vice President shall immediately assume the powers and duties of the office as Acting President.

Thereafter, when the President transmits to the President pro tempore of the Senate and the Speaker of the House of Representatives his written declaration that no inability exists, he shall resume the powers and duties of his office unless the Vice President and a majority of either the principal officers of the executive department or of such other body as Congress may by law provide, transmit within four days to the President pro tempore of the Senate and the Speaker of the House of Representatives their written declaration that the President is unable to discharge the powers and duties of his office. Thereupon Congress shall decide the issue, assembling within 48 hours for that purpose if not in session. If the Congress, within 21 days after receipt of the latter written declaration, or, if Congress is not in session, within 21 days after Congress is required to assemble, determines by two-thirds vote of both houses that the President is unable to discharge the powers and duties of his office, the Vice President shall continue to discharge the same as Acting President; otherwise, the President shall resume the powers and duties of his office.

Amendment XXVI
[Adopted 1971]

Section 1

The right of citizens of the United States, who are 18 years of age or older, to vote shall not be denied or abridged by the United States or any state on account of age.

Section 2

The Congress shall have the power to enforce this article by appropriate legislation.

Amendment XXVII
[Adopted 1992]

No law, varying the compensation for the services of the Senators and Representatives shall take effect, until an election of Representatives shall have intervened.

Presidential Elections

Year	Candidates	Parties	Popular Vote	Electoral Vote	Voter Participation
1789	**George Washington**		*	69	
	John Adams			34	
	Others			35	
1792	**George Washington**		*	132	
	John Adams			77	
	George Clinton			50	
	Others			5	
1796	**John Adams**	Federalist	*	71	
	Thomas Jefferson	Democratic-Republican		68	
	Thomas Pinckney	Federalist		59	
	Aaron Burr	Dem.-Rep.		30	
	Others			48	
1800	**Thomas Jefferson**	Dem.-Rep.	*	73	
	Aaron Burr	Dem.-Rep.		73	
	John Adams	Federalist		65	
	C. C. Pinckney	Federalist		64	
	John Jay	Federalist		1	
1804	**Thomas Jefferson**	Dem.-Rep.	*	162	
	C. C. Pinckney	Federalist		14	
1808	**James Madison**	Dem.-Rep.	*	122	
	C. C. Pinckney	Federalist		47	
	George Clinton	Dem.-Rep.		6	
1812	**James Madison**	Dem.-Rep.	*	128	
	De Witt Clinton	Federalist		89	
1816	**James Monroe**	Dem.-Rep.	*	183	
	Rufus King	Federalist		34	
1820	**James Monroe**	Dem.-Rep.	*	231	
	John Quincy Adams	Dem.-Rep.		1	
1824	**John Quincy Adams**	Dem.-Rep.	108,740 (30.5%)	84	26.9%
	Andrew Jackson	Dem.-Rep.	153,544 (43.1%)	99	
	William H. Crawford	Dem.-Rep.	46,618 (13.1%)	41	
	Henry Clay	Dem.-Rep.	47,136 (13.2%)	37	
1828	**Andrew Jackson**	Democratic	647,286 (56.0%)	178	57.6%
	John Quincy Adams	National Republican	508,064 (44.0%)	83	
1832	**Andrew Jackson**	Democratic	687,502 (55.0%)	219	55.4%
	Henry Clay	National Republican	530,189 (42.4%)	49	
	John Floyd	Independent		11	
	William Wirt	Anti-Mason	33,108 (2.6%)	7	
1836	**Martin Van Buren**	Democratic	765,483 (50.9%)	170	57.8%
	William Henry Harrison	Whig		73	
	Hugh L. White	Whig	739,795 (49.1%)	26	
	Daniel Webster	Whig		14	
	W. P. Magnum	Independent		11	
1840	**William Henry Harrison**	Whig	1,274,624 (53.1%)	234	80.2%
	Martin Van Buren	Democratic	1,127,781 (46.9%)	60	
	J. G. Birney	Liberty	7069	—	

*Electors selected by state legislatures.

Year	Candidates	Parties	Popular Vote	Electoral Vote	Voter Participation
1844	**James K. Polk**	Democratic	1,338,464 (49.6%)	170	78.9%
	Henry Clay	Whig	1,300,097 (48.1%)	105	
	J. G. Birney	Liberty	62,300 (2.3%)	—	
1848	**Zachary Taylor**	Whig	1,360,967 (47.4%)	163	72.7%
	Lewis Cass	Democratic	1,222,342 (42.5%)	127	
	Martin Van Buren	Free-Soil	291,263 (10.1%)	—	
1852	**Franklin Pierce**	Democratic	1,601,117 (50.9%)	254	69.6%
	Winfield Scott	Whig	1,385,453 (44.1%)	42	
	John P. Hale	Free-Soil	155,825 (5.0%)	—	
1856	**James Buchanan**	Democratic	1,832,955 (45.3%)	174	78.9%
	John C. Frémont	Republican	1,339,932 (33.1%)	114	
	Millard Fillmore	American	871,731 (21.6%)	8	
1860	**Abraham Lincoln**	Republican	1,865,593 (39.8%)	180	81.2%
	Stephen A. Douglas	Democratic	1,382,713 (29.5%)	12	
	John C. Breckinridge	Democratic	848,356 (18.1%)	72	
	John Bell	Union	592,906 (12.6%)	39	
1864	**Abraham Lincoln**	Republican	2,213,655 (55.0%)	212[*]	73.8%
	George B. McClellan	Democratic	1,805,237 (45.0%)	21	
1868	**Ulysses S. Grant**	Republican	3,012,833 (52.7%)	214	78.1%
	Horatio Seymour	Democratic	2,703,249 (47.3%)	80	
1872	**Ulysses S. Grant**	Republican	3,597,132 (55.6%)	286	71.3%
	Horace Greeley	Dem.; Liberal Republican	2,834,125 (43.9%)	66[†]	
1876	**Rutherford B. Hayes ‡**	Republican	4,036,298 (48.0%)	185	81.8%
	Samuel J. Tilden	Democratic	4,300,590 (51.0%)	184	
1880	**James A. Garfield**	Republican	4,454,416 (48.5%)	214	79.4%
	Winfield S. Hancock	Democratic	4,444,952 (48.1%)	155	
1884	**Grover Cleveland**	Democratic	4,874,986 (48.5%)	219	77.5%
	James G. Blaine	Republican	4,851,981 (48.2%)	182	
1888	**Benjamin Harrison**	Republican	5,439,853 (47.9%)	233	79.3%
	Grover Cleveland	Democratic	5,540,309 (48.6%)	168	
1892	**Grover Cleveland**	Democratic	5,556,918 (46.1%)	277	74.7%
	Benjamin Harrison	Republican	5,176,108 (43.0%)	145	
	James B. Weaver	People's	1,041,028 (8.5%)	22	
1896	**William McKinley**	Republican	7,104,779 (51.1%)	271	79.3%
	William Jennings Bryan	Democratic People's	6,502,925 (47.7%)	176	
1900	**William McKinley**	Republican	7,207,923 (51.7%)	292	73.2%
	William Jennings Bryan	Dem.-Populist	6,358,133 (45.5%)	155	
1904	**Theodore Roosevelt**	Republican	7,623,486 (57.9%)	336	65.2%
	Alton B. Parker	Democratic	5,077,911 (37.6%)	140	
	Eugene V. Debs	Socialist	402,283 (3.0%)	—	
1908	**William H. Taft**	Republican	7,678,908 (51.6%)	321	65.4%
	William Jennings Bryan	Democratic	6,409,104 (43.1%)	162	
	Eugene V. Debs	Socialist	420,793 (2.8%)	—	
1912	**Woodrow Wilson**	Democratic	6,293,454 (41.9%)	435	58.8%
	Theodore Roosevelt	Progressive	4,119,538 (27.4%)	88	
	William H. Taft	Republican	3,484,980 (23.2%)	8	
	Eugene V. Debs	Socialist	900,672 (6.0%)	—	
1916	**Woodrow Wilson**	Democratic	9,129,606 (49.4%)	277	61.6%
	Charles E. Hughes	Republican	8,538,221 (46.2%)	254	
	A. L. Benson	Socialist	585,113 (3.2%)	—	
1920	**Warren G. Harding**	Republican	16,152,200 (60.4%)	404	49.2%
	James M. Cox	Democratic	9,147,353 (34.2%)	127	
	Eugene V. Debs	Socialist	919,799 (3.4%)	—	

[*]Eleven secessionist states did not participate.
[†]Greeley died before the electoral college met. His electoral votes were divided among the four minor candidates.
[‡]Contested result settled by special election.

Year	Candidates	Parties	Popular Vote	Electoral Vote	Voter Participation
1924	**Calvin Coolidge**	Republican	15,725,016 (54.0%)	382	48.9%
	John W. Davis	Democratic	8,386,503 (28.8%)	136	
	Robert M. La Follette	Progressive	4,822,856 (16.6%)	13	
1928	**Herbert Hoover**	Republican	21,391,381 (58.2%)	444	56.9%
	Alfred E. Smith	Democratic	15,016,443 (40.9%)	87	
	Norman Thomas	Socialist	267,835 (0.7%)	—	
1932	**Franklin D. Roosevelt**	Democratic	22,821,857 (57.4%)	472	56.9%
	Herbert Hoover	Republican	15,761,841 (39.7%)	59	
	Norman Thomas	Socialist	881,951 (2.2%)	—	
1936	**Franklin D. Roosevelt**	Democratic	27,751,597 (60.8%)	523	61.0%
	Alfred M. Landon	Republican	16,679,583 (36.5%)	8	
	William Lemke	Union	882,479 (1.9%)	—	
1940	**Franklin D. Roosevelt**	Democratic	27,244,160 (54.8%)	449	62.5%
	Wendell L. Willkie	Republican	22,305,198 (44.8%)	82	
1944	**Franklin D. Roosevelt**	Democratic	25,602,504 (53.5%)	432	55.9%
	Thomas E. Dewey	Republican	22,006,285 (46.0%)	99	
1948	**Harry S Truman**	Democratic	24,105,695 (49.5%)	304	53.0%
	Thomas E. Dewey	Republican	21,969,170 (45.1%)	189	
	J. Strom Thurmond	State-Rights Democratic	1,169,021 (2.4%)	38	
	Henry A. Wallace	Progressive	1,156,103 (2.4%)	—	
1952	**Dwight D. Eisenhower**	Republican	33,936,252 (55.1%)	442	63.3%
	Adlai E. Stevenson	Democratic	27,314,992 (44.4%)	89	
1956	**Dwight D. Eisenhower**	Republican	35,575,420 (57.6%)	457	60.6%
	Adlai E. Stevenson	Democratic	26,033,066 (42.1%)	73	
	Other	—	—	1	
1960	**John F. Kennedy**	Democratic	34,227,096 (49.9%)	303	62.8%
	Richard M. Nixon	Republican	34,108,546 (49.6%)	219	
	Other	—	—	15	
1964	**Lyndon B. Johnson**	Democratic	43,126,506 (61.1%)	486	61.7%
	Barry M. Goldwater	Republican	27,176,799 (38.5%)	52	
1968	**Richard M. Nixon**	Republican	31,770,237 (43.4%)	301	60.6%
	Hubert H. Humphrey	Democratic	31,270,533 (42.7%)	191	
	George Wallace	American Indep.	9,906,141 (13.5%)	46	
1972	**Richard M. Nixon**	Republican	47,169,911 (60.7%)	520	55.2%
	George S. McGovern	Democratic	29,170,383 (37.5%)	17	
	Other	—	—	1	
1976	**Jimmy Carter**	Democratic	40,828,587 (50.0%)	297	53.5%
	Gerald R. Ford	Republican	39,147,613 (47.9%)	241	
	Other	—	1,575,459 (2.1%)	—	
1980	**Ronald Reagan**	Republican	43,901,812 (50.7%)	489	52.6%
	Jimmy Carter	Democratic	35,483,820 (41.0%)	49	
	John B. Anderson	Independent	5,719,722 (6.6%)	—	
	Ed Clark	Libertarian	921,188 (1.1%)	—	
1984	**Ronald Reagan**	Republican	54,455,075 (59.0%)	525	53.3%
	Walter Mondale	Democratic	37,577,185 (41.0%)	13	
1988	**George H. W. Bush**	Republican	48,886,000 (53.4%)	426	57.4%
	Michael S. Dukakis	Democratic	41,809,000 (45.6%)	111	
1992	**William J. Clinton**	Democratic	43,728,375 (43%)	370	55.0%
	George H. W. Bush	Republican	38,167,416 (38%)	168	
	H. Ross Perot	Independent	19,237,247 (19%)	—	
1996	**William J. Clinton**	Democratic	45,590,703 (50%)	379	48.8%
	Robert Dole	Republican	37,816,307 (41%)	159	
	H. Ross Perot	Reform	7,866,284		
2000	**George W. Bush**	Republican	50,456,167 (47.88%)	271	51.2%
	Al Gore	Democratic	50,996,064 (48.39%)	266*	
	Ralph Nader	Green	2,864,810 (2.72%)	—	
	Other		834,774 (< 1%)	—	

*One District of Columbia Gore elector abstained.

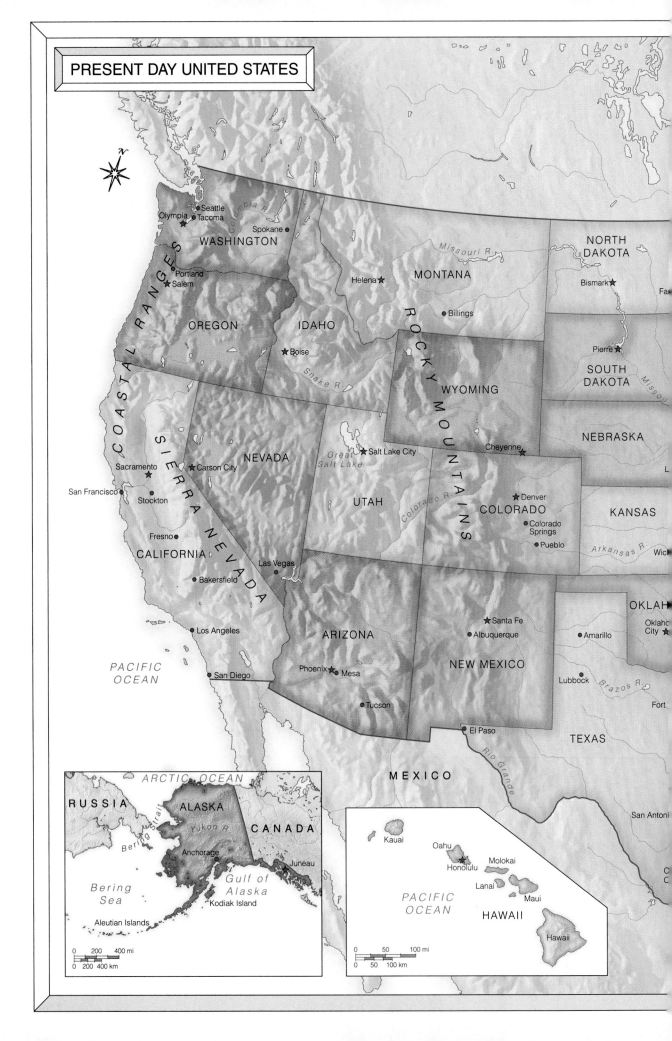

PRESENT DAY UNITED STATES

WASHINGTON
- Seattle
- Olympia ★
- Tacoma
- Spokane
- Portland
- Salem ★

OREGON

COASTAL RANGES

SIERRA NEVADA

IDAHO
- Boise ★

MONTANA
- Helena ★
- Billings

ROCKY MOUNTAINS

WYOMING
- Cheyenne ★

NORTH DAKOTA
- Bismark ★
- Fa

SOUTH DAKOTA
- Pierre ★

NEBRASKA

NEVADA
- Carson City ★

Sacramento ★
- San Francisco
- Stockton

Great Salt Lake
- Salt Lake City ★

UTAH

Colorado R.

COLORADO
- Denver ★
- Colorado Springs
- Pueblo

KANSAS

Arkansas R.
- Wich

Fresno

CALIFORNIA
- Las Vegas
- Bakersfield

- Los Angeles

PACIFIC OCEAN

- San Diego

ARIZONA
- Phoenix ★ Mesa

- Tucson

Santa Fe ★
- Albuquerque

NEW MEXICO

- El Paso

OKLAH

OKLAHO
- Oklaho City ★

- Amarillo

- Lubbock
Brazos R.

TEXAS

Fort

MEXICO

Rio Grande

San Antoni

Missouri R.

Snake R.

Columbia R.

ALASKA inset

ARCTIC OCEAN

RUSSIA

ALASKA

CANADA

Bering Strait

Yukon R.

- Anchorage
- Juneau

Bering Sea

Gulf of Alaska
- Kodiak Island

Aleutian Islands

| 0 | 200 | 400 mi |
| 0 | 200 | 400 km |

HAWAII inset

- Kauai
- Oahu
- Honolulu ★
- Molokai
- Lanai
- Maui

PACIFIC OCEAN

HAWAII

- Hawaii

| 0 | 50 | 100 mi |
| 0 | 50 | 100 km |

A-20

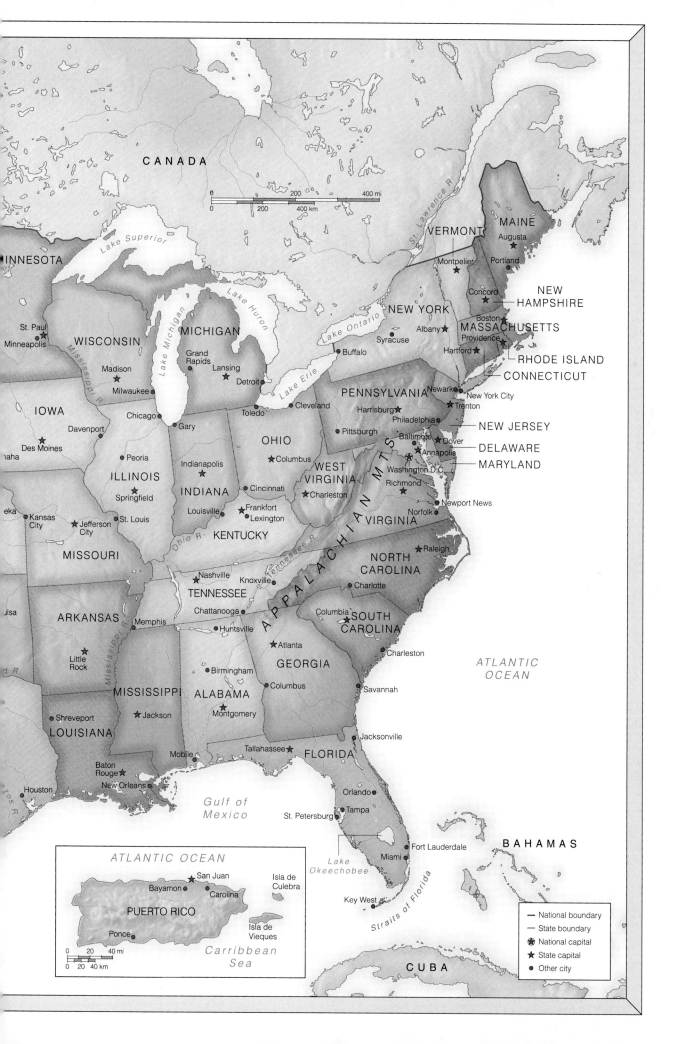

CANADA

Lake Superior

200   400 mi
0
200   400 km

St. Lawrence R.

MINNESOTA

Lake Michigan

Lake Huron

MAINE
Augusta ★

VERMONT

Montpelier ★

Portland ●

NEW YORK

Concord ★

NEW
HAMPSHIRE

St. Paul ★
Minneapolis ●

WISCONSIN

MICHIGAN

Grand
Rapids ●

Lansing ★

Syracuse ●

Albany ★

Boston ★
Providence ★

MASSACHUSETTS

Madison ★

Detroit ★

Lake Ontario

Buffalo ●

Hartford ★

RHODE ISLAND

Milwaukee ●

Lake Erie

CONNECTICUT

IOWA

Mississippi R.

Chicago ●

Toledo ●

Cleveland ●

PENNSYLVANIA

Newark ●

New York City

Davenport ●

Gary ●

Harrisburg ★

Trenton ★

NEW JERSEY

maha ●

Des Moines ★

Peoria ●

OHIO

Columbus ★

Pittsburgh ●

Philadelphia ●

Baltimore ●

Dover ★

DELAWARE

ILLINOIS

Indianapolis ★

WEST
VIRGINIA

Annapolis ★

MARYLAND

Springfield ★

INDIANA

Cincinnati ●

Washington D.C.

ka ●

Kansas
City ●

St. Louis ●

Louisville ●

Frankfort ★

Lexington ●

Charleston ★

Richmond ★

Newport News ●

Jefferson
City ★

KENTUCKY

Ohio R.

VIRGINIA

Norfolk ●

MISSOURI

Tennessee R.

Raleigh ★

NORTH
CAROLINA

Nashville ★

Knoxville ●

APPALACHIAN MTS.

Charlotte ●

lsa ●

TENNESSEE

ARKANSAS

Chattanooga ●

Columbia ★

SOUTH
CAROLINA

Memphis ●

Huntsville ●

Atlanta ★

Charleston ●

Little
Rock ★

Birmingham ●

GEORGIA

ATLANTIC
OCEAN

Mississippi R.

Columbus ●

Savannah ●

MISSISSIPPI

ALABAMA

Shreveport ●

Jackson ★

Montgomery ★

LOUISIANA

Mobile ●

Tallahassee ★

FLORIDA

Jacksonville ●

Baton
Rouge ★

Houston ●

New Orleans ●

Gulf of
Mexico

Orlando ●

Tampa ●

BAHAMAS

St. Petersburg ●

s R.

ATLANTIC OCEAN

San Juan ★
Bayamon ●   Carolina ●

Isla de
Culebra

Fort Lauderdale ●

Lake
Okeechobee

Miami ●

PUERTO RICO

Isla de
Vieques

Key West ●

Ponce ●

0   20   40 mi
0   20   40 km

Carribean
Sea

Straits of Florida

CUBA

— National boundary
— State boundary
⊛ National capital
★ State capital
● Other city

A-21

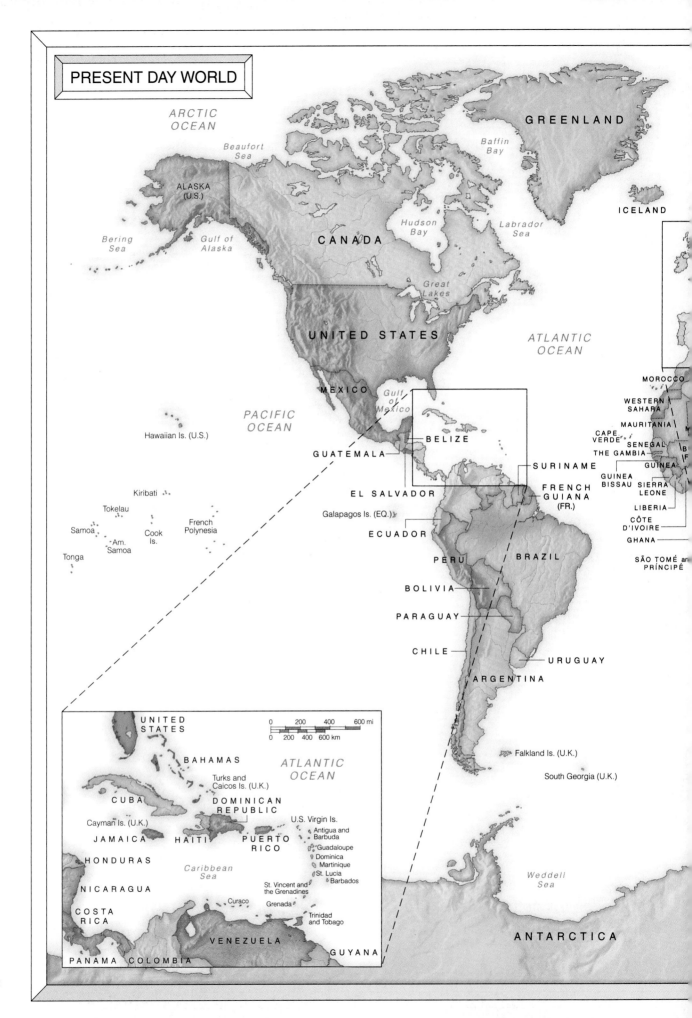

PRESENT DAY WORLD

ARCTIC
OCEAN

GREENLAND

Beaufort
Sea

Baffin
Bay

ICELAND

ALASKA
(U.S.)

Hudson
Bay

Labrador
Sea

Bering
Sea

Gulf of
Alaska

CANADA

ATLANTIC
OCEAN

MOROCCO

UNITED STATES

WESTERN
SAHARA

MAURITANIA

MEXICO

Gulf
of
Mexico

PACIFIC
OCEAN

CAPE
VERDE
SENEGAL

Hawaiian Is. (U.S.)

BELIZE

THE GAMBIA

GUINEA

B
F

GUATEMALA

SURINAME

GUINEA
BISSAU

SIERRA
LEONE

EL SALVADOR

FRENCH
GUIANA
(FR.)

LIBERIA

Galapagos Is. (EQ.)

CÔTE
D'IVOIRE

Kiribati

GHANA

Tokelau

ECUADOR

SÃO TOMÉ an
PRÍNCIPE

Samoa

Cook
Is.

French
Polynesia

PERU

BRAZIL

Am.
Samoa

Tonga

BOLIVIA

PARAGUAY

CHILE

URUGUAY

ARGENTINA

Falkland Is. (U.K.)

South Georgia (U.K.)

UNITED
STATES

0   200   400   600 mi

0   200 400 600 km

BAHAMAS

ATLANTIC
OCEAN

Turks and
Caicos Is. (U.K.)

CUBA

DOMINICAN
REPUBLIC

Cayman Is. (U.K.)

U.S. Virgin Is.

Antigua and
Barbuda

JAMAICA

HAITI

PUERTO
RICO

Guadaloupe

Dominica

Martinique

HONDURAS

Caribbean
Sea

St. Lucia

Barbados

NICARAGUA

St. Vincent and
the Grenadines

Weddell
Sea

COSTA
RICA

Curaco

Grenada

PANAMA   COLOMBIA

VENEZUELA

Trinidad
and Tobago

GUYANA

ANTARCTICA

Svalbard Is. (NOR.)   Novaya Zemlya

Barents Sea   *Kara Sea*   *Laptev Sea*   New Siberian Is.   *ARCTIC OCEAN*   *East Siberian Sea*

RUSSIA

Lake Baikal   *Sea of Okhotsk*   Sakhalin

KAZAKHSTAN   *Aral Sea*   *Lake Balkhash*   MONGOLIA   N. KOREA   JAPAN   *PACIFIC OCEAN*

AFGHAN.   PAKISTAN   PEOPLE'S REPUBLIC OF CHINA   S. KOREA   *East China Sea*

TUNISIA   ISRAEL   IRAQ   JORDAN   IRAN   NEPAL   BHUTAN

LIBYA   EGYPT   BAHRAIN   QATAR   U.A.E.   BANG.   BURMA (MYANMAR)   TAIWAN   MACAO   *Philippine Sea*   Northern Mariana Is.

SAUDI ARABIA   OMAN   INDIA   LAOS   VIETNAM   PHILIPPINES

CHAD   ERITREA   YEMEN   *Arabian Sea*   *Bay of Bengal*   THAILAND   *South China Sea*   Marshall Is.

SUDAN   DJIBOUTI   CAMBODIA

CENT. AFRICAN REP.   SOMALIA   ETHIOPIA   SRI LANKA   MALAYSIA   BRUNEI

CAMEROON   EQUA. GUINEA   UGANDA   KENYA   SINGAPORE   PAPUA NEW GUINEA   Nauru

DEM. REP. OF CONGO   RWANDA   INDONESIA   Solomon Is.   Tuvalu

BURUNDI   TANZANIA   *INDIAN OCEAN*

ANGOLA   MALAWI   *Coral Sea*   Vanuatu   Fiji

ZAMBIA   MADAGASCAR   MAURITIUS   New Caledonia (FR.)

ZIMB.   AUSTRALIA   *Tasman Sea*

BOTSWANA   MOZAMBIQUE

SOUTH AFRICA   SWAZILAND   *N*

LESOTHO   NEW ZEALAND

NORWAY   FINLAND   SWEDEN   ESTONIA

IRELAND   *North Sea*   DENMARK   LATVIA   LITHUANIA   RUSSIA   *Baltic Sea*

UNITED KINGDOM   NETHERLANDS   POLAND   BELARUS   *ATLANTIC OCEAN*   BELGIUM   GERMANY   CZECH REPUBLIC   UKRAINE   LUX.   LIECHT.   SLOVAKIA   FRANCE   SWITZ.   AUSTRIA   HUNGARY   MOLDOVA   SLOVENIA   ROMANIA   *Caspian Sea*   CROATIA   BOSNIA HERZ.   SERBIA   BULGARIA   *Black Sea*   GEORGIA   PORTUGAL   SPAIN   ITALY   *Adriatic Sea*   MACEDONIA   ARMENIA   AZERBAIJAN   ALBANIA   GREECE   TURKEY   *Aegean Sea*   CYPRUS   SYRIA   IRAQ   *Mediterranean Sea*   LEBANON

0   1000   2000   3000 mi
0   1000   2000   3000 km

0   200   400   600   800 mi
0   200   400   600   800 km

Credits

Chapter 15

Page 510: From "Post-Bellum Southern Rental Contracts" by Rosser H. Taylor from *Agricultural History,* Volume 17, Number 2, April 1943. Published by The Agricultural History Society.

Page 523 (Table 15-3): From *Americans and Their Forests: A Historical Review* by Michael Williams. Copyright © 1989 by Cambridge University Press. Reprinted by permission of Cambridge University Press.

Page 530 (Table 15-4): From *Beyond Equality: Labor and the Radical Republicans, 1862–1872* by David Montgomery. New York: Alfred Knopf, 1967.

Part Six Timeline

Page 536: (Top) Michael Freeman Photography; (bottom) Courtesy, Janice L. and David Frent

Page 537: (Top) From the HUC Skirball Cultural Center, Museum Collection, Los Angeles, CA. Gift of Brenda Grossman Spivack in memory of Godina Eisenstein Schwartz. Clothes and Textiles: Gift of Harold Brill and Regina Starr Brill. HUCSM 31.194. Photography by Susan Einstein; (bottom) Fair Street Pictures

Chapter 16

Page 545 (Table 16-1): From *Americans and Their Forests: A Historical Review* by Michael Williams. Copyright © 1989 by Cambridge University Press. Reprinted by permission of Cambridge University Press.

Page 547 (Table 16-2): From "How Indians Used the Buffalo" adapted from *The Native American Almanac* by Arlene B. Hirschfelder and Martha Kreipe de Montano. Copyright © 1998. Reprinted by permission of Hungry Minds.

Page 549 (Map 16.2): Adapted from "Population of Foreign Birth by Region, 1880" in *Historical Atlas of the United States* by Clifford L. Lord & Elizabeth H. Lord. New York: Holt, 1953.

Page 551 (Map 16.3): From *Chinese in the Post–Civil War South* by Lucy Cohen. Copyright © 1984 by Louisiana State University Press. Reprinted by permission of Louisiana State University Press.

Page 568: From "The Gospel of Wealth" by Andrew Carnegie from *North American Review,* No. CCCXCL (June 1889).

Chapter 17

Page 579 (Map 17.1): From "Farm Tenancy, by Counties, 1880" in *Historical Atlas of the United States* by Clifford L. Lord & Elizabeth H. Lord. New York: Holt, 1953.

Page 582 (Map 17.2): From *The Atlas of African-American History and Politics: From the Slave Trade to Modern Times* by Arwin D. Smallwood with Jeffrey M. Elliot. McGraw-Hill, 1998.

Page 585 (Map 17.3): From *American History Atlas,* revised edition by Martin Gilbert. London: Weidenfeld & Nicolson, 1969.

Chapter 18

Page 609 (Map 18.1): From *Atlas of American History* by Kenneth T. Jackson and James T. Adams. New York: Charles Scribner's Sons. 1985.

Page 610 (Map 18.2): From "Population Density, 1890" in *Historical Atlas of the United States* by Clifford L. Lord & Elizabeth H. Lord. New York: Holt, 1953.

Page 613 (Map 18.3): From Paullin and Wright, *Atlas of the Historical Geography of the United States,* 1932.

Page 616 (Map 18.4): From "Compulsory School Attendance, 1890" and Compulsory School Attendance, 1900" in *Historical Atlas of the United States* by Clifford L. Lord & Elizabeth H. Lord. New York: Holt, 1953.

Pages 632–633 (Map 18.6): Adapted from Spanish-American War in the Pacific and Spanish-American War in the Caribbean in Kenneth T. Jackson and James T. Adams, *Atlas of American History.* New York: Charles Scribner's Sons. 1985.

Pages 634–635: From Proceedings of the Congressional Committee on the Philippines—Testimony of Robert P. Hughes and Charles S. Riley, 1902.

Part Seven Timeline

Page 638: (Top) From the Collections of Henry Ford Museum & Greenfield Village; (middle) Courtesy, The Lilly Library, Indiana University, Bloomington, Indiana; (bottom) Courtesy, Military Antiques & Museum, Petaluma, CA

Page 639: (Top) Fair Street Pictures; (middle) Courtesy, Janice L. and David Frent; (bottom) From the Collections of Ford Museum & Greenfield Village

Chapter 19

Page 645 (Map 19.1): From *Historical Atlas of the United States* by Clifford L. Lord & Elizabeth H. Lord. New York: Holt, 1953.

Page 646 (Figure 19.1): "Immigration by Decade, 1821–1990" from Immigration and Naturalization Service.

Page 648 (Map 19.2): Adapted from "Areas Restricted by Chinese Exclusion Acts" in *Atlas of American Migration* by Stephen A. Flanders. New York: Facts on File, 1998.

Page 651 (Map 19.3): Adapted from "Italian and Russian Immigrants in the United States, 1910" in *Atlas of American Migration* by Stephen A. Flanders. New York: Facts on File, 1998.

Chapter 20

Page 693: From Addie W. Hunton & Kathryn M. Johnson, *Two Colored Women with the American Expeditionary Forces.* Brooklyn, NY: Brooklyn Eagle Press, 1920.

Chapter 21

Page 706 (Figure 21.1): From *Brought to Bed: Childbearing in America, 1750–1950* by Judith Walzer Leavitt, copyright © 1986 by Judith Walzer Leavitt. Used by permission of Oxford University Press, Inc.

Page 708 (Figure 21.2): From U.S. Immigration, 1891–1940.

Page 712 (Figure 21.4): "Changes in Farm and Nonfarm Populations: 1880–1980" from *America's Northern Heartland: An Economic and Historical Geography of the Upper Midwest* by John R. Borchert. Copyright © 1987, published by the University of Minnesota Press. Used by permission.

Page 730: From *The Fortunate Pilgrim* by Mario Puzo. New York: Antheneum, 1965.

Part Eight Timeline

Page 734: (Top) Courtesy, Janice L. and David Frent; (middle) Nationalmuseet, Copenhagen/The Bridgeman Art Library International Ltd.; (bottom) Gift of Mr. and Mrs. Jim Kawaminami, Japanese American National Museum. Photo by Norman Sugimoto

Page 735: (Top) Fair Street Pictures; (middle) Courtesy, The United Nations; (bottom) Joseph Sohm; ChromoSohm Inc./CORBIS

Chapter 23

Page 789: Interview with Zelda Anderson in R. T. King, ed., from *War Stories: Veterans Remember World War II.* Published by the University of Nevada Oral History Program, 1995. Used by permission of Zelda Anderson and the University of Nevada Oral History Program.)

Chapter 24

Page 825: From NSC-68: United States Objectives and Programs for National Security (April 14, 1950).

Part Nine Timeline

Page 832: (Top) Library of Congress; (bottom) Roger Ressmeyer/CORBIS

Page 833: (Top) Library of Congress; (middle) Tamiment/Wagner Poster and Broadside Collection, Tamiment Library, New York University; (bottom) TimePix

Chapter 25

Page 857: From *Silent Spring* by Rachel Carson. Boston: Houghton Mifflin, 1962.

Page 863: Martin Luther King, Jr., "I Have a Dream" (speech delivered August 28, 1963, Washington, D.C.) Reprinted by arrangement with The Heirs to the Estate of Martin Luther King Jr., c/o Writers House, Inc as agent for the proprietor. Copyright 1963 by Martin Luther King Jr., copyright renewed 1991 by Coretta Scott King.

Chapter 26

Page 882: "A Time to Break Silence" by Martin Luther King, Jr. Reprinted by arrangement with the Estate of Martin Luther King Jr., c/o Writers House as agent of the proprietor. Copyright 1963 by Martin Luther King Jr., copyright renewed 1991 by Coretta Scott King.

Chapter 27

Page 920: Interim Report of the U.S. Senate Select Committee to Study Government Operations (November 20, 1975).

Part Ten Timeline

Page 934: (Top) Courtesy, Janice L and David Frent; (bottom) W. Cody/CORBIS

Page 935: (Top) Justin Sullivan/AP/Wide World; (bottom) Amy E. Conn/AP/Wide World

Chapter 28

Pages 954–955: From *Listen America* by Jerry Falwell, copyright © 1980 by Jerry Falwell. Used by permission of Doubleday, a division of Random House.

Page 955: "The Need for a Moral Minority" by Robert McAfee Brown. Reprinted by permission of the estate of Robert McAfee Brown.

Chapter 29

Pages 976 (Map 29.1) and 983 (Map 29.2): From *Atlas of American Migration* by Stephen A. Flanders. New York: Facts on File, 1998.

Page 980: From the Vermont Civil Union Law (April 26, 2000.)

Chapter 30

Page 1022: The Slow Food Manifesto (Nov. 9, 1989) of The Slow Food Movement (http://www.slowfood.com)

Index

Entries followed by *f, t, m,* and *i* refer to figures, tables, maps, and illustrations, respectively

A

Abalone Alliance, 916
Abbey, Edward, 915, 1005
Aberdeen Saturday Pioneer, 562
ABM treaty, 906
Abortion
    early 20th century, 678
    in 1940s, 817
    in 1950s, 855
    in 1960s, 888
    in 1970s, Medicaid funds and, 930
    in 1980s, debate over, 953, 954
    in 1990s: anti-abortion violence, 984–985; Clinton policies on, 988; debate over, 984–985, 985i
    Bolsheviks and, 697
Abstract expressionism, 854, 854i
Acheson, Dean, 809, 812, 827
Acquired immunodeficiency syndrome. *See* AIDS
ACT-UP. *See* AIDS Coalition to Unleash Power
Adams, Ansel, 872i
Adams, Henry, 582
Adams, John, on wealth, 950
Adamson Act (1916), 683
Addams, Jane, 598, 657, 660, 662, 685
Advertising
    in 1920s, 725, 725i
    late 19th century: mass merchandising, 560–563; minorities and, 541
    late 20th century, 1018
    history of, 561, 562–563, 563i
    and minorities, 562–563

AEF. *See* American Expeditionary Force
Affirmative action
    debate over, 1025
    Reagan administration and, 956
    Supreme Court on, 931
Afghanistan
    Soviet invasion of, 938, 939–940, 959, 1030
    Taliban regime in, 995, 1021, 1030
    U.S. intervention in (2001), 1030
AFL. *See* American Federation of Labor
Africa
    Africa American return to, early 20th century, 709
    Carter policy in, 922, 923m
    European imperialism in, late 19th century, 628
Africa American women
    late 19th century, reform movements and, 526–527, 624–625
    early 20th century, suffrage movement and, 661
    in 1920s, 714i
    in 1930s: employment, 744; New Deal and, 761
    in 1990s, first in Congress, 981
    in World War I, 693, 693i
    in World War II, 783, 788, 789
    post–World War II: employment, 817; role and status of, 843–844
African Americans
    post–Civil War: aspirations of, 501, 503–504, 508; challenges facing, 503–504; citizenship of, 506; class divisions among, 511; education and, 500i, 501, 502i, 504; employment and, 553; marriage and family, 508,

512–513, 512t; political organization, 511–513, 515; rights of, 511, 516, 532; sharecropping system, 510–511, 510i, 579m, 580t; voting rights, 504, 506, 507, 511, 513m, 514–515, 516–517; white efforts to control, 501, 506, 507, 532
    late 19th century: aspirations of, 615; education, 599, 612–614; efforts to control, 580, 611; military service, 581–582, 582m; religion, 582–584, 583i; resistance to discrimination, 575, 610, 614; social class among, 580; Social Darwinism and, 568; in Spanish-American War, 632; temperance movement and, 599; unions and, 529, 530, 592–593; voting rights, 526–527, 601, 611
    20th century: as cowboys, 523; U.S. culture and, 1018
    early 20th century: businesses, 561; citizenship and, 654; culture of, 656, 658; first White House meeting, 664; Great Migration of, 638, 683–685, 684m, 690; migrations north, 728; mortality rate for, 652; Progressivism and, 683; role and status of, 671, 676–677; unions and, 662, 698
    in World War I: migration to cities in, 638; as soldiers, 690, 692i, 693; support for, 690
    mid-20th century: entrepreneurs, 844i; middle class status, 843–844; service organizations and, 840i; violence against, 698

I-1